The Vietnam Reader

By Stewart O'Nan

In the Walled City
Snow Angels
The Names of the Dead
The Speed Queen
A World Away

As Editor

On Writers and Writing by John Gardner

The Definitive Collection of American Fiction and Nonfiction on the War

ANCHOR BOOKS
DOUBLEDAY
New York   London   Toronto
Sydney   Auckland

The

Vietnam

Reader

Edited by
STEWART O'NAN

AN ANCHOR BOOK
PUBLISHED BY DOUBLEDAY
a division of Bantam Doubleday Dell Publishing Group, Inc.
1540 Broadway, New York, New York 10036

ANCHOR BOOKS, DOUBLEDAY, and the portrayal of an anchor are
trademarks of Doubleday, a division of Bantam Doubleday Dell
Publishing Group, Inc.

The editor would like to thank the contributors for their work and their invaluable help
in tracking down other contributors. I'd also like to thank David Gernert for selling this
book; Bruce Tracy for buying it; Peternelle van Arsdale for her editing; Siobhan Adcock
for her forbearance and Matt Williams for his; and, for her endless legwork and indefat-
igable cheer in the face of rejection, Amy Williams.

Library of Congress Cataloging-in-Publication Data

The Vietnam reader: the definitive collection of American fiction and
nonfiction on the war / Edited by Stewart O'Nan.
p.   cm.
Includes bibliographical references (p.   ) and index.
1. Vietnamese Conflict, 1961–1975. 2. Vietnamese Conflict,
1961–1975—Personal narratives, American. 3. Vietnamese Conflict,
1961–1975—Literature and the conflict. 4. Vietnamese Conflict,
1961–1975—Motion pictures and the conflict. 5. American
literature—20th century. I. O'Nan, Stewart, 1961–   .
DS557.7.V5625   1998
959.704′3—dc21   98-15575
CIP

ISBN 0-385-49118-2

3 5 7 9 10 8 6 4 2

Contents

13 · THE WALL · 675

The Vietnam Reader

June 1963. To protest South Vietnamese President Diem's anti-Buddhist policies, a monk immolates himself in the middle of a busy Saigon street.

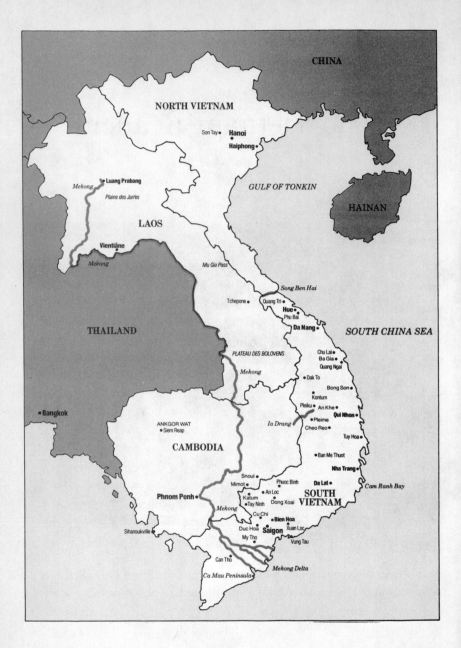

Introduction

A few years ago when I began teaching the American literature of the Vietnam War, I tried to find an anthology my students could use—a book that collected all the major work in one place. This didn't seem far-fetched; the war had been over for twenty years, and thousands of books had been written about it. But as I searched through libraries and catalogues, new- and used-book shops, I discovered there wasn't one.

Yes, there were anthologies, but most were out of print and none put together all the pieces I considered essential. Some were fitted together like polemics, others relied too heavily on dull reportage. There were solid poetry anthologies, most notably W. D. Ehrhart's *Carrying the Darkness*, but few books had tried to collect everything— the fiction, the oral histories, the memoirs, the films, the photos—and those that did inevitably had gaps. Imagine a comprehensive Vietnam anthology without the work of Michael Herr or Tim O'Brien or Larry Heinemann, without a healthy sampling of the oral histories, without a single mention of *Platoon*, without Ronald Haeberle's famous picture of the ditch at My Lai.

Instead of ordering a single volume and sending my students to the campus store, I began digging through the individual novels and poetry collections, poring over the photographic essays, watching the films, taking notes, making photocopies. I haunted the used-book stores for sadly out-of-print work, borrowed books from colleagues, sat in the stacks of libraries. What I finally came up with was a course packet weighing in at around six pounds, the permissions for which were impossible to secure in time for the semester.

While I've cut a great deal from that original manuscript, this book remains true to its core. I believe I've chosen and hunted down the elusive permissions for the best and best known works about the war, selections that will give the reader both an essential overview and a deep understanding of how America has seen its time in Vietnam over the past thirty years.

Any Vietnam anthology should bring its reader closer to the war, and in teaching my course I found that one way to accomplish that, beyond presenting students with the usual literature, was to include such powerful and immediate material as photographs, films, and popular songs. They bring the war home inescapably, in the same way they inflamed and informed the public when they first appeared. It's one thing to tell a class that the average age of the combat soldier in Vietnam was nineteen, another to show them a roomful of recruits no older than themselves. By examining the films and songs, my students gained a deeper appreciation for how the war, and its representation, has always been debated in a charged, extremely public forum, and how that debate has changed over the years. As with the literary selections, the photos, songs, and films I've chosen to include are the best and best known, some, like Haeberle's shot of My Lai, practically iconic at this point.

The Vietnam Reader is organized according to two chronological schemes. The first is the typical arc of the Vietnam narrative and traces the tour of duty from induction all the way through returning stateside. The second scheme is the timeframe during which these books and films were released. In certain chapters (such as the popular songs) I found it did more justice to the material to collect works that span a great deal of time but are similar in either theme or genre, thereby illustrating how trends in representing Vietnam echoed the changes in American popular and political culture. This combination of approaches is intended to give the reader a better sense of how both the soldiers' and the public's attitudes toward Vietnam have changed as the years pass.

An important point to keep in mind is that this anthology isn't concerned with the Vietnamese or French points of view, which have produced an equal if not greater number of insightful and important works. Instead, this volume is restricted to American views of the war. One remarkable aspect of America's involvement is that its literature focuses almost solely on the war's effect on the American soldier and American culture at large. In work after work, Vietnam and the Vietnamese are merely a backdrop for the drama of America confronting itself. To balance American views with others' here—in retrospect—would be to rewrite history and to present a false portrait of America's true concerns.

A number of themes run through these works or can be read into them, the most obvious the representation of the American soldier, since he (most decidedly he) is usually the main character. In Vietnam literature, even more so than in the literature of previous American wars, the hero is the combat infantryman, whether he's regular Army, Special Forces, or a Marine; there are few pieces concerned with Navy or Air Force personnel, and only a smattering deal with support troops. The soldier and later the vet are often given to the reader as types, if not stereotypes already familiar to the casual reader or viewer. Here's a brief list: professional warrior, reluctant draftee, terrified new guy, hardened grunt, psycho killer/psycho vet, deluded lifer, bumbling ROTC lieutenant, disabled protest vet, troubled/addicted vet. Of course these end up being reductive if not outright slanderous clichés, but the reader will recognize variations on all these characters throughout this book and should be aware of them, and also of who on that list is eligible to play the American hero, and why.

Another major concern in these works is their view of the American presence in Vietnam—that is, the question that tortured all of America back then and still troubles some now: Was the war right or wrong? And was the American presence simply an extension of the American character, and not an anomaly? That is, can (should) the war be related to the larger cultural forces that produced it? Most of these works comment overtly on these questions, though some operate more subtly. Every author (filmmaker, photographer, songwriter) has his or her view of the war, and it's rare when that view doesn't surface in the work. The stances of some—say, Ron Kovic in *Born on the Fourth of July*—are unequivocally critical of U.S. involvement, while an alternative viewpoint can be found in the way James Webb's *Fields of Fire* passes judgment on those who opposed the war. What, the reader should ask at this point, is the relationship between subjectivity and war literature? How can the author's politics *not* influence his or her depiction of the war? Does this extend beyond the political to the personal—that is, the emotional relationship the author has with his or her experience, especially if it's traumatic? This takes us back to the basic philosophical question of what is true and how we as readers can tell. It's a sticky question, especially since the final authority for portraying this war—unlike any other American war—has been by default ceded to the individual participants. Instead of a monolithic history of the war, a mural painted by seemingly trustworthy official historians, what Americans have to sort through is an infinite number of puzzle pieces, few of which seem to fit, and some of which seem to be negatives of each other.

How the author or character perceives the military is a constant theme, as is the culpability of the government with respect to the war, the military, and the individual soldier. Questions of truth and responsibility often take the form of a struggle between private thought and public speech, usually in the form of lies, silence, or a tacit acceptance of the unacceptable. Several pieces highlight the use and misuse of language, whether by the media, the government, or the troops themselves. Matters of race and gender as well as class pop up in these accounts, often as a consequence of the soldier or civilian questioning his or her position not merely in the war but in American society. The fact that the war is being debated back in America is inescapable for soldiers in Vietnam, and returning vets quickly realize that the country has changed as drastically as they have. The Vietnam era witnessed the most sweeping and rapid social change in American history, and naturally the writings and films reflect the flashpoints of the culture. The only thing missing, it seems, is the Vietnamese.

On a more literary level, academic critics find the different forms and styles used by Vietnam writers interesting, most championing more technically adventurous work and decrying realism as plodding and incapable of getting the true feel of the war. General audiences, on the other hand, tend to prize the documentary, wanting to trust in the authenticity of what they're being shown. Other critics question various authors' use of the *bildungsroman* form, wondering whether the tour of duty can be so neatly squeezed into the German learning-novel, the youth's positive movement from innocence to experience. Some have even labeled the typical Vietnam narrative an anti-*bildungsroman*, wherein the lesson learned is destructive and leads not to wisdom but confusion. Others denounce the very process by which a chaotic, often formless experience is presented by the artist in formal dramatic terms; these critics look for new styles and forms springing organically from the war, not the tired formula fiction and films of the World War II era.

How America sees and has seen Vietnam across time depends on a number of volatile, not always reliable factors such as the overall political climate and the individual reader or viewer's politics—and in some cases personal relationship to the war. Above and beyond these concerns is the very basic proposition, put forth endlessly by veterans and civilians alike, that you can't know what it was like if you weren't there. Add the difficulty of relating the chaos of war through a struc-tured form (the plotted novel or conventional drama), and it seems impossible that the reader could understand the experience.

This is what I call the "gap" between veterans and civilians, even civilians who were there (Michael Herr has some interesting things to say about this in *Dispatches*), and we see it crop up repeatedly in these selections. Civilians don't or won't understand; veterans shut them-selves off or refuse to talk because they feel distant, different. Much of the drama in these accounts of the war and its aftermath—and cer-tainly much of the despair—comes from a self-conscious recognition of the gap. How America sees the veteran and how the veteran sees America are views, as it were, from the opposite sides of the gap.

Part of the gap has to do with the elusive nature of truth. In a war smothered in lies, silence, and misinformation (even now, well after the fact), how does a writer or screenwriter claim to be the bearer of truth? In American Vietnam literature, as perhaps nowhere else, it often seems the author's authority comes not from his or her work but simply from being there, with the strange corollary that nonfiction's spurious claim to the status of objectivity is extended to fiction written by veterans. The latter is particularly an issue given the pronounced split in methods or modes of portraying the war. While some authors choose a documentary realism, others, hoping to come closer to the emotional and intellectual effect of the experience, shoot for a more poetic or metaphorical truth, employing wild satire (Stephen Wright), magical realism (Larry Heinemann), or absurd allegory (David Rabe). When an author purposefully mixes real and metaphorical forms, the result can leave the reader with more questions than answers. As readers will see from Tim O'Brien's great metafiction "How to Tell a True War Story" and Michael Cimino's *The Deer Hunter*, this can be a valuable thing.

So how, against these odds, does the artist bridge the gap, send his or her work sparking across it so readers and viewers feel that, briefly, they understand what it must have truly been like in Vietnam? One provocative answer is that the Vietnam artist does it the same way any artist does it, using point of view, concrete detail, and the power of language and image, sound and vision—all of the artist's sharpest tools—to transport the reader or viewer there. Another answer is that it's impossible. Regardless, year after year, American artists—vets and otherwise—try. This book is a testament to how well they've done.

Chronology of the War

2nd Century B.C. The Chinese conquer Vietnam.

939 Vietnam expels the occupying Chinese armies.

1500s French missionaries and traders arrive.

1857 Unable to gain trade concessions, the French attack Da Nang.

1867 The French officially make Southern Vietnam (Cochin China) their colony.

1883 The French capture Hanoi and divide the North into two regions, Annam and Tonkin.

1890 Birth of Ho Chi Minh.

1919 Vietnamese living in Paris try to meet with Woodrow Wilson at Versailles to discuss independence. They're turned away.

1940 Japan occupies Vietnam but lets French rule continue.

1945 The Japanese surrender Saigon to British troops; Ho Chi Minh declares Vietnamese independence, but the British impose martial law and return power to the French.

1946 The Viet Minh attack the French, beginning the Indochina War.

1950 The United States sends the French mission economic and military aid.

1954 The French surrender at Dien Bien Phu leads to the Geneva Accords, by which Vietnam is partitioned along the 17th Parallel.

1959 A communist attack on Bien Hoa kills two U.S. military advisers.

1961 President Kennedy sends Green Berets and military advisers to train South Vietnamese troops.

1963 A coup overthrows Vietnamese President Diem with tacit U.S. approval. Diem is assassinated. Less than a month later, JFK is assassinated.

1964 North Vietnamese torpedo boats allegedly attack two U.S. warships. Congress passes the Tonkin Gulf resolution, giving the military the means of protecting itself from Vietnamese aggression.

February 1965 Operation Rolling Thunder. The United States begins sustained aerial bombing of the North.

March 1965 First battalion of U.S. ground troops arrives at Da Nang.

October 1965 The Ia Drang Valley. First major battle between U.S. and Northern forces.

January–February 1968 The Tet Offensive, a massive countrywide attack by Viet Cong forces. While a crushing defeat for the VC, it turned American public opinion against the war. Though the Marines weathered the seventy-seven-day siege of Khe Sanh, it was perceived by the media and the public as a defeat.

March 1968 My Lai. Lt. William Calley and his troops murder an entire South Vietnamese village, killing hundreds.

March 1968 President Johnson announces he will not seek reelection.

May 1968 First formal peace talks.

October 1968 LBJ stops the bombing of the North.

March 1969 President Nixon authorizes the secret, illegal bombing of Cambodia.

June 1969 First U.S. troop withdrawals.

September 1969 Ho Chi Minh dies.

May 1970 In the United States, students stage massive protests against the bombing of Cambodia. National Guardsmen kill four demonstrators at Kent State University.

1970–71 Troop withdrawals continue.

January 1972 Nixon announces that his national security adviser, Henry Kissinger, has been conducting secret peace talks since 1969.

March–April 1972 The Easter Offensive. Northern forces attack bases in the South.

August 1972 Last American ground troops leave Vietnam.

November 1972 Nixon reelected.

April–December 1972 Major bombing of the North.

January 1973 Peace treaty reached. Cease-fire begins.

January 1974 The war between the North and South resumes without U.S. intervention.

April 1975 Saigon falls. U.S. trade embargo imposed. In neighboring Cambodia, Phnom Penh falls to Communist rebels.

January 1977 President Carter grants amnesty to draft evaders.

1977 The Khmer Rouge, the new rulers of Cambodia, attack the Vietnamese border.

1978 Vietnam invades Cambodia.

1979 Vietnam defeats the Khmer Rouge, installs a friendly government in Phnom Penh. China invades northern Vietnam but is repelled.

1982 Dedication of the Vietnam Veterans Memorial in Washington, D.C.

1989 Last Vietnamese troops withdraw from Cambodia.

1994 President Clinton lifts trade embargo on Vietnam.

1

Green

At an induction center, draftees join the U.S. Army.

These three pieces are meant to introduce the reader to the portrayal of the American soldier in Vietnam across time. Robin Moore's *The Green Berets* appeared early in America's involvement and cleaves to the government's line; the soldiers are exemplary—strong, smart and heroic. O'Brien's *If I Die in a Combat Zone* saw publication in the last year of the war, and reflects the confusion and idealism of that era. Appearing in the late seventies, O'Brien's *Going After Cacciato* is more playful in its humor but equally damning. All three revolve around the soldier as hero and how he feels about the war.

Like the green recruit, the reader has to make sense of these conflicting views of Vietnam, learn the language, be careful of whom and what to trust. The various attitudes the authors, narrators, and characters take toward the war and how it's being fought in these pieces seemingly can't be reconciled. Likewise, precisely what constitutes a hero, a man, or a rational response is debatable. In their tone and focus, in their portrayal of Americans and Vietnamese, even in their charged descriptions of the settings, Moore and O'Brien appear to be covering completely different wars.

Robin Moore's *The Green Berets* caused a sensation when it was first published in 1965. As he states in his preface, Moore, a free-lance journalist, wanted to write a nonfiction account of the U.S. Special Forces, but did such a good job of getting close to his subject that he suddenly knew too much sensitive information—so much that the

Pentagon asked for a look at the manuscript and then told Crown, his publisher, that they couldn't release the book as it was. Moore agreed to change facts and call the book a fiction (it's not technically a novel, more a collection of related pieces). The effect of the Pentagon's interference (and tacit admission that Moore knew the real truth) on the book's sales is impossible to gauge, but the hardcover was licensed by the Book of the Month Club, and the paperback climbed the bestseller list. "The Ballad of the Green Berets," a song inspired by the book and cowritten by Moore, shot to the top of the charts. In a neat tie-in, paperbacks from 1966 bear the face of the song's co-author and singer, Sergeant Barry Sadler.

Later, John Wayne bought the movie rights to *The Green Berets* and directed and starred in the film version. Paradoxically, Lyndon Johnson's administration directed the Army to give Wayne whatever technical support he needed, and they did. The resulting film (1968), which Gustav Hasford ridicules in *The Short-Timers* (1979), does in fact contain a scene in which the sun sets in the east. The movie was a tremendous flop, not because Wayne was so out of vogue but because in the three years since the book had come out, mainstream American attitudes toward the war had changed.

Tim O'Brien's *If I Die in a Combat Zone* (1973) is nonfiction. O'Brien served as an infantryman in the Army's Americal Division in 1970–71, and his book impressionistically describes his tour of duty from when he receives his induction notice until he returns home. Sections read like fiction, however, due to O'Brien's novelistic technique; later he would become an acclaimed literary novelist, and some reprints of *If I Die* are actually mislabeled and shelved as fiction. The book was well received by critics; it was widely hailed as the best of the first prose efforts by veterans to describe the GI's life in Vietnam. The piece included in this section details O'Brien's indecisiveness in the face of his induction, a subject he addressed again nearly twenty years later in the award-winning short story "On the Rainy River" in *The Things They Carried.*

In 1978, O'Brien's second novel, *Going After Cacciato*, established him as a major American writer. The book is a heavily sectioned metafiction. One narrative line follows Paul Berlin (a riff on Paul

Baumer from *All Quiet on the Western Front*, and also a reference to the Allies' final destination in World War II) and his squadmates as they chase a fellow grunt, Cacciato, across Asia and Europe. Cacciato (in Italian, the hunter or hunted) has quit the war and is walking to Paris. A second narrative line recounts the everyday boredom and terror of the war. The time scheme is jumbled (the war scenes jumping all over the place, the road to Paris linear), and the storylines speak to each other metaphorically without becoming obvious or heavy-handed. The two narratives are mediated by sections in which Paul Berlin is keeping a lonely watch in a tower; he may be dreaming the Cacciato story to temporarily escape the present. The novel is at once frightening and hilarious, as O'Brien leavens the tragedy of the war with zany plot twists and slapstick humor. Critics were amazed by his mix of the real and the fantastic and gave *Going After Cacciato* the National Book Award. The section that appears here shows Paul Berlin during his first few days in-country. It's typical O'Brien, a combination of realism and telling metaphor.

The Green Berets

ROBIN MOORE

1965

The Green Berets is a book of truth. I planned and researched it originally to be an account presenting, through a series of actual incidents, an inside informed view of the almost unknown marvelous undercover work of our Special Forces in Vietnam and countries around the world. It was to be a factual book based on personal experience, firsthand knowledge and observation, naming persons and places. But it turned out that there were major obstacles and disadvantages in this straight reportorial method. And so, for the variety of reasons mentioned below, I decided I could present the truth better and more accurately in the form of fiction.

You will find in these pages many things that you will find hard to believe. Believe them. They happened this way. I changed details and names, but I did not change the basic truth. I could not tell the basic truth without changing the details and the names. Here's why.

Many of the stories incorporate a number of events which if reported merely in isolation would fail to give the full meaning and background of the war in Vietnam. Saigon's elite press corps, and such excellent feature writers as Jim Lucas of Scripps-Howard, Jack Langguth of *The New York Times*, and Dickey Chappell of *The Reader's Digest* have reported the detailed incidents in the war. I felt that my job in this book was to give the broad overall picture of how Special Forces men operate, so each story basically is representative of a different facet of Special Forces action in wars like the one in Vietnam.

Also, as will be seen, Special Forces operations are, at times, highly unconventional. To report such occurrences factually, giving names, dates, and locations, could only embarrass U.S. planners in Vietnam and might even jeopardize the careers of invaluable officers. Time and again, I promised harried and heroic Special Forces men that their confidences were "off the record." To show the kind of men they are, to present an honest, comprehensive, and informed picture of their activities, one must get to know them as no writer could who was bound to report exactly what he saw and heard.

Moreover, I was in the unique—and enviable—position of having official aid and assistance without being bound by official restrictions. Even though I always made it clear I was in Vietnam in an unofficial capacity, under these auspices much was shown and told to me. I did not want to pull punches; at the same time I felt it wasn't right to abuse those special privileges and confidences by doing a straight reporting job.

The civic action portion of Special Forces operations can and should be reported factually. However, this book is more concerned with special missions, and I saw too many things that weren't for my eyes—or any eyes other than the participants' themselves—and assisted in too much imaginative circumvention of constricting ground rules merely to report what I saw under a thin disguise. The same blend of fact and "fiction" will be found in the locations in the book, many of which can be found on any map, while others are purely the author's invention.

So for these reasons *The Green Berets* is presented as a work of fiction.

1

THE GREEN BERET—ALL THE WAY

The headquarters of Special Forces Detachment B-520 in one of Vietnam's most active war zones looks exactly like a fort out of the old West. Although the B detachments are strictly support and administrative units for the Special Forces A teams fighting the Communist Viet Cong guerrillas in the jungles and rice paddies, this headquarters had been attacked twice in the last year by Viet Cong and both times had sustained casualties.

I was finally keeping my promise to visit the headquarters of Major (since his arrival in Vietnam, Lieutenant Colonel) Train. I deposited my combat pack in the orderly room and strode through the open door into the CO's office.

"Congratulations, Colonel."

Lieutenant Colonel Train, looking both youthful and weathered, smiled self-assuredly, blew a long stream of cigar smoke across his desk, and motioned for me to sit down.

Major Fenz, the operations officer, walked into the office abruptly. "Sorry to interrupt, sir. We just received word that another patrol out of Phan Chau ran into an ambush. We lost four friendlies KIA."

I sat up straight. "Old Kornie is getting himself some action."

Train frowned thoughtfully. "Third time in a week he's taken casualties." He drummed his fingertips on the top of his desk. "Any enemy KIA, or captured weapons?"

"No weapons captured. They think they killed several VC from blood found on the foliage. No bodies."

"I worry about Kornie," Train said, with a trace of petulance. "He's somehow managed to get two Vietnamese camp commanders relieved in the four months he's been here. The new one is just what he wants, pliable. Kornie runs the camp as he pleases."

"Kornie has killed more VC than any other A team in the three weeks since we've taken over here," Fenz pointed out.

"Kornie is too damned independent and unorthodox," Train said.

"That's what they taught us at Bragg, Colonel," I put in. "Or did I spend three months misunderstanding the message?"

"There are limits. I don't agree with all the School teaches."

"By the way, Colonel," I said before we could disagree openly, "one reason I came down here was to get out to Phan Chau and watch Kornie in action."

Train stared at me a moment. Then he said, "Let's have a cup of coffee. Join us, Fenz?"

We walked out of the administration offices, across the parade ground and volleyball court of the B-team headquarters, and entered the club which served as morning coffeehouse, reading and relaxing room, and evening bar. Train called to the pretty Vietnamese waitress to bring us coffee.

There were a number of Special Forces officers and sergeants lounging around. It was to the B team that the A-team field men came on their way to a rest and rehabilitation leave in Saigon. Later they returned to the B team to await flights back to their A teams deep in Viet Cong territory.

Lieutenant Colonel Train had been an enigma to me ever since I first met him as a major taking the guerrilla course at Fort Bragg. His background was Regular Army. In World War II he had seen two years of combat duty in the Infantry, rising to the rank of staff sergeant when the war ended. Since his high-school record had been outstanding and his Army service flawless, he received an appointment to West Point. From the Point to Japan to Korea, Train had served with distinction as an Infantry officer, and in 1954 he applied for jump school at Fort Benning and became a paratrooper.

Almost nine years later, in line with Train's interest in new developments, he had indicated that he would accept an assignment with Special Forces. I met him at Fort Bragg just after he had moved down Gruber Avenue from the 82nd Airborne Division to Smoke Bomb Hill, the Special Warfare Center.

It was obvious to those close to Train that he did not accept wholeheartedly the doctrines of unconventional warfare. But President Kennedy's awareness of the importance of this facet of the military had made unconventional or special warfare experience a must for any officer who wanted to advance to top echelons.

As Train and I chatted and drank our coffee my interest grew in whether this dedicated officer was going to change and how he would operate in the guerrilla war in Vietnam.

"So you want to go to Phan Chau?" Train asked.

"I'd like to see Kornie in action," I said. "Remember him at Bragg? He was the guerrilla chief in the big maneuvers."

"Kornie has been one of the Army's characters for ten years," Train said sternly. "Of course I remember him. I'm afraid you'll get yourself in trouble if you go to Phan Chau."

"What do you mean by trouble?"

"I don't want the first civilian writer killed in Vietnam to get it with my command."

As I expected, Train was going to be a problem. "You think I stand a better chance of cashing in with Kornie than with some of the other A teams?"

Train took a long sip of coffee before answering. "He does damned dangerous things. I don't think he reports everything he does even to me."

"You've been here for three weeks, Colonel. The last B team had him four months. What did Major Grunner say about him?"

Fenz, a Special Forces officer for six years, concentrated on his coffee. Train gave me a wry smile. "The last B team was pretty unorthodox even by Special Forces standards. Major Grunner is a fine officer; I'm not saying anything against him or the way he operated this B detachment." Train looked at me steadily. "But he let his A teams do things I won't permit. And of course he and Kornie were old friends from the 10th Special Forces Group in Germany." Train shook his head. "And that's the wildest-thinking bunch I ever came across in my military career."

Neither Fenz nor I made any reply. We sipped our coffee in silence. Train was one of the new breed of Special Forces officers. Unconventional warfare specialists had proven their ability to cope with the burgeoning Communist brand of limited or guerrilla wars so conclusively that Special Forces had been authorized an increase in strength. Several new groups were being added to the old 1st in Okinawa, 10th in Bad Tölz, Germany, and the 5th and 7th at Fort Bragg.

New officers were picked from among the most outstanding men in airborne and conventional units. Since every Special Forces officer and enlisted man is a paratrooper, it was occasionally necessary to send some "straight-leg" officers to jump school at Fort Benning, Georgia, before they could attend the Special Warfare School at Fort Bragg prior to being assigned to a Special Forces group.

This new group of basically conventional officers in Special Forces were already beginning to make their influence felt early in 1964. Lieutenant Colonel Train was clearly going to be a hard man to develop into a "Green Beret—All the Way!"

I broke the silence, directing a question at Major Fenz. "When can you get me out to Phan Chau?"

Fenz looked to Train for guidance. Train smiled at me wryly. "We've got to let you go if you want to. But do us all a favor, will you? Don't get yourself killed. I thought you'd had it on the night jump in Uwarrie . . ."

He turned to Fenz and told him the story. "They dropped our teams together on the ten-day field training exercise."

Fenz nodded; the ten-day field training exercise was a bond shared by all Special Warfare School graduates.

"The School picked us a drop zone in Uwarrie National Forest near Pisgah—that was something else. It was a terrible night," Train recalled. "Cold. And the wind came up before we reached the DZ. An equipment bundle got stuck in the door for six seconds so we had to make two passes. Our friend here was held at the door by the jump master and was first man out on the second pass. We were blown into the trees over a mile from the DZ. I got hung up, had to open my emergency chute and climb down the shroud lines to get on the ground. We had three broken legs and several other injuries on that DZ."

Train looked at me and smiled. "Our civilian, of course, came out best. Landed in a field the size of the volleyball court, threw his air items in the bag and helped pull his team together."

I looked out the window across the rice paddies where every peasant could be and probably was a Viet Cong. "At least they didn't have shit-dipped pungi stakes waiting for us in North Carolina," I said.

Train frowned briefly at my language. "I guess you and Kornie will get along fine, at that. As I remember, you pulled a few tricks on that exercise that weren't even in the books."

Fenz took this as his cue to volunteer the information that there was an Otter flying down to Phan Chau that afternoon with an interpreter to replace the one killed a few days before on patrol.

"You might as well take it," Train said. "How long do you want to stay?"

"Can't I just play it by ear, Colonel?"

"Certainly. If it looks like there's going to be serious trouble I'll get you evacuated."

"Negative! Please?"

Train stared at me; I met the look. Train gave a shrug. "OK, I'll go along with you, but I still don't—"

"No sweat. I don't want to get myself greased any more than you do."

"OK, get your gear together. Got your own weapon?"

"If you could lend me a folding-stock carbine and a few banana clips, that's all I need."

"Fenz, can you fix him up?"

"Yes, sir. The Otter takes off at 1300 hours."

"One thing," Train cautioned. "Kornie is upset because we transferred two companies of Hoa Hao troops from his camp on orders from the Vietnamese division commander, General Co. You know about the Hoa Hao?"

"They're supposed to be fierce fighters, aren't they?"

"That's right. They're a religious sect in the Mekong Delta with slightly different ethnic origins from the Vietnamese. General Co didn't like having two companies of Hoa Hao fighting together."

"You mean with coup fever raging, he was afraid the Hoa Hao might get together and make a deal with one of his rival generals?"

"We try to keep out of politics," Train said testily. "General Co's reasoning is not my concern."

"But it would concern Kornie to find himself on the Cambodian border in the middle of VC territory suddenly minus two companies of his best fighting men."

Train snorted in exasperation. "Just don't take Kornie's opinions on Vietnamese politics too seriously."

"I'll use discretion in anything I say," I promised.

"I hope so." It sounded like a threat.

Looking down at the sere-brown rice paddies, I felt a sense of quickening excitement as the little eight-place single-engine plane closed on Phan Chau in a hilly section along the Cambodian border. Across from me sat the thin, ascetic-looking young Vietnamese interpreter.

I thought of Steve Kornie. His first name was Sven actually. He was, at forty-four, a captain, as compared to Train, who was a lieutenant colonel at thirty-nine.

Kornie, originally a Finn, fought the Russians when they invaded his native land. Later he had joined the German Army and miraculously survived two years of fighting the Russians on the eastern front. After the war came a period in his life he never talked about. His career was re-entered on the record book when, under the Lodge Act of the early fifties, which permitted foreign nationals who joined in the United States Army in Europe to become eligible for U.S. citizenship after five years service, Kornie enlisted.

In a barroom brawl in Germany in 1955, Kornie and some of his more obstreperous GI companions had committed the usually disastrous error of tangling with several soldiers wearing green berets with silver Trojan horse insignias on them. The blue-eyed Nordic giant, after decking twice his weight in berets, finally agreed to a truce.

Suspiciously he allowed these soldiers, who in spite of their alien headdress proclaimed themselves Americans, to buy him a drink. In his career with several armies he had never fought such tough bare-handed fighters. As the several victims of Kornie's fists and flathanded chops came to, shook their heads, found their berets and replaced them on their heads, it became clear to Kornie that they were asking him to join their group. To his surprise and horror he discovered that one man he had knocked over the bar was a major.

Before the evening was over Kornie discovered the existence of the 10th Special Forces Group at Bad Tölz, had given the major his name, rank and serial number, and had been promised that he would soon be transferred to the elite, highly trained, virtually secret unit of the U.S. Army to which these men in green berets so proudly belonged.

When Special Forces realized the extent of Sven Kornie's combat experience and language capabilities, the commanding officer at Bad Tölz believed his claim that he had gone to the military college for almost three years in Finland, although his academic records had been lost in the war and he could not prove his educational qualifications. Kornie was sent to Officer Candidate School, and Special Forces was waiting to reclaim him immediately upon graduation. He performed many covert as well as overt missions in Europe as a Special Forces officer, several times on loan to the CIA, and finally, having reached the grade of captain, he was shipped to the 5th Special Forces Group at the Special Warfare Center, Fort Bragg.

In his early forties he knew his chances of ever making field grade were slim. For one thing, while in uniform he had killed a German civilian he knew to be a Russian agent with a single punch. Extenuating circumstances had won him an acquittal at his court-martial; nevertheless the affair was distasteful, particularly to conservative old line officers on promotion boards. There was also Kornie's inability to prove any higher education.

Sven Kornie was the ideal Special Forces officer. Special Forces was his life; fighting, especially unorthodox warfare, was what he lived for. He had no career to sacrifice; he had no desire to rise from operational to supervisory levels. And not the least of his assets, he was unmarried and had no attachments to anyone or anything in the world beyond Special Forces.

My thoughts of Kornie and speculations as to what fascinating mischief he would be up to were interrupted by the interpreter.

"Are you posted to Phan Chau?"

I shook my head, but he had an explanation coming. I wore the complete Special Forces uniform, the lightweight jungle fatigues and my highly prized green beret which an A team had given me after a combat mission.

"I will visit Phan Chau for maybe a week. I am a writer. A journalist. You understand?"

The interpreter's face lit up. "Ah, journalist. Yes. What journal you write for?" Hopefully: *"Time* magazine? Maybe *Newsweek? Life?"*

He couldn't disguise his disappointment when he learned what a free-lance writer was.

We were getting close to Phan Chau. I recognized the area from several parachute supply drops I had flown to familiarize myself with the terrain.

The little Otter began circling. Only a few miles off I could look into Cambodia, the border running down the middle of the rough, rocky terrain. A dirt landing-strip appeared below and in moments the plane was bumping along it.

I threw my combat pack out on the ground, and when the small plane had come to a complete stop jumped out after it. I saw a green beret among the camouflage-capped Vietnamese strike-force troopers milling around, and went up to the American sergeant and told him who I was. He recognized my name and mission, but I was surprised to hear Kornie wasn't expecting me.

"Sometimes we can't read the B team for half a day," the sergeant explained. "The old man will be glad to see you. He's been wondering when you were coming."

"I guess I missed some action this morning."

"Yeah, it was a tough one. Four strikers KIA. We usually don't get ambushed so close to camp." The sergeant introduced himself to me

as Borst, the radio operator. He was a well-set young man, his cropped
hair below the green beret yellow, and his blue eyes fierce. I wondered if Kornie had collected an all-Viking A team. Anything unusual,
with flair and color, would be typical Kornie.

"The old man is working out some big deal with Sergeant
Bergholtz, he's our team sergeant, and Sergeant Falk, intelligence."

"Where's Lieutenant Schmelzer?" I asked. "I knew him at Bragg
last year while you were all in mission training."

"He's still out with the patrol that was ambushed. They sent back
the bodies and the wounded, and then kept going."

Sergeant Borst picked up my combat pack, carried it to the truck,
and threw it in back with the strikers and the new interpreter. He
motioned me into the front seat, looked behind to make sure the
mounted .30-caliber machine gun was manned, and drove off as soon
as the Otter was airborne.

The low, white buildings with dark roofs which rose above the mud
walls of Phan Chau, and the tall steel fire-control tower were visible
from the airstrip. Beyond them, directly west, loomed the rocky foothills which spilled along both sides of the Vietnam-Cambodia border.
There were more hills and a scrub-brush jungle north of Phan Chau.
To the south the land was open and bare. The airstrip was only a mile
east of the camp.

"This the new camp?"

"Yes, sir," Borst answered. "The old one next to the town of Phan
Chau was something else. Hills on all sides. We called it little Dien
Bien Phu. Here at least we've got some open fields of fire and the VC
can't drop mortar fire on us from above."

"From what I hear, you're out of that old French camp just in
time."

"That's what I figure. They'd clobber us in there. When this one is
finished we'll be able to hold off about anything they can throw at us."

As we drove into the square fort, with sandbagged mud walls studded with machine-gun emplacements and surrounded with barbed
wire, I could see men working on the walls and putting out more
barbed wire. "Do you still have much work to do?"

"Quite a bit, sir. We're sure hoping we don't get hit in the next few days. The camp isn't secure yet."

Borst stopped before the Vietnamese Special Forces headquarters to let off the strikers and the new interpreter, and then drove me another twenty feet to a cement-block building with a wooden roof. He pulled to a stop and jumped out. Borst beat me inside and I heard him announce me.

It took a moment for my eyes to get used to the cool interior grayness after the hot, bright sunlight. The big form of Sven Kornie came toward me. He had a large grin on his lean, pleasant face and his blue eyes snapped. His huge hand enveloped mine as he welcomed me to Phan Chau. He introduced me to Sergeant Bergholtz, and I sensed my guess was correct that a Germanic-Viking crew had indeed been transported intact to the Vietnam-Cambodia border.

"Well, well," Kornie boomed cheerfully. "You come here at a dangerous time."

"What's happening?"

"By God damn! Those Vietnamese generals—stupid! Dangerous stupid. Two hundred fifty my best men that sneak-eyed yellow-skin bastard corps commander take out of here yesterday—and our big American generals? Politics they play while this camp gets zapped."

"What are you talking about, Steve?"

"Two hundred fifty Hoa Hao fighting men I had. The best. Now General Co decides he don't want any Hoa Hao companies fighting together because maybe they get together under their colonel and pull another coup. So he breaks up the best fighting units in the Mekong Delta. God damn fool! And Phan Chau, what happens? We get more Vietnamese strikers we don't know if they fight for us or VC. You better go back to the B team," he finished lugubriously.

"Too late now," I said. "What action have you got going?"

"Two actions. The VC got one action and we got one. Tell him, Bergholtz."

The team sergeant began his briefing. "The VC have been making ladders for a couple of weeks now in all their villages. They're also making caskets. That means they figure on hitting us sometime soon. The ladders they use to throw across the barbed wire and the mine fields and later as stretchers to carry away the dead and wounded. The VC fight better when they know they're going to get a funeral and a nice wood box if they're killed. They see the coffins, it makes their morale go up."

"We are not ready for attack," Kornie said, "so it probably comes soon."

"What's Schmelzer's patrol doing?"

Kornie's deep laugh boomed out. "Schmelzer is looking for KKK."

"KKK? I thought we were in South Vietnam, not South Carolina."

"The KKK are Cambodian bandits. They fight only for money. They are very bad boys. Tell him, Bergholtz."

"Yes, sir." The team sergeant turned his rugged face to me. "The KKK—that's what everyone calls them—live around these hills. They even attack our patrols for the weapons if they are strong enough. We figure the ambush today may have been KKK. Last week four Buddhist monks went through here to Cambodia to buy gold leaf for their temple. All the local Buddhists kicked in to buy the stuff. You can't buy gold in Vietnam." Bergholtz paused. "We told the monks they better stay home but they said Buddha would protect them."

Kornie finished the story. "Three days ago I was leading a patrol in KKK area. We find the monks. They are lying on the trail, each has his head under his left arm. The KKK got them and their gold."

"And Schmelzer is going to get the KKK?" I asked.

"He is only trying to locate them. Maybe they will be useful to us on the operation we plan."

I gave him full attention, unslinging my carbine and leaning it against the wall.

"We get tired of the VC hitting us and running across the border to Cambodia where we can't get them," Kornie said. "This team of mine, we got only one month left before we go back to Fort Bragg. Garrison duty." Kornie growled. "Two cowardly Vietnamese camp commanders in a row we get. Sometimes is a week between good VC contact."

"But this time I hear you have a good counterpart."

"This one *is* good," Kornie conceded. "He maybe don't like patrols himself, but if the Americans want to kill themselves and only a rea-

sonable number of strikers, that's our business by him. Come, follow
me. I will show you what we are going to do." He led me out of the
teamhouse, down the mud road and on past several cement barracks
with wood and thatch roofs. We stopped at one and a guard saluted.
His dark skin and imprecise features marked the striker in tiger-stripe
camouflage as a Cambodian. Kornie returned the salute and walked
inside. There must have been about 50 men in the barracks. They
were cleaning their rifles, making up packs, and apparently readying
themselves to go out on a combat operation.

"These Cambodes good boys," Kornie boomed. "Loyal to the
Americans who pay them and feed them. Not like the KKK."

The Cambodes evidently liked the captain, for Kornie lustily
shouted some indistinguishable words and got back an enthusiastic
response. "I ask them if they are ready to kill Communists anywhere,
even in Cambodia. They are ready." He gave them a cheerful wave
and we left.

"Let's go to the radio room and see what we hear from Schmelzer."

Borst was at the radio, earphones on, scribbling on a sheet of paper
in front of him. He looked up as Kornie came in.

"Sir, Lieutenant Schmelzer is standing by on voice."

"Good!" Kornie exclaimed, taking the mike. "Handy, Handy," he
called. "This is Grant, Grant. Come in Handy."

"Grant, this is Handy," came back over the receiver. "Made contact
with bandits at BP 236581." On the map above the radio Kornie
located the position of his executive officer from the coordinates. It
was eight miles north of Phan Chau, almost straddling the border.

Schmelzer continued. "Our assets now having friendly talk with
bandits. Believe you can go ahead with operation. That is all. Handy
out."

"Grant out," Kornie said, putting down the mike. He turned to me.
"Our plans are coming along well. Now if the Viet Cong give us
tonight without attacking, we will buy another few days to finish the
camp's defenses. Then"—Kornie grinned—"they can throw a regiment at us and we kill them all."

Kornie led the way back to the operations room where Sergeant
Bergholtz was waiting for him. As we walked in the sergeant said,

"Falk just got another agent report. There are about 100 VC hiding in Chau Lu, resting and getting food. Less than half live there, the rest must be hard-core just come over from Cambodia."

"That is good, that is good," Kornie said, nodding. "Now, I will explain everything. Here." He pointed to the map. "You see the border running north and south? Our camp is three miles east from Cambodia. Four miles north of us is this nasty little village of Chau Lu right on the border near which we were ambushed this morning. Four more miles north of Chau Lu, still on the border, is where Schmelzer is right now, talking to the KKK."

"I'm with you so far," I said.

"Good. Now, in Cambodia, exactly opposite Chau Lu, ten miles in is a big VC camp. They got a hospital, barracks, all the comforts of a major installation. The attack on us will be launched from this big Communist camp. The VC will cross the border and build up in Chau Lu, like they do now. When they're ready, they hit us. If we try to hit their buildup on our side of the border they only got to run a hundred meters and they're back in Cambodia where we can't kill them. Even if we go over after them they pull back to their big camp where we get zapped and cause big international incident."

Kornie watched me intently for a reaction. I began to get a vague idea of what he had in mind. "Keep talking, Steve. I've always wanted to go inside Cambodia."

The big Viking laughed hugely. "Tonight, my Cambodes, 100 of them, cross the border and take up blocking positions two miles inside Cambodia between Chau Lu and the big VC camp. There is a river parallel to the border in there. My Cambodes put their backs to the river and ambush the VC who are running from Chau Lu, which we attack just before sunrise tomorrow morning. At the river my boys can see and kill any VC from the main camp who try to cross it and get behind them."

I had to laugh, the thinking was so typically Kornie, and just what Lieutenant Colonel Train, who was so scrupulous about international politics, was afraid of.

Kornie continued. "If the VC are suddenly cut to little pieces right where they think they are safe, in Cambodia, they will be careful for a while. Maybe they think they get attacked again in this sanctuary our politicians give them."

"They'll know you did it, Steve," I said soberly. "And then they'll raise international hell."

"Yes, they know we do it," Kornie agreed. "This will scare them. But international incident? No. They don't prove we have anything to do with it."

"Well, somebody had to ambush those VC," I pointed out. "If there's a bunch of shot-up bodies nobody's going to believe Cambodian-government troops did it to their Communist friends."

Kornie's blue eyes sparkled with humor and excitement. "Oh yes. But we got what you call, fall guys. Come, let's go back to the radio room."

Just after dark I accompanied Kornie and Sergeant Bergholtz as they led the company of cocky, spoiling-for-action Cambodians to the border where a rally point was established with a squad guarding it. This was the point at which the Cambodians would cross back to the Vietnam side of the border after their mission. Kornie wanted Bergholtz and every one of his Cambodians to be familiar with the place. It was at the base of one of the many hills along this section of the border. For positive identification Kornie sent another squad to the top of the hill. There they would start firing flares a few minutes after the shooting started and keep it up until all the Cambodians had found their way back to the rally point and were accounted for.

With the return point on the border clearly defined, Kornie, Bergholtz, I, and the company of Cambodians stealthily moved northward on the Vietnam side of the border. We carefully gave the Viet Cong village of Chau Lu a wide berth an hour later and kept pushing north two more miles. Halfway between Chau Lu and the KKK camp we stopped.

Kornie shook Bergholtz by the hand and silently clapped him on the back. Bergholtz made a sign to the Cambodian leader and they started due west across the ill-defined border into Cambodia. Kornie watched them until they melted into the dark, rugged terrain. In two and a half miles they would come to the river and follow it back south until they were squarely between Chau Lu and the Viet Cong camp.

They would straddle the east-west road and bridge connecting the two Communist bases and set up blocking positions.

Kornie and I and a security squad walked the six miles back to camp, arriving about 3:00 A.M. We made straight for the radio room and Kornie called Schmelzer.

Schmelzer was handling his operation well. Fifty KKK bandits were already crossing into Cambodia. They would penetrate a mile and staying that far inside Cambodia walk south until they were opposite Chau Lu. Here, according to instructions, they would stop until sunrise. Then they would proceed another mile south. At the point where a needle of rock projected skyward they would cross back into Vietnam and report all they had observed to the Americans.

The KKK leader realized that the Americans had to know what the Viet Cong were doing. He also knew they couldn't send patrols across the border to find out. He was glad to mount an easy reconnaissance patrol in return for the equivalent of $10 a man plus five rifles and five automatic weapons.

Half the agreed-upon money and weapons Schmelzer had already presented to the KKK leader at the time his men began crossing the border. The balance would be forthcoming the moment the men crossed back into Vietnam at the needle-shaped rock and gave their reports.

In the radio room Kornie chortled as his operation began to tighten. "Schmelzer is good boy," he said. "Takes guts to deal with KKK. If they think for a minute they can take Schmelzer and his men, they do it."

"Aren't you afraid they'll use those automatic weapons against you some day?" I asked.

Kornie shrugged. "Most of those KKK and their weapons will never get back from this mission."

He looked at his watch. It was 4:00 A.M. Kornie smiled at me and patted my shoulder. "Now is the time to start out for Chau Lu. We will drive the VC straight into the KKK at 0545, and Bergholtz and the Cambodes will cut both the KKK and VC to pieces and be out of there by 0600 hours." His laugh resounded in the radio shack. "Give me just a few more days and a regiment couldn't overrun Phan Chau."

There was a snapping of static and then the radio emitted Schmelzer's voice. "Grant, Grant, this is Handy. Come in, Grant."

Kornie picked up the mike. "This is Grant. Go ahead, Handy."

"Last of the bandits across. We are ready to carry out phase two. Is 0545 hours still correct?"

"Affirmative, Handy. But wait for us to start our little party off."

"Roger, Grant. We will be in position. When you open up, we'll let go too. Leaving now. Handy out."

"Grant out," Kornie said into the mike and put it down. He walked out of the radio room, and on the parade ground we could sense more than see the company of Vietnamese strikers. Two Vietnamese Special Forces officers, the camp commander, Captain Lan, and his executive officer were standing in front of the company of civilian irregulars waiting for Kornie. They saluted him as he stood in the light flooding from the door of the radio room.

Kornie saluted back. "Are you ready to go, Captain Lan?"

"The men are ready," the Vietnamese commander said. "Lieutenant Cau and Sergeant Tuyet will lead them. I must stay in camp. Maybe B team need talk to me."

"Very good thinking, Captain," Kornie complimented his counterpart. "Yes, since I go out, very good you guard camp."

Pleased, Captain Lan turned his men over to Kornie and departed. "Lieutenant Cau, let's get these men on the move," Kornie urged. "You know the objective."

"Yes, sir. Chau Lu." In the dim light from the radio shack Kornie and I could just make out the broad grin on Cau's face. "We will clobber them, sir," he said, proud of his English slang.

Kornie nodded happily. "Right. We massacre them." To me he said, "Cau here is one of the tigers. If they had a few hundred more like him we could go home. He went through Bragg last year. Class before yours, I think."

For the second time that night we started north toward Chau Lu. Kornie seemed to be an inexhaustible tower of energy. Walking at the head of the column he kept up a brisk pace, but we had to stop frequently to let the short-legged Vietnamese catch up. It took exactly the estimated hour and a half to cover the almost five miles to the positions we took up south and east of the VC village. At 5:45 A.M. two companies of strikers were in place ready to attack Chau Lu. Schmelzer's men were ready to hit from the north.

Lieutenant Cau glanced from his wristwatch to the walls of the village one hundred yards away. He raised his carbine, looked at Kornie who nodded vigorously, and blasted away on full automatic. Instantly from all around the village the strike force began firing. Lieutenant Cau shrilled his whistle and his men moved forward. Fire spurted back at us from the village, incoming rounds whining. Instinctively I wanted to throw myself down on the ground but Cau and his men advanced into the fire from the village shouting and shooting. From the north Schmelzer's company charged in on the village also. Within moments the volume of return fire from the Viet Cong village faded to nothing.

"They're on their way now, escaping to their privileged sanctuary," Kornie yelled. "Cease fire, Lieutenant Cau."

After repeated blasts on the whistle the company gradually, reluctantly, stopped shooting. Schmelzer's people had also stopped and there was a startled silence.

The two companies entered the village and routed the civilians out of the protective shelters dug in the dirt floors of their houses.

Kornie looked at Lieutenant Cau in the pale light of dawn. Disappointment was clearly written on his face as his men herded civilians into the center of town. Cau had not been told about the rest of his operation. After a few minutes of preliminary questioning Cau came to Kornie.

"The people say no men in this village. All drafted into the Army. Just old men, women, and children."

Kornie glanced at his watch. 5:53. His infectious grin puzzled the Vietnamese officer. "Lieutenant Cau, you tell the people that in just a few minutes they'll know exactly where their men are."

Cau looked at Kornie, still puzzled. "They run across into Cambodia." He pointed across the town toward the border. "I would like to take my men after them." He smiled sadly. "But I think maybe I do my country more good if I am not in jail."

"You're so right, Cau. Now search the town. See if you can find any hidden arms."

"We are searching, sir, but why would the VC hide guns here when just two hundred meters away they can keep them in complete safety."

Before Kornie could answer, a sudden, steadily increasing crackling of gunfire resounded through the crisp air of dawn. Kornie cocked an ear happily. The noise became louder and more scattered. Automatic weapons, the bang of grenades, sharp rifle reports and then the whooshing of hot air followed by the shattering explosions of recoil-less-rifle rounds echoed up and down the border.

"Bergholtz is giving them hell," Kornie shouted gleefully, thumping me on the back. I tried to get out from under his powerful arms. "My God! I wish I was with Bergholtz and the Cambodes." A sharp burping of rounds which suddenly terminated with the explosion of a grenade caused Kornie to yell at Schmelzer, who was approaching us.

"Hey, Schmelzer. That was one of those Chinese machine guns we gave the KKK. Did you hear it jam?"

"I heard a grenade get it," Schmelzer answered.

The faces of the old men, women, and children were masks of sudden fear, confusion, and panic. They stole looks at we three Americans and a slow comprehension began to show in their eyes. Then their features twisted into sheer hatred.

The fire-fight raged for fifteen minutes as the sun was rising. To the south a steady series of flares spurted from the top of the hill, marking the rally point where Bergholtz and his Cambodians would cross back into Vietnam.

Kornie took a last look around the village. "OK, Schmelzer, let's go pay off the KKK. Give the ones that come back a nice bonus. If they complain about being attacked by their good friends the VC, tell them"—Kornie grinned—"we're sorry about that."

He gave his executive officer a hearty slap on the back that would have sent a smaller man tumbling. "Be sure that your whole company has weapons at the ready," Kornie cautioned. "They might think we slipped it to them on purpose and do something naughty." Kornie was thoughtful for a moment. "Maybe I take a platoon of Lieutenant Cau's men and go with you. If we meet no trouble I'll go on south, find Bergholtz, and see how he did."

Leaving Lieutenant Cau the dreary task of searching the village and questioning the inhabitants, we started south. It was only a mile walk to the needle of rock, and a band of about 15 KKK were already there. Schmelzer, well covered by a platoon of his best riflemen, approached the KKK leader who was dressed in khaki pants and a black pajama shirt—two bandoleers of ammunition crossing his shoulders. An interpreter walked beside Schmelzer, and Kornie and I edged forward, being careful not to get between our riflemen and the KKK. Both Schmelzer and Kornie gave the thoroughly mean- and suspicious-looking bandit leader friendly smiles. Schmelzer reached inside his coat and produced a thick wallet. The sight of the money seemed to have a slightly calming effect on the KKK chief.

"When all your men are back I give you the other 25,000 piastres," Schmelzer said, counting the money.

The translator came back with the chief's retort. "Maybe my men do not all come back. Who they fight over there?"

"The VC of course," Schmelzer answered innocently. "Your men are friends of the Americans and Vietnamese aren't they?"

The KKK chief scowled, but he did not take his eyes off the money as Schmelzer counted it out. There was an uncomfortably long wait in a highly hostile atmosphere until the rest of the KKK started to arrive at needle rock from across the border.

Kornie and Schmelzer impassively watched the wounded, bloody men straggling in. Those who couldn't walk were helped by others. One or two carried shattered bodies.

"Remember how those monks looked with their heads under the arms?" Kornie asked Schmelzer, who nodded grimly.

Of the 50 KKK who had gone out, 30 were alive, only 10 un-wounded. They brought back only six bodies.

The KKK chief, regarding his broken force, turned toward Kornie, his hand twitching at the trigger guard of the Chinese submachine gun Schmelzer had given him.

There was no doubt that the KKK knew they had been tricked by the Americans. Still, Kornie and Schmelzer played the game, expressing condolences at the number of KKK killed and wounded.

"Tell the chief," Schmelzer said, "we will pay a bounty of 500 piastres for each VC killed."

The chief's visage grew blacker as he walked to the survivors. The interpreter listened, turning his head sidewise to the KKK leader.

"He says," came the translation, "that his men were attacked from two directions at once. He says that first the shooting came from inside Cambodia and then from the VC running from the attack we made on Chau Lu. His men fired in both directions but killed mostly the men running from Chau Lu because they were easier to see. He says he wants to be paid for killing 100 VC. His men had no time to take ears or hands for proof. He says we tricked him, we did not tell him about Chau Lu."

"Tell him it was a very unfortunate misinterpretation of orders," Kornie said. "We'll pay him 500 piastres each for 25 VC dead, and we'll give him a 1,000 piastres for each of the men he lost KIA."

Schmelzer's company of Vietnamese irregulars sensed the hatred of the KKK for us and shifted their weapons uneasily; but the chief was in no position to instigate violence. His eyes glowed malevolently as he estimated our strength and then accepted the deal.

"Why do you pay him anything?" I asked. "He's going to try and get you anyway first chance that comes along."

Kornie grinned. "If a battle across the border is reported I think Saigon would accept the proposition that I paid a bunch of Cambodian bandits to break up the VC in Cambodia long enough to make my camp secure." To Schmelzer he said, "Get receipts from the leader for the money and get photographs of him accepting it."

The interpreter called to Kornie as he and I were about to leave with a security platoon. "Sir, KKK chief say he lose three automatic weapons and two rifles. He want them replaced."

"You tell him I'm sorry about that. We gave him the guns. If he can't hold on to them, that's his fault." Kornie waited until his words had been translated. He stood facing the chief, staring down bleakly at the sinister little brown bandit. The KKK chief realized he had been accorded all the concessions he could expect and avoided Kornie's steady gaze. Schmelzer and his sergeant continued counting out the money for the Cambodian bandits.

The groans of the wounded men attracted Kornie's attention. He walked over to where they were sitting or lying in the dirt. After examining some of the more seriously wounded he straightened up.

"Schmelzer, before you go, ask the Vietnamese medics to help these men. They may be bandits fighting us tomorrow, looting merchants and monks the next day, but they do us a big service today— even though they do not mean to.

"And when you finish here go directly back to Phan Chau. And keep an alert rear guard all the time." Kornie grinned goodnaturedly at the scowling group around the KKK leader. "Those boys have big case of the ass with us."

Kornie and I and his platoon left the needle-rock rendezvous and walked south for two miles to our Cambodians' rally point, covering the distance in less than an hour.

Sergeant Falk and his security squad were just welcoming the returned Cambodians as we arrived. Sergeant Ebberson, the medic, had the tools of his trade spread out and ready. Stretchers and bearers were waiting.

Bergholtz, grinning from ear to ear, was waiting for us. "How goes, Bergholtz?" Kornie called, striding toward his big sergeant.

"We greased the shit out of them, sir," Bergholtz cried joyfully. "These Cambodes never had so much fun in their lives." The little dark men in tiger-striped suits bounced around happily, chattering to each other and displaying bloody ears, proof of the operation's success.

"How many VC killed in action?"

"Things were pretty confused, sir. From Chau Lu the VC walked right into us and the KKK. There was a lot of shooting going on in front of us. I think they killed as many of each other as we did in. Then the KKK and the VC both concentrated on us and our Cambodes flat-ass massacred everything that lived in front of us. If there aren't 60 dead VC lying out there I'll extend another six months.

We lost a few dead and maybe 8 or 10 wounded but we didn't leave a body behind, sir."

Kornie's eyes glistened with pride. "By God damn, Bergholtz. We got the best camp in Vietnam. I volunteer us all to stay another six months. What do you say?"

"Well, sir, we still have one more month left of our tour to burn the asses off the VC. This operation we made it out just in time. When we moved the VC were barreling down the road from the big camp, shooting like mad."

Kornie watched as two Cambodians deposited the gore-smeared body of a comrade on the ground beside two other bodies. Sergeant Ebberson was working on the wounded as they were dragged and assisted in. Even the wounded were in good spirits. They had won a victory and the fact that it had been won by going illegally across the border only made the triumph more satisfying.

Kornie threw a massive arm around my shoulder, another around Bergholtz, and started us in the direction of Phan Chau. "Let's go back, men. Maybe the VC call Phnom Penh and the Cambodian government will be screaming border violation. We must get immediate report to Colonel Train."

We walked at the head of the security platoon for a few minutes and then Kornie said to me, "You are friend of Colonel Train. How much of what happened today can I tell him? If the VC attack us tonight we might not be able to hold. But they won't hit us now."

"I guess he'd understand that, Steve. Wouldn't look good for him to lose a camp. But he's still not really an unconventional warfare man."

Kornie nodded in dour agreement.

"Too bad he couldn't spend a week with you," I went on. "That would make a Sneaky Pete out of him if anything ever could."

"He would court-martial me out of the Army after a week with me," Kornie declared. I tended to agree.

If I Die in a Combat Zone

TIM O'BRIEN

1973

BEGINNING

The summer of 1968, the summer I turned into a soldier, was a good time for talking about war and peace. Eugene McCarthy was bringing quiet thought to the subject. He was winning votes in the primaries. College students were listening to him, and some of us tried to help out. Lyndon Johnson was almost forgotten, no longer forbidden or feared; Robert Kennedy was dead but not quite forgotten; Richard Nixon looked like a loser. With all the tragedy and change that summer, it was fine weather for discussion.

And, with all of this, there was an induction notice tucked into a corner of my billfold.

So with friends and acquaintances and townspeople, I spent the summer in Fred's antiseptic cafe, drinking coffee and mapping out arguments on Fred's napkins. Or I sat in Chic's tavern, drinking beer with kids from the farms. I played some golf and tore up the pool table down at the bowling alley, keeping an eye open for likely-looking high school girls.

Late at night, the town deserted, two or three of us would drive a car around and around the town's lake, talking about the war, very seriously, moving with care from one argument to the next, trying to make it a dialogue and not a debate. We covered all the big questions: justice, tyranny, self-determination, conscience and the state, God and war and love.

41

College friends came to visit: "Too bad, I hear you're drafted. What will you do?"

I said I didn't know, that I'd let time decide. Maybe something would change, maybe the war would end. Then we'd turn to discuss the matter, talking long, trying out the questions, sleeping late in the mornings.

The summer conversations, spiked with plenty of references to philosophers and academicians of war, were thoughtful and long and complex and careful. But, in the end, careful and precise argumentation hurt me. It was painful to tread deliberately over all the axioms and assumptions and corollaries when the people on the town's draft board were calling me to duty, smiling so nicely.

"It won't be bad at all," they said. "Stop in and see us when it's over."

So to bring the conversations to a focus and also to try out in real words my secret fears, I argued for running away.

I was persuaded then, and I remain persuaded now, that the war was wrong. And since it was wrong and since people were dying as a result of it, it was evil. Doubts, of course, hedged all this: I had neither the expertise nor the wisdom to synthesize answers; most of the facts were clouded, and there was no certainty as to the kind of government that would follow a North Vietnamese victory or, for that matter, an American victory, and the specifics of the conflict were hidden away—partly in men's minds, partly in the archives of government, and partly in buried, irretrievable history. The war, I thought, was wrongly conceived and poorly justified. But perhaps I was mistaken, and who really knew, anyway?

Piled on top of this was the town, my family, my teachers, a whole history of the prairie. Like magnets, these things pulled in one direction or the other, almost physical forces weighting the problem, so that, in the end, it was less reason and more gravity that was the final influence.

My family was careful that summer. The decision was mine and it was not talked about. The town lay there, spread out in the corn and watching me, the mouths of old women and Country Club men poised in a kind of eternal readiness to find fault. It was not a town,

not a Minneapolis or New York, where the son of a father can sometimes escape scrutiny. More, I owed the prairie something. For
twenty-one years I'd lived under its laws, accepted its education, eaten
its food, wasted and guzzled its water, slept well at night, driven across
its highways, dirtied and breathed its air, wallowed in its luxuries. I'd
played on its Little League teams. I remembered Plato's *Crito*, when
Socrates, facing certain death—execution, not war—had the chance
to escape. But he reminded himself that he had seventy years in
which he could have left the country, if he were not satisfied or felt
the agreements he'd made with it were unfair. He had not chosen
Sparta or Crete. And, I reminded myself, I hadn't thought much
about Canada until that summer.

The summer passed this way. Gold afternoons on the golf course, a
comforting feeling that the matter of war would never touch me,
nights in the pool hall or drug store, talking with towns-folk, turning
the questions over and over, being a philosopher.

Near the end of that summer the time came to go to the war. The
family indulged in a cautious sort of Last Supper together, and afterward my father, who is brave, said it was time to report at the bus
depot. I moped down to my bedroom and looked the place over,
feeling quite stupid, thinking that my mother would come in there in
a day or two and probably cry a little. I trudged back up to the kitchen
and put my satchel down. Everyone gathered around, saying so long
and good health and write and let us know if you want anything. My
father took up the induction papers, checking on times and dates and
all the last-minute things, and when I pecked my mother's face and
grabbed the satchel for comfort, he told me to put it down, that I
wasn't supposed to report until tomorrow.

After laughing about the mistake, after a flush of red color and a
flood of ribbing and a wave of relief had come and gone, I took a long
drive around the lake, looking again at the place. Sunset Park, with its
picnic table and little beach and a brown wood shelter and some
families swimming. The Crippled Children's School. Slater Park,
more kids. A long string of split-level houses, painted every color.

The war and my person seemed like twins as I went around the town's lake. Twins grafted together and forever together, as if a separation would kill them both.

The thought made me angry.

In the basement of my house I found some scraps of cardboard and paper. With devilish flair, I printed obscene words on them, declaring my intention to have no part of Vietnam. With delightful viciousness, a secret will, I declared the war evil, the draft board evil, the town evil in its lethargic acceptance of it all. For many minutes, making up the signs, making up my mind, I was outside the town, I was outside the law, all my old ties to my loves and family broken by the old crayon in my hand. I imagined strutting up and down the sidewalks outside the depot, the bus waiting and the driver blaring his horn, the *Daily Globe* photographer trying to push me into line with the other draftees, the frantic telephone calls, my head buzzing at the deed.

On the cardboard, my strokes of bright red were big and ferocious looking. The language was clear and certain and burned with a hard, defiant, criminal, blasphemous sound. I tried reading it aloud.

Later in the evening I tore the signs to pieces and put the shreds in the garbage can outside, clanging the gray cover down and trapping the messages inside. I went back into the basement. I slipped the crayons into their box, the same stubs of color I'd used a long time before to chalk in reds and greens on Roy Rogers' cowboy boots.

I'd never been a demonstrator, except in the loose sense. True, I'd taken a stand in the school newspaper on the war, trying to show why it seemed wrong. But, mostly, I'd just listened.

"No war is worth losing your life for," a college acquaintance used to argue. "The issue isn't a moral one. It's a matter of efficiency: what's the most efficient way to stay alive when your nation is at war? That's the issue."

But others argued that no war is worth losing your country for, and when asked about the case when a country fights a wrong war, those people just shrugged.

Most of my college friends found easy paths away from the problem, all to their credit. Deferments for this and that. Letters from doctors or chaplains. It was hard to find people who had to think much about the problem. Counsel came from two main quarters, pacifists and veterans of foreign wars.

But neither camp had much to offer. It wasn't a matter of peace, as the pacifists argued, but rather a matter of when and when not to join others in making war. And it wasn't a matter of listening to an ex-lieutenant colonel talk about serving in a right war, when the question was whether to serve in what seemed a wrong one.

On August 13, I went to the bus depot. A Worthington *Daily Globe* photographer took my picture standing by a rail fence with four other draftees.

Then the bus took us through corn fields, to little towns along the way—Lismore and Rushmore and Adrian—where other recruits came aboard. With some of the tough guys drinking beer and howling in the back seats, brandishing their empty cans and calling one another "scum" and "trainee" and "GI Joe," with all this noise and hearty farewelling, we went to Sioux Falls. We spent the night in a YMCA. I went out alone for a beer, drank it in a corner booth, then I bought a book and read it in my room.

By noon the next day our hands were in the air, even the tough guys. We recited the proper words, some of us loudly and daringly and others in bewilderment. It was a brightly lighted room, wood paneled. A flag gave the place the right colors, there was some smoke in the air. We said the words, and we were soldiers.

I'd never been much of a fighter. I was afraid of bullies. Their ripe muscles made me angry: a frustrated anger. Still, I deferred to no one. Positively lorded myself over inferiors. And on top of that was the matter of conscience and conviction, uncertain and surface-deep but pure nonetheless: I was a confirmed liberal, not a pacifist; but I would have cast my ballot to end the Vietnam war immediately, I would have voted for Eugene McCarthy, hoping he would make peace. I was not soldier material, that was certain.

But I submitted. All the personal history, all the midnight conversations and books and beliefs and learning, were crumpled by abstention, extinguished by forfeiture, for lack of oxygen, by a sort of sleepwalking default. It was no decision, no chain of ideas or reasons, that steered me into the war.

It was an intellectual and physical stand-off, and I did not have the energy to see it to an end. I did not want to be a soldier, not even an observer to war. But neither did I want to upset a peculiar balance between the order I knew, the people I knew, and my own private world. It was not that I valued that order. But I feared its opposite, inevitable chaos, censure, embarrassment, the end of everything that had happened in my life, the end of it all.

And the stand-off is still there. I would wish this book could take the form of a plea for everlasting peace, a plea from one who knows, from one who's been there and come back, an old soldier looking back at a dying war.

That would be good. It would be fine to integrate it all to persuade my younger brother and perhaps some others to say no to wars and other battles.

Or it would be fine to confirm the odd beliefs about war: it's horrible, but it's a crucible of men and events and, in the end, it makes more of a man out of you.

But, still, none of these notions seems right. Men are killed, dead human beings are heavy and awkward to carry, things smell different in Vietnam, soldiers are afraid and often brave, drill sergeants are boors, some men think the war is proper and just and others don't and most don't care. Is that the stuff for a morality lesson, even for a theme?

Do dreams offer lessons? Do nightmares have themes, do we awaken and analyze them and live our lives and advise others as a result? Can the foot soldier teach anything important about war, merely for having been there? I think not. He can tell war stories.

Going After Cacciato

TIM O'BRIEN

1978

HOW THEY WERE ORGANIZED

Even before arriving at Chu Lai's Combat Center on June 3, 1968, Private First Class Paul Berlin had been assigned by MACV Computer Services, Cam Ranh Bay, to the single largest unit in Vietnam, the Americal Division, whose area of operations, I Corps, constituted the largest and most diverse sector in the war zone. He was lost. He had never heard of I Corps, or the Americal, or Chu Lai. He did not know what a Combat Center was.

It was there by the sea.

A staging area, he decided. A place to get acquainted. Rows of tin huts stood neatly in the sand, connected by metal walk-ways, surrounded on three sides by wire, guarded at the rear by the sea.

A Vietnamese barber cut his hair.

A bored master sergeant delivered a Re-Up speech.

A staff sergeant led him to a giant field tent for chow, then another staff sergeant led him to a hootch containing eighty bunks and eighty lockers. The bunks and lockers were numbered.

"Don't leave here," said the staff sergeant, "unless it's to use the piss-tube."

Paul Berlin nodded, afraid to ask what a piss-tube was.

In the morning the fifty new men were marched to a wooden set of bleachers facing the sea. A small, sad-faced corporal in a black cadre helmet waited until they settled down, looking at the recruits as if searching for a lost friend in a crowd. Then the corporal sat down in the sand. He turned away and gazed out to sea. He did not speak. Time passed slowly, ten minutes, twenty, but still the sad-faced corporal did not turn or nod or speak. He simply gazed out at the blue sea. Everything was clean. The sea was clean, the sand was clean, the air was warm and pure and clean. The wind was clean.

They sat in the bleachers for a full hour.

Then at last the corporal sighed and stood up. He checked his wristwatch. Again he searched the rows of new faces.

"All right," he said softly. "That completes your first lecture on how to survive this shit. I hope you paid attention."

During the days they simulated search-and-destroy missions in a friendly little village just outside the Combat Center. The villagers played along. Always smiling, always indulgent, they let themselves be captured and frisked and interrogated.

PFC Paul Berlin, who wanted to live, took the exercise seriously.

"You VC?" he demanded of a little girl with braids. "You dirty VC?"

The girl smiled. "Shit, man," she said gently. "You shittin' me?"

They pitched practice grenades made of green fiberglass. They were instructed in compass reading, survival methods, bivouac SOPs, the operation and maintenance of the standard weapons. Sitting in the bleachers by the sea, they were lectured on the known varieties of enemy land mines and booby traps. Then, one by one, they took turns making their way through a make-believe minefield.

"Boomo!" an NCO shouted at any misstep.

It was a peculiar drill. There were no physical objects to avoid, no obstacles on the obstacle course, no wires or prongs or covered pits to detect and then evade. Too lazy to rig up the training ordnance each morning, the supervising NCO simply hollered *Boomo* when the urge struck him.

Paul Berlin, feeling hurt at being told he was a dead man, complained that it was unfair.

"Boomo," the NCO repeated.

But Paul Berlin stood firm. "Look," he said. "Nothing. Just the sand. There's nothing there at all."

The NCO, a huge black man, stared hard at the beach. Then at Paul Berlin. He smiled. " 'Course not, you dumb twirp. You just fucking *exploded* it."

Paul Berlin was not a twirp. So it constantly amazed him, and left him feeling much abused, to hear such nonsense—twirp, creepo, butter-brain. It wasn't right. He was a straightforward, honest, decent sort of guy. He was not dumb. He was not small or weak or ugly. True, the war scared him silly, but this was something he hoped to bring under control.

Late on the third night he wrote to his father, explaining that he'd arrived safely at a large base called Chu Lai, and that he was taking now-or-never training at a place called the Combat Center. If there was time, he wrote, it would be swell to get a letter telling something about how things went on the home front—a nice, unfrightened-sounding phrase, he thought. He also asked his father to look up Chu Lai in a world atlas. "Right now," he wrote, "I'm a little lost."

It lasted six days, which he marked off at sunset on a pocket calendar. Not short, he thought, but getting shorter.

He had his hair cut again. He drank Coke, watched the ocean, saw movies at night, learned the smells. The sand smelled of sour milk. The air, so clean near the water, smelled of mildew. He was scared, yes, and confused and lost, and he had no sense of what was expected of him or of what to expect from himself. He was aware of his body. Listening to the instructors talk about the war, he sometimes found himself gazing at his own wrists and legs. He tried not to think. He stayed apart from the other new guys. He ignored their jokes and chatter. He made no friends and learned no names. At night, the big hootch swelling with their sleeping, he closed his eyes and pretended it was not a war. He felt drugged. He plodded through the sand, listened while the NCOs talked about the AO: "Real bad shit," said the youngest of them, a sallow kid without color in his eyes. "Real

tough shit, real bad. I remember this guy Uhlander. Not such a bad
dick, but he made the mistake of thinkin' it wasn't so bad. It's bad.
You know what bad is? Bad is evil. Bad is what happened to Uhlander. I don't wanna scare the bejasus out of you—that's not what I
want—but, shit, you guys are gonna *die*."

2

Early Work

Hue, Vietnam, 1968. Marines play cards on the destroyed wall of a cemetery during the Tet Offensive.

Most of the books that came out during the war were nonfiction and political in nature—anti- or prowar tracts, position papers and studies of the larger forces involved in the region. With the notable exception of *The Green Berets*, nearly all the Vietnam fiction and poetry of note that came out between 1965 and 1973 was antiwar, and most appeared after 1968, when even such an establishment figure as trusted evening newscaster Walter Cronkite conceded on air that the war was unwinnable. As on campus, the climate in serious American literature was staunchly antiwar, with marquee writers like Norman Mailer, Mary McCarthy, and Robert Bly stridently denouncing first the Johnson and then the Nixon administrations. War supporters John Steinbeck and Jack Kerouac were seen as traitors to their more socially committed roots and reprimanded in print.

Like much of the socially conscious literature of the period, the works in this chapter look at the moral choices individuals make or refuse to make in relation to some larger group (the Army, America as a whole, humanity), questioning individuality and the consequences of conformity. To many people, the reality of the war seemed an affront to American political and moral ideals; it seemed un-American. Other opponents of the war noted similarities to earlier U.S. conquests, most often the near-eradication of the Native Americans. It was business as usual, they claimed. In the early work, as in all the work, authors examine claims of American innocence and evil, reaching back into history for evidence. Home-front America shows up here as well. There's an attempt to bring the war home, or at least to contrast the daily hardships and brutality of the war with America's fatuous affluence. Again, the portrayal of the Vietnamese is interesting across these pieces, as is the view of the older generation, though, as usual, the final identification the authors ask the reader to make is with the U.S. soldier, to understand his conflicted position.

Of all the major American novels about Vietnam, David Halberstam's *one very hot day* (1967) is singular in that it's the only one with Vietnamese point-of-view characters. Halberstam was a high-profile journalist assigned to the region in the early years of the U.S. buildup and has written insightfully about the war in both fiction and nonfiction. *one very hot day* is written in a plain, realistic style. Like *The Green Berets*, it was picked up by the Book of the Month Club; as of 1998 it's still in print.

Chapter VII of Tim O'Brien's *If I Die in a Combat Zone* (1973) brings the green reader into Vietnam in the second person, then switches to "us," and finally "I" as new guy O'Brien shows us a number of Army personnel and their differing views of Vietnam. The flat, economical Hemingway style only emphasizes how strange and frightening his new surroundings are, and the portraits he draws of his fellow soldiers are decidedly unheroic.

While American poets had been writing antiwar poetry for years, Michael Casey's *Obscenities* (1972) was the first major collection written by a veteran. It won the 1972 Yale Younger Poets Prize and earned glowing notices in the *New York Times Book Review* and elsewhere. Casey served as an MP along Highway 1 in 1969–70. His work here is plainspoken, lightly ironic, and sneakily deep, and few American writers have so successfully drawn the difficult relationship between American soldiers and the Vietnamese civilians around them.

Vet David Rabe's play *Sticks and Bones* was first produced by a university theater in 1969, but was later chosen for a major Broadway production in 1971 by the powerful director Joseph Papp. It's a confrontational piece, extravagant in its effects—including ghosts, onstage violence, absurd humor, and blatantly emblematic characters. The family is patterned after the plastic Nelson family from 1950s TV, and

American denial of the war and protestations of innocence are thoroughly shredded.

On the heels of Michael Casey's *Obscenities*, small presses across the United States published a number of important collections of veterans' poetry. Vets Jan Barry and W. D. Ehrhart gathered the finest pieces from these as well as uncollected poems for their anthology *Demilitarized Zones* (1976). Typical of the early period, much of the strongest work in the book examines the difficulty of conveying the experience of the war to an uncaring America.

Authors of the period often responded to that difficulty by trying innovative forms or strategies, breaking away from the realistic or at least showing it in a strange light. In much of the early work, ironic, often disturbing humor provided both a relief and a way of confronting the horrible facts. Authors used the impact of war on the body to prompt a visceral rather than intellectual response, with interesting results. Rabe's tactic of contrasting the stark terror of the war with plastic popular culture is shocking, whereas O'Brien and Casey use a more subtle, deadpan humor.

While these early works were well received, none was widely read beyond a small intelligensia. It would not be until the mid-seventies, well after the fall of Saigon, that Americans as a whole looked back and rediscovered the war.

one very hot day

DAVID HALBERSTAM

1967

At eleven thirty they were moving haphazardly along the canal, one of those peaceful moments when earlier fears were forgotten, and when it was almost as if they were in some sort of trance from the heat and the monotony, when they were fired on. Three quick shots came from the left, from the other side of the canal. They appeared to hit short, and they landed near the center of the column, close to where Lieutenant Anderson was. He wheeled toward the bullets, spoke quickly in Vietnamese, taking three men with him and sending a fourth back to tell Thuong what he was doing—not to send anyone unless it was clearly a real fight, and he could hear automatic weapon fire; they were taking no automatic weapons, Anderson said.

He sensed that it was not an ambush; you trip an ambush with a full volley of automatic weapons fire—to get the maximum surprise firepower and effect, you don't trip it with a few shots from an M-1 rifle; the fact that the sniper had fired so quickly, Anderson thought, meant that there was probably one man alone who wanted to seem like more than one man. But damn it, he thought, you never really know here, you tried to think like them and you were bound to get in trouble: you thought of the obvious and they did the unique. He brought his squad to the canal bank, and two more bullets snapped near them. *Ping, snap. Ping, snap.*

He told one of the Viets to go above him on the canal bank, and one to stay below him, and one to stay behind him as he waded the canal. They were to cover him as he crossed, and they were not to cross themselves until he was on the other side; he didn't want all four of them bogged down in mid-canal when they found out there was an automatic weapon on the other side. They nodded to him. Do you understand me, he asked in Vietnamese. He turned to one of them and asked him to repeat the instructions. Surprisingly the Vietnamese repeated the instructions accurately.

"The Lieutenant swims?" the Viet added.

"The Lieutenant thinks he swims," Anderson said, and added, "do you swim?"

The man answered: "We will all find out."

Anderson waited for a third burst of fire, and when it came, closer this time, he moved quickly to the canal bank and into the water, sinking more than waist high immediately. As he moved he kept looking for the sniper's hiding place; so far he could not tell where the bullets were coming from. He sensed the general direction of the sniper, but couldn't judge exactly where the sniper was. He was all alone in the water, moving slowly, his legs struggling with the weight of the water and the suck of the filth below him. He knew he was a good target, and he was frightened; he moved slowly, as in a slow-motion dream; he remembered one of the things they had said of the VC in their last briefings. ("The VC infantryman is tenacious and will die in position and believes fanatically in the ideology because he has been brain-washed all his life since infancy, but he is a bad shot, yes, gentlemen, he is not a good shot, and the snipers are generally weak, because you see, men, they need glasses. The enemy doesn't get to have glasses. The Communists can't afford 'em, and our medical people have checked them out and have come up with studies which show that because of their diet, because their diet doesn't have as much meat and protein, their eyes are weak, and they don't get glasses, so they are below us as snipers. Brave, gentlemen, but nearsighted, remember that.") He remembered it and hoped it was true.

Ahead of him all he could see was brush and trees. Remember, he thought, he may be up in the trees: it was another one of the briefings: "Vietcong often take up positions in the tops of trees, just like the

Japanese did, and you must smell them out. Remember what I'm telling you, it may save your life. You will be walking along in the jungle, hot and dirty. And you hear a sniper, and because your big fat feet are on the ground, you think that sniper's feet are on the ground too. But you're wrong, he's sitting up there in the third story, measuring the size of your head, counting your squad, and ready to ruin your headgear. They like the jungle, and what's in the jungle? Trees. Lots of 'em. Remember it, gentlemen, smell them in the trees."

Anderson had left the briefing thinking all Vietcong were in the trees; even now as he walked, he kept his eye on the trees more than on the ground.

Behind him he heard the Viets firing now, but there was still no fire from the sniper. He reached the middle of the canal where the water was deepest; only part of his neck, his head, and his arms and weapons were above water now. He struggled forward until he reached the far side of the canal. He signaled to the Viets to hold fire, and then, holding his weapon in one hand (he did not want to lay it on the canal bank, suppose someone reached out from behind a bush and grabbed it), he rolled himself up on the canal edge, but there was still no fire. He punched through the first curtain of brush, frightened because he did not know what would be there (Raulston had once done this, pushed through and found to his surprise a Vietcong a few feet away; they had looked at each other in total surprise, and the Vietcong had suddenly turned and fled—though Beaupre in retelling the story claimed that it was Raulston who had fled, that the Vietcong had lost face by letting him escape, had lied to his superiors, and that Raulston was now listed on Vietcong rolls as having been killed in action, and that Raulston was now safe because they didn't dare kill him again).

He moved past the canal and into the dense brush, found what looked like a good position, and fired off a clip to the left, right in front of him, most of the clip to his right, and finally, for the benefit of his instructors, for Fort Benning, the last one into a tree nest. Nothing happened and he reloaded and moved forward. Then there were two little pings, still in front of him, though sounding, perhaps it was his imagination, further away. But the enemy was there, and so, encouraged, he began to move forward again, his senses telling him that the sniper was slightly to his right. He was alone, he had kept the others back at the canal bank; they would be no help here, for they would surely follow right behind him and he would be in more trouble for the noise they would make and for being accidentally shot from behind, that great danger of single-file patrolling; yet going like this, he sensed terribly how alone he was—he was in *their* jungle, they could see him, know of him, they could see things he couldn't see, there might be more of them. He moved forward a few yards, going slowly both by choice and necessity in the heavy brush. If there had been a clock on the ground, where he left the canal and entered the jungle, it would have been six o'clock, and he was now moving slowly toward one o'clock. He kept moving, firing steadily now. From time to time he reversed his field of fire. Suddenly there was a ping, landing near him, the sound closer, but coming from the left, from about eleven o'clock. The shot sounded closer, and more excited and frightened now, he moved quickly in that direction, feeling the brush scratch his arms and his face (he couldn't use his hands to protect his face, they were on his weapon); now he squeezed off another clip, two quick ones, three quick ones, the last three spaced out, a musical scale really.

There was no answer and he pressed forward, the jungle still around both of them. Then he was answered again, the mating call, two little pings, the VC's weapon had a lower pitch than his, and the sound.—and this made him angry—was coming from the right, near one o'clock, where he had just been. He cursed under his breath, and moved quickly to his right, realizing even as he pushed ahead that he was doing a foolish thing, that he was violating all the rules he had been taught, that he was offering an American officer to a trap that he might be taken prisoner; at Benning they had warned against that, don't be captured, there was too much psychological advantage the VC could take, showing him around in the villages.

Still he pressed on, angry, frustrated. He thought the VC was mocking him, playing a game with him; you didn't do that in war, war was not a game, you didn't screw around, play jokes with rifles. He fired off another clip toward one o'clock and moved there. Then there was a ping from the left, back at ten o'clock. He moved a little to his left, but he didn't fire. A few minutes passed while the Vietcong finally grasped his message, that Anderson for the time being was not going to fire. Finally there was a ping, from eight o'clock this time; the sniper was behind him. But he couldn't fire in that direction or he might hit one of his own men. He waited and waited and then charged toward six o'clock, ready to fire at point-blank range. But nothing happened.

Suddenly there was a ping ping from eleven o'clock. He turned and fired angrily, shouting: "Come out, you sonofabitch, come on, come on out. Fight. Come on, I'm waiting, I'm here."

He waited but nothing happened. Did he hear a giggle? He made the same challenge in Vietnamese, but it sounded foolish to him. No giggle this time. There were no more shots. He checked his watch. He had been gone ten minutes. He waited two minutes more, and nothing happened. Still angry, he went back to the canal bank, and collected the other Viets.

"Sometimes," said one of them, "Vietcong are like the pederasts. Don't feel so badly. It is their game."

Anderson nodded grimly, and they crossed the canal in single file; Anderson much taller than the Viets, his head barely above water, was amazed; just as much of them showed above water as of him.

"The war is good for the leeches in the canal," said one of the Viets, "that is all. A full meal for them today."

He nodded, and then moved back to the main path. At least they would be able to move quickly, while catching up with the rest of the unit.

Anderson came upon them quicker than he expected. They had stopped and were gathered around a very small Vietnamese. They had formed a circle and the Vietnamese was standing with his hands up and his back to a tree; Dang was standing in front of him, towering over him, and Beaupre was behind Dang, towering over him. They get smaller and smaller, Anderson thought. As he approached, he heard Dang say, "Murderer, we have caught the murderer. VC dog. The dog."

"Got to be one of theirs," Beaupre said. "Doesn't weigh more than fifty pounds. All ours weigh more than that."

Dang was in charge of the interrogation. "A Communist VC," he said to Anderson, "part of the ambush plot against us."

"He means the little scouting party you just went on," Beaupre whispered.

"Proceed with the interrogation of the Communist Vietcong prisoner," Dang told Thuong. "I will assist when necessary."

The suspect said he was Hung Van Trung.

"Of course that's his name," Beaupre told Anderson, "they all have that name, that or Trung Van Hung or Hung Van Hung." His age was fifty-eight.

"The Communist is probably lying about his age," Dang said, "these people lie about everything."

Suspect said he owned a water buffalo: "Rich bastard, eh," Beaupre said when Anderson translated, "usually they don't even own a goddamn chicken by the time we catch them."

He came from the village of Ap Xuan Thong.

"Is he a Communist? Ask him if he is a Communist." Dang shouted and the prisoner began to mumble, a rambling guttural chant which seemed half song and half prayer.

"Tell him we are interested in his relationship with Ho Chi Minh and not his relationship with Buddha," Dang said.

A corporal slapped the prisoner. He was loyal to the government, he insisted, he was sometimes a government agent.

"Knees are too bony for one of ours," Beaupre told Anderson. In fact the prisoner said he was in trouble because the local Communist cadre which was headed by Thuan Han Thuan ("How can the VC chief have the same name as our man there?" Beaupre said), suspected that he worked for the government and had taken his wife away last night when the Communists had come; when he mentioned the cadre chief's name, he paused as if expecting that this would confirm his story.

Dang asked him for his identification card, and he could produce none, and Dang slapped him. He claimed the Communists had taken it and he was slapped again. They asked him about children. He said he had three sons, and mentioned daughters, but seemed unsure of the number. Of the sons, he said, one had died of a disease. Which disease, he was asked; the yellow disease, he answered, and they all nodded *yes, the yellow disease, that one*, though later it turned out they were unsure exactly what the yellow disease was.

"Yellow disease," Beaupre said when told, "everybody in this god-damn country's got that. How the hell can you die from it?"

Two of the other sons had served with the government forces; he believed one was dead and one was alive.

"What units?" Thuong asked, the tone of his voice reflecting his boredom with the interrogation. The prisoner said he did not know the units, but they fought against the Vietminh, he was sure of that.

"Tell him that it is not the Vietminh, it is the Vietcong," Dang said, and the corporal slapped him again.

"Now tell us what happened," Thuong said, "and try to make it as honest as you can. Show us your heart is pure."

The prisoner nodded and began: he had worked long that day and had gone to bed early. It was the rainy season and there was more to be done this year because of last year's drought.

"Ask him what he had for breakfast," Beaupre told Anderson, "go ahead. Speed up the interrogation."

The prisoner was interrupted by Thuong who told him to hurry up with the story if he wanted to live to finish it. He had gone to bed early when he was called by Thuan Van Thuan.

"Is he a neighbor?" asked Thuong.

"No, he lives three houses away," said the prisoner.

"Sweet Jesus," said Beaupre. "The prisoner said he knew it was trouble right away."

"Why," demanded Dang, "because he knew all his Communist friends were coming? All the dogs were coming?"

"No," said the prisoner, "because Thuan's voice was loud and commanding"; he stopped, and it appeared for a second that he was going to say, commanding, like the Captain's, but then he continued. Usually Thuan's voice was soft and supplicating, an attitude he did not trust because Thuan was not honest. He claimed to have an electric box, the only one in the village from which he received special messages from Saigon and Paris and Hanoi; the prisoner was sure it was a false electric box. Thuan had been arrogant and had demanded they come to a meeting; Thuan had insisted that his wife come too, which upset him since she had been sick and coughing and had finally fallen asleep, but Thuan had given them no choice and so they were taken to the center of the hamlet, where lamps had been lit, and where there were twelve visitors, all men. He knew right away they were soldiers.

"Did they have any weapons?" Thuong asked.

"I didn't see any," he said, "but he knew they were there."

"How does he know?" Dang asked, "because he is one of them."

"Because of the way the men behaved," he said, "men who have guns behave one way and men who do not behave another."

He seemed puzzled that they did not understand the distinction, and asked Thuong: "You have never talked with a man with a gun when you don't have one?"

"Good question," Beaupre said, "the sonofabitch is telling the truth."

The suspect stopped as if waiting for someone to stop him; he said the men had talked about politics and said that the long noses (he looked embarrassed at Anderson and Beaupre) were coming to the village the next day and would try to kill all the people. Then they had served tea. He himself had taken two glasses. He had wanted to take only one, but had been afraid if he took one, this might offend the Vietminh.

"Vietcong," Dang corrected, less angrily this time.

Some of the others had taken three cups.

"See how many cups he'll take from us," Beaupre said when Anderson translated this.

The next day he had been told to go north from the village, because the Americans were coming from the south, east and west, and for that reason he had slipped away and gone south. Thuong asked him about his wife; she had been kept by the Communists as a bearer and as a hostage. Thuong continued to ask questions about the enemy, and Beaupre pulled Anderson aside and told him to get on the American radio and quickly call the information in; he did not trust the

Viets; if it were left to them, the intelligence might not reach the CP until the next day.

"He was telling the truth, wasn't he?" Anderson said.

Beaupre didn't say anything for a minute. "Yes," he finally answered, "he's telling the truth. That's the worst thing about it. Makes you long for the usual ones, who've never seen a VC, never heard of the war."

He walked on a few yards. "A rock and hard place. That's where we are, between a rock and a hard place."

He felt dry and thirsty and a little nervous; he had mocked this operation from the start, and most of his fear had disappeared with the selection of Big William for the helicopters. Now he was becoming frightened again, aware of his age and the senselessness of the war—not the killing but the endless walking each day and the returning to My Tho with nothing done, nothing seen, nothing accomplished, nothing changed, just hiking each day with death, taking chances for so very little, wondering if he were going to be sold out, wondering whom you could trust. He had not distrusted people in World War II. He had been assigned to an infantry regiment and he had fought with a variety of men, some had been good soldiers, some weak, some brave, and some cowardly, some who had loved the war, and most who had hated it, but whatever, there had never been a quality of distrust. It had been simpler there, even in Germany, where you hated everyone, but once you entered the villages, you were not loved and kissed, you were not ambushed or tricked or betrayed. The distrust had begun in Korea when suddenly it was more than a matter of fighting and killing, instead it was a matter of wondering where you were going, and whose intelligence had set it up and who was paying, was it only one side: a matter of looking into the face of the man when you finally met him, and perhaps looking for too much, seeing things which didn't exist, and looking for things which had no right to exist, which probably had never existed. "Don't expect our Korean agents to have blue eyes and blond hair and friendly smiles," they had told him, "they don't. They don't look like Marines. They look like gooks because they are gooks. Don't you worry about who they are or the way they look. You let us do the worrying. All you have to do is keep the goddamn loose change out of your pockets because it makes too much noise on cold winter nights out there, that and trust your compass and your own good common sense. We don't expect you to like the Koreans, that's not your job." But compared to this country, Korea was simple: here you began with distrust, you assumed it about everything, even things you thought you knew. Even the Americans seemed different to him now, and he trusted them less; in order to survive in this new world and this new Army, they had changed. Yes was no longer exactly yes, no was no longer exactly no, maybe was more certainly maybe.

"I think we may be getting ourselves sold out," he said, and then added to Anderson, one of the few kind things he said that day or any other, "you be a little careful now. Hear?"

There was a terrible quality of truth to what Thuong had just heard and he did not like it; he had not liked the operation from the start and he had always disagreed with Headquarters and Staff over the area. Staff called it a blue area (the Americans, he decided, loved maps even more than the French and had taught them about red, white and blue areas; the Americans loved to change the colors, to turn red into white and white into blue, to put red pins on white spots and blue pins on red spots) and blue was supposed to be secure, but Thuong had never liked the area; he did not operate there often and so he tended to accept the Headquarters' version of the area as being secure, only to find once they were in the area that it was not quite what it seemed, that it was always a little more hostile than the authorities claimed. He suspected that it was a Communist area where the guerrillas did little in the way of challenging the government and were content to rest somewhat tranquil on the surface, using it as a communications path. The Arvin recruited, Thuong remembered, few government soldiers from the area, and the young men they did take showed a higher desertion rate than might have been expected.

He walked beside the suspect, near the rear of the column. "I believe you have told us the truth," he told the prisoner.

The man did not look up at him.

"Perhaps you will be free by the end of the day," Thuong said.

"Perhaps we will all be dead by the end of the day," the prisoner said a little bitterly.

"Would you like some of my water?" Thuong asked.

The prisoner said no, but then asked if Thuong would do him a favor: "You believe me and know what I say is true." Thuong said yes, he would do the favor, if he could, depending on what it was.

"Would you tie my hands together?" the prisoner asked. "You see if they see me walking with you . . ."

"I know," Thuong said, and ordered his hands bound; the Americans, he thought, should have asked this peasant whether he thought the area was blue or red. Perhaps they should explain that it was safe to walk free, that it was blue.

"You are not from here, are you?" the prisoner asked.

"No," said the Lieutenant, "I come from the north."

"I know, but you are not like the other northerners, you are nicer than them."

"Only because you are more honest than the other southerners," he said.

Thuong trusted the man although he did not trust southerners in general; he thought of them as dishonest, a little too lazy for their own good, a little too willing to tell you what you wanted to hear, always dependent on their women to do their work (almost, he thought, a pride in this, the best man was the one whose woman worked the hardest). He thought of northerners as being more honest, although the northerners who had come south like himself were no longer particularly honest; they had to bend enough themselves in order to survive.

Thuong was thirty-one, though, like most Vietnamese, he looked younger to foreign eyes. He was slim and his face seemed almost innocent; he had been in the Government Army too long to be innocent, eight years, and all of them either as aspirant or lieutenant. His lack of advancement was no particular reflection on his ability, indeed, those few superiors who took the time to monitor his file, such as it was with more papers missing than enclosed, were surprised at the degree of achievement and ability; having achieved this surprise, however, they did not feel obligated to increase his rank or command. Indeed the older he got, and the more papers there were in praise of him—including, dangerously American praise—the more it tended to mitigate against him; here after all was a man of ability who had not gotten ahead. Therefore, there must be something wrong, something unseen but known, something political; his superiors were in particular surprised by his father's choice of religion. His father, having associated with foreigners in the north, did not choose to convert; he worked closely with foreigners and dutifully accepted their pay and their orders, but not their religion. This was unusual for the time; there were, after all, many Vietnamese who began to dress like the French, eat like the French, and talk like the French. His father referred to them all as the "mustache-Vietnamese" in honor of their copying French-style mustaches. Thuong had once gently asked his father about this, why he had never taken their faith, and his father had said simply that he was paid for his manual contributions, not his spiritual ones. Nevertheless, he was closely associated with foreigners and during the beginning of the French war, he had continued to work for them, as much by accident as by decision (he did not particularly like them, but he had a vague feeling that since everyone else was deserting the foreigners, it was improper for him to do it as well); one of his objections after all to the French had been the contempt they had showed toward Vietnamese people and their obvious belief that all Vietnamese were cowards, to leave now would be to confirm all the worst things the French had said. When the foreigners by their stupidity, which his father could not have been expected to have foreseen, lost the war, thereby proving to the French that all Vietnamese were not cowards and making his father's original reason somewhat obsolete, it was decided to split up the family and come to the south, splitting up into small groups so that they wouldn't be stopped by the local Vietminh bands.

The way had been difficult from the start and Thuong's grandmother, who was in his charge, had nearly died from exhaustion. (Later Thuong remembered trying to find water for her, giving her all his water, and the terrible thirst that had stayed with him for days at a time. When he thought of the division of the country, he thought of his own thirst.) When they finally arrived in the south, they turned out to be among the few Buddhists who had made the trip, and were immediately placed in a camp for Catholic refugees. There they shared the difficult position of the Catholics of being unwanted immigrants in the south, without sharing either their faith or their protection.

On the basis of his father's connections, he had managed to attend a military school, after first lingering on the waiting list for a year and a half. There he quickly discovered that he was a northerner in the south, a Buddhist among Catholics, and thus at almost any given time lacked the proper credentials. The southerners did not trust him because he was a northerner, the Catholics did not trust him because he was a Buddhist. In a country shorn of idealism and reeking of cynicism and opportunism, he was an object of suspicion. So he remained a lieutenant; as they remained suspicious of him, so he in turn became distrustful and cynical about them. He accepted the legacy of being his father's son with the same fatalism, largely because he could think of no real alternative to it and because if it offered nothing else, it offered him a certain sense of privacy and individualism. He went along with their rules but he tried to remain himself. He envied the Communists their self-belief, their ideology, their certainty, even their cruelty; the Catholics, their convictions and connections; the Americans, their intensity and idealism; and his father, his gentleness and enduring innocence (his father, embarrassed and uneasy and unworldly, periodically would ask him if he *had* to be a soldier, wasn't there something else he could do; his father knew, of course, that it paid well . . .); he doubted what he did and he suspected that the war would probably be lost. It was not that he wished to be on the other side—that would be easy to do, a short walk away during an operation—nor that he thought the other side more just: the Communists, after all, had killed an uncle, just as the French had stupidly managed to kill a cousin, wiping out a village (until then pro-French) as the Vietminh had planned for them to do. The Vietminh side was as cruel as the French, and lacked only the corruption of the French.

He suspected that ten years of power would improve their sense of corruption (depending, he thought, on the degree of success of their system; they would need a certain amount of success to be corrupt. If their system failed, they could retain their integrity). The danger of going over, he thought, would not be that he had been fighting them all these years and had killed many of their people (they, unlike the Arvin, would have real records and they would know who he was, and who he had killed); nor that after the minimal comfort of My Tho, with its soda pop and iced beer, that life would be too rigorous. It was simply that he knew he was too cynical for the passion and commitment their life took. To gain religion in Vietnam, he thought, you must start very young; to retain it, he thought, you have to be very lucky.

So he did his best at being a lieutenant. He told Anderson, the young American, that he was twenty-five instead of thirty-one in order to avoid embarrassing the young American; Anderson had been surprised, he had thought Thuong much younger. Thuong took a certain limited pride in what he did; more, almost in what he did not do, in that he did not play the game of promotion and did not attach himself like a barnacle to his superior officers, did not call in prolonged artillery barrages on villages before the assault. But the dominant feature of his life remained his fatalism. As his father had somehow made these fatal flaws, deciding at one strange moment to keep a false sense of integrity (false, thought Thuong, because both he and his father had made so many other demeaning decisions and accepted so much other fraud during their lifetimes), Thuong had continued relentlessly and recklessly down the same deserted path: there had been, after all, chances to convert. Others did; it had been suggested to him. There were many new Catholics in his class at the Academy, and now several were captains, and one was a major; but there was for him in conversion a sense of surrender, he had admired the Catholics when they were the minority in the north, but now that they had come to the south they had changed. What had struck him as quiet courage, now often seemed to him to be arrogance, and the converts were inevitably the worst.

So he continued his own way: he did not desert because it would hurt his parents (and also because it would make no difference to him) and so his life had made him a very old lieutenant. The particular reward that he now enjoyed for his fatalism was Captain Dang. The Captain was a year younger than Thuong and had been in the army for a shorter time, and was soon to be a major, according to Dang himself. He was well connected in Saigon and was aware of this; he visited Saigon frequently, and he often referred to the dinners and parties he had just attended. He frequently praised Thuong (in front of Thuong, implying that he had also praised Thuong in those same great halls); he talked of promotion for Thuong, something, Thuong was virtually sure, if it ever came, would come in spite of Dang. Dang did not know the name of anyone in the unit below the rank of corporal; he cheated on the ranks, regularly turning in more men than he actually had, failing to report losses (the advantage being that he was not reprimanded for losing men, and at the same time continued to draw their pay. The result was that the company which should have been understrength by ten men was usually understrength about two dozen, and the pressure on the men was even greater than it should have been). Thuong had compensated for this in part by commandeering an extra light machine gun from a friend in another company: the company had lost it, then captured it back in a long battle with the Vietcong battalion. Since it had already been reported lost, it was surplus on the rolls and Thuong had been owed a major favor by his friend—he had lent them three men during a key inspection. Thuong was careful to pay as little attention as possible to Dang's corruption; Dang, indeed, was convenient for Thuong. He fitted Thuong's own view of what an officer was, what the system was, and made his own lack of promotion easier to bear; it would have been more bitter were Dang a real soldier. But for two years and a half now, he had despised Dang over one incident. It was a time just before the American helicopters had arrived with their remarkable ability to bring in reinforcement, and there was still a terrible isolation to battle: you were hit and you stayed there alone and fought it out. There had been an ambush, a brief and bitter one, and Thuong at first had been paralyzed like everyone else, sure that he was going to die there; but he had in those first minutes seen something he would never forgive and never forget (particularly since when he saw it, he expected it to be one of the last things he ever saw): Dang taking off his officer's pips. If you are going to wear the pips in the great halls of Saigon, he thought, you must wear them in the U Minh forest.

If I Die in a Combat Zone

TIM O'BRIEN

1973

ARRIVAL

First there is some mist. Then, when the plane begins its descent, there are pale gray mountains. The plane slides down, and the mountains darken and take on a sinister cragginess. You see the outlines of crevices, and you consider whether, of all the places opening up below, you might finally walk to that spot and die. In the far distance are green patches, the sea is below, a stretch of sand winds along the coast. Two hundred men draw their breath. No one looks at the others. You feel dread. But it is senseless to let it go too far, so you joke: there are only 365 days to go. The stewardess wishes you luck over the loudspeaker. At the door she gives out some kisses, mainly to the extroverts.

From Cam Ranh Bay another plane takes you to Chu Lai, a big base to the south of Danang, headquarters for the Americal Division. You spend a week there, in a place called the Combat Center. It's a resortlike place, tucked in alongside the South China Sea, complete with sand and native girls and a miniature golf course and floor shows with every variety of the grinding female pelvis. There beside the sea you get your now-or-never training. You pitch hand grenades, practice walking through mine fields, learn to use a minesweeper. Mostly, though, you wonder about dying. You wonder how it feels, what it looks like inside you. Sometimes you stop, and your body tingles. You feel your blood and nerves working. At night you sit on the beach and watch fire fights off where the war is being fought. There are movies at night, and a place to buy beer. Carefully, you mark six days off your pocket calendar; you start a journal, vaguely hoping it will never be read.

Arriving in Vietnam as a foot soldier is akin to arriving at boot camp as a recruit. Things are new, and you ascribe evil to the simplest physical objects around you: you see red in the sand, swarms of angels and avatars in the sky, pity in the eyes of the chaplain, concealed anger in the eyes of the girls who sell you Coke. You are not sure how to conduct yourself—whether to show fear, to live secretly with it, to show resignation or disgust. You wish it were all over. You begin the countdown. You take the inky, mildew smell of Vietnam into your lungs.

After a week at the Combat Center, a truck took six of us down Highway One to a hill called LZ Gator.

A sergeant welcomed us, staring at us like he was buying meat, and he explained that LZ Gator was headquarters for the Fourth Battalion, Twentieth Infantry, and that the place was our new home.

"I don't want you guys getting too used to Gator," he said. "You won't be here long. You're gonna fill out some forms in a few minutes, then we'll get you all assigned to rifle companies, then you're going out to the boonies. Got it? Just like learning to swim. We just toss you in and let you hoof it and eat some C rations and get a little action under your belts. It's better that way than sitting around worrying about it.

"Okay, that's enough bullshit. Just don't get no illusions." He softened his voice a trifle. "Of course, don't get too scared. We lose some men, sure, but it ain't near as bad as '66, believe me, I was in the Nam in '66, an' it was bad shit then, getting our butts kicked around. And this area—you guys lucked out a little, there's worse places in the Nam. We got mines, that's the big thing here, plenty of 'em. But this ain't the delta, we ain't got many NVA, so you're lucky. We got some mines and local VC, that's it. Anyhow, enough bullshit, like I say, it ain't all that bad. Okay, we got some personnel cards here, so fill 'em out, and we'll chow you down."

Then the battalion Re-Up NCO came along. "I seen some action. I got me two purple hearts, so listen up good. I'm not saying you're gonna get zapped out there. I made it. But you're gonna come motherfuckin' close, Jesus, you're gonna hear bullets tickling your asshole. And sure as I'm standing here, one or two of you men are gonna get your legs blown off. Or killed. One or two of you, it's gotta happen."

He paused and stared around like a salesman, from man to man, letting it sink in. "I'm just telling you the facts of life, I'm not trying to scare shit out of you. But you better sure as hell be scared, it's gotta happen. One or two of you men, your ass is grass.

"So—what can you do about it? Well, like Sarge says, you can be careful, you can watch for the mines and all that, and, who knows, you might come out looking like a rose. But careful guys get killed too. So what can you do about it then? Nothing. Except you can re-up."

The men looked at the ground and shuffled around grinning. "Sure, sure—I know. Nobody likes to re-up. But just think about it a second. Just say you do it—you take your burst of three years, starting today; three more years of army life. Then what? Well, I'll tell you what, it'll save your ass; that's what, it'll save your ass. You re-up and I can get you a job in Chu Lai. I got jobs for mechanics, typists, clerks, damn near anything you want, I got it. So you get your nice, safe rear job. You get some on-the-job training, the works. You get a skill. You sleep in a bed. Hell, you laugh, but you sleep in the goddamn monsoons for two months on end, you try that sometime, and you won't be laughing. So. You lose a little time to Uncle Sam. Big deal. You save your ass. So, I got my desk inside. If you come in and sign the papers—it'll take ten minutes—and I'll have you on the first truck going back to Chu Lai, no shit. Anybody game?" No one budged, and he shrugged and went down to the mess hall.

LZ Gator seemed a safe place to be. You could see pieces of the ocean on clear days. A little village called Nuoc Man was at the foot of the hill, filled with pleasant, smiling people, places to have your laundry done, a whorehouse. Except when on perimeter guard at night, everyone went about the fire base with unloaded weapons. The atmosphere was dull and hot, but there were movies and floor shows and sheds-ful of beer.

I was assigned to Alpha Company.

"Shit, you poor sonofabitch," the mail clerk said, grinning. "Shit. How many days you got left in Nam? 358, right? 357? Shit. You poor mother. I got twenty-three days left, twenty-three days, and I'm sorry but I'm gone! Gone! I'm so short I need a step ladder to hand out mail. What's your name?"

The mail clerk shook hands with me. "Well, at least you're a lucky sonofabitch. Irish guys never get wasted, not in Alpha. Blacks and spics get wasted, but you micks make it every goddamn time. Hell, I'm black as the colonel's shoe polish, so you can bet your ass I'm not safe till that ol' freedom bird lands me back in Seattle. Twenty-three days, you poor mother."

He took me to the first sergeant. The first sergeant said to forget all the bullshit about going straight out to the field. He lounged in front of a fan, dressed in his underwear (dyed green, apparently to camouflage him from some incredibly sneaky VC), and he waved a beer at me. "Shit, O'Brien, take it easy. Alpha's a good square-shooting company, so don't sweat it. Keep your nose clean and I'll just keep you here on Gator till the company comes back for a break. No sense sending you out there now, they're coming in to Gator day after tomorrow." He curled his toe around a cord and pulled the fan closer. "Go see a movie tonight, get a beer or something."

He assigned me to the third platoon and hollered at the supply sergeant to issue me some gear. The supply sergeant hollered back for him to go to hell, and they laughed, and I got a rifle and ammunition and a helmet, camouflage cover, poncho, poncho liner, back pack, clean clothes, and a box of cigarettes and candy. Then it got dark, and I watched Elvira Madigan and her friend romp through all the colors, get hungry, get desperate, and stupidly—so stupidly that you could only pity their need for common sense—end their lives. The guy, Elvira's lover, was a deserter. You had the impression he deserted for an ideal of love and butterflies, balmy days and the simple life, and that when he saw he couldn't have it, not even with blond and blue-eyed Elvira, he decided he could never have it. But, Jesus, to kill because of hunger, for fear to hold a menial job. Disgusted, I went off to an empty barracks and pushed some M-16 ammo and hand grenades off my cot and went to sleep.

In two days Alpha Company came to LZ Gator. They were dirty, loud, coarse, intent on getting drunk, happy, curt, and not interested in saying much to me. They drank through the afternoon and into the night. There was a fight that ended in more beer, they smoked some dope, they started sleeping or passed out around midnight.

At one or two in the morning—at first I thought I was dreaming, then I thought it was nothing serious—explosions popped somewhere outside the barracks. The first sergeant came through the barracks with a flashlight. "Jesus," he hollered. "Get the hell out of here! We're being hit! Wake up!"

I scrambled for a helmet for my head. For an armored vest. For my boots, for my rifle, for my ammo.

It was pitch dark. The explosions continued to pop; it seemed a long distance away.

I went outside. The base was lit up by flares, and the mortar pits were firing rounds out into the paddies. I hid behind a metal shed they kept the beer in.

No one else came out of the barracks. I waited, and finally one man ambled out, holding a beer. Then another man, holding a beer.

They sat on some sandbags in their underwear, drinking the beer and laughing, pointing out at the paddies and watching our mortar rounds land.

Two or three more men came out in five minutes; then the first sergeant started shouting. In another five minutes some of the men were finally outside, sitting on the sandbags.

Enemy rounds crashed in. The earth split. Most of Alpha Company slept.

A lieutenant came by. He told the men to get their gear together, but no one moved, and he walked away. Then some of the men spotted the flash of an enemy mortar tube.

They set up a machine gun and fired out at it, over the heads of everyone in the fire base.

In seconds the enemy tube flashed again. The wind whistled, and the round dug into a road twenty feet from my beer shed. Shrapnel slammed into the beer shed. I hugged the Bud and Black Label, panting, no thoughts.

The men hollered that Charlie was zeroing in on our machine gun, and everyone scattered, and the next round slammed down even closer.

The lieutenant hurried back. He argued with a platoon sergeant, but this time the lieutenant was firm. He ordered us to double-time out to the perimeter. Muttering about how the company needed a rest and that this had turned into one hell of a rest and that they'd rather be out in the boonies, the men put on their helmets and took up their rifles and followed the lieutenant past the mess hall and out to the perimeter.

Three of the men refused and went into the barracks and went to sleep.

Out on the perimeter, there were two dead GI's. Fifty-caliber machine guns fired out into the paddies and the sky was filled with flares. Two or three of our men, forgetting about the war, went off to chase parachutes blowing around the bunkers. The chutes came from the flares, and they made good souvenirs.

In the morning the first sergeant roused us out of bed, and we swept the fire base for bodies. Eight dead VC were lying about. One was crouched beside a roll of barbed wire, the top of his head resting on the ground like he was ready to do a somersault. A squad of men was detailed to throw the corpses into a truck. They wore gloves and didn't like the job, but they joked. The rest of us walked into the rice paddy and followed a tracker dog out toward the VC mortar positions. From there the dog took us into a village, but there was nothing to see but some children and women. We walked around until noon. Then the lieutenant turned us around, and we were back at LZ Gator in time for chow.

"Those poor motherfuckin' dinks," the Kid said while we were filling sandbags in the afternoon. "They should know better than to test Alpha Company. They just know, they *ought* to know anyhow, it's like tryin' to attack the Pentagon! Old Alpha comes in, an' there ain't a chance in hell for 'em, they oughta know *that*, for Christ's sake. Eight to two, they lost six more than we did." The Kid was only eighteen, but everyone said to look out for him, he was the best damn shot in the battalion with an M-79.

"Actually," the Kid said, "those two guys weren't even from Alpha. The two dead GI's. They were with Charlie Company or something. I don't know. Stupid dinks should know better." He flashed a buck-toothed smile and jerked his eyebrows up and down and winked.

Wolf said: "Look, FNG, I don't want to scare you—nobody's trying to scare you—but that stuff last night wasn't *shit!* Last night was a lark. Wait'll you see some really *bad* shit. That was a picnic last night. I almost slept through it." I wondered what an FNG was. No one told me until I asked.

"You bullshitter, Wolf. It's never any fun." The Kid heaved a shovelful of sand at Wolf's feet. "Except for me maybe. I'm charmed, nothing'll get me. Ol' Buddy Wolf's a good bullshitter, he'll bullshit you till you think he knows his ass from his elbow."

"Okay, FNG, don't listen to me, ask Buddy Barker. Buddy Barker, you tell him last night was a lark. Right? We got mortars and wire and bunkers and arty and, shit, what the hell else you want? You want a damn H bomb?"

"Good idea," Kid said.

But Buddy Barker agreed it had been a lark. He filled a sandbag and threw it onto a truck and sat down and read a comic. Buddy Wolf filled two more bags and sat down with Buddy Barker and called him a lazy bastard. While Kid and I filled more bags, Wolf and Barker read comics and played a game called "Name the Gang." Wolf named a rock song and Barker named the group who made it big. Wolf won 10 to 2. I asked the Kid how many Alpha men had been killed lately, and the Kid shrugged and said a couple. So I asked how many had been wounded, and without looking up, he said a few. I asked how bad the AO was, how soon you could land a rear job, if the platoon leader were gung-ho, if Kid had ever been wounded, and the Kid just grinned and gave flippant, smiling, say-nothing answers. He said it was best not to worry.

Obscenities

MICHAEL CASEY

1972

To Sergeant Rock

Gentlemen
One year over there
An you'll age ten
Am I exaggeratin, Sergeant Rock?
You ask Sergeant Rock
If I'm exaggeratin
Sergeant Rock was in the army
Since the day he was born
He was in the war of the babies

A Bummer

We were going single file
Through his rice paddies
And the farmer
Started hitting the lead track
With a rake
He wouldn't stop
The TC went to talk to him
And the farmer
Tried to hit him too
So the tracks went sideways
Side by side
Through the guy's fields
Instead of single file
Hard On, Proud Mary
Bummer, Wallace, Rosemary's Baby
The Rutgers Road Runner
And
Go Get Em—Done Got Em
Went side by side
Through the fields
   If you have a farm in Vietnam
And a house in hell
Sell the farm
And go home

track: tracked vehicle
TC: track commander

For the Old Man

The old man was mumbling
And Delbert was shouting at him
Im! Im! Im!
Until Booboo told Delbert
To shut the fuck up
The old man was skinny
The old man had looked young
With the sand bag
Over his head
Without the bag
The man was old
There was a bump
The size of a grapefruit
On his head
When the bag was taken off
The man
Clasped his hands
In front of him
And bowed to us
Each in turn
To Booboo, Delbert, and me
He kept it up too
He wouldn't stop
His whole body shaking
Shivering with fright
And somehow
With his hands

im: silence

84

Clasped before him
It seemed as if
He was praying to us
It made all of us
Americans
Feel strange

Explanation

My friend with me is National Policeman Hieu
Of the National Police Field Force
Hieu shakes his head and says something
In Vietnamese meaning   of very poor quality
My friend is impressed
Not favorably, I think,
As the Marine Captain
Explains the key chain
On which is a bit of jawbone
With three little teeth
He points to it
"VC" he says

"I could've guessed"
I says, "that a Communist
Would have but three teeth
Three is a number
I never liked"

And the captain
Explains to me
That the thing
Was part of
A larger bone
Containing more
Than three teeth

The LZ Gator Body Collector

See
Her back is arched
Like something's under it
That's why I thought
It was booby trapped
But it's not
It just must have been
Over this rock here
And somebody moved it
After corpus morta stiffened it
I didn't know it was
A woman at first
I couldn't tell
But then I grabbed
Down there
It's a woman or was
It's all right
I didn't mind
I had gloves on then

Learning

I like learning useless things
Like Latin
I really enjoyed Latin
Caesar and the Gallic Wars
Enjoyed his fighting
The Helvetians and Germans
And Gauls
I enjoyed Vietnamese too
The language
Its five intonations
Its no conjugations
A good language to learn
Vietnam is divided in
Three parts too
It makes me wonder
Who will write their book

Sticks and Bones

DAVID RABE

1969

[FROM ACT ONE:]

RICK. Somebody knockin'.

OZZIE. Knockin'?

RICK. The door, Dad.

OZZIE. Oh.

RICK. You want me to get it?

OZZIE. No, no. It's just so late. *(He moves for the door.)*

RICK. That's all right.

OZZIE. Sure.

He opens the door just a crack, as if to stick his head around. But the door is thrust open and a man enters abruptly. He is black or of Spanish descent, and is dressed in the uniform of a sergeant major and wearing many campaign ribbons.

SGT. MAJOR. Excuse me. Listen to me. I'd like to speak to the father here. I'd like to know who . . . is the father? Could . . . you tell me the address?

OZZIE. May I ask who's asking?

SGT. MAJOR. I am. I'm asking. What's the address of this house?

OZZIE. But I mean, who is it that wants to know?

SGT. MAJOR. We called; we spoke. Is this seven-seventeen Dunbar?

OZZIE. Yes.

SGT. MAJOR. What's wrong with you?

Ozzie. Don't you worry about me.

Sgt. Major. I have your son.

Ozzie. What?

Sgt. Major. Your son.

Ozzie. No.

Sgt. Major. But he is. I have papers, pictures, prints. I know your blood and his. This is the right address. Please. Excuse me. *(He pivots, reaches out into the dark.)* I am very busy. I have your father, David.

He draws David in—a tall, thin boy, blond and, in the shadows, wearing sunglasses and a uniform of dress greens. In his right hand is a long, white, red-tipped cane. He moves, probing the air, as the sergeant major moves him past Ozzie toward the couch, where he will sit the boy down like a parcel.

Ozzie. Dave? . . .

Sgt. Major. He's blind.

Ozzie. What?

Sgt. Major. Blind.

Ozzie. I don't . . . understand.

Sgt. Major. We're very sorry.

Ozzie, *realizing.* Ohhhhhh. Yes. Ohhhhh. I see . . . sure. I mean, we didn't know. Nobody said it. I mean, sure, Dave, sure; it's all right—don't you worry. Rick's here, too, Dave—Rick, your brother, tell him hello.

Rick. Hi, Dave.

David, *worried.* You said . . . "father."

Ozzie. Well . . . there's two of us, Dave; two.

David. Sergeant, you said "home." I don't think so.

Ozzie. Dave, sure.

David. It doesn't feel right.

Ozzie. But it is, Dave—me and Rick—Dad and Rick. Harriet! *(Calling up the stairs)* Harriet!

David. Let me touch their faces. . . . I can't see. *(Rising, his fear increasing)* Let me put my fingers on their faces.

Ozzie, *hurt, startled.* What? Do what?

Sgt. Major. Will that be all right if he does that?

OZZIE. Sure. . . . Sure. . . . Fine.

SGT. MAJOR, *helping David to Ozzie.* It will take him time.

OZZIE. That's normal and to be expected. I'm not surprised. Not at all. We figured on this. Sure, we did. Didn't we, Rick?

RICK, *occupied with his camera, an Instamatic.* I wanna take some pictures, okay? How are you, Dave?

DAVID. What room is this?

OZZIE. Middle room, Dave. TV room. TV's in—

HARRIET, *on the stairs.* David! . . . Oh, David! . . . David . . .

And Ozzie, leaving David, hurries toward the stairs and looks up at her as she falters, stops, stares. Rick, moving near, snaps a picture of her.

OZZIE. Harriet . . . don't be upset . . . They say . . . Harriet, Harriet, . . . he can't see! . . . Harriet . . . they say—he—can't . . . see. That man.

HARRIET, *standing very still.* Can't see? What do you mean?

SGT. MAJOR. He's blind.

HARRIET. No. Who says? No, no.

OZZIE. Look at him. He looks so old. But it's nothing, Harriet, I'm sure.

SGT. MAJOR. I hope you people understand.

OZZIE. It's probably just how he's tired from his long trip.

HARRIET, *moving toward him.* Oh, you're home now, David.

SGT. MAJOR, *with a large sheet of paper waving in his hand.* Who's gonna sign this for me, Mister? It's a shipping receipt. I got to have somebody's signature to show you got him. I got to have somebody's name on the paper.

OZZIE. Let me. All right?

SGT. MAJOR. Just here and here, you see? Your name or mark three times.

As they move toward a table and away from Harriet, who is near David.

OZZIE. Fine, listen, would you like some refreshments?

SGT. MAJOR. No.

OZZIE. I mean while I do this. Cake and coffee. Of course, you do.

SGT. MAJOR. No.

OZZIE. Sure.

SGT. MAJOR. No, I haven't time. I've got to get going. I've got trucks out there backed up for blocks. Other boys. I got to get on to Chicago, and some of them to Denver and Cleveland, Reno, New Orleans, Boston, Trenton, Watts, Atlanta. And when I get back they'll be layin' all over the grass; layin' there in pieces all over the grass, their backs been broken, their brains jellied, their insides turned into garbage. One-legged boys and no-legged boys. I'm due in Harlem; I got to get to the Bronx and Queens, Cincinnati, Saint Louis, Reading. I don't have time for coffee. I got deliveries to make all across this country.

DAVID, *with Harriet, his hands on her face, a kind of realization.* Nooooooo . . . Sergeant . . . nooo; there's something wrong; it all feels wrong. Where are you? Are you here? I don't know these people!

SGT. MAJOR. That's natural, Soldier; it's natural for you to feel that way.

DAVID. Nooooo.

HARRIET, *attempting to guide him back to a chair.* David, just sit, be still.

DAVID. Don't you hear me?

OZZIE. Harriet, calm him.

DAVID. The air is wrong; the smells and sounds, the wind.

HARRIET. David, please, please. What is it? Be still. Please . . .

DAVID. GODDAMN YOU, SERGEANT, I AM LONELY HERE! I AM LONELY!

SGT. MAJOR. I got to go. *(And he pivots to leave.)*

DAVID, *following the sound of the sergeant major's voice.* Sergeant!

SGT. MAJOR, *whirling, bellowing.* You shut up. You piss-ass soldier, you shut the fuck up!

OZZIE, *walking to the sergeant major, putting his hand on the man's shoulder.* Listen, let me walk you to the door. All right? I'd like to take a look at that truck of yours. All right?

SGT. MAJOR. There's more than one.

OZZIE. Fine.

SGT. MAJOR. It's a convoy.

OZZIE. Good.

They exit, slamming the door, and Rick, running close behind them, pops it open, leaps out. He calls from off.

RICK. Sure are lots of trucks, Mom!

HARRIET, *as he re-enters.* Are there?

RICK. Oh, yeah. Gonna rain some more too. *(And turning, he runs up the stairs.)* See you in the morning. Night, Dave.

HARRIET. It's so good to have you here again; so good to see you. You look . . . just . . .

(Ozzie has slipped back into the room behind her, he stands, looking.)

fine. You look—

(She senses Ozzie's presence, turns, immediately, speaking.)

He bewilders you, doesn't he?

(And Ozzie, jauntily, heads for the stairs.)

Where are you going?

(He stops; he doesn't know. And she is happily sad now as she speaks—sad for poor Ozzie and David, they are whimsical, so childlike.)

You thought you knew what was right, all those years, teaching him sports and fighting. Do you understand what I'm trying to say? A mother knows *things* . . . a father cannot ever know them. The measles, smallpox, cuts and bruises. Never have you come upon him in the night as he lay awake and staring . . . praying.

OZZIE. I saw him put a knife through the skin of a cat. I saw him cut the belly open.

DAVID. Noooo. . . .

HARRIET, *moving toward him in response.* David, David . . .

DAVID. Ricky!

(There is a kind of accusation in this as if he were saying Ricky did the killing of the cat. He says it loudly and directly into her face.)

HARRIET. He's gone to bed.

DAVID. I want to leave.

There is furniture around him; he is caged. He pokes with his cane.

HARRIET. What is it?

DAVID. Help me. *(He crashes.)*

OZZIE. Settle down! Relax.

DAVID. I want to leave! I want to leave! I want to leave. I . . .

(And he smashes into the stairs, goes down, flails, pounding his cane.)

want to leave.

OZZIE and HARRIET. Dave! David! Davey!

DAVID. . . . to leave! Please.

He is on the floor, breathing. Long, long silence in which they look at him sadly, until Harriet announces the problem's solution.

HARRIET. Ozzie, get him some medicine. Get him some Easy Sleep.

OZZIE. Good idea.

HARRIET. It's in the medicine cabinet; a little blue bottle, little pink pills.

(And when Ozzie is gone up the stairs, there is quiet. She stands over David.)

It'll give you the sleep you need, Dave—the sleep you remember. You're our child and you're home. Our good . . . beautiful boy. *And front door bursts open. There is a small girl in the doorway, an Asian girl. She wears the Vietnamese ao dai, black slacks and white tunic slit up the sides. Slowly, she enters, carrying before her a small straw hat. Harriet is looking at the open door.*

HARRIET. What an awful . . . wind. *(She shuts the door.)*

Blackout. Guitar music.

A match flickers as Harriet lights a candle in the night. And the girl silently moves from before the door across the floor to the stairs, where she sits, as Harriet moves toward the stairs and Ozzie, asleep sitting up in a chair, stirs.

HARRIET. Oh! I didn't mean to wake you. I lit a candle so I wouldn't wake you.

(He stares at her.)

I'm sorry.

OZZIE. I wasn't sleeping.

HARRIET. I thought you were.

OZZIE. Couldn't. Tried. Couldn't. Thinking. Thoughts running very fast. Trying to remember the night David . . . was made. Do you understand me? I don't know why. But the feeling in me that I had to figure something out and if only I could remember that night . . . the mood . . . I would be able. You're . . . shaking your head.

HARRIET. I don't understand.

OZZIE. No.

HARRIET. Good night.

(*She turns and leaves Ozzie sitting there, gazing at the dark. Arriving at David's door, she raps softly and then opens the door. David is lying unmoving on the bed. She speaks to him.*)

I heard you call.

DAVID. What?

HARRIET. I heard you call.

DAVID. I didn't.

HARRIET. Would you like a glass of warm milk?

DAVID. I was sleeping.

HARRIET, *after a slight pause.* How about that milk? Would you like some milk?

DAVID. I didn't call. I was sleeping.

HARRIET. I'll bet you're glad you didn't bring her back. Their skins are yellow, aren't they?

DAVID. What?

HARRIET. You're troubled, warm milk would help. Do you pray at all anymore? If I were to pray now, would you pray with me?

DAVID. What . . . do you want?

HARRIET. They eat the flesh of dogs.

DAVID. I know. I've seen them.

HARRIET. Pray with me; pray.

DAVID. What . . . do . . . you want?

HARRIET. Just to talk, that's all. Just to know that you're home and safe again. Nothing else; only that we're all together, a family. You must be exhausted. Don't worry; sleep. (*She is backing into the hallway. In a whisper*) Good night.

(*She blows out the candle and is gone, moving down the hall. Meanwhile the girl is stirring, rising, climbing from the living room up*) *toward David's room, which she enters, moving through a wall, and David sits up.)*

DAVID. Who's there?

(As she drifts by, he waves the cane at the air.)

Zung? *(He stands.)* Chào, Cô Zung.

(He moves for the door, which he opens, and steps into the hall, leaving her behind him in the room.)

Zung. Chào, Cô Zung.

(And he moves off up the hallway. She follows.)

Zung! . . .

Blackout. Music.

[LATER IN ACT ONE:]

DAVID, *changing, turning.* I have some movies. I thought you . . . knew.

HARRIET. Well . . . we . . . do.

OZZIE. Movies?

DAVID. Yes, I took them.

RICK. I thought you wanted to sing.

OZZIE. I mean, they're what's planned, Dave. That's what's up. The projector's all wound and ready. I don't know what you had to get so angry for.

HARRIET. Let's get everything ready.

OZZIE. Sure, sure. No need for all that yelling.

He moves to set up the projector.

DAVID. I'll narrate.

OZZIE. Fine, sure. What's it about anyway?

HARRIET. Are you in it?

OZZIE. Ricky, plug it in. C'mon, c'mon.

DAVID. It's a kind of story.

RICK. What about my guitar?

DAVID. No.

OZZIE. We oughta have some popcorn, though.

HARRIET. Oh, yes, what a dumb movie house, no popcorn, huh, Rick!

Rick switches off the lights.

OZZIE. Let her rip, Dave.

(Dave turns on the projector; Ozzie is hurrying to a seat.)

Ready when you are, C.B.

HARRIET. Shhhhhhh!

OZZIE, *a little child playing.* Let her rip, C.B. I want a new contract, C.B.

The projector runs for a moment. (Note: In proscenium, a screen should be used if possible, or the film may be allowed to seem projected on the fourth wall; in three-quarter or round the screen may be necessary. If the screen is used, nothing must show upon it but a flickering of green.)

HARRIET. Ohhh, what's the matter? It didn't come out, there's nothing there.

DAVID. Of course there is.

HARRIET. Noooo . . . It's all funny.

DAVID. Look.

OZZIE. It's underexposed, Dave.

DAVID, *moving nearer.* No. Look.

HARRIET. What?

DAVID. They hang in the trees. They hang by their wrists half-severed by the wire.

OZZIE. Pardon me, Dave?

HARRIET. I'm going to put on the lights.

DAVID. NOOOOO! LOOK! They hang in the greenish haze afflicted by insects; a woman and a man, middle aged. They do not shout or cry. He is too small. Look—he seems all bone, shame in his eyes; his wife even here come with him, skinny also as a broom and her hair is straight and black, hanging to mask her eyes.

The girl, Zung, drifts into the room.

OZZIE. I don't know what you're doing, David; there's nothing there.

DAVID. LOOK! *(And he points.)* They are all bone and pain, uncontoured and ugly but for the peculiar melon-swelling in her middle which is her pregnancy, which they do not see—look! these soldiers who have found her—as they do not see that she is not dead but only dying until saliva and blood bubble at her lips. Look . . . Yet . . . she dies. Though a doctor is called in to remove the bullet-shot baby she would have preferred . . . to keep since she was dying and it was dead.

(And Zung silently, drifting, departs.)

In fact, as it turned out they would have all been better off left to hang as they had been strung on the wire—he with the back of his head blown off and she, the rifle jammed exactly and deeply up into her, with a bullet fired directly into the child living there. For they ended each buried in a separate place; the husband by chance alone was returned to their village, while the wife was dumped into an alien nearby plot of dirt, while the child, too small a piece of meat, was burned. Put into fire, as the shattered legs and arms cut off of men are burned. There's an oven. It is no ceremony. It is the disposal of garbage! . . .

Harriet gets to her feet, marches to the projector, pulls the plug, begins a little lecture.

HARRIET. It's so awful the things those yellow people do to one another. Yellow people hanging yellow people. Isn't that right? Ozzie, I told you—animals—Christ, burn them. David, don't let it hurt you. All the things you saw. People aren't themselves in war. I mean like that sticking that gun into that poor woman and then shooting that poor little baby, that's not human. That's inhuman. It's inhuman, barbaric and uncivilized and inhuman.

DAVID. I'm thirsty.

HARRIET. For what? Tell me. Water? Or would you like some milk? How about some milk?

DAVID, *shaking his head.* No.

HARRIET. Or would you like some orange juice? All golden and little bits of ice.

OZZIE. Just all those words and that film with no picture and these poor people hanging somewhere—so you can bring them home like this house is a meat house—

HARRIET. Oh, Ozzie, no, it's not that—no—he's just young, a young boy . . . and he's been through terrible, terrible things and now he's home, with his family he loves, just trying to speak to those he loves—just—

DAVID. Yes! That's right. Yes. What I mean is, yes, of course, that's what I am—a young . . . blind man in a room . . . in a house in the dark, raising nothing in a gesture of no meaning toward two voices who are not speaking . . . of a certain . . . incredible . . . *connection!*

All stare. Rick leaps up, running for the stairs.

RICK. Listen, everybody, I hate to rush off like this, but I gotta. Night.

HARRIET. Good night, Rick.

OZZIE, *simultaneously.* Good night.

David moves toward the stairs, looking upward.

DAVID. Because I talk of certain things . . . don't think I did them. Murderers don't even know that murder happens.

HARRIET. What are you saying? No, no. We're a family, that's all— we've had a little trouble—David, you've got to stop—please—no more yelling. Just be happy and home like all the others—why can't you?

DAVID. You mean take some old man to a ditch of water, shove his head under, talk of cars and money till his feeble pawing stops, and then head on home to go in and out of doors and drive cars and sing sometimes. I left her like you wanted . . . where people are thin and small all their lives. *(The beginning of realization)* Or did . . . you . . . think it was a . . . place . . . like this? Sinks and kitchens all the world over? Is that what you believe? Water from faucets, light from wires? Trucks, telephones, TV. Ricky sings and sings, but if I were to cut his throat, he would no longer and you would miss him—you would miss his singing. We are hoboes! *(And it is the first time in his life he has ever thought these things.)* We make signs in the dark. You know yours. I understand my own. We share . . . coffee!

(There is nearly joy in this discovery: a hint of new freedom that might be liberation. And somewhere in the thrill of it he has whirled, his cane has come near to Ozzie, frightening him, though Harriet does not notice. Now David turns, moving for the stairs, thinking.) I'm going up to bed . . . now . . . I'm very . . . tired.

OZZIE. Well . . . you have a good sleep, Son. . . .

DAVID. Yes, I think I'll sleep in.

OZZIE. You do as you please. . . .

DAVID. Good night.
HARRIET. Good night.
OZZIE. Good night.
HARRIET. Good night. *(Slight pause.)* You get a good rest. *(Silence.)* Try . . .

[FROM ACT TWO:]

David descends with Zung behind him. Calmly he speaks, growing slowly happy.
DAVID. Do you know how north of here, on farms, gentle loving dogs are raised, while in the forests, other dogs run wild? And upon occasion, one of those that's wild is captured and put in among the others that are tame, bringing with it the memory of when they had all been wild—the dark and the terror—that had made them wolves. Don't you hear them?
And there is a rumbling.
RICK. What? Hear what?
It is windlike, the rumbling of many trucks.
DAVID. Don't you hear the trucks? They're all over town, lined up from the center of town into the country. Don't you hear? They've stopped bringing back the blind. They're bringing back the dead now. The convoy's broken up. There's no control . . . they're walking from house to house, through the shrubbery, under the trees, carrying one of the dead in a bright blue rubber bag for which they have no papers, no name or manner. No one knows whose it is. They're at the Jensens' now. Now Al Jensen's at the door, all his kids behind him trying to peek. Al looks for a long, long time into the open bag before he shakes his head. They zipper shut the bag and turn away. They've been to the Mayers', the Kellys', the Irwins' and the Kresses'. They'll be here soon.
OZZIE. Nooo.
DAVID. And Dad's going to let them in. We're going to let them in.
HARRIET. What's he saying?
DAVID. He's going to knock.
OZZIE. I DON'T KNOW.

DAVID. Yes. Yes.

A knocking sound. Is it David knocking with his fist against the door or table?

OZZIE. Nooooo.

RICK. Mom, he's driving Dad crazy.

Knocking loud: it seems to be at the front door.

OZZIE. David, will I die?

He moves toward the door.

HARRIET. Who do you suppose it could be so late?

RICK, *intercepting Ozzie, blocking the way to the door.* I don't think you should just go opening the door to anybody this time of the night, there's no telling who it might be.

DAVID. We know who it is.

OZZIE. Oh, David, why can't you wait? Why can't you rest?

But David is the father now, and he will explain. He loves them all.

DAVID. Look at her. See her, Dad. Tell her to go to the door. Tell her yes, it's your house, you want her to open the door and let them in. Tell her yes, the one with no name is ours. We'll put it in that chair. We can bring them all here. I want them all here, all the trucks and bodies. There's room. *(Handing Rick the guitar)* Ricky can sing. We'll stack them along the walls . . .

OZZIE. Nooo . . .

DAVID. Pile them over the floor . . .

OZZIE. No, no . . .

DAVID. They will become the floor and they will become the walls, the chairs. We'll sit in them; sleep. We will call them "home." We will give them as gifts—call them "ring" and "pot" and "cup." No, no; it's not a thing to fear. . . . We will notice them no more than all the others.

He is gentle, happy, consoling to them.

OZZIE. What others? There are no others. Oh . . . please die. Oh, wait . . .

(And he scurries to the TV where it sits beneath the stairs.)

I'll get it fixed. I'll fix it. Who needs to hear it? We'll watch it. *(Wildly turning TV channels.)* I flick my rotten life. Oh, there's a good one. Look at that one. Ohhh, isn't that a good one? That's the best one. That's the best one.

DAVID. They will call it madness. We will call it seeing.

Calmly he lifts Ozzie.

OZZIE. I don't want to disappear.

DAVID. Let her take you to the door. We will be runners. You will have eyes.

OZZIE. I will be blind. I will disappear.

Knocking is heard again. Again.

DAVID. You stand and she stands. "Let her go," you say; "she is garbage and filth and you must get her back if you wish to live. She is sickness, I must cherish her." Old voices you have trusted all your life as if they were your own, speaking always friendly. "She's all of everything impossible made possible!"

OZZIE. Ricky . . . noooo! . . .

DAVID. Don't call to Ricky. You love her. You will embrace her, see her and—

OZZIE. He has no right to do this to me.

DAVID. Don't call to Ricky!

OZZIE, *suddenly raging, rushing at David, pushing him.* You have no right to do this.

RICK. Nooooooo!

(Savagely he smashes his guitar down upon David, who crumples.) Let Dad alone. Let him alone. He's sick of you. What the hell's the matter with you? He doesn't wanna talk anymore about all the stupid stuff you talk. He wants to talk about cake and cookies and cars and coffee. He's sick a you and he wants you to shut up. We hate you, goddamn you.

Silence: David lies still.

ZUNG. Chào ông!

(Ozzie pivots, looks at her.)

Chào ông! Hôm nay ông manh không?

OZZIE. Oh, what is it that you want? I'm tired. I mean it. Forgive me. I'm sick of the sight of you, squatting all the time. In filth like animals, talking gibberish, your breath sick with rot. . . . And yet you look at me with those sad pleading eyes as if there is some real thing that can come between us when you're not even here. You are deceit.

(*His hands, rising, have driven to her throat. The fingers close.*)

I'm not David. I'm not silly and soft . . . little David. The sight of you sickens me. YOU HEAR ME, DAVID? Believe me. I am speaking my honest true feelings. I spit on you, the both of you; I piss on you and your eyes and pain. Flesh is lies. You are garbage and filth. You are darkness. I cast you down. Deceit. Animal. Dirty animal.

And he is over her. They are sprawled on the ground. Silence as no one moves. She lies like a rag beneath him.

RICK. I saw this really funny movie last night. This really . . . funny, funny movie about this young couple and they were going to get a divorce but they didn't. It was really funny.

Ozzie is hiding the girl. In a proscenium production, he can drag her beneath the couch; in three-quarters, he covers her with a blanket brought to him by Harriet which matches the rug.

HARRIET. What's that? What's that?

RICK. This movie I saw.

HARRIET. Anybody want to go for groceries? We need Kleenex, sugar, milk.

RICK. What a really funny movie.

OZZIE. I'll go; I'll go.

HARRIET. Good. Good.

OZZIE. I think I saw it on TV.

They are cleaning up the house now, putting the chairs back in order, dumping all of Ozzie's leaflets in the waste can.

HARRIET. Did you enjoy it, Rick?

RICK. Oh, yeh. I loved it.

OZZIE. I laughed so much I almost got sick. It was really good. I laughed.

RICK. I bet it was; I bet you did.

OZZIE. Oh, I did.

Even David helps with the cleaning: he gets himself off the floor and is seated in a chair.

HARRIET. How are you feeling, Ricky?

Rick. Fine.

Harriet. Good.

Rick. How do you feel?

Harriet. Oh, I'm all right. I feel fine.

Ozzie. Me, too. I feel fine, too. What day is it, anyway? Monday?

Harriet. Wednesday.

Rick. Tuesday, Mom.

Now all three are seated on the couch.

Ozzie. I thought it was Monday.

Rick. Oh, no.

Harriet. No, no. You're home now, David. . . .

Rick, *moving to David, who sits alone in a chair.* Hey, Dave, listen, will you. I mean I know it's not my place to speak out and give advice and everything because I'm the youngest, but I just gotta say my honest true feelings and I'd kill myself if I were you, Dave. You're in too much misery. I'd cut my wrists. Honestly speaking, brother to brother, you should have done it long ago.

(David is looking about.)

David. What?

Rick. Nooo. She's never been here. You just thought so. You decided not to bring her, Dave, remember? You decided, all things considered that you preferred to come back without her. Too much risk and inconvenience . . . you decided. Isn't that right? Sure. You know it is. You've always known.

(Silence. Harriet moves to look out the front door.)

Do you want to use my razor, Dave? *(Pulling a straight razor from his pocket)* I have one right here and you can use it if you want. *(David seems to be looking at the razor.)*

Just take it if you want it, Dave.

Harriet. Go ahead, David. The front yard's empty. You don't have to be afraid. The streets, too . . . still and empty.

Rick. It doesn't hurt like you think it will. Go ahead; just take it, Dave.

Ozzie. You might as well.

Rick. That's right.

Ozzie. You'll feel better.

Rick. I'll help you now, Dave, okay?

HARRIET. I'll go get some pans and towels.

RICK, *moving about David, patting him, buddying him.* Oh, you're so confused, you don't know what to do. It's just a good thing I got this razor, Boy, that's all I gotta say. You're so confused. You see, Dave, where you're wrong is your point of view, it's silly. It's just really comical because you think people are valuable or something and, given a chance like you were to mess with 'em, to take a young girl like that and turn her into a whore, you shouldn't, when of course you should or at least might . . . on whim . . . you see? I mean, you're all backwards, Dave—you're upside down. You don't know how to go easy and play—I bet you didn't have any fun the whole time you were over there—no fun at all—and it was there. I got this buddy Gerry, he was there, and he used to throw bags of cement at 'em from off the back a his truck. They'd go whizzin' through those villages, throwin' off these bags a cement. You could kill people, he says, you hit 'em right. Especially the kids. There was this once they knocked this ole man off his bicycle—fifty pounds a dry cement—and then the back a the truck got his legs. It was hysterical—can't you just see that, Dave? Him layin' there howlin', all the guys in the truck bowin' and wavin' and tippin' their hats. What a goddamn funny story, huh?

Harriet has brought silver pans and towels with roosters on them. The towels cover the arms of the chair and David's lap. The pans will catch the blood. All has been neatly placed. David, with Ricky's help, cuts one wrist, and then the other, as they talk.

DAVID. I wanted . . . to kill you . . . all of you.

RICK. I know, I know; but you were hurt; too weak.

DAVID. I wanted for you to need what I had and I wouldn't give it.

HARRIET. That's not possible.

OZZIE. Nooooo.

DAVID. I wanted to get you. Like poor bug-eyed fish flung up from the brief water to the lasting dirt, I would get you.

HARRIET. David, no, no, you didn't want that.

OZZIE. No, no.

RICK. I don't even know why you'd think you did.

OZZIE. We kill you is what happens.

RICK. That's right.

OZZIE. And then, of course, we die, too . . . Later on, I mean. And nothing stops it. Not words . . . or walls . . . or even guitars.

RICK. Sure.

OZZIE. That's what happens.

HARRIET. It isn't too bad, is it?

RICK. How bad is it?

OZZIE. He's getting weaker.

HARRIET. And in a little, it'll all be over. You'll feel so grand. No more funny talk.

RICK. You can shower; put on clean clothes. I've got deodorant you can borrow. After Roses, Dave. The scent of a thousand roses.

He is preparing to take a picture—crouching, aiming.

HARRIET. Take off your glasses, David.

OZZIE. Do as you're told.

RICK *(as David's hands are rising toward the glasses to remove them).* I bet when you were away there was only plain water to wash in, huh? You prob'ly hadda wash in the rain.

(He takes the picture; there is a flash. A slide appears on the screen: A close-up of David, nothing visible but his face. It is the slide that, appearing as the start of the play, was referred to as "somebody sick." Now it hovers, stricken, sightless, revealed.)

Mom, I like David like this.

HARRIET. He's happier.

OZZIE. We're all happier.

RICK. Too bad he's gonna die.

OZZIE. No, no, he's not gonna die, Rick. He's only gonna nearly die. Only nearly.

RICK. Ohhhhhhhhhhhhh.

HARRIET. Mmmmmmmmmmmmm.

And Rick, sitting, begins to play his guitar for David. The music is alive and fast. It has a rhythm, a drive of happiness that is contagious. The lights slowly fade.

From
Demilitarized Zones

J an B arry and
W. D. E hrhart , E ditors

1976

Imagine

W. D. EHRHART

The conversation turned to Vietnam.
He'd been there, and they asked him
what it had been like:
had he been in battle?
Had he ever been afraid?

Patiently, he tried to answer
questions he had tried to answer
many times before.

They listened, and they strained
to visualize the words:
newsreels and photographs, books
and Wilfred Owen tumbled
through their minds. Pulses quickened.

They didn't notice, as he talked,
his eyes, as he talked,
his eyes begin to focus
through the wall, at nothing,
or at something deep inside.

When he finished speaking,
someone asked him
had he ever killed?

War Stories

PERRY OLDHAM

Have you heard Howard's tape?
You won't believe it:
He recorded the last mortar attack.
The folks at home have never heard a real
Mortar attack
And he wants to let them know
Exactly
What it's like.

Every night he pops popcorn
And drinks Dr. Pepper
And narrates the tape:
　　Ka-blooie!
　　Thirty-seven rounds of eighty millimeter—
　　You can count them if you slow down the tape.
　　There's an AK.
　　Those are hand grenades.
　　Here's where the Cobras come in
　　And whomp their ass.

D. C. BERRY

A poem ought to be a salt lick
rather than sugar candy.
A preservative.
Something to make a tongue
tough enough to taste
the full flavor
of beauty and grief.

I would go to the dark
places where the
animals go;

they know
where the salt licks are
far
away from the barbed glitters of neon,
far
away from the bottles of booze
stacked like loaded rifles,
far
away into the gray-bone and
bleached silence.

I would go there now
before the slow explosion of Spring.
Already my tongue bleeds from
the yellow slash of Forsythia
that must be blooming
where you are.

In Celebration of Spring 1976

JOHN BALABAN

Our Asian war is over, squandered, spent.
Our elders who tried to mortgage lies
are disgraced, or dead, and already
the brokers are picking their pockets
for the keys and the credit cards.

In delta swamp in a united Vietnam,
a Marine with a bullfrog for a face
rots in equatorial heat. An eel
slides through the cage of his bared ribs.
At night, on the still battlefields, ghosts,
like patches of fog, lurk into villages
to maunder on doorsills of cratered homes,
while all across the U.S.A. in this 200th year
of revolution and the rights of man,
the wounded walk about and wonder where to go.

And today, in the simmer of lyric sunlight,
a chrysalis pulses in its mushy cocoon
under the bark on a gnarled root of an elm.
In the brilliant creek, a minnow flashes
delirious with gnats. The turtle's heart
quickens its taps in the warm bank sludge.
As she chases a frisbee spinning in sunlight
a girl's breasts bounce full and strong;
a boy's stomach, as he turns, is flat and strong.

Swear by the locust, by dragonflies on ferns,
by the minnow's flash, the tremble of a breast,
by the new earth spongy under our feet:

that as we grow old, we will not grow evil,
that although our garden seeps with sewage,
and our elders think it's up for auction—swear
by this dazzle that does not wish to leave us—
that we will be keepers of a garden, nonetheless.

3

First Wave of Major Work

Vietnam, 1963. Troops land in a field near Tan Hung.

The year 1976 marked America's Bicentennial and the election of President Jimmy Carter, the first President from the Deep South. Carter had been the governor of Georgia, and his status as a Washington outsider appealed to voters tired of the Nixon/Ford administrations' corruption and back-room dealing. Carter's ability to project an honest, down-home image helped him win the election, and for the first time in thirty years, America had a president with no direct tie to the Vietnam War.

American politicians in the mid-seventies naturally would have liked to put the war behind them, just as they would have liked America to forget the Watergate scandal, but the government's abuse of the public trust was still fresh in the nation's memory. During this era, skepticism was rampant, and all institutions were suspect. Carter himself referred to this as "the malaise," and hoped that Americans would regain their faith.

Vietnam veterans had no part in this hopeful new beginning. Living reminders of a war that had split the country, they were rarely seen or heard, and when by chance they were, they seemed to fit stereotypes like the protest vet or psycho vet that were already growing old (see the introduction to Chapter 4 for Hollywood's portrayal of the vet at this time).

The first wave of major works changed this. Between 1976 and 1978, after years of being told by publishing houses that "Vietnam doesn't sell," veterans and journalists with Vietnam experience released powerful and controversial works that not only earned them literary awards and brilliant reviews, but became surprise bestsellers. Part of the first wave's impact came from the fact that the general reader had never seen anything like these accounts. Though it had been years since the war had ended, these books were bringing the reader news, and unlike the institutions that had run and reported the war, the American people were still interested in finding out the truth about America's role in Vietnam.

Ron Kovic's *Born on the Fourth of July* (1976) is a nonfiction account of his stint in the Marines, his disabling injuries, and his struggles with the Veterans Administration. Written in an odd mix of first- and third-person narration, often drifting into stream-of-consciousness, *Born on the Fourth of July* shows Kovic's progression from an idealistic teenager to a scared and bitter patient and finally to a committed political activist. The book was an immediate success; after years of rejection, Oliver Stone finally made it into a popular if not well-received movie in 1989.

Marine lieutenant James Webb's first novel, *Fields of Fire* (1978), was a best-seller. In a realistic, if sometimes overwrought style, the book chronicles the Vietnam experience of several men in a Marine unit. It's stuffed with technical expertise, and the characters are relatively flat and often take a backseat to the action. Critics sometimes label *Fields of Fire* old-fashioned, comparing it to World War II novels such as Norman Mailer's *The Naked and the Dead* in its concentration on unit politics. Webb, a conservative Republican, was later appointed Secretary of the Navy by Ronald Reagan and wrote several other novels, none of which made as great an impact as his first.

Philip Caputo's memoir *A Rumor of War* (1977) was also a best-selling first book. In a high literary style, the former Marine lieutenant and journalist describes his 1965–66 tour of duty, including an incident—a pair of murders—for which he faced a court-martial. This is another piece of nonfiction that reads like a novel in its attention to detail and setting of scenes. Caputo digs deep into important moral issues, and his explanations of the war and his own actions are provocative.

Of all the books to come out of the Vietnam War, journalist Michael Herr's *Dispatches* (1977) is most often cited as the best, capturing the thrills, terror, and madness of the war. Written in a wild, anecdotal style, *Dispatches* nails the absurd contradictions (both moral and material) of the conflict and takes the reader seemingly everywhere in-country by chopper, touching down with Herr in the middle of the first rock 'n' roll war. While Herr is writing nonfiction, he never lets the reader assume his objectivity, often focusing on his own strange, even parasitic role in the proceedings. And the stories that he tells or retells have the feel of legends or tall tales, even jokes. Later Herr would write parts of the scripts for both *Apocalypse Now* and *Full Metal Jacket.*

As mentioned in the introduction to Chapter 2, Tim O'Brien's *Going After Cacciato* (1978) won the National Book Award. Grittily realistic in places, the book also serves up absurd and deadpan humor, earning comparisons to Joseph Heller's *Catch-22*. One section included here, "The Things They Didn't Know," neatly shows the reader the relationship between U.S. troops and Vietnamese civilians, as well as hero Paul Berlin's feelings of guilt and complicity.

While these five pieces use a range of literary styles, they all purport to contain some deep and significant truth about the war. Technically, Kovic, Herr, and Caputo are writing nonfiction, yet all three use novelistic details and tactics, and Herr's language often takes on a jaunty "I dare you to believe this" tone. Webb, while writing fiction, seems to cram as much factual detail about life in the bush into his scenes as they'll hold, relying on the reader's thirst for firsthand knowledge to sustain interest, and O'Brien pointedly undercuts his own grave use of realism with hilarious routines right out of some cosmic vaudeville. Yet no matter how odd the materials they use, these authors pointedly question the reality of the war. Like the American reader of the time, they have a desperate need to find out exactly what happened. What is true and what is a lie? What are the facts, and how did it really feel?

There are any number of instances in these pieces where these veterans attempt to relate their experience in Vietnam to people in America. Again and again, we see the difficulty, perhaps the impossibility, of bridging that gap. Herr, as a bystander, not a true participant, has a great deal of insight on this, as does Kovic, separated from everyone (and maybe even himself) by what he's been through.

It is worthy of note that several of these writers/veterans were in Vietnam for more than one tour, an occurrence less rare than the public, schooled to accept the typical vet as a reluctant draftee, might think. Both Kovic and Caputo comment on the allure of combat and Vietnam, weighing it against their mundane lives in America. Some of Herr's grunts have interesting things to say on this point as well.

Most important, though, like the early works, the first wave is interested in the moral questions surrounding the individual soldier's participation in war—in this particular war, and in war in general. Is there a difference, and if so, what?

Born on the Fourth of July

RON KOVIC

1976

The bus turned off a side street and onto the parkway, then into Queens where the hospital was. For the first time on the whole trip everyone was laughing and joking. He felt himself begin to wake up out of the nightmare. This whole area was home to him—the streets, the parkway, he knew them like the back of his hand. The air was fresh and cold and the bus rocked back and forth. "This bus sucks!" yelled a kid. "Can't you guys do any better than this? I want my mother, I want my mother."

The pain twisted into his back, but he laughed with the rest of them—the warriors, the wounded, entering the gates of St. Albans Naval Hospital. The guard waved them in and the bus stopped. He was the last of the men to be taken off the bus. They had to carry him off. He got the impression that he was quite an oddity in his steel frame, crammed inside it like a flattened pancake.

They put him on the neuro ward. It was sterile and quiet. I'm with the vegetables again, he thought. It took a long while to get hold of a nurse. He told her that if they didn't get the top of the frame off his back he would start screaming. They took it off and moved him back downstairs to another ward. This was a ward for men with open wounds. They put him there because of his heel, which had been all smashed by the first bullet, the back of it blown completely out.

He was now in Ward I-C with fifty other men who had all been recently wounded in the war—twenty-year-old blind men and ampu-

119

tees, men without intestines, men who limped, men who were in wheelchairs, men in pain. He noticed they all had strange smiles on their faces and he had one too, he thought. They were men who had played with death and cheated it at a very young age.

He lay back in his bed and watched everything happen all around him. He went to therapy every day and worked very hard lifting weights. He had to build up the top of his body if he was ever going to walk again. In Da Nang the doctors had told him to get used to the idea that he would have to sit in a wheelchair for the rest of his life. He had accepted it, but more and more he was dreaming and thinking about walking. He prayed every night after the visitors left. He closed his eyes and dreamed of being on his feet again.

Sometimes the American Legion group from his town came in to see him, the men and their wives and their pretty daughters. They would all surround him in his bed. It would seem to him that he was always having to cheer them up more than they were cheering him. They told him he was a hero and that all of Massapequa was proud of him. One time the commander stood up and said they were even thinking of naming a street after him. But the guy's wife was embarrassed and made her husband shut up. She told him the commander was kidding—he tended to get carried away after a couple of beers.

After he had been in the hospital a couple of weeks, a man appeared one morning and handed him a large envelope. He waited until the man had gone to open it up. Inside was a citation and a medal for Conspicuous Service to the State of New York. The citation was signed by Governor Rockefeller. He stuck the envelope and all the stuff in it under his pillow.

None of the men in the wards were civilian yet, so they had reveille at six o'clock in the morning. All the wounded who could get on their feet were made to stand in front of their beds while a roll call was taken. After roll call they all had to make their beds and do a general clean-up of the entire ward—everything from scrubbing the floors to cleaning the windows. Even the amputees had to do it. No one ever bothered him, though. He usually slept through the whole thing.

Later it would be time for medication, and afterward one of the corpsmen would put him in a wheelchair and push him to the shower room. The corpsman would leave him alone for about five minutes, then pick his body up, putting him on a wooden bench, his legs dangling, his toes barely touching the floor. He would sit in the shower like that every morning watching his legs become smaller and smaller, until after a month the muscle tone had all but disappeared. With despair and frustration he watched his once strong twenty-one-year-old body become crippled and disfigured. He was just beginning to understand the nature of his wound. He knew now it was the worst he could have received without dying or becoming a vegetable.

More and more he thought about what a priest had said to him in Da Nang: "Your fight is just beginning. Sometimes no one will want to hear what you're going through. You are going to have to learn to carry a great burden and most of your learning will be done alone. Don't feel frightened when they leave you. I'm sure you will come through it all okay."

I am in a new hospital now. Things are very different than in the last place. It is quiet in the early morning. There is no reveille here. The sun is just beginning to come in through the windows and I can hear the steady dripping of the big plastic bags that overflow with urine to the floor. The aide comes in the room, a big black woman. She goes to Willey's bed across from me, almost stepping in the puddle of urine. She takes the cork out of the metal thing in his neck and sticks the long rubber tube in, then clicks on the machine by the bed. There is a loud sucking slurping sound. She moves the rubber tube around and around until it sucks all the stuff out of his lungs. After she is done she puts the cork back in his throat and leaves the room.

There are people talking down at the end of the hall. The night shift is getting ready to go home. They are laughing very loud and flushing the toilets, cursing and telling jokes, black men in white uniforms walking past my door. I shut my eyes. I try to get back into the dream I was having. She is so pretty, so warm and naked lying next to me. She kisses me and begins to unbutton my hospital shirt. "I love you," I hear her say. "I love you." I open my eyes. Something strange is tickling my nose.

It is Tommy the enema man and today is my day to get my enema. "Hey Kovic," Tommy is saying. "Hey Kovic, wake up, I got an enema for you."

She kisses my lips softly at first, then puts her tongue into my mouth. I am running my hands through her hair and she tells me that she loves that. She is unbuttoning my trousers now and her small hand is working itself deep down into my pants. I keep driving my tongue into her more furiously than ever. We have just been dancing on the floor, I was dancing very funny like a man on stilts, but now we are making love and just above me I hear a voice trying to wake me again.

"Kovic! I have an enema for you. Come on. We gotta get you outta here."

I feel myself being lifted. Tommy and another aide, a young black woman, pick me up, carefully unhooking my tube. They put my body into the frame, tying my legs down with long white twisted sheets. They lay another big sheet over me. The frame has a long metal bar that goes above my head. My rear end sticks out of a slit that I lie on.

"Okay," shouts Tommy in his gravel voice. "This one's ready to go."

The aide pushes me into the line-up in the hallway. There are frames all over the place now, lined up in front of the blue room for their enemas. It is the Six o'Clock Special. There are maybe twenty guys waiting by now. It looks like a long train, an assembly line of broken, twisted bodies waiting for deliverance. It is very depressing, all these bodies, half of them asleep, tied down to their frames with their rear ends sticking out. All these bodies bloated, waiting to be released. Every third day I go for my enema and wait with the long line of men shoved against the green hospital wall. I watch the dead bodies being pushed into the enema room, then finally myself.

It is a small blue room and they cram us into it like sardines. Tommy runs back and forth placing the bedpans under our rear ends, laughing and joking, a cigarette dangling from the corner of his mouth. "Okay, okay, let's go!" he shouts. There is a big can of soapy water above each man's head and a tube that comes down from it. Tommy is jumping all around and whistling like a little kid, running to each body, sticking the rubber tubes up into them. He is jangling the pans, undoing little clips on the rubber tubes and filling the bellies up with soapy water. Everyone is trying to sleep, refusing to admit that this whole thing is happening to them. A couple of bodies in the frames have small radios close to their ears. Tommy keeps running from one frame to the other, changing the rubber gloves on his hands and squirting a tube of lubricant onto his fingers, ramming his hands up into the rear ends, checking each of the bodies out, undoing the little clips. The aide keeps grabbing the bedpans and emptying all the shit into the garbage cans, occasionally missing and splattering the stuff on the floor. She places the empty pans in a machine and closes it up. There is a steam sound and the machine opens with all the bedpans as clean as new.

Oh God, what is happening to me? What is going on here? I want to get out of this place! All these broken men are very depressing, all these bodies so emaciated and twisted in these bedsheets. This is a nightmare. This isn't like the poster down by the post office where the guy stood with the shiny shoes; this is a concentration camp. It is like the pictures of all the Jews that I have seen. This is as horrible as that. I want to scream. I want to yell and tell them that I want out of this. All of this, all these people, this place, these sounds, I want out of this forever. I am only twenty-one and there is still so much ahead of me, there is so much ahead of me.

I am wiped clean and pushed past the garbage cans. The stench is terrible. I try to breathe through my mouth but I can't. I'm trapped. I have to watch, I have to smell. I think the war has made me a little mad—the dead corporal from Georgia, the old man that was shot in the village with his brains hanging out. But it is the living deaths I am breathing and smelling now, the living deaths, the bodies broken in the same war that I have come from.

I am outside now in the narrow hallway. The young black woman is pushing my frame past all the other steel contraptions. I look at her face for a moment, at her eyes, as she pushes my frame up against another. I can hear the splashing of water next door in the shower room. The sun has come up in the Bronx and people are walking through the hallways. They can look into all the rooms and see the men through the curtains that never close. It is as if we are a bunch of cattle, as if we do not really count anymore.

They push me into the shower. The black woman takes a green plastic container and squirts it, making a long thin white line from my head to my legs. She is turning on the water, and after making sure it is not too hot she hoses me down.

It's like a car wash, I think, it's just like a big car wash, and I am being pushed and shoved through with the rest of them. I am being checked out by Tommy and hosed off by the woman. It is all such a neat, quick process. It is an incredible thing to run twenty men through a place like this, to clean out the bodies of twenty paralyzed men, twenty bloated twisted men. It is an incredible feat, a stupendous accomplishment, and Tommy is a master. Now the black woman is drying me off with a big white towel and shoving me back into the hallway.

Oh get me back into the room, get me back away from these people who are walking by me and making believe like all the rest that they don't know what's happening here, that they can't figure out that this whole thing is crazy. Oh God, oh God help me, help me understand this place. There goes the nurse and she's running down the hall, hitting the rubber mat that throws open the big green metal door with the little windows with the wire in them. Oh nurse please help me nurse, my stomach is beginning to hurt again like it does every time I come out of this place and my head is throbbing, pounding like a drum. I want to get out of this hall where all of you are walking past me. I want to get back into my bed where I can make believe this never happened. I want to go to sleep and forget I ever got up this morning.

I never tell my family when they come to visit about the enema room. I do not tell them what I do every morning with the plastic glove, or about the catheter and the tube in my penis, or the fact that I can't ever make it hard again. I hide all that from them and talk about the other, more pleasant things, the things they want to hear. I ask Mom to bring me *Sunrise at Campobello*, the play about the life of Franklin Roosevelt—the great crisis he had gone through when he had been stricken with polio and the comeback he had made, becoming governor, then president of the United States. There are things I am going through here that I know she will never understand.

I feel like a big clumsy puppet with all his strings cut. I learn to balance and twist in the chair so no one can tell how much of me does not feel or move anymore. I find it easy to hide from most of them what I am going through. All of us are like this. No one wants too many people to know how much of him has really died in the war.

At first I felt that the wound was very interesting. I saw it almost as an adventure. But now it is not an adventure any longer. I see it more and more as a terrible thing that I will have to live with for the rest of my life. Nobody wants to know that I can't fuck anymore. I will never go up to them and tell them I have this big yellow rubber thing sticking in my penis, attached to the rubber bag on the side of my leg. I am afraid of letting them know how lonely and scared I have become thinking about this wound. It is like some kind of numb twilight zone to me. I am angry and want to kill everyone—all the volunteers and the priests and the pretty girls with the tight short skirts. I am twenty-one and the whole thing is shot, done forever. There is no real healing left anymore, everything that is going to heal has healed already and now I am left with the corpse, the living dead man, the man with the numb legs, the sexlessman, the sexlessman, the man with the numb dick, the man who can't make children, the man who can't stand, the man who can't walk, the angry lonely man, the bitter man with the nightmares, the murder man, the man who cries in the shower.

In one big bang they have taken it all from me, in one clean sweep, and now I am in this place around all the others like me, and though I keep trying not to feel sorry for myself, I want to cry. There is no shortcut around this thing. It is too soon to die even for a man who has died once already.

I try to keep telling myself it is good to still be alive, to be back home. I remember thinking on the ambulance ride to the hospital that this was the Bronx, the place where Yankee Stadium was, where Mickey Mantle played. I think I realized then also that my feet would never touch the stadium grass, ever again; I would never play a game in that place.

. . .

The wards are filthy. The men in my room throw their breadcrumbs under the radiator to keep the rats from chewing on our numb legs during the nights. We tuck our bodies in with the sheets wrapped around us. There are never enough aides to go around on the wards, and constantly there is complaining by the men. The most severely injured are totally dependent on the aides to turn them. They suffer the most and break down with sores. These are the voices that can be heard screaming in the night for help that never comes. Urine bags are constantly overflowing onto the floors while the aides play poker on the toilet bowls in the enema room. The sheets are never changed enough and many of the men stink from not being properly bathed. It never makes any sense to us how the government can keep asking money for weapons and leave us lying in our own filth.

Briggs throws his bread over the radiator.

"There he goes again," says Garcia. "That goddamn rat's been there for the last two months."

Briggs keeps the rats in our room well fed. "It's a lot better than having the bastards nibble at your toes during the night," he says with a crazy laugh.

The nurse comes in and Garcia is getting real excited. "I think I pissed in my pants again," he cries. "Mrs. Waters, I think I pissed in my pants."

"Oh Garcia," the pretty nurse scolds, "don't say *piss*, say *urine*. *Urine* is much nicer."

Garcia tells her he is sorry and will call it urine from here on out.

Willey is clicking his tongue again and the nurse goes over to see. "What do you want?" she says to Willey. He is the most wounded of us all. He has lost everything from the neck down. He has lost even more than me. He is just a head. The war has taken everything.

He clicks three times. The nurse knows he wants the stuff sucked out of his lungs, so she does it. Garcia's radio is playing in the background. She slurps all of the stuff out, then walks out of the room. Now Briggs is getting the whiskey bottle out of his top drawer, taking big gulps and cursing out the rats that are still running under the radiator.

Someone please help me understand this thing, this terrible thing that's happening to me. I'm a brave man and I want to be brave even with this wound. I want to understand how I can live with it and with everything else that happened over there, the dead corporal from Georgia and all the other crazy things.

I find a place on the side of the hospital where the old men sit. The grass is very green and they feed the birds from their wheelchairs. They are the old men from the First World War, I am sure of that, and I sit next to them and feed the birds too. I just want to slow down, the whole thing has been moving much too fast, like some wild spinning top, and now I am trying to catch my breath, I am trying to figure out what this whole terrible thing is about.

I read the paper every morning and it always says the war is going on and the president is sending more troops, and I still tell people, whoever asks me, that I believe in the war. Didn't I prove it by going back a second time? I look them all right in the eye and tell them that we are winning and the boys' morale is high. But more and more what I tell them and what I am feeling are becoming two different things. I feel them tearing, tearing at my whole being, and I don't want to talk about the war anymore. I feed the birds and the squirrels. I want things to be simple again, things are just too confusing. The hospital is like the whole war all over again.

The aides, the big tall black guys who spit and sit on the toilet bowls all night, they're doing it again, they're picking up the paralyzed drunks from the hallways, they're wheeling them along the halls to the rooms. Now I see them strapping the men into big lifts, hoisting the drunken bodies back into their beds. And the aides are laughing, they're always laughing the way people laugh at a sideshow, it's all pretty funny to them. We are like a show of puppets dancing on strings for them, dancing to maddening music. They're wheeling all the guys in from the halls because it's late and it's time for all of the bodies to be put back in the beds, for all the tubes to be hooked up, and the drip of the piss bags to start all over again.

There's a train in the Bronx, somewhere out over the Harlem River, and it sounds so good, it sounds warm and wonderful like the heater back home, like the Long Island train that I used to hear as a kid. Pat, the new guy, is crying for help. He's puking into the cup again and he's cursing out everybody, he's cursing the place and the nurses, the doctors. He's asking me if I still have my Bible and he's laughing real loud now, he's laughing so loud the other men are telling him to shut up, to be quiet and let them go to sleep. It's a madhouse, it's a crazy house, it's a wild zoo, and we're the animals, we're the animals all neatly tucked into these beds, waking up every morning puking at the green walls and smelling the urine on the floor. We're hurting and we're praying that we can get out of this place. Somebody, give us back our bodies!

And each day I train in an exercise room that is very crowded with broken men, bodies being bent and twisted, put up on the parallel bars. Our therapists, Jimmy and Dick, train us hard. We put on braces and crawl on the floor. We're pissing in our pants and crawling into the bathtub. We're jumping up and down the curb, learning how to use our wheelchairs. There is a big wheel in the corner and they're strapping a puny guy with glasses to it. I'm watching the clock and the kid is trying to spin the big wheel around. There are machines like the wheel all over the place, and there's pain on all the faces. Some of us are trying to laugh, we're talking about the beer that comes into the hospital in the brown paper bags. But you cannot mistake the pain. The kid with the long hair is in the hallway again, the kid who looks in and never does anything but look in.

Now I'm grabbing the weights, twenty-five-pound weights, I'm grabbing them and lifting them up and down, up and down, until my shoulders ache, until I can't lift anymore. I'm still lifting them even after that, I'm still lifting them and Jimmy is talking about his model airplanes and then he and Dick are lifting me up to the high bar. There are newly invented machines sold to the hospital by the government to make the men well, to take all the Willeys and the Garcias and make them well again, to fix these broken bodies. There are machines that make you stand again and machines that fix your hands again, but the only thing is that when it's all over, when the guys are pulled down from the machines, unstrapped from them, it's the same body, the same shattered broken man that went up on the rack moments before, and this is what we are all beginning to live with, this is what the kid standing in the hallway is saying with his eyes.

It's early in the afternoon. I'm standing on my braces, holding on to the parallel bars. My mother and little sister have just come through the doorway. It is the first chance for them to see me try to stand again. My mother is frightened, you can tell by the look on her face, and my sister is standing next to her trying to smile. They are holding each other's hands.

My legs are shaking in terrible spasms. They're putting thick straps around my waist and around my legs and now my arms start to shake furiously. My mother and sister are still standing in the hallway. They haven't decided to come into the room yet. Jimmy is strapping my arms along the pole and my big oversized blue hospital pants are falling down below my waist. My rear end is sticking out and Jimmy is smiling, looking over to my mother in the corner.

"See," says Jimmy, "he's standing."

I start throwing up all over the place, all over the blue hospital shirt and onto the floor, just below the machine. Jimmy quickly undoes the straps and puts me back in the chair. My sister and my mother are clutching each other, holding real tight to each other's hands.

"It's really a great machine," Jimmy says. "We have a couple more coming in real soon."

I turn the chair toward the window and look out across the Harlem River to where the cars are going over the bridge like ants.

Fields of Fire

JAMES WEBB

1978

From the air they would have been barely visible, a half-mile string of burdened green ants, struggling up a kidney-shaped, foliated anthill.

In the weeds where the wind would not blow, Bagger sweated freely into his flak jacket, shirtless underneath it, and adjusted one of his pack straps. It was cutting deep into a shoulder. "If this is Tuesday," he drawled wryly to no one in particular, knocking a branch out of his way, "it must be Phu Phong four."

The ville, designated on American maps as the fourth hamlet in the village of Phu Phong, and hence Phu Phong (4), was one of many frequent perimeters used by the Marines in their random wanderings across the valley floor. Four hundred meters across at its widest point, it sat on a high, kidney-shaped mound, covered with trees and shrubs and high weeds, scarred by years of bombing, and dotted with ragged, straw-thatched hootches.

From the heights of Phu Phong (4), Hodges got his first clear look at the layout of the Arizona Valley. To the west, beyond three other similar mounds that made a bumpy line toward the village, was the only prominent terrain feature in the valley: Razorback Ridge jutted bald and high and rounded, like the back of a huge pink hog, out from the blue-green gloominess of the wall of western mountains. In all other directions from the village there were wide seas of rice paddies, brown with harvest rice, dotted with lower villages and occasional treelines that floated like islands in the rice.

Far to the south, over the wide cut of an oozing river, Hodges could just make out the brick-red trail of dust that was puffing up from east to west, as if someone was skywriting on the Basin floor. The morning convoy from Da Nang, twenty-five miles west and north, was grinding its way toward the regimental combat base at An Hoa. Far southwest there were the red scarred hills, the high claydust mist of An Hoa itself. Three, perhaps four miles away, but unreachable and thus irrelevant, except when it came time for resupply or artillery support.

The Arizona Valley was a veritable island. A northern river separated it from the calmer Dai Loc District, where there was access to Da Nang. The southern river cut it off from the rest of the An Hoa Basin, where there were two artillery bases—at Liberty Bridge and An Hoa—a Vietnamese Popular Force compound at Duc Duc near An Hoa, and a road capable of transporting the convoy. The northern and southern rivers came together at the eastern tip of the valley, where Liberty Bridge sat just beyond their confluence. And to the west, as all around the larger basin that held the valley, canopied mountains rose like foliated skyscrapers, unpopulated barriers that stretched all the way to distant Laos. The North Vietnamese owned the mountains.

Phu Phong (4) was the highest village in the valley, and an ideal fighting perimeter for the Marines. Hedges and holes would provide good cover and concealment. The draws of the hill, and the open, sweeping paddies would give good fields of fire if they were attacked.

The company went on line and swept toward the far edge of the hill, moving slowly past ragged hedges, clumps of hootches, clusters of junk and dented cooking pans, torn straw matting, stench-filled waterbull pens, and staring, stolid villagers. Hodges noticed the evidences of other warring units as they swept. There were dozens of fighting holes along the fringes of the hill, many so old that weeds had claimed them. There were old mortar pits, and dozens of burn holes and straddle trenches. Worn portions of the villagers' thatch roofs were often patched with C-ration boxes or strips of American ponchos.

As the company dug into its new positions Hodges strode the hill, examining it. At its very crest was a long, Z-shaped trench, chest-deep and as wide as a man's body. It was perfectly sculpted, the walls of the trench absolutely parallel. In the middle of the trench, just to one side of it, was a large, circular hole, four feet deep and about six feet across, with the earth left in the middle of it as a perfectly cylindrical post. It seemed to him to be a work of engineering genius.

He called Snake to the trench. "What is this? I've never seen anything like it."

Snake scratched a tattoo, bronzed and shirtless in the heat. "Everybody likes this hill, Lieutenant. That's the way the gooks set up." Snake jumped into the trench, demonstrating. "They don't need any circle. They don't need to protect all those radios and shit. If a man stands in this trench he can blow you away no matter which side of the hill you come charging up."

Hodges pointed to the circular post. "What about that?"

"That's a machine-gun post. Prob'ly a fifty-cal. Maybe a twelve-seven. You put a tripod on the post and get down in that hole and you can fire three-sixty degrees, keep a bead on a jet coming and going, hardly even expose yourself."

"That's stomp-down amazing."

"Hey, Lieutenant." Snake measured his new Brown Bar carefully, not yet accepting him. "Old Luke the Gook don't screw around."

Snake sat comfortably at the edge of the NVA trench, peering steadily at Hodges. Finally he grimaced. "You shouldn't of made Flaky burn that boot. Sir. Bad style. It stunk."

"It would've stunk anyway."

"My new man Senator threw up."

"I was sick of looking at it. What a mess. Don't you ever clean up?" Hodges studied the man who had already showed himself to be the most proficient member of his platoon. "What would you have done?"

"I'da buried it."

"Then why didn't you?"

"Sir?"

"Why didn't you? You had the CP for half a day. You sat up there with all those flies and shit. You were acting platoon commander. If it pissed you off so bad, why didn't *you* bury it?"

Snake smiled slightly, surveying Hodges with fresh interest.

" 'Cause I don't like dead stuff. I never touch dead stuff. I just leave it alone."

"Well, I don't like dead stuff, either." Hodges' eyebrows lifted and he offered Snake a grin. "That's why I burn it."

Snake shrugged, satisfied. "O.K. Lieutenant. I just never seen it before. It made my man Senator get sick, I told you."

"Yeah." Hodges sat across from Snake. He took out a pocketknife and cut himself a plug of chewing tobacco that had come in a Supplementary Pack, along with cigarettes, candy, and writing gear in the resupply. He pulled his map from a lower trouser pocket, and studied it, then looked to Snake.

"We're gonna ambush Nam An two tonight. Half the platoon. Your squad and a gun team and me."

Snake lit a cigarette, staring coolly at Hodges. "Did you think this up yourself, Lieutenant?"

"Are you crazy? I got nothing against Nam An two." The two men smiled at each other with a tentative fraternity. "Know any good places?"

Snake took out his own map, pondered it, then peered down the hill into the paddies, scanning the narrow string of trees across from them that marked a heavily used speed trail. Nam An two was one mile down the trail. "There's a little cemetery just off the speed trail, maybe a hundred meters from the ville. We could put a gun on the trail. Easy to defend in the cemetery. Might make a Number One ambush." He eyed his new Lieutenant. "Long as we gotta go."

"Yeah. Well, we do. Skipper's breaking me in, or something. Says we'll have a good shot at the gooks if they move down the trail toward the company tonight. Hell, I don't know. Says we should have first shot."

"He's all heart, ain't he?" Snake watched Hodges spit a stream of brown tobacco juice into the dirt. "You really chewing that SP tobacco, sir?"

Hodges nodded casually. "It ain't that bad."

"Bagger says he wouldn't give it to his horse for worms. If he *had* a horse. And it *had* the worms." They laughed together. "Only thing that ragweed's good for is feeding gooks who don't answer questions.

Fucks them up, Lieutenant! One swallow of that and they sing like stoolies." Hodges shook his head, amused at Snake's quick humor.

Snake reached into his lower trouser pocket and pulled out a pack of Marlboros. "Here, Lieutenant. Have a smoke."

"I've been trying to cut back. Bad for your wind."

"You gonna worry about that out *here?* Hey, Lieutenant. We are *all* sucking wind."

Hodges shook his head, still amused, and took a Marlboro. He spat out the chewing tobacco and rinsed his mouth with canteen water. "Bagger's right. It tastes terrible." He casually placed the remainder of the plug into his low trouser pocket.

"You *keeping* the rest of it?"

" 'Course I am." Hodges grinned, his amused face thanking Snake for teaching him this latest Lesson Learned in Vietnam. "For gooks."

Phu Phong (4) had three good wells, deep concrete holes with raised portions of earth at the base. The French had built them for the villagers. They sat at the base of the village's steep hill, equally spaced along a wide, dusty trail that ringed the village on a paddy dike. The dike itself was thick and high, separating the village from the surrounding fields. Hundreds of smaller, lower dikes latticed the paddies into a maze that somehow held deep certainties to farmers.

Marines flocked to the wells in groups of twos and threes, refilling canteens and washing. Village children gathered and gazed somberly at their frolics, standing off of the trail in the dry bush. The babysans were sickly and unwashed.

Goodrich leaned over a concrete hole, drawing water out of it with a half-gallon can that had once held apple juice supplied to the Marines. The can was left by some other company that used Phu Phong, and made into a bucket by the villagers. Goodrich worked the rope, pulling the can of clear, sweet water from the black hole, and poured it over his face, drinking thirstily. The move to the Phu Phongs had exhausted him.

He then turned to Speedy, handing him the can. "I really think those kids hate us." Goodrich spoke as though the feasibility had never crossed his mind.

Speedy tossed the can into the well and let it sink, then drew it back up. He found Goodrich's comments perplexing, naive. "We try to kill their papa, Senator. This whole valley VC." Speedy gorged himself on village water.

"That's a hell of a note." Goodrich forced a winsome smile. "It'll take a little getting used to. I just hadn't expected to be hated. Not by them."

Speedy drew another pail of water, mildly irritated. "Ah. It don't mean nothing, Senator." His wide, brown face went orgasmic as cool water poured over it again. "We get over to the Phu Nhuans, on the other side of the river, the kids are better. They hustle for you. Fill canteens, help wash you, stuff like that. We give 'em C-rats and cigarettes for it. It's all right." He attempted to console Goodrich, himself unconcerned with staring children. "It's better over there. You'll see."

Speedy scrutinized Goodrich, who was still studying the children, apparently lost in thought. It appeared that Goodrich was becoming upset. Speedy finally ran at the babysans, throwing his arms out threateningly. "*Didi*, you little fuckers! *Didi mau len!*"

The children stared at their attacker for an unfrightened moment, then turned and walked solemnly through the brush, back up the hill. Goodrich held the water can over one of his canteens, filling it.

"You didn't have to do that, Speedy. I didn't *mind* them, really. I just can't help feeling sorry for them."

Speedy's flat face cocked curiously and he grimaced to Goodrich. "Make up your *mind*, Senator." He looked back through the brush. "Those little sons of bitches'll *do* your ass, I mean it." He took the bucket from Goodrich and tossed it back into the black hole of the well. "Don't feel sorry for 'em, Senator. You give 'em chow, their old man eats it tomorrow night. You turn your back"—the brown face splashed with water again—"they steal everything you got. Grenades. Everything."

Speedy took a long drink, then peered philosophically at Goodrich. "Those little babysans are devils, man. No shit. Devils."

"I still can't help it. I mean it. None of this is *their* fault."

"Well, none of this is *our* fault, either." Speedy stared solemnly at Goodrich. "Do yourself a favor, Senator. Frag yourself and get the hell outa here before you crack up. You don't belong here. Know what I mean?"

The stand of trees loomed like a low black cloud in front of them. Goodrich watched it grow larger, strained to find some light or movement that would disclose the great chimera that sat among the sun-baked branches, waiting to scorch him dead. The column seemed to jet along through the knee-deep rice. Goodrich fought reluctantly to keep the pace. Too fast, he mused loudly, the thought echoing through the chambers of his fear. We'll walk right into them and when we get five feet away they'll kill us all. I've heard the stories. Who the hell's on point? Doesn't he know they'll kill us all? What will I do? Can't hear anything but clonks of LAAWs and bandoleers and rice swish on my legs I'm thirsty need a drink. What if I just take out a grenade and pull the pin and hold it so when they start to kill us I can throw it at them how will I know where to throw it I can't see a fucking *thing* not even Burgie and I could reach out and touch Burgie he's that close look at the trees now we're so close we could die at any moment who the hell is walking *point*?

Thud. Goodrich tripped over Ottenburger, who was squatting in the rice. He fell down next to him, the echoes of his bandoleers a scream inside the ear horn that was his helmet. Burgie grasped him quickly and held him to the earth.

"Lay chilly, Senator. They're peeping out the treeline."

Goodrich sat very still, then turned his head slowly toward the trees. The whole column was kneeling, motionless, frozen like a picture, swallowed by rice. It was so quiet he could hear the distant booms of artillery shooting out of An Hoa with a clarity that seemed to come from just on the other side of the looming trees.

Four silhouettes crept soundlessly from the treeline then, rifles ready, moving toward the column. Goodrich felt his eyebrows raise and pointed his M-16. Burgie pressed the rifle back into the rice.

"Take it *easy*, Senator. That's Cat Man."

Cat Man set his team in at the edge of the treeline and moved to a low dike where Snake and Hodges were kneeling. He knelt next to them, pushed his helmet back, and leaned over. He addressed Snake, ignoring Hodges.

"Too much shit in there, man."

Hodges whispered. "It's the right trail, ain't it? We follow it for a click and we're there."

Cat Man shook his head. Snake looked coolly at Hodges. "Cat Man's right, Lieutenant. We take the trail, we may never make it there. Too many dogs and water bulls, shit like that. They'll start barking and grunting and the gooks'll hear us coming, blow our asses away. Don't take that treeline, sir."

Hodges nodded, acquiescing. Then, as an afterthought: "You can find the cemetery all right from the paddy?"

Cat Man measured him without emotion. Starting from a known point, his mind was its own map. "Yes, sir."

The column cut quickly through the trees. Goodrich moved inside them, was enveloped by the black haunt of empty hootches, mushroom trees, thick high sawgrass where every inch a shadowed ghoul lurked, waiting. Will I die tonight? How embarrassing that would be: to die on my first patrol. He softly clicked his weapon off "safe," then thought of tripping over Ottenburger again and accidentally killing him, and clicked it back.

Finally back into the open paddy again. He felt the welcome scrape of rice along his legs, waited briefly for the monster to attack and kill him from behind, then focused his fear to the front once more. The whole black night was a laughing killer, waiting for its moment.

Goodrich's ears were filled with clonking metal, whispered curses, and his own stomps from stumbles into potholes and low unseen dikes. Finally they reached the low mounds of the cemetery. He viewed its haunting isolation as a haven from the swishing madness.

Hodges placed the machine gun quickly on the mound nearest the trail. Snake began to position his squad behind various graves, making a tight perimeter.

Across the trail, a hundred meters distant, was a clump of trees shot with a dozen scraggly hootches. It was off the trail, an island in more rice, laced to the other villes by another narrow treeline. Nam An (2). Hodges peered intently at the ville. A small mote of light flickered inside the dark shadows of trees and hootches. He remembered that no lights were to be on in villages after sunset. The villagers know that, he mused.

Hodges approached Snake, who was setting in two men behind a mound. "That light mean anything?"

Snake squinted. His hands grasped clumps of grass on the mound. He bolted toward the unpositioned squad members.

"*Open fire on that ville!*"

The cemetery erupted as tracers reached toward Nam An (2). Rounds poured furiously for a few quick seconds, then there was a moment of silence: in their excitement, all had emptied the first magazine of ammo at the same time.

Hodges caught up with Snake. "What's going on?"

But now the ville responded, answering Hodges' question. Muzzle flashes by the hootches, high cacophony of AK bullets overhead, flashbooms of B-40 rockets, their large grenades a rash of second booms around the cemetery. A .50-caliber machine gun tore ragged holes in slow, heavy bursts above their heads.

"*Fire the LAAW!*" Speedy cut loose. There was a belch of fire on his shoulder, then a boom in the ville. "*Fire the LAAW!*" Another belch, another boom. A hootch in the ville was now in flames. Hodges could see urgent shadows near the flames, creeping to new places. What do you know, he marveled. Gooks.

Snake now had the whole patrol in place, firing steadily at the treeline with a slow, well-aimed pressure. Hodges peered at the ville for another moment, entranced. I never would have known. Then he remembered that he had an on-call target right on top of it.

Radio. He turned for Flaky. Flaky was gone. "*Fairchild!*" Hodges searched for a moment and found him lying flat behind a mound, calmly oblivious in his cowardice. "Come on. Hurry up." Flaky came sullenly, like a dog with his tail tucked. Hodges grabbed the handset off the radio.

"Fire Alpha Delta four-oh-seven!"

A mocking hiss, unanswering, on the other end. Finally, "Who is this?"

Hodges swore. "Come on, goddamn it. This is Three Actual. Give me Six. Somebody. Hurry up. Contact mission." The .50-cal bullets cut lower now, just above the mounds.

The company commander came on the net. "Whatcha got, Three Actual?"

Hodges peered into the village again. Two hootches burned. Figures scampered near the flames. Two more LAAWs boomed in the cemetery. His machine gun poured tracers into the village in a low, steadily sweeping line. Be cool, he told himself. "I don't know." He thought another moment. "Gooks in a ville. I got an on-call on top of it. Alpha Delta four-oh-seven."

The company commander was crisp, professional, removed. "Roger, understand four-zero-seven. Got a direction on that?"

Direction. Damn. "Wait one." He pulled his compass out and peered carefully over a grave, shooting an azimuth at a flaming hootch. He tried to read the luminous dial under the hootch's burn. South. Something like that. He thought to shoot a more accurate azimuth but a B-40 rocket slammed onto the trail just down from him and he ducked behind the mound again. South is fine. "Thirty-two hundred. Danger close."

"Roger, understand thirty-two hundred, danger close. How close?"

The .50-cal just above his head. Be cool. "*Real* close." Not good enough. " 'Bout a hundred meters."

"Roger. Stand by."

"Could you hurry?"

No answer. The radio was once more a silent hiss.

Goodrich half-lay, half-crouched behind a grave, reloading magazines. He pulled a clip from his bandoleer, fit the charger guide into the magazine, then clumsily dropped the ammunition. He searched frantically in the high, brittle grass for the lost bullets, but felt naked stooping away from the sanctum of his mound, and abandoned his search. He pulled out another clip and jammed it down the charger guide, bending the clip in his petrified fury, and ten bullets bounced like pearls from a broken necklace through his lap, lost among the high weeds in the darkened night. He leaned over, trying to catch the last of them, and stared up at two spindly, tattooed arms that hung down from a crouching frame.

Snake grimaced impatiently, shaking his head. "You stupid shit. What the hell you doing? You shoulda loaded those before. Hurry up. Quit bagging it, Senator."

An AK-47 burst cracked on top of the grave, four digging rounds that threw up puffs of dust. Snake moved off to check the other positions. He took a couple of steps, then turned back to Goodrich. "*C'mon*, Senator. Put out rounds."

Hiss of the radio was finally broken. "Three, Six. Stand by for shot."

Hodges keyed the handset, peeping the ville. "Roger, Six." He screamed to the patrol. "Stand by for shot!"

"Shot out."

"Shot out!" A metallic double bang floated across the fields from An Hoa. They crouched low in the graves and in one instant a phosphorescent flash erupted just on the other side of the mounds, joined by another that smoked whitely twenty meters down the trail. The patrol was frozen behind the mounds now, staring uneasily at Hodges: you trying to *kill* us?

"Ah—add a hundred. Fire for effect."

An eternity that was perhaps two minutes. "Stand by for shot."

"Roger." Hodges screamed, "*Stand by for shot!*" The patrol hugged the bottom of the mounds this time, fearful of Hodges' talents.

The rounds impacted with steady earnest crunches that began just outside the ville and spanned its width. They threw up cloudlets of dust, pieces of flashing hootches. Snake and Phony nudged each other from behind one mound.

Snake nodded toward the ville. Another series of rounds dug into it. "See. I *told* you."

Phony popped a wad of gum, nodding judiciously with approval. "Well, whatta you know. Get some, Lieutenant Hodges."

Three repeats on the ville. Explosions saturated the trees, filling the air with a low layer of dust that had raised from riven fields among the hootches. The firing from the ville ceased. Hodges gloated.

Then there was a heavy burst, a dozen AKs spitting angrily far to the right. Across three hundred meters of reaching rice, another village rose on a low hill thick with trees and squatting bushes. Dai Khuong (4).

Snake tightened the perimeter into two-man positions and ordered them all to hold their fire. Then he crept over to Hodges.

"Hey, Lieutenant. We could really be in the shit. We better lay chilly til we scope 'em out. They could be moving on us. Might really do us if they get the drop on us."

"Anybody hit?"

"Wild Man. Tee-Tee. He's grooving on it. No sweat."

Hodges nodded. The AKs started from Dai Khuong again and he remembered he had an on-call on that village, too. Man, I am a *thorough* son of a bitch, he gloated.

On the radio, Dai Khuong was a repeat of Nam An (2). And, later in the night, Nam An (1), three hundred meters to the north, directly on the other side of the patrol from their first encounter in Nam An (2). The patrol passed the night under high, sporadic bursts from three sides, one man up and one sleeping at each position.

When Nam An (1) opened up Snake crawled casually to Hodges. It was the key he had been waiting for. "No sweat, Lieutenant. They're just screwing with us." It was three o'clock. "If they were really gonna try and *do* us they wouldn't be up there. It's too late. They gotta make their hat most ricky-tick." He allowed Hodges a small grin. "Nice job on the art'y. Sir."

"You ain't seen nothing yet."

Deep blue slivers in the eastern sky, mosquito slaps and grunts, weapons wet with dew. The last round of security checks on the radio. In the near ville an early rooster crowed lonesomely. Dawn. Hodges listened to the rooster, wondering how it had survived the artillery of the night before. Then he smiled a bit perversely to himself: let's see if it makes it through *this*.

Flaky lay against the bottom of a mound, helmet forward over his eyes, the radio handset stuck inside the helmet. There was a muffled squawk and he reached languidly for the handset and keyed it, speaking sleepily.

"Go, six." Short pause. "Roger that." He turned to Hodges, who was watching the ville emerge eerily in front of the bluing sky, as if a great TV picture tube were slowly warming up. "Guns up on the T.O.T., Lieutenant."

"Tell 'em to go ahead."

"Yes, sir." Flaky keyed the handset again, still sprawled against the mound. "Six, three." Pause. "Let 'er eat."

Hodges strode to the rear of the cemetery and awakened Snake, who had curled up on the high grass inside his poncho liner. "Saddle 'em up. Let's go."

Steady thunks from miles away, a rhythm, interminable, of mortars popping out of tubes. Deep blue had surrendered to a mix of gray: the sun lurked just beyond the edge of the world. Nam An (2) became saturated with explosions, mixes of phosphorous and high-explosive shells that rained down like a steady hailstorm, raising jets of dirt like water spurts. Round after round, like the explosions of cylinders in a slowly idling engine.

The thunking tubes in the distance ceased, the last rounds still latent in the air, and the patrol moved out. Snake's squad made a wide line and Hodges and the gun team followed in trace. Snake paced just behind his squad, dispersing the advancing men, controlling the rate, keeping them on line. They advanced toward the ville, twenty meters apart, weapons pointed forward.

The last mortar exploded inside the trees and there was a moment of nerve-shattering silence. The patrol moved cautiously toward the gloomy mist of smoke and dust, watching for movement. In the ville the rooster crowed again, tentatively, as if his earlier effort had beckoned a falling sky. Hodges smiled tightly: how the hell did it make it?

Goodrich watched the phosphorescent fog anxiously, his weapon pointing forward from his waist. The gloom of the village prepared to envelop him. Twenty meters. Behind him, Snake chanted tersely.

"If they hit us it'll be most ricky-tick. If it moves blow it away. If it moves blow it away."

Something stirred in the brush to his right. Phony laced it with a short, perfunctory burst, not even breaking stride. It was a dog. It moaned like a fading record. OWW-W-w-ww. Phony chuckled softly and grinned. Ten meters from the outer trees.

In front of Goodrich a pajama-clad figure rustled and then crouched, on the porch of a burnt-out hootch. Goodrich saw a black sleeve and inhaled sharply, startled, then fired three quick rounds. The figure ran to the corner of the hootch. Goodrich fired a full magazine, spraying the entire hootch without aiming, and dropped heavily behind a near dike. The whole patrol then opened up on the village. This is it, thought Goodrich. Five feet away they'll kill us all now no using mortars on them no getting out of it we're *dead*.

The patrol had fired on full automatic, and all firing stopped as the squad changed magazines in unison. The gun team jogged cautiously up to a dike and prepared to fire. The ville was silent. No return fire. Snake called to the patrol. "Hold your fire!" He crawled over to Goodrich. "Whatcha shoot at, Senator?"

"In the hootch. Black pajamas. I dunno."

The patrol lay flat along the edge of the village, peering into it. Snake called loudly to the hootch. "*Lai day! Lai day, you mother-fucker!*"

No movement. Snake screamed again and fired a round into the hootch. There was a whimpered answer from the hootch's corner. Mumble mumble mumble whimper *Khong biet* whimper mumble.

Snake called to Hodges. "It's a mamasan, Lieutenant."

"Move out, then. Be careful, though."

The patrol picked up, rushing past the first hootches, and set up security. Hodges put the machine gun on top of one family bunker, covering a tree-lined path, and walked into the burnt-out hootch. Goodrich and Snake were busily searching for contraband through random piles of burnt matting, pots, and mackerel cans.

The wounded woman was curled in a corner, weeping, holding one shoulder. Her coarse black hair was pulled into a loose bun and her lips were stained red by betel nut, making her look as if she had begun to paint herself up for a welcoming party. Her teeth were purplish-black after years of chewing the numbing betel nut. She turned pained eyes up from her lined, puffy face and pleaded with the hulking figures that stared down at her. Mumble mumble mumble whisper *khong biet* mumble *honcho* mumble *bac se.*

Snake leaned over threateningly. *"Dung Lai!"* She stopped talking, continued to whimper. "What did you expect, Mamasan? You heard all the racket. You know—*bac bac* VC? *Khong biet?* What the hell did you leave your bunker for?" He shook his head, feigning anger. "You lucky old bitch! You should be dead! That's right!"

Goodrich knelt next to her, mortified. A pool of blood leaked down from her shoulder in a steady rivulet, dripping off her elbow to the dirt floor of the hootch. "I'm sorry, Mamasan. Really." He reached out to her, intending to examine the wound and wrap it for her. She shrank back immediately, mumbling rapidly to him. He cringed from her. "Goddamn, Mamasan. I'm really sorry. *Really.*" He began to unbutton the pajama top and she grasped it shut, terrified.

Snake nudged Goodrich with a boot. "Don't be sorry, Senator. She knows the rules. She shoulda been in her bunker. It's her own fault."

Goodrich shook his head, his chubby face sagging in its grief. He looked down at the bleeding, decrepit creature whose most recent misery emanated from his very trigger, and neared tears. "I should have looked more closely. I was scared. It was crazy to shoot like that."

Snake scoffed contemptuously. "Oh, bullshit, Senator. Don't turn yourself all around—"

Speedy interjected from the other corner of the hootch, where he was going through mamasan's fireplace with an intrenching tool. "Senator crying again?"

"—She coulda been a gook. She knew she was wrong. Look twice and you're dead, Senator."

Speedy eyed his new charge with disbelief. "You're a case, Senator. They going to carry you out of here in a strait jacket."

Hodges yelled to the hootch from across the weed path. "Forget mamasan. We'll take her back and have a doc check her out. Search the rest of the ville. I'm tired as hell."

The patrol moved through the village in a floating perimeter, two hootches at a time, following a tedious, standard practice. Call the villagers out of their earthen family bunkers, where they've spent their latest night in hell. Throw grenades into the bunkers to ensure there are no enemies still hiding in them. Then search them out. Check hootch areas and bushes for bodies, weapons, and contraband.

Bagger discovered a pair of bright blue pin-striped shorts in one hootch, a unique find. He held them daintily in his huge hands, his red face grinning mischievously, and walked over to the hootch's eldest occupant, a mamasan of perhaps thirty who stood under the thatch with five small children.

"Where's your old man, Mamasan? Huh? *O dau Papasan?*"

Mamasan smiled tightly, humoring the invader. "*Khong biet.*" I don't know.

"Oh, I'll bet my ass you dunno, with all them babysans." Bagger loomed over her, grinning meanly. "Well, if you dunno, I s'pose it's all right for me to souvenir his britches, huh?" The stocky man laughed devilishly. "Gotcha, Mamasan. Catch Twenty-two. If he's around, you better tell us where, so we can liberate his ass. If he ain't, what do you care about his old shorts, anyway?"

Snake noticed Bagger, and called to him. "Bagger."

Bagger stuffed the shorts into his flak-jacket pocket. "Oh, I'll bet old papasan was humping a B-forty last night. Ain't that right, Mamasan."

"Bagger. Give 'em back."

Bagger finally acknowledged Snake. "I'm gonna wear 'em, man, instead of tiger shorts."

"It's against the rules. You know that. Give 'em back."

"So what do you care? Huh? You talking like a goddamn lifer, Snake. What's the rules to a pair of shorts?"

Cannonball called from the top of a nearby family bunker, where he was standing security. "Man, you know Snake, he goan' be a lifer. I been telling you that."

"Ah, screw you, Cannonball." Snake walked up to Bagger. "I ain't gonna get in trouble because of any damn shorts." He looked around for Hodges. "I ain't having any new Lieutenant or somebody run me in because you want a pair of shorts. Now give 'em back to the lady. Hurry up."

Bagger fished them out of his pocket. "Oh. Now she's a *lady*, too. Cannonball's right. My man Snake is gonna be a lifer."

· · ·

One hootch over, Cat Man and Phony were patiently standing in front of an old man who was gesturing wildly in the air. They both grinned, shaking their heads in perfect time with the gestures. Hodges walked over to them, curious at the mimic pantomime of it, as if all elements were prerehearsed.

"What the hell . . . ?"

Phony eyed Hodges pleasantly. "Hey, Lieutenant. You can shoot some art'y, you know? Not bad. Oh. *Him?* He lost his *can cuoc.*" Phony noted that the phrase did not register with Hodges. "His I.D. card." He put his arm around the old man's shoulders. "It's a lifer game. Find a dude without his *can cuoc* and he's s'posed to be VC or something, 'cause he ain't registered with the gov'mint."

Snake had joined the group. He addressed Hodges. "So every time we find a dude without one, we're s'posed to run him in. But it's like everything out here, Lieutenant. Nothing's what it's s'posed to be. All the VC have *can cuocs.* Half the villagers don't, cause when you lose it, you have to pay a goddamn fortune to get a new one. So *can cuocs* don't mean nothing, really. It's just a game." He grinned, poking the old man playfully in the chest. "But every villager has the same story. We ask where it is and they point up to the sky and tell us how the bombs blew it up, so we'll feel sorry for 'em and think it's our own fault. That right, Papasan?"

The old man smiled earnestly, his electric, beady eyes communicating as he ran frail hands through the air, simulating an air strike, then brought them together in front of himself and threw them up and apart, indicating the exploding bomb.

"And anyway," Phony shrugged absently, "they're all VC. Every ville out here is VC. Them *can cuocs* don't mean a goddamn thing."

Cat Man agreed. He nodded shyly, his delicate features intense, and addressed Hodges with carefully chosen words. "Wait till you sweep into a ville and it's flying a VC flag for you, Lieutenant. Papasan grins 'cause he thinks we're gonna stick him. If we were just moving through, he wouldn't even wave."

They found no bodies in the ville. There were numerous blood trails, a blend of blood that joined in a drag line toward the western mountains, a half-dozen dropped grenades, and one abandoned AK-47 rifle, lost in the dark as the enemy retreated.

Hodges was slightly disappointed. No victories without tangible monuments. He was also amazed at the lack of damage to the village. Two burnt hootches, several dozen new pockmarks in the dried earth, and one bleeding mamasan. All those mortar rounds, he marveled. And even the rooster came away unscathed.

The company perimeter was more than a mile away. Speedy and Burgie pulled a bamboo pole off one rended hootch, found a parachute that had once floated down above a huge Basketball flare, and fashioned a hammocklike carrying device for the whimpering mamasan. The patrol then straggled back across the sunbaked valley, walking in the sanctum of the treelines because it was daylight and there would be snipers, then finally cut across the wide, parched paddy that led to the southern tip of Phu Phong (4). Hodges radioed ahead, and a small patrol met them at the base of the hill, near one of the wells. The company corpsman, one of the Vietnamese Kit Carson Scouts, and a fire team for security awaited them in the scrubby shade of the well.

They filed up to the well, the patrol finished. Some walked immediately to it and doused themselves, cooling off from the hump. Others dropped into the shade, greeting the fire team, which was from the other squad in their platoon. Still others moved up to the perimeter without pausing, anxious to eat.

A dozen Marines ambled down from the perimeter when the patrol returned, curious about the previous night's happenings, calling and jibing friends from the returning patrol.

They gathered around the moaning mamasan. The corpsman took her pajama top and ripped it at the shoulder, then wrapped her wound with a battle dressing. She winced mightily, still whimpering.

The Kit Carson Scout sauntered slowly over and peered down unemotionally at the woman. Snake put his hand on the man's shoulder, pointing to the mamasan. "Dan. Ask her why she wasn't in the bunker. Why she in fucking hootch when Marines *bac bac* VC."

Dan nodded solemnly, thinking for a moment, then asked her a question in Vietnamese that came out as a song. Mamasan whimpered, responding in a weakened rapid fire, a long, gesturing explanation. Dan pondered the answer, still emotionless, then sent her into tears with a short retort.

Snake leaned in front of Dan, smiling amusedly to him. "What did she say, Dan?"

Dan still stared down at her. His expression had not changed. "She say, Marines, VC *bac-bac boo coo* long time, she in bunker, gotta take shit. She say, wait all night, go outside to take shit, got *boo coo* bombs. Go back fucking hootch, Marine come, shoot her."

The crowd nodded, muttering judiciously. Mamasan still whimpered. Snake nudged Dan. "So, what did you say?"

Dan shrugged absently. "I say, now on, shit in bunker."

The crowd applauded in appreciation of Dan's wisdom. Dan smiled back impishly, acknowledging the praise. Then he coolly, persistently questioned the weary mamasan, prodding her, trying to discover information about the North Vietnamese unit that had been in her village the night before.

Goodrich watched Dan and the others and, attempting to understand and rationalize their callousness, discovered a basic truth about himself. Even as he searched for some humorous remark that would write off the incident, he knew that he could not accept it. He could understand, condone the massive use of force, but the terrors of its particularizations horrified him. A hundred NVA deaths tallied in a newspaper column would draw an absent nod, but one stinking, suffering old wretched woman who bled from his own bullet, who would be flown by helicopter to an air-conditioned hospital and saved, turned his stomach.

Whoo boy, he fretted, walking by himself up the hill. Only 387 more days of this. Time sure flies when you're having fun.

The mail had arrived on the resupply helicopter and there was a letter from Mark. Goodrich dropped his gear next to his poncho hootch and lit a cigarette, reading it.

You wouldn't believe the faces of my friends when I told them my old college roomy was a Marine! I think they believe I'm an FBI plant! It is kind of funny, you know—me *here* and you *there*. I see pictures of the patrols burning down homes, things like that and I just can't picture you there. But if anything I feel a little good, if you insist on making an ass out of yourself. It injects the tiniest bit of credibility to the holocaust. I mean, I sure can't see *you* burning people, or standing by while someone else does. *Pot*, maybe, but definitely not *people*.

The letter was the touch that bottomed out Goodrich's depression. He turned to Ottenburger, who was napping under his poncho hootch. "Hey, Burgie. Where do I turn in my letter of resignation?"

"Say what, Senator?"

Goodrich attempted a smile. "Where do I quit, man?"

Ottenburger snorted. "Talk to Bagger. He knows all about it. He quits at least once a day."

Speedy overheard them and called almost derisively, fed up with Goodrich. "Tonight, Senator, I'll give you a grenade. You pull your own pin. No sweat. One hand up in the air, *boom*, bye-bye Senator."

Goodrich grinned miserably. "Tempting. Tempting. But it might hurt."

A Rumor of War

PHILIP CAPUTO

1977

PROLOGUE

In thy faint slumbers I by thee have watch'd
And heard thee murmur tales of iron wars. . . .
—Shakespeare, *Henry IV, Part I*

This book does not pretend to be history. It has nothing to do with politics, power, strategy, influence, national interests, or foreign policy; nor is it an indictment of the great men who led us into Indochina and whose mistakes were paid for with the blood of some quite ordinary men. In a general sense, it is simply a story about war, about the things men do in war and the things war does to them. More strictly, it is a soldier's account of our longest conflict, the only one we have ever lost, as well as the record of a long and sometimes painful personal experience.

On March 8, 1965, as a young infantry officer, I landed at Danang with a battalion of the 9th Marine Expeditionary Brigade, the first U.S. combat unit sent to Indochina. I returned in April 1975 as a newspaper correspondent and covered the Communist offensive that ended with the fall of Saigon. Having been among the first Americans to fight in Vietnam, I was also among the last to be evacuated, only a few hours before the North Vietnamese Army entered the capital.

Although most of this book deals with the experiences of the marines I served with in 1965 and 1966, I have included an epilogue briefly describing the American exodus. Only ten years separated the two events, yet the humiliation of our exit from Vietnam, compared to the high confidence with which we had entered, made it seem as if a century lay between them.

For Americans who did not come of age in the early sixties, it may be hard to grasp what those years were like—the pride and overpowering self-assurance that prevailed. Most of the thirty-five hundred men in our brigade, born during or immediately after World War II, were shaped by that era, the age of Kennedy's Camelot. We went overseas full of illusions, for which the intoxicating atmosphere of those years was as much to blame as our youth.

War is always attractive to young men who know nothing about it, but we had also been seduced into uniform by Kennedy's challenge to "ask what you can do for your country" and by the missionary idealism he had awakened in us. America seemed omnipotent then: the country could still claim it had never lost a war, and we believed we were ordained to play cop to the Communists' robber and spread our own political faith around the world. Like the French soldiers of the late eighteenth century, we saw ourselves as the champions of "a cause that was destined to triumph." So, when we marched into the rice paddies on that damp March afternoon, we carried, along with our packs and rifles, the implicit convictions that the Viet Cong would be quickly beaten and that we were doing something altogether noble and good. We kept the packs and rifles; the convictions, we lost.

The discovery that the men we had scorned as peasant guerrillas were, in fact, a lethal, determined enemy and the casualty lists that lengthened each week with nothing to show for the blood being spilled broke our early confidence. By autumn, what had begun as an adventurous expedition had turned into an exhausting, indecisive war of attrition in which we fought for no cause other than our own survival.

Writing about this kind of warfare is not a simple task. Repeatedly, I have found myself wishing that I had been the veteran of a conventional war, with dramatic campaigns and historic battles for subject matter instead of a monotonous succession of ambushes and firefights. But there were no Normandies and Gettysburgs for us, no epic clashes that decided the fates of armies or nations. The war was mostly a matter of enduring weeks of expectant waiting and, at random intervals, of conducting vicious manhunts through jungles and swamps where snipers harassed us constantly and booby traps cut us down one by one.

The tedium was occasionally relieved by a large-scale search-and-destroy operation, but the exhilaration of riding the lead helicopter into a landing zone was usually followed by more of the same hot walking, with the mud sucking at our boots and the sun thudding against our helmets while an invisible enemy shot at us from distant tree lines. The rare instances when the VC chose to fight a set-piece battle provided the only excitement; not ordinary excitement, but the manic ecstasy of contact. Weeks of bottled-up tensions would be released in a few minutes of orgiastic violence, men screaming and shouting obscenities above the explosions of grenades and the rapid, rippling bursts of automatic rifles.

Beyond adding a few more corpses to the weekly body count, none of these encounters achieved anything; none will ever appear in military histories or be studied by cadets at West Point. Still, they changed us and taught us, the men who fought in them; in those obscure skirmishes we learned the old lessons about fear, cowardice, courage, suffering, cruelty, and comradeship. Most of all, we learned about death at an age when it is common to think of oneself as immortal. Everyone loses that illusion eventually, but in civilian life it is lost in installments over the years. We lost it all at once and, in the span of months, passed from boyhood through manhood to a premature middle age. The knowledge of death, of the implacable limits placed on a man's existence, severed us from our youth as irrevocably as a surgeon's scissors had once severed us from the womb. And yet, few of us were past twenty-five. We left Vietnam peculiar creatures, with young shoulders that bore rather old heads.

My own departure took place in early July 1966. Ten months later, following a tour as the CO of an infantry training company in North Carolina, an honorable discharge released me from the Marines and the chance of dying an early death in Asia. I felt as happy as a condemned man whose sentence has been commuted, but within a year I began growing nostalgic for the war.

Other veterans I knew confessed to the same emotion. In spite of everything, we felt a strange attachment to Vietnam and, even stranger, a longing to return. The war was still being fought, but this desire to go back did not spring from any patriotic ideas about duty, honor, and sacrifice, the myths with which old men send young men off to get killed or maimed. It arose, rather, from a recognition of how deeply we had been changed, how different we were from everyone who had not shared with us the miseries of the monsoon, the exhausting patrols, the fear of a combat assault on a hot landing zone. We had very little in common with them. Though we were civilians again, the civilian world seemed alien. We did not belong to it as much as we did to that other world, where we had fought and our friends had died.

I was involved in the antiwar movement at the time and struggled, unsuccessfully, to reconcile my opposition to the war with this nostalgia. Later, I realized a reconciliation was impossible; I would never be able to hate the war with anything like the undiluted passion of my friends in the movement. Because I had fought in it, it was not an abstract issue, but a deeply emotional experience, the most significant thing that had happened to me. It held my thoughts, senses, and feelings in an unbreakable embrace. I would hear in thunder the roar of artillery. I could not listen to rain without recalling those drenched nights on the line, nor walk through the woods without instinctively searching for a trip wire or an ambush. I could protest as loudly as the most convinced activist, but I could not deny the grip the war had on me, nor the fact that it had been an experience as fascinating as it was repulsive, as exhilarating as it was sad, as tender as it was cruel.

This book is partly an attempt to capture something of its ambivalent realities. Anyone who fought in Vietnam, if he is honest about himself, will have to admit he enjoyed the compelling attractiveness of combat. It was a peculiar enjoyment because it was mixed with a commensurate pain. Under fire, a man's powers of life heightened in proportion to the proximity of death, so that he felt an elation as extreme as his dread. His senses quickened, he attained an acuity of consciousness at once pleasurable and excruciating. It was something like the elevated state of awareness induced by drugs. And it could be just as addictive, for it made whatever else life offered in the way of delights or torments seem pedestrian.

I have also attempted to describe the intimacy of life in infantry battalions, where the communion between men is as profound as any between lovers. Actually, it is more so. It does not demand for its sustenance the reciprocity, the pledges of affection, the endless reassurances required by the love of men and women. It is, unlike marriage, a bond that cannot be broken by a word, by boredom or divorce, or by anything other than death. Sometimes even that is not strong enough. Two friends of mine died trying to save the corpses of their men from the battlefield. Such devotion, simple and selfless, the sentiment of belonging to each other, was the one decent thing we found in a conflict otherwise notable for its monstrosities.

And yet, it was a tenderness that would have been impossible if the war had been significantly less brutal. The battlefields of Vietnam were a crucible in which a generation of American soldiers were fused together by a common confrontation with death and a sharing of hardships, dangers, and fears. The very ugliness of the war, the sordidness of our daily lives, the degradation of having to take part in body counts made us draw still closer to one another. It was as if in comradeship we found an affirmation of life and the means to preserve at least a vestige of our humanity.

There is also the aspect of the Vietnam War that distinguished it from other American conflicts—its absolute savagery. I mean the savagery that prompted so many American fighting men—the good, solid kids from Iowa farms—to kill civilians and prisoners. The final chapter of this book concentrates on this subject. My purpose has not been to confess complicity in what, for me, amounted to murder, but, using myself and a few other men as examples, to show that war, by its nature, can arouse a psychopathic violence in men of seemingly normal impulses.

There has been a good deal of exaggeration about U.S. atrocities in Vietnam, exaggeration not about their extent but about their causes. The two most popularly held explanations for outrages like My Lai have been the racist theory, which proposes that the American soldier found it easy to slaughter Asians because he did not regard them as human beings, and the frontier-heritage theory, which claims he was inherently violent and needed only the excuse of war to vent his homicidal instincts.

Like all generalizations, each contains an element of truth; yet both ignore the barbarous treatment the Viet Cong and ARVN often inflicted on their own people, and neither confront the crimes committed by the Korean division, probably the most bloody-minded in Vietnam, and by the French during the first Indochina war.

The evil was inherent not in the men—except in the sense that a devil dwells in us all—but in the circumstances under which they had to live and fight. The conflict in Vietnam combined the two most bitter forms of warfare, civil war and revolution, to which was added the ferocity of jungle war. Twenty years of terrorism and fratricide had obliterated most reference points from the country's moral map long before we arrived. Communists and government forces alike considered ruthlessness a necessity if not a virtue. Whether committed in the name of principles or out of vengeance, atrocities were as common in the Vietnamese battlefields as shell craters and barbed wire. The marines in our brigade were not innately cruel, but on landing in Danang they learned rather quickly that Vietnam was not a place where a man could expect much mercy if, say, he was taken prisoner. And men who do not expect to receive mercy eventually lose their inclination to grant it.

At times, the comradeship that was the war's only redeeming quality caused some of its worst crimes—acts of retribution for friends who had been killed. Some men could not withstand the stress of guerrilla-fighting: the hair-trigger alertness constantly demanded of them, the feeling that the enemy was everywhere, the inability to distinguish civilians from combatants created emotional pressures which built to such a point that a trivial provocation could make these men explode with the blind destructiveness of a mortar shell.

Others were made pitiless by an overpowering greed for survival. Self-preservation, that most basic and tyrannical of all instincts, can turn a man into a coward or, as was more often the case in Vietnam, into a creature who destroys without hesitation or remorse whatever poses even a potential threat to his life. A sergeant in my platoon, ordinarily a pleasant young man, told me once, "Lieutenant, I've got a wife and two kids at home and I'm going to see 'em again and don't care who I've got to kill or how many of 'em to do it."

General Westmoreland's strategy of attrition also had an important effect on our behavior. Our mission was not to win terrain or seize positions, but simply to kill: to kill Communists and kill as many of them as possible. Stack 'em like cordwood. Victory was a high body-count, defeat a low kill-ratio, war a matter of arithmetic. The pressure on unit commanders to produce enemy corpses was intense, and they in turn communicated it to their troops. This led to such practices as counting civilians as Viet Cong. "If it's dead and Vietnamese, it's VC," was a rule of thumb in the bush. It is not surprising, therefore, that some men acquired a contempt for human life and a predilection for taking it.

Finally, there were the conditions imposed by the climate and country. For weeks we had to live like primitive men on remote outposts rimmed by alien seas of rice paddies and rain forests. Malaria, blackwater fever, and dysentery, though not the killers they had been in past wars, took their toll. The sun scorched us in the dry season, and in the monsoon season we were pounded numb by ceaseless rain. Our days were spent hacking through mountainous jungles whose immensity reduced us to antlike pettiness. At night we squatted in muddy holes, picked off the leeches that sucked on our veins, and waited for an attack to come rushing at us from the blackness beyond the perimeter wire.

The air-conditioned headquarters of Saigon and Danang seemed thousands of miles away. As for the United States, we did not call it "the World" for nothing; it might as well have been on another planet. There was nothing familiar out where we were, no churches, no police, no laws, no newspapers, or any of the restraining influences without which the earth's population of virtuous people would be reduced by ninety-five percent. It was the dawn of creation in the Indochina bush, an ethical as well as a geographical wilderness. Out there, lacking restraints, sanctioned to kill, confronted by a hostile country and a relentless enemy, we sank into a brutish state. The descent could be checked only by the net of a man's inner moral values, the attribute that is called character. There were a few—and I suspect Lieutenant Calley was one—who had no net and plunged all the way down, discovering in their bottommost depths a capacity for malice they probably never suspected was there.

Most American soldiers in Vietnam—at least the ones I knew—could not be divided into good men and bad. Each possessed roughly equal measures of both qualities. I saw men who behaved with great compassion toward the Vietnamese one day and then burned down a village the next. They were, as Kipling wrote of his Tommy Atkins, neither saints "nor blackguards too / But single men in barricks most remarkable like you." That may be why Americans reacted with such horror to the disclosures of U.S. atrocities while ignoring those of the other side: the American soldier was a reflection of themselves.

This book is not a work of the imagination. The events related are true, the characters real, though I have used fictitious names in some places. I have tried to describe accurately what the dominant event in the life of my generation, the Vietnam War, was like for the men who fought in it. Toward that end, I have made a great effort to resist the veteran's inclination to remember things the way he would like them to have been rather than the way they were.

Finally, this book ought not to be regarded as a protest. Protest arises from a belief that one can change things or influence events. I am not egotistical enough to believe I can. Besides, it no longer seems necessary to register an objection to the war, because the war is over. We lost it, and no amount of objecting will resurrect the men who died, without redeeming anything, on calvaries like Hamburger Hill and the Rockpile.

It might, perhaps, prevent the next generation from being crucified in the next war.

But I don't think so.

CHAPTER FOURTEEN

In such condition there is . . . no account of time; no arts; no
letters; no society; and which is worst of all, continual fear and
danger of violent death; and the life of man, solitary, poor, nasty,
brutish and short.
—Hobbes, *Leviathan*

In late October an enemy battalion attacked one of our helicopter
bases, inflicted fifty casualties on the company guarding it, and destroyed or damaged over forty aircraft. Two nights later, another Viet
Cong battalion overran an outpost manned by eighty marines from A
Company, killing twenty-two and wounding fifty more. The usual
ambushes and booby traps claimed daily victims, and the medevac
helicopters flew back and forth across the low, dripping skies.

The regiment's mood began to match the weather. We were a long
way from the despair that afflicted American soldiers in the closing
years of the war, but we had also traveled some emotional distance
from the cheery confidence of eight months before. The mood was
sardonic, fatalistic, and melancholy. I could hear it in our black jokes:
"Hey, Bill, you're going on patrol today. If you get your legs blown off
can I have your boots?" I could hear it in the songs we sang. Some
were versions of maudlin country-and-western tunes like "Detroit
City," the refrain of which expressed every rifleman's hope;

I wanna go home, I wanna go home,
O I wanna go home.

Other songs were full of gallows humor. One, "A Belly-full of War," was a marching song composed by an officer in A Company.

Oh they taught me how to kill,
Then they stuck me on this hill,
I don't like it anymore.
For all the monsoon rains
Have scrambled up my brains.
I've had a belly-full of war.

Oh the sun is much too hot,
And I've caught jungle rot,
I don't like it anymore.
I'm tired and terrified,
I just want to stay alive,
I've had a belly-full of war.

So you can march upon Hanoi,
Just forget this little boy,
I don't like it anymore.
For as I lie here with a pout,
My intestines hanging out,
I've had a belly-full of war.

There was another side to the war, about which no songs were sung, no jokes made. The fighting had not only become more intense, but more vicious. Both we and the Viet Cong began to make a habit of atrocities. One of 1st Battalion's radio operators was captured by an enemy patrol, tied up, beaten with clubs, then executed. His body was found floating in the Song Tuy Loan three days after his capture, with the ropes still around his hands and feet and a bullet hole in the back of his head. Four other marines from another regiment were captured and later discovered in a common grave, also tied up and with their skulls blasted open by an executioner's bullets. Led by a classmate from Quantico, a black officer named Adam Simpson, a twenty-eight-man patrol was ambushed by two hundred VC and almost annihilated. Only two marines, both seriously wounded, lived through it. There might have been more survivors had the Viet Cong not made a systematic massacre of the wounded. After springing the ambush, they went down the line of fallen marines, pumping bullets into any body that showed signs of life, including the body of my classmate. The two men who survived did so by crawling under the bodies of their dead comrades and feigning death.

We paid the enemy back, sometimes with interest. It was common knowledge that quite a few captured VC never made it to prison camps; they were reported as "shot and killed while attempting to escape." Some line companies did not even bother taking prisoners; they simply killed every VC they saw, and a number of Vietnamese who were only suspects. The latter were usually counted as enemy dead, under the unwritten rule "If he's dead and Vietnamese, he's VC."

Everything rotted and corroded quickly over there: bodies, boot leather, canvas, metal, morals. Scorched by the sun, wracked by the wind and rain of the monsoon, fighting in alien swamps and jungles, our humanity rubbed off of us as the protective bluing rubbed off the barrels of our rifles. We were fighting in the cruelest kind of conflict, a people's war. It was no orderly campaign, as in Europe, but a war for survival waged in a wilderness without rules or laws; a war in which each soldier fought for his own life and the lives of the men beside him, not caring who he killed in that personal cause or how many or in what manner and feeling only contempt for those who sought to impose on his savage struggle the mincing distinctions of civilized warfare—that code of battlefield ethics that attempted to humanize an essentially inhuman war. According to those "rules of engagement," it was morally right to shoot an unarmed Vietnamese who was running, but wrong to shoot one who was standing or walking; it was wrong to shoot an enemy prisoner at close range, but right for a sniper at long range to kill an enemy soldier who was no more able than a prisoner to defend himself; it was wrong for infantrymen to destroy a village with white-phosphorous grenades, but right for a fighter pilot to drop napalm on it. Ethics seemed to be a matter of distance and technology. You could never go wrong if you killed people at long range with sophisticated weapons. And then there was that inspiring order issued by General Greene: kill VC. In the patriotic fervor of the Kennedy years, we had asked, "What can we do for our country?" and our country answered, "Kill VC." That was the strategy, the best our best military minds could come up with: organized butchery. But organized or not, butchery was butchery, so who was to speak of rules and ethics in a war that had none?

In the middle of November, at my own request, I was transferred to a line company in 1st Battalion. My convictions about the war had eroded to nothing; I had no illusions, but I had volunteered for a line company anyway. There were a number of reasons, of which the paramount was boredom. There was nothing for me to do but count casualties. I felt useless and a little guilty about living in relative safety while other men risked their lives. I cannot deny that the front still held a fascination for me. The rights or wrongs of the war aside, there was a magnetism about combat. You seemed to live more intensely under fire. Every sense was sharper, the mind worked clearer and faster. Perhaps it was the tension of opposites that made it so, an attraction balanced by revulsion, hope that warred with dread. You found yourself on a precarious emotional edge, experiencing a headiness that no drink or drug could match.

The fear of madness was another motive. The hallucination I had had that day in the mess, of seeing Mora and Harrison prefigured in death, had become a constant, waking nightmare. I had begun to see almost everyone as they would look in death, including myself. Shaving in the mirror in the morning, I could see myself dead, and there were moments when I not only saw my own corpse, but other people looking at it. I saw life going on without me. The sensation of not being anymore came over me at night, just before falling asleep. Sometimes it made me laugh inside; I could not take myself seriously when I could already see my own death; nor, seeing their deaths as well, could I take others seriously. We were all the victims of a great practical joke played on us by God or Nature. Maybe that was why corpses always grinned. They saw the joke at the last moment. Sometimes it made me laugh, but most of the time it was not at all humorous, and I was sure that another few months of identifying bodies would land me in a psychiatric ward. On staff, there was too much time to brood over the corpses; there would be very little time to think in a line company. That is the secret to emotional survival in war, not thinking.

Finally, there was hatred, a hatred buried so deep that I could not then admit its existence. I can now, though it is still painful. I burned with a hatred for the Viet Cong and with an emotion that dwells in most of us, one closer to the surface than we care to admit: a desire for retribution. I did not hate the enemy for their politics, but for murdering Simpson, for executing that boy whose body had been found in the river, for blasting the life out of Walt Levy. Revenge was one of the reasons I volunteered for a line company. I wanted a chance to kill somebody.

Jim Cooney, my old roommate on Okinawa, was brought up from 3d Battalion to replace me. And it was with a sense of achievement that I gave him casualty files several times thicker than the ones that had been given to me in June.

Kazmarack drove me out to One-One's headquarters. Sergeant Hamilton saw me off. I would miss him, for his humor had helped me maintain at least an outward semblance of sanity during the previous five months: Hamilton, who suffered constantly from gastroenteritis, running into the colonel's head, then telling the officer who chewed him out, "For Christ's sake, sir, I've got Ho Chi Minh's revenge. What do you expect me to do, dump a load in my pants just because my turds don't have a colonel's eagles on them? Shit and death are no respecters of rank, sir."

Battalion HQ, awash in mud, was a cluster of tents and bunkers near the French fort. There I followed the usual Stations of the Cross: to the adjutant's tent to have my orders endorsed, to the battalion aid station to drop off my health records, back to the adjutant's to have the transfer entered in my service record book, then to a meeting with the CO, a rangy lieutenant colonel named Hatch. He told me I was to be given a platoon in C Company, Walt Levy's old company. Captain Neal was the Skipper and McCloy, who had extended his tour, was the executive officer. When the chat with the colonel was over, I went back to the adjutant's to wait for Charley Company's driver to pick me up. It was raining hard. It had been raining day and night for two weeks.

The driver, PFC Washington, pulled up in a mud-slathered jeep. Like all company drivers, Washington was eager, cheerful, and helpful. Drivers who were eager, cheerful, and helpful got to remain drivers, while lazy, dour, unhelpful drivers were given rifles and sent back to the line. We drove down the road that cut through the Dai-La Pass, the rain lashing our faces because there was no windshield. The road, which had been churned into a river of mud, meandered through villages stinking of buffalo dung and nuocmam. Flooded rice paddies and rows of banana trees whose broad leaves bowed in the rain lined the road. Putting the gears in low, Washington gunned the jeep up a gentle hill, the wheels spinning, the jeep fishtailing as it went over the top of the rise. From there, I could see a T-junction about half a mile ahead, a clump of dark trees shading a hamlet, then the rice paddies and foothills, which rose in tiers toward the black mountains. The plumes of mist rising through the jungle canopy made the mountains look menacing and mysterious. We went down the hill, and the road became like reddish-brown pudding two feet deep. Several farmers stood by a village well, washing their legs and feet. Far away, a machine gun was firing in measured bursts. Washington turned onto a side road just short of the T-junction, passing a cement house whose walls were pocked with bullet and shrapnel holes. A section of 81-mm mortars, emplaced in a field near the house, was shelling a hill in the distance. The shells made gray puffs on the crest of the hill, which was also gray, as gray as slag in the rain. Running along the edge of an overgrown ravine, the side road led into a stretch of low, worn-looking hills. C Company's base camp lay just ahead. The tents were pitched randomly beside a one-oh-five battery, whose candy-stripe aiming stakes looked strangely festive against the background of tents, guns, mud, and rain-swept hills. A squad of marines slogged up the track that led from the base camp to the front line. They walked slowly and in single file, heads down, long, hooded ponchos billowing in the wind. The stocks of their rifles, slung muzzle-down against the rain, bulged under the backs of the ponchos; hooded and bowed, the marines resembled a column of hunchbacked, penitent monks.

Captain Neal was sitting behind his desk in the headquarters tent. A wirily built man with bleak eyes and taut, thin lips, he resembled one of those stern schoolmasters seen in sketches of old New England classrooms. I handed him my orders. He looked up from his paperwork and all I could see in his eyes was their color, pale blue.

"Lieutenant Caputa, been expecting you," he said.

"Caputo, sir."

"Welcome aboard." He attempted to smile, and failed.

"I'm giving you second platoon, Mister Caputa. They've been without an officer since Mister Levy was killed."

"I was at Quantico with Mister Levy, skipper."

"Third and weapons platoons don't have officers, either."

He stood up, unfolded a map, and briefed me on the situation. The battalion, the whole division in fact, was now on the defensive. Our job was to prevent another VC attack on the airfield by holding the main line of resistance. No offensive operations of any kind were being conducted, except squad- and platoon-sized patrols, and even those were not to venture farther than two thousand yards from the MLR.

The company's frontage extended from the T-junction south along the road to the Song Tuy Loan River, a distance of nearly a mile; that is, three times the distance a full-strength company could defend adequately, and this company was considerably understrength. The gaps in the line were covered by artillery barrages. The company followed a set routine: two platoons, less the squads on ambush patrol, manned the MLR at night. A third platoon held Charley Hill, a combat outpost about seven hundred yards forward. In the morning, a twenty-five-percent alert was maintained on the line, while the rest of the men hiked the half-mile back to base camp to eat a hot meal, clean their rifles, and rest. In the afternoon, they relieved the morning watch, worked on their positions, or went out on daylight patrols. In the evening, the routine began again.

Mines and booby traps accounted for almost all of the company's casualties. There was some sniping and, rarely, a mortar shelling. I was to keep a sharp look-out for immersion foot in my platoon. The men were constantly wet. They were also tired, and sometimes hungry because they subsisted almost exclusively on cold C rations. *But I was not to give them any slack.* Give 'em slack and they'd start thinking about home, and the worst thing an infantryman could do was think. Did I understand all that? Yes. Did I have any questions? No.

"Good. You're going up to the line tonight, so draw your gear now, Mister Caputa."

"Caputo, sir. As in *toe*."

"Whatever. You'll be going up tonight."

"Yes, sir," I said, thinking that he was absolutely the most humorless man I had ever met.

Evening vespers began about seven o'clock, when the howitzers and mortars started firing their routine harassment missions. With my new platoon, I sloshed up to the line. The shells ripped the air over our heads and the rain, slanting before a high monsoon wind, pelted our faces. The platoon moved up the track at the steady, plodding pace that is one of the signs of veteran infantry. And they were veterans if they were anything. Looking at them, it was hard to believe that most of them were only nineteen or twenty. For their faces were not those of children, and their eyes had the cold, dull expression of men who are chained to an existence of ruthless practicalities. They struggled each day to keep dry, to keep their skin from boiling up with jungle rot, and to stay alive. In the sodden world they inhabited, the mere act of walking, an act almost as unconscious as breathing, could bring death. The trails they had to patrol were sown with mines. One misstep, and you were blasted to bits or crippled for life. One misstep or a lax moment where your eyes wandered and failed to notice the thin strand of wire stretched across the trail.

We reached the road that marked the front line. I crawled into the platoon command post—a foxhole ringed with sandbags and covered by a leaky poncho. Jones, the radioman, Brewer, the platoon runner, and a corpsman crawled in with me. The CP was on a grassy hillock just behind the road. A pool of cold water lay at the bottom of the foxhole. We bailed it out with our helmets and, spreading a poncho over the mud, sat down to smoke a last cigarette before darkness fell.

Jones slipped the heavy, ancient PRC-10 radio from his back, propping it against one side of the hole.

"Charley Six, this is Charley Two. Radio check," he said into the handset. "How do you read me, Six?"

"Two, this is Six. Read you loud and clear. Six Actual says to advise your actual that Alpha Company taking some mortar fire."

"Roger, Six. If no further traffic, this is Two out."

"Six out."

"Did you hear that, sir?" Jones said.

I said that I had.

The wind was blowing hard, and the rain came sweeping horizontally across the paddies to strike the hooch like buckshot. I listened for the mortars, but could not hear anything over the wind, the rain, and the dry-rattling branches of the bamboo trees around us. The last of my platoon were filing through the gray dusk toward their positions. Heavy-legged, they walked along the line—which was not a line, but a string of isolated positions dug wherever there was solid ground—and dropped off by twos into the foxholes. The coils of concertina wire in front of the positions writhed in the wind.

I had the first radio watch. Jones and the others lay down to sleep, curling up into the fetal position. Looking out, I tried to familiarize myself with the landscape. Second platoon's part of the line followed the course of the road, skirted a hamlet that was guarded by some Popular Forces—village militia—and ended at the river. Altogether, we held a frontage of seven hundred yards, normally the frontage for a company, and there were dangerously wide gaps between positions. One such position, called the "schoolhouse" because of the cement-walled school that stood there, was separated from the next, a knoll near the river, by about two hundred yards of flooded rice paddy. The two positions were like islands in an archipelago. Out front were more paddies, a stream with jungle-covered banks, then the gray-green foothills. Charley Hill stood there, a muddy, red little knob that stuck out of the surrounding hills like an inflamed sore. In the dimming light, I could just see the olive-drab patches of the hooches and the small figures of our men. There was nothing in front of the outpost but more hills, then the mountains, rising into the clouds. Compared to that place, the front line was the center of civilization. Charley Hill was at the ragged edge of the earth.

It was soon dark. I still could not hear anything but the wind and crackling branches, and now I could see nothing except varying shades of black. The village was a pitch-colored pool in the gray-black paddies. Beyond the inky line of the jungle bordering the stream, the Cordillera was so black that it looked like a vast hole in the sky. Even after my eyes adjusted, I could not see the slightest variation in color. It was absolutely black. It was a void, and, staring at it, I felt that I was looking into the sun's opposite, the source and center of all the darkness in the world.

The wind kept blowing, relentless and numbing. Soaked through, I started to shiver. It was difficult to hold the hand-set steady, and I stammered when I called in the hourly situation report. I could not remember having been so cold. A flare went up, revealing the silhouettes of palm trees tossing in the wind and sheets of rain falling from scudding clouds. A strong gust knifed into the foxhole, tugged at the hooch, and tore one side of it from its moorings. Rubbery and wet, the poncho slapped against my face, and Brewer said "Goddamn" as the rain sluiced into the now exposed hole. Then a stream of water guttered down from the hilltop and seeped through cracks in the sandbags, almost flooding us out. The poncho was still flapping like a sail loosed from its sheets. "Goddamn motherfuckin' Nam."

"Jones, Brewer, get that thing pegged down," I said, bailing again with my helmet. The rain fell into my collar and poured down the sleeves of my jacket as if they were drainpipes.

"Yes, sir," said Jones. He and Brewer climbed out, got hold of the poncho and pegged it down, pounding the metal stakes with the butt ends of their bayonets. The corpsman and I bailed, and the work warmed us a little. There was still an inch of water in the foxhole when we settled down again. I turned the radio over to Jones. It was his watch. Lying on my side, knees drawn up, I tried to sleep, but the puddles and chilling wind made it impossible.

Around midnight, automatic-rifle fire spattered into one of the positions near the hamlet. The squad leader called me on the field phone and said that twenty rounds had been fired into his right flank, but without causing any casualties. There was another burst.

"He's at it again, Two Actual," said the voice on the phone. "I think he's in the tree line along that stream."

"Roger. Give him a couple of M-79s. I'll be right down."

Taking a rifleman along for security, I went down the road and through the village. Two M-79 grenades exploded in the tree line. The mud on the road was ankle deep. We could not see anything except a lamp burning in one of the huts. Staying close to the culvert at the roadside in case we had to take cover quickly, we reached the position that had taken the fire. There were a couple of bullet holes in the marines' hooch. It began to rain harder, although that did not seem possible. Huddling down next to the riflemen, I tried to see something in the black tree line a hundred yards across the rice paddies. The paddies had been turned into a miniature lake, and wind-driven waves lapped the dike in front of us. Then a white-orange light winked in the gloom. Bullets streamed past us with that vicious, sucking sound, and I went down on my belly in the mud.

"See you now, you cocksucker," one of the riflemen said, pumping rapid fire at the sniper's muzzle-flash. Three or four more grenades, flashing brightly, crashed into the trees.

"That should give him something to think about, if it didn't blow his shit away," said the rifleman who had done the firing.

We waited for perhaps half an hour. When nothing more happened, my guard and I headed back toward the CP. The wind had let up finally, and in the quiet air mosquitoes hummed. Two mortar shells hit far behind us, where the road climbed and curved around a bend in the river. They exploded near D Company's lines, bursting in showers of lovely red sparks. In the opposite direction, One-Three, newly returned to Vietnam with all unseasoned troops, was having a fire-fight with figments of its imagination. We passed the hut where the lamp was burning. "Hey, GI," someone whispered. "GI, you come." A middle-aged farmer stood in the doorway, waving us inside. The marine brought his rifle up, just in case, and we went into the hut. It reeked of garlic, woodsmoke, and rotten fish-sauce, but it was dry and we were grateful for even a few moments out of the rain. I lit a cigarette, grateful for that, too. I drew the smoke deep into my lungs, feeling it calm my nerves.

The farmer had meanwhile taken some photographs out of an oil-skin packet. They were photos of Vietnamese whores and American soldiers making love in various positions. The farmer hissed and chuckled as he showed us each a picture. "Good, huh?" he said. "Number one, no? Want buy? You buy. Number one."

"Jesus Christ, you old pervert, no," I said. "Khoung. No buy."

"No buy?" the farmer asked in the surprised tone of all salesmen when met by a customer's refusal.

"Khoung. Chao Ong."

"Chao Ong, dai-uy." (Good night, captain.)

"No dai-uy. Trung-uy." (Lieutenant.)

"Ah. Ah. Trung-uy. Hokay. Chao trung-uy."

"How do you like that shit, lieutenant," said the rifleman when we were outside. "We're supposed to be fighting for these people. We're getting soaked and our asses shot at and he's in there whacking off at dirty pictures."

"Life is full of injustices."

"If you're a grunt, that's no lie, sir."

We slept fitfully for the rest of the night and woke up to a drizzling dawn. Dazed, the platoon hiked back to base camp, leaving one squad behind to guard the line. The rice paddies were underwater and filled with snakes. We could see the wakes they made as they slithered just beneath the surface. One fireteam, marooned on an island of high ground, had to borrow sampans from the villagers to get back to the road. Like prisoners in a labor gang, the marines marched toward camp joylessly and without expectation that the new day would bring anything different or better. Shivering myself warm, I felt more tired than I had ever felt before. I was worn out after only one night on the line, and I wondered how the platoon felt, after months on the line. I found out soon enough: they felt nothing, except occasional stabs of fear.

It went like that for the rest of the month. It was a time of little action and endless misery. I was given command of 1st platoon for a week, while its officer was absent. Our sole casualty that week was the squad leader who ended up hospitalized with a centipede bite. The real fighting had shifted to the Ia Drang Valley in the Central Highlands, where the Seventh Cavalry, of Little Bighorn fame, was fighting the North Vietnamese in what was then the biggest battle of the war. But it was quiet at Danang. Almost every hour of every night, the radio operators chanted, "All secure. Situation remains the same." I took out two or three patrols, but there was no contact except for the usual snipers. All secure. Situation remains the same. The company lost two machine-gunners to a mine. All secure. Situation remains the same. We trudged up to the line and back again, patrolled the booby-trapped trails, dug foxholes and redug them when they were collapsed by the rain. It rained all the time. We slept, when we slept, in the mud. We shivered through our nervous night watches, calling in reports every hour: All secure. Situation remains the same. A sentry from B Company was killed one morning by infiltrators. And still it rained. The Viet Cong lobbed a few shells at us, but they fell short, exploding in the paddies a long way from our wire, gray smoke blossoming, water and clods of mud geysering. Charley Six observed six enemy mortar rounds six-oh millimeters two hundred meters from this position. No casualties. All secure. Situation remains the same.

At the end of the month, the Viet Cong staged a small attack on the village. The rain that night was falling lightly. It leaked from the swollen sky like pus from a festering wound. The second squad leader, Sergeant Coffell, who had been transferred to One-One from another battalion, and I were on watch in a murky foxhole, talking to each other to keep awake. We talked about home, women, and our fears. A heavy mist lay in the jungle along the stream in front of us. The trees appeared to be standing in a bank of deep snow. Coffell was whispering to me about his dread of Bouncing Betties: mines that sprang out of the ground and exploded at waist level. He was going to take a patrol out in the morning and said he hoped they did not trip any Bouncing Betties. His last company commander had been hit by one.

"It tore one of his legs off at the thigh, sir. His femur artery was cut and the blood was pouring out of it like out of a hose. We couldn't stop it. We didn't know what the hell to do, so we just started packing mud into it, from out of the rice paddy. We kept slapping mud into the stump, but it didn't do any good. No, sir, those Bouncing Betties, goddamn, I hate those things."

An automatic rifle thumped in the village behind us. One of the Popular Force militiamen fired a burst from his carbine.

"Goddamn PFs shooting at shadows again," Coffell said.

"Shadows don't carry automatic rifles. That sounded like an AK to me."

Then came a crackling as of a dry brush pile set alight. Hand grenades exploded and tracers were glowing redly above our heads. A couple of rounds whacked into the sandbags of a nearby position, narrowly missing a machine-gunner. Crouching low, I picked up the field phone and called Dodge, the platoon sergeant. He was with another squad at the schoolhouse position, on the opposite side of the village. I asked if he could see where the fire was coming from.

"No, sir. We're pinned down here. Can't even lift our heads. We got automatic-weapons fire hitting the schoolhouse. It's coming from near the ville, but I can't say exactly."

"Then Charlie's behind us. Anyone hit?"

"No, sir, but old watash almost got it between the running lights. Four, five rounds hit the wall next to me. Got sprayed with a lot of plaster . . ."

The line went dead as two more grenades burst.

"Dodge, are you reading me?" I asked, clicking the receiver button several times. There was no answer. The grenades had cut the landline; so now I had one squad pinned down and no communications with them.

Rolling over the parapet of the foxhole, I crawled up the road embankment to see if I could spot the enemy's muzzle-flashes. I could. The Viet Cong were in the village, shooting in every direction. A line of red light appeared above the road. It was moving rapidly toward me, and one of the tracers cracked past my ear, close enough for me to feel the shock wave. With the sick feeling that comes when you are receiving fire from your rear, I rolled back down the embankment.

"Coffell, they're behind us. Face your people about. Face 'em toward the road and tell 'em to drop anything that moves on that road."

"Yes, sir."

Sliding on my belly toward the radio, I heard my heart drumming against the wet earth. "Charley Six, this is Charley Two Actual," I said, trying to reach Neal. "Do you read me?" I was answered by static. "Six, this is Two requesting illumination on concentration one. Are you reading me, Six?" The static hissed in the receiver. A rifleman was lying next to me, his M-14 pointed at the road. He had turned his head to face me. I could not tell who he was. In the darkness, I could only see his hollow, haggard eyes staring from beneath his helmet's brim. "Six, this is Two. If you are receiving me, I have Victor Charlies in the ville behind me. One squad pinned down by automatic-weapons fire and landlines cut by grenades. Request illumination on concentration one." Mockingly, the static hissed. I hit the radio with my fist. Discards from World War II, the PRC-10s could always be relied on to break down in a crisis.

After trying for nearly fifteen minutes, I got through to company HQ. Neal said he knew nothing about a fire-fight.

"It's going on right behind me. Or was. It's just about over now."

"I don't hear anything," he said.

"Six, that's because it's almost over. They were really going at it before. Can you give me some illumination on concentration one? Maybe we can spot the VC pulling out."

"I didn't hear anything before, Charley Two."

"In the village, Six! The Victor Charlies are in the ville behind me, engaged with the PFs. My first squad is pinned down."

I knew why Captain Neal had not heard anything: he was in the company's base camp, half a mile behind the line. He slept there, or in the command bunker, most every night. "I really felt bad about sleeping in my tent while you guys were out there," he told me after one particularly wretched night. "Yes, sir," I said. "We felt pretty bad about it, too."

"Charley Two, have you got any casualties?"

"Negative."

"Do you think you can handle the situation?"

"Roger. A little illumination would help."

"Keep me informed. This is Six Actual out."

"Two out."

So, I would get no illumination. I was not to be illuminated.

The skirmish had ended by the time I finished talking with Neal. We made contact with the PF commander, who said, "Now, hokay. VC di-di."

I called Neal again. "Victor Charlies have pulled out, Six. No casualties. We searched area with negative results."

"Roger. How's your situation now?"

"All secure," I said. "Situation remains the same."

In the company mess the next morning, I sat with my numbed hands wrapped around a mug of coffee. I had not slept after the firefight. None of us had slept. We had been put on full alert because an enemy battalion was reported to be moving in our direction. We waited, and, waiting, fought off sleep. A sniper teased us now and then, the rain fell incessantly, but nothing happened. At dawn, we moved back to base camp, except for those who had to stay on the line or go on patrol.

It was still raining while I sat in the mess across from Captain Neal. Outside, a line of marines shuffled past the immersion burners, each dipping his mess kit into the boiling water. I wanted to sleep. I wanted four or five hours of dry, unbroken sleep, but I had to lay communications wire to a new position. That would take most of the day. I also had to inspect the police of my platoon's sector. Neal had found a pile of empty C-ration tins near the schoolhouse, which upset him. He liked to keep a tidy battlefield. So I would have to make sure the men buried the tin cans. I mustn't forget to do that, I thought. It's important to the war effort to pick up our garbage. A voice inside my head told me I was being overly bitter. I was feeling sorry for myself. No one had forced me to join the Marines or to volunteer for a line company. I had asked for it. That was true, but recognizing the truth of it did not solve my immediate problem: I was very tired and wanted to get some sleep.

Neal said he had been looking at my service record and noticed that I had been in Vietnam for nine months without an R-and-R.

There was an opening on a flight to Saigon the next morning. Would I like to go to Saigon for three days' R-and-R? Yes, I said without hesitating. Oh yes yes yes.

The green and brown camouflage C-130 landed at Tan Son Nhut airport in the early evening. We rode into Saigon on a bus that had wire screens on its windows, to deflect terrorist grenades. It pulled up in front of the Meyercourt, a hotel reserved for soldiers on R-and-R. The high wall surrounding the hotel was topped with barbed wire, and an MP armed with a shotgun stood by the door in a sand-bagged sentry booth. Out on the balcony of my eighth-floor room, I watched a flare-ship dropping flares over the marshlands south of the city. Shellfire flickered on the horizon, the guns booming rhythmically. So, even in Saigon there was no escape from the war. But the room was clean and cheap. It had a shower and a bed, a real bed with a mattress and clean sheets. I took a hot shower, which felt wonderful, lay down, and slept for fifteen hours.

I found escape from the war the next morning. It was in a quiet quarter of the city, where tall trees shaded the streets and I could walk for a long way without seeing soldiers, whores, or bars; just quiet, shady streets and whitewashed villas with red tile roofs. There was a sidewalk café on one of the side streets. I went inside for breakfast. The café was cool and fresh-smelling in the early morning, and the only other customers were two lovely Vietnamese girls wearing orange ao-dais. The waiter handed me a menu. A *menu.* I had a choice of what to eat, something I had not had in months. I ordered juice, café au lait, and hot croissants with jam and butter. After eating, I sat back in the chair and read a collection of Dylan Thomas. The book, a gift from my sister, took me a long way from Vietnam, to the peaceful hills of Wales, to the rocky Welsh coasts where herons flew. I liked "Fern Hill" and "Poem in October," but I could not read "And Death Shall Have No Dominion." I didn't know much about Dylan Thomas's life, but I guessed that he had never been in a war. No one who had seen war could ever doubt that death had dominion.

As I was leaving, an old woman with one arm came up to me begging. She handed me a note which read, "I am fifty years old and lost my left arm in an artillery bombardment. My husband died in a battle with the Viet Cong in 1962. Please give me 20 piasters." I gave her a hundred; she bowed and said, "Cam Ong." Tell her, Dylan, that death has no dominion.

On my second day in Saigon, I met an Indian silk-merchant in one of the city's noisy, enclosed market places, and he asked how I liked Saigon. I said that I liked it very much. It was a beautiful city, a magnificent city when you compared it to the mess in the country-side. "Yes, you are right," he said sadly. "There is something wrong with this country. I think it is the war."

In the evening, I had dinner on the terrace of the Continental Palace Hotel. The Palace was a very old French hotel, where waiters behaved with a politeness that was not fawning and with a dignity that was not haughtiness. I sat at one of the linen-covered tables on the terrace, beside an archway that looked out on the street. A few French plantation owners, old colonials who had stayed on in Indochina, were sitting across from me. Suntanned men dressed in cotton shirts and khaki shorts, they were drinking cold white wine, and eating and gesturing as if they were on the Champs Elysées or the Left Bank. They were enjoying themselves. It occurred to me that it had been a long time since I had seen anyone enjoying himself.

A waiter came up and asked for my order.

"Chateaubriand avec pommes frites, s'il vous plaît."

The waiter, an old Vietnamese man with the bearing of a village elder, winced at my accent. "Pardonnez-moi monsieur. Le chateaubriand est pour deux."

"I know, I want it anyway." I said switching back to English.

"Bien. Vin Rouge?"

"Oui, rouge. A bottle."

"But there is only you."

"I'll drink it. Don't worry."

He wrote on his pad and walked off.

Waiting for the wine, I looked at the Frenchmen talking, gesturing, and laughing at some joke or other, and I began to feel light-headed. It had something to do with the relaxed manner of those men, with their laughter and the sound their forks made against the plates. The

wine heightened the sensation. Later, after finishing the chateaubri-
and and half the bottle of red wine, I realized what the feeling was:
normality. I had had two nights of solid sleep, a bath, an excellent
dinner, and I felt normal—I mean, I did not feel afraid. I had been
released from that cramped land of death, the front, that land of
suffering peasants, worn soldiers, mud, rain, and fear. I felt alive again
and in love with life. The Frenchmen across from me were living, not
just surviving. And for the time being, I was a part of their world. I had
temporarily renewed my citizenship in the human race.

I drank more of the wine, loving the way the sweating bottle looked
on the white linen tablecloth. The thought of deserting crossed my
mind. It was a deliciously exciting thought. I would stay in Saigon and
live life. Of course, I knew it was impossible. Physically, it was impossible. I was white, several inches taller and about seventy pounds
heavier than the biggest Vietnamese. The MPs could not miss me.
But I was also constrained by the obligation I had toward my platoon.
I would be deserting them, my friends. That was the real crime a
deserter committed: he ran out on his friends. And perhaps that was
why, in spite of everything, we fought as hard as we did. We had no
other choice. Desertion was unthinkable. Each of us fought for himself and for the men beside him. The only way out of Vietnam,
besides death or wounds, was to fight your way out. We fought to live.
But it was pleasant to toy with the idea of desertion, to pretend I had a
choice.

Twenty or thirty of us were standing on the tarmac when the C-130
taxied to a stop. Our three days of freedom were over. An old gunnery
sergeant stood next to me, entertaining the crowd with his jokes. He
knew more jokes than a stage comedian, and he told them one after
another. He had fought on Iwo Jima and in Korea and had been in
Vietnam for seven months. He was a veteran, and with his brown,
lined face, he looked it. His rapid-fire jokes kept us laughing, kept us
from thinking about where we were going. Perhaps he was trying to
keep himself from thinking. But the jokes and laughter stopped when
the hatch of the C-130 opened and they brought the bodies off. The
corpses were in green rubber body-bags. We knew what they were by

the humps the boots made in the bags—and why was that always such a painful sight, the sight of a dead man's boots?

The mood changed. No one spoke. Silently we watched the crewmen carry the dead down the ramp and into an ambulance parked near the aircraft. And I felt it come back again, that old, familiar, cold, cramping fear. The humorous gunnery sergeant, veteran of three wars, shook his head. "Goddamn this war," he said. "Goddamn this war."

FROM CHAPTER EIGHTEEN

I slept briefly and fitfully in the bunker and woke up agitated. Psychologically, I had never felt worse. I had been awake for no more than a few seconds when I was seized by the same feeling that had gripped me after my nightmare about the mutilated men in my old platoon: a feeling of being afraid when there was no reason to be. And this unreasoning fear quickly produced the sensation I had often had in action: of watching myself in a movie. Although I have had a decade to think about it, I am still unable to explain why I woke up in that condition. I had not dreamed. It was a quiet day, one of those days when it was difficult to believe a war was on. Yet, my sensations were those of a man actually under fire. Perhaps I was suffering a delayed reaction to some previous experience. Perhaps it was simply battle fatigue. I had been in Vietnam for nearly a year, and was probably more worn-out than I realized at the time. Months of accumulated pressures might have chosen just that moment to burst, suddenly and for no apparent reason. Whatever the cause, I was outwardly normal, if a little edgier than usual; but inside, I was full of turbulent emotions and disordered thoughts, and I could not shake that weird sensation of being split in two.

Thinking fresh air might help, I climbed out of the musty bunker. I only felt worse, irritated by the pain that came each time my trousers tore loose from the ulcers. The sores itched unbearably, but I couldn't scratch them because scratching would spread the disease. The late-afternoon air was oppressive. Heat came up from the baked earth and pressed down from the sky. Clouds were beginning to build in gray towers over the mountains, threatening more rain. Rain. Rain. Rain. When would it stop raining? From the heads rose the stench of feces, the soupy deposits of our diseased bowels. My need for physical activity overcame my discomfort and I set out to walk the perimeter. Around and around I walked, sometimes chatting with the men, sometimes sitting and staring into the distance. A few yards outside the perimeter, the walls of a half-ruined building shone bright white in the sun's glare. It made me squint to look at them, but I did anyway. I looked at them for a long time. I don't know why. I just remember staring at them, feeling the heat grow more oppressive as the clouds piled up and advanced across the sky. The building had been a temple of some kind, but it was now little more than a pile of stones. Vines were growing over the stones and over the jagged, bullet-scarred walls, which turned from white to hot-pink as the sun dropped into the clouds. Behind the building lay the scrub jungle that covered the slopes of the hill. It smelled of decaying wood and leaves, and the low trees encircled the outpost like the disorderly ranks of a besieging army. Staring at the jungle and at the ruined temple, hatred welled up in me; a hatred for this green, moldy, alien world in which we fought and died.

My thoughts and feelings over the next few hours are irretrievably jumbled now, but at some point in the early evening, I was seized by an irresistible compulsion to do something. "Something's got to be done" was about the clearest thought that passed through my brain. I was fixated on the company's intolerable predicament. We could muster only half of our original strength, and half of our effectives had been wounded at least once. If we suffered as many casualties in the next month as we had in the one past, we would be down to fifty or sixty men, little more than a reinforced platoon. It was madness for us to go on walking down those trails and tripping booby traps without any chance to retaliate. *Retaliate.* The word rang in my head. *I will retaliate.* It was then that my chaotic thoughts began to focus on the two men whom Le Dung, Crowe's informant, had identified as Viet

Cong. My mind did more than focus on them; it fixed on them like a heat-seeking missile fixing on the tailpipe of a jet. They became an obsession. I would get them. I would get them before they got any more of us; before they got me. I'm going to get those bastards, I said to myself, suddenly feeling giddy.

"I'm going to get those bastards," I said aloud, rushing down into the bunker. Jones looked at me quizzically. "The VC, Jones, I'm going to get them." I was laughing. From my map case, I took out an overlay of the patrol route which 2d squad was to follow that night. It took them to a trail junction just outside the village of Giao-Tri. It was perfect. If the two VC walked out of the village, they would fall into the ambush. I almost laughed out loud at the idea of their deaths. If the VC did not leave the village, then the squad would infiltrate into it, Crowe guiding them to the house Le Dung had pointed out, and capture them—"snatch," in the argot. Yes, that's what I would do. A snatch patrol. The squad would capture the two VC and bring them to the outpost. I would interrogate them, beat the hell out of them if I had to, learn the locations of other enemy cells and units, then kill or capture those. I would get all of them. But suppose the two guerrillas resisted? The patrol would kill them, then. Kill VC. That's what we were supposed to do. Bodies. Neal wanted bodies. Well, I would give him bodies, and then my platoon would be rewarded instead of re- proved. I did not have the authority to send the squad into the village. The patrol order called only for an ambush at the trail junction. But who was the real authority out on that isolated outpost? *I* was. I would take matters into my own hands. Out there, I could do what I damned well pleased. And I would. The idea of taking independent action made me giddier still. I went out to brief the patrol.

In the twilight, Allen, Crowe, Lonehill, and two other riflemen huddled around me. Wearing bush hats, their hands and faces black- ened with shoe polish, they looked appropriately ferocious. I told them what they were to do, but, in my addled state of mind, I was almost incoherent at times. I laughed frequently and made several bloodthirsty jokes that probably left them with the impression I wouldn't mind if they summarily executed both Viet Cong. All the time, I had that feeling of watching myself in a film. I could hear myself laughing, but it did not sound like my laugh.

"Okay, you know what to do," I said to Allen, the patrol leader. "You set in ambush for a while. If nobody comes by, you go into the ville and you get them. *You get those goddamned VC.* Snatch 'em up and bring 'em back here, but if they give you any problems, kill 'em."

"Sir, since we ain't supposed to be in the ville, what do we say if we have to kill 'em?"

"We'll just say they walked into your ambush. Don't sweat that. All the higher-ups want is bodies."

"Yes, sir," Allen said, and I saw the look in his eyes. It was a look of distilled hatred and anger, and when he grinned his skull-like grin, I knew he was going to kill those men on the slightest pretext. And, knowing that, I still did not repeat my order that the VC were to be captured if at all possible. It was my secret and savage desire that the two men die. In my heart, I hoped Allen would find some excuse for killing them, and Allen had read my heart. He smiled and I smiled back, and we both knew in that moment what was going to happen. There was a silent communication between us, an unspoken understanding: blood was to be shed. There is no mystery about such unspoken communication. Two men who have shared the hardships and dangers of war come to know each other as intimately as two natural brothers who have lived together for years; one can read the other's heart without a word being said.

The patrol left, creeping off the outpost into the swallowing darkness. Not long afterward, I began to be teased by doubts. It was the other half of my double self, the calm and lucid half, warning that something awful was going to happen. The thought of recalling the patrol crossed my mind, but I could not bring myself to do it. I felt driven, in the grip of an inexorable power. Something had to be done.

And something was done. Allen called on the radio and said that they had killed one of the Viet Cong and captured the other. They were coming in with the prisoner. Letting out a whoop, I called Neal on the field phone. He said he had monitored Allen's radio transmission. He congratulated me:

"That's good work your men did out there."

I was elated. Climbing out of the bunker, I excitedly told Coffell "They got both of 'em! Both of 'em! Yeeeah-hoo!" The night was hot and still. Off to the west, heat-lightning flashed like shellfire in the clouds that obscured the sky above the mountains. It was clear directly overhead, and I could see the fixed and lofty stars.

Waiting by the perimeter for the patrol to return, I heard a burst of rifle fire and the distinctive roar of Crowe's shotgun. Allen called on the radio again: the prisoner had whipped a branch in Crowe's face and tried to escape. They had killed him.

"All right, bring the body in. I want to search it," I said.

They came in shortly. The five men were winded from their swift withdrawal and a little more excited than such veterans should have been. Allen was particularly overwrought. He started laughing as soon as he was inside the perimeter wire. Perhaps it was the release from tension that made him laugh like that, tinny, mirthlessly. When he calmed down, he told me what had happened:

"We sneaked into the ville, like you told us, sir. Crowe guided us to the house where he'd talked to the informant. It was empty, so we went to the hooch where the VC lived. Me, Crowe, and Lonehill went inside. The other two stayed on the trail to guard our rear. It was dark in the house, so Crowe turned on his flashlight and there's the two Cong, sleepin' in their beds. Lonehill goes into the other room and this girl in there starts screamin'. 'Shut her up,' I said and Lonehill cracks her with his rifle barrel." Allen started to laugh again. So did Crowe and a few of the men who were listening. I was laughing, too. How funny. Old Lonehill hit her with his rifle. "So about then, one of the Cong jumps up in his bed and the broad starts screamin' again. Crowe went in and slapped her and told her to keep her damned mouth shut. Then he comes back into the room and pops the Cong sittin' up with his forty-five. The dude jumps up and runs—he was hit in the shoulder—and Crowe runs after him. He was runnin' around outside yellin' 'Troi Oi! Troi Oi!' " (Oh God) "and then Crowe greased him and he didn't do no more yellin'. The other dude made a break for the door, but Lonehill grabbed him. 'Okay, let's take him back,' I said, and we moved the hell out. We was right at the base of the hill when the gook whipped the branch in Crowe's face. Somebody said, 'He's makin' a break, grease the motherfucker,' and Lonehill greased him and Crowe blasted him with the shotgun. I mean, that dude was *dead.*" Madly and hysterically, we all laughed again.

"Okay," I said, "where's the body?"

"Right outside the wire, sir."

The dead man was lying on his belly. The back of his head was blown out, and, in the beam of my flashlight, his brains were a shiny gray mass. Someone kicked the body over onto its back and said, "Oh, excuse me, Mr. Charles, I hope that didn't hurt," and we all doubled over with laughter. I beamed the flashlight on the corpse's face. His eyes were wide and glowing, like the eyes in a stuffed head. While Coffell held the flashlight, I searched the body. There was something about the dead man that troubled me. It was not the mutilation—I was used to that. It was his face. It was such a young face, and, while I searched him, I kept thinking, He's just a boy, just a boy. I could not understand why his youth bothered me; the VC's soldiers, like our own, were all young men.

Tearing off his bloodstained shirt, shredded, like his chest, by shotgun pellets, I looked for his papers. Someone quipped, "Hey, lieutenant, he'll catch cold." Everyone laughed again. I joined in, but I was not laughing as hard as before.

There were no documents in the boy's pockets, no cartridge belt around his waist. There was nothing that would have proved him to be Viet Cong. That troubled me further. I stood up and, taking the flashlight from Coffell, held it on the boy's dead face.

"Did you find anything on the other one?" I asked Allen.

"No, sir."

"No documents or weapons?"

"No, sir. Nothing."

"How about the house? Did you find anything that looked like booby-trap gear in the house?"

"No, sir."

"And no forged papers or anything like that?"

"No, sir. We didn't find nothing."

The laughter had stopped. I turned to Crowe.

"Are you *sure* that this was one of the two that kid pointed out?"

"Yes, sir," Crowe said, but he looked away from me.

"Tell me again why you shot him."

"Whipped a branch in my face, like Allen said." Crowe would not look at me. He looked at the ground. "He whipped a branch in my face and tried to make a break, so we wasted him."

The air seemed charged with guilt. I kept looking at the corpse, and a wave of horror rolled through me as I recognized the face. The sensation was like snapping out of a hypnotic trance. It was as jarring as suddenly awakening from a nightmare, except that I had awakened from one nightmare into another.

"Allen, is that how it happened?" I asked. "The prisoner tried to escape, right?"

"As far as I know, yes sir. Crowe shot him."

He was already covering himself. "Okay, if anyone asks you about this, you just say both these guys walked into your ambush. That's what you'll say, and you stick to that, all of you. They walked into your ambush and you killed one and captured the other. Then the prisoner tried to escape, so you killed him, too. Got that? You don't tell anybody that you snatched him out of the village."

"Yes, sir," Allen said.

"Shove off and pass that on to the others. You too, Crowe."

"Yes, sir," Crowe said, hanging his head like a naughty child.

They walked off. I stayed for a while, looking at the corpse. The wide, glowing, glassy eyes stared at me in accusation. The dead boy's open mouth screamed silently his innocence and our guilt. In the darkness and confusion, out of fear, exhaustion, and the brutal instincts acquired in the war, the marines had made a mistake. No, not they; *we*. We had killed the wrong man. That boy's innocent blood was on my hands as much as it was on theirs. I had sent them out there. My God, what have we done? I thought. I could think of nothing else. My God, what have we done. Please God, forgive us. What have we done?

Clicking off the flashlight, I told Coffell to get a burial party together. I did not know what else to do with the body of Crowe's informant, the boy named Le Dung.

. . .

The typewriters in the quonset hut began to click promptly at eight o'clock, when the legal clerks came in to begin another routine day of typing up routine reports. The red light on the electric coffee pot glowed and the electric fans on the clerks' desks stirred the warm, dense air. Having slept undisturbed for eight hours, as they did every night, and breakfasted on bacon and eggs, as they did every morning except when the division HQ served pancakes, the clerks were happy, healthy-looking boys. They appeared slightly bored by their dull work, but were content in the knowledge that their rear-echelon jobs gave them what their contemporaries in the line companies lacked: a future.

Sitting in one corner of the hut with my defense counsel, Lieutenant Jim Rader, I looked at the clerks and wished I were one of them. How pleasant it would be to have a future again. A crowd of witnesses milled around outside: marines and Vietnamese villagers, the latter looking utterly bewildered by the courtroom drama in which they would soon play their assigned roles. One of the clerks muttered a curse as a fan blew some papers off his desk. The artificial gust blew against the wall behind him, rustling the pages of his short-timer's calendar. The calendar was graced by a pornographic drawing, beneath which the word *June* was flanked by the numbers 1966. All the dates had been crossed off except today's, the 30th, the day on which Lance Corporal Crowe was to be tried on two counts of premeditated murder.

I was to appear as a witness for the prosecution. There was an absurdity in that, as I was to be tried on the same charges by the same prosecutor the following morning. But then, the fact that we had been charged in the first place was absurd. They had taught us to kill and had told us to kill, and now they were going to court-martial us for killing.

A bound sheaf of papers as thick as a small-town phone book and entitled "Investigating Officer's Report" sat on Rader's desk. It was the product of five months' labor on the part of various military lawyers, and the two top forms—DD457 and DD458—contained the charges against me: ". . . in that First Lieutenant Philip J. Caputo . . . did murder with premeditation Le Dung, a citizen of the Republic of Vietnam. In that First Lieutenant Philip J. Caputo . . . did murder with premeditation Le Du . . ." There was a third charge, resulting from my panicked attempt to deny that I had tried to cover up the killings: "In that First Lieutenant Philip J. Caputo . . . did subscribe under lawful oath a false statement in substance as follows: 'I did not tell them to stick by their statements,' which statements he did not then believe to be true."

There was a lot of other stuff—statements by witnesses, inquiry reports, and so forth—but one square on form DD457 was conspicuously blank. It was the square labeled EXPLANATORY OR EXTENUATING CIRCUMSTANCES ARE SUBMITTED HEREWITH. Early in the investigation, I wondered why the investigating officer had not submitted any explanatory or extenuating circumstances. Later, after I had time to think things over, I drew my own conclusion: the explanatory or extenuating circumstance was the war. The killings had occurred in war. They had occurred, moreover, in a war whose sole aim was to kill Viet Cong, a war in which those ordered to do the killing often could not distinguish the Viet Cong from the civilians, a war in which civilians in "free-fire zones" were killed every day by weapons far more horrible than pistols or shotguns. The deaths of Le Dung and Le Du could not be divorced from the nature and conduct of the war. They were an inevitable product of the war. As I had come to see it, America could not intervene in a people's war without killing some of the people. But to raise those points in explanation or extenuation would be to raise a host of ambiguous moral questions. It could even raise the question of the morality of American intervention in Vietnam; or, as one officer told me, "It would open a real can of worms." Therefore, the five men in the patrol and I were to be tried as common criminals, much as if we had murdered two people in the course of a bank robbery during peacetime. If we were found guilty, the Marine Corps' institutional conscience would be clear. Six criminals, who, of course, did not represent the majority of America's fine fighting sons, had been brought to justice. Case closed. If we were found innocent, the Marine Corps could say, "Justice has taken its course, and in a court-martial conducted according to the facts and the rules of evidence, no crime was found to have been committed." Case closed again. Either way, the military won.

"I was talking to your old skipper outside," Rader said. "He told me you seemed nervous."

"Well, how the hell do you expect me to feel? By tomorrow night, I could be on my way to Portsmouth for life." Portsmouth, the U.S. Naval prison, is a penal institution that was said to combine the worst aspects of Marine boot camp and a medieval dungeon. Nevertheless, a life sentence there was better than the alternative—execution by firing squad. That possibility had been hanging over our heads until only a few weeks before, when it was ruled that our case would be tried as noncapital. We were not to be shot if found guilty. A boon!

"Look, I don't want you thinking that way," Rader said. "I'm confident about what the outcome'll be. Even if you're convicted, we'll appeal. All the way up to the President if we have to."

"Terrific. Meanwhile I'll have brig guards playing the drums on my head with billy clubs. Christ, you've heard what it's like in that place. Can you imagine what they'll do to a busted officer?"

"I don't want you getting bitter. I want you to do well on that stand today. I can tell you that I admire you for the way you've borne up under all this. Don't mess it up now. Really, I would've cracked long ago."

"Well, I don't break, Jim. That's one thing I'm not going to do. I broke once and I'm never going to break again."

"Hell, when did you ever break?"

"That night. The night I sent those guys out there. I just cracked. I couldn't take it anymore. I was frustrated as hell and scared. If I hadn't broken, I would've never sent those guys out."

"Oh, that. We've been over that a dozen times. No drama, okay? This is the real world. We've been over that, over and over. You told them to capture those Vietnamese and to kill them if they had to. You didn't order an assassination. That's what you'll say on the stand and you'll say it because it's the truth."

Rader and I had argued the point before. We had argued it from the day that he was appointed my defense counsel. That had been in February, after several villagers from Giao-Tri lodged a complaint with their village chief, who went to the district chief, a Vietnamese Army colonel, who took the matter to the American military authorities in Danang. Two young men from Giao-Tri, both civilians, had been assassinated by a marine patrol. The investigation got under way. The battalion was meanwhile establishing new permanent positions forward of the old front line. The Viet Cong protested the intrusion into their territory with land mines, infiltrators, mortars, and snipers. My platoon lost several more men, including Jones, who was seriously wounded by a booby trap. The other two platoons suffered about sixteen casualties between them, and C Company became so short-handed that Neal had to make riflemen out of the mortar crews attached to the company, leaving no one to man the eighty-ones.

It was in this depressing atmosphere of steady losses that the five marines and I were called to battalion HQ to be questioned about what came to be known as "the incident at Giao-Tri."

Most of the particulars of that long and complicated inquiry have faded from memory. What remains most vividly is the mind-paralyzing terror that came over me when the investigating officer told me I was under suspicion of murder. *Murder.* The word exploded in my ears like a mortar shell. *Murder.* But they were Viet Cong, I told the IO, a hearty lawyer-colonel from the division legal section. At least one of them was. No, he said, they did not appear to be VC. That had been confirmed by the village police chief and the village chief. *Murder.* I knew we had done something wrong, but the idea of homicide had never occurred to me. Bewildered and frightened, I answered the colonel's questions as best I could, but when he asked, "Did you tell your men to stick to their statements?" I blurted out "No!"

Accompanied by his reporter, a lance corporal who had tapped out my answers on a transcript machine, the colonel left a few minutes later with his papers, case books, and machine, all the paraphernalia from the tidy world of Division HQ, the world of laws, which are so easy to obey when you eat well, sleep well, and do not have to face the daily menace of death.

I was badly shaken afterward, so badly I thought I was going to break in two. It was not only the specter of a murder charge that tormented me; it was my own sense of guilt. Lying in a tent at HQ, I saw that boy's eyes again, and the accusation in their lifeless stare. Perhaps we had committed homicide without realizing it, in much the same way McKenna had. Perhaps the war had awakened something evil in us, some dark, malicious power that allowed us to kill without feeling. Well, I could drop the "perhaps" in my own case. Something evil had been in me that night. It was true that I had ordered the patrol to capture the two men if at all possible, but it was also true that I had wanted them dead. There was murder in my heart, and, in some way, through tone of voice, a gesture, or a stress on *kill* rather than *capture*, I had transmitted my inner violence to the men. They saw in my overly aggressive manner a sanction to vent their own brutal impulses. I lay there remembering the euphoria we had felt afterward, the way we had laughed, and then the sudden awakening to guilt. And yet, I could not conceive of the act as one of premeditated murder. It had not been committed in a vacuum. It was a direct result of the war. The thing we had done was a result of what the war had done to us.

At some point in this self-examination, I realized I had lied to the investigating officer. Walking over to the adjutant's tent, I called the colonel and said I wanted to amend my statement and to exercise my right to counsel. He returned to battalion HQ with Rader, a tall redhead in his late twenties.

"Sir," I said, "that part in my statement where I said that I didn't tell the men to stick by their statements? Well, that isn't true. I wasn't thinking straight. I'd like it deleted and replaced with the truth."

Sorry, he said, that statement had been made under oath. It could not be deleted. That was the law. If I wished to say something else, fine, but the original statement would remain in the record. The colonel smiled, quite pleased with himself and the inexorable logic of his precious law. He had me on another charge. I made another statement.

Afterward, Rader and I had the first of our many long interviews. He asked me to describe everything that had happened that night.

"All right," I said, "but before I do, I want you to read this. I wrote it while I was waiting for you and the colonel to get here."

I handed him a turgid essay on front-line conditions. In a guerrilla war, it read, the line between legitimate and illegitimate killing is blurred. The policies of free-fire zones, in which a soldier is permitted to shoot at any human target, armed or unarmed, and body counts further confuse the fighting man's moral senses. My patrol had gone out thinking they were going after enemy soldiers. As for me, I had indeed been in an agitated state of mind and my ability to make clear judgments had been faulty, but I had been in Vietnam for eleven months. . . .

Rader crumpled up my literary ramblings and said, "This is all irrelevant, Phil."

"Why? It seems relevant to me."

"It won't to a court-martial."

"But *why*? We didn't kill those guys in Los Angeles, for Christ's sake."

Rader replied with a lecture on the facts of life. I cannot remember exactly what he said, but it was from him that I got the first indication that the war could not be used to explain the killings, because it raised too many embarrassing questions. We were indeed going to be charged as if we had killed both men on the streets of Los Angeles. The case was to be tried strictly on the facts: who said what to whom; what was done and who did it. A detective story. The facts, Rader said, are what he wanted. He did not want philosophy.

"Did you order your men to assassinate the two Vietnamese?" he asked.

"No."

"Did you say they were to capture them, or to shoot first and ask questions later?"

"No. They were supposed to capture them, kill them if they had to. But the thing is, I must have given them the impression that I wouldn't mind if they just killed them. Jim, I wasn't right in the head that night . . ."

"Don't try temporary insanity. There's a legal definition for that, and unless you were bouncing off the walls, you won't fit it."

"I'm not saying I was crazy. What I'm saying is that I was worn-out as hell. And scared. Goddamnit, I admit it. I was scared that one of those damned mines was going to get me if I didn't do something.

You've got to realize what it's like out there, never knowing from one minute to the next if you're going to get blown sky-high."

"Look, a court-martial isn't going to care about what it's like out there. You've got to realize that. This isn't a novel, so drop the dramatics. Nothing would've happened if those villagers hadn't complained. But they did and that started an investigation. Now the machine's in gear and it won't stop until it's run its course. Now, did anyone else hear you brief the patrol?"

"Yeah, Sergeant Coffell and the platoon sergeant were there."

"So, in other words, you gave orders to capture if possible, kill if necessary, or words to that effect. That's what you said, and there are two witnesses who'll corroborate you. Right?"

"That's what I said. I'm not sure if I completely meant it. I had this feeling that night . . . a sort of violent feeling . . ."

"Feelings aren't admissible evidence. I'm not worried about your psyche. The important thing is whether or not you ordered your men to commit an assassination."

"Damnit, Jim. It keeps coming back to the war. I wouldn't have sent those guys out there and they would never have done what they did if it hadn't been for this war. It's a stinking war and some of the stink rubs off on you after a while."

"Will you please drop that. If you ordered an assassination, tell me now. You can plead guilty and I'll try to get you a light sentence—say, ten to twenty in Portsmouth."

"I'll tell you this. I'll have a helluva time living with myself if those guys get convicted and I get off."

"Do you want to plead guilty to murder?"

"No."

"Why?"

"Because it wasn't murder. Whatever it was, it wasn't murder. And if it was murder, then half the Vietnamese killed in this war have been murdered."

"No. You don't want to plead guilty because you're innocent as charged. You did not order an assassination."

"All right. I'm innocent."

"So, what we have is this: you gave orders to a patrol to capture two

Viet Cong suspects who were to be killed only if necessary. That's a lawful order in combat. And there are two NCOs who'll support you on that, right?"

"You're the boss. Whatever you say. Just get me out of this mess."

"Don't give me that 'you're the boss' routine. Are those the facts or aren't they?"

"Yes, those are the facts."

And so I learned about the wide gulf that divides the facts from the truth. Rader and I had a dozen similar conferences over the next five months. "Preparing testimony," it was called. With each session, my admiration for Rader's legal skills increased. He prepared my case with the hard-minded pragmatism of a battalion commander preparing an attack on an enemy-held hill. In time, he almost had me convinced that on the night of the killings, First Lieutenant Philip Caputo, in a lucid state of mind, issued a clear, legitimate order that was flagrantly disobeyed by the men under his command. I was fascinated by the testimony that was produced by our Socratic dialogues. Rader had it all written on yellow legal tablets, and I observed that not one word of it was perjured. There were qualifying phrases here and there—"to the best of my recollection," "if I recall correctly," "words to that effect"—but there wasn't a single lie in it. And yet it wasn't the truth. Conversely, the attorneys for the enlisted men had them convinced that they were all good, God-fearing soldiers who had been obeying orders, as all good soldiers must, orders issued by a vicious killer-officer. And that was neither a lie nor the truth. The prosecution had meanwhile marshaled facts to support its argument that five criminal marines, following the unlawful orders of their criminal platoon leader, had cold-bloodedly murdered two civilians whom they then tried to claim as confirmed Viet Cong to collect the reward their captain had offered for enemy dead, a reprehensible policy not at all in keeping with the traditions of the U.S. Marine Corps. And that was neither a lie nor the truth. None of this testimony, none of these "facts" amounted to the truth. The truth was a synthesis of all three points of view: the war in general and U.S. military policies in particular were ultimately to blame for the deaths of Le Du and Le Dung.

That was the truth and it was that truth which the whole proceeding was designed to conceal.

Still, I was not without hope for an acquittal. Throughout the investigation, a number of officers told me: "What's happened to you could've happened to anybody in this war." In their eyes I was a victim of circumstances, a good officer unjustly charged. I had an above-average service record, and was normal to outward appearances. Those other officers saw in me a mirror image of themselves. I was one of them.

And the enlisted men were all good soldiers. There wasn't a mark on their records, not even for AWOL. Four of the five had been honorably wounded in combat. Two—Allen and Crowe—were family men. And yet, paradoxically, they had been accused of homicide. If the charges were proved, it would prove no one was guaranteed immunity against the moral bacteria spawned by the war. If such cruelty existed in ordinary men like us, then it logically existed in the others, and they would have to face the truth that they, too, harbored a capacity for evil. But no one wanted to make that recognition. No one wanted to confront his devil.

A verdict of innocent would solve the dilemma. It would prove that no crime had been committed. It would prove what the others wanted to believe: that we were virtuous American youths, incapable of the act of which we had been accused. And if we were incapable of it, then they were too, which is what they wanted to believe of themselves.

It was nine o'clock. Witnesses began to file into the neighboring hut, where the court-martial was being held. In our hut, the clerks continued to peck at their typewriters. Rader and I again went over my testimony. He told me how to behave on the stand: use a firm, but not strident, tone of voice; look at the six officers who were to be my judges when I answered questions; appear earnest and forthcoming.

I was called sometime in the late afternoon. Crowe, sitting at the defendant's table, looked very small. I confess I don't remember a word of what I said on the stand. I only recall sitting there for a long time under direct and cross-examination, looking at the six-man court as I had been instructed to do and parroting the testimony I had rehearsed a hundred times. I must have sounded like Jack Armstrong, all-American boy. Later, during a recess, I heard the prosecutor congratulating Rader. "Your client did very well on the stand today, Mister Rader." I felt pleased with myself. I was good for something. I was a good witness.

The trial dragged on to its conclusion. In my tent awaiting the verdict, I felt in limbo, neither a free man nor a prisoner. I could not help thinking about the consequences of a guilty verdict in my own case. I would go to jail for the rest of my life. Everything good I had done in my life would be rendered meaningless. It would count for nothing.

I already regarded myself as a casualty of the war, a moral casualty, and like all serious casualties, I felt detached from everything. I felt very much like a man who has lost a leg or an arm, and, knowing he will never have to fight again, loses all interest in the war that has wounded him. As his physical energies are spent on overcoming his pain and on repairing his bodily injuries, so were all of my emotional energies spent on maintaining my mental balance. I had not broken during the five-month ordeal. I would not break. No matter what they did to me, they could not make me break. All my inner reserves had been committed to that battle for emotional and mental survival. I had nothing left for other struggles. The war simply wasn't my show any longer. I had declared a truce between me and the Viet Cong, signed a personal armistice, and all I asked for now was a chance to live for myself on my terms. I had no argument with the Viet Cong. It wasn't the VC who were threatening to rob me of my liberty, but the United States government, in whose service I had enlisted. Well, I was through with that. I was finished with governments and their abstract causes, and I would never again allow myself to fall under the charms and spells of political witch doctors like John F. Kennedy. The important thing was to get through this insane predicament with some degree of dignity. I would not break. I would endure and accept whatever happened with grace. For enduring seemed to me an act of penance, an inadequate one to be sure, but I felt the need to atone in some way for the deaths I had caused.

Lying there, I remembered the South Vietnamese insurrection that had begun three months before and ended only in May. That insurrection, as much as my own situation, had awakened me to the senselessness of the war. The tragifarce began when General Thi, the commander of I Corps, was placed under arrest by the head of the Saigon government, Nguyen Cao Ky. Ky suspected him of plotting a coup. Thi's ARVN divisions in I Corps rallied to his support. There were demonstrations and riots in Danang, where Thi's headquarters were located. This prompted Ky to declare that Danang was in the hands of Communist rebels and to send his divisions to the city to "liberate it from the Viet Cong." Soon, South Vietnamese soldiers were fighting street battles with other South Vietnamese soldiers as the two mandarin warlords contended for power.

And while the South Vietnamese fought their intramural feud, we were left to fight the Viet Cong. In April, with the insurrection in full swing, One-Three suffered heavy casualties in an operation in the Vu Gia Valley. Because of the investigation, I had been transferred from the battalion to regimental HQ, where I was assigned as an assistant operations officer. There, I saw the incompetent staff work that had turned the operation into a minor disaster. Part of the battalion was needlessly sent into a trap, and one company alone lost over one hundred of its one hundred and eighty men. Vietnamese civilians suffered too. I recalled seeing the smoke rising from a dozen bombed villages while our artillery pounded enemy positions in the hills and our planes darted through the smoke to drop more bombs. And I recalled seeing our own casualties at the division hospital. Captain Greer, the intelligence officer, and I were sent there from the field to interview the survivors and find out what had gone wrong. We knew what had gone wrong—the staff had fouled up—but we went along with the charade anyway. I can still see that charnel house, crammed with wounded, groaning men, their dressings encrusted in filth, the cots pushed one up against the other to make room for the new wounded coming in, the smell of blood, the stunned faces, one young platoon leader wrapped up like a mummy with plastic tubes inserted in his kidneys, and an eighteen-year-old private, blinded by shellfire, a bandage wrapped around his eyes as he groped down the aisle between the cots. "I can't find my rack," he called. "Can somebody help me find my rack?"

Meanwhile, the armies of Thi and Ky continued to spar in Danang. One morning in May, after I had been sent to division HQ, I led a convoy of marine riflemen into the city. They were part of a security detachment that was to guard American installations—not against the VC, but against the rebelling South Vietnamese troops. I returned to HQ in the afternoon. Division's command post was on Hill 327, which gave us a ringside seat. Looking to the west, we could see marines fighting the VC; to the east, the South Vietnamese Army fighting itself. Early that evening, I saw tracers flying over the city, heard the sound of machine-gun fire, and then, in utter disbelief, watched an ARVN fighter plane strafing an ARVN truck convoy. It was incredible, a tableau of the madness of the war. One of the plane's rockets fell wide of the mark, exploding near an American position and wounding three marines. The prop-driven Skyraider roared down again, firing its rockets and cannon once more into the convoy, packed with South Vietnamese soldiers. And I knew then that we could never win. With a government and an army like that in South Vietnam, we could never hope to win the war. To go on with the war would be folly—worse than folly: it would be a crime, murder on a mass scale.

The insurrection ended on May 25. General Walt sent a message to all Marine units in I Corps. In it, he said that the "rebellion" had been crushed and that we could "look forward to an era of good relations with our South Vietnamese comrades-in-arms."

The message shocked me. Even Lew Walt, my old hero, was blind to the truth. The war was to go on, senselessly on.

A few days later, my antiwar sentiments took an active form. The division HqCo commander ordered me to take part in a parade in honor of some visiting dignitary. I refused. He said I could not refuse to obey an order. I replied, yes, I could and would. I thought the whole thing was a mess, a folly and a crime, and I was not going to participate in some flag-waving sham. I was in no position to make such statements, he said. Oh yes I was. I was already up for the most serious crime in the book—one more charge made no difference to me. He could get somebody else to strut around to Sousa marches. Much to my surprise, I won.

It was then that I tried to do a bit of proselytizing among the clerks in the HqCo office. The war, I said, was unwinnable. It was being fought for a bunch of corrupt politicians in Saigon. Every American life lost was a life wasted. The United States should withdraw now, before more men died. The clerks, their patriotism unwavering, having never heard a shot fired in anger, looked at me in disbelief. I wasn't surprised. This was 1966 and talk such as mine was regarded as borderline treason.

"Sir," said a lance corporal, "if we pulled out now, then all our efforts up to now would have been in vain."

"In other words, because we've already wasted thousands of lives, we should waste a few thousand more," I said. "Well, if you really believe that 'not in vain' crap, you should volunteer for a rifle company and go get yourself killed, because you deserve it."

Rader walked into the tent in the early evening. "Phil," he said, "they've come in with a verdict on Crowe. Not guilty on all counts."

I sat up and lit a cigarette, not sure what to think. "Well, I'm happy for him. He's got a wife and kids. But how does that make it look for us?"

"Well, I think it looks good. Just hang loose until tomorrow. You go up at oh-nine-hundred."

Curiously, I slept very well that night. Maybe it was my sense of fatalism. Worrying could do no good. Whatever was going to happen, I could do nothing about it. The next morning, I ate an enormous breakfast and managed a few quips about the condemned man's last meal. Then, long before I was due, I walked to the quonset hut, feeling much as I had before going into action: determined and resigned at the same time. I waited in the hut for about an hour, watching the same clerks sitting at the same desks typing the same reports. The red light on the coffee pot glowed and the fans whirred, rustling the pages of the calendar, which was now turned to July. The same crowd of witnesses milled around outside. Captain Neal was there. He looked worn and old. I went out and offered him a cigar. Smoking it, his eyes fixed on the ground, he shook his head and said, "We lost half the company. I hope they realize that. We'd lost half the company then."

At a quarter to nine, Rader called me back inside.

"Here's the situation. The general is thinking of dropping all charges against the rest of you because Crowe was acquitted. In your own case, you'd have to plead guilty to the third charge and accept a letter of reprimand from the general. What do you want to do?"

"You mean if I plead guilty to charge three, there's no court-martial?"

"Unless you want one."

"Of course I don't want one. Okay, I'm guilty."

"All right," Rader said ebulliently, "wait here. I'll let them know and get back to you."

I paced nervously for fifteen or twenty minutes. It looked as if my instincts had been right: the higher-ups wanted this case off their backs as much as I wanted it off mine. Wild thoughts filled my head. I would atone in some way to the families of Le Du and Le Dung. When the war was over, I would go back to Giao-Tri and . . . and what? I didn't know.

Rader returned grinning. "Congratulations," he said, pumping my hand. "The charges have been dropped. The general's going to put a letter of reprimand in your jacket, but hell, all that'll do is hurt your chances for promotion to captain. You're a free man. I also heard that the adjutant's cutting orders for you. You'll be going home in a week, ten days at most. It's all over."

We stood waiting in the sun at the edge of the runway. There were about a hundred and fifty of us, and we watched as a replacement draft filed off the big transport plane. They fell into formation and tried to ignore the dusty, tanned, ragged-looking men who jeered them. The replacements looked strangely young, far younger than we, and awkward and bewildered by this scorched land to which an indifferent government had sent them. I did not join in the mockery. I felt sorry for those children, knowing that they would all grow old in this land of endless dying. I pitied them, knowing that out of every ten, one would die, two more would be maimed for life, another two would be less seriously wounded and sent out to fight again, and all the rest would be wounded in other, more hidden ways.

The replacements were marched off toward the convoy that waited to carry them to their assigned units and their assigned fates. None of them looked at us. They marched away. Shouldering our seabags, we climbed up the ramp into the plane, the plane we had all dreamed about, the grand, mythological Freedom Bird. A joyous shout went up as the transport lurched off the runway and climbed into the placid sky. Below lay the rice paddies and the green, folded hills where we had lost our friends and our youth.

The plane banked and headed out over the China Sea, toward Okinawa, toward freedom from death's embrace. None of us was a hero. We would not return to cheering crowds, parades, and the pealing of great cathedral bells. We had done nothing more than endure. We had survived, and that was our only victory.

Dispatches

MICHAEL HERR

1977

BREATHING IN

There was a map of Vietnam on the wall of my apartment in Saigon and some nights, coming back late to the city, I'd lie out on my bed and look at it, too tired to do anything more than just get my boots off. That map was a marvel, especially now that it wasn't real anymore. For one thing, it was very old. It had been left there years before by another tenant, probably a Frenchman, since the map had been made in Paris. The paper had buckled in its frame after years in the wet Saigon heat, laying a kind of veil over the countries it depicted. Vietnam was divided into its older territories of Tonkin, Annam and Cochin China, and to the west past Laos and Cambodge sat Siam, a kingdom. That's old, I'd tell visitors, that's a really old map.

If dead ground could come back and haunt you the way dead people do, they'd have been able to mark my map CURRENT and burn the ones they'd been using since '64, but count on it, nothing like that was going to happen. It was late '67 now, even the most detailed maps didn't reveal much anymore; reading them was like trying to read the faces of the Vietnamese, and that was like trying to read the wind. We knew that the uses of most information were flexible, different pieces of ground told different stories to different people. We also knew that for years now there had been no country here but the war.

The Mission was always telling us about VC units being engaged and wiped out and then reappearing a month later in full strength, there was nothing very spooky about that, but when we went up against his terrain we usually took it definitively, and even if we didn't keep it you could always see that we'd at least been there. At the end of my first week in-country I met an information officer in the headquarters of the 25th Division at Cu Chi who showed me on his map and then from his chopper what they'd done to the Ho Bo Woods, the vanished Ho Bo Woods, taken off by giant Rome plows and chemicals and long, slow fire, wasting hundreds of acres of cultivated plantation and wild forest alike, "denying the enemy valuable resources and cover."

It had been part of his job for nearly a year now to tell people about that operation; correspondents, touring congressmen, movie stars, corporation presidents, staff officers from half the armies in the world, and he still couldn't get over it. It seemed to be keeping him young, his enthusiasm made you feel that even the letters he wrote home to his wife were full of it, it really showed what you could do if you had the know-how and the hardware. And if in the months following that operation incidences of enemy activity in the larger area of War Zone C had increased "significantly," and American losses had doubled and then doubled again, none of it was happening in any damn Ho Bo Woods, you'd better believe it . . .

I

Going out at night the medics gave you pills, Dexedrine breath like dead snakes kept too long in a jar. I never saw the need for them myself, a little contact or anything that even sounded like contact would give me more speed than I could bear. Whenever I heard something outside of our clenched little circle I'd practically flip, hoping to God I wasn't the only one who'd noticed it. A couple of rounds fired off in the dark a kilometer away and the Elephant would be there kneeling on my chest, sending me down into my boots for a breath. Once I thought I saw a light moving in the jungle and I caught myself just under a whisper saying, "I'm not ready for this, I'm not ready for this." That's when I decided to drop it and do something else with my nights. And I wasn't going out like the night ambushers did, or the Lurps, long-range recon patrollers who did it night after night for weeks and months, creeping up on VC base camps or around moving columns of North Vietnamese. I was living too close to my bones as it was, all I had to do was accept it. Anyway, I'd save the pills for later, for Saigon and the awful depression I always had there.

I knew one 4th Division Lurp who took his pills by the fistful, downs from the left pocket of his tiger suit and ups from the right, one to cut the trail for him and the other to send him down it. He told me that they cooled things out just right for him, that he could see that old jungle at night like he was looking at it through a starlight scope. "They sure give you the range," he said.

This was his third tour. In 1965 he'd been the only survivor in a platoon of the Cav wiped out going into the Ia Drang Valley. In '66 he'd come back with the Special Forces and one morning after an ambush he'd hidden under the bodies of his team while the VC walked all around them with knives, making sure. They stripped the bodies of their gear, the berets too, and finally went away, laughing. After that, there was nothing left for him in the war except the Lurps.

"I just can't hack it back in the World," he said. He told me that after he'd come back home the last time he would sit in his room all day, and sometimes he'd stick a hunting rifle out the window, leading people and cars as they passed his house until the only feeling he was aware of was all up in the tip of that one finger. "It used to put my folks real uptight," he said. But he put people uptight here too, even here.

"No man, I'm sorry, he's just too crazy for me," one of the men in his team said. "All's you got to do is look into his eyes, that's the whole fucking story right there."

"Yeah, but you better do it quick," someone else said. "I mean, you don't want to let him catch you at it."

But he always seemed to be watching for it, I think he slept with his eyes open, and I was afraid of him anyway. All I ever managed was one quick look in, and that was like looking at the floor of an ocean. He wore a gold earring and a headband torn from a piece of camouflage parachute material, and since nobody was about to tell him to get his hair cut it fell below his shoulders, covering a thick purple scar. Even at division he never went anywhere without at least a .45 and a knife, and he thought I was a freak because I wouldn't carry a weapon.

"Didn't you ever meet a reporter before?" I asked him.

"Tits on a bull," he said. "Nothing personal."

But what a story he told me, as one-pointed and resonant as any war story I ever heard, it took me a year to understand it:

"Patrol went up the mountain. One man came back. He died before he could tell us what happened."

I waited for the rest, but it seemed not to be that kind of story; when I asked him what had happened he just looked like he felt sorry for me, fucked if he'd waste time telling stories to anyone dumb as I was.

His face was all painted up for night walking now like a bad hallucination, not like the painted faces I'd seen in San Francisco only a few weeks before, the other extreme of the same theater. In the coming hours he'd stand as faceless and quiet in the jungle as a fallen tree, and God help his opposite numbers unless they had at least half a squad along, he was a good killer, one of our best. The rest of his team were gathered outside the tent, set a little apart from the other division units, with its own Lurp-designated latrine and its own exclusive freeze-dry rations, three-star war food, the same chop they sold at Abercrombie & Fitch. The regular division troops would almost shy off the path when they passed the area on their way to and from the mess tent. No matter how toughened up they became in the war, they still looked innocent compared to the Lurps. When the team had grouped they walked in a file down the hill to the lz across the strip to the perimeter and into the treeline.

I never spoke to him again, but I saw him. When they came back in the next morning he had a prisoner with him, blindfolded and with his elbows bound sharply behind him. The Lurp area would definitely be off limits during the interrogation, and anyway, I was already down at the strip waiting for a helicopter to come and take me out of there.

"Hey what're you guys, with the USO? Aw, we thought you was with the USO 'cause your hair's so long." Page took the kid's picture, I got the words down and Flynn laughed and told him we were the Rolling

Stones. The three of us traveled around together for about a month that summer. At one lz the brigade chopper came in with a real foxtail hanging off the aerial, when the commander walked by us he almost took an infarction.

"Don't you men salute officers?"

"We're not men," Page said. "We're correspondents."

When the commander heard that, he wanted to throw a spontaneous operation for us, crank up his whole brigade and get some people killed. We had to get out on the next chopper to keep him from going ahead with it, amazing what some of them would do for a little ink. Page liked to augment his field gear with freak paraphernalia, scarves and beads, plus he was English, guys would stare at him like he'd just come down off a wall on Mars. Sean Flynn could look more incredibly beautiful than even his father, Errol, had thirty years before as Captain Blood, but sometimes he looked more like Artaud coming out of some heavy heart-of-darkness trip, overloaded on the information, the input! The input! He'd give off a bad sweat and sit for hours, combing his mustache through with the saw blade of his Swiss Army knife. We packed grass and tape: Have You Seen Your Mother Baby Standing in the Shadows, Best of the Animals, Strange Days, Purple Haze, Archie Bell and the Drells, "C'mon now everybody, do the Tighten Up. . . ." Once in a while we'd catch a chopper straight into one of the lower hells, but it was a quiet time in the war, mostly it was lz's and camps, grunts hanging around, faces, stories.

"Best way's to just keep moving," one of them told us. "Just keep moving, stay in motion, you know what I'm saying?"

We knew. He was a moving-target-survivor subscriber, a true child of the war, because except for the rare times when you were pinned or stranded the system was geared to keep you mobile, if that was what you thought you wanted. As a technique for staying alive it seemed to make as much sense as anything, given naturally that you were there to begin with and wanted to see it close; it started out sound and straight but formed a cone as it progressed, because the more you moved the more you saw, the more you saw the more besides death and mutilation you risked, and the more you risked of that the more you would have to let go of one day as a "survivor." Some of us moved around the war like crazy people until we couldn't see which way the run was even taking us anymore, only the war all over its surface with occasional, unexpected penetration. As long as we could have choppers like taxis it took real exhaustion or depression near shock or a dozen pipes of opium to keep us even apparently quiet, we'd still be running around inside our skins like something was after us, ha ha, La Vida Loca.

In the months after I got back the hundreds of helicopters I'd flown in began to draw together until they'd formed a collective meta-chopper, and in my mind it was the sexiest thing going; saver-destroyer, provider-waster, right hand-left hand, nimble, fluent, canny and human; hot steel, grease, jungle-saturated canvas webbing, sweat cooling and warming up again, cassette rock and roll in one ear and door-gun fire in the other, fuel, heat, vitality and death, death itself, hardly an intruder. Men on the crews would say that once you'd carried a dead person he would always be there, riding with you. Like all combat people they were incredibly superstitious and invariably self-dramatic, but it was (I knew) unbearably true that close exposure to the dead sensitized you to the force of their presence and made for long reverberations; long. Some people were so delicate that one look was enough to wipe them away, but even bone-dumb grunts seemed to feel that something weird and extra was happening to them.

Helicopters and people jumping out of helicopters, people so in love they'd run to get on even when there wasn't any pressure. Choppers rising straight out of small cleared jungle spaces, wobbling down onto city rooftops, cartons of rations and ammunition thrown off, dead and wounded loaded on. Sometimes they were so plentiful and loose that you could touch down at five or six places in a day, look around, hear the talk, catch the next one out. There were installations as big as cities with 30,000 citizens, once we dropped in to feed supply to one man. God knows what kind of Lord Jim phoenix numbers he was doing in there, all he said to me was, "You didn't see a thing, right Chief? You weren't even here." There were posh fat air-conditioned camps like comfortable middle-class scenes with the violence tacit, "far away"; camps named for commanders' wives, LZ Thelma, LZ Betty Lou; number-named hilltops in trouble where I didn't want to stay; trail, paddy, swamp, deep hairy bush, scrub, swale, village, even city, where the ground couldn't drink up what the action spilled, it made you careful where you walked.

Sometimes the chopper you were riding in would top a hill and all the ground in front of you as far as the next hill would be charred and pitted and still smoking, and something between your chest and your stomach would turn over. Frail gray smoke where they'd burned off the rice fields around a free-strike zone, brilliant white smoke from phosphorous ("Willy Peter/Make you a buh liever"), deep black smoke from 'palm, they said that if you stood at the base of a column of napalm smoke it would suck the air right out of your lungs. Once we fanned over a little ville that had just been airstruck and the words of a song by Wingy Manone that I'd heard when I was a few years old snapped into my head, "Stop the War, These Cats Is Killing Themselves." Then we dropped, hovered, settled down into purple lz smoke, dozens of children broke from their hootches to run in toward the focus of our landing, the pilot laughing and saying, "Vietnam, man. Bomb 'em and feed 'em, bomb 'em and feed 'em."

Flying over jungle was almost pure pleasure, doing it on foot was nearly all pain. I never belonged in there. Maybe it really was what its people had always called it, Beyond; at the very least it was serious, I gave up things to it I probably never got back. ("Aw, jungle's okay. If you know her you can live in her real good, if you don't she'll take you down in an hour. Under.") Once in some thick jungle corner with some grunts standing around, a correspondent said, "Gee, you must really see some beautiful sunsets in here," and they almost pissed themselves laughing. But you could fly up and into hot tropic sunsets that would change the way you thought about light forever. You could also fly out of places that were so grim they turned to black and white in your head five minutes after you'd gone.

That could be the coldest one in the world, standing at the edge of a clearing watching the chopper you'd just come in on taking off again, leaving you there to think about what it was going to be for you now: if this was a bad place, the wrong place, maybe even the last place, and whether you'd made a terrible mistake this time.

There was a camp at Soc Trang where a man at the lz said, "If you come looking for a story this is your lucky day, we got Condition Red here," and before the sound of the chopper had faded out, I knew I had it too.

"That's affirmative," the camp commander said, "we are *definitely* expecting rain. Glad to see you." He was a young captain, he was laughing and taping a bunch of sixteen clips together bottom to bottom for faster reloading, "grease." Everyone there was busy at it, cracking crates, squirreling away grenades, checking mortar pieces, piling rounds, clicking banana clips into automatic weapons that I'd never seen before. They were wired into their listening posts out around the camp, into each other, into themselves, and when it got dark it got worse. The moon came up nasty and full, a fat moist piece of decadent fruit. It was soft and saffron-misted when you looked up at it, but its light over the sandbags and into the jungle was harsh and bright. We were all rubbing Army-issue nightfighter cosmetic under our eyes to cut the glare and the terrible things it made you see. (Around midnight, just for something to do, I crossed to the other perimeter and looked at the road running engineer-straight toward Route 4 like a yellow frozen ribbon out of sight and I saw it move, the whole road.) There were a few sharp arguments about who the light really favored, attackers or defenders, men were sitting around with Cinema-scope eyes and jaws stuck out like they could shoot bullets, moving and antsing and shifting around inside their fatigues. "No sense us getting too relaxed, Charlie don't relax, just when you get good and comfortable is when he comes over and takes a giant shit on you." That was the level until morning, I smoked a pack an hour all night long, and nothing happened. Ten minutes after daybreak I was down at the lz asking about choppers.

A few days later Sean Flynn and I went up to a big firebase in the Americal TAOR that took it all the way over to another extreme, National Guard weekend. The colonel in command was so drunk that day that he could barely get his words out, and when he did, it was to say things like, "We aim to make good and goddammit sure that if *those guys* try *anything cute* they won't catch us with our pants down." The main mission there was to fire H&I, but one man told us that their record was the worst in the whole Corps, probably the whole country, they'd harassed and interdicted a couple of sleeping civilians and Korean Marines, even a couple of American patrols, but hardly any Viet Cong. (The colonel kept calling it "artillerary." The first time he said it Flynn and I looked away from each other, the second time we blew beer through our noses, but the colonel fell in laughing right away and more than covered us.) No sandbags, exposed shells, dirty pieces, guys going around giving us that look, "We're cool, how come you're not?" At the strip Sean was talking to the operator about it and the man got angry. "Oh *yeah*?" Well fuck *you*, how tight do you think you want it? There ain't been any veecees around here in three months."

"So far so good," Sean said. "Hear anything on that chopper yet?"

But sometimes everything stopped, nothing flew, you couldn't even find out why. I got stuck for a chopper once in some lost patrol outpost in the Delta where the sergeant chain-ate candy bars and played country-and-western tapes twenty hours a day until I heard it in my sleep, some sleep, *Up on Wolverton Mountain* and *Lonesome as the bats and the bears in Miller's Cave* and *I fell into a burning ring of fire*, surrounded by strungout rednecks who weren't getting much sleep either because they couldn't trust one of their 400 mercenary troopers or their own hand-picked perimeter guards or anybody else except maybe Baby Ruth and Johnny Cash, they'd been waiting for it so long now they were afraid they wouldn't know it when they finally got it, *and it burns burns burns*. . . . Finally on the fourth day a helicopter came in to deliver meat and movies to the camp and I went out on it, so happy to get back to Saigon that I didn't crash for two days.

Airmobility, dig it, you weren't going anywhere. It made you feel safe, it made you feel Omni, but it was only a stunt, technology. Mobility was just mobility, it saved lives or took them all the time (saved mine I don't know how many times, maybe dozens, maybe none), what you really needed was a flexibility far greater than anything the technology could provide, some generous, spontaneous gift for accepting surprises, and I didn't have it. I got to hate surprises, control freak at the crossroads, if you were one of those people who always thought they had to know what was coming next, the war would cream you. It was the same with your ongoing attempts at getting used to the jungle or the blow-you-out climate or the saturating strangeness of the place which didn't lessen with exposure so often as it fattened and darkened in accumulating alienation. It was great if you could adapt, you had to try, but it wasn't the same as making a discipline, going into your own reserves and developing a real war metabolism, slow yourself down when your heart tried to punch its way through your chest, get swift when everything went to stop and all you could feel of your whole life was the entropy whipping through it. Unlovable terms.

The ground was always in play, always being swept. Under the ground was his, above it was ours. We had the air, we could get up in it but not disappear in *to* it, we could run but we couldn't hide, and he could do each so well that sometimes it looked like he was doing them both at once, while our finder just went limp. All the same, one place or another it was always going on, rock around the clock, we had the days and he had the nights. You could be in the most protected space in Vietnam and still know that your safety was provisional, that early death, blindness, loss of legs, arms or balls, major and lasting disfigurement—the whole rotten deal—could come in on the freakyfluky as easily as in the so-called expected ways, you heard so many of those stories it was a wonder anyone was left alive to die in firefights and mortar-rocket attacks. After a few weeks, when the nickel had jarred loose and dropped and I saw that everyone around me was carrying a gun, I also saw that any one of them could go off at any time, putting you where it wouldn't matter whether it had been an accident or not. The roads were mined, the trails booby-trapped, satchel charges and grenades blew up jeeps and movie theaters, the VC got work inside all the camps as shoeshine boys and laundresses and honey-dippers, they'd starch your fatigues and burn your shit and then go home and mortar your area. Saigon and Cholon and Danang held such hostile vibes that you felt you were being dry-sniped every time someone looked at you, and choppers fell out of the sky like fat poisoned birds a hundred times a day. After a while I couldn't get on one without thinking that I must be out of my fucking mind.

Fear and motion, fear and standstill, no preferred cut there, no way even to be clear about which was really worse, the wait or the delivery. Combat spared far more men than it wasted, but everyone suffered the time between contact, especially when they were going out every day looking for it; bad going on foot, terrible in trucks and APC's, awful in helicopters, the worst, traveling so fast toward something so frightening. I can remember times when I went half dead with my fear of the motion, the speed and direction already fixed and pointed one way. It was painful enough just flying "safe" hops between firebases and lz's; if you were ever on a helicopter that had been hit by ground fire your deep, perpetual chopper anxiety was guaranteed. At least actual contact when it was happening would draw long raggedy strands of energy out of you, it was juicy, fast and refining, and traveling toward it was hollow, dry, cold and steady, it never let you alone. All you could do was look around at the other people on board and see if they were as scared and numbed out as you were. If it looked like they weren't you thought they were insane, if it looked like they were it made you feel a lot worse.

I went through that thing a number of times and only got a fast return on my fear once, a too classic hot landing with the heat coming from the trees about 300 yards away, sweeping machine-gun fire that sent men head down into swampy water, running on their hands and knees toward the grass where it wasn't blown flat by the rotor blades, not much to be running for but better than nothing. The helicopter pulled up before we'd all gotten out, leaving the last few men to jump twenty feet down between the guns across the paddy and the gun on the chopper door. When we'd all reached the cover of the wall and the captain had made a check, we were amazed to see that no one had even been hurt, except for one man who'd sprained both his ankles jumping. Afterward, I remembered that I'd been down in the muck worrying about leeches. I guess you could say that I was refusing to accept the situation.

"Boy, you sure get offered some shitty choices," a Marine once said to me, and I couldn't help but feel that what he really meant was that you didn't get offered any at all. Specifically, he was just talking about a couple of C-ration cans, "dinner," but considering his young life you couldn't blame him for thinking that if he knew one thing for sure, it was that there was no one anywhere who cared less about what *he* wanted. There wasn't anybody he wanted to thank for his food, but he was grateful that he was still alive to eat it, that the motherfucker hadn't scarfed him up first. He hadn't been anything but tired and scared for six months and he'd lost a lot, mostly people, and seen far too much, but he was breathing in and breathing out, some kind of choice all by itself.

He had one of those faces, I saw that face at least a thousand times at a hundred bases and camps, all the youth sucked out of the eyes, the color drawn from the skin, cold white lips, you knew he wouldn't wait for any of it to come back. Life had made him old, he'd live it out old. All those faces, sometimes it was like looking into faces at a rock concert, locked in, the event had them; or like students who were very heavily advanced, serious beyond what you'd call their years if you didn't know for yourself what the minutes and hours of those years were made up of. Not just like all the ones you saw who looked like they couldn't drag their asses through another day of it. (How do you feel when a nineteen-year-old kid tells you from the bottom of his heart that he's gotten too old for this kind of shit?) Not like the faces of the dead or wounded either, they could look more released than overtaken. These were the faces of boys whose whole lives seemed to have backed up on them, they'd be a few feet away but they'd be looking back at you over a distance you knew you'd never really cross. We'd talk, sometimes fly together, guys going out on R&R, guys escorting bodies, guys who'd flipped over into extremes of peace or violence. Once I flew with a kid who was going home, he looked back down once at the ground where he'd spent the year and spilled his whole load of tears. Sometimes you even flew with the dead.

Once I jumped on a chopper that was full of them. The kid in the op shack had said that there would be a body on board, but he'd been given some wrong information. "How bad do you want to get to Danang?" he'd asked me, and I'd said, "Bad."

When I saw what was happening I didn't want to get on, but they'd made a divert and a special landing for me, I had to go with the chopper I'd drawn, I was afraid of looking squeamish. (I remember, too, thinking that a chopper full of dead men was far less likely to get shot down than one full of living.) They weren't even in bags. They'd been on a truck near one of the firebases in the DMZ that was firing support for Khe Sanh, and the truck had hit a Command-detonated mine, then they'd been rocketed. The Marines were always running out of things, even food, ammo and medicine, it wasn't so strange that they'd run out of bags too. The men had been wrapped around in ponchos, some of them carelessly fastened with plastic straps, and loaded on board. There was a small space cleared for me between one of them and the door gunner, who looked pale and so tremendously furious that I thought he was angry with me and I couldn't look at him for a while. When we went up the wind blew through the ship and made the ponchos shake and tremble until the one next to me blew back in a fast brutal flap, uncovering the face. They hadn't even closed his eyes for him.

The gunner started hollering as loud as he could, "Fix it! Fix it!," maybe he thought the eyes were looking at him, but there wasn't anything I could do. My hand went there a couple of times and I couldn't, and then I did. I pulled the poncho tight, lifted his head carefully and tucked the poncho under it, and then I couldn't believe that I'd done it. All during the ride the gunner kept trying to smile, and when we landed at Dong Ha he thanked me and ran off to get a detail. The pilots jumped down and walked away without looking back once, like they'd never seen that chopper before in their lives. I flew the rest of the way to Danang in a general's plane.

II

You know how it is, you want to look and you don't want to look. I can remember the strange feelings I had when I was a kid looking at war photographs in *Life*, the ones that showed dead people or a lot of dead people lying close together in a field or a street, often touching, seeming to hold each other. Even when the picture was sharp and cleanly defined, something wasn't clear at all, something repressed that monitored the images and withheld their essential information. It may have legitimized my fascination, letting me look for as long as I wanted; I didn't have a language for it then, but I remember now the shame I felt, like looking at first porn, all the porn in the world. I could have looked until my lamps went out and I still wouldn't have accepted the connection between a detached leg and the rest of a body, or the poses and positions that always happened (one day I'd hear it called "response-to-impact"), bodies wrenched too fast and violently into unbelievable contortion. Or the total impersonality of group death, making them lie anywhere and any way it left them, hanging over barbed wire or thrown promiscuously on top of other dead, or up into the trees like terminal acrobats, *Look what I can do.*

Supposedly, you weren't going to have that kind of obscuration when you finally started seeing them on real ground in front of you, but you tended to manufacture it anyway because of how often and how badly you needed protection from what you were seeing, had actually come 30,000 miles to see. Once I looked at them clumped together nearest the wire, then in smaller numbers but tighter groups midway, fanning out into lots of scattered points nearer the treeline, with one all by himself half into the bush and half out. "Close but no cigar," the captain said, and then a few of his men went out there and kicked them all in the head, thirty-seven of them. Then I heard an M-16 on full automatic starting to go through clips, a second to fire, three to plug in a fresh clip, and I saw a man out there, doing it. Every round was like a tiny concentration of high-velocity wind, making the bodies wince and shiver. When he finished he walked by us on the way back to his hootch, and I knew I hadn't seen anything until I saw his face. It was flushed and mottled and twisted like he had his face skin on inside out, a patch of green that was too dark, a streak of red running into bruise purple, a lot of sick gray white in between, he looked like he'd had a heart attack out there. His eyes were rolled up half into his head, his mouth was sprung open and his tongue was out, but he was smiling. Really a dude who'd shot his wad. The captain wasn't too pleased about my having seen that.

There wasn't a day when someone didn't ask me what I was doing there. Sometimes an especially smart grunt or another correspondent would even ask me what I was *really* doing there, as though I could say anything honest about it except "Blah blah blah cover the war" or "Blah blah blah write a book." Maybe we accepted each other's stories about why we were there at face value: the grunts who "had" to be there, the spooks and civilians whose corporate faith had led them there, the correspondents whose curiosity or ambition drew them over. But somewhere all the mythic tracks intersected, from the lowest John Wayne wetdream to the most aggravated soldier-poet fantasy, and where they did I believe that everyone knew everything about everyone else, every one of us there a true volunteer. Not that you didn't hear some overripe bullshit about it: Hearts and Minds, Peoples of the Republic, tumbling dominoes, maintaining the equilibrium of the Dingdong by containing the ever encroaching Doodah; you could also hear the other, some young soldier speaking in all bloody innocence, saying, "All that's just a *load*, man. We're here to kill gooks. Period." Which wasn't at all true of me. I was there to watch.

Talk about impersonating an identity, about locking into a role, about irony: I went to cover the war and the war covered me; an old story, unless of course you've never heard it. I went there behind the crude but serious belief that you had to be able to look at anything, serious because I acted on it and went, crude because I didn't know, it took the war to teach it, that you were as responsible for everything you saw as you were for everything you did. The problem was that you didn't always know what you were seeing until later, maybe years later, that a lot of it never made it in at all, it just stayed stored there in your eyes. Time and information, rock and roll, life itself, the information isn't frozen, you are.

Sometimes I didn't know if an action took a second or an hour or if I dreamed it or what. In war more than in other life you don't really know what you're doing most of the time, you're just behaving, and afterward you can make up any kind of bullshit you want to about it, say you felt good or bad, loved it or hated it, did this or that, the right thing or the wrong thing; still, what happened happened.

Coming back, telling stories, I'd say, "Oh man I was scared," and "Oh God I thought it was all over," a long time before I knew how scared I was really supposed to be, or how clear and closed and beyond my control "all over" could become. I wasn't dumb but I sure was raw, certain connections are hard to make when you come from a place where they go around with war in their heads all the time.

"If you get hit," a medic told me, "we can chopper you back to base-camp hospital in like twenty minutes."

"If you get hit real bad," a corpsman said, "they'll get your case to Japan in twelve hours."

"If you get killed," a spec 4 from Graves promised, "we'll have you home in a week."

TIME IS ON MY SIDE, already written there across the first helmet I ever wore there. And underneath it, in smaller lettering that read more like a whispered prayer than an assertion, *No lie, GI.* The rear-hatch gunner on a Chinook threw it to me that first morning at the Kontum airstrip, a few hours after the Dak To fighting had ended, screaming at me through the rotor wind, "You *keep* that, we got *plenty*, good *luck!*" and then flying off. I was so glad to have the equipment that I didn't stop to think where it had to have come from. The sweatband inside was seasoned up black and greasy, it was more alive now than the man who'd worn it, when I got rid of it ten minutes later I didn't just leave it on the ground, I snuck away from it furtive and ashamed, afraid that someone would see it and call after me, "Hey numbnuts, you forgot something. . . ."

That morning when I tried to go out they sent me down the line from a colonel to a major to a captain to a sergeant who took one look, called me Freshmeat, and told me to go find some other outfit to get myself killed with. I didn't know what was going on, I was so nervous I started to laugh. I told him that nothing was going to happen to me and he gave my shoulder a tender, menacing pat and said, "This ain't the fucking movies over here, you know." I laughed again and said that I knew, but he knew that I didn't.

Day one, if anything could have penetrated that first innocence I might have taken the next plane out. Out absolutely. It was like a walk through a colony of stroke victims, a thousand men on a cold rainy airfield after too much of something I'd never really know, "a way you'll never be," dirt and blood and torn fatigues, eyes that poured out a steady charge of wasted horror. I'd just missed the biggest battle of the war so far, I was telling myself that I was sorry, but it was right there all around me and I didn't even know it. I couldn't look at anyone for more than a second, I didn't want to be caught listening, some war correspondent, I didn't know what to say or do, I didn't like it already. When the rain stopped and the ponchos came off there was a smell that I thought was going to make me sick: rot, sump, tannery, open grave, dumpfire—awful, you'd walk into pockets of Old Spice that made it even worse. I wanted badly to find some place to sit alone and smoke a cigarette, to find a face that would cover my face the way my poncho covered my new fatigues. I'd worn them once before, yesterday morning in Saigon, bringing them out of the black market and back to the hotel, dressing up in front of the mirror, making faces and moves I'd never make again. And loving it. Now, nearby on the ground, there was a man sleeping with a poncho over his head and a radio in his arms, I heard Sam the Sham singing, "Lil' Red Riding Hood, I don't think little big girls should, Go walking in these spooky old woods alone. . . ."

I turned to walk some other way and there was a man standing in front of me. He didn't exactly block me, but he didn't move either. He tottered a little and blinked, he looked at me and through me, no one had ever looked at me like that before. I felt a cold fat drop of sweat start down the middle of my back like a spider, it seemed to take an hour to finish its run. The man lit a cigarette and then sort of slobbered it out, I couldn't imagine what I was seeing. He tried again with a fresh cigarette. I gave him the light for that one, there was a flicker of focus, acknowledgment, but after a few puffs it went out too, and he let it drop to the ground. "I couldn't spit for a week up there," he said, "and now I can't fucking stop."

ILLUMINATION ROUNDS

We were all strapped into the seats of the Chinook, fifty of us, and something, someone was hitting it from the outside with an enormous hammer. How do they do that? I thought, we're a thousand feet in the air! But it had to be that, over and over, shaking the helicopter, making it dip and turn in a horrible out-of-control motion that took me in the stomach. I had to laugh, it was so exciting, it was the thing I had wanted, almost what I had wanted except for the wrenching, resonant, metal-echo; I could hear it even above the noise of the rotor blades. And they were going to fix that, I knew they would make it stop. They had to, it was going to make me sick.

They were all replacements going in to mop up after the big battles on Hills 875 and 876, the battles that had already taken on the name of one great battle, the battle of Dak To. And I was new, brand new, three days in-country, embarrassed about my boots because they were so new. And across from me, ten feet away, a boy tried to jump out of the straps and then jerked forward and hung there, his rifle barrel caught in the red plastic webbing of the seat back. As the chopper rose again and turned, his weight went back hard against the webbing and a dark spot the size of a baby's hand showed in the center of his fatigue jacket. And it grew—I knew what it was, but not really—it got up to his armpits and then started down his sleeves and up over his shoulders at the same time. It went all across his waist and down his

217

legs, covering the canvas on his boots until they were dark like every-thing else he wore, and it was running in slow, heavy drops off his fingertips. I thought I could hear the drops hitting the metal strip on the chopper floor. Hey! . . . Oh, but this isn't anything at all, it's not real, it's just some *thing* they're going through that isn't real. One of the door gunners was heaped up on the floor like a cloth dummy. His hand had the bloody raw look of a pound of liver fresh from the butcher paper. We touched down on the same lz we had just left a few minutes before, but I didn't know it until one of the guys shook my shoulder, and then I couldn't stand up. All I could feel of my legs was their shaking, and the guy thought I'd been hit and helped me up. The chopper had taken eight hits, there was shattered plastic all over the floor, a dying pilot up front, and the boy was hanging forward in the straps again, he was dead, but not (I knew) really dead.

It took me a month to lose that feeling of being a spectator to something that was part game, part show. That first afternoon, before I'd boarded the Chinook, a black sergeant had tried to keep me from going. He told me I was too new to go near the kind of shit they were throwing up in those hills. ("You a reporter?" he'd asked, and I'd said, "No, a writer," dumbass and pompous, and he'd laughed and said, "Careful. You can't use no eraser up where you wanna go.") He'd pointed to the bodies of all the dead Americans lined in two long rows near the chopper pad, so many that they could not even cover all of them decently. But they were not real then, and taught me nothing. The Chinook had come in, blowing my helmet off, and I grabbed it up and joined the replacements waiting to board. "Okay, man," the sergeant said. "You gotta go, you gotta go. All's I can say is, I hope you get a clean wound."

The battle for Hill 875 was over, and some survivors were being brought in by Chinook to the landing strip at Dak To. The 173rd Airborne had taken over 400 casualties, nearly 200 killed, all on the previous afternoon and in the fighting that had gone on all through the night. It was very cold and wet up there, and some girls from the Red Cross had been sent up from Pleiku to comfort the survivors. As the troops filed out of the helicopters, the girls waved and smiled at them from behind their serving tables. "Hi, soldier! What's your name?" "Where you from, soldier?" "I'll bet some hot coffee would hit the spot about now."

And the men from the 173rd just kept walking without answering, staring straight ahead, their eyes rimmed with red from fatigue, their faces pinched and aged with all that happened during the night. One of them dropped out of line and said something to a loud, fat girl who wore a Peanuts sweatshirt under her fatigue blouse and she started to cry. The rest just walked past the girls and the large, olive-drab coffee urns. They had no idea of where they were.

A senior NCO in the Special Forces was telling the story: "We was back at Bragg, in the NCO Club, and this schoolteacher comes in an' she's real good-lookin'. Dusty here grabs her by the shoulders and starts runnin' his tongue all over her face like she's a fuckin' ice-cream cone. An' you know what she says? She says, 'I like you. You're different.'"

At one time they would have lighted your cigarette for you on the terrace of the Continental Hotel. But those' days are almost twenty years gone, and anyway, who really misses them? Now there is a crazy American who looks like George Orwell, and he is always sleeping off his drinks in one of the wicker chairs there, slumped against a table, starting up with violence, shouting and then going back to sleep. He makes everyone nervous, especially the waiters; the old ones who had served the French and the Japanese and the first American journalists and OSS types ("those noisy bastards at the Continental," Graham Greene called them) and the really young ones who bussed the tables and pimped in a modest way. The little elevator boy still greets the guests each morning with a quiet "*Ça va?*" but he is seldom answered, and the old baggage man (he also brings us grass) will sit in the lobby and say, "How are you tomorrow?"

"Ode to Billy Joe" plays from speakers mounted on the terrace's corner columns, but the air seems too heavy to carry the sound right, and it hangs in the corners. There is an exhausted, drunk master sergeant from the 1st Infantry Division who has bought a flute from the old man in khaki shorts and pith helmet who sells instruments along Tu Do Street. The old man will lean over the butt-strewn flower boxes that line the terrace and play "Frère Jacques" on a wooden stringed instrument. The sergeant has brought the flute, and he is playing it quietly, pensively, badly.

The tables are crowded with American civilian construction engineers, men getting $30,000 a year from their jobs on government contracts and matching that easily on the black market. Their faces have the look of aerial photos of silicone pits, all hung with loose flesh and visible veins. Their mistresses were among the prettiest, saddest girls in Vietnam. I always wondered what they had looked like before they'd made their arrangements with the engineers. You'd see them at the tables there, smiling their hard, empty smiles into those rangy, brutal, scared faces. No wonder those men all looked alike to the Vietnamese. After a while they all looked alike to me. Out on the Bien Hoa Highway, north of Saigon, there is a monument to the Vietnamese war dead, and it is one of the few graceful things left in the country. It is a modest pagoda set above the road and approached by long flights of gently rising steps. One Sunday, I saw a bunch of these engineers gunning their Harleys up those steps, laughing and shouting in the afternoon sun. The Vietnamese had a special name for them to distinguish them from all other Americans; it translated out to something like "The Terrible Ones," although I'm told this doesn't even approximate the odium carried in the original.

There was a young sergeant in the Special Forces, stationed at the C Detachment in Can Tho, which served as the SF headquarters for IV Corps. In all, he had spent thirty-six months in Vietnam. This was his third extended tour, and he planned to come back again as soon as he possibly could after this current hitch was finished. During his last tour he had lost a finger and part of a thumb in a firefight, and he had been generally shot up enough times for the three Purple Hearts which mean that you don't have to fight in Vietnam anymore. After all that, I guess they thought of him as a combat liability, but he was such a hard charger that they gave him the EM Club to manage. He ran it well and seemed happy, except that he had gained a lot of weight in the duty, and it set him apart from the rest of the men. He loved to horse around with the Vietnamese in the compound, leaping on them from behind, leaning heavily on them, shoving them around and pulling their ears, sometimes punching them a little hard in the stomach, smiling a stiff small smile that was meant to tell them all that he was just being playful. The Vietnamese would smile too, until he turned to walk away. He loved the Vietnamese, he said, he really *knew* them after three years. As far as he was concerned, there was no place in the world as fine as Vietnam. And back home in North Carolina he had a large, glass-covered display case in which he kept his medals and decorations and citations, the photographs taken during three tours and countless battles, letters from past commanders, a few souvenirs. The case stood in the center of the living room, he said, and every night his wife and three kids would move the kitchen table out in front of it and eat their dinner there.

At 800 feet we knew we were being shot at. Something hit the underside of the chopper but did not penetrate it. They weren't firing tracers, but we saw the brilliant flickering blips of light below, and the pilot circled and came down very fast, working the button that released fire from the flex guns mounted on either side of the Huey. Every fifth round was a tracer, and they sailed out and down, incomparably graceful, closer and closer, until they met the tiny point of light coming from the jungle. The ground fire stopped, and we went on to land at Vinh Long, where the pilot yawned and said, "I think I'll go to bed early tonight and see if I can wake up with any enthusiasm for this war."

A twenty-four-year-old Special Forces captain was telling me about it. "I went out and killed one VC and liberated a prisoner. Next day the major called me in and told me that I'd killed fourteen VC and liberated six prisoners. You want to see the medal?"

There was a little air-conditioned restaurant on the corner of Le Loi and Tu Do, across from the Continental Hotel and the old opera house which now served as the Vietnamese Lower House. Some of us called it the Graham Greene Milk Bar (a scene in *The Quiet American* had taken place there), but its name was Givral. Every morning they baked their own baguettes and croissants, and the coffee wasn't too bad. Sometimes, I'd meet there with a friend of mine for breakfast.

He was a Belgian, a tall, slow-moving man of thirty who'd been born in the Congo. He professed to know and love war, and he affected the mercenary sensibility. He'd been photographing the Vietnam thing for seven or eight years now, and once in a while he'd go over to Laos and run around the jungles there with the government, searching for the dreaded Pathet Lao, which he pronounced "Paddy Lao." Other people's stories of Laos always made it sound like a lotus land where no one wanted to hurt anyone, but he said that whenever he went on ops there he always kept a grenade taped to his belly because he was a Catholic and knew what the Paddy Lao would do to him if he were captured. But he was a little crazy that way, and tended to dramatize his war stories.

He always wore dark glasses, probably even during operations. His pictures sold to the wire services, and I saw a few of them in the American news magazines. He was very kind in a gruff, offhanded sort of way, kindness embarrassed him, and he was so graceless among people, so eager to shock, that he couldn't understand why so many of us liked him. Irony was the effect he worked for in conversation, that and a sense of how exquisite the war could be when all of its machinery was running right. He was explaining the finish of an operation he'd just been on in War Zone C, above Cu Chi.

"There were a lot of dead VC," he said. "Dozens and dozens of them! A lot of them were from that same village that has been giving you so much trouble lately. VC from top to bottom—Michael, in that village the fucking *ducks* are VC. So the American commander had twenty or thirty of the dead flown up in a sling load and dropped into the village. I should say it was a drop of at least two hundred feet, all those dead Viet Congs, right in the middle of the village."

He smiled (I couldn't see his eyes).

"Ah, Psywar!" he said, kissing off the tips of his fingers.

• • •

Bob Stokes of *Newsweek* told me this: In the big Marine hospital in Danang they have what is called the "White Lie Ward," where they bring some of the worst cases, the ones who can be saved but who will never be the same again. A young Marine was carried in, still unconscious and full of morphine, and his legs were gone. As he was being carried into the ward, he came out of it briefly and saw a Catholic chaplain standing over him.

"Father," he said, "am I all right?"

The chaplain didn't know what to say. "You'll have to talk about that with the doctors, son."

"Father, are my legs okay?"

"Yes," the chaplain said. "Sure."

By the next afternoon the shock had worn off and the boy knew all about it. He was lying on his cot when the chaplain came by.

"Father," the Marine said, "I'd like to ask you for something."

"What, son?"

"I'd like to have that cross." And he pointed to the tiny silver insignia on the chaplain's lapel.

"Of course," the chaplain said. "But why?"

"Well, it was the first thing I saw when I came to yesterday, and I'd like to have it."

The chaplain removed the cross and handed it to him. The Marine held it tightly in his fist and looked at the chaplain.

"You lied to me, Father," he said. "You cocksucker. You lied to me."

His name was Davies, and he was a gunner with a helicopter group based at Tan Son Nhut airport. On paper, by the regulations, he was billetted in one of the big "hotel" BEQ's in Cholon, but he only kept his things there. He actually lived in a small two-story Vietnamese house deeper inside of Cholon, as far from the papers and the regulations as he could get. Every morning he took an Army bus with wire-grille windows out to the base and flew missions, mostly around War Zone C, along the Cambodian border, and most nights he returned to the house in Cholon where he lived with his "wife" (whom he'd found in one of the bars) and some other Vietnamese who were said to be the girl's family. Her mamma-san and her brother were always there, living on the first floor, and there were others who came and went. He seldom saw the brother, but every few days he would find a pile of labels and brand names torn from cardboard cartons, American products that the brother wanted from the PX.

The first time I saw him he was sitting alone at a table on the Continental terrace, drinking a beer. He had a full, drooping mustache and sharp, sad eyes, and he was wearing a denim workshirt and wheat jeans. He also carried a Leica and a copy of *Ramparts*, and I just assumed at first that he was a correspondent. I didn't know then that you could buy *Ramparts* at the PX, and after I'd borrowed and returned it we began to talk. It was the issue that featured left-wing Catholics like Jesus Christ and Fulton Sheen on the cover. "*Catholique?*" one of the bar girls said later that night. "*Moi aussi*," and she kept the magazine. That was when we were walking around Cholon in the rain trying to find Hoa, his wife. Mamma-san had told us that she'd gone to the movies with some girlfriends, but Davies knew what she was doing.

"I hate that shit," he said. "It's so uncool."

"Well, don't put up with it."

"Yeah."

Davies' house was down a long, narrow alley that became nothing more than a warren at the end, smelling of camphor smoke and fish, crowded but clean. He would not speak to Mamma-san, and we walked straight up to the second floor. It was one long room that had a sleeping area screened off in an arrangement of filmy curtains. At the top of the stairs there was a large poster of Lenny Bruce, and beneath it, in a shrine effect, was a low table with a Buddha and lighted incense on it.

"Lenny," Davies said.

Most of one wall was covered with a collage that Davies had done with the help of some friends. It included glimpses of burning monks, stacked Viet Cong dead, wounded Marines screaming and weeping, Cardinal Spellman waving from a chopper, Ronald Reagan, his face halved and separated by a stalk of cannabis; pictures of John Lennon peering through wire-rimmed glasses, Mick Jagger, Jimi Hendrix,

Dylan, Eldridge Cleaver, Rap Brown; coffins draped with American flags whose stars were replaced by swastikas and dollar signs; odd parts clipped from *Playboy* pictures, newspaper headlines (FARMERS BUTCHER HOGS TO PROTEST PORK PRICE DIP), photo captions (*President Jokes with Newsmen*), beautiful girls holding flowers, showers of peace symbols; Ky standing at attention and saluting, a small mushroom cloud forming where his genitalia should have been; a map of the western United States with the shape of Vietnam reversed and fitted over California and one large, long figure that began at the bottom with shiny leather boots and rouged knees and ascended in a microskirt, bare breasts, graceful shoulders and a long neck, topped by the burned, blackened face of a dead Vietnamese woman.

By the time Davies' friends showed up, we were already stoned. We could hear them below, laughing and rapping with Mama, and then they came up the stairs, three spades and two white guys.

"It sure do smell *peculiar* up here," one of them said.

"Hi, you freaky li'l fuckers."

"This grass is Number Ten," Davies said. "Every time I smoke this grass over here it gives me a bad trip."

"Ain' nuthin' th'matter with that grass," someone said. "It ain't the grass."

"Where's Hoa?"

"Yeah, Davies, where's your ole lady at?"

"She's out hustling Saigon tea, and I'm fucking sick of it." He tried to look really angry, but he only looked unhappy.

One of them handed off a joint and stretched out. "Hairy day today," he said.

"Where'd you fly?"

"Bu Dop."

"Bu Dop!" one of the spades said, and he started to move toward the joint, jiving and working his shoulders, bopping his head. "Bu Dop, budop, bu dop dop *dop!*"

"Funky funky Bu Dop."

"Hey, man, can you OD on grass?"

"I dunno, baby. Maybe we could get jobs at the Aberdeen Proving Grounds smokin' dope for Uncle Sugar."

"Wow, I'm stoned. Hey, Davies, you stoned?"

"Yeah," Davies said.

It started to rain again, so hard that you couldn't hear drops, only the full force of the water pouring down on the metal roof. We smoked a little more, and then the others started to leave. Davies looked like he was sleeping with his eyes open.

"That goddamn pig," he said. "Fuckin' whore. Man, I'm paying out all this bread for the house and those people downstairs. I don't even know who they are, for Christ's sake. I'm really . . . I'm getting sick of it."

"You're pretty short now," someone said. "Why don't you cut out?"

"You mean just split?"

"Why not?"

Davies was quiet for a long time.

"Yeah," he finally said. "This is bad. This is really bad. I think I'm going to get out of here."

A bird colonel, commanding a brigade of the 4th Infantry Division: "I'll bet you always wondered why we call 'em Dinks up in this part of the country. I thought of it myself. I'll tell you, I never *did* like hearing them called Charlie. See, I had an uncle named Charlie, and I liked him too. No, Charlie was just too damn good for the little bastards. So I just thought, What are they *really* like? and I came up with rinky-dink. Suits 'em just perfect, Rinky-Dink. 'Cept that was too long, so we cut it down some. And that's why we call 'em Dinks."

One morning before dawn, Ed Fouhy, a former Saigon bureau chief for CBS, went out to 8th Aerial Port at Tan Son Nhut to catch the early military flight to Danang. They boarded as the sun came up, and Fouhy strapped in next to a kid in rumpled fatigues, one of those soldiers you see whose weariness has gone far beyond physical exhaustion, into that state where no amount of sleep will ever give him the kind of rest he needs. Every torpid movement they make tells you that they are tired, that they'll stay tired until their tours are up and the big bird flies them back to the World. Their eyes are dim with it, their faces almost puffy, and when they smile you have to accept it as a token.

There was a standard question you could use to open a conversation with troops, and Fouhy tried it. "How long you been in-country?" he asked.

The kid half lifted his head; that question could *not* be serious. The weight was really on him, and the words came slowly.

"All   fuckin'   day," he said.

"You guys ought to do a story on me suntahm," the kid said. He was a helicopter gunner, six-three with an enormous head that sat in bad proportion to the rest of his body and a line of picket teeth that were always on show in a wet, uneven smile. Every few seconds he would have to wipe his mouth with the back of his hand, and when he talked to you his face was always an inch from yours, so that I had to take my glasses off to keep them dry. He was from Kilgore, Texas, and he was on his seventeenth consecutive month in-country.

"Why should we do a story about you?"

" 'Cause I'm so fuckin' good," he said, " 'n' that ain' no shit, neither. Got me one hunnert 'n' fifty-se'en gooks kilt. 'N' fifty caribou." He grinned and stanched the saliva for a second. "Them're all certified," he added.

The chopper touched down at Ba Xoi and we got off, not unhappy about leaving him. "Lis'n," he said, laughing, "you git up onna ridge-line, see y' keep yer head down. Y'heah?"

"Say, how'd you get to be a co-respondent an' come ovah to this raggedy-ass motherfucker?"

He was a really big spade, rough-looking even when he smiled, and he wore a gold nose-bead fastened through his left nostril. I told him the nose-bead blew my mind, and he said that was all right, it blew everybody's mind. We were sitting by the chopper pad of an lz above Kontum. He was trying to get to Dak To, I was headed for Pleiku, and we both wanted to get out of there before nightfall. We took turns running out to the pad to check the choppers that kept coming in and taking off, neither of us was having any luck, and after we'd talked for half an hour he laid a joint on me and we smoked.

"I been here mor'n eight months now," he said. "I bet I been in mor'n twenny firefights. An' I ain' hardly fired back once."

"How come?"

"Shee-it, I go firin' back, I might kill one a th' Brothers, you dig it?"

I nodded, no Viet Cong ever called *me* honky, and he told me that in his company alone there were more than a dozen Black Panthers and that he was one of them. I didn't say anything, and then he said that he wasn't just a Panther; he was an agent for the Panthers, sent over here to recruit. I asked him what kind of luck he'd been having, and he said fine, real fine. There was a fierce wind blowing across the lz, and the joint didn't last very long.

"Hey, baby," he said, "that was just some shit I tol' you. Shit, I ain' no Panther. I was just fuckin' with you, see what you'd say."

"But the Panthers have guys over here. I've met some."

"Tha' could be," he said, and he laughed.

A Huey came in, and he jogged out to see where it was headed. It was going to Dak To, and he came back to get his gear. "Later, baby," he said. "An' luck." He jumped into the chopper, and as it rose from the strip he leaned out and laughed, bringing his arm up and bending it back toward him, palm out and the fist clenched tightly in the Sign.

One day I went out with the ARVN on an operation in the rice paddies above Vinh Long, forty terrified Vietnamese troops and five Americans, all packed into three Hueys that dropped us up to our hips in paddy muck. I had never been in a rice paddy before. We spread out and moved toward the marshy swale that led to the jungle. We were still twenty feet from the first cover, a low paddy wall, when we took fire from the treeline. It was probably the working half of a crossfire that had somehow gone wrong. It caught one of the ARVN in the head, and he dropped back into the water and disappeared. We made it to the wall with two casualties. There was no way of stopping their fire, no room to send in a flanking party, so gunships were called and we crouched behind the wall and waited. There was a lot of fire coming from the trees, but we were all right as long as we kept down.

And I was thinking, Oh man, so this is a rice paddy, yes, wow! when I suddenly heard an electric guitar shooting right up in my ear and a mean, rapturous black voice singing, coaxing, "Now c'mon, baby, stop actin' so crazy," and when I got it all together I turned to see a grinning black corporal hunched over a cassette recorder. "Might's well," he said. "We ain' goin' *no*where till them gunships come."

That's the story of the first time I ever heard Jimi Hendrix, but in a war where a lot of people talked about Aretha's "Satisfaction" the way other people spoke of Brahms' Fourth, it was more than a story; it was Credentials. "Say, that Jimi Hendrix is my main man," someone would say. "He has *de*finitely got his shit together!" Hendrix had once been in the 101st Airborne, and the Airborne in Vietnam was full of wiggy-brilliant spades like him, really mean and really good, guys who always took care of you when things got bad. That music meant a lot to them. I never once heard it played over the Armed Forces Radio Network.

I met this kid from Miles City, Montana, who read the *Stars and Stripes* every day, checking the casualty lists to see if by some chance anybody from his town had been killed. He didn't even know if there was anyone else from Miles City in Vietnam, but he checked anyway because he knew for sure that if there *was* someone else and they got killed, he would be all right. "I mean, can you just see *two* guys from a raggedy-ass town like Miles City getting killed in Vietnam?" he said.

The sergeant had lain out near the clearing for almost two hours with a wounded medic. He had called over and over for a medevac, but none had come. Finally, a chopper from another outfit, a LOH, appeared, and he was able to reach it by radio. The pilot told him that he'd have to wait for one of his own ships, they weren't coming down, and the sergeant told the pilot that if he did not land for them he was going to open fire from the ground and fucking well *bring* him down. So they were picked up that way, but there were repercussions.

The commander's code name was Mal Hombre, and he reached the sergeant later that afternoon from a place with the call signal Violent Meals.

"God *damn* it, Sergeant," he said through the static, "I thought you were a professional soldier."

"I waited as long as I could, Sir. Any longer, I was gonna lose my man."

"This outfit is perfectly capable of taking care of its own dirty laundry. Is that clear, Sergeant?"

"Colonel, since when is a wounded trooper 'dirty laundry'?"

"At ease, Sergeant," Mal Hombre said, and radio contact was broken.

There was a spec 4 in the Special Forces at Can Tho, a shy Indian boy from Chinle, Arizona, with large, wet eyes the color of ripe olives and a quiet way of speaking, a really nice way of putting things, kind to everyone without ever being stupid or soft about it. On the night the compound and the airstrip were hit, he came and asked me if there was a chaplain anywhere around. He wasn't very religious, he said, but he was worried about tonight. He'd just volunteered for a "suicide squad," two jeeps that were going to drive across the airstrip with mortars and a recoilless rifle. It looked bad, I had to admit it; there were so few of us in the compound that they'd had to put me on the reaction force. It might be bad. He just had a feeling about it, he'd seen what always happened to guys whenever they got that feeling, at least he *thought* it was that feeling, a bad one, the worst he'd ever had.

I told him that the only chaplains I could think of would be in the town, and we both knew that the town was cut off.

"Oh," he said. "Look, then. If I get it tonight . . ."

"It'll be okay."

"Listen, though. If it happens . . . I think it's going to . . . will you make sure the colonel tells my folks I was looking for a chaplain anyway?"

I promised, and the jeeps loaded and drove off. I heard later that there had been a brief firefight, but that no one had been hurt. They didn't have to use the recoilless. They all drove back into the compound two hours later. The next morning at breakfast he sat at another table, saying a lot of loud, brutal things about the gooks, and he wouldn't look at me. But at noon he came over and squeezed my arm and smiled, his eyes fixed somewhere just to the right of my own.

For two days now, ever since the Tet Offensive had begun, they had been coming by the hundreds to the province hospital at Can Tho. They were usually either very young or very old or women, and their wounds were often horrible. The more lightly wounded were being treated quickly in the hospital yard, and the more serious cases were simply placed in one of the corridors to die. There were just too many of them to treat, the doctors had worked without a break, and now, on the second afternoon, the Viet Cong began shelling the hospital.

One of the Vietnamese nurses handed me a cold can of beer and asked me to take it down the hall where one of the Army surgeons was operating. The door of the room was ajar, and I walked right in. I probably should have looked first. A little girl was lying on the table, looking with wide dry eyes at the wall. Her left leg was gone, and a sharp piece of bone about six inches long extended from the exposed stump. The leg itself was on the floor, half wrapped in a piece of paper. The doctor was a major, and he'd been working alone. He could not have looked worse if he'd lain all night in a trough of blood. His hands were so slippery that I had to hold the can to his mouth for him and tip it up as his head went back. I couldn't look at the girl.

"Is it all right?" he said quietly.

"It's okay now. I expect I'll be sick as hell later on."

He placed his hand on the girl's forehead and said, "Hello, little darling." He thanked me for bringing the beer. He probably thought that he was smiling, but nothing changed anywhere in his face. He'd been working this way for nearly twenty hours.

The Intel report lay closed on the green field table, and someone had scrawled, "What does it all mean?" across the cover sheet. There wasn't much doubt about who had done that; the S-2 was a known ironist. There were so many like him, really young captains and majors who had the wit to cut back their despair, a wedge to set against the bitterness. What got to them sooner or later was an inability to reconcile their love of service with their contempt for the war, and a lot of them finally had to resign their commissions, leave the profession.

We were sitting in the tent waiting for the rain to stop, the major, five grunts and myself. The rains were constant now, ending what had been a dry monsoon season, and you could look through the tent flap and think about the Marines up there patrolling the hills. Someone came in to report that one of the patrols had discovered a small arms cache.

"An arms cache!" the major said. "What happened was, one of the grunts was out there running around, and he tripped and fell down. That's about the only way we ever find any of this shit."

He was twenty-nine, young in rank, and this was his second tour. The time before, he had been a captain commanding a regular Marine company. He knew all about grunts and patrols, arms caches and the value of most Intelligence.

It was cold, even in the tent, and the enlisted Marines seemed uncomfortable about lying around with a stranger, a correspondent there. The major was a cool head, they knew that; there wasn't going to be any kind of hassle until the rain stopped. They talked quietly among themselves at the far end of the tent, away from the light of the lantern. Reports kept coming in: reports from the Vietnamese, from recon, from Division, situation reports, casualty reports, three casualty reports in twenty minutes. The major looked them all over.

"Did you know that a dead Marine costs eighteen thousand dollars?" he said. The grunts all turned around and looked at us. They knew how the major had meant that because they knew the major. They were just seeing about me.

The rain stopped, and they left. Outside, the air was still cool, but heavy, too, as though a terrible heat was coming on. The major and I stood by the tent and watched while an F-4 flew nose-down, released its load against the base of a hill, leveled and flew upward again.

"I've been having this dream," the major said. "I've had it two times now. I'm in a big examination room back at Quantico. They're handing out questionnaires for an aptitude test. I take one and look at it, and the first question says, 'How many kinds of animals can you kill with your hands?' "

We could see rain falling in a sheet about a kilometer away. Judging by the wind, the major gave it three minutes before it reached us.

"After the first tour, I'd have the goddamndest nightmares. You know, the works. Bloody stuff, bad fights, guys dying, *me* dying . . . I thought they were the worst," he said. "But I sort of miss them now."

Going After Cacciato

TIM O'BRIEN

1978

GOING AFTER CACCIATO

It was a bad time. Billy Boy Watkins was dead, and so was Frenchie
Tucker. Billy Boy had died of fright, scared to death on the field of
battle, and Frenchie Tucker had been shot through the nose. Bernie
Lynn and Lieutenant Sidney Martin had died in tunnels. Pederson
was dead and Rudy Chassler was dead. Buff was dead. Ready Mix was
dead. They were all among the dead. The rain fed fungus that grew in
the men's boots and socks, and their socks rotted, and their feet turned
white and soft so that the skin could be scraped off with a fingernail,
and Stink Harris woke up screaming one night with a leech on his
tongue. When it was not raining, a low mist moved across the paddies,
blending the elements into a single gray element, and the war was
cold and pasty and rotten. Lieutenant Corson, who came to replace
Lieutenant Sidney Martin, contracted the dysentery. The tripflares
were useless. The ammunition corroded and the foxholes filled with
mud and water during the nights, and in the mornings there was
always the next village and the war was always the same. The monsoons were part of the war. In early September Vaught caught an
infection. He'd been showing Oscar Johnson the sharp edge on his
bayonet, drawing it swiftly along his forearm to peel off a layer of
mushy skin. "Like a Gillette Blue Blade," Vaught had said proudly.
There was no blood, but in two days the bacteria soaked in and the
arm turned yellow, so they bundled him up and called in a dustoff,

and Vaught left the war. He never came back. Later they had a letter from him that described Japan as smoky and full of slopes, but in the enclosed snapshot Vaught looked happy enough, posing with two sightly nurses, a wine bottle rising from between his thighs. It was a shock to learn he'd lost the arm. Soon afterward Ben Nystrom shot himself through the foot, but he did not die, and he wrote no letters. These were all things to joke about. The rain, too. And the cold. Oscar Johnson said it made him think of Detroit in the month of May. "Lootin' weather," he liked to say. "The dark an' gloom, just right for rape an' lootin'." Then someone would say that Oscar had a swell imagination for a darkie.

That was one of the jokes. There was a joke about Oscar. There were many jokes about Billy Boy Watkins, the way he'd collapsed of fright on the field of battle. Another joke was about the lieutenant's dysentery, and another was about Paul Berlin's purple biles. There were jokes about the postcard pictures of Christ that Jim Pederson used to carry, and Stink's ringworm, and the way Buff's helmet filled with life after death. Some of the jokes were about Cacciato. Dumb as a bullet, Stink said. Dumb as a month-old oyster fart, said Harold Murphy.

In October, near the end of the month, Cacciato left the war.

"He's gone away," said Doc Peret. "Split, departed."

THE OBSERVATION POST

Cacciato's round face became the moon. The valleys and ridges and fast-flowing plains dissolved, and now the moon was just the moon.

Paul Berlin sat up. A fine idea. He stretched, stood up, leaned against the wall of sandbags, touched his weapon, then gazed out at the strip of beach that wound along the curving Batangan. Things were dark. Behind him, the South China Sea sobbed in against the tower's thick piles; before him, inland, was the face of Quang Ngai.

Yes, he thought, a fine idea. Cacciato leading them west through peaceful country, deep country perfumed by lilacs and burning hemp, a boy coaxing them step by step through rich and fertile country toward Paris.

It was a splendid idea.

Paul Berlin, whose only goal was to live long enough to establish goals worth living for still longer, stood high in the tower by the sea, the night soft all around him, and wondered, not for the first time, about the immense powers of his own imagination. A truly awesome notion. Not a dream, an idea. An idea to develop, to tinker with and build and sustain, to draw out as an artist draws out his visions.

It was not a dream. Nothing mystical or crazy, just an idea. Just a possibility. Feet turning hard like stone, legs stiffening, six and seven and eight thousand miles through unfolding country toward Paris. A truly splendid idea.

He checked his watch. It was not quite midnight.

For a time he stood quietly at the tower's north wall, looking out to where the beach jagged sharply into the sea to form a natural barrier against storms. The night was quiet. On the sand below, coils of barbed wire circled the observation tower in a perimeter that separated it from the rest of the war. The tripflares were out. Things were in their place. Beside him, Harold Murphy's machine gun was fully loaded and ready, and a dozen signal flares were lined up on the wall, and the radio was working, and the beach was mined, and the tower itself was high and strong and fortified. The sea guarded his rear. The moon gave light. It would be all right, he told himself. He was safe.

He lit a cigarette and moved to the west wall.

Doc and Eddie and Oscar and the others slept peacefully. And the night was peaceful. Time to think. Time to consider the possibilities.

Had it ended there on Cacciato's grassy hill, flares coloring the morning sky? Had it ended in tragedy? Had it ended with a jerking, shaking feeling—noise and confusion? Or had it ended farther along the trail west? Had it ever ended? What, in fact, had become of Cacciato? More precisely—as Doc Peret would insist it be phrased— more precisely, what part was fact and what part was the extension of fact? And how were facts separated from possibilities? What had really happened and what merely might have happened? How did it end?

The trick, of course, was to think through it carefully. That was Doc's advice—look for motives, search out the place where fact ended and imagination took over. Ask the important questions. Why had Cacciato left the war? Was it courage or ignorance, or both? Was it even possible to combine courage and ignorance? How much of what happened, or might have happened, was Cacciato's doing and how much was the product of the biles?

That was Doc's theory.

"You got an excess of fear biles," Doc had said one afternoon beneath the tower. "We've all got these biles—Stink, Oscar, everybody—but you've got yourself a whole bellyful of the stuff. You're oversaturated. And my theory is this: Somehow these biles are warping your sense of reality. Follow me? Somehow they're screwing up your basic perspective, and the upshot is you sometimes get a little mixed up. That's all."

Doc had gone on to explain that the biles are a kind of glandular substance released during emotional stress. A perfectly normal thing. Like adrenaline, Doc had said. Only instead of producing quick energy, the biles act as a soothing influence, quieting the brain, numbing, counteracting the fear. Doc had listed the physical symptoms: numbness of the extremities in times of extremity; a cloudiness of vision; paralysis of the mental processes that separate what is truly happening from what only might have happened; floatingness; removal; a releasing feeling in the belly; a sense of drifting; a lightness of head.

"Normally," Doc had said, "those are healthy things. But in your case, these biles are . . . well, they're overabundant. They're leaking out, infecting the brain. This Cacciato business—it's the work of the biles. They're flooding your whole system, going to the head and fucking up reality, frying in all the goofy, weird stuff."

So Doc's advice had been to concentrate. When he felt the symptoms, the solution was to concentrate. Concentrate, Doc had said, until you see it's just the biles fogging things over, just a trick of the glands.

Now, facing the night from high in his tower by the sea, Paul Berlin concentrated.

The night did not move. On the beach below, the barbed wire sparkled in moonlight, and the sea made its gentle sounds behind him. The men slept peacefully. Now and then one of them would stir, turning in the dark, but they slept without stop. Oscar slept in his mesh hammock. Eddie and Doc and Harold Murphy slept on the tower floor. Stink Harris and the lieutenant slept side by side, their backs touching. They could sleep and sleep.

Paul Berlin kept the guard. For a long time he looked blankly into the night, inland, concentrating hard on the physical things.

True, he was afraid. Doc was right about that. Even now, with the night calm and unmoving, the fear was there like a kind of background sound that was heard only if listened for. True. But even so, Doc was wrong when he called it dreaming. Biles or no biles, it wasn't dreaming—it wasn't even pretending, not in the strict sense. It was an idea. It was a working out of the possibilities. It wasn't dreaming and it wasn't pretending. It wasn't crazy. Blisters on their feet, streams to be forded and swamps to be circled, dead ends to be opened into passages west. No, it wasn't dreaming. It was a way of asking questions. What became of Cacciato? Where did he go, and why? What were his motives, or did he have motives, and did motives matter? What tricks had he used to keep going? How had he eluded them? How did he slip away into the deep jungle, and how, through the jungle, had they continued the chase? What happened, and what might have happened?

THE OBSERVATION POST

The issue, of course, was courage. How to behave. Whether to flee or fight or seek an accommodation. The issue was not fearlessness. The issue was how to act wisely in spite of fear. Spiting the deep-running biles: that was true courage. He believed this. And he believed the obvious corollary: the greater a man's fear, the greater his potential courage.

Below, the tower's moon shadow stretched far to the south.

Nearly two fifteen now, but he was not tired. Lightheaded, he faced inland and listened. He could recite the separate sounds—a rolling breeze off the sea, the incoming tide, the hum of the radio. The others slept. Stink Harris slept defensively, knees tucked up and arms curled about his head like a beaten boxer. Oscar slept gracefully, spread out, and Eddie Lazzutti slept fitfully, turning and sometimes muttering. Their sleeping was part of the night.

He bent down and did PT by the numbers, counting softly, loosening up around his arms and neck and legs, then he walked twice around the tower's small platform. He was not tired, and not afraid, and the night was not moving.

Leaning against the wall of sandbags, he lit another of Doc's cigarettes. After the war he would stop smoking. Quit, just like that.

He inhaled deeply and held it and enjoyed the puffy tremor it set off in his head.

Yes, the issue was courage. It always had been, even as a kid. Things scared him. He couldn't help it. Noise scared him, dark scared him. Tunnels scared him: the time he almost won the Silver Star for valor. But the real issue was courage. It had nothing to do with the Silver Star . . . Oh, he would've liked winning it, true, but that wasn't the issue. He would've liked showing the medal to his father, the heavy feel of it, looking his father in the eye to show he had been brave, but even that wasn't the real issue. The real issue was the power of will to defeat fear. A matter of figuring a way to do it. Somehow working his way into that secret chamber of the human heart, where, in tangles, lay the circuitry for all that was possible, the full range of what a man might be. He believed, like Doc Peret, that somewhere inside each man is a biological center for the exercise of courage, a piece of tissue that might be touched and sparked and made to respond, a chemical maybe, or a lone chromosome that when made to fire would produce chain reactions of valor that even the biles could not drown. A filament, a fuse, that if ignited would release the full energy of what might be. There was a Silver Star twinkling somewhere inside him.

UPON ALMOST WINNING
THE SILVER STAR

They heard the shot that got Frenchie Tucker, just as Bernie Lynn, a minute later, heard the shot that got himself.

"Somebody's got to go down," said First Lieutenant Sidney Martin, nearly as new to the war as Paul Berlin.

But that was later, too. First they waited. They waited on the chance that Frenchie might come out. Stink and Oscar and Pederson and Vaught and Cacciato waited at the mouth of the tunnel. The others moved off to form a perimeter.

"This here's what happens," Oscar muttered. "When you search the fuckers 'stead of just blowing them and moving on, this here's the final result."

"It's a war," said Sidney Martin.

"Is it really?"

"It is. Shut up and listen."

"A war!" Oscar Johnson said. "The man says we're in a war. You believe that?"

"That's what I tell my folks in letters," Eddie said.

"A war!"

They'd all heard the shot. They'd watched Frenchie go down, a big hairy guy who was scheduled to take the next chopper to the rear to have his blood pressure checked, a big guy who liked talking politics; a great big guy, so he'd been forced to go slowly, wiggling in bit by bit.

"Not me," he'd said. "No way you get me down there. Not Frenchie Tucker."

"You," said Sidney Martin.

"Bullshit," Frenchie said. "I'll get stuck."

"Stuck like a pig," said Stink Harris, and some of the men murmured.

Oscar looked at Sidney Martin. "You want it done," he said, "then do it yourself. Think how good you'll feel afterward. Self-improvement an' all that. A swell fuckin feeling."

But the young lieutenant shook his head. He gazed at Frenchie Tucker and told him it was a matter of going down or getting himself court-martialed. One or the other. So Frenchie swore and took off his pack and boots and socks and helmet, stacked them neatly on a boulder, cussing, taking time, complaining how this would screw up his blood pressure.

They watched him go down. A big cussing guy who had to wiggle his way in. Then they heard the shot.

They waited a long while. Sidney Martin found a flashlight and leaned down into the hole and looked.

And then he said, "Somebody's got to go down."

The men filed away. Bernie Lynn, who stood near the lip of the tunnel, looked aside and mumbled to himself.

"Somebody," the new lieutenant said. "Right now."

Stink Harris shrugged. "Maybe Frenchie's okay. Give him time, you never can tell."

Pederson and Vaught agreed. The feeling of hope caught on, and they told one another it would be all right, Frenchie could take care of himself. Stink said it didn't sound like an AK, anyway. "No crack," he said. "That wasn't an AK."

"Somebody," the lieutenant said. "Somebody's got to."

No one moved.

"Now. Right now."

Stink turned and walked quickly to the perimeter and took off his helmet, threw it down hard and sat on it. He lit a cigarette. Eddie and

Vaught joined him. They all lit cigarettes. Doc Peret opened his medic's pouch and began examining the contents, as if doing inventory, and Pederson and Buff and Rudy Chassler slipped off into the hedges.

"Look," Sidney Martin said. He was tall. Acne scars covered his chin. "I didn't invent this sorry business. But we got a man down there and somebody's got to fetch him. Now."

Stink made a long hooting noise. "Send down the gremlin."

"Who?"

"The gremlin. Send Cacciato down."

Oscar looked at Cacciato, who smiled broadly and began removing his pack.

"Not him," Oscar said.

"Somebody. Make up your mind."

Paul Berlin stood alone. He felt the walls tight against him. He was careful not to look at anyone.

Bernie Lynn swore violently. He dropped his gear where he stood, just let it fall, and he entered the tunnel headfirst. "Fuck it," he kept saying, "fuck it." Bernie had once poured insecticide into Frenchie's canteen. "Fuck it," he kept saying, going down.

His feet were still showing when he was shot. The feet thrashed like a swimmer's feet. Doc and Oscar grabbed hold and yanked him out. The feet were still clean, it happened that fast. He swore and went down headfirst and then was shot a half inch below the throat; they pulled him out by the feet. Not even time to sweat. The dirt fell dry off his arms. His eyes were open. "Holy Moses," he said.

THE THINGS THEY DIDN'T KNOW

"Lui lai, Lui lai!" Stink would scream, pushing them back. *"Lui lai,* you dummies . . . Back up, move!" Teasing ribs with his rifle muzzle, he would force them back against a hootch wall or fence. *"Coi chung!"* he'd holler. Blinking, face white and teeth clicking, he would kick the stragglers, pivot, shove, thumb flicking the rifle's safety catch. "Move! *Lui lai* . . . Move it, go, go!" Herding them together, he would watch to be sure their hands were kept in the open, empty. Then he would open his dictionary. He would read slowly, retracing the words several times, then finally look up. *"Nam xuong dat,"* he'd say. Separating each word, trying for good diction, he would say it in a loud, level voice. "Everybody . . . *nam xuong dat.*" The kids would just stare. The women might rock and moan, or begin chattering among themselves like caged squirrels, glancing up at Stink with frazzled eyes. "Now!" he'd shout. *"Nam xuong dat* . . . Do it!" Sometimes he would fire off a single shot, but this only made the villagers fidget and squirm. Puzzled, some of them would start to giggle. Others would cover their ears and yap with the stiff, short barking sounds of small dogs. It drove Stink wild. *"Nam xuong* the fuck down!" he'd snarl, his thin lips curling in a manner he practiced while shaving. "Lie down! *Man len,* mama-san! Now, goddamn it!" His eyes would bounce from his rifle to the dictionary to the cringing villagers. Behind him, Doc Peret and Oscar Johnson and Buff would be grinning

at the show. They'd given the English-Vietnamese dictionary to Stink as a birthday present, and they loved watching him use it, the way he mixed languages in a kind of stew, ignoring pronunciation and grammar, turning angry when words failed to produce results. "*Nam thi xuong dat!*" he'd bellow, sweating now, his tongue sputtering over the impossible middle syllables. "*Man len,* pronto, you sons of bitches! Haul ass!" But the villagers would only shake their heads and cackle and mill uncertainly. This was too much for Stink Harris. Enraged, he'd throw away the dictionary and rattle off a whole magazine of ammunition. The women would moan. Kids would clutch their mothers, dogs would howl, chickens would scramble in their coops. "*Dong* fuckin' *lat thit!*" Stink would be screaming, his eyes dusty and slit like a snake's. "*Nam xuong dat!* Do it, you ignorant bastards!" Reloading, he would keep firing and screaming, and the villagers would sprawl in the dust, arms wrapped helplessly around their heads. And when they were all down, Stink would stop firing. He would smile. He would glance at Doc Peret and nod. "See there? They understand me fine. *Nam xuong dat* . . . Lie down. I'm gettin' the hang of it. You just got to punctuate your sentences."

Not knowing the language, they did not know the people. They did not know what the people loved or respected or feared or hated. They did not recognize hostility unless it was patent, unless it came in a form other than language; the complexities of tone and tongue were beyond them. Dinkese, Stink Harris called it: monkey chatter, bird talk. Not knowing the language, the men did not know whom to trust. Trust was lethal. They did not know false smiles from true smiles, or if in Quang Ngai a smile had the same meaning it had in the States. "Maybe the dinks got things mixed up," Eddie once said, after the time a friendly-looking farmer bowed and smiled and pointed them into a minefield. "Know what I mean? Maybe . . . well, maybe the gooks cry when they're happy and smile when they're sad. Who the hell knows? Maybe when you smile over here it means you're ready to cut the other guy's throat. I mean, hey . . . didn't they tell us way back in AIT that this here's a different culture?" Not knowing the people, they did not know friends from enemies. They did not know if it was a popular war, or, if popular, in what sense. They did not know if the people of Quang Ngai viewed the war stoically, as it sometimes seemed, or with grief, as it seemed other times, or with bewilderment or greed or partisan fury. It was impossible to know. They did not know religions or philosophies or theories of justice. More than that, they did not know how emotions worked in Quang Ngai. Twenty years of war had rotted away the ordinary reactions to death and disfigurement. Astonishment, the first response, was never there in the faces of Quang Ngai. Disguised, maybe. But who knew? Who ever knew? Emotions and beliefs and attitudes, motives and aims, hopes—these were unknown to the men in Alpha Company, and Quang Ngai told nothing. "Fuckin beasties," Stink would croak, mimicking the frenzied village speech. "No shit, I seen hamsters with more feelings."

But for Paul Berlin it was always a nagging question: Who were these skinny, blank-eyed people? What did they want? The kids especially—watching them, learning their names and faces, Paul Berlin couldn't help wondering. It was a ridiculous, impossible puzzle, but even so he wondered. Did the kids *like* him? A little girl with gold hoops in her ears and ugly scabs on her brow—did she feel, as he did, goodness and warmth and poignancy when he helped Doc dab iodine on her sores? Beyond that, though, did the girl *like* him? Lord knows, he had no villainy in his heart, no motive but kindness. He wanted health for her, and happiness. Did she know this? Did she sense his compassion? When she smiled, was it more than a token? And . . . and what *did* she want? Any of them, what did they long for? Did they have secret hopes? His hopes? Could this little girl—her eyes squinting as Doc brushed the scabs with iodine, her lips sucked in, her nose puckering at the smell—could she somehow separate him from the war? Even for an instant? Could she see him as just a scared-silly boy from Iowa? Could she feel sympathy? In it together, trapped, you and me, all of us: Did she feel that? Could she understand his own fear, matching it with hers? Wondering, he put mercy in his eyes like lighted candles; he gazed at the girl, full-hearted, draining out suspicion, opening himself to whatever she might answer with. Did the girl see the love? Could she understand it, return it? But he didn't know. He did not know if love or its analogue even existed in the vocabulary of Quang Ngai, or if friendship could be translated. He simply did not know. He wanted to be liked. He wanted them to understand, all of them, that he felt no hate. It was all a sad accident, he would have told them—chance, high-level politics, confusion. He had no stake in the war beyond simple survival; he was there, in Quang Ngai, for the same reasons they were: the luck of the draw, bad fortune, forces beyond reckoning. His intentions were benign. By God, yes! He was snared in a web as powerful and tangled as any that victimized the people of My Khe or Pinkville. Sure, they were trapped, just as injured. He would have told them that. He was no tyrant, no pig, no Yankee killer. He was innocent. Yes, he was. He was innocent. He would have told them that, the villagers, if he'd known the language, if there had been time to talk. He would have told them he wanted to harm no one. Not even the enemy. The enemy! A word, a crummy word. He *had* no enemies. He had wronged no one. If he'd known the language, he would have told them how he hated to see the villages burned. Hated to see the paddies trampled. How it made him angry and sad when . . . a million things, when women were frisked with free hands, when old men were made to drop their pants to be searched, when, in a ville called Thin Mau, Oscar and Rudy Chassler shot down ten dogs for the sport of it. Sad and stupid. Crazy. Mean-spirited and self-defeating and wrong. Wrong! He would have told them this, the kids especially. But not me, he would have told them. The others, maybe, but not me. Guilty perhaps of hanging on, of letting myself be dragged along, of falling victim to gravity and obligation and events, but not—not!—guilty of wrong intentions.

After the war, perhaps, he might return to Quang Ngai. Years and years afterward. Return to track down the girl with the gold hoops through her ears. Bring along an interpreter. And then, with the war ended, history decided, he would explain to her why he had let himself go to war. Not because of strong convictions, but because he didn't know. He didn't know who was right, or what was right; he didn't know if it was a war of self-determination or self-destruction, outright aggression or national liberation; he didn't know which speeches to believe, which books, which politicians; he didn't know if nations would topple like dominoes or stand separate like trees; he didn't know who really started the war, or why, or when, or with what motives; he didn't know if it mattered; he saw sense in both sides of the debate, but he did not know where truth lay; he didn't know if Communist tyranny would prove worse in the long run than the tyrannies of Ky or Thieu or Khanh—he simply didn't know. And who did? Who really did? He couldn't make up his mind. Oh, he had read the newspapers and magazines. He wasn't stupid. He wasn't uninformed. He just didn't know if the war was right or wrong. And who did? Who really *knew*? So he went to the war for reasons beyond knowledge. Because he believed in law, and law told him to go. Because it was a democracy, after all, and because LBJ and the others had rightful claim to their offices. He went to the war because it was expected. Because not to go was to risk censure, and to bring embarrassment on his father and his town. Because, not knowing, he saw no reason to distrust those with more experience. Because he loved his country and more, more than that, because he trusted it. Yes, he did. Oh, he would rather have fought with his father in France, knowing certain things certainly, but he couldn't choose his war, nobody could. Was this so banal? Was this so unprofound and stupid? He would look the little girl with gold earrings straight in the eye. He would tell her those things. He would ask her to see the matter his way. What would *she* have done? What would *anyone* have done, not knowing? And then he would ask the girl questions. What did she want? How did she see the war? What were her aims—peace, any peace, peace with dignity? Did she refuse to run for the same reasons he refused—obligation, family, the land, friends, home? And now? Now, war ended, what did she want? Peace and quiet? Peace and pride? Peace with mashed potatoes and Swiss steak and vegetables, a full-tabled peace, indoor plumbing, a peace with Oldsmobiles and Hondas and skyscrapers climbing from the fields, a peace of order and harmony and murals on public buildings? Were her dreams the dreams of ordinary men and women? Quality-of-life dreams? Material dreams? Did she want a long life? Did she want medicine when she was sick, food on the table and reserves in the pantry? Religious dreams? What? What did she *aim* for? If a wish were to be granted by the war's winning army—any wish—what would she choose? Yes! If

LBJ and Ho were to rub their magic lanterns at war's end, saying, "Here is what it was good for, here is the fruit," what would Quang Ngai demand? Justice? What sort? Reparations? What kind? Answers? What were the questions: What did Quang Ngai want to know?

In September, Paul Berlin was called before the battalion promotion board.

"You'll be asked some questions," the first sergeant said. "Answer them honestly. Don't for Chrissake make it complicated—just good, honest answers. And get a fuckin haircut."

It was a three-officer panel. They sat like squires behind a tin-topped table, two in sunglasses, the third in skintight tiger fatigues.

Saluting, reporting with his name and rank, Paul Berlin stood at attention until he was told to be seated.

"Berlin," said one of the officers in sunglasses. "That's a pretty fucked-up name, isn't it?"

Paul Berlin smiled and waited.

The officer licked his teeth. He was a plump, puffy-faced major with spotted skin. "No bull, that's got to be the weirdest name I ever run across. Don't sound American. You an American, soldier?"

"Yes, sir."

"Yeah? Then where'd you get such a screwy name?"

"I don't know, sir."

"Sheeet." The major looked at the captain in tiger fatigues. "You hear that? This trooper don't know where he got his own name. You ever promoted somebody who don't know how he got his own fuckin name?"

"Maybe he forgot," said the captain in the tiger fatigues.

"Amnesia?"

"Could be. Or maybe shell shock or something. Better ask again."

The major sucked his dentures halfway out of his mouth, frowned, then let the teeth slide back into place. "Can't hurt nothin'. Okay, soldier, one more time—where'd you find that name of yours?"

"Inherited it, sir. From my father."

"You crappin' me?"

"No, sir."

"And just where the hell'd he come up with it . . . your ol' man?"

"I guess from his father, sir. It came down the line sort of." Paul Berlin hesitated. It was hard to tell if the man was serious.

"You a Jewboy, soldier?"

"No, sir."

"A Kraut! Berlin . . . by jiminy, that's a Jerry name if I ever heard one!"

"I'm mostly Dutch."

"The hell, you say."

"Yes, sir."

"Balls!"

"Sir, it's not—"

"Where's Berlin?"

"Sir?"

The major leaned forward, planting his elbows carefully on the table. He looked deadly serious. "I asked where Berlin is. You heard of fuckin Berlin, didn't you? Like in East Berlin, West Berlin?"

"Sure, sir. It's in Germany."

"Which one?"

"Which what, sir?"

The major moaned and leaned back. Beside him, indifferent to it all, the captain in tiger fatigues unwrapped a thin cigar and lit it with a kitchen match. Red acne covered his face like the measles. He winked quickly—maybe it wasn't even a wink—then gazed hard at a sheaf of papers. The third officer sat silently. He hadn't moved since the interview began.

"Look here," the major said. "I don't know if you're dumb or just stupid, but by God I aim to find out." He removed his sunglasses. Surprisingly, his eyes were almost jolly. "You're up for Spec Four, that right?"

"Yes, sir."

"You want it? The promotion?"

"Yes, sir, I do."

"Lots of responsibility."

Paul Berlin smiled. He couldn't help it.

"So we can't have shitheads leadin' men, can we? Takes some brains. You got brains, Berlin?"

"Yes, *sir*."

"You know what a condom is?"

Paul Berlin nodded.

"A condom," the major intoned solemnly, "is a skullcap for us swingin' dicks. Am I right?"

"Yes, sir."

"And to lead men you got to be a swingin' fuckin dick."

"Right, sir."

"And is that you? You a swingin' dick, Berlin?"

"Yes, sir!"

"You got guts?"

"Yes, sir. I—"

"You 'fraid of gettin' zapped?"

"No, sir."

"Sheeet." The major grinned as if having scored an important victory. He used the tip of his pencil to pick a speck of food from between his teeth. "Dumb! Anybody not scared of gettin' his ass zapped is a dummy. You know what a dummy is?"

"Yes, sir."

"Spell it."

Paul Berlin spelled it.

The major rapped his pencil against the table, then glanced at his wristwatch. The captain in tiger fatigues was smoking with his eyes closed; the third officer, still silent, stared blankly ahead, arms folded tight against his chest.

"Okay," said the major, "we got a few standard-type questions for you. Just answer 'em truthfully, no bullshit. You don't know the answers, say so. One thing I can't stand is wishy-washy crap. Ready?"

"Yes, sir."

Pulling out a piece of yellow paper, the major put his pencil down and read slowly.

"How many stars we got in the flag?"

"Fifty," said Paul Berlin.

"How many stripes?"

"Thirteen."

"What's the muzzle velocity of a standard AR-15?"

"Two thousand feet a second."

"Who's Secretary of the Army?"

"Stanley Resor."

"Why we fightin' this war?"

"Sir?"

"I say, why we fightin' this fuckin-ass war?"

"I don't—"

"To win it," said the third, silent officer. He did not move. His arms remained flat across his chest, his eyes blank. "We fight this war to win it, that's why."

"Yes, sir."

"Again," the major said. "Why we fightin' this war?"

"To win it, sir."

"You sure of that?"

"Positive, sir." His arms were hot. He tried to hold his chin level.

"Tell it loud, trooper. Why we fightin' this war?"

"To win it."

"Yeah, but I mean *why*?"

"Just to win it," Paul Berlin said softly. "That's all. To win it."

"You know that for a fact?"

"Yes, sir. A fact."

The third officer made a soft, humming sound of satisfaction. The major grinned at the captain in tiger fatigues.

"All right," said the major. His eyes twinkled. "Maybe you aren't so dumb as you let on. *Maybe.* We got one last question. This here's a cultural-type matter . . . listen up close. What effect would the death of Ho Chi Minh have on the population of North Vietnam?"

"Sir?"

Reading slowly from his paper, the major repeated it. "What effect would the death of Ho Chi Minh have on the population of North Vietnam?"

Paul Berlin let his chin fall. He smiled.

"Reduce it by one, sir."

·   ·   ·

In Quang Ngai, they did not speak of politics. It wasn't taboo, or bad luck, it just wasn't talked about. Even when the Peace Talks bogged down in endless bickering over the shape and size of the bargaining table, the men in Alpha Company took it as another bad joke—silly and sad—and there was no serious discussion about it, no sustained outrage. Diplomacy and morality were beyond them. Hardly anyone cared. Not even Doc Peret, who loved a good debate. Not even Jim Pederson, who believed in virtue. This dim-sighted attitude enraged Frenchie Tucker. "My God," he'd sometimes moan in exasperation, speaking to Paul Berlin but aiming at everyone, "it's your *ass* they're negotiating. Your ass, my ass . . . Do we live or die? That's the issue, by God, and you blockheads don't even talk about it. Not even a lousy *opinion*! Good Lord, doesn't it piss you off, all this Peace Talk crap? Round tables, square tables! Idiotic diplomatic etiquette, power plays, maneuvering! And here we sit, suckin' air while those mealy-mouthed sons of bitches can't even figure out what kind of table they're gonna sit at. Jesus!" But Frenchie's rage never caught on. Sometimes there were jokes, cynical and weary, but there was no serious discussion. They fought the war, but no one took sides.

They did not even know the simple things: a sense of victory, or satisfaction, or necessary sacrifice. They did not know the feeling of taking a place and keeping it, securing a village and then raising the flag and calling it a victory. No sense of order or momentum. No front, no rear, no trenches laid out in neat parallels. No Patton rushing for the Rhine, no beachheads to storm and win and hold for the duration. They did not have targets. They did not have a cause. They did not know if it was a war of ideology or economics or hegemony or spite. On a given day, they did know where they were in Quang Ngai, or how being there might influence larger outcomes. They did not know the names of most villages. They did not know which villages were critical. They did not know strategies. They did not know the terms of the war, its architecture, the rules of fair play. When they took prisoners, which was rare, they did not know the questions to ask, whether to release a suspect or beat on him. They did not know how to feel. Whether, when seeing a dead Vietnamese, to be happy or sad or relieved; whether, in times of quiet, to be apprehensive or content; whether to engage the enemy or elude him. They did not know how to feel when they saw villages burning. Revenge? Loss? Peace of mind or anguish? They did not know. They knew the old myths about Quang Ngai—tales passed down from old-timer to newcomer—but they did not know which stories to believe. Magic, mystery, ghosts and incense, whispers in the dark, strange tongues and strange smells, uncertainties never articulated in war stories, squandered on ignorance. They did not know good from evil.

4

First Wave
of Major Films

Eddie Adams's Pulitzer Prize–winning photo of South Vietnamese
general Nguyen Ngoc Loan executing a suspected Viet Cong.

While TV and the print media made the war inescapable, and in fact, a staple of their daily coverage, during the actual fighting Hollywood pointedly ignored Vietnam. Between the Marines landing at Da Nang in 1965 and the final withdrawal of ground troops in 1973, the major studios released exactly one Vietnam combat film, John Wayne's *The Green Berets.*

Unlike its source, Robin Moore's novel, *The Green Berets* (1968) is an unashamedly gung-ho melodrama that justifies the U.S. presence and methods on the grounds of a single VC atrocity. It is, in a sense, an old-style John Wayne Western with the Viet Cong playing the role of the savage and justly defeated Indians. The American soldiers are tough, gutsy, and heroic, the South Vietnamese incompetents and victims, the Communists vicious, good only for cannon fodder. As in his World War II films, Wayne is portrayed as the professional soldier, even more so than Robin Moore's portrait of the character Sven Kornie.

The mode of storytelling the film purports to use is documentary realism, though big production Hollywood style. Through LBJ himself, Wayne secured the help of the Army in making the film, hoping, one supposes, that their consultants and hardware would give the film an authenticity impossible to match. And it's true that some of the action sequences look good. But the movie is cliché-ridden, right down to the cute orphan Wayne befriends, and by 1968 the American media—if not the public at large—understood that the war wasn't a matter of circling the wagons and breaking out superior firepower. The movie met a scathing critical reception, and though the theme song, Barry Sadler's "The Ballad of the Green Berets," topped the *Billboard* chart for a few weeks, the movie was widely picketed, generally vilified and quickly forgotten. Gustav Hasford's ironic treatment of the film in his book *The Short-Timers* is completely deserved.

The Vietnam War inspired no *Casablanca*, nor even a *Pork Chop Hill*. Hollywood's silence was notable, broken only rarely by allegories disguised as politically enlightened westerns (*Little Big Man*) or as other wars (*M*A*S*H, Catch-22, Patton*). Perhaps the studios thought America could no longer be sold war as adventure or war as a moral duty in the same way World War II and even Korea were sold. At the same time, they were too timid to try an outright anti-Vietnam war movie, and so through the mid-seventies, the only movies that dealt in any way with the Vietnam War were a series of schlock films about crazed returned vets, usually linked in some way to motorcycle gangs. Whether heroes like Billy Jack or antiheroes like *Taxi Driver's* Travis Bickle, in the end these vets let loose their rage and skills in a bloody and satisfying climax, just as Rambo would a decade later. It was an easy demonization of vets, portraying them as outsiders prone to violence, sometimes implicitly blaming them for the loss of the war, and for years after, this stereotype would hold sway.

Some critics, most notably John Hellman in *American Myth and the Legacy of Vietnam*, have argued that the *Star Wars* trilogy (beginning 1977) can be read as an analogy for the younger generation trying to regain American innocence and power from their corrupt fathers. Others cite Akira Kurosawa's *The Hidden Fortress* (1958) as George Lucas's source for the series, laying out an interesting list of similarities between post-war Japan and America after the fall of Saigon and the need to replace irreparably damaged national myths. How much of the possible allegory was actually apprehended by moviegoers, or is now, a year after the triumphant first run of the re-released trilogy, is another question.

But back then, after the shame of Nixon, the conciliation of Ford, and the hoopla of the Bicentennial, the climate of the Carter administration was decidedly self-analytic, if not self-loathing, as the first wave of major books attests. A colder self-regard replaced the confusion and ardor of the late sixties and early seventies. The economy stumbled. American foreign policy was less strident, matching that of the Russians, whose offer of détente the State Department cautiously embraced, all the while keeping an eye on (and a hand in) El Salvador, Nicaragua, and Afghanistan. The loudest policy decision the Carter administration made with respect to Vietnam was to extend amnesty to draft resisters, a rare official admission that perhaps the war was wrong. That Carter could implement this policy over the objections of the military only a few years after the final withdrawal of ground troops—while veterans' health concerns such as Agent Orange were routinely ignored—is a rough barometer of popular opinion. In this relatively anti-Vietnam, antiwar, antimilitary climate, the long-awaited first wave of major films arrived.

After the war, the first major studio release directly addressing Vietnam was supposed to be Francis Ford Coppola's *Apocalypse Now*. At the time Coppola was riding high, coming off *The Conversation*, *The Godfather*, and *Godfather II*, as well as producing *American Graffiti*. Technically brilliant as well as a reasonably aware social critic, Coppola seemed equal to the task. In the spring of 1976 he took his entire cast and crew into the Philippine jungle, expecting to emerge by fall with his adaptation of Joseph Conrad's *Heart of Darkness*, a major statement about Man and Evil and The War.

Months passed. Coppola fired his star, Harvey Keitel, and replaced him with Martin Sheen. He was already millions over budget when a typhoon struck, destroying his major sets. The helicopters he'd rented from dictator Ferdinand Marcos's air force regularly heeled off during shots, called away to fight the Communist rebels in the south. United Artists refused to bankroll him anymore, and Coppola himself had to raise the cash to keep going. The monsoons came, and still it wasn't done. Sheen had a heart attack. Rumor was, Coppola didn't have an ending, that he was improvising, hoping to stumble onto something. The messy epic became an industry joke, *Apocalypse Later*, *Apocalypse Never*.

Meanwhile, Michael Cimino delivered *The Deer Hunter* to Universal, who rushed it into theaters. An ex-Marine (though not a Vietnam vet), Cimino had previously cowritten the second Dirty Harry film, *Magnum Force*, with John Milius (who shares writing credits with Coppola for *Apocalypse Now*), and directed another Clint Eastwood vehicle, *Thunderbolt and Lightfoot*. With these meager credits, he seemed an unlikely candidate to pull off an ambitious and thoughtful film about Vietnam, and yet *The Deer Hunter* became—nearly immediately—the best known and most widely talked about Vietnam film until *Platoon*.

The Deer Hunter follows three friends—Michael (Robert DeNiro, who played Travis Bickle), Nick (Christopher Walken), and Steven (John Savage)—from their hometown of Clairton, Pennsylyania, to the jungles of Vietnam and back home again. Surprisingly little time is spent in Vietnam; rather, Cimino and his scenarist, Deric Washburn, concentrate on how these men fit into the community before and after their part in the war.

The film opens on a truck barreling through the early-morning darkness, its smokestacks throwing sparks. Cimino then takes us into the fiery violence of a steel mill, all noise and heat. The shift ends, and our major players emerge from the bawdy male camaraderie of the locker room into the parking lot, where they pile into Michael's white whale of a Cadillac. Cut to Steven's bride, Angela (Rutanya Alda), in her gown, looking at herself in a mirror; she turns in profile, smooths the fabric over her growing belly. Steven's mother makes a veiled complaint about this to a priest, who ignores her.

The storyline seems simple: After Steven and Angela's wedding, the other men are going to go deer hunting with their friends one last time before shipping off to Vietnam. But rather than briefly summarize these events—say, with a montage—Cimino walks us through the wedding preparations, then the wedding itself, the reception (a huge, bravura set piece in which we see Michael's attraction to Nick's girlfriend Linda [Meryl Streep]), and, in the same basic sequence, the preparations for the hunt, the hunt itself, and the aftermath. By the time we segue to Vietnam (through the same match-on-action ceiling fan Coppola opens *Apocalypse Now* with), the major concerns of the film are solidly in place.

The Vietnam section opens with a chaotic assault on a village. Michael watches as a VC kills a bunkerful of helpless villagers. In a scene that recalls the iconography of World War II, Michael torches him with a flamethrower. The fighting ends, and by coincidence, Nick and Stevie show up; Michael walks right by them, oblivious.

The three men are captured by the VC and kept in half-submerged tiger cages. The VC force them to play Russian roulette, and Michael, following his dictum of "there's no such thing as a sure thing," gambles with their lives and wins, though at a high price for both Nick and Stevie. They escape, though Nick is so damaged by his experience that he can't bring himself to get back in touch with Linda. He wanders Tu Do Street until he finds a paying game of Russian roulette run by a sinister Frenchman.

Michael returns home alone. Linda has organized a party for him, but, like Nick, Michael can't seem to reconnect, and asks the taxi driver to go on. The next morning, when all his friends have left, Michael visits Linda, and the two awkwardly try to comfort each other. We find out Steven is in a VA hospital and refuses to come home, and that Angela is nearly catatonic with grief. Michael tries to blend in with the old gang, except he's different now ("I feel a lot of distance") and wears his dress greens everywhere. Everyone still looks to him as the leader, the hero, but when the men go hunting again, Michael seems to relinquish his "one shot" philosophy of hunting (and life), calling "Okay" to the sky as he stands by a thundering waterfall.

After this, Linda succeeds in taking Michael to bed, and soon Michael tries to bring first Stevie and then Nick back from their separate limbos. Stevie flatly tells him, "I don't want to go home. I don't fit." Nick seems to be in Hell; Michael has to take a punt through flaming water to reach the final game of Russian roulette. When he gets there, Nick doesn't recognize him. Michael begs him to "come home . . . home," and talks about "the trees," which Nick earlier said were what he liked about the hunt: "the way the trees are." For an instant it seems Nick remembers, but what he remembers is Michael's now outmoded philosophy. Nick smiles and says, "One shot," and blows his brains out. From this Cimino cuts to actual footage of Hueys being tossed over the side of an aircraft carrier to make room for more refugees. The war—for America, at least—is over.

Back home, we go to Nick's funeral, the mill chuffing out clouds in the background, only a single spindly tree in the churchyard. At the bar, John (George Dzundza), who has always brought the community together with food and drink and song, cooks them breakfast. Tearfully, he breaks into "God Bless America," and the rest sing along with him. The End.

Emotionally, the movie is undeniably powerful. The Clairton scenes are shot with a patient and gritty realism, which makes Cimino's melodramatic Vietnam scenes all the more strange. Two of the most gripping scenes in the film involve Russian roulette, first as a form of torture by the VC, and second as a spectacle or game run in the back streets of Saigon. Neither has any historical validity, and so it seems apparent that Cimino is using it as a metaphor for U.S. involvement in Vietnam, both collectively and individually. He also substitutes the snow-capped Cascades for the hills of western Pennsylvania and gives us the wrong kind of deer for the area; in addition, the time scheme is a wreck, Michael going back as Saigon falls (1975), meaning he's been wearing his dress greens for at least two years. Surely Cimino was invoking poetic license, yet contemporary critics were baffled by these slips, asking for a monolithic realism. Even more worrisome to them was Cimino's portrayal of the Vietnamese.

In *The Deer Hunter*, the VC are plainly evil, killing civilians and playing games with American lives, and the South Vietnamese aren't much better. We see them as whores and black marketeers, allies unworthy of our help. The movie, critics said, seems to blame Vietnam for what it's done to America rather than vice versa, and in this they saw *The Deer Hunter* as apologist and prowar. Furthermore, with its allusion to James Fenimore Cooper's *The Deerslayer*, the film thrusts Michael into the role of frontier hero, lone protector of society from the savage natives, half outcast himself. They saw the Russian roulette torture sequence and escape as part of an overall captivity narrative, in which the Americans—especially Nick—are martyred.

(Others see it as a Western, with the escape a card game turned shootout, the wedding reception some kind of saloon, complete with dance-hall girls.) Some went on to say that the innocent, close-knit, religious-based community Cimino gives us is false and idealized, that Cimino seems to be celebrating—especially in the final "God Bless America" scene—a sentimentalized America that simply doesn't exist. Where are the protesters? they asked.

Now, twenty years later, it's hard to understand how critics missed what Cimino is trying to say about the individual and community. The institutions he's accused of celebrating are all exposed, at best, as precarious. Linda is beaten by her drunken father. The priest refuses to listen to Steven's mother, and so the church sanctifies a marriage in which the bride is pregnant by another man. Stan punches his girlfriend at the wedding reception. Michael is forced to admit that his hunter's philosophy of "one shot" (possibly a metaphor for American foreign policy) doesn't work. Linda and Michael together are unfaithful to Nick. Michael's big-finned Cadillac, a stand-in for American prestige, slowly rusts and falls apart. In brief exteriors, we're shown lonely people drinking outside the church, shut-ins peering from their windows. Throughout the film, we're given examples of characters separated from the community (including all three friends), their exile often self-imposed. With all the talk about "home," almost no scenes actually take place in someone's home. And the version of "God Bless America" the friends sing in the end is a dirge, with all of the characters painfully aware of the price they've paid.

As for being a prowar film, certainly the fate of the three friends refutes that. Like the frontier hero and the United States, Michael discovers that his power to beat the odds—his mastery—has limits. Michael wins every game he plays, including, tragically, his final round of Russian roulette with Nick. The charges of being anti-Vietnamese may stick; Cimino, like so many other American authors and directors, isn't concerned with the Vietnamese, only the war's effect on America. It could be said that, like Caputo in *A Rumor of War*, Cimino paints his three heroes as innocents who can't bear the evil that Vietnam is. And yet, in his portrayal of Tu Do Street and the Wall Street–like pit of the Russian roulette arena (the men in Western suits, boxes of Kimbies piled in the background), Cimino appears to accuse America of contaminating Vietnamese culture. As usual, the viewer is left to determine whether *The Deer Hunter* celebrates or tests our national myths.

In terms of types, Cimino gives us a few veterans we've seen before. Michael fits the professional soldier category early on, and the troubled loner vet later. Stevie is at first the reluctant soldier and later the disabled vet, and Nick, in the end, is a bona fide psychotic and drug addict. All are portrayed as victims of the war, an improvement from the crazed bikers of the early-seventies films. But despite the fine performances of DeNiro and Walken, they still seem rather two-dimensional, emblems rather than fully rounded characters.

The common storyline of the vet trying to return to society through the love of a woman is present in Linda and Michael, with the interesting variation that Linda is the instigator. This is neatly underlined by the mismatch of Angela and Stevie. Axel's caveman routine and Stan's ridiculous notions of masculinity fit well into an examination of what it means to be a man or a woman in this society. *The Deer Hunter* takes on a great deal beyond the obvious metaphor of the hunt. Other themes include the correlation of luck and gambling, nature versus technology, fire and water, music as a communal bond, religious ritual, and the various uses of alcohol. If Cimino sometimes strays too far from realism—say, in Michael's descent into hell with the satanic Frenchman—his extended metaphors also dramatize many of the complexities of the war.

While some critics panned *The Deer Hunter* on political or aesthetic grounds, the movie did well at the box office and impressed most people as a serious (perhaps too serious) and thoughtful if muddled attempt to put the war into perspective. Reaction from veterans was mixed; some found the Vietnam sequences unconvincing, if not ridiculous. Yet one veteran, Jan Scruggs, found the movie so compelling that after seeing it he decided to build a monument to the men and women who served; only four years later, he presided over the dedication of the Vietnam Veterans' Memorial in Washington, D.C.—what we now call the Wall. Even liberal Hollywood realized *The Deer Hunter*'s strengths. It won the Oscar for best picture,

Cimino won for best director, and Christopher Walken won for best supporting actor. It could have won more—DeNiro and Streep were both strong nominees—except that suddenly 1978 had become the year of the Vietnam movie; the best actor and actress awards were taken by Jon Voight and Jane Fonda, the stars of the unabashedly antiwar *Coming Home.*

While *The Deer Hunter* focuses on small-town America and community using what could be misinterpreted as a realistic slice-of-life approach, Hal Ashby's *Coming Home* looks at a typical Hollywood subject, the individual looking for a true self through loving another in a scenic, even fairy-tale locale.

Coming Home starts with a roomful of disabled vets playing pool in a VA hospital. Many of the actors in the scene were in fact disabled vets—another attempt to establish authenticity. Their seemingly aimless conversation rolls around to the question "Would you go back?" They all agree that they wouldn't, that there was no point—all but one man (a professional actor, notably), whose hesitant and half-formed explanations move no one. He's easily refuted and ridiculed by the others.

Cut to Bob (Bruce Dern) jogging through an Army base to the Stones' "Out of Time" ("You're obsolete, my baby."). We crosscut between the embittered, wise vets and Bob, finally ending up in the officers' club, where Bob smarmily tells a friend who's shipping out to Vietnam with him that his wife, Sally (Jane Fonda), "doesn't understand it all." Bob, an officer, sees the war as "an opportunity." An acquaintance's death is "an embarrassment," presumably to the Army as a whole. The scene, juxtaposed with the disabled vets, indicts the Army in general and more specifically the career officer for being out of touch.

As Bob leaves for Vietnam, Sally gives him a ring, which he vows he'll never take off. The buses pull out, and Sally is left behind with Vi (Penelope Milford), the girlfriend of Bob's buddy. They have a drink, and we see how square Sally is compared to the unmarried, somewhat hip Vi. Vi's only here because her brother Billy's in the VA hospital; he went crazy in Vietnam.

Inspired by Vi, and with nothing else to do, Sally volunteers to work at the hospital. She meets Luke (Jon Voight), a paraplegic vet we've seen in the opening shot. He's feisty and bitter, and, as fate would have it, he was the quarterback and big man on campus at Sally's high school. He's cool where Sally's uptight. They quarrel over Luke's attitude, but soon, because of how uncaring the VA hospital staff are, Sally becomes friends with him, and she begins to understand the plight of these men and how awful the war is. Meanwhile, she's moved off the base to a beach house and bought a Porsche roadster; even her hair has become frizzy and more natural, no longer the coiffed bonnet of the Army wife. In short, she's becoming hip, something we know will be a problem when square old Bob comes back.

Quickly, Sally and Luke fall in love. But Sally's torn; she's always been faithful. Bob writes and tells her and Vi to meet him and his buddy in Hong Kong for R&R, but Vi can't leave her brother, so Sally goes alone. Bob's buddy is furious. Much is made of the difference between being a girlfriend (free-willed) and a wife (seemingly a piece of property, under orders).

In a classic laying-out of the gap between vets and civilians, Bob goes on about how he's tired of hearing "all this bullshit about Nam," and dutiful Sally says, "I'd like to know what's it's like." "TV shows what it's like," Bob mutters. "It sure as hell don't show what it is." Later, in the hotel room, Bob incredulously tells Sally how his men chopped off heads and stuck them on poles to scare the VC. Sally's mute response as the Stones play "Sympathy for the Devil" seems to seal the gap.

Back in the United States, Luke is about to indulge his wounded manhood in a hooker when he gets a call from the hospital. Vi's brother Billy, whom Luke befriended earlier (in an example of only fellow vets understanding what another vet has been through), is attempting to commit suicide by shooting air into his veins. Luke races over in his Mustang GT, but he's too late. In protest, he chains himself and his wheelchair to the gate of the Marine depot.

Meanwhile, Vi has found out about Billy and—in her sorrow— heads off to a go-go club with Sally, where the two get picked up by two nerdy guys. Vi gets drunk and nearly does a striptease in the men's hotel room before breaking down weeping. In the lobby, they see Luke on the news. Sally is so moved that she spends the night with Luke. He's nervous, she's tender, and Sally has her first orgasm.

It's love, and the two, sometimes with Vi in tow, frolic along the beach. Sally takes Luke into her beach house, and Luke lets Sally look at his slides of Vietnam. He shows her tunnels, a buddy who didn't make it, a picture of some Vietnamese kids ("They're a pretty people," he says.) Suddenly, the sheltered Army wife is braless and drinking beer on the beach.

But the FBI has them under surveillance because of Luke's protest, and Bob is coming back because he's been shot in the leg. Luke warns Sally that "whatever he says it's a hundred times worse than what he can tell you."

The lovers part, and Bob returns, hobbling. "What the hell did you do to your hair?" he asks, though the Porsche impresses him. As in *The Deer Hunter*, a banner welcomes the hero home, but the party never starts. Vi wants Bob to tell the story of his leg wound, but Bob refuses. It's boring, "just like this whole fucking war is boring." He gets angry, claiming that he tripped and shot himself; "It was an accident!" he says, and we're left to decide whether he actually did it to leave the war. He goes out to drink with some Army buddies, then brings them back hours later, smashed. They sit around the beach house making brutal jokes about women.

The FBI summons Bob and tells him about Sally and Luke. Enraged, he comes back to the beach house and fixes a bayonet in the garage before hunting down Sally. First Bob and Sally face off, Sally stalling with "I've been wanting to talk to you. You seem so far away from me since you've been back." Bob counters with "How can they give you a medal for a war they don't even want you to fight?" as well as "I don't belong here," and "Get back, slope cunt."

Luke arrives to intervene. "I can understand," he says, "because I'm a brother." And later, "I'm not the enemy. Maybe the enemy is the fucking war." And "You've got enough ghosts to carry around."

"I'm fucked," Bob says, then whines, "I just wanna be a hero, that's all."

Later, Bob receives his apparently unearned Purple Heart. Meanwhile, Luke's TV appearance has made him a local celebrity, and a high school asks him to speak on the war. A spit-and-polish Marine precedes him, then Luke comes on and tells the kids how it really is.

Cut to Bob on the beach, wearing his dress uniform, staring blankly at the waves. Crosscut back to Luke. Bob starts to strip as Tim Buckley's maudlin "Once I Was a Soldier" plays. Luke gets emotional, tells the kids, "I'm tellin' ya it ain't like in the movies," and Bob takes off his ring and runs naked toward the waves. "There's a lot of shit that I did over there that I find fucking hard to live with," Luke says. "I don't feel sorry for myself. All I'm saying is there's a choice to be made here." Bob swims away. The last shot is Sally and Vi going into a supermarket, a cigarette-ad sticker on the door ironically saying *Lucky OUT*.

Coming Home was a massive success on all counts, reaping solid reviews, doing well at the box office, and garnering its stars the best actor and actress Oscars. While some critics took issue with its use of melodrama, few if any argued with its politics or its representation of the veteran.

The mode here is a strict—even dull—Hollywood realism. Present again are the themes of bitterness and alienation, the gap, the return to society through the love of a woman (and the enlightenment of a woman through the love of an antiwar veteran). At times the feminist message of the film overshadows its concerns about Vietnam. Sally's character is the only one with choices, her self-realization the real arc of the narrative. Bruce Dern's Bob is dim before the war and psychotic after. Luke is too typically the disabled protest vet, his situation copied, it seems, from Kovic's *Born on the Fourth of July*, but with fulfilling sex and a pat validation of his antiwar philosophy. In a film that ends with a major character telling us there's a choice to be made, the moral and political issues of the war are mostly ignored.

But perhaps most striking is the appearance of Jane Fonda in a fiction film about Vietnam. During the war she was a vocal opponent of U.S. policy—maybe *the* most visible celebrity protestor—even touring Hanoi. Her posing by North Vietnamese antiaircraft guns and her statements read over Radio Hanoi made her a widely reviled figure among veterans, many of whom still boycott her films and products today, their cars sporting I'M NOT FONDA JANE bumper stickers. For some vets, *Coming Home* was the ultimate slap in the face, a polemic completely void of subtlety. More than a few recent critics have noted the irony inherent in Sally's change from rigid Army wife to liberated, antiwar lover, saying it should be no surprise to the viewer that by the end of the movie she becomes, in essence, Jane Fonda.

The reaction to *Coming Home* is perhaps more indicative of the cultural climate of 1978 than the aesthetic quality of the film. The same ultimately cannot be said of 1979's *Apocalypse Now*.

At Cannes, where *Apocalypse Now* premiered, Francis Ford Coppola uttered the same basic line every author who has taken on Vietnam at some time utters. "My film is not about Vietnam," he said. "My film *is* Vietnam. It's what it was really like."

At the time, this claim wasn't as unfortunate as it might sound now. Like the Americans in Vietnam, critics noted, Coppola and his crew had gone into the jungle unprepared and with muddled intentions, encountered unexpected and devastating setbacks, and returned years later, humbled and bankrupt. So at Cannes perhaps Coppola was projecting himself into the role of America, acknowledging how easy it is to fall victim to one's obsessions.

But movies are not life, and losing one's film company because of shortsightedness, bad luck, and self-indulgence is not an apt metaphor for the deaths of millions of people. Over the years Coppola has been hammered for this quote again and again; it's commonly hauled out as proof of his overall pretentiousness as well as that of *Apocalypse Now*, both of which are amply documented in Eleanor Coppola's *Notes* and the 1991 documentary fashioned from her location footage, *Hearts of Darkness*.

Beyond the metaphor of Coppola in the jungle and the massive hype both the filming and the release of the movie attracted, *Apocalypse Now* was burdened with fleshing out—dramatically fulfilling, that is—one of English literature's finest allegories for colonial domination and the evil in men's souls, Joseph Conrad's *Heart of Darkness*. In Conrad's novella, the seaman Marlow begins his tale by imagining what it must have been like for a Roman captain to take his ship up the Thames, surrounded by darkness, forest, savages; he goes on to relate the story of his encounter with Mr. Kurtz, the chief of the Inner Station, deep in the Congo. Mr. Kurtz's section produces four times more ivory than any other, yet something's amiss. The company has sent Marlow to investigate another matter, but as he winds his way upriver, he becomes more and more intrigued with the figure of Kurtz as a representative of European imperialism gone mad. Rumors abound at each stop: His methods are strange, the natives worship him, he's a wise man, he's a devil. Marlow eventually finds Kurtz— near death—and the strange society he's gathered around him. It seems that Kurtz at first tried to bring Western enlightenment to the natives, but soon gave in to baser impulses, setting himself up as a vengeful god. Marlow is horrified and tries to bring Kurtz back down-river—for everyone's sake—but Kurtz dies, whispering, "The horror, the horror." It's Marlow's job to report his fate to Kurtz's intended, and he finds he cannot tell her the awful truth.

Coppola and his cowriter John Milius use Marlow's journey upriver to illustrate both America's involvement in Vietnam and Man's journey into his uncivilized Self. Marlow is now Willard (Martin Sheen), a fallen CIA operative who, like Kurtz (Marlon Brando), is serving at least his second tour of duty, having found nothing at home in the States. While in *Heart of Darkness* Marlow tells his tale to a group of men, Willard delivers a spare voice-over written by Michael Herr, the author of *Dispatches*, which echoes the hard-boiled *noir* thrillers of the late forties, another genre that posits Evil at the heart of human affairs.

The film's first words, ironically, are "This is the end," sung by Jim Morrison as a napalm strike silently engulfs a jungle, Hueys and Loaches dipping across the screen in slow motion. A shot of Willard's face, upside down, is superimposed on this, a Buddha's stone face opposite him, rightside up.

We're in Willard's hotel room in Saigon. He sleeps with a gun under his pillow, and he's been drinking brandy. As in *The Deer Hunter*, a ceiling fan revolves with the bap-bap-bap of rotor blades. "Saigon," the voice-over goes. "Shit, I'm still only in Saigon. Every time I go to sleep I think I'm going to wake up back in the jungle."

He tells us about going back to the World. "I hardly said a word to my wife until I said yes to a divorce. When I was here I wanted to be there, when I was there I wanted to get back to the jungle."

We watch Willard, stumbling drunk, punch a mirror and cut his hand. Naked, he seems mad, savage, already fallen to the weird core of his Self. When a pair of Army messengers appears, he asks, "What are the charges? What did I do?" As the men dunk him under a shower, the voice-over says, "I was going to the worst place in the world and I didn't know it yet," and, after mentioning Kurtz: "If his story is a confession, so is mine."

Willard is an assassin, though it seems he's lost the heart for it, and a group of Army higher-ups want him to find the mysterious Kurtz. "His ideas, methods," one says, "became . . . unsound." They try to come up with reasons. "In this war, things get confused out there— power, ideals, the old morality and practical military necessity. There's a conflict in every human heart. Between the rational and the irrational, between good and evil." Willard is instructed to terminate Kurtz's command "with extreme prejudice," after which Willard comments in his best tough-guy voice-over, "Charging a man with murder in this place was like handing out speeding tickets at the Indy 500."

Willard hooks up with a Navy patrol boat going up the river. "The crew were mostly just kids, rock 'n' rollers with one foot in the grave." It's a hip crew. They smoke dope and waterski to the Stones's "Satisfaction," swamping the Vietnamese washerwomen and fishermen on the banks.

They meet up with the 1st Cav, which has "cashed in its horses for choppers," though Col. Kilgore (Robert Duvall) still wears a cowboy hat and a bugler sends them off. As they approach a fishing village, Willard and company pass a TV crew led by Coppola himself. It's a shot echoed by Kubrick in *Full Metal Jacket,* among others. "It's for the television," Coppola shouts. "Don't look at the camera, just go by like you're fighting." This is followed by a massive, brilliantly staged assault on the seaside hamlet; it's at once exhilarating and terrible, a true, pleasing spectacle for the eye even as it tacitly decries what it's showing us (Kilgore is taking the village only so they can surf a desirable stretch of beach). After a girl sapper destroys a medevac chopper,

Kilgore mutters, "Fucking savages," then later asks Lance (Sam Bottoms), "What do you think?" Kilgore means the surf, but Lance thinks he means the assault, or Vietnam in general. "It's really exciting," Lance says. Kilgore goes on to utter his famous line, "I love the smell of napalm in the morning. Smells like . . . vict'ry." Then he adds sadly, as if it's something the men should all ponder, "Someday this war's gonna end."

Willard comments acidly on everything, never forgetting—like Herr in *Dispatches* and Walter Neff (Fred MacMurray) in the *noir* classic *Double Indemnity*—that he's implicated as well. "Home . . . we knew it didn't exist anymore." "Murder and insanity—there was enough to go around." "Never get off the boat, unless you're going all the way." "The bullshit piled up so fast in Vietnam you needed wings to stay above it."

Finally we head upriver, and Coppola stages a number of set pieces to show the strangeness—the unique madness—of the war. A USO show featuring a trio of Playboy bunnies dressed as cowboys and Indians turns into a riot. The crew of the patrol boat accidentally massacres a sampan full of innocent civilians. Night at Do Long bridge is an absurd, trippy circus (Willard: "Who's the commanding officer here?" Crazy gunner: "Ain't you?"). The next day, Lance writes back to a friend at home that Vietnam is "better than Disneyland."

They cross into Cambodia and find Kurtz, attended by his legions and his yes-man, a spaced-out photojournalist (Dennis Hopper). Everywhere are heads on pikes, bodies hung from trees. Like the fawning Russian in *Heart of Darkness*, the photojournalist has fallen under Kurtz's spell, thinks he's a genius. He tells Willard, "You don't judge the colonel," although, "Sometimes he goes too far. He forgets himself."

Willard is taken to Kurtz (the bald, ruminant Brando), who knows precisely why Willard is there. "Are my methods unsound?" he asks. Willard carefully replies, "I don't see any method at all, sir."

Kurtz imprisons Willard and butchers one of his two remaining crewmen. The photojournalist admits that "The man is clear in his mind, but his soul is mad." He worries about how Kurtz will be remembered. "What are they going to say? He was a kind man? He was a wise man? He had plans?" He puts the future burden of explaining exactly who Kurtz was on Willard: "Look at me, am I going to set them straight? No. *You.*"

Kurtz lets Willard out of his cage, brings him into the inner sanctum, where he recites Eliot's *The Hollow Men.* "I've never seen a man so ripped apart," Willard tells us. "You have no right to judge me," Kurtz says, and in a speech that directly addresses the gap: "It's impossible for words to describe what is necessary to those who do not know what horror means."

Kurtz relates the story of a VC atrocity, explaining how he became this way, lauding strength of will over morality. "It's judgment that defeats us." And, repeating what Willard has said earlier, "There's nothing more I detest than the stench of lies." With that, Kurtz lays on Willard the responsibility of telling his son what happened.

Night comes down, the torches are lit, a water buffalo prepared for ritual slaughter. Drums thunder (percussion led by Mickey Hart of the Grateful Dead), and then on top of that, the Doors' "The End." Willard rises wraithlike from the dark, smoking water, his face painted like Kurtz's when he killed the crewman. As the Doors pound out the crescendo of "The End," Coppola crosscuts between the ritual slaughter of the buffalo and Willard murdering Kurtz. "The horror," Kurtz whispers as he dies, "the horror." Scrawled across Kurtz's humanitarian treatise on the natives (another element lifted from *Heart of Darkness*) is *Drop the bomb, exterminate them all.* The deed done, Willard's face merges with that of the stone Buddha, and once more we hear Kurtz's last words. Then fade to the sound of rain.

Apocalypse Now is an epic in the grandiosity of its ambitions, the brilliance of its imagery, and the sheer pompousness of the statements it makes about Man and the war. This is a double-layered allegory—a beautiful cartoon, as some critics put it. Only the merest lip service is paid to realism. The symbolism is heavyhanded and constant, the characters grotesques. Everything is in capital letters—Good, Evil, Will, Morality—and the imagery that Coppola uses to bring us his psychodrama is utterly indulgent and at times marvelous. While the storyline sags under the weight of the set pieces, the overall dramatic frame of the journey or mission works well; the mapping of *Heart of*

Darkness onto the war seems apt in that it gives the viewer not only a plot to follow but a lens through which we can judge, historically, the American involvement.

That said, it's important to note that Coppola made this choice and then shot the movie to fulfill it. Implicitly he's criticizing the American involvement with almost no attempt to interpret the complexity of the actual events or the role of the men and women who fought the war. The representation of the American military as bumbling and aimless and the view of individual soldiers as drug-addled and out of control are enormously clichéd, and it could easily be argued that characters like Kilgore and Kurtz are cheap shots. As a metaphor for the madness of the war, as well as a grim comedy indicting perceived U.S. policy, *Apocalypse Now* succeeds, but it's certainly not a thoughtful investigation of what happened and why.

Themes we've seen before (and will see again) include Caputo's assertion that moral decay is implicit in war; the internal struggle between good and evil; the gap between America at large and Vietnam, also between REMF and combat soldier; the perverse attraction or beauty of war; the role of the media; the climate of lies; Vietnam as a physical embodiment of madness; the tendency of the military (and perhaps America) to see the war as a Western; race and class relations; the inhuman treatment of the Vietnamese (especially women and children); the stilted use of American and VC atrocities; and the mapping of a fixed Hollywood genre onto the war (in this case, the *noir* detective thriller, where for *Coming Home* it was the romantic melodrama).

That Cannes awarded the film its *Palme d'Or* says perhaps more about French attitudes and Coppola's talent than the movie's coherence and incisiveness. Like *Coming Home*, *Apocalypse Now* is packed with prevailing contemporary U.S. attitudes toward both the war and the American soldier, and while this did not please veterans or critics, who seemed to agree it was an empty fantasy, it sold well at the box office. None of the principal performances won Oscars (Duvall was nominated for his over-the-top Kilgore), though the lush cinematography earned Vittorio Storaro an award, and the sound crew picked up another.

Twenty years later, these judgments seem keen. The movie still looks and sounds good, and Coppola's eye serves him well. As the documentary *Hearts of Darkness* crows at the end, *Apocalypse Now* has grossed over 150 million dollars and is generally considered an excellent and important film. It's a compelling story: An artist puts his career on the line with an audacious, nearly impossible work, survives innumerable setbacks, unkind critics, and in the end is vindicated by the public. In this at least, Coppola escaped the fate of America's involvement in Vietnam. Still, *Apocalypse Now* continues to mesmerize viewers not because of what it says but how it says it.

This is one of the great paradoxes or challenges every artist faces when taking on Vietnam, but especially filmmakers: The audience's addiction to the raw sensation of aestheticized violence, combined with the difficulty of (and political and cultural opposition to) relating the experience, can easily lead to a falsification of presentation—an emphasis on the spectacle of war or simplistic judgments upon it rather than its political intricacies and the emotional truths of those involved. And that appears to be what happened with *The Deer Hunter, Coming Home,* and *Apocalypse Now,* but with one interesting and important result. The failure of these three widely accepted and highly decorated films to navigate such seemingly impossible demands would inspire, almost immediately, a large number of vets themselves to speak out and try, once again, to set the record straight.

5

Songs

October 1967. During a march on the Pentagon, a protester sticks a carnation in the barrel of a National Guardsman's rifle.

Popular music has always had the ability to react immediately to historical events and sway the public. During previous American wars, sentimental and patriotic songs such as "Over There" and "I'll Be Home for Christmas" cheered the troops and those left behind. After World War II, American music changed drastically, the big bands giving way to bop, hard bop, and the cool school. Rock 'n' roll grew from a mix of blues, gospel, country, and boogie-woogie and quickly displaced the crooners of the war years. Possibly most important, the folk and Beat movements collided in coffeehouses and on campus, taking a cue from left-leaning songwriters like Woody Guthrie, Pete Seeger, and Phil Ochs. By the mid-sixties, three major styles ruled popular music—folk, rock, and soul. Their voices were loud; as record-company earnings soared, artists' celebrity grew, and so did their power to influence the mainstream media's depiction of the war. A good example: in the early seventies, ex-Beatle John Lennon released two antiwar anthems with his Plastic Ono Band—"Christmas (War is Over)" and "Give Peace a Chance"; both are still sung today. By the war's end in 1973, all three branches of popular music had made strong antiwar statements. Only country-western, which held sway in the conservative South and rural West, continued to offer prowar songs.

The single prowar song included here, "The Ballad of the Green Berets" by Special Forces Sgt. Barry Sadler, is something of an anomaly. Its style is a stiff ballad, the lyrics mostly spoken over a lush and sentimental bed of instrumentation. Its success may be a good indication that people did support the war, if only because as a piece of music it's ridiculously old-fashioned. In 1966 when it came out, The Beatles were well past *Rubber Soul* and into *Revolver*.

The folk scene contributed protest songs from the late fifties on, its best-known artists Phil Ochs, Joan Baez, Odetta, and Bob Dylan before his notorious defection to the pop scene in 1965. After Dylan's success, Buffalo Springfield and The Byrds combined folk and rock artfully, scoring a string of hits. Country Joe and the Fish's "I-Feel-Like-I'm-Fixin'-to-Die Rag" (1967) comes from a scruffier blend of the two, and became an anthem, along with the group's "The Fish Cheer," at Woodstock. The song's jaunty gallows humor pokes fun at American foreign policy's inability to come up with a clear and compelling goal in Vietnam.

Creedence Clearwater Revival's lean, clean, bluesy sound earned them pop stardom. John Fogerty's "Fortunate Son" (1969) takes on the common (and correct) perception that the rich and privileged weren't serving in Vietnam but were all too happy to make others go.

Fronted by the legendary Jim Morrison, The Doors played literate acid-pop. "The Unknown Soldier" (1968) contrasts the anonymous death of a grunt with the material comfort and apathy of Americans back home and points up the uselessness of the war.

Motown, along with Stax/Volt the most influential African American labels, shied away from antiwar statements until late in the war. In 1971 Marvin Gaye had to fight to get "What's Going On" released; it became a huge hit, as did a flood of other socially conscious tunes out of Motown, including Edwin Starr's only hit "War" (1970), which has since been covered by any number of bands.

During the war, the pop and rock explosion that swept America kept a steady stream of hits with antiwar themes coming. Armed Forces Radio in-country played many of them; some, like The Animals' "We Gotta Get Out of This Place"—whose lyrics were not actually about the war—were banned. Films dealing with the war often cram their soundtracks full of these tunes, most notably *Good Morning, Vietnam* and *Forrest Gump*.

After 1973, there was no need for anti–Vietnam War songs, and few if any tracks about veterans were released. This changed with the dedication of the Wall. Bruce Springsteen's "Born in the U.S.A." (1984) became a rock anthem and was appropriated by both presidential candidates that year, even though its downbeat lyrics could be drawn from some typical hard-luck vet's oral history. Other pop artists such as Charlie Daniels and Billy Joel also cashed in on America's sudden sympathy for the vet.

10,000 Maniacs' "The Big Parade" (1989) is a late entry, telling the story of one son's journey to the Wall at the behest of his mother to commemorate his brother's death. Like many of the later novels and memoirs, Natalie Merchant's lyrics show the crowd at the Memorial and the different generations' connections with the dead and the unsettled past.

The Ballad of the Green Berets

BARRY SADLER AND ROBIN MOORE

1966

Fighting soldiers from the sky,
Fearless men who jump and die.
Men who mean just what they say,
The brave men of The Green Beret.

Silver wings upon their chests,
These are men, America's best.
One hundred men we'll test today,
But only three win The Green Beret.

Trained to live off nature's land,
Trained to combat, hand to hand.
Men who fight by night and day,
Courage take from The Green Beret.

Silver wings upon their chests,
These are men, America's best.
One hundred men we'll test today,
But only three win The Green Beret.

Back at home a young wife waits
Her Green Beret has met his fate.
He has died for those oppressed,
Leaving her his last request.

Put silver wings on my son's chest,
Make him one of America's best.
He'll be a man they'll test one day,
Have him win The Green Beret.

I-Feel-Like-I'm-Fixin'-to-Die Rag

COUNTRY JOE MCDONALD

1965

Come on all of you big strong men,
Uncle Sam needs your help again;
He's got himself in a terrible jam
Way down yonder in Viet Nam;
So put down your books and pick up a gun,
We're gonna have a whole lot of fun!

Chorus:

And it's one two three,
What are we fighting for?
Don't ask me, I don't give a damn,
Next stop is Vietnam.
And it's five six seven,
Open up the Pearly Gates;
There ain't no time to wonder why,
Whoopie—we're all gonna die!

Come on, generals, let's move fast,
Your big chance has come at last;
Now you can go out and get those Reds,
The only good Commie is one that's dead;
You know that peace can only be won,
When we've blown 'em all to kingdom come!

(Chorus)

Come on, Wall Street, don't be slow,
Why, man, this is war Au-go-go;

There's plenty good money to be made,
Supplying the army with tools of the trade;
Just hope and pray if they drop the Bomb,
They drop it on the Viet Cong!

(Chorus)

Come on, mothers, throughout the land,
Pack your boys off to Vietnam;
Come on, fathers, don't hesitate,
Send your sons off before it's too late;
You can be the first one on your block
To have your boy come home in a box.

(Chorus)

Fortunate Son

CREEDENCE CLEARWATER REVIVAL/
JOHN FOGERTY
1969

Some folks are born made to wave the flag;
ooh, they're red, white and blue.

And when the band plays "Hail to the chief,"
they point the cannon right at you.

 It ain't me, it ain't me—I ain't no senator's son.
 It ain't me, it ain't me;—I ain't no fortunate one. one. one.

Some folks are born, silver spoon in hand;
Lord, don't they help themselves.

But when the tax man comes to the door,
Lord, the house looks like a rummage sale.

 It ain't me, it ain't me—I ain't no millionaire's son.
 It ain't me, it ain't me;—I ain't no fortunate one. one. one.

Some folks inherit star spangled eyes;
ooh, they send you down to war.

And when you ask them, "How much should we give?"
they only answer More! more! more!

It ain't me, it ain't me—I ain't no military son.
It ain't me, it ain't me;—I ain't no fortunate one. one. one.

The Unknown Soldier

THE DOORS/JIM MORRISON

1968

Wait until the war is over
and we're both a little older
The unknown soldier

Breakfast where the news is read
television children fed
unborn living, living dead
bullet strikes the helmet's head
and it's all over for the unknown soldier
it's all over for the unknown soldier

(barked out): Hup two three four
Company, halt.
Present arms.

Make a grave for the unknown soldier
nestled in your hollow shoulder
the unknown soldier

Breakfast where the news is read
television children fed
bullet strikes the helmet's head
and it's all over
the war is over
it's all over
war is over
it's all over
all over
all over
all over

What's Going On

MARVIN GAYE

1971

(background talk: What's happening? Solid. Right on, etc.)

Mother, mother, there's too many of you crying.
Brother, brother, brother, there's far too many of you dying.
You know, we've got to find a way
to bring some loving here today.

Father, father, we don't need to escalate.
You see, war is not the answer
for only love can conquer hate.
You know, we've got to find a way
to bring some loving here today.

Picket lines (sister)
and picket signs. (sister)
Don't punish me (sister)
with brutality. (sister)
Talk to me (sister)
so you can see
Oh, what's goin' on (What's goin' on)
What's goin' on (What's goin' on)
What's goin' on (What's goin' on)
What's goin' on (What's goin' on)

(background talk: Right on, brother. Right on.)

Mother, mother, everybody thinks we're wrong.
Aw, but who are they to judge us

simply cause our hair is long.
You know, we've got to find a way
to bring some understanding here today.

Picket lines (brother)
and picket signs. (brother)
Don't punish me (brother)
with brutality. (brother)
Come on, talk to me (brother)
so you can see
What's goin' on (What's goin' on)
Yeah, what's goin' on (What's goin' on)
Tell me what's goin' on (What's goin' on)
I'll tell you what's goin' on (What's goin' on)

(background talk, etc.)

War

Edwin Starr

1970

War!
Hunh! Yeah
What is it good for?
Absolutely nothing.

(repeat twice)

Oh, war I despise
cause it means destruction of innocent life.
War means tears from thousands of mothers' eyes
when their sons go off to fight and lose their lives.
I said:

(chorus twice)

War, it ain't nothin' but a heartbreaker
Friend only to the undertaker.
War is an enemy to all mankind.
The thought of war blows my mind.
War has caused unrest within the younger generation.
Induction, then destruction—who wants to die?

(chorus twice)

War, it ain't nothin' but a heartbreaker.
It's got one friend, that's the undertaker.
Oh, war has shattered many young man's dreams,
made him disabled, bitter and mean.

Life is too short and precious to spend fighting war these days.
War can't give life, it can only take it away.

(chorus three times)

Peace, love and understanding,
is there no place for them today?
They say we must fight to keep our freedom
But Lord I know there's got to be a better way.

(chorus, with sound of marching)

Born in the U.S.A.

BRUCE SPRINGSTEEN

1984

Born down in a dead man's town
The first kick I took was when I hit the ground
You end up like a dog that's been beat too much
Till you spend half your life just covering up

> Born in the U.S.A.
> I was born in the U.S.A.
> I was born in the U.S.A.
> Born in the U.S.A.

Got in a little hometown jam so they put a rifle in my hand
Sent me off to a foreign land to go and kill the yellow man

> Born in the U.S.A.
> I was born in the U.S.A.
> I was born in the U.S.A.
> I was born in the U.S.A.
> Born in the U.S.A.

Come back home to the refinery
Hiring man says "son if it was up to me"
Went down to see my V.A. man
He said "son don't you understand now"

Had a brother at Khe Sanh fighting off the Viet Cong
They're still there, he's all gone
He had a woman he loved in Saigon
I got a picture of him in her arms now

Down in the shadow of the penitentiary
Out by the gas fires of the refinery
I'm ten years burning down the road
Nowhere to run ain't got nowhere to go

> Born in the U.S.A.
> I was born in the U.S.A.
> Born in the U.S.A.
> I'm a long gone Daddy in the U.S.A.
> Born in the U.S.A.
> Born in the U.S.A.
> Born in the U.S.A.
> I'm a cool rocking Daddy in the U.S.A.

The Big Parade

10,000 MANIACS/NATALIE MERCHANT

1989

Detroit to D.C. night train, Capitol, parts East. Lone young man takes a seat. And by the rhythm of the rails, reading all his mother's mail from a city boy in a jungle town postmarked Saigon. He'll go live his mother's dream, join the slowest parade he'll ever see. Her weight of sorrows carried long and carried far. "Take these, Tommy, to The Wall."

Metro line to the Mall site with a tour of Japanese. He's wandering and lost until a vet in worn fatigues takes him down to where they belong. Near a soldier, an ex-Marine with a tattooed dagger and eagle trembling, he bites his lip beside a widow breaking down. She takes her Purple Heart, makes a fist, strikes The Wall. All come to live a dream, to join the slowest parade they'll ever see. Their weight of sorrows carried long and carried far, taken to The Wall.

It's 40 paces to the year that he was slain. His hand's slipping down The Wall for it's slick with rain. How would life have ever been the same if this wall had carved in it one less name? But for Christ's sake, he's been dead over 20 years. He leaves the letters asking, "Who caused my mother's tears, was it Washington or the Viet Cong?" Slow deliberate steps are involved. He takes them away from the black granite wall toward the other monuments so white and clean.

O Potomac, what you've seen. Abraham had his war too, but an honest war. Or so it's taught in school.

6

The Oral History Boom

February 1968. A Marine awaits evacuation after the Battle of Hue.

After the mainstream success of the late-seventies fiction films such as *The Deer Hunter* and *Apocalypse Now*, Vietnam veterans felt that their story had been stolen and bastardized—that their true story still hadn't been told and probably never would. The oral history boom of the early eighties provided a corrective to the movies' exaggerations and omissions. Here, finally (or so the publishers' publicity claimed) was the vets' real story in their own words—nothing less than the truth. In the spirit of Studs Terkel's popular oral histories *Working* and *Division Street*, the Vietnam oral history, it was said, would give America an objective, grass-roots view of the war that so far was missing.

The difficulty with this idea is that subjects interviewed about their own experience often lie, forget, or fictionalize their lives (exaggeration being one great pleasure of the oral tradition), especially those interviewed ten to fifteen years after traumatic events. On top of that, the editor of such a book decides what that book is finally going to say. The editor, like the writer, practices a conscious selectivity, choosing subjects, what part of an interview to include, what to cut, and how to structure or sequence material for maximum dramatic impact. While the testimony of the subject may or may not be certifiable or valid, the oral history is just as easily manipulated as any other form, but the public commonly accepts it (even more so than other nonfiction) as absolutely true. The problem of authority—supposedly a nonissue here—becomes that much more complex, simply because readers naturally assume complete authority and total disclosure.

The success of these oral histories in the marketplace was in some part due to the sudden and belated recognition of the Vietnam vet by Americans. With the demise of the Carter administration and the rise to power of archconservative Ronald Reagan, the country was encouraged to see its Vietnam policy, as Reagan himself put it, as "a noble cause." In November 1982, amid great controversy (see the introduction to Chapter 13), the Vietnam Veterans Memorial was dedicated, and the ensuing national celebration of America's forgotten heroes lasted several years. The veteran, according to official sources, had finally come home.

Nonveteran Mark Baker's *Nam* (1981) was the first major oral history, and promptly became a bestseller. The veterans whose stories comprise the book are never named. In fact, there's no frame of reference; the only clues to their service branch, years in Vietnam, and areas of operation are those included in their own words (though their voices sound nearly identical section to section). In addition, Baker has cut their stories into bite-size pieces and ordered them chronologically in groups to fit a typical tour of duty—induction, basic training, first day in-country, operations, return home.

Wallace Terry's *Bloods* (1984) avoids this anonymity by concentrating on one subject at a time and giving the reader the soldier's occupation, unit, area, and duration of his tour of duty. Terry, a journalist who spent several years in Vietnam for *Time*, interviewed African American soldiers both while he was in-country and later when he returned to America. His transcription of their voices changes markedly with each participant. The selections are artfully sequenced, and comment as much on race relations in the United States and the abuse of the truth by the media as they do about Vietnam.

Keith Walker's *A Piece of My Heart* (1985) works similarly, focusing on women veterans. It tends to include more about its subjects' lives after Vietnam than other oral histories, and therefore has much to say about the gap between the veteran and America, though this time giving us the rare and strikingly different (yet in some respects familiar) perspective of the female veteran. Vet Al Santoli's *Everything We Had* (1981) follows the same basic format.

Bernard Edelman's *Dear America* (1985) is different from the other books in this chapter in that it employs letters written during the war to portray the lives of American soldiers. It's not always easy to make out the context of these letters—that is, why the writer is mentioning this or that particular issue—and the brief biographical sketches sometimes add an inordinate weight to a piece, telling the reader that a few weeks after this hopeful, idealistic letter was mailed, its nineteen-year-old author was killed. The letters themselves were gathered as part of the design process of the New York Vietnam Veterans Memorial; later, HBO produced a film version of the book, matching home movies shot by veterans to the letters, now read by professional actors.

While the subjects' views of the war and its conduct may disagree, all of these accounts focus on typical issues: the individual versus the group or the individual caught in the system; the problems of guilt or innocence; the struggle to throw off stereotypes about the vet. In fact, much of what we see here is familiar—we've already met most of these people (by type) in the earlier fiction, except now we get the chance to see them looking back and judging what happened, and that judgment often comes against American society and its institutions, especially the military. In a way, many of these testimonies become protests after the fact.

The form some of these accounts take, as critics have noted, is the *Bildungsroman*, the education-novel, showing the movement of a young person from innocence to experience through a trying event. Through their testimony, the subjects of these oral histories provide a last chapter to their own stories, telling us what they've learned. Their words have the ring of finality, of wisdom earned at a high price. It's important to remember that these lessons, like those in the most absurd fiction, are not raw but have been selected and constructed for dramatic impact.

Nam

MARK BAKER

1981

*You want to hear a gen-u-ine war story? I only understand Viet-
nam as though it were a story. It's not like it happened to me.*

❏

I GOT INTO the Marines because the Army wouldn't take me. I was
seventeen, hanging out in the neighborhood in Brooklyn with nothing to do. I knew I had to go to court sooner or later for some shit I
was into. The Army recruiter didn't even want to look at me since
they didn't get involved with court problems or seventeen-year-olds.
Forget the Navy and the Air Force. They had intelligence tests and I
didn't have any.

One of the big boys who remembered me as a kid on the streets
found out I was having a hard time getting into the service. He put his
arm around my shoulder and took me down to talk to the Marine
recruiter.

This big Marine takes one look at me and says, "This guy's a pussy.
We don't want you. Get out of here." So I stand on a chair and get in
his face and say, "Tell me about your big, bad Marine Corps."

"How old are you?"

"I'm only seventeen."

"Will your mother sign for you?"

"She ain't around."

The recruiter gave me ten dollars and said, "See that lady standing right over there? Go give her the money and I'm sure she'll sign for you." I was in this big courthouse in Queens, huge, with columns and the whole bit. She was standing next to a candy counter where they sold newspapers and stuff. So I go over and say, "Hey, I'm trying to get into the Marines. Will you sign for me?" No problem. She must have been doing this for a living.

That weekend I was in the Marines. I had to leave a note for my mother: "Mom, I went to Parris Island. I'll be back in a couple of months." I had no idea what I was getting into.

❑

I WAS IN Johns Hopkins Medical School at the time. As a prank, somebody cut one of the fingers off the cadaver I was working on and kept it. When I went to turn in the cadaver, I couldn't account for the finger.

I knew who'd done it. So the next day, while he was doing a dissection on the leg, I took the arm off his cadaver and snuck it out. I put it in an ice chest and drove out to the Beltway around Baltimore. At a toll-booth, I stuck the frozen arm out the window and some money in the hand and left the toll attendant with the arm.

This got back to the president of the school, who was Dwight Eisenhower's brother, Milton, a real fucking hawk. He told me to take a leave of absence to reconsider my commitment to medical school. I thought that was probably a good idea. I said, "Great." A week later I had my draft notice. They turned me right in to the Board.

❑

I HAD WENT down to the Draft Board originally just for the physical to get my classification and a draft card, the regular eighteen-year-old thing. This woman came in and said, "I want you to take this written test." I was late coming in anyways, and they were putting me through a long song and dance. I figured, "Okay, I took the physical, I'm here, I'll take their test, too. It ain't no big thing."

These guys I was taking the test with was just wild. The whole crew was making noise and they was throwing the pencils. Half of them was banged up high as kites. And I'm laughing, because the woman lieutenant who was supposed to be running things couldn't control the group.

"Well, I got something for you," she says, and she walks out of the room. These big Marines come in the door, right? A major with about four sergeants.

They went around and collected all the test papers. The major says, "Seeing as you want to give the lieutenant such a hard way to go, all of y'all just passed the test. You will be leaving in two days . . . *Or* you could leave in thirty days if you come into the Marine Corps."

We get up. "Oh, come on, you jiving."

"No, I'm serious. Everyone of you just passed the test and y'all leaving. If you keep going through all these changes, we have the right to pull y'all out of here right now and put you on the bus to boot camp."

Everybody got kind of quiet. Wait a minute, where they coming from with this? I was talking to this guy next to me and he said, "Yeah, well, I could stand a little extra time before they grab my ass."

About fifteen of us stood up and said we'll go in the Marine Corps, get us a little extra time.

Going through the paperwork the guy was talking in terms of three years. Then all of a sudden he says, "You know, when you enlist, you go for four years." That was when they told me that I was enlisting.

I was young, stupid, ignorant, along with all the other clowns. Man, we signed up for four years not thinking, "Hey, if I go in with the Army, I'll be going in for two. Here I am signing up for four years just to get an extra thirty days before they take me." Which I didn't get thirty days anyway.

That's not really the whole story. My brother had died that same year and I was ready to get out of the house because we had always shared the same room. All of a sudden, after eighteen years—*whoom*—he's not there no more. My older brothers, they didn't really live with us, so it was all right when they weren't around. But the one who lived close with me, I was missing him too much. I was breaking ties with a lot of friends, because when I saw them coming down the block, I was expecting to see my brother with them, popping up whistling to let me know he was there.

So it was good for me to leave home when I did. I didn't think in terms of what I did to my mother. She had just lost one son, and here's another one going off to some stupid war. Much later, after I thought about it, I had the chance to apologize. But she said she understood, that it was okay.

❑

I CAME from San Jose, California. I grew up in the suburbs and went to public school. I lived on the last block of a new development surrounded on three sides by apricot orchards and vineyards.

The high school was typically middle class. There were very few blacks. We had warm weather and cars. Most of the kids' dads were engineers at Lockheed or they worked at IBM. Most of my friends were preparing for a college degree.

From San Jose, people would go up to San Francisco for concerts. Smoking dope was just coming in at the time and psychedelic music. Some of the kids I knew were involved with that. They weren't pioneers: They were the ones who joined, who wanted to be the first to do this or that—the trendy group.

Then I was conservative. I hadn't experienced any inequality in the social system. Things looked pretty hunky-dory to me. Plus I had read all the war fiction. It never had a particular fascination for me, but it implanted this idea in my mind that war was a place for you to discover things.

I saw older people, World War II age, who weren't in that war. When they were asked about it and what they were doing then, they had to say, "Oh, well, I was in college." It was a major historical event that convulsed the world, and yet they missed it. I was the perfect age to participate in Vietnam and I didn't want to miss it, good or bad. I wanted to be part of it, to understand what it was.

Why should I take the God damn SATs and go off to college? Everybody was going to San Jose State College right there in town. And who wants to do what everybody else does anyway?

I joined the Army at the end of my senior year in high school with delayed induction. I would leave for basic training at the end of the summer when everybody else went away to college. I spent the last summer at home, playing a lot of basketball, riding around with my friends in an old '54 Ford. Nobody's picked up on their adult life. *American Graffiti.*

❏

AFTER I GRADUATED from nursing school, I was looking to go somewhere and do something. Hospitals aren't too gung-ho to hire you if you don't have a master's degree or experience of any kind. I checked into the Army. They were willing to guarantee me my choice of duty stations if I would enlist. Terrific, I'll go to Hawaii.

While I was in basic training, I heard all these people just back from Nam talking about how exciting it was. Professionally, it was the chance of a lifetime. I have two brothers and I grew up in a neighborhood where I was the only girl my age. I used to play guns with the boys all the time. I figured I could manage in Vietnam.

❏

I CAME from a town called Wilcox in the heart of one of the richest counties in the United States—at least that's what they told me. Mine was an ideal childhood. Everything around me was "nice." The schools were good. Everybody was responsible. There were no derelicts in town. Everybody lived in a "nice" house with a "nice" yard. I played Little League Baseball and lived the standard American experience. *Happy Days*, only without the Fonz. There was a part of town where there were a few hoody guys, but I always kept my distance. When I went to college, I was really an innocent coming from this background.

In my sophomore year I had had it with school. I didn't know what the hell I wanted to do. School was boring as hell and I was floating along in a state of limbo. About Christmas, I got word from home that Johnny Kane had been killed over in Vietnam. I couldn't believe it.

Johnny was the All-American boy. He held the state record for the high hurdles. He was the quarterback of the Wilcox High School football team who led Wilcox to an undefeated season and the Class C championship. He was about three years older than me. Even though I was just a punk kid, he was always nice to me. I really liked Johnny Kane.

Johnny and I ended up going to state colleges that were rivals, so I got to see him play football in college. After he graduated, he went into the Marine Corps, became a second lieutenant and then went overseas.

For some reason, his death really affected me. I said to hell with it. Instead of going to class one day, I went down to the Army recruiter and talked to him. I was totally unimpressed. The guy was promising me the world and I couldn't believe it. So I went over to the Marine Corps recruiter. This guy was everything you thought a Marine was supposed to be. All creases, squared away, he looked like a rock.

"Well, I'll tell you quite frankly," he said, "you join us, you're going to Vietnam. No bones about it." I figured that was true for the Army, too, but the Army recruiter wouldn't tell me.

I also had been kind of brainwashed since I was a kid. My father had been a Marine in the South Pacific during World War II. Although he never talked about it all that much, when I was in the second grade I had his web belt and his Marine Corps insignia. I always felt the Marines were elite. If you're going to do something, you go with the best—like playing for Wilcox High. We always had a reputation for being smaller than the other teams, but we were faster and our attitudes were better. We beat people on attitude.

What am I going to do? I'd rather be over there with motivated people, people who've got their shit together, as opposed to being in a paddy with a bunch of zeroes who don't even want to be there.

Not that I really wanted to be there. Yet when I found myself right in the prime age and a war was going on, I knew that I had to be part of it. It was my destiny. It had always been meant for me to do this thing. It sounds strange, but once it happened, I knew somehow, somewhere the handwriting was on the wall.

❏

I COME from a conservative Republican area. I was brought up in a strict, anonymous, nomadic suburban environment, where privilege was part of our legacy. We had our boats. We had our recreation. We had our stability. We had our fifteen-thousand-dollar-a-year jobs guaranteed to us as soon as we got out of college.

I never felt I belonged there, but I never imagined I'd end up in Vietnam. I was in undergraduate school and my deferment ran out. I'd spent some time in Brazil—my junior year abroad. I had thought I was going to get a full year of credits and I didn't get them. During the extra year of college I had to go through, my Draft Board advised me that they had changed my classification from 2S to 1A.

So I thought, I'll just go back to Brazil or I'll join the Peace Corps. But I really got hung up on finishing school. I had it in my head that if I went off then I'd never come back to school and get my degree. It was a real adolescent attitude. That degree was my working papers, my union card.

ROTC on campus had started a new crash program for guys who had never taken ROTC, but who wanted to go into the service as officers. All I had to do was stick around for one more year and take nothing but ROTC courses, and I'd get a commission. I said to myself, "Fuck it, I don't want to go in and peel potatoes. I don't want to be some private. I'm basically antisocial and I hate authority. If I go in that position, I'll just get in trouble and end up in jail. I might as well get myself a little autonomy, a little anonymity." I wanted to be left alone and to have my own way. So my last year in college I was an ROTC major.

I was a fuck-up. My hair was always too long, my uniform was always dirty. I wasn't consciously rebellious. I just couldn't take it seriously. I couldn't sit in class and talk about war the way they were talking about it. It wasn't that I was an intellectual or into politics. I had a strong moral upbringing with my Catholic background. I was very influenced by the lives of the saints, and by Christ, his example—more than I'd like to admit probably. I believed it in a way, you know? I'd talk about the Geneva Convention and how absurd it was to try to talk about the legality of war. I thought it was silly to try to reduce what was essentially an immoral experience into a question of legislation.

I remember having to go out to this athletic field and march around in a baggy uniform, feeling like a complete asshole. Older than the other guys, not taking it seriously, I was very aware of my expedient motives in the whole thing. I was afraid of the experience of being just an average grunt. I was doing what I had pretty much done all my life, using my wits to get over. I had this kind of contempt for the other guys going through all the military paces, who were seeking this power and leadership, who wanted to move other guys around like chess pieces on a board.

Out of the corner of my eye, I saw this small delegation of campus SDS outside the gate of the track field. I felt a tremendous affinity for them. That day, I had a very strong image of me literally slogging through the field, dragging my ass, going through the paces, but having a secret identification with those demonstrators. But they came from an entirely different world than me. For better or worse, I was part of the American experience and I thought there was no way I could bridge the gap. I guess I felt that I wouldn't be accepted, that I was a different species.

After I graduated, I went to the ROTC summer training camp. Essentially, I tried to be invisible most of the time. I failed the marksmanship requirement. I hated guns. I pledged to myself that no matter what position I was in, I would never use a gun, I would never kill anybody. I didn't try to fail, I was just disinterested.

Everybody else in my company was a junior in college. They had to go back and finish their last year and then they would get their commission at the graduation ceremony. I was going to get my commission after camp. I was able to use the officer's club which was a special privilege. A buddy of mine from college who was already a first lieutenant in the signal corps would come by after the day's training and pick me up in his Oldsmobile convertible—a big, fat luxury car, a real meat wagon. I used to feel real cocky. The other guys would be down there polishing the floors and doing all that shit. I'd put on my Madras blazer, my jeans, my tassel loafers and no socks, my buddy the lieutenant would pull up and there was nobody who would say me nay.

It was fucked in a way, it was really fucked. I was never aware until recently how lonely I was, disengaged from my life. How alienated I was from other people, from society and community. Some kind of weird Jesuit.

◻

I GRADUATED from college three days after Robert Kennedy was shot, two months and three days after Martin Luther King was assassinated, an incredible double whammy. The war was hanging there like a sword over everybody. I had been reclassified in the middle of my senior year from 2S to 1A and gone through about six solid months of really examining my feelings about the war. Chiefly, I read a lot of pacifist literature to determine whether or not I was a conscientious objector. I finally concluded that I wasn't, for reasons that I'm still not sure of.

The one clear decision I made in 1968 about me and the war was that if I was going to get out of it, I was going to get out in a legal way. I was not going to defraud the system in order to beat the system. I wasn't going to leave the country, because the odds of coming back looked real slim. I was unwilling to give up what I had as a home. Spending two years in jail was as dumb as going to war, even less productive. I wasn't going to shoot off a toe. I had friends who were starving themselves to be underweight for their physicals. I wasn't going to do it—probably because it was "too far to walk." I wasn't stupidly righteous, there was a part of me that was real lazy at the same time. I wanted to be acted on, and it was real hard for me to make a choice of any kind. Making no choice was a choice.

With all my terror of going into the Army—because I figured that I was the least likely person I knew to survive—there was something seductive about it, too. I was seduced by World War II and John Wayne movies. When I was in high school, I dreamed of going to Annapolis. I was, on some silly level, really disturbed when the last battleship was decommissioned. One of my fantasies as a kid was to be in command of a battleship in a major sea battle, and having somewhere in my sea chest Great-uncle Arthur's Naval dress sword from the eighteenth century.

One way or another in every generation when there was a war, some male in the family on my father's side went to it. I had never had it drilled into me, but there was a lot of attention paid to the past, a lot of not-so-subtle "This is what a man does with his life" stuff when I was growing up. I had been, as we all were, victimized by a romantic, truly uninformed view of war.

I got drafted at the end of the summer. I went into a state of total panic for days. What the fuck am I going to do? I went running off to recruiters to see if I could get into the Coast Guard or the Navy or the Air Force. No way.

There were probably some strings that I could have pulled. One of the things that is curious to me, as I look back on it, is that I had all the information, all the education and all the opportunity that a good, middle-class, college-educated person could have to get out of it . . . and I didn't make a single choice that put it anywhere but breathing down my neck. Even in the midst of the terror after the induction notice came, there was a part of me that would lie in bed at night and fantasize about what it would be like if I went.

The long and the short of the story is that at least half of my emotions were pulled to going. I couldn't get into any other branch of the service, so my final choice was to enlist in the Army. They had a delayed enlistment option. It was August when I got drafted and I figured, "Shit, I don't want to go until October." I took the option. I spent that time at a cottage in Maine, enjoying the wonderful weather, reading books and writing dramatic farewell letters.

❑

I'M FROM BAKERSFIELD. It's pretty hicky, but a lot of America is pretty hicky. I was born and raised there and that's where I went off to the service from.

When I was in high school, I knew I wasn't going to college. It was really out of the question. Even graduating from high school was a big thing in my family. We were originally from Mexico. My dad was a laborer. He had gone to the third grade, I think. He died when I was five. My mom had to bring us up. I have two brothers and three sisters.

I enlisted a couple of years after high school. At the time I was young and innocent and I was under the impression that enlisting was the All-American thing to do.

❏

IT'S JUST A little town where I grew up. I played some football and baseball like everybody else. I was kind of a hard-ass in school. I didn't know how good I had it then. I took little odd jobs and saved up enough money to buy an electric guitar and amplifier. I started playing in a band.

Near the end of high school, everybody's saying, "What you going to do? What you going to do?" I didn't know. I said, "I'm going to join the service." After I graduated, I went into the Marine Corps. They were supposed to be the best. To me, they were. They helped me grow up. I grew up in Vietnam.

❏

MY OLD MAN, when the war came, he says, "Oh, go. You'll learn something. You'll grow up to be a man. Go."

Shit, if my folks had to send their little poodle, they would have cried more tears over that than over me. But I'm supposed to go, because I'm a man.

❏

THE BUS pulls into the receiving area. There's a guy with a Smokey Bear hat out there really looking lean and mean. He gets on the bus and starts reading this stuff off, "All right, you'll grab your bag. You'll get off the bus. You'll fall into the yellow footprints painted on the pavement . . ."

It was really funny, a take-off from *Gomer Pyle*. The guy within arm's reach of the Marine was laughing just like everybody else. Smokey Bear whipped around and smacked him right in the face, knocked him halfway through the window. His head bounced off the luggage rack and he reeled back out in the aisle.

Smiles froze on faces. My heart stopped. We realized, "Hey, this guy isn't fooling around. He's going to come through this bus and kick all our asses." People started flying out of the door.

I came down with a couple of guys who were Puerto Rican street gang material from the big city and they thought they were bad news. They fell down the steps on top of me. We all stumble into the right footprints on the ground and Smokey marches us into some barracks and stands us at attention. He's yelling and screaming, really intimidating. You dumped all of your stuff out on a table and he went by and just threw everything away. We were too scared to say anything to him.

I was next to this big Puerto Rican dude. Smokey catches the dude looking at him out of the corner of his eye. He says, "Are you eye-fucking me, boy? I don't want your scuzzy eyes looking at me. You think this is funny? I hope you fuck up. I hate you Puerto Rican cocksuckers."

Eyes in the back of his head. Smokey sees a guy's eyes flick and he's there to punch him in the chest, five feet to the wall and back again. My knees were shaking. "What the fuck have I gotten myself into?"

Then they march us into some barracks. Bare mattresses and springs. It's like a concentration camp. They turn the lights on and leave us there. My stomach is in a knot. I'm lying there thinking, "What happened to my world?" Reality has suddenly turned to liquid shit before my very eyes. Kids were crying, rolling in their bunks. I'm so depressed, I can't believe this is happening to me.

We're there for a couple of hours. You're in your civilian clothes and you've been in them for a couple of days. You feel like shit. When they march you out, all of a sudden it's by the numbers. All your hair's gone. You don't even know who you are. You get a duffel bag and they're dumping things in it. Everybody hates you and they're fucking with you left and right. You get your shots. You stand at attention. People are passing out on their feet. Going rigid and falling on their faces and the corpsmen are laughing at them. Nobody talks to you, they scream. Nothing they give you fits. You look like shit and you feel like shit. A bunch of drill instructors put you back in receiving and that's when the shit really hits the fan.

❑

THEY STRIP YOU, first your hair. I never saw myself bald before. Not just your goatee, but your hair. Oh, shit, no hair. I'd had a mustache, must have been since I was thirteen years old. I *always* had a mustache. All of a sudden, no hair on my lip, no hair on my chin, no hair on my head.

Guys I had been talking to not an hour before—we was laughing and joking—I didn't recognize no more. I'm looking over there at my friend, "Joe? Is that Joe?"

"Yeah, is that you, James?"

"Yeah. Oh, shit." It was weird how different people look without their hair. That's the first step.

❑

VERY QUICKLY the situation becomes primitive. The leaders are automatically the biggest, the people who can physically enforce their demands. As soon as you get in the Army, they want squad leaders. A sergeant comes by and picks out the biggest guys, because he knows these are the people who can intimidate you into doing something. Everybody understands brute force. Somebody six-foot-two, 275 pounds, is your new squad leader and no matter how dumb he is, he's in charge. The sergeant is the authority figure in the background and this big kid is the bully on the block.

For a long time, I was lost in the shuffle. Everything is relegated to strength and I only weighed 150 pounds. There were very few people smaller than me in the pecking order. It was a shock. I never really got my bearings.

The people in the Army were not intellectuals. Most of them were from working class backgrounds. A lot of them were Southerners. It was my first contact with blacks and they tended to stick together. Certain economic groups like blue-collar kids and city kids adjusted very quickly to the Army. Most of the middle-class kids like me didn't fit into what was going on. We hadn't had to do much on our own before. We grew up in a secure environment where a lot of things were taken for granted.

One of the ways to establish who you were—at least the way that was open for me—was language. I could speak standard English and had a large vocabulary. That made me an outsider because people didn't like it, especially this one older guy with a heavy accent from Georgia.

I don't know exactly why, but I got in several fights with this guy. But I didn't have any peer group pressure. I wasn't well liked. I wasn't actively disliked, but nobody would step in to help me. I was on my own. This kid was quite a bit bigger than me, plus I had really lost my bearings and was sort of helpless. So there were fistfights which were quickly broken up—nothing much really happened. But the feeling of being an outsider was reinforced, because I had this antagonist all the time looking for an opportunity to get at me. I had to be on my toes. It was a whole new education.

❏

THEY HAVE YOU JUMP. You never get up in the morning like normal folk. You know, turn on the light. Okay, get up out of the racks now.

Every morning it was garbage cans going down the middle of the barracks, guys' racks being flipped over. You panic. You got two minutes to get dressed, make your rack and fall out.

The first time that happened, you've gone to sleep and forgotten where you're at. When you wake up, the lights are glaring and you hear this noise like a bomb going off. There's yelling and screaming. You jump in front of your racks. I'm looking, man, and there's all these little puddles. A bunch of guys had peed on themselves, they were so scared.

After a while I knew every morning we're going to go through this routine, so I figured I'd be partially dressed. I'd get up a half hour ahead of time and get my boots on and my pants. Pretty soon, everybody was doing it. Then they would tell us, "Get undressed, get back in the racks and start all over again."

❏

"THE ONLY WAY I'm going to get through this," I said to myself, "is to do everything right and not cause any trouble." That's what I tried to do, but you can't help but get into trouble. "What'd you do in college, boy? Learn to push a pencil?"

"Yessir."

"What do you mean by that?"

"Nossir."

"You like me, don't you, boy?"

"Yessir."

"You're queer for me."

"Nossir."

"You don't like me?"

"Yessir. Nossir."

"All right, ladies. You look like shit, so we're going to do a little PT now. Bends and motherfuckers. Many, many, many of them. Begin. One, two. One, two. One, two, one, two onetwo-onetwo-onetwo-onetwo.

"Up-downs. Get up, get down. Get up, get down. On your backs. On your bellies. Get up, get down.

"Knuckle push-ups. Ready, begin. One, two. One, two. Onetwo-onetwo-onetwo-onetwo. Side straddle hops. Ready, begin . . ."

Then they'd make you march around the barracks. When you'd get a couple hundred yards away, they'd say, "Get back to your rack. Do it!" There'd be a knot of people at the center of the door, clawing their way through to get back to their rack and stand at attention.

When you weren't going through that, you had your recruit regs held up in front of your face memorizing your eleven general orders. It was a real mind fuck.

We had one guy drank a can of Brasso. After they pumped his stomach, they sent him away to psychiatric care. I saw a couple of guys snap. But by the time you get to the end of that whole process, you feel like you're the baddest thing that ever walked the earth. When they call you Marine in the graduation ceremony, there's tears in your eyes. You are thoroughly indoctrinated.

❑

I FOOLISHLY WENT into the Army thinking, "Hey, with a few years of college under my belt, they're not going to put me in the infantry." I didn't see anything wrong with going to Vietnam. The only part I thought was wrong was my fear of being killed. I felt that somehow or other that shouldn't have been part of it. And I couldn't really picture myself killing people. I had flash images of John Wayne films with me as the hero, but I was mature enough even then to realize that wasn't a very realistic picture.

In boot camp I didn't meet very many patriots. They were guys that a judge had told, "Either you go in the Army, or it's two years for grand theft auto." Or they were schmucks like me who managed to lose their deferments. Or they were people who really had decided that the Army would be good for them in the long run.

To discourage us from going AWOL and deserting, all the new draftees were told that only 17 percent of us were going to Vietnam. And of that small percentage, only 11 percent would actually be combat troops. That eased my mind a great deal. Hey, there's still a chance that I won't have to go and get my guts blown out. Terrific.

At the end of our training, with only three exceptions—one fool who had gone Airborne, one guy who kept fainting and another kid who had a perforated eardrum—every single one of us went to Vietnam—200 guys.

❑

AFTER WE GOT in boot camp, they ask you to put down on some form why you joined the Marine Corps. I put down, "To Kill." In essence, that's what the fuck I wanted to do. But I didn't want to kill every fucking body. I wanted to kill the bad guy.

You see the baddies and the goodies on television and at the movies. I wanted to get the bad guy. I wasn't a patriot. I didn't join for the country. I mean, I love this country, but I could have given a fuck for the country then. I wanted to kill the bad guy.

They beat the shit out of me for that in boot camp. "Who is this fucking hawg who wants to KIIILLL?" Then they'd get me. They made me go see two head shrinks. The second shrink I talked to asked me all these questions like, "Did you ever kill as a child?" I told him I had a B-B gun and I killed a couple of birds. What the fuck?

It was just harassment. Why does someone join the military but to defend the country which more often than not means to kill?

I wound up in the Philadelphia Naval Yard of all places. I got to watch wet paint dry. I started putting in requests to go to Vietnam, but I kept being turned down. I kept telling them I wanted to go overseas, so finally they decided to let me go.

I had a couple of accidents before I could leave though. I got stabbed in the heart at a black cabaret and ended up in the Philly Naval Hospital. Right through the cardial sac, nicked my lung. While I was in the hospital, I saw all these amputees coming back from the Nam. Even that didn't stop me. I still wanted to go.

❑

I WAS RAISED a Roman Catholic. When I was about sixteen I became a follower of Elijah Mohammed as a Nation of Islam, a Black Muslim. When I was drafted, I tried to explain to the Army that I did not believe in the government as a whole. I didn't believe in the system. Why should I go out and fight for the system when my people are catching a lot of chaos from being under it—the slave mentality that our people are in?

They sent me up to see a light colonel. The Muhammad Ali decision was sitting in the Supreme Court. The colonel told me point-blank, "Either you raise your right hand or you will go to jail. One of the two. On the spot." I'll never forget his face, he didn't even crack a smile.

"I don't want to go to jail," I told him. "I never been to jail in my life."

"Don't worry," he says. "Once you're in the service and you tell them that you're a Muslim, you shouldn't have to go overseas. You will stay in the States." So I raised my right hand.

From there I went down to Ft. Jackson, South Carolina. That's when the crap started for me. A lot of officers as well as the NCOs was from the South, so they could not understand what a Black Muslim was doing in the U.S. Army, even if he *was* drafted.

I was harassed, called names. "People like you shouldn't be in the service." I feared for my life out on the rifle range. Sergeants told me, "Guys like you should be dead." So naturally, you got to stop and ask yourself, "Is this guy for real or not?" The pressure was on me.

As a Muslim, we're not supposed to eat pork. We're not even supposed to handle pork, touch it. They would assign me to clean the grease trap on the kitchen grill. In the grease trap you had beef, lamb, fish and all sorts of fried foods—plus pork. I told them I didn't mind pulling KP. I would peel all the potatoes to be peeled in the United States Army, but I didn't want to touch pork. They did it to put me in a spot where I would have to disobey an order for my religious beliefs. I would have been brought up on charges.

Luckily, I found a Protestant chaplain who understood. He intervened and said, "Put the man on K, but let him not mess with pork. It's his right as an individual." The whole company couldn't understand that.

After basic training I was supposed to stay in the States as a supply clerk or something. My orders came down for the infantry. All of us, we all went to the infantry.

Ft. Polk, Louisiana, is where they sent us for advanced infantry training. I had the same hassles all over again—"Oh, I see you're a Muslim." Deeper in the South I was treated like a Russian spy. They literally stood me in front of a whole company and told everybody what my religion was. "This guy is a Muslim. He cannot be trusted. If you are in training with him, watch your back."

I tried to protest it, but there's nobody to talk to. As soon as I say I'm a Black Muslim, everybody looks at me strange. I was sent to Army intelligence. The officers had to interview me, because they figured I was a traitor. "Are you a Commie? Are you trying to persuade black GIs to turn against the United States of America?"

Naturally, I was preaching Islam to the brothers and sisters that was there. Some of them were very interested and wanted to know a little more about what Islam was. I pulled them together a little bit. That's what the Army didn't like. They considered me a threat because I was always trying to pull the brothers together. I asked them, why should we fight in a war which we don't even understand?

Once everybody finished AIT, they were sending them directly to

Nam after their leave. After my leave, I ended up back in Ft. Polk. I
was under investigation by Army intelligence. They had to clear me
for going overseas. They pulled me out of my company and put me in
a special headquarters company.

I was a duty soldier, assigned to the orderly room, to the supply
room, like putting rifles together. I was a security risk but I was putting
the rifles together. Plus I was doing anything nasty they could think of
for me to do. I was picking up butts off the street. They gave me a rifle
bore used for cleaning the M-16 and they sent me around to clean out
all the little holes in the urinals. I had to take my hand without no
glove and clean out the urinal holes for each and every urinal in the
company. You know how stinking a urinal is? But I did it with a smile.
I said, "It's not pork, is it."

They said, "He's a psycho." They sent me to the doctors. The
shrink said, "He's no psycho. The man just believes."

I started agitating the Army. That was my biggest thing. I carried
around a book by Karl Marx, just for the hell of it. They brought the
MPs in one time to raid my locker, trying to find books from the
Soviet Mission or something. The only thing they found was that
book by Karl Marx, that you can get in any library. In fact, I got it
from the library right there on the post. They returned it with apolo-
gies.

They kept me under surveillance. I had to report once a week to
Army intelligence. And there was an FBI agent there on base who was
like my probation officer. It didn't bother me going to see him. At
least I got out of work. I'd tell the guy, "Please don't send me back out
there, I'll sit in here all day long and we can talk."

After duty hours I would preach Marxism and Islam. I was a young-
blood at the time, nineteen years old. I was serious about picking up a
gun and letting the fight be here. Not so much a race fight as a social
type of struggle. The system was against my people. If I had to pick up
a gun, let me pick it up and turn it on the system, not on somebody in
Vietnam who I know nothing about. I was dedicated and serious
about dying . . . but I didn't know what death really was.

I had to go up and see the post commander, some two-star jerk. I laid out my beliefs for him and told him I was willing to die for what I believed in.

"Well," he said, "you're going to die all right. But to hell with this fighting and dying in the streets. You're going to die in Vietnam." Intelligence had cleared me and my orders were cut for me to go directly to the Nam.

The assistant to the general told me, "Since you love the Vietnamese people and the Communist way so much, you are going to go out there and be with them. Boy, we going to make sure you die in Vietnam." Everybody smiled. I was the biggest joke in Ft. Polk. Send the Commie to Vietnam.

❏

IN THE MIDDLE of my thirty-day leave before shipping to Vietnam, I was sitting at home in St. Louis watching television. The news flash came on that the Tet Offensive had broken out.

One of the last speeches the Army made to us before we went on leave was, "Listen, it's pretty civilized over there. You'll have swimming pools and snack bars and like that. You won't have to run off the plane and form a defensive perimeter around the air base in Saigon." But that's exactly what the "enemy" was shooting at on the TV. People were being blown away at Ton Son Nhut Air Base.

Friends of mine were saying, "You've got to be crazy. You're going to go there? Michael, think it over." People offered to loan me the money to go to Canada. But I was a little crazy. I was already into it too far.

I spent a few days by myself in San Francisco before I had to report. I must have had a good time. I'd wake up with all my money gone, but without any bruises or gouges on my body. Nobody had hurt me, but the evening would be a real blank. I spent every last dime of several hundred dollars. I had just enough money to catch the bus to Oakland Air Force Base.

❏

WHEN I CAME HOME from training, my family couldn't deal with me. My girl friend was saying, "Oh, wow, Jim. You're so patriotic. Where you coming from? They cut your hair and took your brain, too." The Marine Corps had me believing this war was right. She says, "Yeah, but you weren't ever like that before."

I couldn't relate that I had changed. But everybody I knew couldn't figure me out. "Hey, what is this? Patriotic Jim all of a sudden, going to this great war—doesn't know what for."

Bloods

WALLACE TERRY

1984

Private First Class Reginald "Malik" Edwards
Phoenix, Louisiana
Rifleman
9th Regiment
U.S. Marine Corps
Danang
June 1965–March 1966

I'm in the Amtrac with Morley Safer, right? The whole thing is getting ready to go down. At Cam Ne. The whole bit that all America will see on the *CBS Evening News*, right? Marines burning down some huts. Brought to you by Morley Safer. Your man on the scene. August 5, 1965.

When we were getting ready for Cam Ne, the helicopters flew in first and told them to get out of the village 'cause the Marines are looking for VC. If you're left there, you're considered VC.

They told us if you receive one round from the village, you level it. So we was coming into the village, crossing over the hedges. It's like a little ditch, then you go through these bushes and jump across, and start kickin' ass, right?

Not only did we receive one round, three Marines got wounded right off. Not only that, but one of the Marines was our favorite

Marine, Sergeant Bradford. This brother that everybody loved got shot in the groin. So you know how we felt.

The first thing happened to me, I looked out and here's a bamboo snake. That little short snake, the one that bites you and you're through bookin'. What do you do when a bamboo snake comin' at you? You drop your rifle with one hand, and shoot his head off. You don't think you can do this, but you do it. So I'm rough with this snake, everybody thinks, well, Edwards is shootin' his ass off today.

So then this old man runs by. The other sergeant says, "Get him, Edwards." But I missed the old man. Now I just shot the head off a snake. You dig what I'm sayin'? Damn near with one hand. M-14. But all of a sudden, I missed this old man. 'Cause I really couldn't shoot him.

So Brooks—he's got the grenade launcher—fired. Caught my man as he was comin' through the door. But what happened was it was a room full of children. Like a schoolroom. And he was runnin' back to warn the kids that the Marines were coming. And that's who got hurt. All those little kids and people.

Everybody wanted to see what had happened, 'cause it was so fucked up. But the officers wouldn't let us go up there and look at what shit they were in. I never got the count, but a lot of people got screwed up. I was telling Morley Safer and his crew what was happening, but they thought I was trippin', this Marine acting crazy, just talking shit. 'Cause they didn't want to know what was going on.

So I'm going on through the village. Like the way you go in, you sweep, right? You fire at the top of the hut in case somebody's hangin' in the rafters. And if they hit the ground, you immediately fire along the ground, waist high, to catch him on the run. That's the way I had it worked out, or the way the Marines taught me. That's the process.

All of a sudden, this Vietnamese came runnin' after me, telling me not to shoot: "Don't shoot. Don't shoot." See, we didn't go in the village and look. We would just shoot first. Like you didn't go into a room to see who was in there first. You fired and go in. So in case there was somebody there, you want to kill them first. And we was just gonna run in, shoot through the walls. 'Cause it was nothin' to shoot through the walls of a bamboo hut. You could actually set them on fire if you had tracers. That used to be a fun thing to do. Set hootches on fire with tracers.

So he ran out in front of me. I mean he's runnin' into my line of fire. I almost killed him. But I'm thinking, what the hell is wrong? So then we went into the hut, and it was all these women and children huddled together. I was gettin' ready to wipe them off the planet. In this one hut. I tell you, man, my knees got weak. I dropped down, and that's when I cried. First time I cried in the 'Nam. I realized what I would have done. I almost killed all them people. That was the first time I had actually had the experience of weak knees.

Safer didn't tell them to burn the huts down with they lighters. He just photographed it. He could have got a picture of me burning a hut, too. It was just the way they did it. When you say level a village, you don't use torches. It's not like in the 1800s. You use a Zippo. Now you would use a Bic. That's just the way we did it. You went in there with your Zippos. Everybody. That's why people bought Zippos. Everybody had a Zippo. It was for burnin' shit down.

I was a Hollywood Marine. I went to San Diego, but it was worse in Parris Island. Like you've heard the horror stories of Parris Island— people be marchin' into the swamps. So you were happy to be in San Diego. Of course, you're in a lot of sand, but it was always warm.

At San Diego, they had this way of driving you into this base. It's all dark. Back roads. All of a sudden you come to this little adobe-looking place. All of a sudden, the lights are on, and all you see are these guys with these Smokey the Bear hats and big hands on their hips. The light is behind them, shining through at you. You all happy to be with the Marines. And they say, "Better knock that shit off, boy. I don't want to hear a goddamn word out of your mouth." And everybody starts cursing and yelling and screaming at you.

My initial instinct was to laugh. But then they get right up in your face. That's when I started getting scared. When you're 117 pounds, 150 look like a monster. He would just come screaming down your back, "What the hell are you looking at, shit turd?" I remembered the time where you cursed, but you didn't let anybody adult hear it. You were usually doing it just to be funny or trying to be bold. But these people were actually serious about cursing your ass out.

Then here it is. Six o'clock in the morning. People come in bangin' on trash cans, hittin' my bed with night sticks. That's when you get really scared, 'cause you realize I'm not at home anymore. It doesn't look like you're in the Marine Corps either. It looks like you're in jail. It's like you woke up in a prison camp somewhere in the South. And the whole process was not to allow you to be yourself.

I grew up in a family that was fair. I was brought up on the Robin Hood ethic, and John Wayne came to save people. So I could not understand that if these guys were supposed to be the good guys, why were they treating each other like this?

I grew up in Plaquemines Parish. My folks were poor, but I was never hungry. My stepfather worked with steel on buildings. My mother worked wherever she could. In the field, pickin' beans. In the factories, the shrimp factories, oyster factories. And she was a house-keeper.

I was the first person in my family to finish high school. This was 1963. I knew I couldn't go to college because my folks couldn't afford it. I only weighed 117 pounds, and nobody's gonna hire me to work for them. So the only thing left to do was go into the service. I didn't want to go into the Army, 'cause everybody went into the Army. Plus the Army didn't seem like it did anything. The Navy I did not like 'cause of the uniforms. The Air Force, too. But the Marines was bad. The Marine Corps built men. Plus just before I went in, they had all these John Wayne movies on every night. Plus the Marines went to the Orient.

Everybody laughed at me. Little, skinny boy can't work in the field going in the Marine Corps. So I passed the test. My mother, she signed for me 'cause I was seventeen.

There was only two black guys in my platoon in boot camp. So I hung with the Mexicans, too, because in them days we never hang with white people. You didn't have white friends. White people was the aliens to me. This is '63. You don't have integration really in the South. You expected them to treat you bad. But somehow in the Marine Corps you hoping that's all gonna change. Of course, I found out this was not true, because the Marine Corps was the last service to integrate. And I had an Indian for a platoon commander who hated

Indians. He used to call Indians blanket ass. And then we had a Southerner from Arkansas who like to call you chocolate bunny and Brillo head. That kind of shit.

I went to jail in boot camp. What happened was I was afraid to jump this ditch on the obstacle course. Every time I would hit my shin. So a white lieutenant called me nigger. And, of course, I jumped the ditch farther than I'd ever jumped before. Now I can't run. My leg is really messed up. I'm hoppin'. So it's pretty clear I can't do this. So I tell the drill instructor, "Man, I can't fucking go on." He said, "You said what?" I said it again. He said, "Get out." I said, "Fuck you." This to a drill instructor in 1963. I mean you just don't say that. I did seven days for disrespect. When I got out of the brig, they put me in a recon. The toughest unit.

We trained in guerrilla warfare for two years at Camp Pendleton. When I first got there, they was doing Cuban stuff. Cuba was the aggressor. It was easy to do Cuba because you had a lot of Mexicans. You could always let them be Castro. We even had Cuban targets. Targets you shoot at. So then they changed the silhouettes to Vietnamese. Everything to Vietnam. Getting people ready for the little gooks. And, of course, if there were any Hawaiians and Asian-Americans in the unit, they played the roles of aggressors in the war games.

Then we are going over to Okinawa, thinking we're going on a regular cruise. But the rumors are that we're probably going to the 'Nam. In Okinawa we was trained as raiders. Serious, intense jungle-warfare training. I'm gonna tell you, it was some good training. The best thing about the Marine Corps, I can say for me, is that they teach you personal endurance, how much of it you can stand.

The only thing they told us about the Viet Cong was they were gooks. They were to be killed. Nobody sits around and gives you their historical and cultural background. They're the enemy. Kill, kill, kill. That's what we got in practice. Kill, kill, kill. I remember a survey they did in the mess hall where we had to say how we felt about the war. The thing was, get out of Vietnam or fight. What we were hearing was Vietnamese was killing Americans. I felt that if people were killing Americans, we should fight them. As a black person, there wasn't no problem fightin' the enemy. I knew Americans were preju-

diced, were racist and all that, but, basically, I believed in America
'cause I was an American.

I went over with the original 1st Battalion 9th Marines. When we
got there, it was nothing like you expect a war to be. We had seen a
little footage of the war on TV. But we was on the ship dreaming
about landing on this beach like they did in World War II. Then we
pulled into this area like a harbor almost and just walked off the ship.

And the first Vietnamese that spoke to me was a little kid up to my
knee. He said, "You give me cigarette. You give me cigarette." That
really freaked me out. This little bitty kid smokin' cigarettes. That is
my first memory of Vietnam. I thought little kids smokin' was the
most horrible thing that you could do. So the first Vietnamese words I
learned was *Toi khong hut thuoc lo.* "I don't smoke cigarettes." And
Thuoc la co hai cho suc khoe. "Cigarettes are bad for your health."

Remember, we were in the beginning of the war. We wasn't dealing with the regular army from the North. We was still fightin' the
Viet Cong. The NVA was moving in, but they really hadn't made
their super move yet. So we were basically runnin' patrols in and out
of Danang. We were basically with the same orders that the Marines
went into Lebanon with. I mean we couldn't even put rounds in the
chambers at first.

It was weird. The first person that died in each battalion of the 9th
Marines that landed was black. And they were killed by our own
people. Comin' back into them lines was the most dangerous thing
then. It was more fun sneakin' into Ho Chi Minh's house than comin'
back into the lines of Danang. Suppose the idiot is sleeping on watch
and he wake up. All of a sudden he sees people. That's all he sees.
There was a runnin' joke around Vietnam that we was killing more of
our people than the Vietnamese were. Like we were told to kill any
Vietnamese in black. We didn't know that the ARVN had some black
uniforms, too. And you could have a platoon commander calling the
air strikes, and he's actually calling on your position. It was easy to get
killed by an American.

They called me a shitbird, because I would stay in trouble. Minor
shit, really. But they put me on point anyway. I spent most of my time
in Vietnam runnin'. I ran through Vietnam 'cause I was always on

point, and points got to run. They can't walk like everybody else. Specially when you hit them open areas. Nobody walked through an open area. After a while, you develop a way to handle it. You learned that the point usually survived. It was the people behind you who got killed.

And another thing. It's none of that shit, well, if they start shootin' at you, now all of a sudden we gonna run in there and outshoot them. The motherfuckers hit, you call in some air. Bring in some heavy artillery, whatever you need to cool them down. You wipe that area up. You soften it up. Then you lay to see if you receive any fire. An' *then* you go on in.

I remember the first night we had went out on patrol. About 50 people shot this old guy. Everybody claimed they shot him. He got shot 'cause he started running. It was an old man running to tell his family. See, it wasn't s'posed to be nobody out at night but the Marines. Any Vietnamese out at night was the enemy. And we had guys who were frustrated from Korea with us. Guys who were real gung ho, wanted a name for themselves. So a lot of times they ain't tell us shit about who is who. People get out of line, you could basically kill them. So this old man was running like back towards his crib to warn his family. I think people said, "Halt," but we didn't know no Vietnamese words.

It was like shootin' water buffaloes. Somebody didn't tell us to do this. We did it anyway. But they had to stop us from doing that. Well, the water buffaloes would actually attack Americans. I guess maybe we smelled different. You would see these little Vietnamese kids carrying around this huge water buffalo. That buffalo would see some Marines and start wantin' to run 'em down. You see the poor little kids tryin' to hold back the water buffalo, because these Marines will kill him. And Marines, man, was like, like we was always lookin' for shit to go wrong. Shit went wrong. That gave us the opportunity.

I remember we had went into this village and got pinned down with a Australian officer. When we finally went on through, we caught these two women. They smelled like they had weapons. These were all the people we found. So the Australian dude told us to take the women in. So me and my partner, we sittin' up in this Amtrac with these women. Then these guys who was driving the Amtrac come in there and start unzippin' their pants as if they gonna screw the women. So we say, "Man, get outta here. You can't do it to our prisoners." So they get mad with us. Like they gonna fight us. And we had to actually lock and load to protect the women. They said, "We do this all the time."

One time we had went into this place we had hit. We was takin' prisoners. So this one guy broke and ran. So I chased him. I ran behind him. Everybody say, "Shoot him. Shoot him." 'Cause they was pissed that I was chasin' him. So I hit him. You know I had to do something to him. I knew I couldn't just grab him and bring him back. And his face just crumbled. Then I brought him back, and they said, "You could have got a kill, Edwards."

The first time we thought we saw the enemy in big numbers was one of these operations by Marble Mountain. We had received fire. All of a sudden we could see people in front of us. Instead of waiting for air, we returned the fire, and you could see people fall. I went over to this dude and said, "Hey, man, I saw one fall." Then everyone started yelling, "We can see 'em fall. We can see 'em fall." And they were fallin'. Come to find out it was Bravo Company. What the VC had done was suck Bravo Company in front of us. 'Cause they attacked us and Bravo Company at the same time. They would move back as Bravo Company was in front of us. It was our own people. That's the bodies we saw falling. They figured out what was happening, and then they ceased fire. But the damage was done real fast. I think we shot up maybe 40 guys in Bravo Company. Like I said, it was easy to get killed by an American.

The first time I killed somebody up close was when we was tailing Charlie on a patrol somewhere around Danang. It was night. I was real tired. At that time you had worked so hard during the day, been on so many different details, you were just bombed out.

I thought I saw this dog running. Because that white pajama top they wore at night just blend into that funny-colored night they had over there. All of a sudden, I realized that somebody's runnin'. And before I could say anything to him, he's almost ran up on me. There's nothing I can do but shoot. Somebody get that close, you can't wait to check their ID. He's gonna run into you or stop to shoot you. It's got to be one or the other. I shot him a bunch of times. I had a 20-round clip, and when he hit the ground, I had nothing. I had to reload. That's how many times he was shot.

Then the sergeant came over and took out the flashlight and said, "Goddamn. This is fucking beautiful. This is fucking beautiful."

This guy was really out of it. He was like moanin'. I said, "Let me kill him." I couldn't stand the sound he was makin'. So I said, "Back off, man. Let me put this guy out of his misery." So I shot him again. In the head.

He had a grenade in his hand. I guess he was committing suicide. He was just runnin' up to us, pullin' a grenade kind of thing. I caught him just in time.

Everybody was comin' congratulatin' me, saying what a great thing it was. I'm tryin' to be cool, but I'm really freakin' out. So then I start walking away, and they told me I had to carry the body back to base camp. We had a real kill. We had one we could prove. We didn't have to make this one up.

So then I start draggin' this body by the feet. And his arm fell off. So I had to go back and get his arm. I had to stick it down his pants. It was a long haul.

And I started thinkin'. You think about how it feels, the weight. It was rainin'. You think about the mist and the smells the rain brings out. All of a sudden I realize this guy is a person, has got a family. All of a sudden it wasn't like I was carrying a gook. I was actually carrying a human being. I started feeling guilty. I just started feeling really badly.

I don't feel like we got beat in Vietnam. We never really fought the war. People saying that America couldn't have won that war is crazy.

The only way we could actually win the war was to fight everyday. You couldn't fight only when you felt like it. Or change officers every month. Troops would learn the language, learn the people, learn the area. If you're gonna be fighting in an area, you get to know everybody in the area and you stay there. You can't go rotate your troops every 12 months. You always got new people coming in. Plus they may not get to learn anything. They may die the first day. If you take a guy on patrol and he gets killed the first day, what good is he? See, if you have seasoned troops, you can move in and out of the bush at will. You get the smell of the country on you. You start to eat the food. You start to smell like it. You don't have that fresh smell so they can smell you when you're comin'. Then you can fight a war. Then you can just start from one tip of South Vietnam and work your way to the top. To China. Of course, if we had used the full might of the military, we'd be there now. We could never give the country back up. Plus we'd have to kill millions of Vietnamese. Do we want to do that? What had they done to us to deserve all that? So to do it would have been wrong. All we did was to give our officers the first combat training they had since Korea. It was more like a big training ground. If it was a real war, you either would have come out in a body bag or you would have come out when the war was over.

Sometimes I think we would have done a lot better by getting them hooked on our lifestyle than by trying to do it with guns. Give them credit cards. Make them dependent on television and sugar. Blue jeans works better than bombs. You can take blue jeans and rock 'n' roll records and win over more countries than you can with soldiers.

When I went home, they put me in supply, probably the lowest job you can have in the Marines. But they saw me drawing one day and they said, "Edwards can draw." They sent me over to the training-aids library, and I became an illustrator. I reenlisted and made sergeant.

When I went back to Quantico, my being black, they gave me the black squad, the squad with most of the blacks, especially the militant blacks. And they started hippin' me. I mean I was against racism. I didn't even call it racism. I called it prejudice. And by becoming an illustrator, it gave you more time to think. And I was around people who thought. People who read books. I would read black history where the white guys were going off on novels or playing rock music. So then one day, I just told them I was black. I didn't call them *blanco*, they didn't have to call me Negro. That's what started to get me in trouble. I became a target. Somebody to watch.

Well, there was this riot on base, and I got busted. It started over some white guys using a bunch of profanity in front of some sisters. I was found guilty of attack on an unidentified Marine. Five months in jail, five months without pay. And a suspended BCD. In jail they didn't want us to read our books, draw any pictures, or do anything intellectually stimulating or what they thought is black. They would come into my cell and harass me. So one day I was just tired of them, and I hit the duty warden. I ended up with a BCD in 1970. After six years, eight months, and eight days, I was kicked out of the Corps. I don't feel it was fair. If I had been white, I would never had went to jail for fighting. That would have been impossible.

With a BCD, nothing was happenin'. I took to dressin' like the Black Panthers, so even blacks wouldn't hire me. So I went to the Panther office in D.C. and joined. I felt the party was the only organization that was fighting the system.

I liked their independence. The fact that they had no fear of the police. Talking about self-determination. Trying to make Malcolm's message reality. This was the first time black people had stood up to the state since Nat Turner. I mean armed. It was obvious they wasn't gonna give us anything unless we stood up and were willing to die. They obviously didn't care anything about us, 'cause they had killed King.

For me the thought of being killed in the Black Panther Party by the police and the thought of being killed by Vietnamese was just a qualitative difference. I had left one war and came back and got into another one. Most of the Panthers then were veterans. We figured if we had been over in Vietnam fighting for our country, which at that point wasn't serving us properly, it was only proper that we had to go out and fight for our own cause. We had already fought for the white man in Vietnam. It was clearly his war. If it wasn't, you wouldn't have seen as many Confederate flags as you saw. And the Confederate flags was an insult to any person that's of color on this planet.

I rose up into the ranks. I was an artist immediately for the newspaper. Because of my background in the military, obviously I was able to deal with a lot of things of a security nature. And eventually I took over the D.C. chapter.

At this time, Huey Newton and Bobby Seale were in jail and people sort of idealized them. The party didn't actually fall apart until those two were released, and then the real leader, David Hilliard, was locked up. Spiro Agnew had a lot to do with the deterioration when he said take the Panthers out of the newspapers and then they will go away. And the FBI was harassing us, and we started turning on each other because of what they were spreading. And the power structure started to build up the poverty programs. Nobody was going to follow the Panthers if they could go down to the poverty program and get a check and say they are going to school.

We just didn't understand the times. All we wanted to do was kick whitey's ass. We didn't think about buying property or gaining economic independence. We were, in the end, just showing off.

I think the big trip America put us on was to convince us that having money was somehow harmful. That building businesses and securing our economic future, and buying or controlling areas for our group, our family, our friends like everybody else does, was wrong. Doing that doesn't make you antiwhite. I think white people would even like us better if we had more money. They like Richard Pryor. And Sammy Davis. And Jabbar.

Economically, black folks in America have more money than Canada or Mexico. It's obvious that we are doing something wrong. When people say we're illiterate, that doesn't bother me as much. Literacy means I can't read these books. Well neither does a Korean or a Vietnamese. But where they're not illiterate is in the area of economics. Sure, we're great artists, great singers, play great basketball. But we're not great managers yet. It's pretty obvious that you don't have to have guns to get power. People get things out of this country and they don't stick up America to do it. Look at the Vietnamese refugees running stores now in the black community where I live.

Right now, I'm an unemployed artist, drawing unemployment. I spent time at a community center helping kids, encouraging kids to draw.

I work for the nuclear-freeze movement, trying to convince people nuclear war is insane. Even when I was in the Marine Corps, I was against nuclear war. When I was a child, I was against nuclear weapons, because I thought what they did to Hiroshima and Nagasaki was totally cold. There's nothing any human being is doing on the planet that I could want to destroy the planet for future generations. I think we should confine war to our century and our times. Not to leave the residue around for future generations. The residue of hate is a horrible thing to leave behind. The residue of nuclear holocaust is far worse.

I went to see *Apocalypse Now*, because a friend paid my way. I don't like movies about Vietnam 'cause I don't think that they are prepared to tell the truth. *Apocalypse Now* didn't tell the truth. It wasn't real. I guess it was a great thing for the country to get off on, but it didn't remind me of anything I saw. I can't understand how you would have a bridge lit up like a Christmas tree. A USO show at night? Guys attacking the women on stage. That made no sense. I never saw us reach the point where nobody is in charge in a unit. That's out of the question. If you don't know anything, you know the chain of command. And the helicopter attack on the village? Fuckin' ridiculous. You couldn't hear music comin' out of a helicopter. And attacking a beach in helicopters was just out of the question. The planes and the napalm would go in first. Then, the helicopters would have eased in after the fact. That was wild.

By making us look insane, the people who made that movie was somehow relieving themselves of what they asked us to do over there. But we were not insane. We were not insane. We were not ignorant. We knew what we were doing.

I mean we were crazy, but it's built into the culture. It's like institutionalized insanity. When you're in combat, you can do basically what you want as long as you don't get caught. You can get away with murder. And the beautiful thing about the military is there's always somebody that can serve up as a scapegoat. Like Calley. I wondered why they didn't get Delta Company 1-9 because of Cam Ne. We were real scared. But President Johnson came out and defended us. But like that was before My Lai. When they did My Lai, I got nervous again. I said my God, and they have us on film.

I was in Washington during the National Vietnam Veterans Memorial in 1982. But I didn't participate. I saw all these veterans runnin' around there with all these jungle boots on, all these uniforms. I didn't want to do that. It just gave me a bad feeling. Plus some of them were braggin' about the war. Like it was hip. See, I don't think the war was a good thing. And there's no memorial to Cam Ne, to My Lai. To all those children that was napalmed and villages that were burned unnecessarily.

I used to think that I wasn't affected by Vietnam, but I been livin' with Vietnam ever since I left. You just can't get rid of it. It's like that painting of what Dali did of melting clocks. It's a persistent memory.

I remember most how hard it was to just shoot people.

I remember one time when three of our people got killed by a sniper from this village. We went over to burn the village down. I was afraid that there was going to be shootin' people that day, so I just kind of dealt with the animals. You know, shoot the chickens. I mean I just couldn't shoot no people.

I don't know how many chickens I shot. But it was a little pig that freaked me out more than the chickens. You think you gonna be shootin' a little pig, it's just gonna fall over and die. Well, no. His little guts be hangin' out. He just be squiggling around and freakin' you out.

See, you got to shoot animals in the head. If we shoot you in your stomach, you may just fall over and die. But an animal, you got to shoot them in the head. They don't understand that they supposed to fall over and die.

A Piece of My Heart

KEITH WALKER

1985

ANNE SIMON AUGER

Anne lives in the Pacific Northwest, has been married for fourteen years (to a Vietnam vet), and has two daughters. She is a computer programmer and showroom manager for a manufacturer's representative. She does a great deal of volunteer work in her community using her medical background and is active in her daughters' scouting activities.

She had just come home from work with a big bag of groceries, and chased her husband and daughters out for the evening. We got acquainted in the kitchen as we ate. After that we sat on a couch in front of a large picture window. When she began talking, she put one hand over her eyes, and it stayed there during the entire ninety minutes the tape recorder ran. I remember looking out the window, not having eye contact with her, watching the effects of the sunset on a large, cloudy Pacific Northwest sky.

I remember driving down to Fort Sam Houston with two of the girls who had signed up with me. I can still see us flying down those freeways heading south toward Texas. We felt like we were invincible. We owned the world; we were free, independent. It was really neat.

I remember trying on our combat boots and ponchos and our uniforms; we'd never worn anything so ridiculous in our lives. And we would parade 'round and play games in them and think we were really cool . . . We learned how to march. We thought that was so funny. I remember we had field training. We were given compasses and had to go out and find our way back: we never had so much fun. We got lost twelve times to Tuesday—it didn't matter. We had a little bit of medical training in the field where they would wrap some volunteer up in bandages, put a tag on him saying what was wrong with him, and we had to take care of him. It was totally unrealistic. It was another game. We knew what to do and how to do it from the lesson, but we didn't have any idea of what we were getting ourselves into. We were given weapons training in that they showed us how to fire an M-16, but they wouldn't let us do it. Of course I didn't want to anyway—they were too noisy. They took us through a mock Vietnam village. That was a little scary when they had the punji stick trap come up, but again it was no big deal. And I don't see how the Army could have done any different. I hated them for years for not training me better for Vietnam, but I don't think it could possibly be done. I don't think you can train anybody or teach anybody to experience something that horrible without having them simply live it. . . . Anyway. We got through Fort Sam. It was a lark.

I went to Fort Devons in Massachusetts for six months. I was assigned to the orthopedic ward, and 100 percent of my patients were Vietnam casualties. They were long-term; they had been in Japan before they came to us. I didn't even relate them to Vietnam, and it bothers me now, because they could have been suffering some of the distress that I have, and I didn't recognize it. I know some of them acted really wild and crazy, but I figured it was just because they were kids. While I was there I was dating a psychologist. He was a captain. I'll never forget when I got my orders he was the first one I showed them to, and I was excited. "I'm going to Vietnam!" I told him. He was upset because he was staying there and I was leaving; he thought the man should go. It hadn't dawned on me before that I should be anything but excited. I didn't think to question anything that was going on or to wonder what I was getting myself into. I was just out for experiences at the time, I guess.

So, I remember flying over from Travis. I was the only woman on the plane. There must have been two hundred men on the plane. But everybody was polite and friendly until we got within sight of Vietnam, and then it all just quieted down. Nobody talked; nobody said anything. Everybody had their noses glued to the window. We saw puffs of smoke. The plane took a sudden turn up, and we heard we were being fired on. That was the first time it dawned on me that my life may be in peril. Then I started thinking, "Why would they want to shoot me? I haven't done anything to them." Anyway, we took this steep, real fast dive into Long Binh, and we landed in Vietnam. I remember talking to the nurse in charge of assigning people, and she actually gave me a choice of where I wanted to go. The other nurses with me knew just about where they wanted to go. They all had choices, and I had no idea of one place from another. So I told her to send me wherever she wanted, and she still wouldn't do that. She said, "North or south?" I said, "I don't know." I finally just decided, "Oh hell, send me north. If I'm going to be here I might as well get as close to the North Vietnamese as I can," which is really irrational now, but at the time I didn't know what I was doing. So she assigned me to the 91st Evac.

I was assigned to intensive care and recovery, which is like jumping straight into the fire. I had no preparation for it. I was six months out of nursing school and had worked in a newborn nursery until I joined the Army. It was hectic. It was fast paced. It was depressing. I spent six months there. Two of the incidents that really stand out from those six months: One was when I was working recovery. I had been there a few months, long enough to get numb and build a few walls. This eighteen-year-old GI came into my recovery ward. He had been through surgery. He'd been in an APC that ran over a mine, and I think he was the only survivor. He was just a young kid; I don't even think he had hair on his face yet. And he came out of the anesthesia crying for his mother. I felt so helpless. I was barely older than he was, and he's crying, "Mommy! Mommy! Mommy!" I didn't know what to do. . . . I just held him, and I think that's all I did. It worked, but it was a real experience for me because I certainly wasn't maternal at the time and hadn't thought that that would ever come up. It got me to realize how young and innocent and how naive these poor kids were. And their choices had been taken away from them.

Then the other incident. We had a sergeant, must have been in his mid forties; he was a drinker, an alcoholic. And he wasn't even involved first line in the war—he was a supply sergeant or something. He came into our intensive care unit with a bleeding ulcer. I remember spending two hours pumping ice water into his stomach, pulling it out, and pumping it back in. We were also pumping blood into him. He died, and he had a family back home, and I thought, "My God, it's bad enough to die over here legitimately"—the gunshot wound—but to die that way seemed like such an awful waste.

The patient that chased me off the ward . . . was a lieutenant named . . . I don't remember his last name—his first name was John. He was twenty-one. He'd gotten married before he came to Vietnam. And he was shot in his face. He absolutely lost his entire face from ear to ear. He had no nose. He was blind. It didn't matter, I guess, because he was absolutely a vegetable. He was alive and breathing: tubes and machines were keeping him alive. . . . I just . . . couldn't handle it. To think of how one instant had affected his life. . . . His wife's life was completely changed, his parents, his friends, me—it affected me too. And all because of one split second. I got to realizing how vulnerable everybody was. And how vulnerable I was. I took care of him for a week. They finally shipped him to Japan, and I never heard from him again. I don't know if he's dead or alive. I don't know how his wife or his family are doing. I don't know how he's doing. It seems like every patient on that ward, when they left, took a piece of me with them. They came in, we would treat them for a few hours or a few days, and then we'd send them off and never hear a word. I had this real need to see one GI who'd survived the war after an injury, because I never saw them—never heard from them again. There was one time in Vietnam when I came so close to writing to my mother and asking her to check around and see if she could find one whole eighteen-year-old. I didn't believe we could have any left. After John left I just couldn't handle it any more. We had too many bodies lying in those beds minus arms and legs, genitals, and faces, and things like that can't be put back together again.

I found I'd built up walls real effectively. I was patient and tender with the GIs. I didn't talk to them a lot because I was afraid to—afraid of losing my cool. I was very professional, but I was distant. I worry sometimes about the way I treated those GIs in intensive care (this was an insight I only got a year ago). . . . I was afraid, because I didn't feel I had done my best with them. Because of the walls I'd put up I didn't listen to them, didn't hear what they might be trying to tell me even just in gestures or whatever. I wasn't open to them because I was so closed to myself.

I got out of ICU. I couldn't handle any more. I asked to be transferred to the Vietnamese ward. Everybody had to do that—spend a rotation in the ward. This is where I found out that war doesn't just hit soldiers, that nobody is safe from war. I can still see this little boy—he was about nine months old. He had both of his legs in a cast and one arm in a cast and his entire abdomen bandaged, because he'd gotten in the way. I delivered a baby for a POW, a stillborn baby. It amazed me that life still went on even in a war. Because it seemed like everything should just stop. We had lots of medical problems too when we weren't too busy with war injuries. I had an eight-year-old girl who died of malnutrition. That's something that we only read about in our textbooks. Her mother brought her in, reluctantly, and she said we had twenty-four hours to cure her. She didn't trust us. If we couldn't cure the kid in twenty-four hours, she was taking her away. She did take her away, and the kid died the day after. To come from a background like I did, where everybody has plenty to eat, a lot of security, and to witness what these kids went through. They were older at the age of four than I was at eighteen. And I'll never forget that look on their faces, that old-man look on those young kids' faces, because they'd lived through so much. That still haunts me today.

The POWs. I took a lot of my frustrations out on them—in innocuous ways. I made one POW chew his aspirin when he wanted something for pain because I didn't think he had any right to complain while there were so many GIs injured . . . just on the next ward. One of the POWs attacked me once—tried to choke me—and I hit back at him. But I think before I even made contact with him, the two MPs were all over him. I never saw him again. We had one twelve-year-old NVA who had killed five GIs. Twelve years old! And he would brag about it to me. He would spit at me. I have never seen such hate. To see the loathing that he had in his eyes was frightening.

But at almost the same time, we had a kid on the other side of the ward who was about the same age. He was a scout for the GIs, so he was on "our side." And the GIs just babied him. They thought he was the coolest kid, and he was so tough he scared me.

One of my most traumatic and long-lasting experiences happened to me while working the POW ward. An NVA was admitted with gunshot wounds he got during an ambush on a platoon of GIs. This POW was personally responsible for the deaths of six of those GIs. When he was wheeled into my ward, something snapped. I was overwhelmed with uncontrollable feelings of hate and rage. I couldn't go near this guy because I knew, without any doubt, that if I touched him I would kill him. I was shaking from trying to keep my hands off his neck. This scared me to death, and for twelve years after I was scared of experiencing it again. I discovered that I was capable of killing and of violently hating another human being. I had been raised to be a loving and giving person. As a nurse, I had vowed to help *all* who need it. As a human being I should love my brother, whoever he was. I was forced to confront a side of myself I never dreamed existed before.

After four months on the Vietnamese ward, I asked to be transferred again. So I was put on the GI medical ward. That was more depressing than the first two wards I'd been on. Mostly because the people that I had labeled as cop-outs were on that ward. The drug abusers, the alcoholics, the guys in there with malaria—because rather than go out in the field they would not take their malaria pills so they could come down with malaria. I was really very unsympathetic to them. I didn't try to understand them. After so many months of taking care of "legitimate" injuries, I couldn't handle that. I just figured, "Hell, even I can take this. Why can't you? You're supposed to be braver and stronger than I am, and somehow I'm managing."

We were shelled monthly, at least monthly. The closest call we had was when I was on the medical ward. I remember mortars were falling all around us. I had just gotten my sixty patients under their mattresses, and I dove under a bed myself, finally, and then this GI next to me says, "Hey, you forgot . . ." whatever his name was, and sure enough—he was one of our drug ODs—he was lying on top of his bed singing. I had to get out, crawl over to him, pull him out of bed, and put the mattress over him. I remember screaming at him. I was so mad at him for making me take any more chances. This happened the same day that my sister got married. In fact it was almost the same hour, and I thought, "My God, they're partying, and here I am." We had a sapper attack too when I was on that ward. That's when somebody infiltrates our perimeter. There's a certain siren that goes off. At the time, my corpsman on the ward was a conscientious objector, so he wouldn't handle any firearms. I remember I had to grab the M-16 and stand guard after I had locked the doors. I didn't even know how to fire the damn thing! I finally had to haul one of my patients—he was a lieutenant, I remember—out of bed and had him stand with me in case the gun needed to be fired. Once again, I had the preconception that women were supposed to be taken care of, and it seemed like I was doing all the taking care of.

A lot more happened; I just don't like pulling it out. . . . It's behind me now, and I think what became of me is more important anyway.

I remember on the plane home I held my breath until we were probably a thousand miles from Vietnam, because I was so afraid that something would happen and we'd have to go back. We landed at Sea Tac. I remember getting a hotel room and calling my parents, because they wanted to come out from Michigan to meet me. I ended up going back to the airport to meet them on *my* way home from Vietnam. They wanted to stay for two days in Seattle and sightsee. I can vividly see me sitting on this tour bus, looking out the window at nothing. Feeling up in the air, lost, disoriented. I was still back there. I didn't smile much. They thought I was angry. Well, they didn't know. They were trying to act like things were just the same as always—that a year hadn't gone by and that I hadn't gone anywhere. They were doing that to relax me. . . . I'm sure they were hurting too. I jumped at any noise. I looked at people walking the streets, and there wasn't even fear in their eyes. All I could think was, "If you only knew . . . you wouldn't be so damned complacent." I didn't even feel like going home. I wish I could have gone somewhere for a while—just to be by myself. I was pushed right back into everyday living, when I was still so far away from it and so disjointed that I couldn't possibly fit in. Everybody tried to ignore where I'd been. I guess some people did ask me about Vietnam, and I would say things like "It was okay." Or "Actually it was the pits." That's all I said for ten years.

I got married about six months after I got home. Rick and I had met in Japan. It was my second R&R, and I remember it was a month before I was DEROSing. All I was going to do was have a good time. I felt like I hadn't laughed in months. And I remember getting to the hotel in Osaka and people could just say "Good morning" and I'd start giggling. Everything was funny. I just laughed because I was releasing tension, I know that. But at the time I just couldn't stop laughing. I had no thoughts of commitments. And I met Rick. It was a good thing he was persistent. He's the best thing that's ever happened to me.

After we got married, we lived in Utah for four years. I put him through college. I worked in the local hospital there. I started out working newborn nursery simply because I wanted a happy job. So I worked for six months in the nursery and found I was bored. I was promoted to nursing supervisor after that, which worked out well, because I was in charge of the emergency room. I was coordinating emergency surgeries, assisting with deliveries, running the pharmacy. It was a nice challenge. But still, nobody knew I was a veteran. I had a desire to meet another veteran, but I wasn't broadcasting. I was having periods of real depression at the time—very happily married, a good job, wonderful husband, a beautiful baby—and I would consider suicide. I didn't understand why I was so depressed. I had nightmares, but I didn't attribute them to the war. It took me many, many years to even interpret those nightmares. All of a sudden one day I realized that a lot of them were centered around gooks; I couldn't see a slant-eye without getting upset. And a lot of it was centered on being misinterpreted, being misunderstood, but I didn't realize it at the time. As soon as I woke up, I tried real hard to forget them.

I've pretty much grown out of nursing. My last nursing job was at an ER in a run-down section of Richmond, California. Something happened there that was literally the straw that broke my back. It was six years after Vietnam, and one evening this fifteen-year-old black boy comes in to our ER with a two-inch laceration above his right eye from a street fight. It needed stitching, and soon. At first, he had refused to even come to ER, and after an hour of pleading, his mother finally got him in. But he absolutely, flat out didn't trust any white person touching him. I begged, pleaded, reasoned, and even threatened him, but he wouldn't let me touch him. He ended up walking out with his eye swollen shut, a gaping wound, and full of mistrust and hostility—and he was only fifteen! He took me back to Vietnam. To the hostility I felt from the POWs. To the mistrust I felt for any slant-eye—we could never be sure *who* the enemy was. I saw those young kids again, with their so old faces. And I couldn't handle it. I had one of my worst episodes of depression—it lasted for days. I still can't go back to nursing because I'm afraid of this happening again.

About nine years after I got out of Vietnam, I read an article in the paper about this guy in Oregon who'd gone berserk and shot somebody. At his trial they named his condition delayed stress syndrome. I had never heard of it before. But the article described some of the symptoms. And I kept saying, "That's me, that's me! This is exactly it. I can't believe this!" So that evening I brought the article to Rick and said, "Don't laugh, but . . ." Rick and I are very open about everything, talk about absolutely everything, but I never talked to him about my nightmares or my depressions. I didn't want to burden him, I guess, or I didn't want to talk about it. I'm not sure which. I asked, "Did you ever notice things like that about me and just not say anything?" And he said, "Yeah, exactly, I figured when you were ready to talk about it, you'd talk." He was in Vietnam too, of course, but where he was at was relatively quiet, and he never saw combat. So anyway, I spent six months reading up on delayed stress. And it was a relief just to find out what it was making me do this stuff. But I still had the nightmares; I still had the depression. I'd go through periods of relative calm and serenity, and then I'd turn around and start screaming at the kids, or at Rick, or the dog. I'd ventilate that way for a while, and then we'd go back to serenity again.

I was reading the Sunday paper, and by God there was this article on women Vietnam veterans in it. First one I'd ever seen. I read that article like it was saving my life. It mentioned Lynda Van Devanter and some of the things she'd gone through. It mentioned several psychologists who were interviewed, and they talked about delayed stress in women veterans. It was like a lifeline. I thought, "I've got to talk to Lynda." So I called our local VA. They'd never heard of her, and they'd never heard of women's Vietnam veteran groups. They gave me a number to call—and I got a runaround for three or four different phone calls. So I read the article again. When I read it I knew I wanted help and that something had to be done, but God, I was scared to reach out. But I did it. I made a long-distance call to the vet center in Los Angeles somewhere, asked for the psychologist that was mentioned in the article. I told her I was trying to get ahold of someone I could talk to who was a veteran. And I made it very clear that I wanted to talk to another woman veteran. She didn't know how to help me. She said the only thing she could figure out was that I should call Vietnam Veterans of America in Washington, D.C., and see if they could locate Lynda Van Devanter. I remember sitting down before I lost all my nerve and writing a seven- or eight-page letter. I wrote down all those things I'd been bottling up and wanting to talk about and not being able to. I didn't have to preface anything with explanations or details or justifications. I just wrote it down straight from my heart. She wrote me a real nice, supportive letter back. She sent me a whole bunch of material on other women veterans who had been interviewed, and I remember poring over those and underlining everything that I could identify closely with. I felt literally like she was the lifeline, that I had been sinking in a sea unable to swim and she was holding the rope.

A few months later a friend of mine in Anchorage, Alaska, whose daughter was also a friend of mine down here, had read an article where Jan Ott from the Seattle vet center was interviewed. She cut it out and sent it to my friend to give to me because she thought I'd be interested. And it mentioned that there was a support group being formed. I thought, "There's nothing wrong with me. I'm functioning fine." I called Jan anyway to say I thought what she was doing was a good job. She convinced me that it was just a talk group, there was no therapy, nothing else, it didn't mean there was anything wrong with us. So I said, "Yeah, okay." I figured they needed numbers to make the group go. I sat there with my legs crossed and my arms folded, and I wasn't going to talk; I was going to listen. But they were saying the same things I was thinking. It was hard to sit there because in my head I was going, "Oh yeah. Oh yeah!" And it started coming out. It took me a long time. Some of the ladies there—maybe they'd had more practice, I don't know; maybe they're more open with themselves— but they shared really well. I would share but more superficially. Not because I didn't want to share deeper. I don't think I could have at that time. It was a slow evolving through about twelve weeks of the group. I had something more to think about every week. They'd brought out new things that I hadn't ever thought about before.

I think the turning point in the group came when I watched a certain movie on TV. *Friendly Fire.* I remember being just over-whelmed because the guy who played the part of the GI in that film looked exactly like the guy in my nightmares. He was blond; he was young; he was so innocent and so naive. He went over to Vietnam just like most of us did, thinking he was doing what he should be doing . . . and you could just see him evolve. He went from being naive and innocent through being scared and confused into being hard-nosed and cynical. Exactly the way I had gone through it. The movie was done with such perception; they really had a handle on it. I remember sitting down with my notebook and writing as I was going through this movie—thank God for commercials. I had started out describing him as I just did, and how I could relate so well to that. And then something snapped. At the end of the movie, when he was killed and brought home, another useless death, I didn't even realize what I was doing. My letters were all of a sudden three times as large. I was tearing the paper with my pen! I was writing about how angry and bitter I was. It was because those people, whoever they were, who sent us over there made us do all these terrible things, wasted so many lives, so much time and money, and so many resources, are not ac-countable and will never be really accountable. They've hidden be-hind so many other people that they will never be brought to justice. I felt really frustrated and impotent knowing that they would not be reckoned with. And I remember saying that I hope that their day of reckoning would come.

I got through the movie, and it just opened up so many things that I hadn't thought about. I realized finally where my anger and my hostility were directed. I realized how sad I was and that it would never go away. For twelve years I've wanted it to go away, to get on with life, and not have that thing hanging around my neck. I realized how badly I felt about the way I saw myself treat some of those GI patients in intensive care. How I wasn't perfect with them like I probably should have been, and how much that affected me. I realized how much each of those GIs had taken of me with them. And how much I wanted it back. Everything came all at once. I had written all this down, and I was going to share it with the group.

I remember reading what I had written because I don't think I could have said it straight on. My one hand bled from my nails biting into my palm because I was still so angry. I think that's where most of the tension and frustration and stress went that evening. I really got it out. Then, a week or two later, we had the male GIs come to our group. That was very powerful. It was really great for me to see the whole GIs. But even more important I remember Dan, this great big hunk of a guy. He was big but he was gentle, kind, caring. He started talking about how he tried to injure himself in Vietnam so he wouldn't have to go out on another firefight. And my first reaction was to tense up and say, "Oh, Goddamn you! You had to be one of those, didn't you." But Dan sat there and went through the buildup to how it got so bad he would get almost physically sick at thinking of having to go out there. To wonder where the next shot was coming from, if it was coming for him, was he going to live or die, was he going to have to kill somebody. He said he got to the point where he just couldn't take it anymore. He honestly thought that he may even have gone a little crazy for a while. He had a friend of his take the butt of his rifle and try to break his collar bone so he couldn't carry a gun. His friend did it as hard as he could, and he ended up just bruising Dan. And he said, "That guy probably saved my life, because I don't think I could have lived with myself if it worked. I still humped and it hurt with every step, but it was almost like it was my punishment." And this big, gentle man is sitting there crying, talking about how traumatic that experience was for him. It gave me such an insight into what I had labeled as a cop-out. I saw that we all had our own ways of coping. Where I built my walls and hid behind them, that was my form of copping out. I could not judge anybody else for whatever form they took.

Since that time, when I really got everything together and spit it out to the group, things have really been okay. The nightmares are absolutely gone. The depressions are just about gone. But Lynda Van Devanter said it better than I could ever say it again: "The war does not control me anymore. I control it." I know the depressions will still come, but I can handle them because I know why they're there and that they'll go away. I know that I can't forget those experiences, but I understand why I have them and that they're a part of my life. I also know that I'm a better person, actually, for having lived them.

Probably my two biggest goals now are, I'll do my damndest to keep something like that from ever happening again, and if I can help even one other woman veteran to work it through as I have, then it's all worth it. I'm not normally an outgoing person, but I'll spill everything if I have to, if that will help just one other person. Because nobody needs to live through this. . . .

From Dear America
Letters Home from Vietnam

BERNARD EDELMAN, EDITOR
1985

Sept. 7th [1969]

We're all scared. One can easily see this emotion in the eyes of each individual. One might hide it with his mouth, while another might hide it with his actions, but there is no way around it—we are all scared.

They say when fear is in a man, he is prepared for anything. When fear possesses the man, he is prepared for nothing.

As of now, fear is in me. I hope I can keep it from possessing me.

This journal entry was written by PFC William A. Maguire, Jr., of Short Hills, New Jersey, who died on 28 September 1969, two days after contracting a fever while on patrol near the DMZ with the 2nd Battalion, 5th Regiment, 1st Marine Division. He was 20 years old. He had been in Vietnam only four weeks.

❑

Dear Madeline,

Hello my dear sister.

Boy, I sure feel close to you. Since your last letter, I almost feel as if you are my sister. It's good to have someone to tell your troubles to. I can't tell them to my parents or Darlene because they

351

worry too much, but I tell you truthfully I doubt if I'll come out of this alive.

In my original squad I'm the only one left unharmed. In my platoon there's only 13 of us. It seems every day another young guy 18 and 19 years old like myself is killed in action. Please help me, Mad. I don't know if I should stop writing my parents and Darlene or what.

I'm going on an operation next month where there is nothing but VC and VC sympathizers. The area is also very heavily mined. All of us are scared cause we know a lot of us won't make it. I would like to hear what you have to say about it, Madeline, before I make any decisions.

Oh, and one more favor. I'd like the truth now. Has Darlene been faithful to me? I know she's been dating guys, but does she still love me best? Thanks for understanding. See ya if it's God's will. I have to make it out of Vietnam, though, cause I'm lucky. I hope. Ha ha.

Miss ya,

Love,
Ray

PFC Raymond C. Griffiths went to Vietnam just after Christmas in 1965 and was assigned to Company A, 1st Battalion, 9th Marines, 3rd Marine Division. He wrote this letter to Madeline Velasco, a friend from high school in San Francisco, California, in June 1966. He was killed a few weeks later, on the Fourth of July. He was 19 years old.

❑

Dec. 18, 1971

Hi, Frank

Do you still remember me? Well I'm Roger, the one who sent the Christmas stuff to you. Well now you know me I'll finish the rest of my letter.

I liked your letter but Frank why did you join the war? I'm sorry about your friends who died. And I hope they let you get out this Christmas.

And Frank I will pray for you and your friends.

I might get to send you another present if my mother lets me. Have a nice Christmas to and I hope you get some presents.

And have a nice time to won't you.

Have you had snow yet? Well we have and we got three snowmobiles. Last year me and my little brother rode the snowmobiles and every time I turned the corner real fast I tipped the snowmobile and then I looked back and he was laying on the ground.

> Well, by and have fun
> Roger David Barber

Sp/4 Frank Russo received this second letter from his pen pal, eight-year-old Roger Barber, a week before he left Vietnam.

❑

> 6 Dec. '69
> 1230 hr.

Dear Gail:

Hi, doll. How's my girl today? I hope you are not feeling too blue. Well, we are on the move again. We got the word to pack our stuff, and we are going to Ban Me Thuot. We are not going to the village itself, but to the airfield. I think we are going to guard the airfield for a while. From what we have heard, we can get showers there and we can even get sodas or beer. Boy, we have not had anything cold to drink in a long time. It does get us mad that we have to move again. We just got our bunkers built—it took us about 1,000 sandbags to build [them]—and now some other company is coming in and using them. That's the way it seems to be all the time. We do all the hard work and then we have to move. Well, that's the Army for you.

I remember in one of your letters you said you were surprised that I said I don't mind being here. Well in a way, that's true. Sure

I want to be home with you and have all the things we dream about. But yet being here makes a man feel proud of himself—it shows him that he is a man. Do you understand? Anyone can go in the Army and sit behind a desk, but it takes a lot to do the fighting and to go through what we have to. When we go home, we can say, "Yes, I was in Vietnam. Yes, I was a line dog." To us it means you have gone to hell and have come back. This is why I don't mind being here, because we are men. . . .

Love,
Pete

Sp/4 Peter H. Roepcke, from Glendale, New York, served as a "line dog"—an infantryman—with Company A, 3rd Battalion, 506th Infantry, 101st Airborne Division, from September 1969 until April 1970, operating in I Corps, when he broke his leg while jumping from a helicopter. He died of a heart attack in October 1981.

❑

Lament

Mother.
I am cursed.
I was chosen
trained to kill
asked to die
I could not vote
I can't ask why

Mother
I am cursed
spit on
and shunned
by long-haired doves

Mother
I am cursed.
I'm a soldier

in an age
when soldiers aren't in fashion.
—Tom Oathout

Sgt. Thomas Oathout served with the 172nd Military Intelligence Detachment, assigned to the 173rd Airborne Brigade, operating in II Corps, from August 1970 through July 1971. He lives in Bear, Delaware, and works in Philadelphia as a salesman for a publishing company.

❑

Feb 14th 66

Dear Mom,
   . . . I've seen some things happen here lately that have moved me so much that I've changed my whole outlook on life. I'll be the same in actions I guess, but inside I'll be changed. I feel different now after seeing some horrible things, and I'll never forget them. It makes you glad you're just existing. I can't say what I mean, but some of the things you see here can really change a man or turn a boy into a man. Any combat GI that comes here doesn't leave the same. I don't mean the cooks, clerks or special service workers, but the fighting man. I doubt if anybody realizes what combat is really like. I *thought* I knew until a few days ago when I started facing harsh realities and forgetting TV and movie interpretations. I never had much respect for GIs even after I was in for a while, but since I've seen what his real job is, I have more respect for him than any man on earth. To shoot and kill somebody, turn your head and walk away isn't hard, it's watching him die that's hard, harder than you could imagine and even harder when it's one of your own men.
   I've said enough about it. Don't ask any questions. When I come home, if I feel like talking about it I will, but otherwise don't ask. It may sound dramatic, and I'll tell you it is. It's just something you don't feel like discussing and can't begin to write about.
   Well, Mom, I'll sign off. Be careful driving.

Love,
George

PFC George Robinson was assigned to the Recon Platoon, Headquarters and Headquarters Company, 2nd Battalion, 28th Infantry, 1st Infantry Division, based at Di An, when he was wounded on 11 June 1966. He lives in North Massapequa, New York, and teaches history at Roslyn Junior High School.

❏

March 2 [1969]

Darling,

I love you so very, very much. Finally it's over for a while and I can write. I don't know where to begin or what to say or how. I guess I'll just try to tell you how I feel, which is mostly proud, sad, tired and relieved. After all these endless days and nights, they gave me and the platoon 36 hours off. I spent today going to memorial services for my people, doing wash, catching up on work in my office and writing up people for medals.

Oh, Darling, it's been so unreal. I'm not going to go into detail—it would only scare, depress or worry you. Just be convinced I'm fine, it's over and all I have to complain of now is a bad cold and a lot of fatigue. These last days were just so filled with fighting, marching, thinking, all the time thinking, "Am I doing it right? Is this what they said at Quantico? How can I be sure I haven't led us into a trap and the NVA are waiting?" etc., etc., until I became so exhausted just by worrying. I'm just so grateful (to whom?). I "only" lost six men (I *know* how awful that sounds)! I had a seventh guy fall off a cliff and get a bad cut and concussion, but he'll be OK.

I'm so confused. At the service today they were talking about God protecting people and eternal life and I felt so desolate, so despairing. I know there is no reward waiting for them or any hope. I began crying I felt so awful and hopeless, but somehow held it back and it just looked like I was sniffling from my cold. (See! How awful my ego and pride that I couldn't even let myself weep for those poor, poor kids!) All I can say is that considering how awful it was, I'm so lucky I didn't lose more.

I said I was proud. Mostly of them. I'm putting 10 of them in for decorations. Enclosed are some of the rough drafts of citations. Don't read them if you don't want to. Just save them for me. I guess I should be honest. I've been nominated, I hear, for the Silver Star, the third highest medal. Please don't get upset. I didn't try to win it—I was just trying to keep my people alive and doing the best I could. I may not even get it, 'cause the reviewing board might knock it down to a Bronze Star. You know me so well, you know I'm lying if I say I'm not pleased. I am, I'm proud, but only the worst part of me. My better part is just so sad and unhappy this whole business started.

Again, though it may be foolish, I'll keep my word and be honest. The post-Tet offensive isn't over. All intelligence points to a return bout. However, my platoon is 1,000% better than it was, we have so much support now—like a family, really. We'll all watch out for each other. Also we don't believe they'll hit again near here, so whatever happens, I'll be OK. That's the truth too, honey. I have fantastic good luck, as strange as that may sound, and what's US is too good and too strong for any badness.

Love,

Brian

Brian Sullivan, a lieutenant assigned to the 4th Battalion, 11th Regiment, 1st Marine Division, was a field artillery officer and infantry platoon commander in the area around Da Nang from June 1968 to June 1969. He is now an associate professor of history at Yale University and lives in New York City. This letter was written to his then-wife Tobie.

❑

Saturday

14 Oct 67

Dear Mom and Dad,

Well, the day after tomorrow we go on Operation Golden Fleece. All we do is go out and make sure that no one steals the rice from the harvest. All it is is a lot of walking and cold nights and hot days. I'm writing in the dark with only a candle for light, so please forgive the handwriting.

Well, I've got the 3rd Platoon—44 different, completely different, men. Some small, some big, some only 18 and some 24. Each one has his own problems, and what I've become is a mother hen watching over her brood all the time, day and night. I'm the first up, the last down at night.

It seems like a long time until I get home, but the days go by quickly. I have a platoon sergeant who keeps my head down for me. He says he doesn't want to lose me so I let him have his way. They haven't had any enemy contact here since June, and the men become hard to handle, too cocky and sure of themselves. There sure is a lot to think about here, and so much to do, really. Tonight I had a 19-year-old come to me for help and advice. He is married to an 18-year-old, and he was having problems. If he knew I was only 20, I wonder if he would have come. I think I helped him—he seemed happy.

Well, how are you both and Jeanene, Bob and Billy and Vallette and Sam and the kids? I do hope they're all doing well. I hope to get some mail from all of you soon.

Well, not much more. It is raining again. *Mud!*

Love,
Don

2Lt. Don Jacques, Co. B, 1/26th Reg., 3rd Mar. Div., Khe Sanh, 1967–1968, KIA 25 February 1968.

❑

18 October 1967

Dear Sue—

Well, I've been transferred to another section. River Section 522. I didn't really want to leave 533. I'd grown attached to the men in the section. My crews found it pretty hard to say good-by. I did,

BERNARD EDELMAN · *Dear America*   359

too. After all, we'd seen a lot of action together. When you've been under fire with the same people enough times, you don't even have to think about what they're going to do or wonder if what they do will be right. You work as a team. Torres, before he went home to Hawaii, told me he could tell by the look in my eyes what I wanted them to do. I didn't have to say a thing.

I got that letter from my mother. I'm trying to think of the best way to answer it. I know she only wants me to come back home alive and without battle scars—as you and everyone else [do]. But I can't be anything less than I am out there. You know that. I suppose it's because I'm a perfectionist in everything I do, including waging war. If I have a chance to shoot it out with the enemy, I'm not going to turn tail and run. I'm not [the] fool she thinks I am. I gambled and won. I killed at least one of the enemy and didn't lose a man, whether because of blind luck, or God, or ability to handle myself in a tight situation. There are too many armchair quarterbacks in this war, whether they're sitting in the States or a safe chair here in Vietnam. You have to be in the war to understand it and be able to make judgments on the actions of men in war. My ex-CO in 533 never went out on the river, except for an occasional special operation. Yet he had the balls to stand up before commanders, etc., and tell them which were the bad canals and what kind of weapons this or that VC company used—all of it based on information I'd brought back or actions I'd been in. I could tell you the name of the man who lives in the last house on the east bank near the broken bridge where I've been ambushed twice and give you a description of the man I've seen him meeting on the other side of the bridge. I keep book on my patrol areas. He couldn't even tell you the name of the sector the canal is located in. All he's thinking about are his promotion to lieutenant commander and the medals he's going to put himself in for. And he—like the commanders and captains above him—are afraid some obscure ensign is going to upset all of that. . . .

· · ·

28 October 1967

Dear Susan—

The war is getting worse. The bastards are getting more and better weapons, and are making use of them. For the first week I was down here on the Ham Luong, the monotonous quiet of the river lulled us into a false sense of contentment that we had the Viet Cong on the run. The only way we could get him to fight was by going into his backyard. However, we went into his backyard once too often. During the previous night, a VC platoon (as near as I can figure) overran an outpost next to the riverbank almost directly across from the heart of the city of Ben Tre and set up an ambush for our PBRs. The battle was terrible. They hit the boats with recoilless rifles (like bazookas from WW II), wounding every man and completely destroying one of the boats. Fortunately the patrol officer had the sense to have his men bail out after the first two rounds hit the lead boat. No sooner had they jumped over the side than five more rounds hit. The men swam for it, and as they scrambled ashore, helping one another through the barbed wire, the VC fired the rockets after them. One man, having lost three fingers and much blood from numerous wounds, was about to collapse on the shoreline. The patrol officer was screaming at him to keep going and trying to haul the man (who was twice my size) over the fence, when a round exploded ten yards from them. The wounded man leaped completely over the barbed wire without any help—that was all the incentive he needed. All Americans are now well on their way to recovery.

Sue, I thought about keeping this whole thing secret until I got home. But I can't. I have to tell you people back home what this war is like. It's worse than any war the U.S. has fought to date. I know most people back home are wondering why we're even bothering to stick it out. I'm no superpatriot, as you know. And I'm no Navy stooge. It's just that for the hundred garbage-pickers you meet over here who have no belly for fighting the VC, I meet a couple of people I like and respect, who are my friends and who stick up for their rights, and I don't want to see them get killed by the VC. I've come to evaluate things as a soldier. I'm closer to life and death every day than the majority of men are on their last day on earth. And I tend to form my values about one simple axiom: Life.

Love,
Dick

LT. J.G. Dick Strandberg, River Patrol Sections 533 and 522, Mekong Delta, 1967–1968.

❑

Hue–Phu Bai
29 June 68

Mom,

Today I received your letter in reply to my extension letter. You replied as I knew you would—always the mother who tries to put her son's wishes before her own, even when she is not sure it is best for his welfare. It made me sad. I want so much to make you proud. I want so much to make you happy. At the same time I have my life to lead with my own dreams, goals, and outlook. And I know all these things cannot be compatible—particularly over the short run.

But understand that I love my family more than anyone or anything in the world. March 1969 is not so very far away. I have been in Vietnam more than 11 months. I have only eight more months in the country. My chances of coming away unhurt improve every month because I know so much more than I did as a beginner. I know much better when to take a chance and when not to. Please trust my judgment. Try to understand that you raised a son who likes the excitement and challenge he finds here, and these qualities will see him through the opportunities he will face in the 1970s.

Know that I dream of that day when I return home to you and Dad, and hold you in my arms again. Sometimes I get lonely. Sometimes I want nothing more than to sit down at the dinner table, see before me roast beef, corn on the cob, mashed potatoes, bow my head for the blessing, and look up and see my mother— pretty and smiling—searching for any way she can [to] make her son more comfortable. Know that it is hard to turn your back on these things.

It is not easy to say I opt for six more months of heat, sand, and shooting. I know there will [be] the nights that I suffer the loss of another friend. And nothing can make a man feel so alien or alone as [a] walk by the seashore as he tries to adjust to the loss of another friend in this godforsaken country. But that is part of the draw, the attraction, the challenge. Here there is a job to be done. There are moral decisions made almost every day. My experience is invaluable. This job requires a man of conscience. The group of men that do this job *must* have a leader with a conscience. In the last three weeks we killed more than 1,500 men on a single operation. That reflects a lot of responsibility. I am needed here, Mom. Not that I am essential or indispensable. But my degree of proficiency is now undisputed as the best in 1st Marine Division. The young men coming in need the leadership of an older hand. I am that hand. I relish the opportunity.

I am sorry I have hurt you. But if I thought I was needed at home more than here, I would come home. Things are going well at home. So where do I belong? This is an unusual time in our nation's history. The unrest around the world is paralleled only a handful of times in history. Young men are asking questions—hard questions. Much of the focus of the entire world is on Vietnam. The incompetency and the wrongs committed in Vietnam are staggering. But through it all I see a little light. Some men choose to fight on the streets. Some choose to fight in the universities. Some choose to fight in the parliaments. My choice is between two options—fight in Vietnam or shut up. I choose Vietnam. If I am to contribute, it must be Vietnam. And when I get home, you too will see that little light.

Your son,
Rod

Capt. Rodney R. Chastant, from Mobile, Alabama, served with Marine Air Group 13, 1st Marine Air Wing, based at Da Nang. Although his 13-month tour in Vietnam was up in September 1968, he extended for an additional six months. He was killed on 22 October 1968. He was 25 years old.

❑

October 20, 1966

Dear Aunt Fannie,

This morning, my platoon and I were finishing up a three-day patrol. Struggling over steep hills covered with hedgerows, trees, and generally impenetrable jungle, one of my men turned to me and pointed a hand, filled with cuts and scratches, at a rather distinguished-looking plant with soft red flowers waving gaily in the downpour (which had been going on ever since the patrol began) and said, "That is the first plant I have seen today which didn't have thorns on it." I immediately thought of you.

The plant, and the hill upon which it grew, was also representative of Vietnam. It is a country of thorns and cuts, of guns and marauding, of little hope and of great failure. Yet in the midst of it all, a beautiful thought, gesture, and even person can arise among it waving bravely at the death that pours down upon it. Some day this hill will be burned by napalm, and the red flower will crackle up and die among the thorns. So what was the use of it living and being a beauty among the beasts, if it must, in the end, die because of them, and with them? This is a question which is answered by Gertrude Stein's "A rose is a rose is a rose." You are what you are what you are. Whether you believe in God, fate, or the crumbling cookie, elements are so mixed in a being that make them what he is, his salvation from the thorns around him lies in the fact that he existed at all, in his very own personality. There once was a time when the Jewish idea of heaven and hell was the thoughts and opinions people had of you after you died. But what if the plant was on an isolated hill and was never seen by anyone? That is like the question of whether the falling tree makes a sound in the forest primeval when no one is there to hear it. It makes a sound, and the plant was beautiful and the thought was kind, and the person was humane, and distinguished and brave, not merely because other people recognized it as such, but because it is, and it is, and it is.

The flower will always live in the memory of a tired, wet Marine, and has thus achieved a sort of immortality. But even if we had never gone on that hill, it would still be a distinguished, soft, red, thornless flower growing among the cutting, scratching plants, and that in itself is its own reward.

Love,
Sandy

On 11 November 1966, less than three weeks after he wrote this letter to his great-aunt Mrs. Louis Adoue, Marine 2Lt. Marion Lee Kempner, from Galveston, Texas, was killed by a mine explosion near Tien Phu. After he disarmed one mine, another was tripped by one of his men. Although wounded by shrapnel, Lt. Kempner ordered the corpsman to take care of the other wounded man first. He died aboard a medevac en route to the hospital. He was 24 years old.

Everything We Had

AL SANTOLI

1981

Robert Santos
Rifle Platoon Leader
101st Airborne Division
Hue
November 1967–November 1968

MY MEN

I was drafted in March 1966. It wasn't my intention to go into combat, but to go to Officer Candidate School, and quit a month before OCS ended. It wouldn't be held against me and I'd have less than a year left. But the way it worked out, a friend did that ahead of me and he went to 'Nam, anyway. So I decided that based on what I had seen and my own feelings about myself, I should complete OCS.

I went over to 'Nam with two other guys as part of an advance party for the 101st Airborne, mainly to handle logistics and to make sure all the equipment was there. The rumors were that advance parties were being wiped out. When my company got there, they were under the impression that I had already died, which was a really weird feeling, to meet the company commander, who I didn't get along with, and the first words out of his mouth are "I thought you were dead." My response was "Too bad, huh?"

The 101st were mostly West Point officers. I was the first guy to

come there from OCS, and was not well received. They had a camaraderie. Most of the lieutenants out of West Point graduated from the
same class. They graduated through Airborne school, Ranger school,
and all came there as a unit.

We were part of the Hue liberation force in the Tet offensive. The
North Vietnamese Army had taken the city. So the Marine Corps, the
South Vietnamese, the 101st and the 1st Cavalry went in from differ-
ent angles to liberate the city.

I was twenty-one. But I was young in terms of commanding men in
combat. I didn't know anything. I was the kind of lieutenant that
they'd say, "Oh, shit, here's another green lieutenant." That's what I
was. You don't know what to do, your mind races over the training
you've taken in how to deal with these kinds of situations. I was naïve
and really took what they said at face value.

We operated for maybe two weeks with only minor contact. I was
working the whole time, spreading the platoon out, doing it right. I
was lead platoon on our way into Hue. We came past the paddies, the
trees, came around the green. I looked up and saw an NVA flag flying
over the next open space. I couldn't believe it. I just . . . I guess I
just freaked. I got on the horn right away and called the CO. I was
stuttering and stammering: "I see it. I see the flag! I . . . My God,
they're finally there."

All I knew at that point was "My God! I'm scared shitless. Holy shit.
This is the real thing." I never expected to see a flag. I expected to get
shot at. But they were so brazen. They were there. Dug in. The CO
said, "Move out." I've heard that before: "Follow me." But I was in
the bottom of the infantry. He didn't say "Follow me," he said "Move
out." I said, "Now I know what 'Follow me' means—Lieutenant says
'Follow me'." And that's what we did.

The strange thing about war, there's always humor. Prior to that,
when I was walking around I was your typical "asshole lieutenant."
Everyplace I walked something got caught. You know, guys could
walk right through a bush. My helmet would fall off, my pack would
get snagged. And although no one ever told me, I had a reputation as
the wait-a-minute-lieutenant. "Hold up, hold up, the lieutenant's
caught." Here you're trying to lead men in combat and be a tough

guy. Most of the guys were bigger than me. I weighed like 130 pounds. And really, always getting snagged was embarrassing.

I remember walking through the rice paddies that opened up and the small stream and the green on both sides. We were walking down the right side, near the trail, and there was another company on my left flank. All of a sudden all hell opened up. You have to understand, I've never been a Boy Scout, I've never been a Cub Scout. The closest I came to that was going to my sister's Campfire Girl meetings. I grew up in New York City and Long Island. Watched a lot of movies and read a lot of books. I never fired a weapon. I never got into fights with my buddies. My RTO was from East Wenatchee, Washington. Grew up a hunter. They opened up fire and Wes started going down. You make a connection real quick that someone's been shot and someone's getting hurt.

The first thing I did was yell, "Follow me," and I turned to the right for cover. There was a bamboo thicket. I couldn't walk through a jungle, an open field, without tripping. Somehow I made a hole through those bushes that everyone in the platoon could go through side by side. Got on the other side—my hat was on my head, my rifle was in my hands, I'd lost nothing. There were guys from another platoon that didn't know what they were doing. Everyone was running around crazy.

I said, "Come with me. Follow me." And I didn't know what I was doing. I knew I was supposed to go toward the enemy. I was trained not to stand still. Don't stand in the killing zone. Don't get shot. Move. So I moved, and as I ran forward I heard these noises. Kind of like *ping, ping*—no idea what that noise was. I finally jumped down behind this mound of dirt that turned out to be a grave, which I didn't know at that time. So I jumped behind this mound of dirt with my RTO and we're all kind of hid behind this stuff. I said, "Just climb up, tell them we're in place and we're hooked up with the left flank and the enemy is in front of us." And I started playing the game. I got up and I ran around yelling "Move this machine gun over here" and "Do this over there." I mean, all this noise is going past me. I still didn't know what this noise was. *Ping.* Just a little weird, something new. I finally got back after running around, sat down next to the RTO, and he said, "What the fuck you doing?" I said, "What do you mean?" He said, "Don't you know what's going on?" I said, "Yeah, goddamnit. I know what's going on. Who do you think I am?" He says, "Don't you know what that noise is?" I said no. He said, "That's the bullets going over your head." I never knew it. I mean, if I'd known it I probably would've just buried myself and hid. But I didn't know it. I just didn't know it.

The NVA were in the thicket. There was a stream between us and them, and they were dug in on the opposite side. And they nailed us. They had us pinned down all over the place. Everything that day was done by the book. Just incredible. I don't know how I survived that day, because lieutenants had a very short life expectancy and the reason is because they're jerks and they run out and do stupid stuff by the book. That day we took our first casualties in our platoon. Sergeant Berringer, I think his name was, next to me got shot in the arm. And I remember the training again. Here you were a medic. Look for the bullet's exit. So I found the exit and patched him up with his bandage. Then I realized that there's also an entrance. So I took my bandage out. This is a mistake. You're not supposed to take out your bandage and patch someone else up. But I had to do it. I turned around and called the medic, but he was all freaked out. The bullet that went through Berringer's arm killed the guy next to him. It was a very traumatic day for all of us.

I had told that guy's squad leader that morning, "Tell him to stay behind with the gear and the chopper will bring him forward later." But he wanted to go out. To this day I still think you can tell ahead of time when someone's going to die. Whether they know it or not, I'm convinced that I can tell. It's not something deliberate. Kind of a blankness comes over their face. It's not like they're already dead. It's like a distance and a softness to their features.

But he died and it was a really bad day. We found out how heavy a dead guy can be. The biggest guy in our platoon couldn't pick him up and carry him. So I picked him up, took about three steps, and I couldn't go much farther. But by that time the big guy realized that he could pick him up—It was just mental. We were freaked. And eventually we got out of that mess.

From that first time we made contact we proceeded to keep sweeping toward the city. The way the 101st operated, we sometimes moved as a battalion, but generally the company split off and we did that whole anvil/hammer bit. So although you were working in the battalion operation, you were functioning as a company and sometimes as small a unit as a platoon.

I think it's funny how you can rationalize everything while you're there. Everything is justifiable in terms of survival, which is unfortunate. I can criticize people today, like at law school when I went there, for being so competitive, so survival-oriented. They were called "gunners," would do things just to make sure they got a better grade. Seems to me today's perception of how unimportant that all is . . . Whereas you go back there and you're justifying killing someone. I'm not sure which one's worse—whether it's unimportant or the means by which you compete. It's really crazy. But we would chase them every day, they'd shoot at us and we'd shoot at them, never making contact. And then every day, almost like clockwork, in the late afternoon they'd stop and make a stand and we'd fight. Went on for months, literally for months. Even after the city was retaken, they still operated in the area.

We overran a base camp on the way into Hue. We called it a base camp, but it probably wasn't but a staging area—there were packs just like ours lined up on the ground. It's a really freaky thing to think you're chasing someone and then to suddenly show up and there they are taking a break for exercise or going inside a barracks for a class—I don't know what they did. But psychologically it really shook us because shit, they're just as disciplined and efficient as we are. They're so confident they can just walk away and leave their stuff like it was a field exercise, training. Maybe it was. Maybe that's what I was to them. But this time we were using live fire. We opened up their packs and they had sets of civilian clothes, military clothes, personal effects. I really wondered if they were at war, except to know that we fought with them every day.

North Vietnamese, that's all I fought. I went into Hue and saw the civilian bodies lined up. I know I didn't kill them. Americans don't shoot people from a distance and then line the bodies up. So when you walk in and find them lined up there on their stomachs with their hands tied behind their backs, you know it was the NVA who did that. I know no Americans did that because we were the first ones to enter that portion of the village. They killed the water buffalo, everything.

It was civil war and we were in there and they were killing us as we killed them. I mean, the poor victims who had relatives in the North and relatives in the South . . . The only equivalent I can imagine was I was sent to the Detroit riots with the 101st before I went to 'Nam. Coming back, my biggest fear was going to Fort Dix, because even though I wanted to be close to home, I didn't want to be stuck on riot duty. I said, "I'll be damned if I come all the way back here from Vietnam to go on riot duty and have someone throw a bottle or a brick and split my head open." What's your reaction going to be? Pull that trigger? Shoot my own countrymen?

Patriotism is just loyalty to friends, people, families . . . I didn't even know those guys in Vietnam until I got there, and it wouldn't have mattered if you came to my platoon tomorrow—if we got hit, I would go out and try to save your ass just as I would've done for anyone else I'd been with for a month, two months, three months. Instant bonding.

One thing I did find out after I went to Hue and came back, which I didn't know at the time because of the cultural gap, was the significance of the pine trees in the middle of the jungle. Every time someone died that was relatively famous, they'd plant a pine tree in his honor so his spirit would live on. I had a teacher who was Vietnamese when I went to school after getting out of the service. His father was a poet laureate of Hue who had a tree planted for him. I never had the heart to tell the teacher, who was a friend, that I used to sling a poncho on those trees. I mean, I thought it was a great place to sleep because the pine needles were nice and it was always clean. I didn't make the connection that there was something special about the area. We used the needles to help start our fires. Dig little holes in the hedges around it—dig in. Sacrilege. In some sense his father's spirit gave me shelter, which is kind of ironic.

It was really a break for us to go to rice hovels because we hadn't cooked for so many months. A little boy came out and wanted some C-rations. When they want C-rations, you know they're hurting, the food's just terrible. He was going to share his dinner with us and he brought out some fish. The hottest damn thing I ever had. I can still to this day remember them being fuming hot. We shared our food and we asked him where he lived. He pointed to this house in the clearing. He said he was there with his sister, and we said, "Well, why doesn't your sister come out and join us for dinner?" And he said, "She can't. The VC will see her with us, they'll kill her." We said, "What about you? They'll see you." He said it didn't matter because they know he's getting food.

So it's just like everything else: you leave and they're back, and people have to live with that. They have to deal with the fact that we're going to be gone and leave them behind. But what struck me that day was I was looking at that kid—and I didn't know how old he was, but he had to be under ten—was that all his life he knew war. And then when we're gone he's going to know that Americans may have come through and raped his sister. The VC may have raped his sister because she allowed the Americans to do this. And if the Americans had conceivably seen her with the VC, they would've . . . the whole thing was just . . . it was certainly a statement. It was a tragedy and it was so horrifying. I tried to think of what I would be like if this took place in my hometown. This may have been a turning point in my life, at least in the terms of the war.

When we operated around Hue we didn't stay in the populated areas. We were in the mountains and in the dry season and wet season in different places. I remember having to cross a river at night to set up a blocking force for what we called a major invasion the next day in what we termed VC-controlled territory. The VC controlled one side of the river and the ARVNs controlled the other side. We always operated with the South Vietnamese, we figured there must be VC sympathizers there. And the ARVNs we worked with refused to cross the river. Now, that told me two things: either they were waiting for us to get shot at or they were telling me, "Look, this isn't worth it. They don't bother us and we don't bother them." And that was a great way of living. Survival, right? But we were forced to cross that damn river.

I had to send my platoon across. To say I was pissed and confused would not be adequate. But we did it and it happened all the time. Whenever you went on an ambush with the ARVN they made so much noise that no one would ever walk through your ambush site. So it was safe. You never got hit, but then again, you never carried out your mission either, which was not clear to the American soldiers. And what became confusing was the ARVNs didn't want to fight for their country. Why should we? If you want us to go out and defend ourselves, don't stick us with those guys, because they're going to run away. They're not going to fight.

There were a couple of units, the South Vietnamese marines, the rangers and the paratroopers, who would stand and fight for the most part, but working with regular ARVNs or the Popular Forces or police — that was a liability.

Also, whenever you worked with them you were subject to S-5 [U.S. military intelligence] coming down and asking how you're doing. They were trying to win the hearts and minds of the people, which I could never fully understand because I didn't think there was anything to win. I thought we should just leave. There was confusion from a military standpoint and, of course, from a psychological standpoint.

I remember going on an operation and being attached to the 1st Cavalry. We had full security for a mine-sweep team down the road. Well, out there was a command-detonation mine team. As the truck went over the bridge, that mine team detonated the mine. My men were in the truck. I watched the VC run into a village, and after taking care of what we had to take care of, we went after them.

There was nobody in the village, only an old couple, and there's all this VC literature. It made no sense, absolutely no sense to me. Why this village was there, why this old couple was there, why they were killing . . . I mean I know it made sense, but I just couldn't put it together. I did the whole thing I learned in training. You go to the fire and scrape off the top ash to see if there were hot coals underneath.

Everything was warm. The pots were warm, warm embers underneath. And my men were obviously upset. One of our men had died and a couple others were wounded, engineers as well. They just went right up in the air and that was it.

When the explosion went off. An object was moving through the air towards us. I'm thinking clear. How long will it take? Not very long, I thought. But it was like a long time coming and it was high in the air and this dark object was moving and I was watching it. I was transfixed by it. It was almost hypnotic. Here were two seasoned combat veterans standing there in a crouch watching something come through the air at us. I thought calmly, "It's gonna hit me." We watched it and we watched it and we watched it. It came closer and closer and closer. And at some point I suspect we both realized that it wasn't a bomb, it wasn't . . . it was part of a body. And we stood there, he and I, about three feet apart. It landed between us. It was a boot with the leg in it sheered at the top of the boot. It landed fucking upright and it was like a goddamn movie.

But we didn't shoot at the village. I had seen these two guys running and then when we got to the village and found the old couple I knew it was obviously utilized by the enemy. I was trying to deal with my men and find out what I could do. So I decided to—from purely military standpoint—try to close my men psychologically. We would burn down the hootches except the old couple's, who remained for one reason or another—we left their property alone. We just burned down, denied the enemy that kind of shelter, although they could build them again; they were just grass and weeds. In the process of burning down the village a major from the 1st Cav came by. I never wore rank in the field and he was looking for it. He says, "Who's in charge here?" I said, "I am." He said, "Who are you?" And I told him I was Lieutenant Santos. He says, "Were you doing this here?" I said, "Yeah. We were looking for the men that detonated the mine. They ran into this village. We came in and looked for them. This is a VC village and . . ."

It's not so much that we missed them as the frustration of having been blown up from a distance and the old people standing there saying, "No VC here, no VC." And everything around them says someone just left. What do you do? My responsibility would be, I think, somewhat complex. I had to uphold the traditions of military America, all that crap. I had to worry about my men. And I felt that responsibility goes down rather than up. I owed no allegiance to America. I owed no allegiance to the S-5 or the 1st Cav and all of that crap. I had to make sure that these thirty guys—which were never really thirty; eighteen or twenty-two—had to keep their head in line. And the men burning down a few grass huts which would kill no one and hurt no one but deny the enemy shelter in the rain, which they had no problem finding, was worth it.

That was very confusing. We thought we did what we had to do and they would understand that. But apparently we upset the winning of the hearts and the minds of the people. I told them, "What are you talking about, hearts and minds? Look what they just did to us. I mean, I should risk my men every day so you can come in and tell me that these people believe in America?"

These S-5 guys were from base camp. They operated out of planes, dropping those propaganda leaflets. Those leaflets mean nothing to you when you pick one up next to a dead American. They operated in a vacuum. They operated more in a vacuum than I did. I went there with some ideals. These guys were just stupid.

I ended up going there . . . It sounds corny, but this is what I felt when I went into the service: that if I didn't go, someone else would have to go in my place. I couldn't possibly be responsible knowing that someone else may have died because I didn't want to go. It was a question of having enough confidence or being sure enough of my convictions that it would be the right thing and my job would be to permit someone else not to go. So I went.

At the nitty-gritty it was only survival. It was only to come home and see your friends, your family, not to shame them, not to hurt them. Come back to America. And it wasn't like, "America the great, the land of the beautiful." I mean, I didn't grow up in an area like Pennsylvania—it's beautiful out there—but I came back to Long Island and New York City. Traffic, people, noise. I just wanted to come home. And I think that the one thing that people lost track most of was their families. I mean, you realized that you die . . . My philosophy is, and I used to tell people this, they'd come to my platoon and I'd say it was the best platoon in the battalion. Probably the best battalion in the brigade, the best brigade in the division and all that bullshit.

I said, "Only two things can happen to you. You can get wounded and go home early. Or you can die. And then you really don't give a shit. You're just dead. I'm planning to go home, and I think when it's your turn to go home, the best way to go home is whole. If you stick with me, stick it out and learn from the guys who are here, you won't get wounded. You won't die. If you stick the whole fucking year out here and go home, that's the worst possible thing that can happen, and that's what you should look forward to." I believed it. I really believed it. And that's what we did. We really tried to do that.

You didn't want to get close to anyone over there. I was trained not to get close to my men. I was trained to keep a distance. And it wasn't simply because they would lose respect for you, but because you would never be able to control them, you would never be objective in your decisions if you had friends. You'd stay with them, it's only logical. That was really hard, being an officer. I mean, it's just a title, being an officer. And it's a strange thing that the men hate you, but when the bullet goes off, they look to you: "What now, Lieutenant?" Everyone wants to say, "Get down. Let's not do anything." In the field you always look to the leaders. In the military it just so happens that they're preordained by rank—not necessarily by skill or competence or anything else for that matter. I mean, one of the things is realizing that because somebody has more rank or is older than you, it doesn't make him any smarter.

Another thing I learned after going to Vietnam. I grew up and was in the kind of crowd in high school that was the all-American bunch. But back there I didn't realize that having the last name of Santos made me different, until I found out later on that it had an effect on me in the Army in how people treated me. Having a Hispanic surname—I didn't even think about it. I just thought I was white like everyone else. I grew up in a clique that ran the school, the officers of all the clubs. We were the athletes, all that bullshit.

I mean, I was in the Airborne. Airborne guys are tough and all that bullshit, and they're the best outfit. So I looked around for some kind of support. Of course, I looked at the guys who I thought identified with me: "Oh, he went to college. Hey, you're an athlete. Hey, you're this. Great." Well, they're not all from New York City, much less from Long Island. They're from all parts of the country.

I found out that bullshit is not an indicator of what you're going to do under stress. It's so artificial, the world we live in. And in the service, tall, short, thin, fat, good-looking, homely, ugly—it didn't matter. Name, color—it meant nothing under combat. Bullets have no discrimination. And I think some of the smallest guys carried more weight than the biggest guys because they could psychologically do it. They could take more abuse physically, mentally, because they were stronger.

For me it really wasn't a limit of confidence. I was determined. And part of my determination came out of the fact that I was responsible for bringing these guys home. Eight of my men died over there and two got wounded. All I was determined to do was protect us. I wrote very few letters home because there was nothing to talk about. And I would watch the mail come in. The mail was dropped off at the CP [command post] and I'd watch. Let's say Jones got letters this week and then I noticed there was a break in his mail. I'd watch the guy to see if it had an effect on him, would depress him. And if in the second mail call he got nothing again, then I would go sit down with him.

Or I always had a three-man point and I was always number three because I felt I couldn't ask the men to do something that I wouldn't do. So I would be first. If I died, then they knew better to do it themselves. Right? It was kind of a sick psychology, but I think it was appropriate for my position by virtue of survival and fairness. But I'd go along on point with the guy and say, "Damnit, I didn't get a letter again." Kind of compassion by identification. And within a couple of steps, the guy would lay the whole story out on me, what happened, if it was important. If it wasn't important I'd just move on. But if the guy was really hurting, I'd stay.

I was like a father and a mother to these guys, even though they didn't know that. They carried more ammo or weapons than anybody else. A lot of times in between when you need it, it's just a pain in the ass to carry all of it around. But I wanted to bring back thirty guys. I didn't. I remember when they died. I remember their names periodically, but I can't remember all eight at the same time. But I do remember them. Still to this day.

I can almost picture my platoon, how tall they were, where they were from, what they did—I mean, who cried and who didn't cry. I had a lot of deep feelings for those people. I say "my men," but the average age of the platoon was around nineteen. We had an old guy, Coogan. He was twenty-eight, "the Old Man."

One time after I got wounded and was waiting in base camp to go back out to the field, this new guy came to me. His name was Peterson. He was a young guy—I mean, he was a kid. They sent him over to me. He wanted to talk to somebody. He didn't want to stay in country. His brother was in the Navy stationed on a ship somewhere, and he wanted to know if this could get him out of Vietnam. I explained to him what I understood the rules to be. I said to him, "As far as I understand it, you're going to be in the field. What company are you assigned to?" He said Charlie Company. I said, "Look, when you get out there, tell them you want to be in the 3rd Platoon. That's the best goddamn platoon out there. They'll take care of you."

He was really upset and he left. I called the field and said this guy's coming out—I wanted him in my platoon. I got out there about two days later. He was sitting down and they were trying to explain things to him. He was a kid.

It wasn't so much that he was younger than us, but he was a kid by our standards. We got old fast. We were exposed to so much shit and you find out so much about yourself—your good, your bad, your strengths and your weaknesses—if you're honest with yourself—so quickly that you might as well have aged. You might as well be eighty years old looking back or looking forward, however you want to talk about it. It's the only way to survive.

I had to know how everyone would be responding because of that old thing: the chain is only as strong as its weakest link. I would always keep my weakest link protected. I would never put my weakest link on point, never put him out on flank. At the same time I made everyone think that the weakest link was pulling his share. So it was very confusing at times, giving orders to the platoon and rotating responsibilities. But Peterson came in March, and I think it was by May—two months later—that Peterson was for all intents and purposes a strack [exemplary] trooper. I mean, this guy had confidence. We had built him. We had taken him in that sense, a guy who was crying and scared, no confidence whatsoever, and made him feel confident. He was in some contact, but the men protected him and kept him away from things. He was so sure of himself, and it was really a pleasure, like watching your kid grow up. Everybody kind of took him along as the kid brother.

Well, it was a day where nothing was going to happen. We hadn't had any contact in a while. He wanted to go on point. I said, "Who's on point?" They said, "Peterson." I said, "What's he doing out there?" He wanted to go on point. I used an unorthodox formation. I was in the middle, so the point he was going on was a right flank because there were people on the trail. We're out in an open area. We're relatively safe. Some of the in-house rules: If you get wounded, don't say a word, don't scream. Sit still. We know where you are. We know where you went down. We'll get there.

There's people on the trail and we were lax, I guess. Shots rang out and somebody yelled, "Peterson." So we immediately went forward. I ran over. I never asked my men to go forward without me. I always went with them. I was up on that trail. Peterson starts screaming. Two more shots rang out. Silence. I just stopped. Peterson's dead. And of course, no one could believe that. We wanted to go forward to get him. I said, "He's dead. Leave him be." We got pinned down going to the left.

The battalion commander was in a chopper right above us. He says, "I don't see you guys." I say, "You're not supposed to see us. That's what we're trained for, to conceal ourselves. I can see you. I know where the chopper's pointing and I'm going to give you a direction on it—a compass reading—to tell you where we are. I see two guys over there. That's them. Hit them." He says, "I can't take a chance. It might be your men." I said, "We're not anywhere near that kind of terrain. You're facing them. Just shoot out of the goddamn chopper, you'll hit them. We're behind you." He refused to do it. We never found those two guys.

We got to Peterson. Since we heard Peterson yell, we knew he was hit twice. The first shot was in the arm. The second shot was in the head. If he hadn't screamed he would've lived. There's no question, he would've lived. He freaked. He broke.

One thing I did over there I think to this day is valid, though I think in one point in time it was one of the most cruel things you could do to someone. After every time someone was wounded or someone was killed, you're psychologically most vulnerable to suggestion. I knew what I was going to say. I pulled the platoon together and told them that the wounded person, the dead person, their buddy, their friend, fucked up because he did something I told him not to do. He did something he was trained not to do. And by virtue of doing that he risked all our lives. Sure, feel sorry for him, but now you know why he died. You want to end up the way he did? You want us to feel about you the way you feel about him? Then go ahead and fuck up. But this is what he did wrong . . .

All I know is that psychologically we had to stay up. And this is when I hit them, when they were most vulnerable, smashed them down—and they might not have liked it, but they never forgot what I said. It was important.

That day when Peterson . . . I asked the platoon to move forward and I left them in the field and I sat down and tried to cry. It was the first time and . . . I moved my platoon forward because in basic training at Fort Hood our drill sergeant was sick one time from the flu. He made the platoon do an about-face while we heard him throw up—timed it so we wouldn't see him. We knew what he was doing. It stuck in my mind. And that day, certainly risking my life, I moved the platoon forward because I knew they knew what I was feeling. I had

Peterson's personal effects, and there was a letter addressed to, I suspect, his girlfriend. He had flowers on the envelope. Nineteen years old. When he arrived he was eighteen. He was a young kid. He was our guy that we were going to take care of. We adopted him in a sense. We were going to bring him through. The one guy we didn't want killed. He didn't belong there any more than we belonged there. He belonged there even less.

See, I never cried in Vietnam. I cried that one time. I cried inside all the time. I was so unhappy. But I never cried. Not because you're a man or not a man, but as an officer you weren't supposed to cry, no emotion.

I didn't know of anybody in my entire platoon that wanted to kill, who ever killed before. There was one guy, Haynor, who was like a cowboy, young, brash: "Hey, this is an adventure." He saved my life and left the field wounded as a result of saving my life. He was the only guy I felt was like that. Man, it was just . . . you become tight or you don't become tight.

I remember freezing at night and wanting to crawl up next to the RTO—we spent ten months together and there was no sexual overtone or anything else. I was freezing. He was someone who had been with me every day, every minute, and I just wanted to hold the two bodies together. I couldn't do it. I couldn't do it because of the fact that I would show weakness. I would become too close psychologically and I would be really upset. What a lonely fucking place.

I was convinced my platoon had to carry more ammo, more weapons, and that I had to carry more ammo than anybody else in my platoon. Because once the company ran out of ammo and we were the only ones left with some, so we held the ground while the other platoons backed off. From then on I was convinced you had to carry it. You never know. What you did saved their lives, but they hate you for it. They're feeling guilty now, but they're living and they're going to hate me for saving their lives. If they're miserable when that took place, they'll hate me for making them miserable. You know, it's that—or I've earned their respect. I'll never—I mean, once or twice people will say something to me and you get the feeling that you earned their respect. But the whole time doing it, it's hard to make decisions that tomorrow . . .

We caught a VC rice harvest and were given a stand-down as our big break. The colonel came down, battalion commander, and said, "The general's coming down to give you a medal." I said, "Well, that's nice. What about my men?" He says, "What about your men?" I say, "Don't they get anything? You can't do it without them." And the lieutenant commander says, "Well, what should we do about his men?" True to form, the colonel said, "Well, sir, they could use some baths and haircuts." And he turned to me—the colonel had been an NCO and got commissioned and worked his way up—and said, "What do you think, Lieutenant?" I said, "Well, I think they could get laid and drunk, personally. A couple of men just died." You don't talk to a colonel like that, but that was my feeling—that was what my men wanted. They didn't give a shit about showers, we washed with rain water plenty of times, we never had showers. The colonel left, the general came. But shortly after the colonel left, two motor scooters came down with cases of beer on the back and women.

The lieutenant commander just looked at it all and said, "Okay, all of the guys get Airborne haircuts." Vietnam? Airborne? I had long hair. So I called all my men together in formation. I said, "All right, you guys, you heard what the captain said. You're getting Airborne haircuts. Now line up. Dress-right-dress."

They were grouching, "Fucking Vietnam. Say, jerk, what's going on?" So I marched them over to the barber chair that was set up. I turned around and pulled the old Sergeant Rock routine. If I had a cigar I would've put it in my mouth. "All right, you guys, you're going to get haircuts just like mine." The guys really thought I flipped. I sat down and told the guy, "Cut it just one snip. That's it." I got back up and said, "All right, next . . . next . . . next . . ." Just like mine. We just didn't want short hair. We always shaved. We were clean. We fought. But any feeling was that if it's going to make us happy, then give it to us. Just give us that one concession. And no one could say anything to me because I happened to have gotten a lot of medals when I first got there. I got a reputation of being a great soldier, leader, combat leader. My platoon got lots of medals. So we did whatever we wanted within bounds and we got away with it. You have long hair—no other platoon has short haircuts. That's stupid, really dumb to cut a guy's hair. Doesn't make you a better soldier. There's one way to go—and that's home.

Before I went there I remember thinking that if I lost anything, a finger, an arm, my face, my teeth, my nose, anything, I'd rather die than come back. After the first casualties I was convinced I wanted to come back. And there are so many things that I thought were important before I went there. I want to do this, I want to do that. I missed this club, I didn't see this movie, read this book. By the time I came back all I wanted to do was see America. I wanted to travel, wanted to see what it was all about. I just wanted to see the rest of life. God, how you value things . . .

When it came to survival, we just avoided stuff. I didn't kick off ambushes when I could have. There was no reason to. Killing them meant nothing. It was just stupid. I mean, they saw us walk past them during the day, they could walk past us at night. I walked in a very distinctive formation. The VC knew who I was, and if they didn't shoot at me during the day, I wouldn't shoot at them at night. We just survived.

When I left the field after being there for ten months, I came to Bien Hoa–Long Binh for the first time. When we came to the gate at Long Binh I was still into carrying my rifle wherever I went. It was a very uncomfortable feeling not to have a rifle with you. We came to this gate, and I'll never forget it, the first thing we saw was a taco stand. Then I saw a soft-ice-cream truck—you know, one of those guys that drives around the streets in the suburbs. And then we got to MACV headquarters. We walked in and they had a water fountain, a cooler. You stand there and you just drink until your body is distended and you faint from all the water. And you're just staring because there are women with round eyes. I don't know where they came from, but they were there. I didn't ask. Didn't matter—I mean, I didn't give a shit, they were there. I couldn't touch them, couldn't talk to them.

Once I went on an in-country R & R to Danang and I had the personal effects of a man to deliver. I was in my fatigues and I went to where I was supposed to stay for three-day R & R. The guard said, "Check your rifle." I responded, "Wait, I want to keep it." Gotta check your rifle, so I checked it. I said, "Well, what are we going to eat?" They gave me directions. One day you're fighting and the next day you're in another sector. It was like living in New York City, where there's poverty and right across the street an opulent town house.

I went down to the river and there was a big barge and these naval officers going to the Marine Corps naval club. It was a special launch for officers. So I remembered from the books, the movies, to salute the flag. I went aboard and thought, "This is ridiculous. I want to be with my men." We never did things separately. We always drank together, ate together. My father was the same way. He was an officer in the Naval Reserve. I met him there in Danang.

The cab to the officers' club was called the Pink Elephant, appropriately so. My XO and I were there together. Jungle fatigues, clean-shaven. We'd been fighting for almost three months. We go in there and see a big buffet, just like my first day in country. The plates were china. No C-rations, no paper plates. This is a naval club.

We sat down and we looked at each other. We didn't say a word. We were shoveling the crap into our mouths. Both of us looked up simultaneously—the plates were clean. I mean, I don't even know what I ate. Clean. We looked at each other, and you didn't have to say anything—you knew. And then there were the stares. I looked around and there were all these Navy officers, Marine Corps officers and some Army officers. Dress whites. Dress uniforms. Women with round eyes. Danang. Blond, blue eyes. And they're looking at us not like you expected—"Ah, there are some men from the field"—but "What is that scum doing in here?" I couldn't believe it. They didn't want us there at all. The only person that was nice to us was an enlisted man who was a waiter, who came over and offered to take us out to the patio for dessert. I said, "Dessert? What dessert? Peaches?" He says, "Well, I recommend the vanilla ice cream with crème de menthe." "I'll take it." I never had ice cream with crème de menthe. My parents don't drink. I never had any alcohol around my house. It was delicious. We got thoroughly plowed and watched them dance. And of course, no one ever came over and asked us to dance with them. They were all escorted.

All these Americans—well, round eyes. I was just totally blown away. And it wasn't like a whorehouse. It wasn't like a Saigon bar or a club upstairs. This was really legit. I mean, I didn't think these guys were fighting. This was maybe how the French fought the war: all the officers standing around the hotel balcony while all the men swept below. They're drinking and talking about the old days, when the war was going to end real quickly and people would come out from Washington and sit on a hill and watch the war going on in the distance.

This was the war and these were the people who controlled the war. This was MACV. It blew me away.

We were told that you could call home. It was on the MARS phone line [military satellite radio]. This was probably a sick way of dealing with something—my uncle had died in Korea. I called home. I hadn't written any letters yet. This is right after Tet, after most of the shit was done. My mother answered the phone, which is not unlikely because my father is never home. He's out at sea all the time. I can tell she's pissed off. "Hello." She sounds like a drill sergeant. I said, "Mother, this is Robert. Now relax. Don't say anything. You have to follow military radio procedures. Now I'll say something, and when I stop I'll say 'Over.' Then you can speak, and when you stop you say 'Over' and that way we can continue. Do you understand it? No, no, no. Try it again. Over." Okay, second try she got it. I said, "Look, I'm fine. I'm healthy. I have no problems. I've been taken as a prisoner of war, but they're treating me real well, Mom." You could feel a thud. You could hear her heart. She didn't want to believe it. "No, no, I'm just joking, Mom. I'm just joking." She was all excited: "Where are you? Where are you?" I told her Danang and I explained the whole bit to her. But I could never tell her up front—I always had to pull a little twist to it. It's my own personality. I always do the reverse, you know, the sick way of doing it, but it was in a sense kind of funny. I thought, "Ho, ho, ho, yeah, she'd think of the worst and then she'd be relieved to find out I'm alive."

Being the kind of guy that I was, not really following orders, I decided, since my first duty there was to deliver personal effects, to go to the fucking morgue. The military term for it was "G.R. Point" [Graves Registration]. I remember walking into it—it was in a hangar in this huge fucking building—I remember walking in and going past a room. It had these contoured fiberglass chairs, like a futuristic barbershop. I looked over and there were guys in these chairs. Dead bodies, all naked. They just had big stitches. I mean, they were like Frankenstein. A guy's face had been blown apart. They just stitched it, a job you wouldn't put on your face for Halloween. But what they did there was put them back together as far as stuff them and—the word escapes me—embalm them. Then they were going to go back and get cosmetic later on.

There was a guy trying to get a ring off a hand, because they stiffen up and everything swells and it's tough. This was like a Gahan Wilson cartoon. These morticians looked like they were embalmed themselves. They were inhaling these fumes, whatever they use to embalm them, and it does something to your skin. Talk about waxy-looking people. The receding hairlines . . . These guys really looked like they were undertakers. They were probably just a bunch of soldiers who got assigned burial duty. And I remember them saying to me, "Hey, take it easy. Nice talking to you. Maybe you'll come around again. See you again." I said, "I doubt it. I hope to God I never see you. And if I do, I'm sure I won't be looking at you. I don't ever want to be here." And I left.

I said, "Look, that ruined my fucking day. They owe me a day." So instead of going back on Tuesday, I went back on Wednesday. I said, "If I get into trouble, I'll just tell them I missed the fucking flight. I tell my men to say that. What the hell."

Tuesday night the company was out in the field, the mountains. My platoon lacked an officer. They sent another platoon out on ambush. This was the thing I didn't realize—my platoon was always sent out on ambush. We were always point platoon when it came to combat or contact. And I think part of it was because my last name was Santos. I had the blacks in my platoon. I had the guys who had been fuck-ups. I just thought we were really good. I thought we were kind of a Dirty Dozen. We had tough guys. We were good.

But they sent this other platoon out. The platoon made a mistake. Instead of holding their perimeter, they went into a horseshoe and were wiped out. I thought my platoon would have been pissed at me for not coming back, but their response was "Boy, we were glad you weren't here. We were really lucky. Because we knew what you would do, where you would sit or where you would dig in when we'd start setting up." My replacement was sitting there, and the first round that came in took him out. We never found him. We just found the book he was reading.

You can't translate it or explain it to people. I try to explain post-Vietnam syndrome by saying, you know, it's trauma. Going through war is trauma. You lose your arm, you lose your uncle, you lose your mother, you lose your father, it's trauma. You go through a period of depression. I mean, it didn't just tell me I lost something. It told me a whole bunch of things about myself I probably never would've found out. I probably in some respects would be far more successful if I'd never known. On the other hand, I'd probably be less developed and less wise. But maybe that's the way I should go through life, ignorantly happy and successful. Instead I struggle and I do what's important and I always have to fight with myself to go out and push Robert. And it's a real pain in the ass.

One of the sad things about being an officer was that you never knew that doing the right job meant that you'd earn the hatred of your men. What you did saved their lives, but they hate you for it. I mean, often I've heard these people talk about how doctors think they're God. I was looking into med school after I got out of the service and I used to hear them talk about this shit, and I said to myself, "You really think it's going to be great. You really think this is going to be something. That you're going to be God, you're going to cure people, save people, and your ego is going to be so inflated and you're going to be so fucking important." But they just don't realize how lonely it is.

I never had the opportunity to directly save lives. My responsibility was to kill and in the process of killing to be so good at it that I indirectly saved my men's lives. And there's nothing, nothing, that's very satisfying about that. You come home with the high body count, high kill ratio. What a fucking way to live your life.

7

Second Wave
of Major Work

1966. American casualties in the field.

The second wave of major work coincides with the dedication of the Wall and the oral history boom. Interest in the war and the veteran peaked here, between 1982 and 1987. In addition to works written by veterans and directly addressing the war and its immediate issues, a surprising number of literary and mainstream novels and story collections by nonveteran writers included veterans as emblematic characters and used the Vietnam experience as either backdrop or backstory. The vet had become an American character in his or her own right, the experience shared with the rest of the country. This of course had its pitfalls, in that the gap between veterans and civilians was still in effect, and often authors unfamiliar with the territory gave the reader the same old clichéd vets and overwrought atrocities, only this time with the understanding that the reader's sympathies would be with the veteran.

The second wave also marks the last time American mainstream publishing would consider Vietnam a viable commercial subject, at least in fiction. After 1988, the number of new Vietnam novels released by major houses dwindled to a trickle. The time to celebrate the veteran and question the war, it seemed, was up.

The 13th Valley, 101st Airborne vet John M. Del Vecchio's first novel, is a large, sometimes sprawling attempt at a realist epic. The book follows the men of Alpha company during a large-scale operation in 1970. A best seller in 1982, it relies on an avalanche of technical detail and a modicum of heavy symbolism. Del Vecchio uses maps and official after-action reports to augment his storyline; he contrasts the unemotional, euphemistic language of the official version with his grunts' ground-level view of combat.

Stephen Wright served in Army Intelligence in 1969–70. His *Meditations in Green* (1983) is a dense, metaphorical novel that looks at the rear-echelon Vietnam experience of Spec. 4 James Griffin and his equally strange existence as a heroin user after the war. This is a self-consciously literary book, an ornate, high-energy performance. Wright's use of both form and language is startling, and Griffin's position and skewed view of the world gives the author space to make funny and cutting observations about America. His first book, *Meditations* immediately established Wright as a literary novelist.

Larry Heinemann, like Oliver Stone a veteran of the Army's 25th Infantry Division, had already published a Vietnam novel before *Paco's Story* (1986). His first book, *Close Quarters* (1977), was for the most part realism, but, like Wright, in *Paco's Story* Heinemann chose a more literary style. The novel follows the horribly scarred Paco, the sole survivor of his platoon, as he travels through small-town America, trying to find a place for himself. He keeps to himself in his rented room, where he's visited nightly by memories of the war. None of this would be remarkable, but Heinemann has chosen for his narrator the dead platoon, speaking like a jive chorus from beyond the grave. It casts Paco's mundane return to the world in both a comic and tragic light, and lets Heinemann—in the combined voices of the dead—tear into the reading audience, openly teasing them with a litany of tall tales and overblown clichés they may believe because they're so gullible. It's a virtuoso performance which earned Heinemann the National Book Award.

The second wave operates differently, in that it assumes its audience has some familiarity with the war—and in Heinemann's case, with the literature of the war. Work in the second wave has to do more than simply contain some truth about the war and a litany of facts. While Del Vecchio overwhelms the reader with the sheer size and scope of his project, Wright gives us a near-hallucinatory vision of both America and Vietnam, a satire of the technological country at war with all of nature. Heinemann goes even further, at once parodying and fulfilling the vet-comes-home story, all the while castigating the reader and America (hilariously) for being so stupid. His opening section is a clever, self-conscious dissection of the very act of telling Vietnam stories—who does it and why, and who does or doesn't want to read them. Most folks will shell out to see artful carnage, his narrator says, and how can we refute him?

The focus here, as usual, is not merely on Vietnam, but on the relationship between the veteran and America, between the war and the American public, and between men and women. By the early eighties, the fictional veteran may still be a loner, but he's trying to find a way to belong, even—as in Paco's case—when he knows he doesn't.

The 13th Valley

JOHN M. DEL VECCHIO

1982

CHAPTER 19
15 AUGUST 1970

It was two hours past midnight. The moon was rising behind fast tumbling clouds and the sky was illuminated with eerie turbulence. The ground fog was thick and sticky. Alpha was in column, moving, stumbling, bitching. They had humped off the east side of the peak, then, following a compass course, they circled the peak to the south then west and finally northwest where they picked up the trail along the flat ridge down through the shallow draw and up toward the isolated peak that 2d Plt had reconned with helicopter at point the previous afternoon. From there until they reached their objective eleven days away the inertia of their forward motion would keep them in motion, never stopping, never slowing, gradually accelerating in their spiral descent into hell.

The path of Alpha's movement was very dark because of the ground mist. The soldiers felt insecure moving in the blackness, feeling their way toward a possible ambush. They bitched. They were tired. They had been working since before dawn. They had stopped long enough to dig in and set up and now they were moving through the unknown.

Night vision is a gift but a gift which each receiver must develop. Brooks had excellent night vision as did Jackson and Numbnuts Willis, who never let anyone know. Part of the ambient knowledge within the infantry was how to exploit the gift. To see at night it is necessary to look NOT directly at the object of sight but to look left or right of it about 15°. That way the image passing through the eye's lens hits the side of the retina where the rods, black/white receptors, are concentrated and not the center of the retina where the cones, color receptors, are clustered. Cherry knew all this but he had never practiced it before and on the night march he was nearly blind. Oh God. Oh God. This is fucked. Oh God, this is fucked. He was shaking.

As important as night vision is kinesthesis, the ability to comprehend the signals of the muscles, tendons and joints and to know the precise location and movement of one's body and bodily components. It is through the understanding of those sensory experiences one knows one's environment and one's position in it. Cherry knew this also. He had had enough psychology and physiology classes to know in detail the theories and even the history of their development. But the knowledge without practice was nearly useless.

Egan had scant knowledge of the theory of night vision and only slightly more knowledge of kinesthesis. But Egan was a mole. He had an immense amount of practice in night moving and he took considerable pride in his ability. He asked, volunteered, cajoled and forced the L-T to allow him to walk point. Behind him was Pop Randalph and behind them the bitching was universal.

The column was in a black cave of unknowns. They groped for the contours of the trail, the slope, the holes, the protruding roots. They stumbled forward in a long line, trying to be silent, listening to the swishing soundlessness of the good infantrymen, listening to the quick slip, topple—"Ooooophs, oh shit! Fuck this, Man"—of the bad. They followed Egan into dips and over crests, generally downward toward the valley then generally upward toward the peak.

As they moved in column Egan thought of the NVA soldiers who would also be moving now. Bitching, he thought, just like these assholes. Every army's made up of assholes. They're the only fuckers dumb enough to fight. It gave him strength because he was not bitching. It made him feel secure and superior and happy. Egan thought about the NVA sergeants and lieutenants who surely had to be leading equally unwilling, lazy, scared NVA soldiers. They're just like us. Egan felt warm. He felt warmth for the bitching assholes he was leading and warmth for the NVA assholes being lead toward him. Only one thing ruined Egan's night march, spider webs. Spider webs seemed to cross his path a hundred times.

Pop Randalph at Egan's slack was oblivious to everything. His body behaved perfectly, mechanically, without his consciousness. His eyes saw nothing but black void and only if the void were disturbed would his mind register. 2d Plt followed, then the company CP, 3d Plt and 1st at rear security. In the middle of 1st Cherry stumbled along swearing, one hand on Lt. Thomaston's ruck before him, one holding his M-16. He could feel the edginess of the others about him, the fear of being ambushed.

Behind Cherry Jackson was raging pissed. What that fuckin Marcus think I ken do? Jax snarled wildly in the dark. He think I ken jest git up an walk away. Where to? Fucka. An who gowin listen ta me if I says, 'Throw down yo weapons Brotha Boonierats. The word has come, Marcus has declared this war ended.' Mothafuckin dinks id love it. Walk right up en fuck everyone a us up. Then whut I got to be proud a? Pap sick, huh? Dat too bad. Aint my fault. Fucka tryin make me feel guilt. Can't that mothafucka Marcus see? Can't he see? Hey! I's somebody. I aint no nigger-slave soldier. I's somebody out here. He jest aint seen them people in Hue or Phu Luong. I am here fightin for freedom an justice an I's somebody. That the difference, Mista Marcus. I's really important here, dig? This the first time I ever been somebody. Every fucka here depend on me, depend on Jax keepin the gooks from comin through his side a the perimeter. That aint no shit. And when I comes home, stand back! That's right Mista. Pap'll be proud. He proud now. I know. An ef the revolution do come, I am ready. I am trained. I am experienced. I am ready to lead my company fo my people gainst any mothafuckin white honky pig.

Cherry entered a tiny clearing. The velvet dark below the canopy was a void: no light, no brush, no breeze, no sound. The column had stopped. The bitching had stopped. He had lost hand contact with Thompson's ruck. No one was holding him from behind. He stood still, exhausted, too tired to be frightened anymore, too tired to make the effort to sit. Everything had vanished. The men of Company A had melted into the mist and moist humus of the trail.

"We're NDPing here," Egan's whisper oozed from the void. "Settle down right there. I'm goina check the squads. Make sure we got everybody."

Cherry nodded. He walked forward several steps and bumped into Thomaston. He stepped back, set his ruck down quietly, removed his helmet and sat down. Egan's whisper oozed from the void again. "Just rest, I got first radio watch. We're set up in a straight line on the trail." Egan grabbed Cherry's right arm, shook it gently. "There's our people behind you"—he pushed Cherry's body—"and up that way." He rocked Cherry back and forth. "This way here or that way there, if you see somebody, shoot em. I'll be back in one-five."

Cherry sat very still. He was very tired and the thick mist had condensed to make him soggy. He was too tired to fear an enemy probe yet a chill ran over his shoulders and across his neck. He closed his eyes. He could see the face of the enemy soldier he had shot. The face would not leave him alone. The soldier moved cautiously, slowly. Cherry stared into the man's dark eyes. Cherry shook his head, looked elsewhere. The eyes stayed before him. The soldier was looking directly back at Cherry. Surely he could see Cherry behind the bush aiming his M-16 directly at the soldier's face. The face came forward, the eyes twinkled, a smile came to the man's lips. The image of the black post of the M-16 sight covered the man's mouth. The man laughed. The face enlarged, the eyes were wild, frenzied. Cherry stared back, growled, slowly squeezed the trigger of his weapon. The gun barked explosively, the muzzle flashing, the soldier's head . . .

"Hey! Cherry!" It was Egan. "Come with me. Bring the radio. L-T wants your radio to the CP."

How can one explain the anticipation, the tremendous suspense and expectation of R&R. It affects every move, every thought. Perhaps the old system of being in for the duration is better. Brooks had been a platoon leader with Bravo Company, 7/402, for five months when he left the boonies for R&R. In those last days of December 1969, it had been for him as if every effort, every night in the monsoon slime, every incoming round was endured solely for the reward of spending six nights away from Nam, six nights with Lila. Brooks had not had any specific expectations before he left, just the general anticipation of his sweet lady in a Hawaiian wonderland.

It began as he expected. He savored the very first passionate kiss in ten months, savored her lips as they embraced. They neither noticed nor would they have cared that the scene was repeated a hundred times about them by a hundred soldiers and soldiers' wives. Brooks was speechless. God, she was warm. They kissed and embraced and kissed and embraced and in the taxi leaving the airport for their hotel they devoured each other, not even noticing the demonstrators greeting the arrivals from Vietnam with their shouted chant:

HEY BABYKILLER, PLEASE
SHOOT YOURSELF, NOT VIETNAMESE.

But in all the anticipation, all the expectation, there is no thought, no preparation. That comes later, after the return to Nam, comes while trying to piece together what happened. For Lieutenant Rufus Brooks it was a dreaded thought with dreamlike qualities but not truly a dream for he would be conscious and he could run from the thoughts and hide in his work. During the night march the thoughts of R&R overpowered the concerns of work, overran the fleeting intellectualizations on conflict. The thought condensed to one day, a repetition of each day of his life as if time were a record with a scratch and on each revolution the needle jumped back to the same day, the same horrid day.

The beginning of the day was glorious. When they finally broke away from each other long enough to speak, Rufus held Lila at arm's length and softly cooed, "Let me look at you." She giggled and breathed back, "And you. You've lost so much weight. Aren't they taking care of you?"

"I'm fine," Rufus said squeezing her again. He wanted to sprint upstairs to their room. He squeezed her tightly and she squeezed him back. He could feel the soft firmness of her breasts through his uniform, the warmth of her thighs against his legs. Rufus had always had a strong hard body but the months of field duty had made his legs tighter, harder, had flattened his belly and made his chest more solid. Lila stroked his arms, his back, his neck. He felt alive again, vibrant.

He held her at arm's length again. "Hey, what's this?" he asked. "What'd you do to your eyes?"

"Do you like them?"

"Hey, they're green. What'd you do? You don't have green eyes."

Lila raised her eyebrows flashing her sparkling eyes at him, smiling, teasing and tempting him. "Colored contacts," she grinned. Rufus pulled her to him, squeezed, then held her at arm's length again and covered her shoulders with his huge hands, massaging gently, lightly feeling the tops of her breasts with his thumbs. Lila's eyes were beautiful but they made him feel uneasy, as if he did not know her.

"Should we, ah, get a drink or something?" he asked anxiously. "Tell me everything that's been happening to you."

"Let's just go upstairs," she whispered coyly. "Let's go upstairs." He ran his hand down her back to her small solid round buttocks. "Ooooh, Rufus! Please! Not here. People are looking. Let's go upstairs and get you out of that uniform. I bought you some clothes this morning."

Upstairs they leaped to the bed. Rufus pulled at Lila's clothes wildly, festively, feverishly. Lila twisted and turned helping him. She covered her breasts with her hands. She stroked her nipples. He ripped his own shirt exposing the strong shoulders and chest, the powerful neck and arms. She ran her hands down her thighs, hungry for him, wanting to feel his weight on her. He pulled at her panties and she raised her thighs, brought her knees up allowing him to whisk the last stitch of cloth away. She covered her body coquettishly, eyes sparkling, smiling, giggling as he tore his pants off. She squealed and squiggled and feinted squeamish shock at his exposure. And they made love. They loved each other over and over.

To her, he had never felt so wonderful, so warm, so light yet so firm. He had never moved so smoothly. He had never touched her in so many places simultaneously. To him her mouth had never been so sweet, her tongue so sensual. Her excitement rose higher, higher, faster, tauter.

"Ooooo," she groaned. "Oooh Rufus, Rufus, Rufus. Oooh Rufus.

Make me pregnant." Love exploded from her. "Make me pregnant. Oooh Rufus. I want all of you."

"Oh my sweet Lila, I love you so. I love you so much. I've missed you so much. Lila. Lila."

Rufus had never been so excited, Lila never so exciting. The nearness of her wonderful glowing body, the newness, renewedness of their love was overwhelming. They relaxed, kissed, lay in the bed. She teased him, tickled his side, kissed his scrotum. Nibbling at him she watched his excitement rise. He ran his fingers down her back onto her ass. He followed his fingers with his tongue. Lila lay on her back and he kissed her body, her proud body. She arched her back as he mouthed her breasts, licked and rolled the nipples with his tongue. Their passion had never known the variety. They loved again and again and then they relaxed.

"It's going to be wonderful," Lila said. "There's so much to see and do. Let's not waste any time doing nothing."

Rufus agreed fully. It was wonderful. It was wonderful having her to make the decisions. He gave himself to her totally, trustingly. "Lila," he confessed, "I've thought about you so much. All the time. You're on my mind all the time." It was as if he needed her to carry him now. "You're everything to me," he said. With the last sentence he felt he had made a mistake, had given too much, even to a wife. Lila did not return his loneliness confession with one of her own.

"It's going to be wonderful," she said laying her head on his chest. They did not say anything for several minutes. Rufus felt pleasantly tired. Yet he was anxious. He thought about his platoon, about each of the men in his platoon. He chose his words carefully, trying to be lighthearted, "I wonder," he said, "where those poor bastards are sleeping tonight?" Lila rose up on her forearms on his chest and looked into his eyes. He avoided her gaze. "This is the first real bed," he chuckled, "I've been in in ten months. I've slept in my clothes on the ground ever since July when I went to the Oh-deuce."

"Is it bad?" Lila asked sympathetically.

"No. That part's not bad," Rufus said. "I was just wondering where they were. It's raining there now and we're in the mountains." He changed his tone to sound more cheerful. "It's wonderful to be here with you."

"Rufus," she asked. He knew what was coming. Every one in Nam who had returned from R&R said wives always asked it on the first night. "Rufus," Lila asked. She put her head down on his chest again. "Have you killed anyone?"

He paused and sighed. He took a deep breath. "Why don't you ask me if I've saved anyone's life?" he said.

"L-T. Bravo's gettin hit." It was El Paso. He had been monitoring all three CP radios while Cahalan and Brown slept. A light rain had begun falling. It was very cool and a shiver ran up Brooks' back. Sporadic rifle shots cracked from across the valley. Bravo Company had been inserted on the north escarpment of the Khe Ta Laou on the 13th, had moved north, uphill and NDPed. On the 14th day they had engaged three NVA soldiers in a brief firefight and had pursued them south across their insertion LZ toward the valley. The Bravo troops had lost the NVA trail and had returned to the LZ for their NDP. They were now north northwest of Alpha by 2½ kilometers with only lower hills and the valley between. More rifles chattered. The NVA were probing Bravo first from one side then another. A few frags exploded.

"Put everyone on alert," Brooks directed El Paso. "Monitor Bravo's internal and have Egan's cherry bring his radio up here."

An illumination flare popped above Bravo's position. Then another and another. Several popped over the center of the valley. The light pierced the canopy and fell eerily upon the boonierats of Company A. Brooks hated calling for illumination. The light fell indiscriminately, silhouetting enemy and friendly forces alike. Usually US forces NDPed on high ground and the illumination actually helped the NVA kill more Americans then vice versa.

El Paso, Cahalan and Brown along with Doc, Minh and FO clustered low close about Brooks. "We're going to run into a lot of shit in this AO," FO said quietly to the RTOs.

"I hope we don't get hit by mortars again," Brown said. "I hate those fucken things."

"Anything comin at you is bad shit," El Paso said. Artillery from Barnett began firing Bravo's DTs.

"Down south," FO said getting everyone's attention, "we used to use a doughnut. We'd use a full brigade to encircle the enemy just before dark. All night long they'd pour in artillery and air strikes. The dinks'd try to move out. In the morning we'd go in and mop up."

Egan and Cherry joined the CP circle. Egan had led Cherry to the CP during a break from the illumination. Cherry slapped at a mosquito. Egan grabbed his hand. "Keep the fuckin noise down," he snarled. Doc handed Cherry a small plastic bottle of insect repellent. Cherry squirted some into his hands and wiped it on his face and neck and passed it back. It passed around the circle. The mosquitos had come out with the rain.

Nine men with four radios sat quietly listening to the valley noises and to the faint rushing air sound of the radios. The probe of Bravo had slackened. It had lasted less than ten minutes. The artillery crews on Barnett ceased shooting illumination and DTs for Bravo and returned to the random H & I fire, the blasts rumbling and echoing in the dark. It seemed peaceful. Cherry had not slept when the column stopped. He had not rested before the night move. With the security of being at the center of the company and surrounded by eight others he tried to close his eyes. It was peaceful.

A new sound entered the night. It was that most horrible of sounds, the light concussion of air non-sound, a mortar being fired. And everyone of them knew it was not friendly mortars. They had no sister units that close, in that direction, below them east in the valley. FO, Egan and Brooks instinctively pulled out lensmatic compasses and fixed on the sound. Everyone else froze. There was no place to move. No holes had been dug. Along the column men, already on the ground, lay flatter, condensed their bodies. Sweat sprouted in beads on foreheads. phaffft. Hearts slowing, eyes widening, balls clinging, climbing, rectums constricting and sphincters clamping down in anticipation. phaffft. phaffft. Ten times. Twelve times. Ears like radar searching the sky. Then lightning bursts in the mist and karrumph . . . karrumph . . . Flashes across the valley. karrumph. karrumph.

Radios crackled lowly. Panicked voices could be heard. "Bravo's

FO is hit," Cahalan reported. Rounds continued to explode at Bravo's location. Twelve, sixteen, twenty times. "They got three dudes hit." Then rifles chattered. AKs, RPD machine guns clattered and were answered by M-16s and M-60s. The fire intensified. Hand grenades and RPGs and thumpers exchanged percussion. The howitzers on Barnett reacted firing Bravo's DTs. "Drop one hundred, left fifty." The caller was working the howitzer rounds around his perimeter.

Amid the explosions and the continuous small arms cacophony came the popping sounds of the NVA mortar tube below Company A. The enemy mortar team was firing furiously. Brooks grabbed Cahalan's handset, threw it back and scrambled for Brown's. He keyed the handset bar furiously, interrupting Bravo's artillery adjustments. "Armageddon Two, Armageddon Two, this is Quiet Rover Four, over." He unkeyed. "Come on you bastard, I got a fix on the tube." Brooks keyed again. "Armageddon . . ." He paused. Everyone else had frozen. The twelve howitzers on Barnett were all firing. The booming from Barnett and the explosions across the valley increased. Brooks violently shoved the handset into FO's hand. "Get Arty. Tell em you hear the tube. Tell em you'll adjust by sound." El Paso covered Brooks with a poncho and Egan produced a flashlight and topo map. They could still hear the NVA mortar rounds being launched. "We are receiving in-coming mortars at our sierra," an RTO in the TOC bunker on Barnett reported. "Firebase gettin hit," FO reported to the group. FO reached the FDC at Barnett. He calmly explained the situation. "Armageddon Two, Rover Four. Fire mission. Over." FO gave the direction and approximate location of the target as Egan and Brooks deciphered the coordinates from the map. FO casually suggested the type of projectile and fuse action and adjustment. Then he added, "Now fo Gawd sakes fire the Gawddamned thing."

"Stand by for shot," the radio rasped.

"Standin by," FO said coolly.

The popping sound had stopped. It now began popping again, popping over and over. Again the boonierats of Alpha clung to the earth. Had the NVA mortar team adjusted to their, Alpha's, position? The small arms fire from Bravo never ceased.

"Shot out," the radio rasped.

"Shot out," FO repeated.

FLASH! KARRUMP! The first NVA mortar rounds exploded, the noise following the flash by half a breath. Flash! KARRUMP! Flash! KARRUMP! Flash! KARRUMP!

"Shee-it," Doc smiled.

The howitzer round from Barnett exploded near to where the sound of the popping tube had come. "Right fifty," FO called. "Yo on the money. Fire for effect."

KARRUMP! The NVA mortar rounds were exploding on Alpha's old NDP, on their locations of three hours earlier. "Shee-it," Doc laughed. He turned to Minh and punched him on the shoulder. Up and down the column troops were breathing easier.

KARABABOOMBOOMBOOMBOOM! Six US 105mm howitzer rounds exploded in the valley very close below Company A. The entire peak rocked. KARABABOOMBOOMBOOMBOOM! Another volley exploded. "Get em, Arty." Another volley. The earth shook. Rifle fire was still clattering from Bravo's position. KARABABOOM-BOOMBOOMBOOM! Silent cheers arose, imaginary banners waved. Silent bands played. The cavalry rode across ninety unseeable TV screens. The pioneers were saved.

The frequency of artillery explosions in the valley increased. The 105s from Barnett were joined by huge 175mm and eight-inch howitzers from distant firebases. The small arms clatter at Bravo ceased, then erupted, then ceased again. It settled down to sporadic crackings in the wet drizzle night sky.

"Bravo's requesting an emergency Dust-Off," Cahalan reported to the group.

"No fucken way, Man," Brown said.

"How in fuck they gonna get them dudes out?" Doc whispered angrily. "How they gonna get a bird inta the middle a dis mothafuck?"

"Their FO's dead," Cahalan said. "They got three urgent, one priority, one tactical urgent. And their FO."

"Oh this fucken valley," El Paso said. "It's socked in tighter en shit in yer ass when hell's rainin down."

Cherry's hands and legs were quivering. He had his radio on company internal freq and monitored the routine sit-reps from his squads and the other platoon CPs. His whole body shook. Oh God. Don't let any of us get blown away. Please God.

The sounds of the valley diminished. The small arms fire at Bravo's location ceased. The NVA mortar tube was silent. US artillery slowed but continued to erupt in the valley. Waiting dragged heavily.

"How will they get the wounded out?" Cherry whispered to Egan.

"They'll get em," Egan said. "Medevac pilots got big brass balls."

Doc Johnson was sick, nauseous. The inability to help, to affect the situation at all, always made him ill with frustration and anger. You trah, trah, trah, Doc thought, an what it get you? You trah bein good, doin right, an it doan change a fucken thing, Mista. Not a fucken thing. It was the same in the rear and the lowlands as it was in the boonies. It was even the same back in the World.

Doc was a large dark brown man, large and heavy for an infantry-man. He had a large head and fuzzy black coarse hair and a scant fuzzy moustache that came to the corners of his mouth and curled back into itself. His chin was covered with coarse stubble. Over his left eye there was a deep scar, pink against his deep brown skin, that ran to the bridge of his nose and obliterated the eyebrow. In all, Doc had a heavy thick look which many people automatically associated with slowness, dullness and dumbness.

Doc, Sergeant Alexander Vernon Johnson, was a city black. He was born and rasied in New York, Manhattan, up at 143d Street with a turf extending from the Hudson River east across all of Harlem, mixed neighborhoods, mixed ghetto of Puerto Ricans and blacks, some whites, old Irish and Jewish remnants. Doc's family had been lured from the South in the 1920s by the prospect of high-paying employ-ment in the factories of the northeast, lured with tens of thousands of southern blacks migrating for a better life. Long before he was born, in 1949, his people had settled into a pattern of male nomadic job searching and broken matriarchal families. Alexander was raised by a woman who was not his mother in a family where the siblings were not blood brothers and sisters in a street culture which was more tribal than cognatic. Alexander had no father but many fathers, no mother but many mothers and no siblings but brothers and sisters everywhere on the turf.

For a boy growing up in the city, the street was a good place, the best place. Inside it was dull, dingy gray close and dirty with age, the kind of dirt cleaning does not affect. Inside was where the winos laid in the hallways, where the roaches spawned in the moisture beneath sinks and behind tipping commodes. Inside the paint had all yellowed and cracked and chipped, and the plaster walls and ceilings had cracks running like veins in science book pictures of the human body. In the street there was handball and stickball and stoopball, and over at the school there was basketball. On the street the buildings had color and the walls carried ads for skin bleach and hair straightener. On the street there was music and dance. The street never, never was completely dark.

Street life connotates a harsh nastiness to the uninitiated but to a boy who knew the street it was communal, pleasant. Alexander knew from very early on that someone or thing would watch out for his welfare by forcing him to school or by rapping with him when he needed a man to talk to or by protecting him when a rival gang invaded his turf. He was an inner-city poor black child who did not know he was poor and who scoffed at the social worker's condescension. For a time he was a city cowboy, a small time street hustler, good friend, bad enemy.

Alexander was the kind of teenager his country calls first when it needs men for war, the kind of man his country, even its military, rejects when there is no need for strong hands to carry rifles and strong backs to carry the dead.

So it was with Alexander Johnson in 1966. At seventeen, his country decided it would like to use his services. Perhaps he was lucky to have had a brother advise him to enlist for a school instead of simply being drafted or perhaps he was wise enough to accept the advice or perhaps it was the vein-cracked walls and the science book diagram, for Alexander signed up for four years and a guarantee of medical corps training. Perhaps that was not luck at all.

When Alexander left New York for basic training in early '67, he thought New York would be an easy place to forget, the kind of place a man turns from easily. But almost immediately he missed his home, his siblings and his sister who was not his sister at all: his delightful little sister Marlena, three months apart in age and always together.

When Alexander came home after basic training and before he was shipped to Texas for twenty-six weeks of medical training, he spent his week's leave on the streets with old friends, but mostly he spent time with Marlena. One evening they had come through the streets and upon a street meeting. There were lots of young children running about and older people on the stoops sitting and talking and some older men sitting together drinking wine and several hard-looking women standing by the curb watching the street. It was late March and it was warm for the first time since the January thaw. Down the block, away from the meeting, Puerto Rican punks were playing stickball with stones, trying to clear the street and hit the windows in the buildings on the far side with their triples and homers.

On the center stoop there were two sisters and three brothers. One sister raised up her arms and started to sing and the others joined in. Marlena's eyes lit as she watched and listened and Alexander watched her as she watched the meeting.

A white couple approached, crossed the street and passed, then recrossed the street and continued on their way. "Look at them folk," Marlena sighed, "all dressed up in their white skin and their threads just so. That make me sad."

"That jus crazy," Alexander said. "White folk is crazy. I'll tell you bout them in Basic. Lena, white folk is a crazy cluster."

Marlena slipped her arm around Alexander's waist and he put his arm about her shoulder and they looked at each other and gave each other a squeeze and she said, "Let's go listen to some sounds and maybe do some boogyin."

The schools for army medics in San Antonio lasted from twelve to forty weeks depending upon the specialty. Draftees with two year commitments generally were run through a short course that concentrated on basic combat first aid—traumatic amputation, sucking chest wounds, shock. Enlistees, Regular Army personnel with more promising service length, were trained in all the various medical fields from operating room technicians to physical therapists. For most, when their schooling was over, their first duty assignment placed them with medical detachments attached to combat units; they became grunt medics. It was thus with Alexander, twenty-six weeks of intensive medical training followed by a month's leave and a year with the First Cavalry Division, November '67 to November '68, in I Corps, the Republic of Vietnam, as a grunt with a big bag of medical supplies.

During the time of his paramedical training it was discovered that Marlena was suffering from a blood disease of the sickle-cell syndrome, a lethal disease where increasing numbers of red blood cells deform, become excessively fragile and finally burst in great numbers releasing toxins into the victim's system. Treating the symptoms can elongate a victim's life but the disease is painful, unstoppable and incurable.

After a year with the Cav, Doc was assigned to the RNV training school at Fort Riley, Kansas, an assignment stimulating at first but terribly isolated and finally completely unacceptable.

In July of '69 Marlena died from untreated internal lung ulcerations and the complications of pneumonia. She died as much from lack of treatment as from the disease. "Died, Mothafucka," Doc had screamed in drunk nauseous vomiting when he'd heard, "cause she was a beautiful black lady inheritin bad genes from some badass fucka seven thousand years ago. Died cause them people, my people, don't yet know that they don't have ta die." On request, Doc was transferred back to Vietnam and in December of '69 he was assigned to the 326th Medical Battalion Detachment attached to the First Brigade of the 101st Airborne Division (Airmobile).

During the early months of his second tour Doc was in charge of the Oh-deuce MEDCAPs, Medical Civil Assistance Program. He and another medic and an interpreter and usually one or two boonierats temporarily in from the bush would go from hamlet to hamlet on a scheduled route. They tried to visit each of their eleven assigned hamlets once every week to ten days. At first that had given Doc Johnson a great deal of satisfaction but then the despair, the depression, the nausea set in. Doc Johnson once described it to El Paso.

"There one thing, Mista, you gotta know first," Doc had said. "It's old age that hold traditional Vietnamese society together. You remember Quay, one fine Marvin de ARVN? Quay was my interpreter for three months. He tell me how the Buddhist and the Taoist and the Confucianist all hold there to be a proper order in the universe. Like that's their religion. Ya know what I mean? Everybody gotta respect the old cause that's their proper place. You doan never be sarcastic to a old papa-san. He is like the man, the key of their social structure.

"We go to a ville like Luong Vinh. There'd be dogs layin outside and baby-sans runnin around naked amongst the grass shacks. We go up to the school buildin which our own engineers built a corrugated steel in the center of the ville and Quay'd look for the village chief.

"Mista, people'd jam inta that tin shack ta see me. They be round the corner standin in line. All a em barefoot. Quay'd go out, explain to em that I'd see all the baby-sans first, then the mamas with small children and then the old. People be standin on tiptoes ta see what I doin. Be jus like a circus tent. I'm maybe about done. Some old lady come up an I know she got TB or pneumonia and she gonna die. So I give her maybe some vitamins or somethin cause I know I can't do nothin fo her. Or an old man come up and talk to Quay and Quay, he say to me, 'Doc, you give this man some medicine. He an old man. He have no money. He need something to trade fo food.' Like that.

"Then I realized it, Mista. You understand what I'm sayin? There a reign a terror in them villes. It aint the Cong. It aint the NVA. It's the cowboys. All these young bucks who aint been drafted yet. They like a gang back on the block cept worse. They approach, little kids dee-dee. Mama-sans run. I give this one old man some *Sing tô*, vitamins, and some nitrofurizone fo ringworm. He leave the school house an four wiseass cowboys take half a what I give'm. They rough him up tee-tee then let'm go. Like a protection racket, Mista. The old man whimper his shit ta some baby-sans but he powerless.

"Cowboys. That's pure Americanization. They take half a everybody's shit an sell it on the black market. All the middle-aged men been drafted. Or killed. They the link between the young and the old. These kids grow up without discipline. They're like animals. The whole social structure fallin apart, Mista. An you know why? You know why, Mista? Nixon pushed Saigon inta passin one hundred percent mobilization an they draft every dude from eighteen to thirty-eight. And they put the seventeen and the thirty-nine ta forty-three-year-olds in the popular forces. Aint nobody left home ta mind the ville and the ville probably a refugee camp tha's overcrowded anyway. Break my heart, Man. It break my fuckin heart."

It was the same feeling Doc Johnson had now, that same feeling he suffered when he had a boonierat brother lying with his intestines on the ground and blood flowing from a dozen holes in his body and the valley's socked in and he could not get a medevac. It made him sick. The frustration went very deep. It went back to his sister's death. Poor Marlena. She could have been helped but he could not, did not, help. It came from being black, from being low class ghetto, from speaking low ghetto English. You trah, Man. You trah, trah, trah. If only I could be a doctor, a real doctor. If only I could go to school, I could be a researcher or a doctor.

Cherry could not stop shaking. His arms and back were quivering with the cold and his teeth chattered. "Maybe I'm coming down with malaria," he whispered to himself. "Oh God, please let us get out of here." Cherry had not been to church in over four years. He had been raised Roman Catholic, been baptized and confirmed and then he had broken away. Before coming to the boonies he had not prayed in years. Now he prayed hard. He thought of every prayer he had ever memorized as a child and he mouthed them. He said *Hail Marys* and *The Lord's Prayer* and the *Act of Contrition*.

"GreenMan's on the horn to Bravo's niner," Cahalan's voice slid into the wet blackness. "They got a Dust-Off comin out." Cahalan reported in short low bursts, listening then speaking then listening.

"Bout fuckin time," Egan said.

"They tried earlier," Cahalan said. "First bird got lost comin up the Sông Bo. Ran low on fuel and returned."

Random artillery had been exploding in the valley. It stopped as the helicopters approached. For a moment everything was completely silent. Then the soft thwack of rotor blades reached the valley and quickly the noise level rose. The birds either had come out without lights on or the rainmist obscured and diffused the light completely. To Alpha they were only noise.

"Little people gonna lay-n-wait fo the evac," FO said.

"They goina want that bird," Egan agreed.

"Oh God," Cherry said aloud.

The sound of the rotor blades slapping the night air caused an eerie sensation. It was difficult to distinguish what had arrived. There were at least two Cobras, one very large bird, possibly a Chinook, and three, maybe four Hueys.

Bravo's Senior RTO, Joe Escalato, was directing the birds to his location by sound. Escalato was well known to the old-timers of Alpha. He had been Lt. Brooks' RTO when the L-T was a platoon leader with Bravo, and Escalato was a good friend of El Paso's. "You can do it, Babe," El Paso quietly cheered him. El Paso monitored Escalato's net. Bravo troops popped two green star clusters, handheld flares that fired vertically a hundred feet then burst like small skyrockets.

"I've two lime stars." The Dust-Off commander identified Bravo's signal. The medical evacuation helicopter began its descent toward Bravo company. The large helicopter circling above began dropping parachute flares. Dozens of them. The burning white phosphorous splashed brightness throughout the valley and sent flat white light down through the canopy to the wet jungle floor. "I've my LZ marked with four reds at the corners," Escalato informed the pilot. The flare ship circled Bravo again, dropping a second ring of flares. The lights rocked gently beneath the parachutes, descended, sputtered and went out. The flare ship renewed the lights with each pass. Alpha troops froze. "Bird's makin a pass," El Paso reported. "The center of my LZ is marked with a strobe," Escalato's voice came from the radio. "Bird's comin in," El Paso informed the group. With all the light from the flares it was not possible for Alpha to see Bravo. The sky glowed like the inside of a frosted light bulb.

When the medevac helicopter was still about 100 meters in the air Bravo company opened up like a mad minute, 16s, 60s, 79s, frags. They showered the jungle with suppressive fire. The intensity slowed as they reloaded. "Bird's in," El Paso said. Loud exploding pops from AKs intermingled with the blasting chatter of the friendly fire. "They're loadin up," El Paso reported. "Bird's comin out." The suppressive fire continued the entire time the helicopter was on the ground and as it lifted, the firing intensified. Sporadic fire came from AKs, as if the NVA were toying with Bravo, simply letting them know their mad minute was a joke. The medevac was up. The helicopters retreated from the valley. The flares sank and went out.

The night was peaceful again. Only the exploding H & I rounds disrupted the black velvet mistdrizzle. At the CP they passed the time softly discussing whatever came to mind. FO told several stories of units he had been with in the Mekong Delta on an earlier tour. El Paso jumped on an opportunity to tell Cherry about the history of Vietnam and Egan added his views of the present political situation. Doc spoke a little about the proper treatment for various wounds he suspected Bravo troops had sustained. No one mentioned Bravo's dead FO. At one point the L-T said a few lines about the causes of war and violence and Cherry said he believed it was genetically predestined by the structure of the brain. "I want to hear more about that," Brooks said. In their exhaustion none of them went into much detail. The GreenMan radioed Brooks and told him to speed up Alpha's movement and get into the valley. "You gotta get in there and hurt those little people," he said. He also congratulated Brooks on evading the NVA mortars. It was Cherry's first CP rap session. He enjoyed it immensely. For the others it was a repeat of many previous nights. Cahalan, Brown, Doc and Minh slept. At 0455 the NVA began a full scale assault on Bravo Company.

"Oh them fuckas," Doc said waking.

Meditations in Green

STEPHEN WRIGHT

1983

If I knew for a certainty that a man was coming to my house with the conscious design of doing me good, I should run for my life.
  —Henry David Thoreau, *Walden*

All God's chillun got guns.
  —The Marx Brothers, *Duck Soup*

MEDITATION IN GREEN: 1

Here I am up in the window, that indistinguishable head you see listing toward the sun and waiting to be watered. Through a pair of strong field glasses you might be able to make out the color of my leaf (milky green), my flower (purple-white), and the poor profile of my stunted growth. In open country with stem and root room I could top four feet. Want a true botanical friend? Guess my species and you can take me home.

The view from this sill is not encouraging: colorless sky, lusterless sun, sooty field of rusted television antennas, the unharvested crop of the city; and below, down a sheer wall, the persistent dead unavoidable concrete.

This is what it means to be torn from your native soil, exiled in a clay pot five stories vertical, a mile and a half horizontal from the nearest uncemented ground. I feel old. I take light through a glass, my rain from a pipe.

Have you talked to a plant today, offered kindnesses to something green? These are crucial gestures. A plant is not free. It does not know the delirium of locomotion, the pyramidical play of consciousness, the agonies of volition. It simply stands in the dirt and grows. Vegetable bliss. But trapped indoors a plant's pleasure becomes dependent upon human hands, clumsy irresponsible hands, hands that pinch and prune, hands that go on vacation, abandon their ferns to northern exposure, cracked beds, stale air, enervations, apathy, loneliness.

Help! My stalk is starting to droop.

Up late and into the street, that was my habit then, the night's residue still sifting softly through my head, I'd wander down to the corner, stand shivering in the sun, waiting for the light to change and my reconnaissance to begin. I was a spook. All my papers were phony. The route was the same every afternoon, a stitching of right angles across the heart of the city where I mingled anonymously with the residents of the day world.

I was under a doctor's care at the time, sixty minutes exercise q.d., an order I probably wouldn't have bothered to honor had not these prescribed walks delivered me into the relief of cacophony and throng. I needed the glow of animate heat, of blood in motion, regular doses of herdlike solidity, curses, jostles, tears, life. I ogled the goodies in the big windows with the other shoppers. I rode express elevators to offices where the receptionists smiled behind bulletproof glass. I burst into violent sidewalk imprecations on the government. Nothing urban was alien to me.

At the end of the day, I'd find myself come to rest atop a public trash can. Same can, same corner, same attitude. I became a fixture of the neighborhood. There were certain faces I learned to recognize, faces I suppose recognized me, but we spoke no words, exchanged no names, in accordance with the rules of metropolitan intimacy. I sat on my can, watching the heads bob up and down the avenue like poppies in a spring meadow until the constant nodding movement turned unreal, the slow agitation of pink marine life swaying in tempo to oceanic tunes. The heart idled, breathing deepened, silver bubbles popped against my ears.

"You're ruining the symmetry," I announced one day to an old derelict tramping unsteadily past. He was walking the street backwards, the rear of his head advancing blindly down the block. His dress was equally distinctive: orange Day-Glo painter's cap, field jacket fastened with safety pins, patched jeans bleached the bluish white of skim milk, purple hightop tennis shoes split at the creases. He turned and his face was that of a young woman ready to be amused. "*You're* sitting on a fucking garbage can," she said.

"I was tired."

She hopped up beside me. "I like it," she said. "Gargoyles."

I saw her fairly often after that. She'd stop by my post to share a pretzel, a carton of orange juice. "Professional interest," she explained. "I'm a part-time social worker." She said her name was Huette Mirandella. The rest of her history was a series of true-false propositions. Her parents had died in a hotel fire or an auto accident or a plane crash or an artful combination of the three. Orphans at ten and four, she and her younger brother were abandoned to the indifferent care of a senile great aunt. Home was boring. School was boring. Staying out late and running away were interesting and then boring. The five universities she attended were universally boring. She drifted. Minor jobs, petty boyfriends. There was an abortion, a botched suicide, a hospital vacation, "the stupid clichés of an unimaginative life," she said. When I met her she was twenty-two years old, she studied Chinese, played electric guitar, read a science fiction novel every two days, practiced a lethal form of martial arts once a week with a garageful of women, painted vast oil abstracts she called soulographs, and speculated that if there was another Renaissance lurking about the bloody horizon of our future then she was a candidate to be its Leonardo—"the smart clichés of a pop life."

We met on the corner for weeks and then came periods when I wouldn't see her at all. She was home, she was at work, a soulograph required a more steely shade of blue. I continued diligently to push the leg uptown and down, in sun and snow, through needles and cramps. It seemed to change size from day to day in phase with its own moods, its own dreams. On bad days, when it dragged behind me like a sea anchor, the blocks telescoped outward, the pavement all slanted uphill, and I'd entertain notions of traveling in style. Imagine commandeering a tank, one of the big ones, forty-seven tons of M48, cast steel hull, 90 mm gun, 7.62 mm MG coaxially mounted in the turret, and running down the boulevard. Imagine the clanking, the honking horns, the cheers of the liberated masses, the flattening of each tiny car beneath the monstrous tread, the squash of automotive cockroaches. Imagine the snap, the crackle, the pop.

One bad gray afternoon I had just reached home and was rounding the turn on the first landing when, "Bang, bang," a voice echoed harshly up. I leaned over the splintered banister. In the gloom at the bottom of the stairwell a face materialized luminous as a toy skull. I could see shining teeth and that chipped incisor that always seemed to be winking at someone over my right shoulder.

"No fair. I had my fingers crossed."

"You're dead," said Huey. "You're lying out on the front steps with the change falling out of your pockets."

"Yeah? Where were you?"

"Sitting right on the stoop."

"What can I say? Come pick out your prize."

Up in my kitchen she dropped a fat brown package onto the table. Dozens of rubber bands of all colors, red, yellow, blue, green, were wound around it like shipping twine.

"That's a mean looking bundle," I said.

"A prize. For you."

"Wonderful," I said, weighing the package in my hand. "Who wrapped this, a paranoid paper boy?"

"Rafer."

The colors of the rubber bands flipped into bright relief like thin neon tubes switched suddenly on. Rafer was her brother, executive officer of a street gang notorious for reckless drug use and dropping bricks on pedestrians from tenement rooftops. We'd once spent an amicable afternoon together, comparing scars, tattoos, chatting about the effects of various arms and pharmaceuticals.

"Three guesses," she said, rattling open a drawer. "This the only knife you've got?"

I took the bayonet and began to saw. It was like cutting into a golf ball, bits of elastic flying about the room. The wrapping paper was a greasy grocery bag. Inside, pillowed upon a golden excelsior of marijuana, lay a large plastic envelope containing a small glassine envelope containing a few spoonfuls of fine white powder. Embossed in red on the large envelope was a pair of lions rampant pawing at a beachball-sized globe of the earth. Indecipherable Oriental ideograms framed the scene except beneath the cats' feet where appeared the figure 100% and below that in English the identification DOUBLEUOGLOBE BRAND.

"What's that?" asked Huey, peering.

"Ancient history."

"It looks like a bag of dope."

"Yes."

"It looks like junk."

I pulled open the glassine envelope, dipped a finger, and sniffed. A line from powder to nostril formed the advancing edge of a fan that spread in regal succession before inturned eyes a lacquered arrangement of glacial rock, green-toothed pine, unbroken snow, then the shimmer, the shiver, the snaking fissures, melting mountains, gray rain, animate forest, the dark, the warm, the still time of mushroom-padded places.

I was amazed. I hadn't seen those magic lions in years. It wasn't often you encountered an adolescent able to weld a connection into the high-voltage Oriental drug terminals.

I began rolling the unfiltered end of a Kool cigarette between thumb and forefinger. Shreds of brown tobacco sprinkled onto the white enamel table.

"What are you doing now," asked Huey, "sleight of hand?"

I emptied out about an inch of cigarette. I poured in the powder. I tamped it down. I twisted the end shut.

"What are you laughing at?" she said.

I struck a match, touched it to the cigarette, and inhaled deeply. A dirty yellow dog ran barking into the red muddy road and beneath the tires of a two-and-a-half ton truck.

"You want any of this?" I offered in a strangled voice, leaning forward, the joint poised in midair between us. A thick strand of smoke slipped snakelike from the moist end, raised itself erect into blue air, smiled, and dissolved without a sound. In the corner the refrigerator began to hum.

This is not a settled life. A children's breakfast cereal, Crispy Critters, provokes nausea; there is a woman's perfume named Charlie; and the radio sound of "We Gotta Get Out Of This Place" (The Animals, 1965) fills me with a melancholy as petrifying as the metal poured into casts of galloping cavalry, squinting riflemen, proud generals, statues in the park, roosts for pigeons. My left knee throbs before each thunderstorm. The sunsets are no damn good here. There are ghosts on my television set. What are we to do when the darkness comes on and we wait for something to happen, as Huey, who never even knew she shared her name with a ten-thousand-pound assault helicopter, sprawls on the floor with her sketchbook, making pastel pictures of floating cities, sleek spaceships, planets of ice, and I, your genial story-teller, wreathed in a beard of smoke, look into the light and recite strange tales from the war back in the long ago time.

❏

A sweltering classroom in Kentucky. Seated, in long orderly rows, a terrorized company of grimy, red-faced trainees. Stage center, on an elevated podium before their fatigued eyes, a sergeant, a captain, a war.

SERGEANT: (Hands poised on hips. Booming voice.) Okay, gentlemens, listen up! This morning your commanding officer will speak on the subject of Vietnam. I'd advise you all to pay close attention to what he has to say. He's been there, I've been there, we've all been there, and since ninety-nine point nine percent of you candy-asses now sitting in this room will also soon be there bawling and yelling for your mamas you might want to know why. So if your memory ain't too good, take notes. And let me warn you, anyone I catch asleep will wish to Christ he was already safe and snug in a nice bronze box with the colors draped over his face. Understand? (Pause.) Ten-HUT! (The company springs up. CAPTAIN, a collapsible pointer tucked under his right arm, strides smartly to the lectern.) Take your seats! (The company falls down.)

CAPTAIN: (Low authoritative manner.) Too slow, sergeant. Have them do it again.

SERGEANT: Yessir! On your feet! (The company springs up.) Now all I want to hear is the sound of one large butt slapping against the bottom of one chair or we spend the afternoon low-crawling through the gravel parking lot. (Pause.) Taaaaake . . . seats! (The company falls down.) Good.

CAPTAIN: Thank you, sergeant. (He steps to stage left, extending pointer to its full length with a brisk snap.) Gentlemen, a map of Southeast Asia. This stub of land (Tap) hanging like a cock off the belly of China is the Indochinese peninsula. Here we have North Vietnam (Tap), South Vietnam (Tap), and Laos, Cambodia, and Thailand (Tap. Tap. Tap.) The Republic of Vietnam occupies the area roughly equivalent to the foreskin, from the DMZ at the seventeenth parallel down along the coast of the South China Sea to the Mekong River in the delta. Today this tiny nation suffers from a bad case of VD or, if you will, VC. (Smiles wanly.) What we are witnessing, of course, is a flagrant attempt on the part of the communist dictatorship of Hanoi to overthrow, by means of armed aggression, the democratic regime in Saigon. (Clears throat.) Now I know the majority of you could give a good goddamn about the welfare of these people or their problems; they live in a land twelve thousand miles away with habits and customs foreign to our own so you assume that their struggles are not yours. Believe me, this is a rather narrow shortsighted view. Consider the human body. What happens if an infection is allowed to go untreated? The bacteria spread, feeding on healthy tissue, until finally the individual dies. Physicians are bound by a moral oath which forbids them to ignore the presence of disease. They cannot callously turn their backs on illness and suffering and neither can we. A sore on the skin of even a single democracy threatens the health of all. Need I remind you that four presidents—I can't emphasize this strongly enough—four presidents have recognized the danger signs and have seen fit to come to the aid of these afflicted people with massive doses of arms, troops, and economic assistance to ensure their continued independence. (Walks methodically back to lectern.) Certainly, we seek no personal gain; we're just pumping in the penicillin, gentlemen, just pumping in the penicillin. (Long pause.) I'm sure we are all aware that this policy of limited intervention has been challenged by large segments of our own population, but just remember one thing, as far as the United States Army is concerned all debate ceased the moment you raised your right hands and took that one step forward. As men in uniform your duty is not to question policy but to carry it out as ordered. (Grips sides of lectern, leans forward menacingly.) Those *are* the facts regarding our present involvement in Vietnam. Are there any questions? (Short pause.) Very good. We've got a movie here, an excellent one as a matter of fact, produced by the State Department, which will explain the historical origins of this conflict in greater detail. And since this is probably the last time I'll see you together as a group, I'd like to leave you with a few words of advice: keep a tight asshole, leave your pecker in your pants, and change your socks twice a day. (He winks.)

SERGEANT: Ten-HUT! (The company springs up, CAPTAIN departs down center aisle.) Take your seats! (The company falls down.)

Lights dim, film begins, images burn through the screen: bursting bombs, dying French, gleaming conference tables, scowling Dulles, golf-shirted Ike, stolid Diem shaking head, Green Berets from the sky, four stars at Kennedy's ear, charred Buddhists, scurrying troops, Dallas, Dallas, destroyers shuddering, Marines in surf, napalm eggs, dour Johnson: let us reason, come let us reason, plunging jets, columns of smoke, beaming Mao, B-52s, UH-1As, 105s, M-16s, Nuremberg cheers, jack-booted Fuehrer, grinning peasants, rubber-sandaled Ho,

Adolf Hitler, Ho Chi Minh, Adolph Hitler, Ho Chi Minh, Adolf Hitler, Ho Chi Minh . . .

❑

Someone flipped a switch and the darkness exploded into geometry. Spheres of light overhead illuminated the angles and planes of an enormous rectangular room. Two rows of bunks faced one another in mirrored perfection and on the last bunk of the left row, a warp in the symmetry, one body, male, inert, semiconscious.

GRIFFIN, JAMES I. 451 55 0366 SP4 P96D2T

USARV TRANS DET APO SF 96384

"Hey, numbnuts, wake up!" yelled a voice slurred with drink. "There's a goddamn war out there."

The lights went rapidly on and off, on and off.

Griffin's eyes blinked once, twice, then closed in defense against the naked one-hundred-watt bulb he could feel even through shut lids bombarding him from above. Planetary-sized spots bloomed on his retina, slid back and forth, black holes in his vision. He hated being awakened like this. It was too sudden, too brutal, it was like being hit on the head from behind. It made him uneasy, subject to disturbing, revelatory thoughts. This is how you will die, said such an interruption, not in the comfortable tranquillity you have always imagined as a natural right, but violently, in shock and confusion, far from home, without preparation or kindness, rudely extinguished by an unexpected light much bigger than your own.

Then a mortar round fell out of the sky into the roof directly over his head.

In the super slow motion of television sports reports Griffin saw the underside slope of the roof shiver into a pattern of stress lines, bow, change color, and had the time to think even this: the barracks is a beer can and we're about to be opened before his eyes and everything in them fizzed up and whooshed out into the warm foreign night. He didn't have time to scream. The smoking rubble of morning yielded one charred finger and a handful of blackened molars

a flap of skin and a torn nail
a left ear, a right hoof
a hambone and the yolk of an eye

He could never decide how to finish. Real death was a phenomenon at once so sober and so silly his imagination tended to go flat
attempting comprehension. Like everyone else he was able to picture
possibilities. The gathered parts, the body bag, the flagged casket,
grief, tears, the world going tritely on, the war too, the sky above an
untarnished blue. These were generalities, accurate but lacking the
satisfaction of the personal detail. Griffin believed that there existed a
proper sequence of final events, which when imagined correctly
would give off a click, dim the room, and shut down at last that
section of his brain which worked for the other side. Meanwhile, he
would learn how to handle these terrible rehearsals that rushed in on
him from nowhere. Maybe they were valuable learning experiences.
Maybe layers of protective hide were being sewn onto his character.
Maybe when the time came he would be brave when bravery was
required, calm when there was an excess of panic. He didn't really
know. Nor did he know where or when he might encounter real
death, but he was sure he didn't ever want to die in a place where in
the corner two drunks argued in loud whispers over the juiciest way to
fuck a gook pussy.

❏

When you go they put you in a shed there until the computer finishes
its shuffle, marked cards, shaved deck, jokers all around. Griffin remained in bed. He chose to pass.

"Got no slots for mattress testers," they said. "We gonna place you
in a right tasty location, way up north maybe, where the only lying
down is of a permanent nature, heehee."

"Do I get a pillow?" asked Griffin. Hoho.

In the bunk to his right was a randy adolescent ripe with virginal
fantasies of wartime sex. He spent hours leafing through pornographic
pictures reading the good parts aloud. On Griffin's left a twenty-six-
year-old baker from Buffalo, New York, who had already received his

orders directed a feverish monologue to the ceiling while scratching anxiously at his groin: "I won't go I tell you, no way, I won't go, they'll have to drag me out of here, those people are animals, fucking animals, they *like* to pull triggers, bayonet babies, I've seen the pictures, strings of ears on a wire, Christ! can you imagine that, what kind of person walks around wearing an ear necklace for God's sake, who would have believed it, airborne, me airborne, why me, huh? there must be thousands of guys itching to go airborne, run around like baboons and get blown away, well I'm the winner, I'm the goddamn lucky winner. I don't need this, I got a wife and two kids, I'll shoot myself in the foot first, I'm not gonna get killed for a bunch of crazy glory hounds, that's insane, know what I mean, fucking sick, YOU KNOW WHAT I MEAN?"

Griffin pulled the sheet up over his head. He lay quite still and soon felt himself sinking into an immense bowl of vanilla pudding. It was peaceful and quiet on the bottom, submerged and fetal. From the surface the slow mournful sound of a distant radio filtered down like weary shafts of sun through an unruffled sea:

> When the train left the station
> It had two lights on behind.
> The blue light was my blues
> And the red light was my mind.

The song faded to be instantly replaced by the manic voice of a Top Forty disc jockey: "This is AFVN, the American Forces Vietnam Network broadcasting from our Tower of Power in Saigon with studios and transmitters in Nha Trang, Qui Nhon, Pleiku, Tuy Hoa, Da Nang, and Quang Tri."

My God, thought Griffin in astonishment. I really am in Vietnam. He had been in the country for two weeks.

MEDITATION IN GREEN: 2

What can go wrong: ants
anthracnose
aphids
Botrytis
caterpillars
chlorosis
cockroaches
compacted soil
crickets
crown and stem rot
cutworms
damping-off disease
earthworms
earwigs
fungus
gnats
improper lighting
improper soil pH
improper temperature
improper watering
insufficient humidity
leaf miners
leaf rollers
leaf spots
mealybugs
mildew
millipedes
mold
nematodes
nutrient deficiencies

Paco's Story

LARRY HEINEMANN

1986

1. The First Clean Fact. Let's begin with the first clean fact, James:
This ain't no war story. War stories are out—one, two, three, and a
heave-ho, into the lake you go with all the other alewife scuz and
foamy harbor scum. But isn't it a pity. All those crinkly, soggy sorts of
laid-by tellings crowded together as thick and pitiful as street cobbles,
floating mushy bellies up, like so much moldy shag rug (dead as rusty-
ass doornails and smelling so peculiar and un-Christian). Just isn't it a
pity, because here and there and yonder among the corpses are some
prize-winning, leg-pulling daisies—some real pop-in-the-oven muf-
fins, so to speak, some real softly lobbed, easy-out line drives.

But that's the way of the world, or so the fairy tales go. The people
with the purse strings and apron strings gripped in their hot and soft
little hands denounce war stories—with perfect diction and practiced
gestures—as a geek-monster species of evil-ugly rumor. (A geek,
James, is a carnival performer whose whole act consists of biting the
head off a live chicken or a snake.) These people who denounce war
stories stand bolt upright and proclaim with broad and timely sweeps
of the arm that war stories put *other* folks to sleep where they sit.
(When the contrary is more to the truth, James. Any carny worth his
cashbox—not dead or in jail or squirreled away in some county
nuthouse—will tell you that most folks will shell out hard-earned,
greenback cash, every time, to see artfully performed, urgently fascinating, grisly and gruesome carnage.)

Other people (getting witty and spry, floor-of-the-Senate, let-me-read-this-here-palaver-into-the-*Congressional-Record*, showboat oratorical) slip one hand under a vest flap and slide one elegantly spit-shined wing-tip shoe forward ever so clever, and swear and be *damned* if all that snoring at war stories doesn't rattle windows for miles around—all the way to Pokorneyville, or so the papers claim. (Pokorneyville, James, is a real place, you understand, a little bit of a town between Wheeling and Half Day at the junction of U.S. route 12 and Aptakisic Road—a Texaco gas station, a Swedish bakery, and Don't Drive Beddie-Bye Motel.)

And a distinct but mouthy minority—book-learned witchcraft amateurs and half-savvy street punks and patriots-for-cash (for some piddling hand-to-mouth wage, James)—slyly hang their heads and secretly insinuate that the snoring (he-honk, he-honk, the way a good, mean, shake-shake-like-a-rag-doll snore snaps at you, James) is nothing if it isn't the Apocalypse itself choking on its own spit, trying to catch its breath for one more go-round.

And the geeks and freaks and sideshow drifters of this world hear the dipstick yokels soaking up a shill like that, well, damned if they don't haul off a belly laugh—haw haw haw. *They* know a prize-winning shuck when they hear one, James. They lean back in their folding lawn chairs, lined up in front of their setups and shacks—the Skil-Thro and Ring Toss and Guess-How-Many-Pennies-in-the-Jar-Bub? and such as that—and slap their thighs hard enough to raise welts, all the while whispering among themselves that the rubes of this world will *never* get the hang of things.

Now, according to some people, folks do not want to hear about Alpha Company—us grunts—busting jungle and busting cherries from Landing Zone Skator-Gator to Scat Man Do (wherever *that* is), humping and *hauling ass* all the way. We used French Colonial maps back then—the names of towns and map symbols and elevation lines crinkled and curlicued and squeezed together, as incomprehensible as the Chiricahua dialect of Apache. We never could cipher a goddamned thing on those maps, so absolutely and precisely where Scat Man Do is tongue cannot tell, but we asked around and followed

Lieutenant Stennett's nose—flashing through some fine firefight possibilities, punji pits the size of copper mines, not to mention hog pens and chicken coops (scattering chickens and chicken feathers like so many wood chips). We made it to the fountain square in downtown Scat Man Do—and back to LZ Skator-Gator—in an afternoon, James, singing snatches of arias and duets from *Simon Boccanegra* and *The Flying Dutchman* at the top of our socks. But what we went there for no one ever told us, and none of us—what was left of us that time—ever bothered to ask.

And some people think that folks do not want to hear about the night at Fire Base Sweet Pea when the company got kicked in the mouth good and hard—street-fight hard—and wound up spitting slivers of brown teeth and bloody scabs for a fortnight. Lieutenant Stennett had us night-laagered in a lumpy, rocky slope down the way from high ground—his first (but by no stretch of your imagination his last) mistake. And you could hawk a gob of phlegm and spit into the woodline from your foxhole, James. And it was raining to beat the band. And no one was getting any sleep. And just after midnight— according to Gallagher's radium-dial watch—some zonked-out zip crawled up sneaky-close in the mangled underbrush and whispered in the pouring rain, "Hey, you! Rich-chard Nick-zun is a egg-suckin' hunk of runny owlshit!" And then Paco and the rest of us heard him and some other zip giggling—tee-hee-hee-hee—as though that was the world's worst thing they could think to say, and would provoke us into rageful anger. But before any of us could wipe the rain out of our eyes, Jonesy raised his head from his rucksack, where he was taking one of his famous naps—fucking the duck, we called it—and stage-whispered right back, "Listen, you squint-eyed spook, you ain' tellin' me annathang ah don' know!" Then they whispered back at us with one voice, as giggly and shivery cute as a couple smart-ass six-year-olds, "GI, you *die* tonight!" and then giggled some more. Paco blinked his eyes slowly, glancing out of the corners as if to say he didn't believe he heard what he *knew* he heard, and shook his head, saying out loud, "What do these zips think this is, some kind of chicken-shit Bruce Dern–Michael J. Pollard–John Wayne movie? '*GI, you die tonight!*' What kind of a fucked-up attitude is that?" Then he leaned over his sopping-wet rucksack in the direction of the smirking giggles, put his hands to his mouth, megaphone-fashion, and said, "Hawkshit," loud enough for the whole company to hear. "Put your money where your mouth is, Slopehead," he said. "Whip it on me!" So later that night they did. They greased half the 4th platoon and Lieutenant Stennett's brand-new radioman, and we greased so many of them it wasn't even funny. The lieutenant got pissed off at Paco for mouthing off and getting his radioman blown away so soon—but that was okay, because the lieutenant wasn't "wrapped too tight," as Jonesy would say.

The next morning we got up, brushed ourselves off, cleared away the air-strike garbage—the firefight junk and jungle junk and the body bags. And the morning after that, just as right as rain, James, we saddled up our rucksacks and slugged off into the deepest, baddest part of the Goongone Forest north of our base camp at Phuc Luc, looking to kick some ass—anybody's ass (can you dig it, James?)—and take some names. Yessiree! We hacked and humped our way from one end of that goddamned woods to the other—crisscrossing wherever our whim took us—no more sophisticated or complicated or elegant than an organized gang; looking to nail any and all of that goddamned giggling slime we came across to the barn door. Then one bright and cheery morning, when our month was up, Private First Class Elijah Raintree George Washington Carver Jones (Jonesy for short, James) had thirty-nine pairs of blackened, leathery, wrinkly ears strung on a bit of black commo wire and wrapped like a garland around that bit of turned-out brim of his steel helmet. He had snipped the ears off with a pearl-handled straight razor just as quick and slick as you'd lance a boil the size of a baseball—snicker-snack—the way he bragged his uncle could skin a poached deer. He cured the ears a couple days by tucking them under that bit of turned-out brim of his steel helmet, then toted them crammed in a spare sock. The night that Lieutenant Stennett called it quits, Jonesy sat up way after dark stringing those ears on that bit of black wire and sucking snips of C-ration beefsteak through his teeth.

And the next afternoon, when we finally humped through the south gate at Phuc Luc, you should have seen those rear-area motherfucking housecats bug their eyes and cringe every muscle in their bodies, and generally suck back against the buildings (you would have been right proud, James). Jonesy danced this way and that—shucking and jiving, juking and high-stepping, rolling his eyes and snapping his fingers in time—twirling that necklace to a fare-thee-well, shaking and jangling it (as much as a necklace of ears will jangle, James) and generally fooling with it as though it were a cheerleader's pom-pom.

And the Phuc Luc base camp Viets couldn't help but look, too. Now, the Viets worked the PX checkout counters (good-looking women who had to put out right smart and regular to keep their jobs), the PX barbershop (where the Viet barbers could run a thirty-five-cent haircut into $6.50 in fifteen minutes), and the stylishly thatched souvenir shack (where a bandy-legged ARVN cripple sold flimsy beer coolers and zip-a-dee-doo-dah housecat ashtrays, and athletic-style jackets that had a map embroidered on the back with the scrolled legend *Hot damn—Vietnam* sewn in underneath). And, James, don't you know they were Viets during the day and zips at night; one zip we body-counted one time couldn't booby-trap a shithouse any better than he could cut hair.

Every Viet in base camp crowded the doorways and screened windows, and such as that, gawking at Jonesy—and the rest of us, too. So he made a special show of shaking those ears at them, witch-doctor-fashion, while booming out some gibberish mumbo jumbo in his best amen-corner baritone and laughing that cool, nasty, grisly laugh of his, acting the jive fool for all those housecats. And the rest of the company—what was left of us *that* time—laughed at him, too, even though we humped those last three hundred meters to the tents (up an incline) on sloppy, bloody blisters, with our teeth gritted and the fraying rucksack straps squeezing permanent grooves in our shoulders. (A body never gets used to humping, James. When the word comes, you saddle your rucksack on your back, take a deep breath, and set your jaw good and tight, then lean a little forward, as though you're walking into a stiff and blunt nor'easter, and begin by putting one foot in front of the other. After a good little while you've got two sharp pains as straight as a die from your shoulders to your kidneys, but there's nothing to do for it but grit your teeth a little harder and keep humping. And swear to God, James, those last uphill three hundred meters were the sorriest, goddamnedest three hundred motherfuckers in all of Southeast Asia. Captain Courtney Culpepper, who never missed a chance to flash his West Point class ring in your face—that ring the size of a Hamilton railroad watch—never once sent the trucks to meet us at the gate: said we had humped that far, might as well hump the rest.)

Nor do people think that folks want to hear what a stone bore (and we do mean *stone*, James) sitting bunker guard could be. Now some troopers called it perimeter guard and some called it berm guard, but it was all the same. The bunkers, James: broad, sloping sandbagged affairs the size of a forty-acre farm on the outside and a one-rack clothes closet inside, lined up every forty meters or so along the perimeter, within easy grenade range of the concertina wire and the marsh. You sit scrunched up, bent-backed, and stoop-shouldered on a plain pine plank, staring through a gun slit the size of a mail slot. And you stare at a couple hundred meters of shitty-ass marsh that no zip in his right mind would try to cross, terraced rice paddy long gone to seed, and a raggedy-assed, beat-to-shit woodline yonder. (That woodline was *all* fucked up, James, because we used to shoot it up every now and again out of sheer fucking boredom.) Well, you stare at all that, and stare at it, until the moonlit, starlit image of weeds and reeds and bamboo saplings and bubbling marsh slime burns itself into the back of your head in the manner of Daguerre's first go with a camera obscura. You peep through that skinny-ass embrasure with your M-16 on full rock and roll, a double armful of fragmentation grenades— frags, we called them—hanging above your head on a double arm's length of tripflare wire, and every hour at the quarter hour you crank up the land-line handphone and call in a situation report—sit-rep, we called it—to the main bunker up the hill in back of you fifty paces or so. "Hell-o? Hell-o, Main Bunker!" you say, extra-friendly-like. "Yez," comes this sleepy, scrawny voice, mellowed by forty meters of land-line commo wire. "This here is Bunker Number 7," you say, and snatch one more glance downrange—everything bone-numb evil and cathedral-quiet. "Everything is okeydokey. Hunky-dory. In-the-pink and couldn't-be-sweeter!" And that sleepy, scrawny voice takes a good long pause, and takes a breath, and drawls right back at you, "Well, okay, cuz!"

And between those calls up the hill—and taking a break every now and again to take a whiz, downrange—you have nothing better to do than stare at that marsh and twiddle your thumbs, and give the old pecker a few tugs for the practice, wet-dreaming about that Eurasian broad with the luscious, exquisite titties who toured with a Filipino trio and turned tricks for anyone of commissioned rank.

Those Filipinos, James, they were extra-ordinary. One guy played a rickety Hawaiian guitar, one guy played a banged-up tenor saxophone, and the third guy played the electric accordion—and that dude could squeeze some *fine* accordion, James. That trio and the woman played every nickel-and-dime base camp, every falling-down mess hall and sleazy, scruffy Enlisted Men's Club south of the 17th Parallel (the DMZ, we called it)—as famous in their own way as Washing Machine Charlie, the legendary night rider of Guadalcanal. So how come they never made the papers, you may ask.

Well, James, reporters, as a gang, acted as though our whole purpose for being there was to entertain them. They'd look at you from under the snappily canted brim of an Abercrombie & Fitch Australian bush hat as much as to say, "Come on, kid, *astonish* me! Say *something* fucked up and quotable, *something* evil, something *bloody* and *nasty*, and be quick about it—I ain't got all day; I'm on a deadline." But mostly you'd see them with one foot on the lead-pipe rail and one elbow on the stained plywood bar of the Mark Twain Lounge of the Hyatt-Regency Saigon, swilling ice-cold raspberry daiquiris and vodka sours by the pitcherful—pussy drinks, bartenders called them. The younger, "hipper" ones popped opium on the sly or sprinkled it on their jays, and chewed speed like Aspergum, but their rap was the same, "Don't these ignorant fucking grunts *die* ugly! It's goddamned *bee-utiful!*" They'd lean sideways against the bar, drugstore-cowboy-style—twiddling their swizzle sticks—and stare down at their rugged-looking L. L. Bean hiking boots or Adidas triple-strip deluxe gym shoes, swapping bullshit lies and up-country war stories. "Say, Jack," would say this dried-up, milky-eyed old sports hack from the

Pokorneyville Weekly Volunteer-Register, "I seen this goofy, wiggy-eyed, light-skinned spade up at Fire Base Gee-Gaw las' week. Had some weird shit scrawled on the back of his flak jacket, Jack: 'Rule 1. Take no shit. Rule 2. Cut no slack. Rule 3. Kill all prisoners.' I ast him if he was octoroon—he looked octoroon to me—and he says (can you beat this?), 'I ain't octoroon, I'm from Philly!' Haw-shit, buddy-boy, some of these nigras is awful D-U-M-B." Then slush-eyes'll take another couple he-man slugs of raspberry daiquiri, smacking his lips and grinning to high heaven.

So, James, listening to conversation like that, how can anyone expect reporters and journalists—and that kind—would appreciate anything as subtle and arcane and pitiful as one three-piece USO band and the snazziest, hot-to-trot honey-fuck to hit the mainland since the first French settlers. Those guys can't be everywhere, now, can they?

Those Filipinos ha-wonked and razza-razzed and pee-winged, sharping and flatting right along for close to three hours down at the lighted end of our company mess hall. The whole charm of their music was the fact that they couldn't hit the same note at the same time at the same pitch if you passed a hat, plunked the money down, put a .45 to their heads, and said, "There! Now, damnit, play!" They played the "Orange Blossom Special" and "Home on the Range" and "You Ain't Nothing but a Hound Dog" and "I Can't Get No Satisfaction," after a fashion. And they played songs like "Good Night, Irene" and "I Wonder Who's Kissing Her Now" and "I Love You a Bushel and a Peck"—music nobody ever heard of but the gray-headed lifers. And that woman, who hardly had a stitch on (and she was one fluffy dish, James), wiggled pretty little titties right in the colonel's mustache—Colonel Hubbel having himself a front-row kitchen chair—and she sure did sit him up straight, *all right*. And the rest of the battalion officers and hangers-on (artillery chaplains and brigade headquarters busybodies on the slum) sat shoulder patch to shoulder patch in a squared-off semicircle just as parade-ground pretty as you please. They crossed their legs to hide their hard-ons, and tried to look as blasé and matter-of-fact—as officer-like and gentlemanly—as was possible, trying to keep us huns away from the honey. And the rest of the company, us grunts, stood close-packed on the floor and the chairs and tables, and hung, one-armed, from the rafters—our tongues hanging out, swilling beer from the meat locker and circle-jerking our brains out. Our forearms just a-flying, James; our forearms just a blur. And that broad shimmied and pranced around near-naked, jiggling her sweaty little titties like someone juggling two one-pound lumps of greasy, shining hamburger, and dry-humping the air with sure and steady rhythmic thrusts of her nifty little snatch—ta-tada-ha-humpa, ta-tada-ha-humpa, ta-tada-ha-humpa, *ha-whoo*! Then a couple black guys from the 3rd platoon's ambush began to clap their hands in time and shout, "Come awn, Sweet Pea, twiddle those goddamn thangs in my mustache! Come awn, Coozie, why don't ya'll sit awn *my* face— yaw haw haw."

(Let's tell it true, James, do you expect you'll ever see that scene in a movie?)

But most particularly, people think that folks do not want to hear about the night at Fire Base Harriette—down the way from LZ Skator-Gator, and within earshot of a ragtag bunch of mud-and-thatch hooches everyone called Gookville—when the whole company, except for one guy, got killed. Fucked-up dead, James; scarfed up. Everybody but Paco got nominated and voted into the Hall of Fame in one fell swoop. The company was night-laagered in a tight-assed perimeter up past our eyeballs in a no-shit firefight with a battalion of headhunter NVA—corpses and cartridge brass and oily magazines and dud frags scattered around, and everyone running low on ammo. Lieutenant Stennett crouched over his radio hoarsely screaming map coordinates to every piece of artillery, every air strike and gunship within radio range, like it was going out of style, when all of a sudden—*zoom*—the air came alive and crawled and yammered and whizzed and hummed with the roar and buzz of a thousand incoming rounds. It was hard to see for all the gunpowder smoke and dust kicked up by all the muzzle flashes, but everyone looked up—GIs *and* zips—and knew it was every incoming round left in Creation, a wild and bloody shitstorm, a ball-busting cataclysm. We knew that the dirt under our bellies (and the woods and the villes and us with it) was going to be pulverized to ash (and we do mean *pulverized*, James), so you could draw a thatch rake through it and not find the chunks; knew by the overwhelming, ear-piercing whine we swore was splitting our heads wide open that those rounds were the size of houses. We don't know what the rest of the company did, or the zips for that matter, but the 2nd squad of the 2nd platoon swapped that peculiar look around that travels from victim to victim in any disaster. We ciphered it out right then and there that we couldn't dig a hole deep enough, fast enough; couldn't crawl under something thick enough; couldn't drop our rifles, and whatnot, and turn tail and beat feet far enough but that this incoming wouldn't catch us by the scruff of the shirt, so to speak, and lay us lengthwise. We looked around at one another as much as to say, "*Oh fuck!* My man, this ain't your average, ordinary, everyday, garden-variety sort of incoming. This one's going to blow everybody down." Swear to God, James, there are those days—no matter how hard you hump and scrap and scratch—when there is simply nothing left to do but pucker and submit. Paco slipped off his bandanna and sprinkled the last of his canteen water on it, wiped his face and hands, then twirled it up again and tied it around his neck—the knot to one side. Jonesy laid himself out, with his head on his rucksack, getting ready to take another one of his famous naps. Most of the rest of us simply sat back and ran our fingers through our hair to make ourselves as presentable as possible. And Gallagher, who had a red-and-black tattoo of a dragon on his forearm from his wrist to his elbow, buttoned his shirt sleeves and brushed himself off, and sat cross-legged, with his hands folded meditatively on his lap. In another instant everyone within earshot was quiet, and a hush of anticipation rippled through the crowd, like a big wind that strikes many trees all at once. Then we heard the air rushing ahead of those rounds the same as a breeze through a cave—so sharp and cool on the face, refreshing and foul all at once—as though those rounds were floating down to us as limp and leisurely as cottonwood leaves. We looked one another up and down one more time, as much as to say, "Been nice. See you around. *Fucking shit!* Here it comes."

And in less than it takes to tell it, James, we screamed loud and nasty, and everything was transformed into Crispy Critters for half a dozen clicks in any direction you would have cared to point; every-

thing smelled of ash and marrow and spontaneous combustion; everything—dog tags, slivers of meat, letters from home, scraps of sandbags
and rucksacks and MPC scrip, jungle shit and human shit—*everything* hanging out of the woodline looking like so much rust-colored
puke.

Yes, sir, James, we screamed our gonads slam-up, squeeze up
against our diaphragms, screamed volumes of unprintable oaths.
When the motherfuckers hit we didn't go *poof* of a piece; rather, we
disappeared like sand dunes in a stiff and steady offshore ocean
breeze—one goddamned grain at a time. We disappeared the same as
if someone had dropped a spot of dirt into a tall, clear glass of water—
bits of mud trailed behind that spot until it finally dissolved and nothing reached bottom but a swirling film. (Not that it didn't smart,
James. Oh, it tickled right smart. First it thumped ever so softly on the
top of our heads—your fat-assed uncle patting you on your hat, leaning way back and bragging his fool head off about how proud he is of
the way you do your chores. But then came the bone-crushing, ball-
busting rush—the senior class's butter-headed peckerwood flashing
around the locker room, snapping the trademark corner of a sopping-
wet shower towel upside everyone's head with a mighty crack.
Whack!)

Whooie! We reared back and let her rip so loud and vicious that all
the brothers and sisters at Parson Doo-dah's Meeting House Revival
fled—we mean *split*, James; we mean they peeled the varnish off the
double front doors in their haste. The good parson was stalking back
and forth in front of the pulpit rail, shouting and getting happy, slapping his big meaty hands together, signifying those sinners—bim-
bam-boom—and calling on the mercy of Sweet Jesus. Well, sir, our
screams hit the roofing tin like the dictionary definition of a hailstorm
and swooped down the coal-stove chimney—*"Ah-shoo!"* Those sinners jumped back a row or two as though Brother Doo-dah had
thrown something scalding in their faces. They threw up their arms,
wiggled and wagged their fingers, shouting to high heaven, "Alle-
lujah!" "A-men!" "Yes, Lord!" "Save me, Jesus!" Then they grabbed
their dog-eared Bibles and hand-crocheted heirloom shawls, and hit
the bricks. Yes, sir, James, plenty of the good brothers and sisters got

right and righteous *that* night. And Brother Doo-dah was left standing in the settling dust slowly scratching his bald, shining head, pondering—wondering—just exactly how did he do that marvelous thing?

Oh, we dissolved all right, everybody but Paco, but our screams burst through the ozone; burst through the rags and tatters and café-curtain-looking aurora borealis, and so forth and suchlike; clean as a whistle; clean as a new car—un-fucked-with and frequency-perfect out into God's Everlasting Cosmos. Out where it's hot enough to shrivel your eyeballs to the shape and color and consistency of raisins; out where it's cold enough to freeze your breath to resemble slab plastic.

And we're pushing up daisies for half a handful of millennia (we're *all* pushing up daisies, James), until we're powder finer than talc, *finer* than fine, as smooth and hollow as an old salt lick—but that blood-curdling scream is rattling all over God's ever-loving Creation like a BB in a boxcar, only louder.

8

Second Wave
of Major Films

1972. A South Vietnamese girl flees a U.S. napalm strike by Highway 1.

During the early years of the Reagan administration, after the artistic success (and excess) of *The Deer Hunter, Coming Home*, and *Apocalypse Now*, Hollywood returned to form, giving America a more familiar, less complex vet, and by extension a simplified view of the war. The years between the two waves of major films were ruled first by Sylvester Stallone's Rambo, the wronged vet on the rampage, and then by the emergence of a related subgenre, the prisoner-of-war adventure film. America, though ready to accept the warrior, still couldn't look hard at the war. The one good serious film that came out during this period dealt with the fallout of the war in Cambodia, Roland Joffe's *The Killing Fields* (1984), and it was British.

In the seventies, the psycho vet on a rampage was a staple of both film and TV, an emblem of America's failure and a perfect catalyst for action. Typically, the vet was a damaged grunt or Green Beret or—more likely—a demolitions expert. In his bitterness against the government for wrongs real or imagined, the disturbed vet took hostages, went on a killing spree, or threatened to bomb public places until the law (our heroes) brought him to justice, often killing him. Rarely, as in the case of Billy Jack, was the vet fighting for an honorable cause. He was a menace, a reminder of how insane and out of control the country had been back in the sixties—in essence, a symptom of a larger sickness the country as a whole had now supposedly overcome.

Like his brothers the earlier psycho vets, in *First Blood* (1982, the year of the Wall) John Rambo comes to a quiet town, runs afoul of the law, declares war on the authorities, and ends up leveling the place with his specialized training. But unlike his predecessors, Rambo is the hero of the film. The town is corrupt, and in contrast to Billy Jack, Rambo's noble cause is not universal brotherhood but merely the acknowledgment that the vet did his part and shouldn't be ostracized for it. Paradoxically, Rambo the psycho vet is supposed to convince the audience of the average vet's humanity and courage. Of course, the level of violence in the film contradicts this, but no matter, in the end we're cheering. Interestingly, like Billy Jack, Rambo turns to both Native American and Far Eastern tactics to win his battle against the corrupt establishment; he becomes a lone guerrilla who's one with the land, very much the frontier hero.

If *First Blood* could possibly be misconstrued as pro-vet, antigovernment and even antiwar, the second installment of the series, *Rambo: First Blood, Part II* (1985), could not. In the sequel Rambo returns to Vietnam to free American prisoners of war being held by both the Viet Cong and a few stray, sinister Russians. Though the mission is sabotaged by a dovish American politician, Rambo succeeds in an orgy of muscles and slow-motion firepower. The film's politics are standard cold-war fare; the Vietnamese civilians are mere bystanders. Rambo—like the stereotypical vet of the period—is a victim who is now empowered to exact a personal revenge and in doing so achieves redemption. "What do you want?" he is asked at the end, and Rambo says, "For our country to love us as much as we love it."

Later, in *Rambo III*, Stallone goes to Afghanistan to take on the whole Soviet Army. Like the other two movies, it's a ridiculous shoot-'em-up with nothing to say, though all three made truckloads of money. The most interesting aspect of the series is surely the position of the vet as prototypical action hero—strong but misunderstood, brave and righteous, a true underdog. After years of fitting bombs together in seedy hotel rooms, the rampaging vet was suddenly someone to cheer.

Meanwhile in 1984, Chuck Norris, a B-movie version of Stallone (and formerly Bruce Lee's sparring partner), launched the first installment of his POW-rescue series *Missing in Action*. Like Rambo, Norris's character is a lone crusader for justice. He returns to Vietnam to find POWs he knows the VC are still holding—in fact are torturing with typical captivity narrative details. Stylized violence ensues. The movies are crude, even stupid, with the Vietnamese captors reminiscent of the evil Japanese guards in World War II films. They die by the bunch and the good guys ride away to big music.

The POW-rescue movies were huge successes as action flicks. While *Uncommon Valor* (1983) was both the first and the best of the lot, its star, Gene Hackman, didn't have the drawing power of Norris or Stallone, and its producers didn't feel it could benefit from a sequel. Still, as a group, the movies are interesting in their use of both the war and the vet. By framing the films (and the war) in terms of the documented Vietnamese mistreatment of POWs, the rescue movie gives American viewers a simplified moral high ground that was decidedly absent during the war. The vet finally gets his chance to reclaim America's lost honor as well as the missing victory.

The Reagan eighties were a strikingly heroic time for the media-created figure of the Vietnam vet. After the dedication of the Wall and the oral history boom, Americans were eager to redress the past and canonize the vet as a forgotten hero. A sympathy that had been withheld for more than a decade burst forth in book after book. In each, the vet was portrayed as a noble victim, someone who'd given up his youth, his body, or his peace of mind for his country. While many of the books were well received—even lauded—by vets, Hollywood's versions of the war were corny and cartoonish, an embarrassment. The real Vietnam was still missing.

Oliver Stone served in the Third Battalion of the Army's 25th Infantry Division in 1967–68. After the war he became interested in film, eventually hooking up, like many young filmmakers, with Roger Corman's production company in the late seventies. His earliest works as a screenwriter and director of B-pictures fit the Corman formula—fast, violent, and sensational. His first mainstream scripts—for Alan Parker's *Midnight Express*, Michael Cimino's *Year of the Dragon* (widely picketed for its treatment of Asian-Americans), and Brian DePalma's *Scarface*—seemed an extension of that sensibility. Only in

Salvador (1986) did Stone begin to include the overt criticisms of the American political system that he's become known for. That same year, he released what is commonly regarded as the best and most realistic film about the American war in Vietnam—*Platoon*.

The storyline of *Platoon* is standard fare. Like many of the oral histories, *Platoon* seems to follow the arc of the *Bildungsroman*. A quote from Ecclesiastes precedes the film—"Rejoice, O young man, in thy youth"—immediately followed by the perfectly green Chris Taylor (Charlie Sheen) arriving on an airport tarmac in Vietnam only to face a trolley of carts hauling body bags and a line of jive-talking short-timers, one with the thousand-yard stare. Like Willard in *Apocalypse Now* (played by Charlie's father, Martin Sheen), Chris tells us his tale in a portentous voice-over, supposedly a letter or series of letters to his grandmother, though this device fades away later, when he tells the audience things his character would never tell his grandma.

We go out on patrol for the first time with Chris, and Stone pours on the realistic details for which the film is known: the jungle, the bugs, the equipment, the lingo, the heat. The focus, as in the oral histories and realistic novels, is on the grunt's daily existence, the everyday life. Suddenly the other greenie who came on board with Chris is killed in an ambush, and quickly we meet the power structure of the platoon: Sgt. Barnes (Tom Berenger), a macho professional soldier whose face is grotesquely scarred; his counterpart Sgt. Elias (Willem Dafoe), who helps Chris lug his extra gear; and the useless ROTC lieutenant who wants to give the orders but doesn't know what to do. No one mourns the dead new guy, they just look at him with disgust. "Man'd be alive if he had a few more days to learn something," Barnes says, pointing up the *Bildungsroman* theme.

"I think I made a big mistake coming here," Chris tells us.

We stand down, head back to the firebase, where Chris shares his personal history with his buddies. Stone's screenplay touches on racial and social inequality here, as well as piling on more sharply drawn details. "You volunteered for this shit?" one guy asks. "You got to be rich in the first place to think like that."

It seems the platoon is split into two groups, the heads and the juicers. Chris finds the heads getting stoned in a bunker (to the Jefferson Airplane's totally overused "White Rabbit"), and Elias, bare-chested and in a hammock, beckons him. "First time?" Elias asks, and then gives him a true shotgun, blowing the smoke down a gun barrel. "Put your mouth on this," Elias says, and Chris does. Cut to Kevin Dillon's character, Bunny, sitting in front of a Confederate flag, swigging a beer and talking garbage with Junior and Rodriguez. Bunny tosses around ethnic slurs and seems stupid and out of touch. Back in the bunker, the heads are slow-dancing with each other.

The platoon goes out and finds a tunnel complex. A booby trap kills a man, and later, in the confusion, another member of the platoon, Manny, turns up missing. They find him dead and staked to a tree, tortured. Barnes is pissed and leads the platoon into the nearest village, where the troops unleash their frustration on civilians. Swept up in the hatred, Chris makes a one-legged man dance, firing at the ground. Right in front of him, Bunny kills a retarded boy with his rifle butt. "Holy shit," he marvels, "you see that fucking head come apart?" This sobers Chris, and soon Elias shows up to put a stop to the slaughter, facing off with Barnes.

The LT comes up and says the captain wants the place torched, and so the village burns to Samuel Barber's syrupy Adagio. Chris regains his humanity, stopping a gang rape, saying, "She's a fucking human being, man!"

Back at base, Elias reports the incident, but though the captain says there'll be a court-martial if there were any "illegal killings," nothing immediate comes of it.

Chris and Elias talk that night. "There's no right or wrong in them," Elias says of the stars.

"Do you believe?" Chris asks him, about the American involvement.

"In '65, yeah. Now, no. We're going to lose this war. We've been kicking people's asses so long, I figure it's time we got ours kicked."

Chris ruminates on the split in the platoon. "I can't believe we're fighting each other when we should be fighting them."

Back in the jungle, the platoon runs into some serious VC. They're in danger of being overrun when Elias volunteers to outflank the enemy. The LT botches his grid coordinates and short rounds fall all around them. They've got to pull back, get the hell out. But Elias is still out there. Barnes says he'll go get him. Instead, when he finds him, Barnes levels his weapon and pumps some rounds into him.

Barnes runs into Chris, who asks him where Elias is. Barnes says he's dead, and they hop into the Hueys and get out of there just as the VC come streaming out of the jungle, Elias a few steps ahead of them, bleeding, stumbling, raising his arms toward the departing liftships. He dies in slow motion with Barber's Adagio going, his arms out, Christlike.

Chris knows Barnes killed him. "When you know, you know," he explains.

Barnes hears his explanation down in the heads' bunker and challenges Chris to do something about it. Barnes sneers at the joint they're sharing. "You smoke this shit to escape from reality? Me, I don't need this shit. I *am* reality." Barnes taunts Chris until Chris attacks him, but Barnes is too strong. Barnes marks his cheek with a knife and walks off.

They're about to be sent back into the jungle. "It felt like we were returning to the scene of the crime," Chris says. Rumor is they're going to see action. Big Harold (Forrest Whitaker) says, "Somewhere out there's the beast, and he's hungry tonight." Getting ready, Bunny says of the village killings, "I don't feel like we done something wrong, but sometimes I get this bad feeling," then invokes the World War II hero Audie Murphy.

That night, they're overrun by the VC, and Stone administers poetic justice, killing Bunny in an over-the-top scene. In the middle of the confusion, Barnes and Chris square off. Barnes is about to kill Chris (his face strikingly like Willard's here) when an airstrike hits and we're blinded by white light.

Chris wakes to a red deer. Barnes is trying to crawl away. "Get me a medic," he says. "Go on, boy." Then when he realizes that Chris means to kill him, Barnes chides him: "Do it."

Chris does.

In the end, good wins out over evil. The stoner dudes live, and Barnes's right-hand man O'Neill gets stuck with the crappy task of leading second platoon. As the medevac lifts off, taking Chris away, Rhah, one of the heads, bangs his chest and lifts his arms in triumph, an echo of Elias's last gesture.

Chris flies off, profile framed in the door of the chopper (again the Adagio), the green mountains of Vietnam (the Philippines) sliding by behind him. "I think now, looking back," he concludes, "we did not fight the enemy; we fought ourselves, and the enemy was in us. The war is over for me now, but it will always be there the rest of my days, as I'm sure Elias will be, fighting with Barnes for what Rhah called the possession of my soul. There are times since I've felt like a child born of those two fathers." Lastly, Chris cites for all veterans "an obligation to build again, to teach to others what we know, and to try with what's left of our lives to find a goodness and a meaning to this life."

The film ends with a placard: "Dedicated to the men who fought and died in the Vietnam War."

With that wrap-up of a speech, it seems *Platoon* can be read as a *Bildungsroman*, as Chris moves from innocence to experience and can make a meaningful lesson of his service that he can use and pass along to others. He's no longer the young man in Ecclesiastes, and while there may be little reason to rejoice, he's survived his trial. He's learned.

Oliver Stone struggled for years to get the backing to make *Platoon*, so it would be wrong to call it an instant success, but upon release the film garnered solid box-office receipts and sterling reviews, becoming something of a phenomenon. It was talked about, lauded, debated. *Time* magazine dedicated seven pages to it. Most critics noted the level of detail as well as the response of many veterans, who thought it the first film that showed what Vietnam was really like. In 1986, *Platoon* was sold and accepted as realism, perhaps even history. Stone had done the impossible, critics said, and the academy agreed. *Platoon* won the Oscar for best picture, and Stone won for best director.

Now, a decade later, it's hard not to see *Platoon*—despite its attention to concrete detail—as an allegory for American society during the war. Chris is given the choice of backing the heads (the antiwar counterculture) or the juicers (the establishment), which, in Stone's view of America, is an easy choice. And the day-to-day moral dilemmas of the American soldier in Vietnam—the grunt's inner life—aren't gone into in any real depth, only sideswiped during big, melodramatic scenes, most of which are, and were at the time, familiar clichés in the literature. The first dead, the U.S. atrocity in the village, the incompetent ROTC LT, Bunny the psycho—all of these would have been old hat to anyone who'd read the novels or the oral histories. But astonishing as this may seem, in 1986, thirteen years after the last U.S. ground troops left Vietnam, the American moviegoer had never seen any of them.

The major films that preceded *Platoon* focused not on combat but the effect of the war on America—the war as a way of understanding America. *Platoon* does this as well, but merely as subtext. On the surface, it deals with combat and the tensions and camaraderie between soldiers, and though it awkwardly twists its plot and characters to set up almost cartoonish good-versus-evil climaxes, it succeeds around the edges, nails the atmosphere, takes us there. In a sense, all the smaller elements of the movie work, while the major pieces fail. What, finally, does *Platoon* tell us that we don't already know? And yet, this is it, this is *the* Vietnam movie. It captured the attention of the nation as no other version of Vietnam has or possibly ever will.

There's no certain answer as to why this happened. By 1986, as evidenced by the *Rambo* and *Missing in Action* films, America was ready to see the Vietnam vet as a hero, and this applied retroactively to the vet as soldier in Vietnam. *Platoon* gave America back the vet as innocent, the vet capable of seeing clearly and making the right choices. Chris Taylor (Christ?) is seen, as the eighties demanded, as a victim of the war, a survivor, and it's his experience that's held up as representative, not, as Chris implies at the end, a mix of Barnes's and Elias's. Chris isn't a professional soldier or a frontier hero type; he's an average middle-class kid, yet he volunteered, hoping "to see something I haven't seen, learn something I don't know yet." It could be said that he's an everyman, a regular guy yet not a reluctant draftee. There's something of the adventurer in him, or the quest hero, which he fulfills by killing the clearly evil figure of Barnes. As in *Apocalypse Now*, the war itself is assumed to be absurd and unwinnable, but the inner struggle for the soul of America doesn't end in an ambiguous tie, as it does with Willard slaying Kurtz and becoming one with the face of the stone Buddha, but in a clear victory for Good, with Chris surviving to bring his message home and teach it to others. For a supposedly gritty, realistic film about the American war in Vietnam, *Platoon* has the form of a melodrama and what could be seen—in a historical context—as an incredibly happy ending.

Just as *The Deer Hunter* beat *Apocalypse Now* into theaters, *Platoon* upstaged Stanley Kubrick's long-awaited *Full Metal Jacket* (1987). Kubrick's previous epics, such as *Spartacus, Dr. Strangelove, A Clockwork Orange,* and *2001,* had established him as one of the finest filmmakers in the world, one with a keen—even cutting—political and cultural sensibility. When early word leaked that he was training his eye on Vietnam, critics wondered if he would be the one to finally "get the war right." Kubrick had enlisted Gustav Hasford and Michael Herr to help him adapt Hasford's *The Short-Timers* to the screen. The talent, it seemed, was in place, and hopes for the film were high; it had been seven years since Kubrick's last release, *The Shining,* and that movie, though obviously brilliant in parts, had been widely met with disappointment. This would be Kubrick's return to form. And so, like *Apocalypse Now, Full Metal Jacket* steamed into theaters both too late and burdened with impossible critical expectations.

The movie opens with recruits being shorn of their locks to a country-western tune, "Good-bye My Darling, Hello Vietnam," and soon it's apparent that we're going to spend a good deal of time (half the film, in fact) going through basic training with this group of Marines. In the barracks, drill instructor Gunny Hartman (Lee Ermey, a real-life DI before taking up acting) berates his charges in an extended and hilarious routine, giving our major players their new names—Joker (Matthew Modine), Cowboy (Arliss Howard), and Gomer Pyle (Vincent D'Onofrio)—and laying out his philosophy of the Corps. His harangue is full of lines like, "Only steers and queers come from Texas. Do you suck dicks? You look like you could suck a golfball through a garden hose. You look like the kind of person who would fuck someone in the ass and not give him the courtesy of a reach-around." He leads his men through PT (physical training), calling obscene cadences and intimidating the fat, hapless Pyle. He instructs the recruits to give their rifle a girl's name and to sleep with it. "No more finger banging Mary Jane Rottencrotch," this is the only pussy they're going to get. In making these boys into men, Hartman stresses the immortality of the Corps, saying "God's got a hard-on for Marines," and in one brutal sequence, he strikes Joker for saying he doesn't love the Virgin Mary. Impressed by Joker's courage in standing up to him, Hartman makes him squad leader.

The training continues, as Joker narrates the change in the men in a flat voice-over. Pyle can't hack it, and Hartman puts Joker in charge of shaping him up. It's no use. Again and again, we see Pyle lagging behind the group, his trousers around his ankles and his thumb in his mouth. When he talks with Joker, it seems he's reverting to childhood; he can't button his shirt, he doesn't know left from right. On the rifle range, Hartman tells them that a Marine needs a hard heart to kill, and later, after Pyle screws up and Hartman punishes the squad for it, Joker becomes at first a reluctant and then a vicious participant in a blanket party as the whole squad beats the sleeping Pyle. In the darkened barracks, Pyle cries like a baby, and Joker plugs his ears with his fingers.

Pyle degenerates further, developing a strange relationship with his rifle, Charlene. On the range, he finds the one thing he can master. Earlier, Hartman cited the marksmanship of Lee Harvey Oswald and Charles Whitman (the University of Texas tower sniper) as products of the Marine Corps. Cowboy and Joker are worried about Pyle, and the night after they graduate and receive their assignments, Joker finds him in the head with his rifle, obviously deranged. He calls for Hartman, who comes in with his usual over-the-top bluster—"What is your major malfunction, numbnuts? Didn't mummy and daddy show you enough attention when you were a child?"—and Pyle blows him away, then eats Charlene and splashes the back of his head all over the clean white tiles.

Cut to Saigon, awash in signage and blatting traffic. A whore cruises Joker, now a combat correspondent, and Rafterman (Kevyn Major-Howard), his green photographer, as Nancy Sinatra belts out

"These Boots are Made for Walkin'." "Me so horny," the whore en-
tices Joker, "Me love you long time." A Saigon cowboy snatches
Rafterman's camera and jumps on a buddy's Honda. Afterward,
Rafterman gripes about the ingratitude of the Vietnamese. "It's just
business," Joker says.

At a *Stars and Stripes* briefing in Da Nang, we see how Joker's out-
of-it editor only wants to publish good news, asking Joker to change
his phrasing ("search and destroy" becomes "sweep and clear") and
even to fabricate stories ("grunts like reading about dead officers"). It's
Tet 1968, and that night in the barracks Rafterman and Joker are
talking about "getting back into the shit" when the VC hit the front
gate to the tune of "The Chapel of Love." Our green heroes rush out
to a bunker, Joker manning a machine gun. "I'm not ready for this
shit," he admits.

The next morning the wire is strung with dead VC. At his *Stars and
Stripes* briefing, Joker mouths off, and his editor assigns him to cover
the enemy occupation of Hue. (This is also the first time we see the
peace sign on Joker's helmet, as well as the motto: BORN TO KILL.)
Rafterman asks if he can come along, and the two take a chopper
north.

In Hue their first stop is a mass grave of civilians executed by either
the VC or NVA, another learning experience for Joker. An officer
comments on the contradictory messages on Joker's helmet, asking if
it's a joke. Joker replies that he's trying to say "something about the
duality of man, sir." The oblivious officer (as loopy as Kilgore in
Apocalypse Now) tells him to jump on the wagon for the big win, and
that "inside every gook there is an American trying to get out."

Joker finds out that his old buddy Cowboy's outfit is in Hue, and
tracks him down. The two have a macho, insult-filled reunion, and
Joker and Rafterman join Cowboy's Lusthog Squad (with Animal
Mother [Adam Baldwin], Eightball [Dorian Harewood], Crazy Earl,
and T.H.E. Rock, among other colorful grunts) as they move through
Hue. At one point, as in *Apocalypse Now*, a camera crew shoots them
during combat. The men mug and wisecrack for the camera: "This is
Vietnam—the movie." "Is that you, John Wayne? Is this me?" "We'll
let the gooks play the Indians."

A surprising amount of time is given to this kind of highly self-conscious criticism of, or simply statements about, the war. In the next sequence a squad member has been killed, and the survivors stand above him, all chipping in their thoughts; and immediately after this is a montage of mock TV interviews (a tactic familiar to viewers of the TV series M*A*S*H) in which the men comment on how little the Vietnamese appreciate their efforts, including the line "We're shooting the wrong gooks." As if to confirm this, in the next episode an ARVN soldier rides up on a Honda with a whore, whom he offers to the men, who are stretched out in an unbolted row of seats in front of a movie theater playing a Western.

Finally the squad moves out on patrol. Crazy Earl is killed by a sniper in a ruined building, leaving the untried Cowboy in charge, hunkered down behind a mound of rubble. Cowboy can't seem to read the map. "What are we," Joker asks, "lost?" Eightball tries to cross a patch of open ground to reach Crazy Earl and is gunned down—in slo-mo—by the sniper. Cowboy can't control Animal Mother, who makes a heroic, John Wayne–like charge to safe cover. Animal Mother spots the sniper and covers the squad as they move up.

But there's a line of fire through the building they're crouched behind, and the sniper takes out Cowboy. He dies in Joker's arms. It's time for some payback.

The squad infiltrates the building, clears the first floor, moves upstairs. Joker is the first person to see the sniper, who wheels around to reveal she's a woman, her braid flying, teeth gritted as she fires. Joker fumbles with his weapon, and is saved only because Rafterman unloads a clip into her. Shaken, Joker joins the circle of grunts standing over her. Rafterman is doing a little victory dance, humping the air. The sniper's not dead, instead she's croaking out a few words none of them understand. "She's praying." "No more boom-boom for this babysan," Animal Mother says.

Joker's worried. What should they do with her? "Fuck her. Let her rot." "Cowboy's wasted," someone reminds him. Joker has to make a choice, and he chooses to kill her—out of mercy, it seems. "Fucking hardcore," Animal Mother says, possibly misinterpreting his motives, and they move out.

It's night and the fires are burning, the men spread out on patrol, stalking through the rubble. Joker's voice-over says that though he's "in a world of shit," "I am not afraid." As we close, the men are singing the theme from the Mickey Mouse Club. Fade out and the credits roll over the Stones' "Paint It, Black."

Initial reaction to *Full Metal Jacket* was cool. Critics called the film aimless, partitioned, episodic, and singled out Matthew Modine's performance as wooden and ineffective. The screenplay was praised for its inventive use of language, but, film being a visual medium, the fact that Kubrick chose to shoot the movie in England rather than the Philippines (the location of choice) completely undermined *Full Metal Jacket*'s authenticity. In the wake of *Platoon*, the release of *Full Metal Jacket* couldn't help but be anticlimactic. Comparisons with Stone's film were inescapable and harsh, as were comparisons with Kubrick's own earlier work. On the very basic level of cinematography, even *The Shining* was more interesting. *Full Metal Jacket* was a disappointment, the critics said, a failure on all counts.

That view of the film hasn't changed. Veterans find the basic training section on target except for Pyle's violence and the Vietnam sections unconvincing. Film critics continue to hold *Full Metal Jacket* up to Kubrick's earlier work as well as to *Platoon* (more realistic) or *Apocalypse Now* (more daring and more interesting visually). Thematically though, the film—like most of Kubrick's work—is chock-full of interesting stuff.

First, the film comments sharply on the Vietnam narrative as *Bildungsroman*. Where *Platoon* affirms the old and romantic idea of war as a crucible that builds men, Kubrick seems to be saying— through Pyle and then Joker and the men of the Lusthog squad—that Vietnam, or simply war, takes these boys not from innocence to experience but to numbness or madness. The ironic use of the Mickey Mouse theme song to close the film is a far cry from Chris Taylor's heroic speechmaking.

Second, throughout the film Kubrick is examining the construction of gender and the institutionalized twining of sex and violence. The extremes to which the recruits have to create a dominant masculine self (violent, sexually potent) at the expense of anything feminine (weak, rotten, helpless) is shockingly reversed in the end, with the revelation that the sniper is a woman, is in fact what Gunny Hartman said they would have to become—a hardhearted killer of many enemies whose weapon is an expression of her will. And yet even then the men (except for Joker, our hero) persist in equating death with sexual domination, standing over her like participants in a gang rape, Rafterman dancing lewdly.

Third—and part of the construction of gender falls under this—in *Full Metal Jacket,* as in *A Clockwork Orange* and *2001,* Kubrick is interested in the institutional and societal shaping or destruction of personality and the mystery of the human capacity for evil, this time playing it off American claims of innocence.

Beyond these conscious, well-developed themes, *Full Metal Jacket* looks at truth versus fiction in the media (especially in the official misuse of language), America as an inherently violent culture, war as business, race relations, and the institution as religion (and vice versa). Critics likewise have investigated Kubrick's ironic use of pop culture and language, the film's view of the Vietnamese, and Kubrick's implementation of Herr's dictum of the beauty or allure of destruction, the spectacle of war (you want to look and you don't want to look).

An insatiable reader and writer, Kubrick fits his movies together like novels. As a literary object—a thing to be read—*Full Metal Jacket* continues to interest academics if not Vietnam vets, general moviegoers, or video renters. The film won't go away, though, as Kubrick's position as an intellectual moviemaker is firmly established, whereas Stone's, like Cimino's, seems to fade with each new release.

The second wave of films includes one other major work of note, John Irvin's *Hamburger Hill* (1987), from a script by veteran James Carabatsos. The movie is remarkable solely for the fact that some vets rank it with or even above *Platoon* in its depiction of combat. While the script is leaden and obvious and the performances weak, the production crew's attention to detail is sometimes impressive. On the whole, the film has little to say, since the action is given almost no context, political or otherwise, and the occasional statement about the war, the media, or America is inevitably old hat—as are, in fact, the details of *Hamburger Hill*. As with *Platoon*, the idea that a movie might get something right about Vietnam—if only the basest physical elements—was impressive to moviegoers (and vets) as late as 1987. As a study of character and war, however, *Hamburger Hill* owes more to the melting-pot platoon movies of World War II than to Vietnam.

Barry Levinson's *Good Morning, Vietnam* (1987) did impressively at the box office, but other than Robin Williams's typical shtick, the film gives us nothing that hasn't already been done—and done better—elsewhere. Its widespread acceptance as a commercial vehicle is a good indicator of Hollywood suddenly embracing Vietnam if not as subject matter then at least as a palatable background.

The great success of the second wave was due almost entirely to *Platoon*, and for the first time, television sought to cash in on that success. In 1987, CBS developed a weekly series called *Tour of Duty*, in which the viewing audience followed the fortunes of a platoon in the Americal Division. Much of the writing was done by veterans, and the young actors involved underwent a less rigorous form of basic training so the details would be right. Though it earned solid reviews, the show lasted only two seasons.

More successful was ABC's 1988 *China Beach*, which introduced us to a group of nurses stationed by the seaside R&R site. The writing and the performances were better than average for TV, and the details, especially in the first year, were handled carefully. Later the show slid into melodrama (some critics have dismissively called it a high-tone soap opera), and with the same anachronistic hindsight used by *M*A*S*H* in its later years contemporary issues such as nurses' PTSD (Post-Traumatic Stress Disorder) were sensitively addressed in the context of the late sixties. Despite—or because of—its obvious debts to *M*A*S*H*, *China Beach* gobbled up solid ratings, established a following, and took home a number of Emmys before being canceled in 1992. For several years it was the only view of Vietnam offered to the average American viewer, and, like *M*A*S*H* and Korea, is probably at this writing—for those too young to remember the nightly newscasts—the most familiar face of the Vietnam War next to that of the hapless *Forrest Gump* (1994).

Since the second wave, a number of major Vietnam films have been released, including Brian De Palma's *Casualties of War* (1989, from a script by vet David Rabe) and the two remaining entries in Oliver Stone's Vietnam trilogy—his adaptations of Ron Kovic's *Born on the Fourth of July* (1989) and Le Ly Hayslip's *Heaven and Earth* (1993). Some have done well—notably *Born on the Fourth*, because of Tom Cruise's star power—but no Vietnam film has captured the American imagination since *Platoon*, and it's likely none will, at least for a while. The latest success was Disney's *Operation Dumbo Drop* (1995), a comedy about a group of misfit, good-at-heart GI's who have to deliver an elephant to a village. Since the second wave, there's been an industry trend of using Vietnam simply as a backdrop for a standard genre film (detective, comedy) or to examine something else—say, women's rights in *China Beach*, or the African American experience in *The Walking Dead* (1995)—not why America was there, what it was doing, and who paid the price. The prospect of a serious new Vietnam film, in 1998, seems remote. The common wisdom now in Hollywood is that Vietnam has been done and is therefore over with. But, like America's view of the war, that will certainly change.

9

Memoirs

1967. On a U.S. firebase, empty boots at a memorial service stand in for the dead.

The memoir, like the oral history, claims to take readers past the lies and obfuscations of the media and the official story of the war and give them the real truth from someone who's been there. The drawbacks of this method are the same as the oral history, maybe to an even greater degree, since there's no supposedly objective intermediary figure like an overall editor or compiler. The reader is asked to buy the author's subjective version of events and has little or nothing with which to compare it.

This was especially true early on, when Ronald J. Glasser, M.D.'s *365 Days* (1971) appeared. Glasser served as an Army doctor in-country, so it's intriguing that in the section here he's chosen to write in the third person about a patrol he doesn't seem to have been on. While the book was marketed as nonfiction, Glasser employs a novelistic technique, a blunt realism mixing clichés with sharply observed details, many rarely seen at the time. A powerful indictment of the war, *365 Days* was well reviewed and continues to be reprinted today.

Army lieutenant Frederick Downs's *The Killing Zone* (1978) belongs to the first wave, yet unlike much of that work, lays out the contradictions of the American experience without drawing any conclusions. His book details his tour leading an infantry platoon and relies on a simple straight-ahead realism, marking off the days. The section here features the interrogation of a prisoner, a common occurrence in the literature.

Chickenhawk (1983), by helicopter pilot Robert Mason, belongs to the second wave, yet dwells on atrocities like an antiwar tract from the early seventies—a rarity both for that time period and this genre. Note Mason's ironic use of quotations at the beginning of the chapter. Again, the mode is realism and the author ticks off the months of his tour. *Chickenhawk* was extremely well received, and Mason later wrote a sequel, *Chickenhawk: Back in the World,* in which he relates his difficulties after coming home.

The Only War We Had (1987) is former Army lieutenant (and later captain) Michael Lee Lanning's first of his four Vietnam books. Based on Lanning's journals, like *The Killing Zone* it follows his outfit from day to day in a flat, realistic style. Lanning's publisher, Ivy Books (a division of Ballantine, itself a division of the giant Random House), has released a whole shelf-ful of this kind of combat memoir, which critics have christened the "tactical duty narrative." In these cheap mass-market paperbacks, combat veterans from specialized units such as SEALs, Marine snipers, or LRRPs let the reader in on the secrets of their professions. These titles sell well at both large chain bookstores (where they make up the majority of Vietnam titles) and, strangely, at airports. Lanning's, like the rest, is somewhat heroic and technically oriented compared to the other memoirs in this section, and shies away from political or moral questions of character, concentrating instead, like an adventure film, on exciting exterior action.

Implicitly or explicitly, each of these works takes a moral stance with respect to the war, seeing it as justified or not. Likewise, each paints the American military and the individual soldier in a certain light, as well as their relationship to the Vietnamese. As in the fiction and films, atrocities and war crimes crop up often, serving as a test case or metaphor for either the war as a whole or this particular soldier's involvement in it.

365 Days

RONALD J. GLASSER, M.D.

1971

SEARCH AND DESTROY

It was 115 degrees in the sun, and what little shade there was offered no relief. A dull, suffocating dryness hung over the paddies, making it almost impossible to breathe. By seven-thirty, the troopers were already covered with a thin, dusty layer of salt. Instead of swallowing their salt pills, they walked along chewing them two or three at a time. A few visibly hunched their shoulders against the heat, but there was nothing to be done about it so they kept walking, trying as well as they could to shelter the metal parts of their weapons from the sun. The sweet smell of marijuana drifted along with them. A little before noon, the point man, plodding along a dusty rise, sweating under his flack vest, stepped on a pressure-detonated 105-mm shell, and for ten meters all around the road lifted itself into the air, shearing off his legs as it blew up around him. The rest of the patrol threw themselves on the ground.

That evening, the company was mortared—two rounds that sent the already exhausted troopers scurrying for shelter. After the attack, those who had been resting found it impossible to get back to sleep. The heat that the sun poured into the Delta during the day continued to hang over them, covering them like a blanket; despite the darkness, it was still over 90 degrees. The troopers lay on the ground, smoking grass or just looking vacantly up at the empty sky. It was the fifth night that week they were hit.

461

Before breakfast, a patrol was sent out to sweep the area around the nearby village. The troopers got up while it was still dark, put on their webbing and flack vests, and without saying a word, went out. All they found were the usual, uncooperative villagers. The patrol, against orders, went into the village, searched a few huts, kicked in a door, and left.

Later that morning, the company began sweeping again. They moved out on line, humping through the gathering heat, chewing salt pills as they had the day before, looking out over the same shimmering landscape. A little after ten o'clock, they began moving through a hedgegrove. A trooper tripped a wire and detonated a claymore set up to blow behind him. It took down three others, killing two right off and leaving the third to die later. The survivors rested around the bodies till the Dust Offs came in and took out the casualties, then started up again.

Before noon, the platoon strung out along a dike had entered a tangled area of burned-over second growth. It wasn't so big that they couldn't have gone around, but the Old Man wanted to kill some gooks, so he sent them through it just in case. Disgusted, they moved into it, and for over two hours pushed their way through the steaming shadowy tangle. The thick overhead filtered out almost all the sunlight, making it difficult to see, while the matting of vines and bushes held onto the heat, magnifying it until the troopers felt they were moving through a breathless oven. The sweat poured off them as they moved cautiously through the suffocating half light. At places the growth was so thick that to get through they had to sling their weapons and pull the vines apart with their bare hands.

"Careful, there . . . hold it, man . . . don't move."

The vines and thorns caught onto their fatigues and equipment, and they had to stop to tear themselves loose.

"Watch it, Smithy . . . hold up, Hank; there, by your foot . . ."

"Fuck . . . I'm caught."

"Watch your step, man . . ."

Scratched and bleeding, they pushed on through the tangle.

"Larry, don't move your arm. Don't move. I think I see a wire."

"It's OK, Frey. It's just a vine."

Suddenly, out on their right someone screamed.

"Don't move!" Crayson yelled. "Just don't move. I'm coming."

"Jesus Christ, I'm on one."

Pulling up short, the others froze.

Crayson and the other corporal stepped carefully through the bushes toward the trooper.

"Don't lift your foot. Freeze, man, just don't lift it."

"EOD, EOD, forward! EOD forward!"

"That fucken bastard, that fucken bastard," the trooper kept repeating, almost hysterically, "that fucken bastard," as the EOD bent down to look at the mine.

"What is it? Jesus!" he said, rigid with fear.

"It's OK," the EOD said, straightening up, wiping the sweat from his eyes. "It's pressure-release. Don't worry, it's not a bouncing betty. Just don't move."

"M-60 carriers, forward! Ammo carriers, forward!"

The EOD slipped off his rucksack, and laying down his weapon got down on his hands and knees, as the troopers came up with the boxes of M-60 ammunition.

"OK, now, just don't move," he said. "I'm gonna stack these ammunition cans on the detonator plate. When I tell you, move your foot a bit, but don't lift it up. OK?" The EOD carefully wiped off the steel plate and placed one forty-pound can on the right side of the plate next to the trooper's foot and another on the left side of the plate.

"OK, man," the EOD said, looking up. "It's OK. Just step off."

Three-quarters of the way through the tangle, a trooper brushed against a two-inch vine, and a grenade slung at chest height went off, shattering the right side of his head and body. The medic, working down in the dim light, managed to stop the major bleeders, but could do nothing about the shattered arm and the partially destroyed skull. Nearby troopers took hold of the unconscious soldier and half carrying, half dragging him, pulled him the rest of the way through the tangle.

The platoon finally came out onto a small dirt road. Shielding their eyes from the sudden glare of sunlight, they dropped their rucksacks and sat down along the slight rise bordering the road, licking the salt off their lips as they waited for the chopper to come in and take out the body.

They were sitting there strung out along the road, when they spotted a small figure putt-putting toward them. They watched disinterestedly while the figure moved toward them, its progress marked by little puffs of grayish smoke, and became an old man driving a scooter. When the scooter was less than fifty meters away from them, the old man began to slow down.

The point, a blank-faced kid, picked up his weapon and got slowly to his feet. Holding up his hand, he walked wearily into the center of the road and stopped there, waiting. The old man slowed to a stop and stared at the trooper, waiting impatiently for him to move. He had a small steel container strapped to the back of his Honda. The point leveled his weapon at the little man's stomach, and, walking around him, motioned for him to open the container. The old man hesitated. The trooper calmly clicked his M-16 to automatic. Holding it with one hand, he carefully opened the container.

"Hey," he said, lowering his weapon. "The dink's got cokes."

The rest of the platoon got to their feet. The point was reaching into the container when the old man grabbed his wrist. Startled, the trooper jumped back.

"Hey!" He pulled his hand away. "What the fuck?"

"Fifty cent," the old man demanded, waving five fingers in the trooper's face. "Fifty cent!"

There was a moment of stunned silence.

"The little fucker steals 'em from us and then wants us to pay," someone said angrily. The point reached in again, only to have the old man slap his hand away.

"Watch it, dink," he said angrily. The Vietnamese, furious, reached for the container top and slammed it shut. From the side of the road there was the metallic click of a round being chambered. The old man turned on his scooter and kicked at the starter.

"Hold it," the corporal said, moving into the road. Others followed him and gathered around in angry, sullen silence. The Vietnamese, head down, ignoring them all, kicked again at his starter.

"I want a coke," one of the troopers said, and swinging his rifle, he knocked the top off the steel container. The Vietnamese spun around and spat at him. The trooper took a small step backward, brought the weapon smoothly up into the crook of his arm and emptied the magazine into him, cutting him off his scooter, then calmly reached into his webbing, took out another clip, and pushed it into his gun. When the chopper came they were standing there drinking the cokes. They sent their own dead home and left the old man sprawled in the middle of the road.

That night, a little after midnight, just as they were getting to sleep, the company was rocketed again. The first 122-mm rocket hit near their flank. The jarring whoosh of its explosion rolled over the camp, and a moment later someone was screaming for a medic.

In the morning, the patrol sweeping the area in front of the village found the partially destroyed cross pieces of a rocket launcher. When they brought it back, the CO examined it and asked permission to hit the village. It was denied. That afternoon, two platoons of the company were ordered out of the area to take part in a combined sweep of a nearby VC stronghold. Brigade sent them some slicks and they were CA'd in.

What was supposed to be a VC stronghold turned out to be an NVA regiment. The slicks on line brought the platoons in downwind of a little group of paddies. Even as the choppers drifted into a hover, they came under fire. While the door gunners swept the tree lines, loaches and cobras swung in and out over the LZ, shooting at anything that looked good.

The troopers, huddled in the doorways of their slicks, were being shot down before they had a chance to jump. The air crackled with passing rounds. One of the slicks was still thirty feet off the ground when a gunship, keeping pace with them, shuddered, wavered a bit, then dropped fifteen feet and exploded, sending great pieces of metal hurtling in all directions. The 1st Platoon's six slicks brought them in closer to the tree line than the other units. Hovering three feet off the ground, the troopers jumped out into the swirling dust while the door gunners shot up the tree lines. Three troopers got hit right off, tumbling over even before they'd got their balance. Those running could hear the sledge hammer sounds of the RPD's slamming into the choppers behind them.

The second platoon was landing off to their right, the chopper's blades flattening down the bushes, while the troopers leaped out. A gunship came in low, right over the slicks, its gunner planted solidly in the door, feet braced against the struts, firing his 60 directly into the tree line. The pilot kept the chopper moving parallel to the troopers rushing the line, while the door gunner, pressing down on the trigger, kept his quad 60's cracking out in one long continuous roar. A slick exploded as it pulled out.

A cobra swept in, running down the whole length of a nearby hedgegrove, cutting it apart with its mini guns. The company charging through the heat took the wood line. Stumbling through the bushes, they overran it, killing everyone they found. Panting, barely able to catch his breath, the platoon's RTO found a wounded NVA, his shoulder and thighs smashed by the mini guns. Unable to move, he lay there, his AK broken beside him. The RTO shot him through the face.

It went on like that until the troopers had cleared the line. With the gunships moving out in front they found themselves on the edge of another paddy. Beyond was a thicker tree line. The platoon's lieutenant, keeping low, moved out ahead.

"OK, OK," he said; "come on, let's go."

No one moved. The med evacs were already coming in behind them.

"Lieutenant," the Sergeant said, "they're waiting."

All along the grove, troopers were stretched out, looking grimly across the open paddy.

"I know, I know," he said, "but the gunships shook them up, and the Major wants us to go. The quicker we get at 'em the better. Don't want them to dig in."

"Shit," one of the troopers mumbled.

A machine gun opened up on their left flank.

"They've been dug in for twenty years," someone else volunteered disgustedly. "Why don't we soften the fucken thing up first."

"Let's go," the lieutenant said flatly. "That's an order."

Bitterly they got up, and the NVA let them get halfway across the field before they hit them. They had to pull back. A gunship coming in to help was hit by an RPD, scattering itself over 200 meters of Nam. Air strikes were finally called in and then, with gunships anchoring their flanks and artillery in rolling barrages, destroying the grove and cutting off any retreat, they moved out again. Another battalion was committed and then another. In the heat of it all, more choppers, flying close support, were shot down. Finally, on the second day, what was left of the 35th NVA regiment left whatever it was they had been fighting for and simply disappeared.

That afternoon the Americans, slinging their weapons, began counting bodies. The brass flew in, and to show how pleased they were, OK'd a policy of claiming a kill for every weapon found, even without a body. The exhausted troops, eighteen- and nineteen-year-old kids, ignored the congratulations and simply went on stacking the bodies, throwing them into countable piles. It was the chopper pilots, though, flying in and out of it, right through the center of an NVA regiment and losing nine choppers, who summed up the bitterness of what had happened. At dusk of that last day of fighting, they flew in a CH-47 flying crane and slung a great cargo net below it. After the counting, they helped the troopers throw the NVA bodies into the net.

They filled the net quickly, and when it was filled, the crane, blowing up great clouds of dust, rose off the flat, pock-marked paddy. When the net had cleared the ground, the crane spun slowly around its center and, carrying its dripping cargo, moved off to drop the bodies on the path of the retreating NVA.

The next morning the two platoons were flown back to the rest of their company. That first night back they were hit again—two mortar rounds. The next day on patrol near the village, the slack stepped on a buried 50-caliber bullet, driving it down on a nail and blowing off the front part of his foot. When the medic rushed to help, he tripped a pull-release bouncing betty, blowing the explosive charge up into the air. It went off behind him, the explosion and shrapnel pitching him forward onto his face. Some of the white hot metal, blowing backwards, caught the trooper coming up behind him.

The men asked to take the village, and that afternoon the company commander, fed up himself, asked Brigade for portable strobe lights so they could section off the village and search it at night. Brigade told him there weren't any available, so the Captain sent a squad to sweep the village before it got dark. The troopers, bitter and angry, found the village equally hostile and antagonistic. The villagers watched sullenly as the troopers, fingers on the triggers of their weapons, walked by their huts. No words were exchanged, nor any sign of recognition; the hate was palpable. Through it all the villagers had enough sense not to move; even the children stood rigidly still. Behind one of the huts, a squad found a rotting NVA medical kit. Without asking for approval they burned down the hut and waited there threateningly till it burned itself to the ground.

Half a kilometer past the village, the patrol was moving along the edge of one of the villager's paddies, trying to shield their eyes from the low-slung sun, when their point was cut down by a burst of automatic fire. Throwing themselves down, they waited for the mortars or machine-gun fire. There wasn't any, and a trooper, looking up, saw something move away from behind the nearest hedgegrove.

"Fuck it," he screamed, the last of his adolescent control gone. In a sudden fury he ripped off his webb gear. Even before it hit the ground he was up and running. He hit the hedgegrove on a dead Iowa run, barely keeping his balance as he burst through it. The rest of the squad was running after him. Carrying their M-16's and M-79's, they raced through the line and out onto the flat behind it. For Nam it was an incredibly abandoned affair. Helmetless, webb gear and flack vests thrown away, these bareheaded Negro and freckle-faced kids, heads down, arms pumping, their boots barely touching the ground, ran on through the shimmering heat, stumbling over the uneven ground. Just past the next grove they caught them—a girl and two men. They caught them out in the open and killed them, shooting them down as they ran. Afterward, they stood around the sprawled bodies, chests heaving, staring in bewilderment at each other. Then they stripped the girl, cut off her nose and ears, and left her there with the other two for the villagers.

That night, a starlight scope picked up movement near the village a few minutes before three rockets hit their lager. The next morning another patrol was sent out. Halfway to the village, one of the troopers stepped on a pressure-release land mine. They were still close enough to carry him back to the base camp. A little before noon, a squad found three of the village water buffalo out grazing. The machine gunner set up his M-60, carefully adjusted the sights, and while the rest of the patrol stood around him, calmly killed each buffalo in turn.

The following day a huge food cache was found buried in the area. The CO asked for a sectioning off and company-size sweep of the village and surrounding area. Brigade sent down a lieutenant colonel. He looked at the size of the food cache, the paths leading to it from the village, listened to the stories about booby traps and injuries, and OK'd a sweep for the next morning.

It was still dark when the men were shaken awake. "I want that fucken village locked in," the CO told the platoon leaders. "I don't want a mouse to get out, and I want every one of those huts searched. I want every floorboard pulled up, every wall knocked open. I want that village clean when we leave it. Is that understood? Clean." They filed out of the lager and waited until it was just light enough to see each other and then closed in. No one was smoking; no one said a word. There wasn't a sound except the soft footfalls of 112 troopers walking silently through the grass.

The Killing Zone

FREDERICK DOWNS

1978

2 November 1967

Our battalion had been ordered into the mountains west of the highway. We were to be relieved today by the 198th Brigade, fresh from the States. Bridge duty was relatively easy and it was thought that the green troops, "new" to Vietnam, should be broken in on the bridges before becoming bloodied in the jungles. The procedure for relieving us would be the same as before, only now, some weeks later, I would be the critical old-timer, scrutinizing the soldiers new to Vietnam.

But with one night remaining for us, there was time for a last mission. The platoon relieving us in the afternoon would allow me to use my complete platoon in an operation Captain Sells and I had been planning for days.

Intelligence had word that the village directly to the east about half a klick had nightly visits from the Cong, coming to see their families and draft new recruits. My platoon would work a coordinated attack by closing the village off on three sides after midnight. The east side, which abutted a large lake, would be covered by gunships in case any of the guerrillas tried to escape by boat. The frosting on the operation would be an MI (Military Intelligence) team, with a Chou-Hoi. The team would fly in at daybreak with an intelligence expert whom I would get to know in the future on other jobs. The man with him would be a dink named Fouel. Fouel had been a guerrilla for many

470

years but, for unknown reasons, he had become a Chou-Hoi. A Chou-Hoi was an enemy who turned himself, and hopefully his weapons, into the hands of the ARVNs or the Americans.

Our air force dropped millions of yellow leaflets urging the enemy to give up by waving the yellow papers at us. When the distraught enemy soldier gave himself up, he would be welcomed by smiling South Vietnamese soldiers into the fold. At least, the Chou-Hoi leaflets showed smiling South Vietnamese soldiers welcoming the enemy soldier. Somewhere there are records which show how many Chou-Hoi came in. I was always skeptical of their effectiveness, but they did work to some extent. If the enemy were getting beat pretty bad, they were more likely to turn themselves in. We never wholly trusted the Chou-Hois. There were many rumors circulating among the American soldiers stating that many Chou-Hois came in only to get information for their commanders in the field. After gaining the trust of the ARVNs or Americans, they would be issued an M-16 and assigned to a unit. When the fighting started, they would bug out back to their side with their new weapons, plenty of ammo, and good intelligence as to what kind, how many, and the disposition of the troops they had just left. True or not, we never trusted Chou-Hois.

Around 1400 hours the platoon relieving us arrived on deuce-and-a-halfs. I quickly briefed Lieutenant Lorbieki, the platoon leader, and went back to planning my operation. The skies were heavily overcast, boding a wet, miserable night; with luck, the rain would hold off. The operation would start from my bridge after dark.

I stood on the bridge facing east toward the village we would attack, seven hundred meters away. The villagers were coming home from their everyday chores. I thought of the many patrols we had conducted through that village in the last two or three weeks; we had found nothing. At night, we took fire from the direction of all the villages and I was slightly wounded.

We gave our equipment a last check. This operation called for web gear only. It meant we would carry only weapons, ammo, canteen, and first-aid packets. All the men had been briefed. The platoon would leave after dark in a single file, going directly across the open rice paddies toward the village. Fifty meters from the village, one squad with Spagg's machine gun would go around to the north and spread itself in a line to the lake, cutting escape to the north. I would stay at the west end with one squad spread in a line across the west end of the village, preventing escape. The third squad, with Indian's M-60, would spread to the south in a line to the lake. We would lie in wait all night until dawn, when the MI team would land by chopper to take us into the village. There was only one blind spot that was not covered, but it couldn't be helped. Starting at the edge of the lake, coming straight out into the rice paddies for two hundred meters, was a string of hills no more than fifty meters high. The village was built along the north side, out to where the hills ended. Some of the villagers had built up into the hills, which were heavily grown over. My squad on the south had those hills between them and the village. We believed the guerrillas would hide in the hills, but since the hills were small we would sweep them out fairly easily.

Lt. Lorbieki's platoon had completed taking over our old positions on the three bridges. My platoon had gathered at my bridge (now Lorbieki's bridge), where the relief men would guard our packs until we returned the next day.

It was dark. Lorbieki wished me luck.

"Saddle up!" I called. Then I gave the order to the point to move out and we filed into the darkness. The point was zigzagging through the paddies, following the small paddy dikes so we could stay in the dry paddies.

The flare was totally unexpected. One second we were dark ghosts drifting through the night; the next second our bodies stood out in stark relief, our shadows sifted into the knee-deep rice. "Down," our voices rasped to each other, needlessly. Our bodies had responded the instant the light flared into existence. I was terrified that we had triggered an ambush. My body and mind prepared to respond to the sound of bullets and explosions. In the next second, however, I realized the light was coming from the sky to the south. We all lay hidden in the rice fields watching the pyrotechnic show. *Puff is working,* we suddenly realized, as two solid red lines reached from the sky to etch the earth. This explained the flares. Above Puff was a flare ship. They were far enough away so their sound didn't carry to us, only the sight of flares and the red lines of tracers. We didn't dare move because the flares would point us out to the guerrillas in the village, who were undoubtedly also watching the show. The RTO had gotten the captain for me and handed the receiver over.

"This is One-six. What the hell is going on? We were caught out in the middle of this rice paddy and almost gave ourselves away! Over."

"This is Delta-Six. Dragon Six said that one of the new units is being attacked by a battalion of dinks. I don't believe it, but their Dragon Six got Puff called in anyway. Just lie low until the show is over, then get into position before any of those guerrillas escape, out."

"Those assholes down the road there are going to get us killed," I whispered to the men around me. The word was passed to let the men know what was happening. I informed the point to move out as soon as the flares quit and those flyboys went home. "Puff the Magic Dragon" was a C-47 loaded with thousands of rounds of ammo with mini-guns or gatling guns bolted to the side door. It was said that a ten-second burst would cover every square foot of a football field. The twin red lines we saw were tracer rounds, every fifth round in a belt of machine gun ammo. Puff was firing so fast that the tracers were two solid lines in the sky. It was a pretty sight, but hardly conducive to our plans.

The flares finally died and darkness returned. Our night sight was also gone, but it would come back. Unfortunately, as we moved forward, Puff also came back. As the first flare lit the sky, we hit the dirt.

"Son-of-a-bitch," I remarked. "If that lieutenant down south isn't being attacked by the dinks, I'll go down there and kill him myself."

The action finally ended and we moved into position fifty meters from the village. The north squad radioed in that they were further away from the village, about a hundred meters. The south squad radioed that they were right next to the small hills separating them from the village. The men with me were lying prone, heads resting on a small dike, bodies for once lying in a dry paddy. We could hear the villagers talking and a few girls giggling.

"Goddamn! Charlie is having a good time, having a family reunion, while we're out here lying in rice paddy shit," Mann mumbled to me.

"He'd better enjoy it while he can because it'll be the last reunion he'll ever have on this planet," Doc whispered over.

"Yeah, when that MI chopper lands and the dinks start deciding to move, I don't want one fucking dink to get away," I stated.

The inevitable rain started falling about 0200 hours. Not a hard, driving rain but a good, steady, ass-soaking rain that the gods unleash on soldiers to remind them who is really in charge. Off to the north the rain-muted sound of a machine gun, ours by the sound of it, muttered a few seconds then quit.

"What the hell? Mann, call Schaldenbrand and find out what happened!"

"Yes, sir. Here's Schaldenbrand."

"One-five, this is One-six. What was that firing all about? Over."

"This is One-five. A dink was trotting down the rice paddy dike out of the village right toward the Mike-60. Spagg opened up on him when he was only a few feet from us. He's deader than hell. His left arm is ripped almost off, out."

The rain stopped about the time the sky started to lighten in the east. All of us were crouched, wary of any movement in the village, ready to move as soon as MI arrived.

The villagers were becoming more active as they prepared for the day. As their movements increased, our tension mounted. Where was that chopper with the MI and his turncoat dink?

The chop-chop of rotor blades beat the early morning air. This was it! Suddenly the chopper came into view. The noise within the village became excited and the dinks started moving faster. The hell with them! My men could hold them. I would set the chopper down. The funny burbling voice of the chopper pilot came over the radio.

"Delta One-six, this is Early Bird with Hawk. Pop smoke, over."

"This is One-six. Affirmative, out."

The man who had popped smoke stood facing the direction the chopper would come from, holding his rifle in a horizontal position with his hands over his head. The pilot would read on the man holding the rifle. As the pilot drew closer, he would watch the rifle to correspond the altitude of his chopper with the altitude of the rifle. Since the man on the ground would be aware of hidden rocks, holes, or obstructions the pilot couldn't see, it was the soldier's duty to act as a guide-in. As the chopper approached the exact spot on which he should land, the soldier would begin to lower the rifle straight out in front of his body. When the set-down spot was reached by the chopper, right in front of the soldier, the soldier would crouch down, bending both elbows together, and act as though he was laying the rifle down at his feet. The pilot would then settle in.

As the chopper landed, the field agent and Fouel jumped out. The pilot immediately headed back to base. I shook hands with the agent and he introduced me to Fouel. Fouel was a typically built Vietnamese, five feet tall and starving. He was wearing black pajamas and carrying an M-2 carbine. He looked just like a Cong in that outfit.

I called the other two squads to warn them not to shoot our own man. One of my men yelled and pointed toward the village with all the activity. It looked like someone had kicked an anthill. Hot damn! There were dinks in there for sure.

We moved on line through the west edge of the village. The villagers stood in groups. This was not going to be just another patrol designed to show strength. This time we had something definite in mind.

A man went into each hootch, ripping apart the rooms and belongings, looking for guns, ammo, anything which the dinks used for weapons or war. The Chou-Hoi, Fouel, was a fanatic. He knew the people in this village personally and he was grabbing certain men and talking very rapidly, pointing his gun at their heads, waving his arms, and just generally stomping around.

Action! The squad on the north side had intercepted about ten or more dinks trying to escape. The dinks had run back into the village on the side facing the lake. The squad stayed on line, causing them to move slower. They called on the radio to say they could see the dinks piling into boats.

I yelled to no one in particular, "Where are those motherfucking gunships? If those dinks get away across that lake . . ."

We couldn't see to the east end of the village but I could hear the firing going on. The right side of the squad on the north could now be seen. Good! Good! The south squad was holding its position on the other side of the hill. When my squad reached the lake, we would swing around and sweep the hills.

I grabbed the radio. "Those gunships show up yet? One-five, what the hell's going on? Over."

"One-six, this is One-five. Those dinks took off in their boats but we shot one boat up pretty bad. Six dinks were on board; all of them had Thompsons [submachine guns]. We zapped five of them and have captured one. Here come the gunships! It's a fucking lick! They have two boats trapped out in the middle of the lake. I'll get back to you, out."

The sound of the gunships was clearly audible. We could catch occasional glimpses as they rose up after completing a firing run. They didn't have to make many passes. The dinks in the boats only fired a few rounds before they were chopped to pieces. My squad had almost reached the edge of the lake and the village and had not run into anything but the hostile stares of the villagers. They wouldn't say anything to Fouel, no matter how much he berated them.

I called again. "One-five, where are you? I've reached the lake, over."

"This is One-five. We're right north of you. We have you in sight. This rain is screwing up visibility." (It had started again.) "We're diving in the lake where the boat flipped over; we want to get some of those Thompsons, over."

"Okay, just don't let that prisoner loose. Have a couple of men bring him over and we'll question him. Out."

My squad had found a clear spot on the side of the hill a little higher than the main village area. The trees formed a kind of shelter and we were sitting in a circle taking a smoke break. I was preparing the plans for the sweep of the hill behind us when two of my men arrived with our prisoner. He was the healthiest dink I had seen up to then, about five feet three inches, very muscular, and well fed. His shirt was khaki, but it was pretty much in shreds. He had on shorts which were common among the lake people.

"Here, sir, we found this on him." My man handed me a billfold and some papers. I couldn't read the papers, but in the billfold was a very clear photograph of a Vietcong squad, complete with weapons.

The prisoner was one of the men in the photograph. Paydirt! This man could lead us to weapons and perhaps other members of the squad. I pointed him out in the picture and pointed to him. He just looked defiant and stuck out his jaw. I tried to get some information out of him, but he could not or would not understand what I was saying. One of the guys gave him a smoke.

The Vietcong squatted down on his haunches with his arms wrapped around his legs, smoking our American cigarettes, waiting for us to take him in. Here was a live enemy squatting there smoking, seemingly unconcerned with us or the fact we had captured him. I wished I could speak his language. I didn't understand why he seemed so unconcerned. Probably because he didn't fear us now. He knew the Americans turn their prisoners over to the ARVNs at which time he would have plenty to worry about. The field agent and Fouel had been nosing around somewhere in the village when the prisoner had been brought to me. Fouel and the agent suddenly burst into the circle of soldiers. Upon spying our prisoner, Fouel yelled a few short words in Vietnamese toward the prisoner. The guerrilla's expression turned from a cool disinterest to one of terror. He obviously knew his adversary.

Fouel ran across the short distance of the circle and kicked the guerrilla as he was rising from his crouch. The guerrilla rolled backward and drew his body up into the fetal position, covering his head with his hands to protect himself from the kicks and slaps which Fouel battered him with. Fouel was screaming the whole time. He would stick his head down and yell what was obviously a question. No response from the guerrilla brought a good kick in the ribs from Fouel. The guerrilla would roll on his other side and Fouel would kick that side for a while. This shock treatment went on for a few minutes to loosen him up. Then Fouel got down to business.

The First Squad had given up diving for the Thompsons and had joined my squad. We all formed a ring around the activities. Fouel grabbed what was left of the guerrilla's shirt to drag him to the center of our ring. The shirt came off as Fouel was dragging him. Fouel immediately whipped the dink with the rag before throwing it to the ground. Fouel made the guerrilla sit up. Fouel's voice had dropped to a serious businesslike manner as he began to question the guerrilla. The black pajamas Fouel was wearing made the scene look eerie, as if one Vietcong were questioning another Vietcong. The only difference was the ring of soldiers, American instead of Oriental. In fact, it was Vietcong questioning Vietcong. Fouel had come from their ranks and obviously knew this man. Fouel had made his hand into a fist, developing a steady, rhythmic beat between the guerrilla's eyes with his knuckles. I had seen the dinks use this on other prisoners. The actual contact of the knuckles against the skull between the eyes was not a swinging blow but delivered from six or eight inches with a smart rap in a continuous manner. We had tried it on each other enough to know it quickly became a painful and irritating process. After a few minutes, Fouel changed tactics by abruptly lashing out with his foot, kicking the guerrilla in the head. The guerrilla let out a howl as he clasped his head and rolled on the ground. Fouel was methodically hitting the guerrilla with the butt of his rifle. Knee, back, kidneys, head, chest, arms, legs—it didn't make any difference. The field agent finally noticed we were taking pictures and ran out into the middle of the circle yelling, "Hey, no pictures, no pictures of this!" He thrust his hands up in front of a few lenses. We put our cameras away with no squawk. What the hell? We could understand his not wanting pictures to go back home showing an MI interrogation team working over a prisoner. We continued to watch the prisoner. After having a few rounds fired at us in the past—perhaps he had planted the land mines—we didn't care if Fouel killed him. My concern was in information that he could give us.

Eventually Fouel ripped his clothes off him and he was naked. Not much blood was on him, but quite a few knots were rising up on his body. He was muddy, bruised, tired, scared, and he started talking. Every time he slowed down, Fouel would rap him between the eyes. Translated, his story was this: He had been recruited into the Vietcong in 1960 from this area. The picture he carried was his squad, the members who lived in this and surrounding villages. When time permitted, they would cross the road at night between our bridges to visit in the villages, recruit members, visit with their relatives, and develop propaganda against the Americans and the current government of

South Vietnam. A year ago he had been picked to go north to a special guerrilla training school near Hanoi. This training lasted about six months. The training involved propaganda procedures, weapons use, both theirs and ours, and recruiting techniques. He had seen some American prisoners in or near Hanoi. After coming back, he had been busy increasing the guerrilla activity in all aspects for this area. After the confession, he sullenly picked up what was left of his shirt and shorts, and got dressed. His hands were then tied behind him. I had kept in contact with Captain Sells during the whole operation. He was particularly happy with the news that we had gotten information from our prisoner. We would finish the operation and bring the prisoner in.

The two squads of men formed a line from the edge of the village at the base of the small hill up to the top. The lake was at our back as we began a sweep back to the west determined to flush out any more dinks hiding on the hill. The south squad was still holding firm at the bottom on the other side. I glanced in both directions to observe that the line was fairly even, cautiously moving forward, halting whenever thick bushes, trees, and grass broke us up and also provided an infinite number of hiding places for the dinks.

Woods, a black man who was an excellent shot, held up his hand. Our section of the line stopped, the anticipation of action guiding our every movement. Woods moved stealthily forward from his position on my left. After advancing about five meters, he stared intently to his front. We stared forward, trying to penetrate the thick growth to see what was in front of him. Suddenly he whirled to his left, bringing his rifle up and firing in one motion. Two meters to his left a dink flopped backward, a bullet through his head. Woods cautiously approached the dink and reached down to search the body. Woods stayed alive by being cautious.

"Jesus-fucking-Christ, Woods, how did you see that son-of-a-bitch? I thought there was something in front of you, not sitting in your left side pocket."

"Yeah, that's what that motherfucker was thinking, too. That motherfucker figured if he kept quiet, I'd pass him by since I was staring in another direction. Out of the corner of my eye I saw that mother watching me so I zapped him before he could think about it."

"Hey! Look at this! Look! It's a picture just like the one that other dink was carrying. Look, it's that dink squad."

Sure enough! It was the same picture of that Vietcong squad.

I held the black and white photo and looked at the dink lying dead on the ground before me, his body twisted in the grotesque frozen dance of death. Yes, there he was in the photo, smiling with his comrades as they all held their weapons in preparation for being immortalized by the photographer.

Well, you poor motherfucker. I hope your folks have a copy of this picture because you belong to the jungle now, I thought to myself. We passed on into the jungle growth to complete our sweep.

We had reached a little clear area surrounded by a hedgerow-like bush common in that part of Vietnam. Those damn bushes grew everywhere and anywhere. The dinks used them as fences. They were thick and bushy with a little red flower growing from every major leaf, it seemed like. The only way through one of these bushes was where the farmers had made a path over many years.

This little area was a good place to take a break. The agent and Fouel were standing next to me when Fouel let out a yell and jumped into a large growth of tangled bushes next to the trail. We wondered what the hell was going on in that thicket. Fouel was yelling like a madman. All of a sudden he popped out of the growth, prodding another guerrilla.

We were surprised as hell. How did Fouel know he was there? Some of my men grabbed the dink and tied him up. I looked at Fouel just as he let out another yell and jumped back into the brush. More yelling and talking produced another soldier. This one was different. Fouel explained this was an NVA soldier. We looked on in astonishment.

"Shit, sir, this ain't nothing but a fucking kid."

The NVA soldier was a boy about fourteen years old. The only thing he had left was his green NVA soldier's jungle fatigues. His baggy jungle shirt hung on him a few sizes too big. With his young face and baggy clothes, he certainly didn't look dangerous.

I forgot him as I called my radioman over to call Captain Sells.

I looked around the little grass-covered clearing. The men were spread out in little groups, smoking C ration cigarettes or eating a can of C rations. It had been a good operation so far and we were ready to go back to the bridge. Just a little longer.

Smack! A rifle butt streaked by my side into the side of the young NVA soldier who had sidled up to me. Fouel had hit him with his rifle butt and was on top of him swinging his fists. My men and I pulled Fouel off.

"What did you hit that kid for?"

Fouel looked at the agent as someone translated what we had said. Fouel looked at me and for an answer reached down and ripped the kid's jungle fatigue shirt back. Strapped to his stomach were two American hand grenades.

"Jesus! Didn't anybody search him?" I exclaimed.

We thought Fouel had searched him and he figured we were going to do it. It hadn't been done.

Fouel explained that the NVA soldier waited until he figured out who the leader was and that he was going to blow both himself and the leader up. The dink had seen me talking on the radio and was preparing to take me with him.

I looked at the young soldier lying on the ground. He was looking back at me just as intently.

My life on this sweet earth had been within a few seconds of its end. Everything had seemed so peaceful, the sweep was almost over, I was enjoying a smoke and congratulating myself on a good operation—and this dink kid had almost zapped me. Never again would I trust any dinks.

The squad coming up the other side of the hill called me on the radio to say they had found a big tunnel. Leaving our three prisoners with one squad, we went over the crest of the hill to see the other squad below us in a large grassy area on the hill.

Partially covered over with grass was a huge well-like hole, at least five feet in diameter and fifteen feet deep. The hole went straight down. The walls were perfectly smooth and at the bottom we could see the holes of five or six tunnels. Where we were standing was not an entrance. There was no way in or out. This hole was an air hole for the tunnel systems which honeycombed the little hill.

None of us was going to lower himself to the bottom to explore the tunnels, so I called Delta Six to report the find. We were not too concerned since Vietnam must have had a million miles of tunnels under everything. I had only been in-country a short time and already tunnels were a feature of the landscape.

We completed the sweep and prepared to go back to the bridges. We wanted to get out of this miserable rain.

The agent informed me that Fouel had convinced the young boy to lead us to a hidden weapon. It would be a good way to end our operation.

Fouel and the kid took out ahead of us, heading for the village next to the bridge. We hurried to catch up as I was anxious to see where a weapon was hidden around there, we had conducted so many patrols without turning up anything.

The kid led Fouel across the road. I told Schaldenbrand to take most of the men with him back to the road while I took a squad with me.

The kid twisted through the farmers in their fields, crossed the stream, and pointed to a pile of wood that we had passed many times in our patrols.

"That's one of the few woodpiles we never pulled apart," Mann said to me.

"Yeah, we had better be careful of booby traps."

Fouel did the work for us, throwing the wood out from the pile as he dug down. With a yell of discovery, he pulled out a rifle wrapped tightly in plastic and tied with cord. The rifle was unwrapped, revealing a delapidated M-1 carbine and magazines with ammo.

We trudged back to the bridge through the rain with our find, proud of the success of the patrol.

Chickenhawk

ROBERT MASON

1983

TELL ME YOU'RE AFRAID

I am sure we are going to win.
—Nguyen Cao Ky, in *U.S. News & World Report*,
August 1, 1966

A Communist military takeover in South Vietnam is no longer
just improbable . . . it is impossible.
—Lyndon Johnson, August 14, 1966 (after conferring
with General Westmoreland at the LBJ Ranch)

July–August 1966
Sleep no longer gave me peace. I had escaped Vietnam with an
R&R to Hong Kong, but I had not escaped my memories.

Twenty-one men lay trussed in a row, ropes at their ankles, hands
bound under their backs—North Vietnamese prisoners. A sergeant
stood at the first prisoner's feet, his face twisted with anger. The North
Vietnamese prisoner stared back, unblinking. The sergeant pointed a
.45 at the man. He kicked the prisoner's feet suddenly. The shock of
the impact jostled the prisoner inches across the earth. The sergeant
fired the .45 into the prisoner's face. The prisoner's head bounced off
the ground like a ball slapped from above, then flopped back into the
gore that had been his brains. The sergeant turned to the next prisoner in the line.

"He tried to get away," said a voice at my side.

"He can't get away; he's tied!"

"He moved. He was trying to get away."

The next prisoner said a few hurried words in Vietnamese as the sergeant stood over him. When the sergeant kicked his feet, the prisoner closed his eyes. A bullet shook his head.

"It's murder!" I hissed to the man at my side.

"They cut off Sergeant Rocci's cock and stuck it in his mouth. And five of his men," said the voice. "After they spent the night slowly shoving knives into their guts. If you had been here to hear the screams. . . . They screamed all night. This morning they were all dead, all gagged with their cocks. This isn't murder; it's justice."

Another head bounced off the ground. The shock wave hit my body.

"They sent us to pick up twenty-one *prisoners*," I pleaded.

"You'll get 'em; you'll get 'em. They'll just be dead, is all."

The sergeant moved down the line stopping prisoners who tried to escape. The line of men grew longer than it had been, and the sergeant grew distant. His face glowed red and the heads bounced. And then he looked up at me.

Forgotten events dogged my sleep.

A wounded VC lay on a stretcher, one end rested on my ship's deck, the other end held by a medic.

"I don't think he appreciates this. I think he'd rather die," said the medic.

The VC stared at me. His black eyes accused me. He lay in a black pajama top—the bottoms were gone. He had a swollen, stinking thigh wound from days before. He'd been hiding in the jungle.

"He's going to lose that leg," said the medic.

The man stared at me. The stretcher grated against the deck as the medic shoved. The crew chief reached across from the other side and pulled. They slid the stretcher up against the cockpit seats. While they shoved and jostled the stretcher, he kept his eyes on mine.

"That fucker either has the clap or he's turned on by us." The crew chief grinned. He pointed to the man's groin. What looked like semen dripped from his penis and glistened on his thigh. I looked away, feeling his hate. I felt his exposure. I looked back to his eyes and they stared, black and hot. The scene stopped. I thought I was waking up. But then it was the human shield I'd seen during LZ Dog.

The eyes blinked and wrinkles formed at their edges. The old woman with black teeth said something to me, then screamed. There was no sound. Her wrinkled hand held a child's smooth arm. The child hung lifeless and dragged the old woman down. She moved slowly, like she was falling through water. The crowd around her gasped silently and flinched and fell. The machine gun stuttered from a distant place. The woman fell slowly to the ground, bounced, dying and dead. The old woman had been saying something. When I saw her lips moving, I knew that she had been saying, "It's okay . . ."

The scene changed again. I sat in my Huey waiting for the grunts to finish inspecting a napalmed village.

"It's okay." A man looked in my cockpit window.

"She's dead!"

"They're all dead. It's okay."

The crowd was gone. I sat in my cockpit while the man talked to me from outside. The place had been a village. The wet ground smoked. Scorched poles and mud-daubed walls and thatch smoldered. Charred people lay twenty feet away. The smell of burnt hair and smoldering charcoal sank into my lungs and brain.

Why was there barbed wire in the village? Was it a pen? A defense perimeter? I couldn't see the scene beyond where the child stuck to the wire.

"This is wrong," I said to the man.

"It's okay. It's the way it is. They had their warning. Everybody else left the village. They're VC."

"She's VC?"

The man looked down. "No. She's unfortunate."

She was burned to the barbed wire. The wire was growing from the charred flesh of her tiny chest. She was bent over the wire, a toddler who had run away from the hell from the sky. The lower half of her two-year-old body was pink from intense heat; her tiny vulva looked almost alive.

"This is not war. It's—"

"It's okay. There's always going to be some innocent victims."

The man talked on, but his voice became silent. The little girl's stark body, half charred death, half pink life, leaned against the wire, almost free. Suddenly I heard ringing.

I awoke hearing my voice echoing off the far wall. The phone was ringing on the night table.

"Hel—" I gulped. "Hello?"

"Your call to the United States will be coming through in fifteen minutes," said the voice.

The call! Of course. The call to Patience. "Thank you."

"We wanted to make sure you would be here for the call, Mr. Mason."

"Yes. Yes, thank you. I'm here."

The phone clicked off and I held the buzzing receiver in my hand for a minute before setting it back on its cradle. I shivered as an air-conditioned breeze chilled me. The sheets were wet and twisted.

I lit a cigarette with shaking hands and sat up to wait for the call. I was having these dreams almost every night. I began to feel better. I was awake, after all, away from the dreams.

After four miserable nights, I decided to cut my leave short and return to Vietnam. The leave had been a disaster. Gary had come to Hong Kong with me, but he left the second day for Taipei. I had bragged about the women there too convincingly, and the call girls in Hong Kong were too experienced, too professional, and too expensive. Resler packed up and left. I was going to follow, but when I tried to get a ticket to Taipei, I was refused because I was a serviceman on leave to Hong Kong, and that's where I'd have to stay. I don't know how Gary slipped through the red tape, but I was alone.

I had not the slightest desire to hire a call girl; I really just wanted to talk.

"I love you. Over," I said.

"I love you too. Are you okay? Over," said Patience. Her voice struggled weakly through the hiss and whistles of the radiophone connection.

"I'm fine. They say I won't have to fly any more combat assaults when I get back. Over."

"No?"

"That's what—"

"The party has not said 'over,' sir."

"Oh," said Patience. "Over."

"That's what the doc said when I left. He said that the Prospectors were going to put their last-month short-timers on ass-and-trash missions. Over."

"Oh, I hope they keep their word. Over."

"They will. These guys are not the Cav. Over."

I listened to the howl and echoes of interfering electronics, sorting out the words. Patience, my son, Jack, and my family had become phantoms. They were dreams, too. When we finally stopped talking, when her voice melted into the static, the tenuous link to my home fantasies broke. "Over," I said.

And there I sat, on the edge of the bed, just like every other dream.

It was very similar to my hometown, Delray Beach. There was a beach; it ran north and south. There were palm trees, sandy roads, salt smells, girls playing in bikinis, and quietly rolling surf. It was late afternoon, almost dusk, and the sun glinted off parts of the heavy wire screen that surrounded the terrace. My table stood near the front of the terrace, allowing me the best view.

Voices chattered quietly behind me. Vietnamese sounds lovely even if you can't understand it.

It did feel like home.

Golden dolls, wearing bikinis so brief they were ribbons of modesty, strolled with pale GIs. As it got darker, the beach crowd broke up, drifting into the town.

"*Manh gioi khoung?* How are you?" said the smiling waitress. I noticed her Vietnamese glance of nerves and felt comforted by familiar behavior. "What would you like?" she asked.

I would like to jump you like a rabbit. "I'll have another beer, please," I said. The girl prompted immediate lust. Perhaps I could find solace in solace. My conscience immediately began to pummel me with shots of raw guilt, delivered at high voltage. "Monster!" it railed. "Married. Short-timer. And not only that, but you're just getting over the clap!" It was mercilessly rational. I succumbed to its barbs.

The waitress bowed and left to get the beer. I smiled as I watched my phantom flit naked from me to the girl, to hump her happily while she leaned over the bar.

She returned, beaming, friendlier, and served my beer. Her arm brushed mine and I felt warm electricity flicker between us. My mind savored salty-sweet smells and orgasmic contractions, hearing her voice as an echo "Would you like . . ."

Her voice was obliterated by the sudden ripping, zipping howl of a stylus skidding across a record. She dropped to the floor and rolled under a table.

At the sound of crashing chairs and breaking glassware, I turned and saw the Vietnamese taking cover. Five men crouched low behind the bar. I sat alone on the porch and took a sip of beer. The girl knocked over a chair as she crawled toward the back of the porch.

All because of a stylus skidding across a record? Damn, they were even jumpier than I was. I looked around the bar. Nothing was happening. There was no fight. People peered from behind the bar and tables, looking up front. It had just been the sound that spooked them. They had absolutely no confidence that their city was secure. They knew the facts. The VC were everywhere.

Cowards, I thought. Anger flushed through me. I felt betrayed, revolted. They're really afraid.

For five minutes I had complete quiet as I watched the surf foam glow in the gathering dusk. At the end of that time, the bar, the customers, the porch, came back to life.

I paid my tab and walked to the room I had rented.

I sat against the wall on the bed, thinking about the panic at the bar. The old question "Why don't the Vietnamese fight the VC like the VC fight the Vietnamese?" seemed very valid. Without the support of the people, we were going to lose. And if they didn't care, why were we continuing to fight? Surely the people who were running this fiasco could see this, too. The signs were obvious. Plans leaked to the

VC, reluctant combatants, mutinies in the ARVN, political corruption, Vietnamese marines fighting Vietnamese marines at Da Nang, and the ubiquitous Vietnamese idea that Ho would eventually win.

I stabbed a cigarette into an ashtray. Without American financial support and military support, the South Vietnamese government would have failed long ago, as a natural result of its lack of popular support.

The whole problem settled on my shoulders. In a few hours, I was going to voluntarily go back into battle and risk my scrawny neck for people who didn't care.

I stayed up and smoked cigarettes all night. I tried to sleep, only to jerk awake, sitting in bed, listening.

I was back at Dak To, home, the next day. Here, the war was simple. We did our job well, beat the VC almost every time, and kept them on the run. Here, I was a member of the honorable side. The reluctant, cowardly Vietnamese were not visible to remind me that they didn't care. I could go on believing that simply by killing more and more Communists we would win. When I crawled into my cot my first night back, I fell instantly asleep.

The next day, Gary and I sat on the deck of our Huey waiting for the grunts to finish eating. Their platoon was one of several that were pushing toward the west, scouting for the VC. We joked in familiar surroundings.

"You shoulda come, you know," said Gary.

"I tried, asshole. They wouldn't let me. How did you get a ticket?"

"I just went to the ticket counter and bought it."

"Well, you must have looked like a civilian, because they wouldn't sell me anything."

"It's really a shame. You missed Grass Mountain."

"What's that?"

"Grass Mountain is packed with geisha houses. Wanna know what it's like to go to a geisha house?"

"No."

"They start off with a bath. Just you and two naked girls. They wash you first, then soak you, then massage you."

"Didn't you hear me?"

"I heard you," Gary said. "The two of them massage you so well you think you're going to crack. Then, at the perfect moment, one of the girls sits on you and puts you out of your misery."

I nodded my head with closed eyes, kicking myself for not getting laid when I had the chance.

"And that's just the beginning."

"Just the beginning?"

"That's right. It takes hours to get out of this place. They give you more baths, and tea and food and massages, to keep you going, and then they pass you down the line to teams of two or three girls who work you over in different ways." Gary's face brightened at his memories.

"I never heard of Grass Mountain when I was there," I lamented.

"Never heard of it? Where the hell were you?"

The next day I was flying with Sky King. In the middle of a laager, a grunt lieutenant came to our ship. "We just had a newsman wounded. Will you guys pick him up?"

"Sure," I said.

"The squad leader with the guy said it was a sniper. They say they've got the place secured."

"No problem. Where are they?"

The lieutenant showed me on his map. They were only a mile away. When I turned to get into the ship, Sky King and the crew chief were all ready to go. I strapped in as Sky King cranked up.

Sky King flew at fifty knots heading for the place.

"Over there," I pointed to four or five soldiers standing around a prone man in a thicket of leafless trees. "You see them?"

"Got 'em."

As we flew by, the men hit the dirt, leaving one man standing. He was aiming a movie camera at us.

"Great place for a landing," said Sky King.

The base of the clearing was wide enough for our ship, but the scrawny branches twenty feet off the ground crowded over the circle, making it too tight to get in.

"Axle One-Six," I radioed. "Can you move to a better clearing?" Sky King circled, looking for a way to get through the trees.

"Negative, Prospector. We're still getting sniper fire, and this guy is wounded pretty bad."

Sky King set up an approach and closed in. As he got to the tree-tops, it became obvious that he was going to hit branches with the main rotor, so he aborted.

When the squad saw us heading across the LZ, they radioed, "Can you make it, Prospector?"

Sky King shook his head. "I can't get in there. You want to try it?"

I nodded and took the controls. While Sky King had approached, I thought I saw a way. "We'll get in, Axle One-Six. Just hang on."

The plan was simple. I would come in ninety degrees to Sky King's last try and then turn sharp. I thought that in a bank the rotors could slip through the narrow slot that Sky King had shot for. I lined up on a tangent to the clearing and let down.

I hit the turn fast, banked hard over, and as we slipped toward the ground, I saw that I was going to hit some stuff anyway. The main rotor smashed some dead branches, sounding like machine-gun fire. I flared for the landing and we were down.

"Great. Now how are you going to get out?" said Sky King.

I didn't answer, because I didn't know how I was going to get out. The grunts grabbed the wounded man. He was unconscious, his fatigue blouse sopping with his blood. At that point I noticed the cameraman standing back filming the whole thing. The grunts were prone beside him, laying out cover fire toward the jungle. When I saw him aim the camera toward the cockpit, I sat a little straighter, and thought cool thoughts, in case those, too, might somehow be recorded. The crew chief called that we were ready, and the cameraman jumped on board.

In fact, there was no acceptable way to get out. There was not enough room to accelerate and bank back out through the slot. Some of the high branches hung over our rotor disk. By the book, we were trapped.

But I had seen rotor blades stand up to incredible stress before, so I decided to take the brute-force option. I picked up to the hover, turned the tail until it matched a slot in the overhanging branches, and then pulled the pitch. We climbed straight up twenty feet before the rotors smashed into cane-thick branches at nearly every point of their circle. It sounded like the rotors were being smashed to pieces. Seconds later we cleared the treetops and I nosed over, accelerating toward the airstrip five miles away.

"Someday you're going to hit a branch that's just a little too big," Sky King said after a long quiet.

"What then?" I asked.

"Then your ship's going to come apart, and you're going to kill yourself and everybody around you."

"Now *that's* frightening," I said. "I think maybe I oughta quit this job and go home."

"This guy's still alive, sir." The crew chief's voice buzzed in my headphones. "The cameraman says he's the *president* of CBS News. Imagine that."

"Ain't that a kick," Sky King said. "I guess he got bored with his nice safe desk job, the dumb shit."

When we landed at the hospital tent at the 101st, the cameraman jumped out and filmed his boss being unloaded. He filmed Gary and me in the cockpit, then put the camera down and gave us a salute.

I nodded, brought the rotors up to operating, and leapt off the pad. As I flew back to retrieve the empty thermos containers we left with the grunts, I recalled the cameraman's salute and felt slightly heroic.

When we shut down that night, Sky King showed me the creases and nicks in the rotors and scolded me. "Look at this. You've ruined them."

"Naw. They're fine. Just creased is all. No holes. Look at the bright side. The guy's alive."

"Yeah, but look at those rotors."

During the second week of July, Operation Hawthorne began winding up. The patrols and reconnaissance companies were getting very little opposition in the battle zone. The NVA had slipped away.

"If they're gone, and we killed two thousand of them, we won," said Gary.

"What did we win? We don't have any more real estate, no new villages are under American control, and it took everything we had to stop them," I said.

"We won the battle. More of them got killed than us. It's that simple."

"Doesn't it bother you that it takes so much equipment and men to beat the NVA? If we were equally equipped, we'd lose."

"Yeah, but we aren't equally equipped, and they lose. Besides that, I have a month to go and I don't give a shit."

"Unless they made you fly assaults during your last month."

"If they do that, then I'll give a shit."

While the First Cav slipped unceremoniously back to An Khe, the 101st decided to end the operation with a parade. There would be no spectators except for the news reporters—unless you want to count the men in the parade as spectators, and of course they were.

Hundreds of bone-weary soldiers gathered at the artillery emplacements and began the five-mile march back to the airstrip. They marched, in parade step, along the dusty road. Insects buzzed in the saturated air. No virgins threw flowers. No old ladies cried. No strong men wept. They marched to their own muffled footsteps.

"I bet they're pissed off," said Gary, leaning against his door window, staring down at the column. "Especially when they look up and see all these empty helicopters flying around."

We flew up and down the column in four V's at 500 feet during the entire march. Supposedly we were generating excitement, or underscoring a memorable event. But according to a grunt, "We wanted to know why you fuckers wouldn't come down and give us a fucking ride."

When the head of the column finally reached the 101st section of the airstrip, the band played, the Hueys whooshed overhead, and the general beamed.

With all the troopers back in camp, noses were counted. Nearly twenty people were unaccounted for. It was presumed that these men were all dead. There would be a search operation to find their bodies in few days.

. . .

The next day, while the missing moldered, the 101st had a party for the survivors. Their camp was within walking distance, but our aviator egos demanded that we fly. After seeing too much death and injury, the survivors celebrated life. We had a boisterously good time to emphasize that we were still alive.

The Only War We Had

MICHAEL LEE LANNING

1987

23 June 1969

Monday

> Set up on side of a mountain tonight
>
> SP4 Garcia and one of the ARVNs talked for an hour—1 in
> Spanish, 1 in Vietnamese—Never could figure it out but they
> seemed to be communicating
>
> Am getting so I can work with the ARVNs

The ARVN seemed relaxed, appearing basically happy with their situation. There would be no end of the war for them after only a year. None of them seemed to be in a hurry, particularly to face the enemy. They liked our C-rations and filled their rucksacks.

We were now deep into the jungle. Brush and vines covered the ground and small trees reached to a height of about six feet. Another layer of trees grew to about twenty-five feet. Yet a final growth of large trees, reaching heights of about a hundred feet, towered above the lower two layers of vegetation. This triple canopy virtually blocked the sunlight.

No breeze penetrated the damp jungle. The dark floor was stifling hot, and the unrelenting smell of rotting vegetation filled the air.

At frequent intervals were thickets of bamboo. Varying from small clumps to patches thirty meters in diameter, their six-inch-thick stalks were impossible to cut through. The inevitable zigzagging around them made navigation difficult.

At least thirst was not the problem it had been in the Delta. Fresh streams of fairly clear water ran at frequent intervals. A purification tablet per canteen made it bitter but safe. Some of the soldiers added packets of Kool Aid to make the water more palatable.

24 June 1969
Tuesday
> Continue mission
> Today we airmobiled to help out Alpha in contact—Had an NVA Regiment on a hill—By the time we got there NVA had left

We were in thick jungle when the radio crackled with Alpha Company's contact followed by Battalion's ordering us to the nearest pick up zone (PZ). Moving as quickly as possible, we still were nearly an hour covering the short kilometer to the PZ.

No sooner had we reached the clearing than the slicks came over the horizon. Their blade noise changed to a distinctive whoop-whoop as they turned toward us. Our loading was SOP as groups of six men sped down the open area with no group containing more than one M-60 or radio. Leaders were careful to get on different choppers. If a bird went down, we did not want to lose a group of critical weapons or leaders.

The flight of eight helicopters carried half the company at a time. Blood was up and running hot. As we jumped from the skids, the men were shouting so loudly that I could hear them over the rotors. Charlie Company wanted part of the action.

When we learned the NVA had broken contact, we were disappointed—and somewhat relieved. Alpha lost one killed, the dinks four. After hearing reports of the fire fight, it was evident that the first word, about a regiment-sized enemy, had been greatly exaggerated.

25 June 1969
Wednesday
    Continue mission

After it was determined that the NVA were no longer in the area, CPT McGinnis received orders for Charlie Company to conduct a reconnaissance in force (RIF) to the south.

Our movement halted about an hour before dusk. The lead platoon leader selected a site for the night defensive position (NDP) and the platoons occupied their sectors based on a clock system. The direction of movement was considered twelve o'clock. From twelve to three was the lead platoon sector, from nine to twelve the next platoon, then from three to six and from six to nine the remaining platoon. The company CP set up near the center of the circle.

Because of thick jungle, the perimeter often was more oval than circular. Claymore mines, trip illumination flares and intersecting fields of machine gun fire were the first priorities. Half of the men remained on alert while the others worked. Trails or other likely avenues of approach were covered by sending out three-man observation/listening posts. Depending on the situation, they might stay in the positions all night or return to the perimeter just before dark.

LT Jong called in nightly artillery defensive concentrations. Marking rounds of aerial smoke bursts were always fired before shooting the high-explosive steel.

We dug holes deep enough to protect a prone man and stacked sandbags and logs for added protection. Then we stretched ponchos on sticks about eighteen inches above the ground with the ends either staked with more sticks or tied to trees or logs with extra boot laces.

The makeshift poncho tents were strictly for sleeping. Soldiers on alert sat outside the poncho hooch so they could hear without the distraction of the rain pelting the fabric.

We slept directly on the ground. The men carried air mattresses but used them only at the fire bases. In the boonies, the soldiers' rolling over on the air-filled pads made too much noise.

After the NDP was completely established, platoon leaders checked their sectors. McGinnis usually made a brief tour, stopping to visit with the grunts as he made his round.

It was now time to eat. A few of the soldiers ate three full meals a day, but the combination of the heat and the monotony of C-rations made most of us rarely hungry.

I usually ate most of a complete C-ration in the evening. After stand-to the next morning, a cup of coffee brewed in an empty C-ration cracker can was breakfast. At noon a can of fruit, a pound cake or pecan nut roll was all I wanted in the heat.

26 June 1969
Thursday
 Jungle
  After moving all day we were ready to set up NDP—2nd plt on point heard gook voices—My plt set up a block in a creek and 2nd moved in—After a brief fire fight we withdrew—Called in arty and set up for night
  One man wounded—Shot through mouth—Had to use hook on chopper to raise him out of jungle

On the battlefield, skill and experience are critical, but at times luck is the deciding factor. If we had halted a few hundred meters earlier, we would not have heard the enemies' voices. If we had not been moving with stealth, they would have escaped or ambushed us, but not all the luck was on our side. Darkness was approaching and we had to make our attack quickly.

McGinnis assembled the platoon leaders, ordering the third platoon to remain on our small hill to secure our rucksacks so we could move in unencumbered. The fourth platoon was to establish a blocking position on a hill two hundred meters to our left. My platoon was to move down a small stream to our right while Little's second platoon proceeded directly toward the voices. Jong plotted artillery to seal off the far side.

About two hundred meters down the stream a trail led from the far side to the water. On the bank a pair of wet black pajama trousers was still dripping. Apparently, a gook doing his laundry had heard our approach.

Just as I called McGinnis to inform him we had been detected, the second platoon opened fire about 150 meters to our left. By the sound of the barrage, they were firing every weapon they had. We could not directly see the enemy through the thick foliage, but we directed our fire at the reports of the AK47s.

As the gooks' fire diminished we pushed up the trail. I had never seen Tom scared. He was shaking so hard that we could barely understand him as he said, "Beaucoup NVA! Beaucoup NVA!"

Artillery was now blasting the jungle. Jong brought it to within a hundred meters of us. Fire from the gooks diminished to sporadic shots by a weapon none of us could identify.

Though it was now completely dark, we all wanted to sweep through the gook camp. McGinnis' order to return to the secured hill was a good one; however, as in the darkness, we might have fought each other rather than the dinks.

Sassner guided each platoon into sector. Little's platoon was the last to return, his medic half-carrying a rifleman who had taken a round through the lower face. Apparently the soldier had his mouth open when the bullet entered. Its exit took out some teeth and a part of the jaw and cheek. He was bleeding heavily.

McGinnis had already called in a dust off while Sassner had secured a bomb crater inside the perimeter that provided enough clearance for the chopper to drop a hook-sling for the casualty.

We began to dig in. DeForrest and I soon discovered that in the darkness we were sharing our position with a large bed of black ants. We withdrew without a fight. The huge ants left red welts from their bites.

Jong continued artillery off and on throughout the night to prevent the gooks' returning to remove bodies or equipment. Some of Little's men reported fighting their way to the edge of bunkers before withdrawing. My platoon had made it far enough for us to see what appeared to be low, thatched hooches.

During the long night I decided not to return to BMB as Hawkins' temporary replacement. I did not want to leave my platoon. McGinnis agreed while rejecting my recommendation that Sassner go instead. He needed us all in the field.

27 June 1969
Friday
> Moved into contact area—Search found:
>> 7 large bunkers
>> 9 hooches
>> 1 cook shack
>> 2 bodies—1 male 1 female—KIA
>> 100 lbs. of various clothing & boots
>> 55 lbs. of rice
>> 1 printing press
>> 1 typewriter
>> 3 large bags of documents—(Later found to have secret
>> info—Also names and addresses of VC supporters in area)
>> Much cooking equipment
>> Sewing gear
>> 1 SKS with ammo
>> 1 US M-2 carbine ammo
>> Misc ammo & misc equipment
>> $160 in VC money—Found by me—Split among 1st plt
>> Medicine—Much

At daylight we went back into the contact area following the same plan as the previous evening. Just beyond the point where we had halted the attack was a latrine and wash area. A few meters later we came to the bunkers. Some had tables built on top, covered with thatched roofs supported by bamboo poles.

Another hut protected a cooking area where a large pot of now burnt rice sat on dying embers. Next to the cook shack lay a dead gook wearing only shorts, sandals and a covering of flies. An SKS rifle was a few feet away.

The body had been hit many times. DeForrest and I noticed a small sack tied around the body's waist at about the same time. We cut the bloody canvas strap and found the roll of South Vietnamese piasters. The paper bills, called "Ps," would buy the platoon beer for awhile.

On the other side of the bunker complex, Little's platoon discovered the source of the odd sounding weapon we had heard the night before. The M-2 carbine lay next to a dead young woman. She was far too bloated for her enlargement to have been the result of the heat. We wondered why a pregnant woman had stayed, fought and died while others were escaping. We joked that the woman and unborn child should count as two bodies. No one expressed any regret about killing her. She had the opportunity to do the same to us. In fact, she had tried very hard to do so.

After the entire complex was secured, we began a more detailed search. Several blood trails led into the jungle between the fourth platoon's blocking position and the artillery barrage. More blood and bandages showed we had killed at least five or six more. We claimed only the two we had weapons in hand for. The others were reported as probable kills.

We ignored the dink bodies after we searched them. Tom, DeForrest and I had our CP within five meters of the male gook. We heated water for coffee and ate our lunch as we discussed how quickly the maggots had begun their work.

The other gooks had escaped with little but their lives. Eating utensils were still on the table. Packs, ammo and food were neatly stacked in nearly every bunker. Rice was in bags and long sack-like cylinders. Tom showed us how these containers could be easily carried around the neck like a loose scarf. We cut open the containers and poured the grain in the creek and the latrine. Equipment and clothing we burnt. Ammo, documents and the small printing press was carried to an LZ a couple of klicks away for transfer to the S-2.

The typewriter contained an unfinished report. Intelligence later sent us an interpretation that said the report was from the commander of the camp, saying new US units were operating in his area. He wrote we would not venture far enough into the jungle to find his headquarters. He had been wrong.

Other documents revealed that we had found a rest area for the

274th NVA Regiment which was composed of NVA and a consolidation of local VC. We presumed the woman was with the latter.

We burned the hooches. They had been camouflaged so well under the triple canopy that they were impossible to spot from the air. From the ground we had to be within ten meters to make out their barest outline.

The two weapons were awarded to the second platoon. They had made the initial contact and had been in the thickest of the fighting. There were sufficient souvenirs for all. McGinnis kept the Vietnamese typewriter because his wife taught high school typing classes back in North Carolina.

We also found several diaries. Neatly drawn pictures of people and animals along with poems adorned the pages. We wanted to keep them but sent them to the S-2 because they might contain some intel value.

In the late afternoon we moved to the LZ from which the documents had been extracted. We felt better setting up our NDP in a place the enemy did not know as well as their camp.

Spirits were high. We had done significant damage to the enemy while only taking one WIA. We had surprised and defeated the enemy on his own turf.

My letter to Linda briefly described the fight. I also asked her if she had any ideas for baby names. Although I had promised her I would give her full details about events in my life, I did not include anything about the rotting body of the pregnant woman we had left in the jungle camp.

10

Masterwork

July 1967. Infantryman, Camp Warrior, Pleiku Province.

Tim O'Brien's *The Things They Carried* (1990) is subtitled not a novel or a collection of stories, but "A Work of Fiction." It's dedicated to the fictional men of Alpha company who inhabit the book, and the epigraph from John Ransom's *Andersonville Diary* is telling:

This book is essentially different from any other that has been published concerning the "late war" or any of its incidents. Those who have had any such experience as the author will see its truthfulness at once, and to all other readers it is commended as a statement of actual things by one who experienced them to the fullest.

With this mysterious blending of the real and the imaginary, O'Brien opens his third major work on Vietnam, and throughout the book he never lets the reader get too comfortable about what is and what isn't real. What is *true*, however, not what is real, is O'Brien's final goal, and he uses all of fiction and metafiction's effects to get there. O'Brien himself presides over the book, illuminating the creation of the stories, letting us know what really happened. Or is it a fictional character named Tim O'Brien, very much like the fictional Jorge Luis Borges who in one of Borges's stories meets his own creator on the banks of the Charles? There's no way of telling, and perhaps that's O'Brien's point—that fiction has a life of its own, and that story-truth, as he says in "How to Tell a True War Story," is more important than happening-truth.

Like his earlier *Going After Cacciato*, *The Things They Carried* alternates between a richly observed realism and fanciful yarn-spinning. There are ghosts and tall tales, shaggy-dog stories, metaphorical anecdotes, and on top of these, O'Brien and his characters comment on how stories operate, sometimes coming up with supposedly unwitting metaphors for that as well. It's a daring performance, especially in an area where stringent realism has commonly been the ultimate goal. O'Brien, both drawing on and disowning his authority as a veteran, seems to be claiming as an ideal the power of fiction rather than that of witness.

The book is fractured, often contradictory. O'Brien loves to give us a ready-made sentimental image and then explode it, throw a different spin on it. Half the time it seems O'Brien is painting his fellow platoon members as innocent kids playing games, the other half as hardened killers. The book is sweet and vicious, deadly serious and whoopie-cushion goofy. Throughout, O'Brien and his characters find they can't make other people understand their stories or their experiences, yet they (and O'Brien, in writing for us) continue to try. As in *If I Die*, there's a split between private thought and public speech that only story can fill. And yet, can story really fill it? O'Brien seems to be saying yes, maybe.

O'Brien's view of the soldier here is complex, and he extends this vision, for the first time, to the enemy, imagining the life and dreams of "The Man I Killed," whose life is strikingly similar to that of the real Tim O'Brien in *If I Die*. His portrait of his fictional self as a vet and his take on the effect of memory are equally thoughtful. "It wasn't a war story," he says at one point. "It was a love story." In making the reader feel the loss of friends and innocence and the resulting confusion of the years gone by, O'Brien gives the war a deeply personal resonance—all the while telling us that it's a fake, a construction, just a story.

The Things They Carried garnered excellent reviews, as all of O'Brien's Vietnam books have, and while it didn't win any of the major literary awards that year (possibly because by 1990 the critics, like the publishers, considered Vietnam over and done with), it has attracted a large following among writers and readers, and is often regarded as the finest single volume of fiction written about the Vietnam War.

The Things They Carried

TIM O'BRIEN

1990

SPIN

The war wasn't all terror and violence. Sometimes things could almost get sweet. For instance, I remember a little boy with a plastic leg. I remember how he hopped over to Azar and asked for a chocolate bar—"GI number one," the kid said—and Azar laughed and handed over the chocolate. When the boy hopped away, Azar clucked his tongue and said, "War's a bitch." He shook his head sadly. "One leg, for Chrissake. Some poor fucker ran out of ammo."

I remember Mitchell Sanders sitting quietly in the shade of an old banyan tree. He was using a thumbnail to pry off the body lice, working slowly, carefully depositing the lice in a blue USO envelope. His eyes were tired. It had been a long two weeks in the bush. After an hour or so he sealed up the envelope, wrote FREE in the upper right-hand corner, and addressed it to his draft board in Ohio.

On occasions the war was like a Ping-Pong ball. You could put fancy spin on it, you could make it dance.

I remember Norman Bowker and Henry Dobbins playing checkers every evening before dark. It was a ritual for them. They would dig a foxhole and get the board out and play long, silent games as the sky went from pink to purple. The rest of us would sometimes stop by to watch. There was something restful about it, something orderly and reassuring. There were red checkers and black checkers. The playing field was laid out in a strict grid, no tunnels or mountains or jungles. You knew where you stood. You knew the score. The pieces were out on the board, the enemy was visible, you could watch the tactics unfolding into larger strategies. There was a winner and a loser. There were rules.

I'm forty-three years old, and a writer now, and the war has been over for a long while. Much of it is hard to remember. I sit at this typewriter and stare through my words and watch Kiowa sinking into the deep muck of a shit field, or Curt Lemon hanging in pieces from a tree, and as I write about these things, the remembering is turned into a kind of rehappening. Kiowa yells at me. Curt Lemon steps from the shade into bright sunlight, his face brown and shining, then he soars into a tree. The bad stuff never stops happening: it lives in its own dimension, replaying itself over and over.

But the war wasn't all that way.

Like when Ted Lavender went too heavy on the tranquilizers. "How's the war today?" somebody would say, and Ted Lavender would give a soft, spacey smile and say, "Mellow, man. We got ourselves a nice mellow war today."

And like the time we enlisted an old poppa-san to guide us through the mine fields out on the Batangan Peninsula. The old guy walked with a limp, slow and stooped over, but he knew where the safe spots were and where you had to be careful and where even if you were careful you could end up like popcorn. He had a tightrope walker's feel for the land beneath him—its surface tension, the give and take of things. Each morning we'd form up in a long column, the old poppa-san out front, and for the whole day we'd troop along after him, tracing his footsteps, playing an exact and ruthless game of follow the leader. Rat Kiley made up a rhyme that caught on, and we'd all be chanting it together: *Step out of line, hit a mine; follow the dink, you're in the pink.* All around us, the place was littered with Bouncing Betties and Toe Poppers and booby-trapped artillery rounds, but in those five days on the Batangan Peninsula nobody got hurt. We all learned to love the old man.

It was a sad scene when the choppers came to take us away. Jimmy Cross gave the old poppa-san a hug. Mitchell Sanders and Lee Strunk loaded him up with boxes of C rations.

There were actually tears in the old man's eyes.

"Follow dink," he said to each of us, "you go pink."

If you weren't humping, you were waiting. I remember the monotony. Digging foxholes. Slapping mosquitoes. The sun and the heat and the endless paddies. Even in the deep bush, where you could die any number of ways, the war was nakedly and aggressively boring. But it was a strange boredom. It was boredom with a twist, the kind of boredom that caused stomach disorders. You'd be sitting at the top of a high hill, the flat paddies stretching out below, and the day would be calm and hot and utterly vacant, and you'd feel the boredom dripping inside you like a leaky faucet, except it wasn't water, it was a sort of acid, and with each little droplet you'd feel the stuff eating away at your important organs. You'd try to relax. You'd uncurl your fists and let your thoughts go. Well, you'd think, this isn't so bad. And right then you'd hear gunfire behind you and your nuts would fly up into your throat and you'd be squealing pig squeals. That kind of boredom.

I feel guilty sometimes. Forty-three years old and I'm still writing war stories. My daughter Kathleen tells me it's an obsession, that I should write about a little girl who finds a million dollars and spends it all on a Shetland pony. In a way, I guess, she's right: I should forget it. But the thing about remembering is that you don't forget. You take your material where you find it, which is in your life, at the intersection of past and present. The memory-traffic feeds into a rotary up in your head, where it goes in circles for a while, and shoots off down a thousand different streets. As a writer, all you can do is pick a street and go for the ride, putting things down as they come at you. That's the real obsession. All those stories.

·   ·   ·

Not bloody stories, necessarily. Happy stories, too, and even a few peace stories.

Here's a quick peace story:

A guy goes AWOL. Shacks up in Danang with a Red Cross nurse. It's a great time—the nurse loves him to death—the guy gets whatever he wants whenever he wants it. The war's over, he thinks. Just nookie and new angles. But then one day he rejoins his unit in the bush. Can't wait to get back into action. Finally one of his buddies asks what happened with the nurse, why so hot for combat, and the guy says, "All that peace, man, it felt so good it *hurt*. I want to hurt it *back*."

I remember Mitchell Sanders smiling as he told me that story. Most of it he made up, I'm sure, but even so it gave me a quick truth-goose. Because it's all relative. You're pinned down in some filthy hellhole of a paddy, getting your ass delivered to kingdom come, but then for a few seconds everything goes quiet and you look up and see the sun and a few puffy white clouds, and the immense serenity flashes against your eyeballs—the whole world gets rearranged—and even though you're pinned down by a war you never felt more at peace.

What sticks to memory, often, are those odd little fragments that have no beginning and no end:

Norman Bowker lying on his back one night, watching the stars, then whispering to me, "I'll tell you something, O'Brien. If I could have one wish, anything, I'd wish for my dad to write me a letter and say it's okay if I don't win any medals. That's all my old man talks about, nothing else. How he can't wait to see my goddamn medals."

Or Kiowa teaching a rain dance to Rat Kiley and Dave Jensen, the three of them whooping and leaping around barefoot while a bunch of villagers looked on with a mixture of fascination and giggly horror. Afterward, Rat said, "So where's the rain?" and Kiowa said, "The earth is slow, but the buffalo is patient," and Rat thought about it and said, "Yeah, but where's the *rain*?"

Or Ted Lavender adopting an orphan puppy—feeding it from a plastic spoon and carrying it in his rucksack until the day Azar strapped it to a Claymore antipersonnel mine and squeezed the firing device.

The average age in our platoon, I'd guess, was nineteen or twenty, and as a consequence things often took on a curiously playful atmosphere, like a sporting event at some exotic reform school. The competition could be lethal, yet there was a childlike exuberance to it all, lots of pranks and horseplay. Like when Azar blew away Ted Lavender's puppy. "What's everybody so upset about?" Azar said. "I mean, Christ, I'm just a *boy*."

I remember these things, too.

The damp, fungal scent of an empty body bag.

A quarter moon rising over the nighttime paddies.

Henry Dobbins sitting in the twilight, sewing on his new buck-sergeant stripes, quietly singing, "A tisket, a tasket, a green and yellow basket."

A field of elephant grass weighted with wind, bowing under the stir of a helicopter's blades, the grass dark and servile, bending low, but then rising straight again when the chopper went away.

A red clay trail outside the village of My Khe.

A hand grenade.

A slim, dead, dainty young man of about twenty.

Kiowa saying, "No choice, Tim. What else could you do?"

Kiowa saying, "Right?"

Kiowa saying, "Talk to me."

Forty-three years old, and the war occurred half a lifetime ago, and yet the remembering makes it now. And sometimes remembering will lead to a story, which makes it forever. That's what stories are for. Stories are for joining the past to the future. Stories are for those late hours in the night when you can't remember how you got from where you were to where you are. Stories are for eternity, when memory is erased, when there is nothing to remember except the story.

HOW TO TELL
A TRUE WAR STORY

This is true.

I had a buddy in Vietnam. His name was Bob Kiley, but everybody called him Rat.

A friend of his gets killed, so about a week later Rat sits down and writes a letter to the guy's sister. Rat tells her what a great brother she had, how together the guy was, a number one pal and comrade. A real soldier's soldier, Rat says. Then he tells a few stories to make the point, how her brother would always volunteer for stuff nobody else would volunteer for in a million years, dangerous stuff, like doing recon or going out on these really badass night patrols. Stainless steel balls, Rat tells her. The guy was a little crazy, for sure, but crazy in a good way, a real daredevil, because he liked the challenge of it, he liked testing himself, just man against gook. A great, great guy, Rat says.

Anyway, it's a terrific letter, very personal and touching. Rat almost bawls writing it. He gets all teary telling about the good times they had together, how her brother made the war seem almost fun, always raising hell and lighting up villes and bringing smoke to bear every which way. A great sense of humor, too. Like the time at this river when he went fishing with a whole damn crate of hand grenades. Probably the funniest thing in world history, Rat says, all that gore,

513

about twenty zillion dead gook fish. Her brother, he had the right attitude. He knew how to have a good time. On Halloween, this real hot spooky night, the dude paints up his body all different colors and puts on this weird mask and hikes over to a ville and goes trick-or-treating almost stark naked, just boots and balls and an M-16. A tremendous human being, Rat says. Pretty nutso sometimes, but you could trust him with your life.

And then the letter gets very sad and serious. Rat pours his heart out. He says he loved the guy. He says the guy was his best friend in the world. They were like soul mates, he says, like twins or something, they had a whole lot in common. He tells the guy's sister he'll look her up when the war's over.

So what happens?

Rat mails the letter. He waits two months. The dumb cooze never writes back.

A true war story is never moral. It does not instruct, nor encourage virtue, nor suggest models of proper human behavior, nor restrain men from doing the things men have always done. If a story seems moral, do not believe it. If at the end of a war story you feel uplifted, or if you feel that some small bit of rectitude has been salvaged from the larger waste, then you have been made the victim of a very old and terrible lie. There is no rectitude whatsoever. There is no virtue. As a first rule of thumb, therefore, you can tell a true war story by its absolute and uncompromising allegiance to obscenity and evil. Listen to Rat Kiley. Cooze, he says. He does not say bitch. He certainly does not say woman, or girl. He says cooze. Then he spits and stares. He's nineteen years old—it's too much for him—so he looks at you with those big sad gentle killer eyes and says *cooze*, because his friend is dead, and because it's so incredibly sad and true: she never wrote back.

You can tell a true war story if it embarrasses you. If you don't care for obscenity, you don't care for the truth; if you don't care for the truth, watch how you vote. Send guys to war, they come home talking dirty. Listen to Rat: "Jesus Christ, man, I write this beautiful fuckin' letter, I slave over it, and what happens? The dumb cooze never writes back."

The dead guy's name was Curt Lemon. What happened was, we crossed a muddy river and marched west into the mountains, and on the third day we took a break along a trail junction in deep jungle. Right away, Lemon and Rat Kiley started goofing. They didn't understand about the spookiness. They were kids; they just didn't know. A nature hike, they thought, not even a war, so they went off into the shade of some giant trees—quadruple canopy, no sunlight at all—and they were giggling and calling each other yellow mother and playing a silly game they'd invented. The game involved smoke grenades, which were harmless unless you did stupid things, and what they did was pull out the pin and stand a few feet apart and play catch under the shade of those huge trees. Whoever chickened out was a yellow mother. And if nobody chickened out, the grenade would make a light popping sound and they'd be covered with smoke and they'd laugh and dance around and then do it again.

It's all exactly true.

It happened, to *me*, nearly twenty years ago, and I still remember that trail junction and those giant trees and a soft dripping sound somewhere beyond the trees. I remember the smell of moss. Up in the canopy there were tiny white blossoms, but no sunlight at all, and I remember the shadows spreading out under the trees where Curt Lemon and Rat Kiley were playing catch with smoke grenades. Mitchell Sanders sat flipping his yo-yo. Norman Bowker and Kiowa and Dave Jensen were dozing, or half dozing, and all around us were those ragged green mountains.

Except for the laughter things were quiet.

At one point, I remember, Mitchell Sanders turned and looked at me, not quite nodding, as if to warn me about something, as if he already *knew*, then after a while he rolled up his yo-yo and moved away.

It's hard to tell you what happened next.

They were just goofing. There was a noise, I suppose, which must've been the detonator, so I glanced behind me and watched

Lemon step from the shade into bright sunlight. His face was suddenly brown and shining. A handsome kid, really. Sharp gray eyes, lean and narrow-waisted, and when he died it was almost beautiful, the way the sunlight came around him and lifted him up and sucked him high into a tree full of moss and vines and white blossoms.

In any war story, but especially a true one, it's difficult to separate what happened from what seemed to happen. What seems to happen becomes its own happening and has to be told that way. The angles of vision are skewed. When a booby trap explodes, you close your eyes and duck and float outside yourself. When a guy dies, like Curt Lemon, you look away and then look back for a moment and then look away again. The pictures get jumbled; you tend to miss a lot. And then afterward, when you go to tell about it, there is always that surreal seemingness, which makes the story seem untrue, but which in fact represents the hard and exact truth as it *seemed.*

In many cases a true war story cannot be believed. If you believe it, be skeptical. It's a question of credibility. Often the crazy stuff is true and the normal stuff isn't, because the normal stuff is necessary to make you believe the truly incredible craziness.

In other cases you can't even tell a true war story. Sometimes it's just beyond telling.

I heard this one, for example, from Mitchell Sanders. It was near dusk and we were sitting at my foxhole along a wide muddy river north of Quang Ngai. I remember how peaceful the twilight was. A deep pinkish red spilled out on the river, which moved without a sound, and in the morning we would cross the river and march west into the mountains. The occasion was right for a good story.

"God's truth," Mitchell Sanders said. "A six-man patrol goes up into the mountains on a basic listening-post operation. The idea's to spend a week up there, just lie low and listen for enemy movement. They've got a radio along, so if they hear anything suspicious—anything—they're supposed to call in artillery or gunships, whatever it takes. Otherwise they keep strict field discipline. Absolute silence. They just listen."

Sanders glanced at me to make sure I had the scenario. He was playing with his yo-yo, dancing it with short, tight little strokes of the wrist.

His face was blank in the dusk.

"We're talking regulation, by-the-book LP. These six guys, they don't say boo for a solid week. They don't got tongues. *All* ears."

"Right," I said.

"Understand me?"

"Invisible."

Sanders nodded.

"Affirm," he said. "Invisible. So what happens is, these guys get themselves deep in the bush, all camouflaged up, and they lie down and wait and that's all they do, nothing else, they lie there for seven straight days and just listen. And man, I'll tell you—it's spooky. This is mountains. You don't *know* spooky till you been there. Jungle, sort of, except it's way up in the clouds and there's always this fog—like rain, except it's not raining—everything's all wet and swirly and tangled up and you can't see jack, you can't find your own pecker to piss with. Like you don't even have a body. Serious spooky. You just go with the vapors—the fog sort of takes you in . . . And the sounds, man. The sounds carry forever. You hear stuff nobody should *ever* hear."

Sanders was quiet for a second, just working the yo-yo, then he smiled at me.

"So after a couple days the guys start hearing this real soft, kind of wacked-out music. Weird echoes and stuff. Like a radio or something, but it's not a radio, it's this strange gook music that comes right out of the rocks. Faraway, sort of, but right up close, too. They try to ignore it. But it's a listening post, right? So they listen. And every night they keep hearing that crazyass gook concert. All kinds of chimes and xylophones. I mean, this is wilderness—no way, it can't be real—but there it *is*, like the mountains are tuned in to Radio fucking Hanoi. Naturally they get nervous. One guy sticks Juicy Fruit in his ears. Another guy almost flips. Thing is, though, they can't report music. They can't get on the horn and call back to base and say, 'Hey, listen, we need some firepower, we got to blow away this weirdo gook rock band.' They can't do that. It wouldn't go down. So they lie there in the fog and keep their mouths shut. And what makes it extra bad, see, is the poor dudes can't horse around like normal. Can't joke it away. Can't even talk to each other except maybe in whispers, all hush-hush, and that just revs up the willies. All they do is listen."

Again there was some silence as Mitchell Sanders looked out on the river. The dark was coming on hard now, and off to the west I could see the mountains rising in silhouette, all the mysteries and unknowns.

"This next part," Sanders said quietly, "you won't believe."

"Probably not," I said.

"You won't. And you know why?" He gave me a long, tired smile. "Because it happened. Because every word is absolutely dead-on true."

Sanders made a sound in his throat, like a sigh, as if to say he didn't care if I believed him or not. But he did care. He wanted me to feel the truth, to believe by the raw force of feeling. He seemed sad, in a way.

"These six guys," he said, "they're pretty fried out by now, and one night they start hearing voices. Like at a cocktail party. That's what it sounds like, this big swank gook cocktail party somewhere out there in the fog. Music and chitchat and stuff. It's crazy, I know, but they hear the champagne corks. They hear the actual martini glasses. Real hoity-toity, all very civilized, except this isn't civilization. This is Nam.

"Anyway, the guys try to be cool. They just lie there and groove, but after a while they start hearing—you won't believe this—chamber music. They hear violins and cellos. They hear this terrific mama-san soprano. Then after a while they hear gook opera and a glee club and the Haiphong Boys Choir and a barbershop quartet and all kinds of weird chanting and Buddha-Buddha stuff. And the whole time, in the background, there's still that cocktail party going on. All these different voices. Not human voices, though. Because it's the mountains. Follow me? The rock—it's *talking*. And the fog, too, and the grass and the goddamn mongooses. Everything talks. The trees talk politics, the monkeys talk religion. The whole country. Vietnam. The place talks. It talks. Understand? Nam—it truly *talks*.

"The guys can't cope. They lose it. They get on the radio and report enemy movement—a whole army, they say—and they order up the firepower. They get arty and gunships. They call in air strikes. And I'll tell you, they fuckin' crash that cocktail party. All night long, they just smoke those mountains. They make jungle juice. They blow away trees and glee clubs and whatever else there is to blow away. Scorch time. They walk napalm up and down the ridges. They bring in the Cobras and F-4s, they use Willie Peter and HE and incendiaries. It's all fire. They make those mountains burn.

"Around dawn things finally get quiet. Like you never even *heard* quiet before. One of those real thick, real misty days—just clouds and fog, they're off in this special zone—and the mountains are absolutely dead-flat silent. Like Brigadoon—pure vapor, you know? Everything's all sucked up inside the fog. Not a single sound, except they still *hear* it.

"So they pack up and start humping. They head down the mountain, back to base camp, and when they get there they don't say diddly. They don't talk. Not a word, like they're deaf and dumb. Later on this fat bird colonel comes up and asks what the hell happened out there. What'd they hear? Why all the ordnance? The man's ragged out, he gets down tight on their case. I mean, they spent six trillion dollars on firepower, and this fatass colonel wants answers, he wants to know what the fuckin' story is.

"But the guys don't say zip. They just look at him for a while, sort of funny like, sort of amazed, and the whole war is right there in that stare. It says everything you can't ever say. It says, man, you got *wax* in your ears. It says, poor bastard, you'll never know—wrong frequency—you don't *even* want to hear this. Then they salute the fucker and walk away, because certain stories you don't ever tell."

You can tell a true war story by the way it never seems to end. Not then, not ever. Not when Mitchell Sanders stood up and moved off into the dark.

It all happened.

Even now, at this instant, I remember that yo-yo. In a way, I suppose, you had to be there, you had to hear it, but I could tell how desperately Sanders wanted me to believe him, his frustration at not quite getting the details right, not quite pinning down the final and definitive truth.

And I remember sitting at my foxhole that night, watching the shadows of Quang Ngai, thinking about the coming day and how we would cross the river and march west into the mountains, all the ways I might die, all the things I did not understand.

Late in the night Mitchell Sanders touched my shoulder.

"Just came to me," he whispered. "The moral, I mean. Nobody listens. Nobody hears nothin'. Like that fatass colonel. The politicians, all the civilian types. Your girlfriend. My girlfriend. Everybody's sweet little virgin girlfriend. What they need is to go out on LP. The vapors, man. Trees and rocks—you got to *listen* to your enemy."

And then again, in the morning, Sanders came up to me. The platoon was preparing to move out, checking weapons, going through all the little rituals that preceded a day's march. Already the lead squad had crossed the river and was filing off toward the west.

"I got a confession to make," Sanders said. "Last night, man, I had to make up a few things."

"I know that."

"The glee club. There wasn't any glee club."

"Right."

"No opera."

"Forget it, I understand."

"Yeah, but listen, it's still true. Those six guys, they heard wicked sound out there. They heard sound you just plain won't believe."

Sanders pulled on his rucksack, closed his eyes for a moment, then almost smiled at me. I knew what was coming.

"All right," I said, "what's the moral?"

"Forget it."

"No, go ahead."

For a long while he was quiet, looking away, and the silence kept stretching out until it was almost embarrassing. Then he shrugged and gave me a stare that lasted all day.

"Hear that quiet, man?" he said. "That quiet—just listen. There's your moral."

In a true war story, if there's a moral at all, it's like the thread that makes the cloth. You can't tease it out. You can't extract the meaning without unraveling the deeper meaning. And in the end, really, there's nothing much to say about a true war story, except maybe "Oh."

True war stories do not generalize. They do not indulge in abstraction or analysis.

For example: War is hell. As a moral declaration the old truism seems perfectly true, and yet because it abstracts, because it generalizes, I can't believe it with my stomach. Nothing turns inside.

It comes down to gut instinct. A true war story, if truly told, makes the stomach believe.

This one does it for me. I've told it before—many times, many versions—but here's what actually happened.

We crossed that river and marched west into the mountains. On the third day, Curt Lemon stepped on a booby-trapped 105 round. He was playing catch with Rat Kiley, laughing, and then he was dead. The trees were thick; it took nearly an hour to cut an LZ for the dustoff.

Later, higher in the mountains, we came across a baby VC water buffalo. What it was doing there I don't know—no farms or paddies—but we chased it down and got a rope around it and led it along to a deserted village where we set up for the night. After supper Rat Kiley went over and stroked its nose.

He opened up a can of C rations, pork and beans, but the baby buffalo wasn't interested.

Rat shrugged.

He stepped back and shot it through the right front knee. The animal did not make a sound. It went down hard, then got up again, and Rat took careful aim and shot off an ear. He shot it in the hindquarters and in the little hump at its back. He shot it twice in the flanks. It wasn't to kill; it was to hurt. He put the rifle muzzle up against the mouth and shot the mouth away. Nobody said much. The whole platoon stood there watching, feeling all kinds of things, but there wasn't a great deal of pity for the baby water buffalo. Curt Lemon was dead. Rat Kiley had lost his best friend in the world. Later in the week he would write a long personal letter to the guy's sister, who would not write back, but for now it was a question of pain. He shot off the tail. He shot away chunks of meat below the ribs. All around us there was the smell of smoke and filth and deep greenery, and the evening was humid and very hot. Rat went to automatic. He shot randomly, almost casually, quick little spurts in the belly and butt. Then he reloaded, squatted down, and shot it in the left front knee. Again the animal fell hard and tried to get up, but this time it couldn't quite make it. It wobbled and went down sideways. Rat shot it in the nose. He bent forward and whispered something, as if talking to a pet, then he shot it in the throat. All the while the baby buffalo was silent, or almost silent, just a light bubbling sound where the nose had been. It lay very still. Nothing moved except the eyes, which were enormous, the pupils shining black and dumb.

Rat Kiley was crying. He tried to say something, but then cradled his rifle and went off by himself.

The rest of us stood in a ragged circle around the baby buffalo. For a time no one spoke. We had witnessed something essential, something brand-new and profound, a piece of the world so startling there was not yet a name for it.

Somebody kicked the baby buffalo.

It was still alive, though just barely, just in the eyes.

"Amazing," Dave Jensen said. "My whole life, I never seen anything like it."

"Never?"

"Not hardly. Not once."

Kiowa and Mitchell Sanders picked up the baby buffalo. They hauled it across the open square, hoisted it up, and dumped it in the village well.

Afterward, we sat waiting for Rat to get himself together.

"Amazing," Dave Jensen kept saying. "A new wrinkle. I never seen it before."

Mitchell Sanders took out his yo-yo. "Well, that's Nam," he said. "Garden of Evil. Over here, man, every sin's real fresh and original."

How do you generalize?

War is hell, but that's not the half of it, because war is also mystery and terror and adventure and courage and discovery and holiness and pity and despair and longing and love. War is nasty; war is fun. War is thrilling; war is drudgery. War makes you a man; war makes you dead.

The truths are contradictory. It can be argued, for instance, that war is grotesque. But in truth war is also beauty. For all its horror, you can't help but gape at the awful majesty of combat. You stare out at tracer rounds unwinding through the dark like brilliant red ribbons. You crouch in ambush as a cool, impassive moon rises over the night-time paddies. You admire the fluid symmetries of troops on the move, the harmonies of sound and shape and proportion, the great sheets of metal-fire streaming down from a gunship, the illumination rounds, the white phosphorous, the purply orange glow of napalm, the rocket's red glare. It's not pretty, exactly. It's astonishing. It fills the eye. It commands you. You hate it, yes, but your eyes do not. Like a killer forest fire, like cancer under a microscope, any battle or bomb-ing raid or artillery barrage has the aesthetic purity of absolute moral indifference—a powerful, implacable beauty—and a true war story will tell the truth about this, though the truth is ugly.

To generalize about war is like generalizing about peace. Almost everything is true. Almost nothing is true. At its core, perhaps, war is just another name for death, and yet any soldier will tell you, if he tells the truth, that proximity to death brings with it a corresponding proximity to life. After a firefight, there is always the immense plea-sure of aliveness. The trees are alive. The grass, the soil—everything. All around you things are purely living, and you among them, and the aliveness makes you tremble. You feel an intense, out-of-the-skin awareness of your living self—your truest self, the human being you want to be and then become by the force of wanting it. In the midst of evil you want to be a good man. You want decency. You want justice and courtesy and human concord, things you never knew you wanted. There is a kind of largeness to it, a kind of godliness. Though it's odd, you're never more alive than when you're almost dead. You recognize what's valuable. Freshly, as if for the first time, you love what's best in yourself and in the world, all that might be lost. At the hour of dusk you sit at your foxhole and look out on a wide river turning pinkish red, and at the mountain beyond, and although in the morning you must cross the river and go into the mountains and do terrible things and maybe die, even so, you find yourself studying the fine colors on the river, you feel wonder and awe at the setting of the sun, and you are filled with a hard, aching love for how the world could be and always should be, but now is not.

Mitchell Sanders was right. For the common soldier, at least, war has the feel—the spiritual texture—of a great ghostly fog, thick and permanent. There is no clarity. Everything swirls. The old rules are no longer binding, the old truths no longer true. Right spills over into wrong. Order blends into chaos, love into hate, ugliness into beauty, law into anarchy, civility into savagery. The vapors suck you in. You can't tell where you are, or why you're there, and the only certainty is overwhelming ambiguity.

In war you lose your sense of the definite, hence your sense of truth itself, and therefore it's safe to say that in a true war story nothing is ever absolutely true.

Often in a true war story there is not even a point, or else the point doesn't hit you until twenty years later, in your sleep, and you wake up and shake your wife and start telling the story to her, except when you get to the end you've forgotten the point again. And then for a long time you lie there watching the story happen in your head. You listen to your wife's breathing. The war's over. You close your eyes. You smile and think, Christ, what's the *point*?

This one wakes me up.

In the mountains that day, I watched Lemon turn sideways. He laughed and said something to Rat Kiley. Then he took a peculiar half step, moving from shade into bright sunlight, and the booby-trapped

105 round blew him into a tree. The parts were just hanging there, so Dave Jensen and I were ordered to shinny up and peel him off. I remember the white bone of an arm. I remember pieces of skin and something wet and yellow that must've been the intestines. The gore was horrible, and stays with me. But what wakes me up twenty years later is Dave Jensen singing "Lemon Tree" as we threw down the parts.

You can tell a true war story by the questions you ask. Somebody tells a story, let's say, and afterward you ask, "Is it true?" and if the answer matters, you've got your answer.

For example, we've all heard this one. Four guys go down a trail. A grenade sails out. One guy jumps on it and takes the blast and saves his three buddies.

Is it true?

The answer matters.

You'd feel cheated if it never happened. Without the grounding reality, it's just a trite bit of puffery, pure Hollywood, untrue in the way all such stories are untrue. Yet even if it did happen—and maybe it did, anything's possible—even then you know it can't be true, because a true war story does not depend upon that kind of truth. Absolute occurrence is irrelevant. A thing may happen and be a total lie; another thing may not happen and be truer than the truth. For example: Four guys go down a trail. A grenade sails out. One guy jumps on it and takes the blast, but it's a killer grenade and everybody dies anyway. Before they die, though, one of the dead says, "The fuck you do *that* for?" and the jumper says, "Story of my life, man," and the other guy starts to smile but he's dead.

That's a true story that never happened.

Twenty years later, I can still see the sunlight on Lemon's face. I can see him turning, looking back at Rat Kiley, then he laughed and took that curious half step from shade into sunlight, his face suddenly brown and shining, and when his foot touched down, in that instant, he must've thought it was the sunlight that was killing him. It was not the sunlight. It was a rigged 105 round. But if I could ever get the story right, how the sun seemed to gather around him and pick him up and lift him high into a tree, if I could somehow re-create the fatal whiteness of that light, the quick glare, the obvious cause and effect, then you would believe the last thing Curt Lemon believed, which for him must've been the final truth.

Now and then, when I tell this story, someone will come up to me afterward and say she liked it. It's always a woman. Usually it's an older woman of kindly temperament and humane politics. She'll explain that as a rule she hates war stories; she can't understand why people want to wallow in all the blood and gore. But this one she liked. The poor baby buffalo, it made her sad. Sometimes, even, there are little tears. What I should do, she'll say, is put it all behind me. Find new stories to tell.

I won't say it but I'll think it.

I'll picture Rat Kiley's face, his grief, and I'll think, *You dumb cooze.*

Because she wasn't listening.

It *wasn't* a war story. It was a *love* story.

But you can't say that. All you can do is tell it one more time, patiently, adding and subtracting, making up a few things to get at the real truth. No Mitchell Sanders, you tell her. No Lemon, no Rat Kiley. No trail junction. No baby buffalo. No vines or moss or white blossoms. Beginning to end, you tell her, it's all made up. Every goddamn detail—the mountains and the river and especially that poor dumb baby buffalo. None of it happened. *None* of it. And even if it did happen, it didn't happen in the mountains, it happened in this little village on the Batangan Peninsula, and it was raining like crazy, and one night a guy named Stink Harris woke up screaming with a leech on his tongue. You can tell a true war story if you just keep on telling it.

And in the end, of course, a true war story is never about war. It's about sunlight. It's about the special way that dawn spreads out on a river when you know you must cross the river and march into the mountains and do things you are afraid to do. It's about love and memory. It's about sorrow. It's about sisters who never write back and people who never listen.

THE MAN I KILLED

His jaw was in his throat, his upper lip and teeth were gone, his one eye was shut, his other eye was a star-shaped hole, his eyebrows were thin and arched like a woman's, his nose was undamaged, there was a slight tear at the lobe of one ear, his clean black hair was swept upward into a cowlick at the rear of the skull, his forehead was lightly freckled, his fingernails were clean, the skin at his left cheek was peeled back in three ragged strips, his right cheek was smooth and hairless, there was a butterfly on his chin, his neck was open to the spinal cord and the blood there was thick and shiny and it was this wound that had killed him. He lay face-up in the center of the trail, a slim, dead, almost dainty young man. He had bony legs, a narrow waist, long shapely fingers. His chest was sunken and poorly muscled—a scholar, maybe. His wrists were the wrists of a child. He wore a black shirt, black pajama pants, a gray ammunition belt, a gold ring on the third finger of his right hand. His rubber sandals had been blown off. One lay beside him, the other a few meters up the trail. He had been born, maybe, in 1946 in the village of My Khe near the central coastline of Quang Ngai Province, where his parents farmed, and where his family had lived for several centuries, and where, during the time of the French, his father and two uncles and many neighbors had joined in the struggle for independence. He was not a Communist. He was a citizen and a soldier. In the village of My Khe,

527

as in all of Quang Ngai, patriotic resistance had the force of tradition, which was partly the force of legend, and from his earliest boyhood the man I killed would have listened to stories about the heroic Trung sisters and Tran Hung Dao's famous rout of the Mongols and Le Loi's final victory against the Chinese at Tot Dong. He would have been taught that to defend the land was a man's highest duty and highest privilege. He had accepted this. It was never open to question. Secretly, though, it also frightened him. He was not a fighter. His health was poor, his body small and frail. He liked books. He wanted someday to be a teacher of mathematics. At night, lying on his mat, he could not picture himself doing the brave things his father had done, or his uncles, or the heroes of the stories. He hoped in his heart that he would never be tested. He hoped the Americans would go away. Soon, he hoped. He kept hoping and hoping, always, even when he was asleep.

"Oh, man, you fuckin' trashed the fucker," Azar said. "You scrambled his sorry self, look at that, you *did*, you laid him out like Shredded fuckin' Wheat."

"Go away," Kiowa said.

"I'm just saying the truth. Like oatmeal."

"Go," Kiowa said.

"Okay, then, I take it back," Azar said. He started to move away, then stopped and said, "Rice Krispies, you know? On the dead test, this particular individual gets A-plus."

Smiling at this, he shrugged and walked up the trail toward the village behind the trees.

Kiowa kneeled down.

"Just forget that crud," he said. He opened up his canteen and held it out for a while and then sighed and pulled it away. "No sweat, man. What else could you do?"

Later, Kiowa said, "I'm serious. Nothing *anybody* could do. Come on, stop staring."

The trail junction was shaded by a row of trees and tall brush. The slim young man lay with his legs in the shade. His jaw was in his throat. His one eye was shut and the other was a star-shaped hole.

Kiowa glanced at the body.

"All right, let me ask a question," he said. "You want to trade places with him? Turn it all upside down—you *want* that? I mean, be honest."

The star-shaped hole was red and yellow. The yellow part seemed to be getting wider, spreading out at the center of the star. The upper lip and teeth and gum were gone. The man's head was cocked at a wrong angle, as if loose at the neck, and the neck was wet with blood.

"Think it over," Kiowa said.

Then later he said, "Tim, it's a *war*. The guy wasn't Heidi—he had a weapon, right? It's a tough thing, for sure, but you got to cut out that staring."

Then he said, "Maybe you better lie down a minute."

Then after a long empty time he said, "Take it slow. Just go wherever the spirit takes you."

The butterfly was making its way along the young man's forehead, which was spotted with small dark freckles. The nose was undamaged. The skin on the right cheek was smooth and fine-grained and hairless. Frail-looking, delicately boned, the young man would not have wanted to be a soldier and in his heart would have feared performing badly in battle. Even as a boy growing up in the village of My Khe, he had often worried about this. He imagined covering his head and lying in a deep hole and closing his eyes and not moving until the war was over. He had no stomach for violence. He loved mathematics. His eyebrows were thin and arched like a woman's, and at school the boys sometimes teased him about how pretty he was, the arched eyebrows and long shapely fingers, and on the playground they mimicked a woman's walk and made fun of his smooth skin and his love for mathematics. The young man could not make himself fight them. He often wanted to, but he was afraid, and this increased his shame. If he could not fight little boys, he thought, how could he ever fight the Americans with their airplanes and helicopters and bombs? It did not seem possible. In the presence of his father and uncles, he pretended to look forward to doing his patriotic duty, which was also a privilege, but at night he prayed with his mother that the war might end soon. Beyond anything else, he was afraid of disgracing himself, and therefore his family and village. But all he could do, he thought, was wait and pray and try not to grow up too fast.

"Listen to me," Kiowa said. "You feel terrible, I know that."

Then he said, "Okay, maybe I *don't* know."

Along the trail there were small blue flowers shaped like bells. The young man's head was wrenched sideways, not quite facing the flowers, and even in the shade a single blade of sunlight sparkled against the buckle of his ammunition belt. The left cheek was peeled back in three ragged strips. The wounds at his neck had not yet clotted, which made him seem animate even in death, the blood still spreading out across his shirt.

Kiowa shook his head.

There was some silence before he said, "Stop *staring.*"

The young man's fingernails were clean. There was a slight tear at the lobe of one ear, a sprinkling of blood on the forearm. He wore a gold ring on the third finger of his right hand. His chest was sunken and poorly muscled—a scholar, maybe. His life was now a constellation of possibilities. So, yes, maybe a scholar. And for years, despite his family's poverty, the man I killed would have been determined to continue his education in mathematics. The means for this were arranged, perhaps, through the village liberation cadres, and in 1964 the young man began attending classes in Saigon, where he avoided politics and paid attention to the problems of calculus. He devoted himself to his studies. He spent his nights alone, would not let himself think about it. He had stopped praying; instead, now, he waited. And as he waited, in his final year at the university, he fell in love with a classmate, a girl of seventeen, who one day told him that his wrists were like the wrists of a child, so small and delicate, and who admired his narrow waist and the cowlick that rose up like a bird's tail at the back of his head. She liked his quiet manner; she laughed at his freckles and bony legs. One evening, perhaps, they exchanged gold rings.

Now one eye was a star.

"You okay?" Kiowa said.

The body lay almost entirely in shade. There were gnats at the mouth, little flecks of pollen drifting above the nose. The butterfly was gone. The bleeding had stopped except for the neck wounds.

Kiowa picked up the rubber sandals, clapping off the dirt, then bent down to search the body. He found a pouch of rice, a comb, a fingernail clipper, a few soiled piasters, a snapshot of a young woman standing in front of a parked motorcycle. Kiowa placed these items in his rucksack along with the gray ammunition belt and rubber sandals.

Then he squatted down.

"I'll tell you the straight truth," he said. "The guy was dead the second he stepped on the trail. Understand me? We all had him zeroed. A good kill—weapon, ammunition, everything." Tiny beads of sweat glistened at Kiowa's forehead. His eyes moved from the sky to the dead man's body to the knuckles of his own hands. "So listen, you best pull your shit together. Can't just sit here all day."

Later he said, "Understand?"

Then he said, "Five minutes, Tim. Five minutes and we're moving out."

The one eye did a funny twinkling trick, red to yellow. His head was wrenched sideways, as if loose at the neck, and the dead young man seemed to be staring at some distant object beyond the bell-shaped flowers along the trail. The blood at the neck had gone to a deep purplish black. Clean fingernails, clean hair—he had been a soldier for only a single day. After his years at the university, the man I killed returned with his new wife to the village of My Khe, where he enlisted as a common rifleman with the 48th Vietcong Battalion. He knew he would die quickly. He knew he would see a flash of light. He knew he would fall dead and wake up in the stories of his village and people.

Kiowa covered the body with a poncho.

"Hey, you're looking better," he said. "No doubt about it. All you needed was time—some mental R&R."

Then he said, "Man, I'm sorry."

Then later he said, "Why not talk about it?"

Then he said, "Come on, man, talk."

He was a slim, dead, almost dainty young man of about twenty. He lay with one leg bent beneath him, his jaw in his throat, his face neither expressive nor inexpressive. One eye was shut. The other was a star-shaped hole.

"Talk," Kiowa said.

AMBUSH

When she was nine, my daughter Kathleen asked if I had ever killed anyone. She knew about the war; she knew I'd been a soldier. "You keep writing war stories," she said, "so I guess you must've killed somebody." It was a difficult moment, but I did what seemed right, which was to say, "Of course not," and then to take her onto my lap and hold her for a while. Someday, I hope, she'll ask again. But here I want to pretend she's a grown-up. I want to tell her exactly what happened, or what I remember happening, and then I want to say to her that as a little girl she was absolutely right. This is why I keep writing war stories:

He was a short, slender young man of about twenty. I was afraid of him—afraid of something—and as he passed me on the trail I threw a grenade that exploded at his feet and killed him.

Or to go back:

Shortly after midnight we moved into the ambush site outside My Khe. The whole platoon was there, spread out in the dense brush along the trail, and for five hours nothing at all happened. We were working in two-man teams—one man on guard while the other slept, switching off every two hours—and I remember it was still dark when Kiowa shook me awake for the final watch. The night was foggy and hot. For the first few moments I felt lost, not sure about directions, groping for my helmet and weapon. I reached out and found three grenades and lined them up in front of me; the pins had already been straightened for quick throwing. And then for maybe half an hour I kneeled there and waited. Very gradually, in tiny slivers, dawn began to break through the fog, and from my position in the brush I could see ten or fifteen meters up the trail. The mosquitoes were fierce. I remember slapping at them, wondering if I should wake up Kiowa and ask for some repellent, then thinking it was a bad idea, then looking up and seeing the young man come out of the fog. He wore black clothing and rubber sandals and a gray ammunition belt. His shoulders were slightly stooped, his head cocked to the side as if listening for something. He seemed at ease. He carried his weapon in one hand, muzzle down, moving without any hurry up the center of the trail. There was no sound at all—none that I can remember. In a way, it seemed, he was part of the morning fog, or my own imagination, but there was also the reality of what was happening in my stomach. I had already pulled the pin on a grenade. I had come up to a crouch. It was entirely automatic. I did not hate the young man; I did not see him as the enemy; I did not ponder issues of morality or politics or military duty. I crouched and kept my head low. I tried to swallow whatever was rising from my stomach, which tasted like lemonade, something fruity and sour. I was terrified. There were no thoughts about killing. The grenade was to make him go away—just evaporate—and I leaned back and felt my mind go empty and then felt it fill up again. I had already thrown the grenade before telling myself to throw it. The brush was thick and I had to lob it high, not aiming, and I remember the grenade seeming to freeze above me for an instant, as if a camera had clicked, and I remember ducking down and holding my breath and seeing little wisps of fog rise from the earth. The grenade bounced once and rolled across the trail. I did not hear it, but there must've been a sound, because the young man dropped his weapon and began to run, just two or three quick steps, then he hesitated, swiveling to his right, and he glanced down at the grenade and tried to cover his head but never did. It occurred to me then that he was about to die. I wanted to warn him. The grenade made a popping noise—not soft but not loud either—not what I'd expected—and there was a puff of dust and smoke—a small white puff—and the young man seemed to jerk upward as if pulled by invisible wires. He fell on his back. His rubber sandals had been blown off. There was no wind. He lay at the center of the trail, his right leg bent beneath him, his one eye shut, his other eye a huge star-shaped hole.

It was not a matter of live or die. There was no real peril. Almost certainly the young man would have passed by. And it will always be that way.

Later, I remember, Kiowa tried to tell me that the man would've died anyway. He told me that it was a good kill, that I was a soldier and this was a war, that I should shape up and stop staring and ask myself what the dead man would've done if things were reversed.

None of it mattered. The words seemed far too complicated. All I could do was gape at the fact of the young man's body.

Even now I haven't finished sorting it out. Sometimes I forgive myself, other times I don't. In the ordinary hours of life I try not to dwell on it, but now and then, when I'm reading a newspaper or just sitting alone in a room, I'll look up and see the young man coming out of the morning fog. I'll watch him walk toward me, his shoulders slightly stooped, his head cocked to the side, and he'll pass within a few yards of me and suddenly smile at some secret thought and then continue up the trail to where it bends back into the fog.

GOOD FORM

It's time to be blunt.

I'm forty-three years old, true, and I'm a writer now, and a long time ago I walked through Quang Ngai Province as a foot soldier.

Almost everything else is invented.

But it's not a game. It's a form. Right here, now, as I invent myself, I'm thinking of all I want to tell you about why this book is written as it is. For instance, I want to tell you this: twenty years ago I watched a man die on a trail near the village of My Khe. I did not kill him. But I was present, you see, and my presence was guilt enough. I remember his face, which was not a pretty face, because his jaw was in his throat, and I remember feeling the burden of responsibility and grief. I blamed myself. And rightly so, because I was present.

But listen. Even *that* story is made up.

I want you to feel what I felt. I want you to know why story-truth is truer sometimes than happening-truth.

Here is the happening-truth. I was once a soldier. There were many bodies, real bodies with real faces, but I was young then and I was afraid to look. And now, twenty years later, I'm left with faceless responsibility and faceless grief.

Here is the story-truth. He was a slim, dead, almost dainty young man of about twenty. He lay in the center of a red clay trail near the village of My Khe. His jaw was in his throat. His eye was shut, the other eye was a star-shaped hole. I killed him.

What stories can do, I guess, is make things present.

I can look at things I never looked at. I can attach faces to grief and love and pity and God. I can be brave. I can make myself feel again.

"Daddy, tell the truth," Kathleen can say, "did you ever kill anybody?" And I can say, honestly, "Of course not."

Or I can say, honestly, "Yes."

11

Homecoming

August 1966. Corporal Peron Shinneman, who lost a leg in
Vietnam, is welcomed home by his wife, Shirley.

Prior to 1981, there were few serious and thoughtful attempts to dramatize the life of the returned veteran. More often, the vet was seen as psychologically and physically damaged, prone to violence and addiction, and all too eager to bring the ugliness of the war home to the United States. This early and unfair picture of the vet has remained with the American public to this day.

While the extent of the veteran's injuries, both physical and mental, has been downplayed in later efforts, there is still a portrait of the vet as a brooding loner, rarely a family man, and never a success. Suicide, alcoholism, and homelessness dog the Vietnam vet, weighed down with the burden of guilt. Even in the following selections—some of the best writing about returned vets, all later than 1983—the reader will see the usual assortment of troubled-vet symptoms. Haunted by the past, the vet stays in his lonely room or drives around his hometown aimlessly, unable to find anyone who will listen to his troubles, sure anyway that no one will understand. A logical but possibly misguided explanation is that compelling fiction (and poetry) is rarely about happy, untroubled people.

In vet Larry Heinemann's National Book Award–winning *Paco's Story* (1986), Paco is tortured nightly by his unrequited desires toward his hallmate, the pretty and innocent Cathy, and by his related memories of his unit's gang rape of a VC. The warrior's return to the civilized world through the love of a woman is a standard trope in homecoming narratives (say, Michael returning to the community of Clairton through Linda in *The Deer Hunter*), and here Heinemann nails down the reasons that this will never happen for Paco. It's shocking, ugly, and sad, and Heinemann's narrator—the dead platoon members—rubs the reader's face in it.

Nonvet and literary writer Louise Erdrich gives us something of a similar story in "A Bridge," from her first novel *Love Medicine* (1984). Henry Lamartine has returned from Nam and runs into Albertine Johnson on the seedy side of Fargo. Like Paco, the drunken Henry flashes back to an atrocity as he tries to bed Albertine in a flophouse. Though this piece flirts with melodrama, its vivid prose shines, and the novel as a whole received overwhelmingly strong reviews and made Erdrich a literary celebrity.

The poets in W. D. Ehrhart's anthology *Carrying the Darkness* (1985) provide another view of the war living on inside its soldiers. John Balaban, a conscientious objector who spent several years in-country doing humanitarian work, uses bizarre horror-movie images in "After Our War" to bring the waste of the war home to the reader. Veteran Steve Hassett takes this a step further, comparing the Hessians hired to fight the Revolutionary War to the American soldier in Vietnam; "Now we bring our dead to supper," he says in "Patriot's Day," and then, in an untitled piece, sends U.S. troops in to search and destroy a typical American home. In contrast, D. C. Berry paints the separation between soldier and citizen directly, noting that for the dying soldier even something as unchanging as the sun "goes down a different way."

First Air Cavalry veteran Bruce Weigl's selections here, taken from three separate collections, show an astonishing range of technique, from the surrealism of "Sailing to Bien Hoa" to the plainspoken "Girl at the Chu Lai Laundry" to the daring collage of "Monkey." "Him, on the Bicycle" is reminiscent of Tim O'Brien's "The Man I Killed" in its empathy but is far more celebratory, while "Anna Grasa" quietly brings the war home.

"Speaking of Courage" comes from Tim O'Brien's *The Things They Carried* (1990) and shows veteran Norman Bowker trying to come to terms with his Vietnam experience while he drives around his small town on the Fourth of July. The idea of the town in its complacency being culpable for what happened to Norman in Vietnam is reminiscent of the storybook country town of Boone's relationship to the outcast Paco. As usual, O'Brien works with a seemingly simple realism while deftly fitting in metaphorical meanings. The accompanying "Notes" throws a different light on the story and its genesis, and gives us an intriguing view of how vets see other vets.

Paco's Story

LARRY HEINEMANN

1986

6. Good Morning to You, Lieutenant. We can stand at the crest of the town's one good hill, James, and pause and get quiet and comfortable and still, and listen to the night sounds. At this late hour of the night the tranquil murmuring hum of the river, cascading over the rock-and-concrete spillway under the bridge, yonder, is almost the only sound to be heard. That constant rush of water is the hush that has lulled many a strapping newborn infant to sleep in its time; the last sobering sound heard suddenly, abruptly, in many a deathbed room, as clean and even and smooth as the curl in the neck of a glass cider jug.

But that is not the only sound to be heard late at night, James. We can sit on the thick slate curb, under the parkway walnuts, and hear the squeak of wicker chairs; the tumble of ice melting to slivers in glasses of Coke and tea and whiskey, the whisper of bedroom conversation that is all hisses, and the snapping and popping of buttons; women flapping and fluttering their summer dress fronts; the shrill squeal of children racing through swirling clouds of fireflies, a game better than tag; someone spitting on dry pavement; the snick-snick-snick of a loose pack of town dogs trotting across the schoolyard blacktop. Then comes the sound that all but stops the others, even the dogs—the step, tap-step, of that gimpy kid wounded in the war, that guy Paco, walking home from the Texas Lunch.

All those night sounds bristle, brushing back and forth under the trees, and everyone who's sitting back, listening, hears. And we hear, don't we, James—the river pouring over the spillway, the ring of jar lids, the giggles, the clear click of the cast-brass tip of Paco's cane.

And the girl with the rooms across the hall from the top of the stairs at the Geronimo Hotel listens, too. The girl, James—her name Cathy, remember—small-breasted and bony-armed, built like a smooth-faced, tallish boy. Nowadays, whenever Paco sees her, she's wearing one of her father's dress shirts with the cuffs rolled a time or two to the middle of her forearms, the shirttails loose around her thighs, with a starched collar as stiff as a military uniform tunic. Nearly every night now (these the deadest, hottest nights in the deadest, hottest weeks of August and September, James), the girl will sit on the broad, dusty sill of the alley window, with her small, clean feet drawn up under her, and lean her cheek against the filthy screen (her spying game done with; "No fun," she'll tell you facetiously, James, in a parody of pouting). She listens the way a meditative person will gaze into a bonfire. She perks her ears with deliberate intent, listening ever so keenly for the sharp click of Paco's black hickory cane on the asphalt, and the sure and steady, slightly off-rhythm of his walk—step, tap-step. Her moist, sparkling eyes will dart this way and that round the room, and she'll glance out the window, rubbing the cool, smooth, nut-brown skin of her knee (her whole body as brown as buttered toast, James), with the breezy heat of the tin-and-tar roof rising in her face, and she'll count the courses of smoothed railroad brick in the alley below. She will stare absentmindedly at her own fingers as she strums a limp gold anklet with manicured fingernails. She will imagine Paco's hands, bleached white and water wrinkled, his sour, sweat-soaked T-shirt clinging to the hard flat of his belly, that glazed-over, glossy look in his eyes—which in most folks is simply work weariness, you understand.

Every night now, when she hears the click of his cane on the asphalt change to the mellow, hollow thump of the hotel stoop, she will uncurl herself and crawl crablike across her bed. She will primp on the move and brush herself down, using her fingers for a whisk, smoothing that lime- or peach- or cocoa-colored dress shirt (opened a couple of buttons at the neck), and strike a pose leaning against the warm wood of her door. Sometimes she will hold the door open just so far, with her head and shoulders poked into the hall as though she's just out of the shower and still wet and doesn't want to drip on the hallway rug, but the front of her shirt will be nearly all unbuttoned, and there will be enough light shining down her front to be teasing, enticing. And sometimes she will put just her head in the light, with her body to one side behind the door, and she'll have a glittering gleam in her eye, as though she doesn't have a stitch on. And you've got to know, James, that some nights she doesn't, but those nights are for *her* benefit, not Paco's, because being buck naked when she smiles that smirk down at him makes her feel so goosy and juicy, and some nights she can't help but giggle. She will wait for Paco to come in the front and stop at the bottom of the stairway, standing stoop-shouldered, leaning so heavily on that goddamned cane some nights it will bow. She will wait for him to raise his eyes, looking up through the railing rungs, and see her in the dim amber light of the several head-high hallway sconces—the light shining on the smooth, browned skin of her legs and face, looking like dry, oval slivers of yellowed antique ivory, the air musty and rich like a bowl of sun-warmed, softening fruit, and the skylight over the deep, high stairwell nearly painted over with roofing tar.

She will stir slightly, waiting to see that look in his eye that is unmistakable in a man who has not been to bed with a woman for a long time. And Paco will nod, almost imperceptibly, and *then* will begin the race, the *new* game, the struggle to get to the top of the stairs before she slips back into her room and closes the door. It is the one solid rule of their game, James. If Paco can get so much as the tip of his cane in the door before she shuts it, he can come in ("You can fuck me, sugar!").

Paco has struggled up those stairs many a warm night, ass-whipped tired, his legs tingling and throbbing, wobbly even, his feet soaked and sore—that goddamned lye-soap rash on his arms as red as rope burns. Washing dishes by hand ain't no pleasure and it ain't no joke, James.

And tonight, just like any other night, getting in Cathy's doorway doesn't happen. She's not there, but he's not interested either. Oh no. Tonight he comes up the street and into the hotel, hits the stairs, and just keeps coming. Tonight Paco has been sitting on the damp, hard clay of the riverbank near the spillway, listening to the skinny-dippers horsing around in the sand-bottomed shallows downriver from the old railroad trestle, drinking quart after quart of decently warm beer fetched from Rita's half the night—waiting for the air to cool—and there's no telling what time it is.

He tops the stairs and limps along the hallway to the left with his skeleton key in one hand and his cane in the other (the roof rafters crackling overhead, cooling; the chain of the HOTEL sign twisting and squeaking—on rainy nights we can hear the neon sizzle and buzz). He works his door open, steps in, and closes it behind him with a slow and heavy click (as firm and final a sound as we are liable to hear in that hotel, James). The hall light vanishes from the room except for that flat, slender sliver under the door, which is no bigger than a piece of oak lath. Paco squeezes his head against the warm wood of the door (the smelly varnish almost gooey to the touch), squeezing his eyes shut with the pure relief of being home, taking a bit of a breather. He's got a still, stuffy, smothering little room, with a crumbling 8×10 linoleum sheet, a ragged mahogany dresser with the veneer shredding to splinters, and a coffee-colored bedstead with a brown bedspread— all that woodwork smelling of solid old age. There is a scum of dust in all the corners, and fuzzy wallpaper you would swear was flocked if you brushed against it in the dark. He rattles around in his darkened room, peeling off his T-shirt, unbuckling his belt and unzipping his fly, scooting his pants down, skivvies and all. Then he flops on his creaking bed, the way drunks do. His head and arms loll this way and that, and his legs hang over the edge of the bed with the balls of his feet brushing the floor. He sets his hands wide on the raspy, graying sheets, stares *hard* at the curling chips of paint above his head, then takes a good long breath, and, with a sudden, sharp exhalation, lifts his legs onto the bed. And it's godawful painful, James. Sometimes the pain shoots right up his legs and thighs into his back and arms (he can hear the pins and screws grinding against the bone some nights; oh, the grimacing squint wrinkles he will have). The very tips of his fingers tingle as though someone has pricked them.

He takes a long moment to settle in—to get his sore, throbbing legs and the small of his back just so among the lumps. The air is hot and heavy all around him, and the sheets are as itchy and scratchy as snapping-dry flannel. (Everything has been warm and sticky and uncomfortable all day, every day and all the night through for weeks now, James. Bread won't rise right. Beer foam looks pale and greasy and slippery. Your clothes bunch thickly at the crotch and cling to your back and down under your arms, for instance, and folks are awkward and bitchy and ill-tempered most of the time.)

We can take a pause now, and lean over Paco's thighs and knees and calves, James, even in the little light of his room; there *is* a slice of moon, a 40-watt back-porch light, and the glow of a yellow hall light reflected into the room under the door—this faint and burdensomely warm and oppressive light that gives his room a welcome and intimate air nonetheless, as still and smothering a place as we are likely to come across these warm and stuffy nights, unrelieved by comfort. If we lean down, we can see the many razor-thin surgical scars, the bone-fragment scars (going every which way) the size of pine-stump splinters, the puckered burn scars (from cooked-off ammunition) looking as though he's been sprayed with a shovelful of glowing cinders, the deadened, discolored ring of skin at the meatiest part of his thigh, where the Bravo Company medic wound the twisted tourniquet, using Paco's own bandanna, though the time for a tourniquet had long passed. The sallow, thin-faced medic slapped the crook of Paco's elbow to get a vein, and Paco and half the company could hear his grumble: "Come *on*, you dumbshit grunt motherfucker, give me a *goddamn* vein," and Paco's arm stung like a son-of-a-bitch—the medic's dog tags jangling in Paco's face. And if we look closely at Paco's arm, we can see the scar of the gouge at the inside of his forearm, the size of a pencil stub, where the catheter ripped loose when those shit-for-brains Bravo Company litter bearers dropped Paco down a rain-slick footpath, litter and all. ("You goddamned bullshit fucking Bravo Company Jesus Christ, I hope you motherfuckers all die shit!" Paco whispered, and cried.)

We could lean down and take a good hard look, and see all that, James, even in this little light. We could back away, now that we know what we're looking at, and those scars will seem to wiggle and curl, snapping languidly this way and that, the same as grubs and night crawlers when you prick them with the barb of a bait hook. But it is only an illusion, James, a sly trick of the eye—the way many a frightful thing in this world comes alive in the dimmest, whitest moonlight, the cleanest lamplight.

Paco lies on his bed, trying to nod off, trying to get as comfortable as the muggy air and sweaty-filthy sheets and teasing, tickling ache will allow, but out the window—kitty-corner to his—Paco hears Cathy honey-fucking the everlasting daylights out of some guy (*Marty-boy,* she calls him). There's no mistaking that sloppy, glucking sound, the bed squeaking effortlessly and meekly, the lovely sounds of their fucking filling the room (the way a cat's purring will fill a room, James). Marty-boy eases in and out of her, his buttocks working, his ankles crossed and the dry bottoms of his feet reaching over the foot of her bed. He bends his head down and licks her pearly breasts; Cathy arching up, holding him to her with her hands and heels, really enjoying all that.

Fucking the girl is something Paco has dreamed about over and over, sprawled spread-eagle on his creaking bed, with his flaccid cock (slashed with scars) flopped to one side of his thighs—oh, how his back would ache on those nights—his pubic hair fluffy and prickly, almost crackling in the heat, like dry grass.

Paco is furiously jealous—Marty-boy's clean haircut and the undulating smoothness of his back (not a mark on the son-of-a-bitch, James); Cathy's vigorous huffing and puffing, with her face squinched up, and her thrashing that fluffy hair from side to side, whipping it across Marty-boy's face; and him squinting severely, his whole body shuddering with the effort. Paco doesn't have to strain any to hear—can practically slide his hand and arm out his windowsill, over the nicotine burns and coffee-cup rings, lean out a little and fingertip-touch the top of her hair. Cathy sighs slowly and calmly and soothingly—content, Paco thinks to himself (his cock getting solid, jerking stiffly in the air)—brimful of peace and pleasure.

Now Cathy heard Paco fiddle with his key in the lock; heard him fumbling around in his dingy little room; smelled the very beer on his breath. And so now with each slippery thrust she stretches her thin little neck and exhales audibly toward the window. She pulls on Marty-boy's pale, shuddering hips—clawlike, with sedately manicured nails—and sways from side to side with her heels spiked into the mattress. Then she's swinging her legs in the air the hairs glittering—now staccato, now languidly, in a fresh surfeit of pleasure; now pummeling the small of his back in a frenzy with the callused points of her heels (with her thin, pinkish tongue between her teeth and a slaphappy grin on her face, as though to say, I got a nice little kick from teasing that gimp, but the fucking is nice and I love it, too).

Paco wishes Marty-boy (some primary-education major from the Wyandotte Teachers College, the same as Cathy) to hell and gone. Paco sweats up a storm trying to wish himself sober, trying to wish himself up from his bed and out of his room (sidestepping down the hallway in purposeful slow motion—toe-heel-toe—his hands skimming flat against the wall for guidance, balance). Paco has the incredible, shivering urge to sneak into Cathy's room and stalk up behind Marty-boy as bold as brass, grab him by the hips and yank him off, shake him out and set him aside, as if he were a mannequin. (Marty-boy would stand there astonished, wiggling like a big old bass snagged at the side of the head with a treble hook and dragged ashore— flabbergasted.) Cathy would be pulling at her own hair by then; grinding her hips into the air, straining her legs and belly, her pussy luminescent with lubrication. Paco imagines that he climbs onto the bed between her legs, stretching out above her. He imagines, too, that he slides into her as easily as a warm, clean hand slips into a greased glove; that she whimpers grotesquely, encircling him at once with her arms and legs, holding him to her like warm covers.

By this time Paco's cock is iron hard and feels as big as a Coke bottle. And he's just a man like the rest of us, James, who wants to fuck away all that pain and redeem his body. By fucking he wants to ameliorate the stinging ache of those dozens and dozens of swirled-up and curled-round, purple scars, looking like so many sleeping snakes and piles of ruined coins. He wants to discover a livable peace—as if he's come up a path in a vast evergreen woods, come upon a comfortable cabin as solid as a castle keep, and approached, calling, "*Hello the house*," been welcomed in, given a hot and filling dinner, then shown a bed in the attic (a pallet of sweet dry grass and slim cedar shavings) and fallen asleep.

Paco lies on his back, smelling the starched linen on her bed, Cathy's eau de cologne and pink talc, the pungent tin-and-tar porch roof—the powerfully rank sweetness of their sweat. Paco stares up at the darkened ceiling and the curled chips of paint that hang down as thick as a shedding winter shag. Then abruptly, he remembers Gallagher's Bangkok R&R tattoo, the red-and-black dragon that covered his forearm from his wrist to his elbow (that tattoo a goddamned work of art, everyone said, a regular fucking masterpiece). He sees the tattoo, then suddenly remembers the rape of the VC girl, and the dreams he has had of the rape.

He winces and squirms; his whole body jerks, but he cannot choose but remember.

Gallagher had this girl by the hair. She wasn't just anybody, you understand, James—not some dirt farmer's wife or one of those godawful ugly camp-following whores; not some poor son-of-a-bitch's tagalong sister pestering everyone with her whining; not some rear-rank slick-sleeve private (who doesn't know dismounted, close-order drill from shit and Shinola), who pushed a pencil or wrapped bandages, and smiled big and pretty when the Swedish journalists shot through on the grand tour. No, James, she was as hard a hardcore VC as they come (by the look of the miles on her face). She had ambushed the 1st platoon's night listening post just shy of first light and shot two of them dead (the third guy had tackled her when she ran, and beat the shit out of her bringing her in), and now the company was hunkered down, wet and sullen, plenty pissed off, waiting for the dust-off and a couple of body bags. Gallagher was nibbling on a bar of Hershey's Tropical Chocolate (the color of dogshit) and sipping heavily chlorinated canteen water, watching her squatting on her haunches, wolfing down a C-ration can of ham and eggs some fucking new guy had given her—wolfing it down with a plastic spoon and her thumb—and finally Gallagher had had enough. The next thing you know, James, he had her by the hair and was swearing up a storm, hauling her this way and that (the spit bubbles at the corners of his mouth slurring his words) through the company to this brick-and-stucco hooch off to one side of the clearing that's roofless and fucked over with mortar and artillery hits up one side and down the other.

Paco sees wiseacre ("Fuck-you-up-boy") Gallagher haul that girl through the night laager; sees this dude and that peel off from their night positions and follow across the hard, bare clay, smacking their lips to a fare-thee-well—there's a bunch of guys in that company want a piece of *that* gook. Gallagher waltzes her into the room at the side, no doubt a bedroom. And the whole time the girl looked at that red-and-black tattoo out of the corners of her eyes like a fretted, hysterical dog. She could see only the slick-sweated tail, curled and twisted and twined around itself, and the stumpy, lizardlike legs; the long, reddish tongue curled around the snout and head and the long, curving neck and forelegs, but she could not see that much because of the way Gallagher had her by the hair.

(Take your hand, James, and reach around the top of your head, grab as much hair as you can grab in one hand and *yank*, then press that arm tight against the side of your head and look over, hard, at your arm out of the corners of your eyes. That's as much of Gallagher's arm as the girl saw.)

The hooch was claustrophobic, with thick walls and small rooms, and smelled like an old wet dog. Gallagher and the rest of us reeked sourly of issue mosquito repellent and camouflage stick and marijuana, sopping-wet clothes and bloody jungle rot (around the crotch and under our arms). The girl smelled of jungle junk and cordite—gunpowder, James—and piss.

(If the zip had been a man, we would not have bothered with the motherfucker, you understand that, don't you? Gallagher, or whoever, would have grabbed that son-of-a-bitch by his whole head of hair—that zip staring at the twined and twisted and curlicued red-and-black tail of that Bangkok R&R tattoo, knowing jolly well it was going to be the last thing he'd be likely to get a good clean look at in *this* life. Gallagher would have dragged him over to the hooch, jerking him clean off his feet every other step, snatching his head this way and that for good measure, grumbling through his teeth about the one and only way to put the chill on gooks. We would have taken him around to the side, held him straight-backed against the beat-to-hell brick-and-stucco hooch wall—the zip's eyes that big and his poor little asshole squeezed tighter than a four-inch wad of double sawbucks. That cocksucker would have been pounded on till his face was beat to shit; till our arms were tired—"Anybody else want a poke at him? Going once. Twice. Three fuckin' times." Then someone would have held him while Jonesy pulled out his pearl-handled straight razor just as slow and catlike and quiet as a barber commencing to trim around your ears. Jonesy would have flicked that sucker open with a flashy snap, showing that puffy-eyed, bloody-faced zip four inches of the goddamnedest Swedish steel he's likely to come across, and then just as slow and calm and cool as you'd have a melon, James, Jonesy would have slit that zip's throat from nine to three. And he wouldn't have cut him the way he snipped ears; wouldn't have cut him the way he whittled booby-trap tripwire stakes for Paco; no, he'd cut him with a slow sweep of the hand and arm, the same as reapers sweep those long-handled scythes—that long, bare-armed motion that makes their sweat pop and the yellow wheat lie back in thick shocks. Beautiful and terrible.

The razor cut would have bled horrible abundance, the zip's life gushing from his neck in terrific spurts, with him watching it, hardly believing—his face wax-white. It would have been as though he'd been garroted, good and proper hard; only, the razor cut would have hissed and bubbled and gurgled the way strangling with a wire simply cannot.

You've got to understand, James, that if the zip had been a man we would have punched on him, then killed him right then and there and left him for dead.)

So Gallagher hauled the woman off by the hair, and she looked as hard as hard can be at that red-and-black tattoo. And she was naked from the waist up, but nothing much to look at, so no one was much looking at her, and she was flailing her arms, trying to gouge Gallagher's eyes out, and swinging her legs, trying to kick him in the balls, but Gallagher was doing a pretty good job of blocking her punches and holding her back (was a wrestler, Gallagher was). She screamed in Viet that no one understood, but could figure out pretty well, "Pig. You *pig*. GI beaucoup number ten goddamned shit-eating fucking pig. I *spit* on you!" Gallagher dodged and bobbed and weaved, and chuckled, saying, "Sure, Sweet Pea, sure!" He pulled her—arms flailing, legs kicking, screaming that hysterical gibberish at the top of her lungs. And everybody in the whole ballpark knew they weren't going in that hooch to argue who can throw the blandest brush-back pitch—Lyle Walsh or Dub Patterson. Even Lieutenant John Ridley Stennett (Dartmouth, 1967) knew, for a refreshing fucking change. Good morning to you, Lieutenant!

We took her into the side room, and there wasn't much of the roof left, but there were chunks of tiles and scraps of air-burst howitzer shrapnel, and the ass end of some bullshit furniture littered around. You walked on the stone parquet floor and the crumbs of terra-cotta roofing tile, and it crunched—like glass would grind and snap and squeak underfoot. That hooch was a ruin, James, a regular stone riot of ruin. Gallagher and the girl, Jonesy and Paco and the rest of us, stood in the brightening overcast (more like intense, hazy glare) that made us squint involuntarily, as though we were reading a fine-print contract.

Jonesy took a long stretch of black commo wire and whipped a handful of it into the open air. It looped high over the ridgepole and came down, smacking Paco in the leg. Gallagher and Paco held the girl down firmly while Jonesy tied her wrists together behind her back, then hauled on that wire the same as if he were hoisting the morning colors, just as crisp and snappy as the book says—*The Manual of Arms*, James, the twenty-two-dash-five, we called it. The girl had to bend over some or dislocate both arms, so she bent down over this raw wood thing about the size of a kitchen table. The girl was scared shitless, chilly and shuddering, glossy and greasy with sweat, and was all but tempted to ask them as one human being to another not to rape her, not to kill her, but she didn't speak English.

There was considerable jostling and arm punching, jawing and grab-ass back and forth, and everyone formed a rough line, so just for a moment Paco got to stand there and take a long look. A peasant girl, not more than fourteen, say, or sixteen. And by the look of her back she had worked, *hard*, every day of her life. She was not beefy, though. None of the Viets were big, but then sharecropping doesn't tend to turn out strapping-big hale-and-hearty offspring. Ask someone who knows shit from shit and Shinola about farming, James, and he will tell you that sharecropping is a long, hard way to get down to business and get some. The dumbest dumbshit on the face of this earth (who knows just enough about farming to follow a horse around with a coal shovel) knows that sharecropping sucks; knows you can't spend your life sharing your crop with *yourself*, much less split it between you and the Man. But who knows, maybe Viets enjoyed being gaunt and rickety, rheumy and toothless. Maybe. They got along well enough on forty-and-found—what they grew and what they scrounged—and it was a long row to hoe, James. Viet sharecroppers ate rice and greens and fish heads, and such as that—whatever they caught, whatever they could lay their bare hands on.

Jonesy stepped up behind the girl, took out his pearl-handled straight razor with a magician's flourish—acting real gaudy and showy the way he could—and slit her flimsy black pants from the cuffs to the waistband, just the same as you'd zip a parka right up to your chin. Then he hauled off and hoisted her up another notch or two for good measure, until her shoulders turned white (clear on the other side of the laager Lieutenant Stennett heard the commo wire squeak against the ridgepole). Then Gallagher stepped up behind her, between her feet, unbuttoned his fly, and eased out his cock. He leaned on her hard, James, rubbing himself up a fine hard-on, and slipped it into her. Then he commenced to fuck her, hard, pressing his big meaty hand into the middle of her back.

Gallagher and Jonesy started to grin and wanted to laugh, and a couple dudes *did* laugh, because no one in the company had had any pussy for a month of Sundays (except for Lieutenant Stennett, who hadn't been in this man's army that long).

And when Gallagher finished, Jonesy fucked her, and when Jonesy was done, half the fucking company was standing in line and commenced to fuck her ragged. The girl bit the inside of her cheek to keep back the rancor. The line of dudes crowded the low and narrow doorway, drinking bitterly sour canteen water and the warm beers

they'd been saving, smoking cigars and jays, and watching one another while they ground the girl into the rubble. Her eyes got bigger
than a deer's, and the chunks and slivers of tile got ground into her
scalp and face, her breasts and stomach, and Jesus-fucking-Christ, she
had her nostrils flared and teeth clenched and eyes squinted, tearing
at the sheer humiliating, grinding pain of it. (Paco remembers feeling
her whole body pucker down; feels her bowels, right here and now,
squeezing as tight as if you were wringing out a rag, James; can see the
huge red mark in the middle of her back; hears her involuntarily
snorting and spitting; can see the broad smudge of blood on the table
as clear as day; hears all those dudes walking on all that rubble.)
Dudes still ambled over to the doorway to watch, to call out coaching,
taking their turns, hanging around the side of the building after—
some getting back in line.

And clean across the clearing—way the hell on the other side of the
laager; way the fuck out in left field on the other side of the moon—
Lieutenant Stennett squatted on his steel pot with his knees up and
his back to the doings in the hooch, making himself a canteen cup of
coffee. The dudes at the quiet end of the line heard the feathery hiss
of the thumb-sized chunk of C-4 plastic explosive, and the clank of
the green bamboo twig he stirred it with, but don't you know, James,
we didn't pay it so much as a never-you-mind. The lieutenant heard
the grinding, raucous laughter behind him; heard the raw-wood table
squeak and creak, creeping across the floor, shoved at and shoved at
the way you might pound at a kitchen table with the heel of your
hand. And if he'd had a mind to, he could have glanced back over his
shoulder and seen that line and that bit of commo wire looped over
the mahogany ridgepole. He knew what was what in that hooch all
right, all right—he might have been a fool, James, but he wasn't a
stone fool. He worked his shoulders, trying to ease that damp, raw-
boned, sticky-sweaty feeling of sleep out of his back. He kept his back
and his head slumped, tending his hissing little C-4 fire, stirring the
caked and lumpy thousand-year-old C-ration instant coffee furiously
with a knotted bamboo stick until you'd have thought he was going to
wear a hole in it, if you didn't know better; studying it like it might be
entrails.

And when everyone had had as many turns as he wanted (Paco fascinated by the huge red welt in the middle of her back), as many turns as he could stand, Gallagher took the girl out behind that bullshit brick-and-stucco hooch, yanking her this way and that by the whole head of her hair (later that afternoon we noticed black hairs on the back of his arm). He had a hold of her the way you'd grab some shrimpy little fucker by the throat—motherfuck-you-up street-mean and businesslike—and he slammed her against the wall and hoisted her up until her gnarled toes barely touched the ground. But the girl didn't much fucking care, James. There was spit and snot, blood and drool and cum all over her, and she'd pissed herself. Her eyes had that dead, clammy glare to them, and she didn't seem to know what was happening anymore. Gallagher slipped his .357 Magnum out of its holster and leaned the barrel deftly against her breastbone. "We gonna play us a little game. We gonna play tag," he said in a clear and resonant voice, "but who's it?" he said, and jerked the girl once, and her eyes snapped. "Who's it? Why, you are, Sweet Pea."

Then he put the muzzle of the pistol to her forehead, between her eyebrows. He held her up stiffly by the hair and worked his finger on it, to get a good grip (a .357 ain't some chickenshit, metal-shop, hand-crank zip gun, James). The girl glared at the red-and-black tattoo of the dragon, and she was almost near enough to his hand to purse her lips and kiss his knuckles. And then in the middle of us jostling and grab-assing, Gallagher squeezed off a round. Boom.

The pistol bucked and Gallagher's whole body shimmered with the concussion; we all eyed him quickly. Some of the fucking new guys flinched, and Lieutenant Stennett positively jerked his arm and splashed himself with scalding coffee. Smoke rose from the pistol and Gallagher's hand in a cloud, in wisps. If you had listened closely, you would have heard the ring of metal on metal, the same as you hear a 105 howitzer ring with that *tang* sound; a sound the same as if you had hauled off and whacked a 30-foot I beam with a 10-pound ball-peen—a sound you feel in every bone of your body from the marrow out.

Her head was so close to the hooch that we heard the shot simultaneously with the clack and clatter of bone chips against the brick and

stucco. The pistol slug and the hard, splintered chips of brick rico-
cheted and struck her in the meatiest part of her back, between her
shoulder blades. Just that quick there was blood all over everything
and everyone, and splinters of bone and brick stuck to our clothes and
the bare skin of our arms and faces. And the girl was dead in that
instant (and we mean *stone* dead, James) and lay in her own abundant
blood. Her hands and arms fluttered the same as a dog's when it
dreams.

Paco remembers the spray of blood, the splatter of brick and bone
chips on Gallagher and Jonesy and *everyone*, as thick as freckles, and
how it sparkled. He remembers that quick, tingling itch of the spray,
like a mist of rain blown through a porch screen. He remembers the
brown bloodstains down the fronts of our trousers for days afterward;
remembers Gallagher turning to the rest of us, still holding her scalp,
and how we made a path for him when he walked away, hearing him
say out loud (the timbre and resonance of his voice reverberating
superbly), as if we were in an auditorium, *"That's* how you put the
cool on gooks."

Some of us shook out of our reverie and walked away, too, but the
rest lingered with resentful and curious fascination, staring down at
the bloody, filthy bottoms of her feet, her slumped head and flat,
mannish face. The whole expression of her body was drawn to the dry,
drooping lips and lolling tongue. We looked at her and ourselves,
drawing breath again and again, and knew that this was a moment of
evil, that we would never live the same. It even began to dawn on
Lieutenant Stennett, the English major from Dartmouth, who'd been
sitting pucker-assed on the other side of the night laager with his back
as round and smooth as a beach pebble, still stirring his C-ration
coffee and minding his Ps and Qs like there was no tomorrow. Good
morning to you, Lieutenant. Ain't you got that coffee fried yet?

Soon enough, we heard the thump-thump-thump, whomp-whomp-
whomp of the dust-off chopper come to pick up the KIAs. It circled
the laager once, coming around upwind, and landed in the middle of
the hooch yard. One by one we backed away from the girl's corpse
and went to help load the body bags, and by that time the girl—
whatever her name was—was still. When the chopper was loaded, it

rose and left. Lieutenant Stennett got word from Colonel Hubbel for us to hit the road for Fire Base Carolyne. We finished breakfast, saddled up our rucksacks, turned our back to that hooch, and left that place—we never went back. Perhaps the girl's body was found later, and buried, but we would never know.

Paco sprawls spread-eagle on his bed in his one-room room, itchy hot and stinking drunk, thinking about Gallagher's red-and-black tattoo and the girl and the rape, and that look the dust-off medics gave us.

There is nothing to do for the squeeze-you-down heat but lie still—it is too oppressive for anything else. Cathy and Marty-boy are still fucking up a storm an arm's length away, their bodies slapping together, Cathy sighing contentedly. Paco's cock is still iron hard and his groin aches—he cannot help his hard-on. And when they finish Cathy says in an exhausted wine-drunk voice, "Oh, Marty-boy, that was just super!" Marty-boy pours the last of their warm Roditys richly into his plastic cold-drink cup, and Paco hears the pat of dry bare feet on the cheap carpet as they share from the cup. Marty-boy stands among the pretzel crumbs and old wine spills, easy and quiet, feeling the bit of cool of the dark drift in the tall front windows, then hustles into his pants, the loose change jangling and keys rattling. He cinches his belt and ties his sneakers, all the while looking at Cathy lazily rolling and curling this way and that—her beautiful body glistening—cuddling herself. Paco hears Marty-boy leave her rooms, step gingerly down the stairway and out the front door of the hotel, easing the screen door back in its jamb (gleaming at his own cleverness). Paco hears him walk down the middle of the street past the Texas Lunch, scuffing the pavement along the dashed white center line as he goes.

Cathy lounges on her bed, murmuring. Paco lies on his bed with his eyes closed, but awake, daydreaming, brushing the fuzzy wallpaper with the back of his hand and waiting for first light, the coolest part of the day.

Love Medicine

LOUISE ERDRICH

1984

A BRIDGE
(1973)

It was the harsh spring that everybody thought would never end. All the way down to Fargo on the Jackrabbit bus Albertine gulped the rank, enclosed, passenger breath as though she could encompass the strangeness of so many other people by exchanging air with them, by replacing her own scent with theirs. She didn't close her eyes to nap even once during travel, because this was the first time she'd traveled anywhere alone. She was fifteen years old, and she was running away from home. When the sky deepened, casting bleak purple shadows along the snow ditches, she went even tenser than when she'd first walked up the ridged stairs of the vehicle.

She watched carefully as the dark covered all. The yard lights of farms, like warning beacons upon the sea or wide-flung constellations of stars, blinked on, deceptively close.

The bus came upon the city and the lights grew denser, reflecting up into the cloud cover, a transparent orange-pink that floated over the winking points of signs and low black buildings. The streets looked slick, deep green, from the windows of the bus.

The driver made a small rasping sound into the microphone and announced their arrival at the Fargo terminal.

Stepping into the bus station, the crowd of people in the hitched, plastic seats looked to Albertine like one big knot, a linked and doubled chain of coats, scarves, black-and-gray Herbst shopping bags, broad pale cheeks and noses. She wasn't sure what to do next. A chair was open. Beside it a standing ashtray bristled with butts, crushed soft-drink cups, flattened straws. Albertine sat down in the chair and stared at the clock. She frowned as though she were impatient for the next bus, but that was just a precaution. How long would they let her sit? This was as far as she had money to go. The compressed bundle of her jeans and underwear, tied in a thick sweater, felt reassuring as a baby against her stomach, and she clutched it close.

Lights of all colors, vaguely darkened and skewed in the thick glass doors, zipped up and down the sides of buildings. She glanced all around and back to the clock again. Minutes passed. Slow fright took her as she sat in the chair; she would have to go out soon. How many hours did she have left? The clock said eight. She sat stiffly, counting the moments, waiting for something to tell her what to do.

Now that she was in the city, all the daydreams she'd had were useless. She had not foreseen the blind crowd or the fierce activity of the lights outside the station. And then it seemed to her that she had been sitting in the chair too long. Panic tightened her throat. Without considering, in an almost desperate shuffle, she took her bundle and entered the ladies' room.

Fearing thieves, she took the bundle into the stall and held it awk-wardly on her lap. Afterward, she washed her face, combed and redid the tin barrette that held her long hair off her forehead, then sat in the lobby. She let her eyes close. Behind her eyelids dim shapes billowed outward. Her body seemed to shrink and contract as in childish fever dreams when she lost all sense of the actual proportion of things and knew herself as bitterly small. She had come here for some reason, but couldn't remember what that was.

As it happened, then, because she didn't have anything particular in mind, the man seemed just what she needed when he appeared.

He needed her worse, but she didn't know that. He stood for an instant against the doors, long enough for Albertine to notice that his cropped hair was black, his skin was pale brown, thick and rough. He wore a dull green army jacket. She caught a good look at his profile, the blunt chin, big nose, harsh brow.

He was handsome, good-looking at least, and could have been an Indian. He even could have been a Chippewa. He walked out into the street.

She started after him. Partly because she didn't know what she was looking for, partly because he was a soldier like her father, and partly because he could have been an Indian, she followed. It seemed to her that he had cleared a path of safety through the door into the street. But when she stepped outside he had disappeared. She faltered, then told herself to keep walking toward the boldest lights.

Northern Pacific Avenue was the central thoroughfare of the dingy feel-good roll of Indian bars, western-wear stores, pawn shops, and Christian Revival Missions that Fargo was trying to eradicate. The strip had diminished under the town's urban-renewal project: asphalt plains and swooping concrete interchanges shouldered the remaining bars into an intricate huddle, lit for action at this hour. The giant cartoon outline of a cat, eyes fringed in pink neon, winked and switched its glittering tail. Farther down the street a cowgirl tall as a building tossed her lariat in slow heart-shaped loops. Beneath her glowing heels men slouched, passing bags crimped back for bottle-necks.

The night was cold. Albertine stepped into the recessed door stoop of a small shop. Its window displayed secondhand toasters. The other side of the street was livelier. She saw two Indian men, hair falling in cowlicks over their faces, dragging a limp, dazed woman between them. An alley swallowed them. Another woman in a tiger-skin skirt and long boots posed briefly in a doorway. A short round oriental man sprang out of nowhere, gesturing emphatically to someone who wasn't there. He went up the stairs of a doorway labeled ROOMS. That was the doorway Albertine decided she would try for a place to sleep, when things quieted down. For now she was content to watch, shifting from foot to foot, arms crossed over her bundle.

Then she saw the soldier again.

He was walking quickly, duffel hoisted up his shoulder, along the opposite side of the street. Again she followed. Stepping from her doorway she walked parallel with him, bundle slung from her hand

and bouncing off her legs. He must have been a little over six feet. She was tall herself and always conscious of the height of men. She stopped when he paused before a windowful of pearl-button shirts, buff Stetsons, and thick-nosed pawned pistols. He stayed there a long time, moving from one display to the next. He was never still. He smoked quickly, jittering, dragging hard and snapping the cigarette against his middle finger. He turned back and forth, constantly aware of who was passing or what was making what noise where.

He knew the girl had been following and watching.

He knew she was watching now. He had noticed her first in the bus station. Her straight brown hair and Indian eyes drew him, even though she was too young. She was tall, strong, twice the size of most Vietnamese. It had been a long time since he'd seen any Indian women, even a breed. He had been a soldier, was now a veteran, had seen nine months of combat in the Annamese Cordillera before the NVA captured him somewhere near Pleiku. They kept him half a year. He was released after an honorable peace was not achieved, after the evacuation. Returning home he had been fouled up in red tape, routinely questioned by a military psychiatrist, dismissed. It had been three weeks, only that, since the big C-141 and Gia Lam airfield.

He examined the pawnshop window again.

Enough of this, he thought. He turned to face her.

Her legs were long, slightly bowed. Jeans lapped her toed-in boots. She'd be good with a horse. One hand was tensed in the pocket of a cheap black nylon parka. Passing headlights periodically lit her face— wide with strong, jutting bones. Not pretty yet, a kid trying to look old. Jailbait. She stared back at him through traffic. She was carrying a knotted bundle.

He had seen so many with their children, possessions, animals tied in cloths across their backs, under their breasts, bundles dragged in frail carts. He had seen them bolting under fire, arms wrapped around small packages. Some of the packages, loosely held the way hers was, exploded. Henry Lamartine Junior carried enough shrapnel deep inside of him, still working its way out, to set off the metal detector in the airport. He had been physically searched there in a small cur-tained booth. When he told the guard what the problem was, the man just looked at him and said nothing, dumb as stone. Henry had wanted to crush that stupid face the way you crumple a ball of wax paper.

The girl did not look stupid. She only looked young. She turned away. He thought that she might walk off carrying that bundle. She could go anywhere. Possibility of danger. Contents of bundle that could rip through flesh and strike bone. It was as much the sense of danger, the almost sweet familiarity he had with risk by now, as it was the attraction for her that made him put his hands out, stopping traffic, and cross to where she stood.

He turned out to be from a family she knew. A crazy Lamartine boy. Henry.

"I know your brother Lyman," she said. "I heard about you. How'd you get loose?"

"I'm like my brother Gerry. No jail built that can hold me either." He grinned when she told him her name.

"Old Man Kashpaw know you're hanging out on NP Avenue?"

Albertine took his arm. "I'm thirsty," she said.

They walked beneath the cowgirl's lariat and found a table in the Round-Up Bar. After two drinks there they moved down the street, and kept moving on. Somewhere later that night, in the whiskey, her hand brushed his. He would not let go.

"You know any bar tricks?" she asked. "Show me one."

He dropped her hand and she made it into a fist and shoved it in her pocket. She still clutched her bundle tight between her feet, under the table. He got three steak knives and two water glasses from the bartender and brought them back to the table. He set the glasses down half a foot apart. Then he interlapped the knives so they made a bridge between the glass lips, a bridge of knives suspended in air.

Albertine looked at the precarious, linked edges.

She was nervous, but she didn't recognize this feeling, because it was part of a whirl in her stomach that was like excitement.

When Henry and Albertine left the bar it was very late, past last call, past closing. The streets were quiet. He put his arm around her and she stumbled once beneath its weight.

. . .

A small black-and-white television flickered on a high shelf behind the hotel desk. President Nixon's face drooped across the screen. The night clerk took Henry's ten-dollar bill, and threw it into the cash drawer and sleepily shoved a pen and lined slip across the counter toward him. The clerk was a mound of flesh tapering into a small thick skull. Waiting for the soldier to sign, he yawned so hugely that tears sprang from his eyes. It did not interest him that the man and girl, both Indian or Mexicans, whatever, signed in as Mr. and Mrs. Howdy Doody and were shacking up for the night. Whatever. He yawned again.

Motherfucker, Henry thought, lazy motherfucker, aren't you? Drunk, he had taken a violent dislike to the man. I could off this fat shit, he told himself. But Albertine was there. "Advise restraint," he said out loud. She didn't seem to hear. The place was well off the avenue, and the short upstairs hall was quiet. Henry steered her easily before him, touching her shoulder blades through the bunched padding in the nylon jacket. He shook the thought of the fat clerk away, far as possible.

"Angel, where's your wings," he whispered into her hair. "They should be here." He pressed the ends of his fingers hard against her jutting bones.

Her laugh was high and soft. He fumbled for the key. He was not used to having keys again and always forgot where he put them. Groping, patting, he fished the room key from his jacket and put it into the lock. She was poised, half turned from what she might see when the door opened. He waved her in. Once she entered and stood in the hard overhead light, he saw that she was bone tired, sagging from the broad sawhorse shoulders down, her hair wrenched in a clump by the barrette. He was drunker than she was. She had stopped after a few and let him go on drinking, talking, until he spilled too many and knew it was time to taper off.

There was no table lamp. He turned off the overhead light and left on the one over the bathroom mirror.

"Wanna use the head?"

At first she shook her head dumbly, no, and looked at the floor.

But then I can close the door and he'll be out there, she thought.

She walked past him. He heard water rush into the sink. The other sounds she tried to hide made him smile. Women are so fucking cute sometimes it hurts. It really hurts.

Don't ever want to come out of here. She leaned her forehead on cool tile.

"When angel showers," he was singing to her closed door, "come your way. They bring the flowers that bloom in May."

He steadied himself on the iron bed rails, tried to pull his boots off, went to his knees.

"Keep looking for a bluebird and listen. . . . I know by God you were pissing in there. I heard you. It sounded like rain on a tin roof."

Then he was beating his chest lightly, like in the cold mission church he had served in when he was eight.

"Mea culpa, mea culpa, I am not worthy that you should come under my roof."

He tried to stand.

Hearing the sounds of a toothbrush he swayed backward, laughing. It sounded ridiculous. Sitting on the floor, stiff legged, he took off his boots and socks, then stood up warily to ease off his pants, unbutton his shirt. He set the bottle of Four Roses on a chair where he could reach it and turned down the covers on the bed. Then he crawled in and watched the crack of light around all four sides of the bathroom door.

"It was rehung a size too small," he said in a loud critical voice. "Or else it shrunk in the frame." He laughed again.

He is out of his mind.

She came through the door, put some clothes down neatly folded, and disappeared again. "If I close my eyes and imagine very hard what you're doing . . ." He addressed the bottle, then unscrewed the top. With his eyes shut he drank the rough whiskey. It left a sweet burn going down, and when he looked again his vision had narrowed.

He said those men took trophies. Skin pressed in the pages of a book.

There was often a stage in his drunkenness where his eyesight tunneled, like looking through the wrong end of binoculars. He had to be very careful now to remember where he was. He did not dare take his eyes from the shrinking door. "Please . . . ," he urged the dark room, "don't . . . ," fearing something might break the concentration. But he kept tight control. Advise restraint. Advise restraint, his brain tapped. He began connecting each loud invisible rustle with a very specific movement that the woman must make as she undressed. From top to bottom. He undressed her mentally with slow deliberation and no desire. Then suddenly, naked. She had even rolled her socks and stuck them in her boots.

She should have come out then, but she didn't. His heart pumped.

Concentration began to slacken. The image of her fled. He rolled from the bed and started to the door, feeling his way along the edge of the mattress until he lost it and had to cross long steps of endless space, where he thought water lapped his ankles. The rustling stopped. Silence warns. He was going to kick and jump aside like in the village back there, but from somewhere he gained a measure of control. He gripped the handle. The door swung in. The light seemed to move around her in sheets, and the tunnel widened.

On the tiny square of floor, still dressed, the bundle she had carried opened and spread all around her, she crouched low.

And he saw her as the woman back there.

How the hell could you figure them?

She looked at him. They had used a bayonet. She was out of her mind. You, me, same. Same. She pointed to her eyes and his eyes. The Asian, folded eyes of some Chippewas. She was hemorrhaging.

Question her.

Sir, she is dying, sir.

"And anyway, what could I have asked? Huh? What the hell?"

Albertine was looking at him, staring at him. He realized he had spoken out loud.

The brown hair swung over her face as she bent, smoothing a red handkerchief into a small square. She was wrapping things back into her bundle. He tucked a gray towel around his waist and lowered himself onto the edge of the stool. Her clothing was spread between them. He bent over and picked up a thin long-waisted pair of cotton underpants, doubled them, put them back.

"I'll help you," he said.

"I don't need any help."

He put his hands in his lap. He wanted cigarettes now, badly, but he didn't want to go back and look for them in the dark where the bed was.

"Would you get me my smokes? I'm drunk."

His voice caught in his throat. She did not answer or look at him but went out of the room.

I shouldn't stay here, she thought. *But all my things are here. He was talking to himself.*

While she was gone he noticed that his face, hands, chest were cold with sweat. His hands trembled when he lighted the Marlboro.

Weak, he thought, holding the smoke in his lungs. But now he was used to the shaking, this kind of shaking, which meant that the tightness was lowering, lowering him. He lit one cigarette from another and dropped the ends in the bowl beneath his hip. As he watched her, his breathing gradually calmed. The blackness edging his vision dropped away. The movements of her hands were humble and certain. She had a long curved back and those jutting shoulder blades, like wings of horn.

How long can I sit here and let him watch me like this? She felt like she was still riding on the bus. Her blood rocked.

"Please," he said finally, when she had put everything in order several times, "can we go to bed? I won't touch you. Too drunk anyhow."

"All right."

He took her hand and led her from the bathroom, half shutting the door.

"I'm going to leave the light on if that's okay with you."

She nodded silently.

She took her jeans, boots, socks off, then slid into bed. She was wearing a long-sleeved shirt and underwear. Once beside him, although she had been half asleep as she folded her clothes, she became completely alert, conscious of his lightest movement.

Good night. *I'm going to shut my eyes and pretend to sleep.*

But the pretense just increased her sensitivity to his breathing, to the way the sheets scratched against his body.

The CREDIT sign across the street ticked on by slow stages until the letters completed, flared three times in silence. She turned to him. She propped herself on her elbow and unbuttoned her shirt. He took her hand away and worked the cloth off her shoulders. She wore a thick cotton brassiere. He put both arms around her and undid the hook. Once she was naked beneath him, he could hold off no longer. In panic, he tried to surge inside of her.

Her fear excited him so much, though, that he came helplessly, pressed against her, before he was even hard. She was quiet, waiting for him to say something. She touched his face, but he did not speak, so she rolled away from him.

Henry was not drunk anymore, not in the least. He knew that in a moment he would want her again, the right way, and in this expectation he listened as she pretended to sleep. Her back curved, a warm slope. The length and breadth of her seemed edgeless. He felt wonder and moved closer. She tensed. Her breathing changed.

She gave off a fetid traveler's warmth, cigarette smoke, bus-seat smell, a winy undertone from what they'd drunk, the crackery smell of snow melted into unwashed hair, a flowery heat from her armpits.

He thought of diving off a riverbank, a bridge.

He closed his eyes and saw the water, the whirling patterns, below. He pushed her over, face down, and pinned her from behind. He spread her legs with his knees and pulled her toward him.

Muffled, slogged in pillows, she gripped the head bars. He pushed into her. She made a harsh sound. Her back was board hard, resistant. Then she gave with a cry. He touched her with the cushioned part of his fingers until she softened to him. She opened. The bones of her pelvis creaked wide, like the petals of a wooden flower, and he thought she came. Then he did, too. Wobbling then surging smoothly forward, he came whispering that he loved her.

Afterward, he let her go, put his face in dark hair behind her ear, and was about to whisper love talk, but she rolled out from under his chest.

She got as far away from him as possible. It was, to Henry, as if she had crossed a deep river and disappeared. He lay next to her, divided from her, just outside and with no way to follow.

At last she slept. Her even breath was a desolate comfort. He wound his hand in a long hank of her hair and, eventually, slept, too.

Near dawn Albertine could not remember where she was. She could not remember about the dull ache between her legs. She turned to the man and made the mistake of touching him in his sleep. His name came back to her. She was about to say his name.

He shrieked. Exploded.

She was stunned on the floor, gasping for breath against the wall before the syllables of his name escaped. Outside their room a door opened and shut. Somewhere in the room she heard his breath, a slow animal wheeze that froze her to the wall. He moved. The scent of his harsh fear hit her first as he came toward her.

In reflex, she crossed her arms before her face. A dark numbing terror had stopped her mind completely. But when he touched her he was weeping.

From

Carrying the Darkness

W. D. ᴇʜʀʜᴀʀᴛ, ᴇᴅɪᴛᴏʀ

1985

After Our War

JOHN BALABAN

After our war, the dismembered bits
—all those pierced eyes, ear slivers, jaw splinters,
gouged lips, odd tibias, skin flaps, and toes—
came squinting, wobbling, jabbering back.
The genitals, of course, were the most bizarre,
inching along roads like glowworms and slugs.
The living wanted them back, but good as new.
The dead, of course, had no use for them.
And the ghosts, the tens of thousands of abandoned souls
who had appeared like swamp fog in the city streets,
on the evening altars, and on doorsills of cratered homes,
also had no use for the scraps and bits
because, in their opinion, they looked good without them.
Since all things naturally return to their source,
these snags and tatters arrived, with immigrant uncertainty,
in the United States. It was almost home.
So, now, one can sometimes see a friend or a famous man talking
with an extra pair of lips glued and yammering on his cheek,
and this is why handshakes are often unpleasant,
why it is better, sometimes, not to look another in the eye,
why, at your daughter's breast thickens a hard keloidal scar.
After the war, with such Cheshire cats grinning in our trees,
will the ancient tales still tell us new truths?
Will the myriad world surrender new metaphor?
After our war, how will love speak?

D. C. BERRY

The sun   goes
         down
      a different way when

                              you
are lungshot in a rice
paddy and you
are taking a drink of
your own unhomeostatic
globules each

Time

you swallow a pail
of air   pumping like you
were

bailing out the whole
world   throw
   ing it in your leak
   ing   collapsible lung
that won't hold even
a good quart   and on
top of that   the sun
goes down

         Bang

ing the lung completely
flat.

Christmas

STEVE HASSETT

The Hessian in his last letter home
said in part

"they are all rebels here
who will not stand to fight
but each time fade before us
as water into sand . . .

the children beg in their rude hamlets

the women stare with hate

the men flee into the barrens at our approach
to lay in ambush

some talk of desertion . . .
were it not for the hatred
they bear us, more would do so

There is no glory here.
Tell Hals he must evade the Prince's levy
through exile or deformity

Winter is hard upon us. On the morrow we enter
Trenton. There we rest till the New Year. . . .

Patriot's Day

STEVE HASSETT

When the young girls rolled into one
and she without a face became
death's ikon,
   , and to the silence of our fathers
seemed to offer as redemption Vietnam,
we went.

Now we bring our dead to supper.

All our women are warriors
and the men burn slowly inward.

STEVE HASSETT

And what would you do, ma,
if eight of your sons step
out of the TV and begin
killing chickens and burning
hooches in the living room,
stepping on booby traps
and dying in the kitchen,
beating your husband and
taking him and shooting
skag and forgetting in
the bathroom?

would you lock up your daughter?
would you stash the apple pie?
would you change channels?

A Romance

1979

The Monkey Wars

1985

What Saves Us

1992

B RUCE W EIGL

Sailing to Bien Hoa

In my dream of the hydroplane
I'm sailing to Bien Hoa
the shrapnel in my thighs
like tiny glaciers.
I remember a flower,
a kite, a mannikin playing the guitar,
a yellow fish eating a bird, a truck
floating in urine, a rat carrying a banjo,
a fool counting the cards, a monkey praying,
a procession of whales, and far off
two children eating rice,
speaking French—
I'm sure of the children,
their damp flutes,
the long line of their vowels.

Surrounding Blues on the Way Down

I was barely in country. December, hot,
We slipped under rain black clouds
Opening around us like orchids.
He'd come to take me into the jungle
So I felt the loneliness
Though I did not yet hate the beautiful war.
Eighteen years old and a man
Was telling me how to stay alive
In the tropics he said would rot me—

Brothers of the heart he said and smiled
Until we came upon a mama san
Bent over from her stuffed sack of flowers.
We flew past her
But he hit the brakes hard,
He spun the tires backwards in the mud.
He did not hate the war either
But other reasons made him cry out to her
So she stopped,
She smiled her beetle black teeth at us,
She raised her arms in the air.

I have no excuse for myself,
I sat in that man's jeep in the rain
And watched him slam her to her knees,
The plastic butt of his M-16
Crashing down on her.
I was barely in country, the clouds
Hung like huge flowers, black
Like her teeth.

Girl at the Chu Lai Laundry

All this time I had forgotten.
My miserable platoon was moving out
One day in the war and I had my clothes in the laundry.
I ran the two dirt miles.
Convoy already forming behind me. I hit
The block of small hooches and saw her
Twist out the black rope of her hair in the sun.
She did not look up at me,
Not even when I called to her for my clothes.

Him, on the Bicycle

There was no light; there was no light at all . . .
   —Roethke

    In a liftship near Hue
    the door gunner is in a trance.
    He's that driver who falls
    asleep at the wheel
    between Pittsburgh and Cleveland
    staring at the Ho Chi Minh trail.

    Flares fall,
    where the river leaps
    I go stiff,
    I have to think, tropical.

    The door gunner sees movement,
    the pilot makes small circles:
    four men running, carrying rifles,
    one man on a bicycle.

    He pulls me out of the ship,
    there's firing far away.
    I'm on the back of the bike
    holding his hips.
    It's hard pumping for two,
    I hop off and push the bike.

    I'm brushing past trees,
    the man on the bike stops pumping,
    lifts his feet,
    we don't waste a stroke.

His hat flies off,
I catch it behind my back,
put it on, I want to live forever!

Like a blaze
streaming down the trail.

Anna Grasa

I came home from Vietnam.
My father had a sign
made at the foundry:
WELCOME HOME BRUCE
in orange glow paint.
He rented spotlights,
I had to squint.
WELCOME HOME BRUCE.

Out of the car I moved
up on the sign
dreaming myself full,
the sign that cut the sky,
my eyes burned.

But behind the terrible thing
I saw my grandmother,
beautiful Anna Grasa.
I couldn't tell her, tell her.

I clapped to myself,
clapped to the sound of her dress.
I could have put it on
she held me so close,
both of us could be inside.

Monkey

Out of the horror there rises a musical ache that is beautiful . . .
  —James Wright

> 1
> I am you are he she it is
> they are you are we are.
> I am you are he she it is
> they are you are we are.
> When they ask for your number
> pretend to be breathing.
> Forget the stinking jungle,
> force your fingers between the lines.
> Learn to get out of the dew.
> The snakes are thirsty.
> Bladders, water, boil it, drink it.
> Get out of your clothes:
> you can't move in your green clothes.
> Your O.D. in color issue.
> Get out the plates and those who ate,
> those who spent the night.
> Those small Vietnamese soldiers.
> They love to hold your hand.
> Back away from their dark cheeks.
> Small Vietnamese soldiers.
> They love to love you.
> I have no idea how it happened,
> I remember nothing but light.

2
I don't remember the hard
swallow of the lover.
I don't remember the burial of ears.
I don't remember
the time of the explosion.
This is the place curses are manufactured:
delivered like white tablets.
The survivor is spilling his bedpan.
He slips a curse into your pocket,
you're finally satisfied.
I don't remember the heat
in the hands,
the heat around the neck.

Good times bad times sleep
get up work. Sleep get up
good times bad times.
Work eat sleep good bad work times.
I like a certain cartoon of wounds.
The water which refused to dry.
I like a little unaccustomed mercy.
Pulling the trigger is all we have.
I hear a child.

3
I dropped to the bottom of a well.
I have a knife.
I cut someone with it.
Oh, I have the petrified eyebrows
of my Vietnam monkey.
My monkey from Vietnam.
My monkey.
Put your hand here.
It makes no sense.
I beat the monkey.

I didn't know him.
He was bloody.
He lowered his intestines
to my shoes. My shoes
spit-shined the moment
I learned to tie the bow.
I'm not on speaking terms
with anyone. In the wrong climate
a person can spoil,
the way a pair of boots slows you down. . . .

I don't know when I'm sleeping.
I don't know if what I'm saying
is anything at all.
I'll lie on my monkey bones.

4
I'm tired of the rice
falling in slow motion
like eggs from the smallest animal.
I'm twenty-five years old,
quiet, tired of the same mistakes,
the same greed, the same past.
The same past with its bleat
and pound of the dead,
with its hand grenade
tossed into a hootch on a dull Sunday
because when a man dies like that
his eyes sparkle,
his nose fills with witless nuance
because a farmer in Bong Son
has dead cows lolling
in a field of claymores
because the VC tie hooks to their comrades
because a spot of blood
is a number

because a woman is lifting
her dress across the big pond.

If we're soldiers we should smoke them
if we have them. Someone's bound
to point us in the right direction
sooner or later.

I'm tired and I'm glad you asked.

5
There is a hill.
Men run top hill.
Men take hill.
Give hill to man.

Me and my monkey
and me and my monkey
my Vietnamese monkey
my little brown monkey
came with me
to Guam and Hawaii
in Ohio he saw
my people he
jumped on my daddy
he slipped into mother
he baptized my sister
he's my little brown monkey
he came here from heaven
to give me his spirit imagine
my monkey my beautiful
monkey he saved me lifted
me above the punji
sticks above the mines
above the ground burning
above the dead above
the living above the

wounded dying the wounded
dying.

Men take hill away from smaller men.
Men take hill and give to fatter man.
Men take hill. Hill has number.
Men run up hill. Run down.

Winter Meditation, 1970

After the war, after the broken
marriage and failed life,
after the too many jobs,
the too many doctors, so sure
of their enchantments,
after the pills, the diving naked
through the window, after the pills,
their long drowning into nothing,
after the other woman,
the thousand years of grief
in her veins, after the loss,
the broken friends, the deaths
all around us like flies,
we are on the earth
and we have somehow come together
my mother, father
descended to the city where I hide,
to make them believe I'm not a ghost
but here somehow,
among the books and strangers,
the woman's clothes hung
indecently over the mirror,
among the prayers we surrender to no one,
somehow here, with a life,
and my father touches my arm
as if to feel the blood
the way you feel the corpse
when the family has departed

in the black limousine,
and my mother kisses me,
all but an illusive breath
of longing gone,
or no longer for me, that love.

The Things They Carried

TIM O'BRIEN

1990

SPEAKING OF COURAGE

The war was over and there was no place in particular to go. Norman Bowker followed the tar road on its seven-mile loop around the lake, then he started all over again, driving slowly, feeling safe inside his father's big Chevy, now and then looking out on the lake to watch the boats and water-skiers and scenery. It was Sunday and it was summer, and the town seemed pretty much the same. The lake lay flat and silvery against the sun. Along the road the houses were all low-slung and split-level and modern, with big porches and picture windows facing the water. The lawns were spacious. On the lake side of the road, where real estate was most valuable, the houses were handsome and set deep in, well kept and brightly painted, with docks jutting out into the lake, and boats moored and covered with canvas, and neat gardens, and sometimes even gardeners, and stone patios with barbecue spits and grills, and wooden shingles saying who lived where. On the other side of the road, to his left, the houses were also handsome, though less expensive and on a smaller scale and with no docks or boats or gardeners. The road was a sort of boundary between the affluent and the almost affluent, and to live on the lake side of the road was one of the few natural privileges in a town of the prairie— the difference between watching the sun set over cornfields or over water.

It was a graceful, good-sized lake. Back in high school, at night, he had driven around and around it with Sally Kramer, wondering if she'd want to pull into the shelter of Sunset Park, or other times with his friends, talking about urgent matters, worrying about the existence of God and theories of causation. Then, there had not been a war. But there had always been the lake, which was the town's first cause of existence, a place for immigrant settlers to put down their loads. Before the settlers were the Sioux, and before the Sioux were the vast open prairies, and before the prairies there was only ice. The lake bed had been dug out by the southernmost advance of the Wisconsin glacier. Fed by neither streams nor springs, the lake was often filthy and algaed, relying on fickle prairie rains for replenishment. Still, it was the only important body of water within forty miles, a source of pride, nice to look at on bright summer days, and later that evening it would color up with fireworks. Now, in the late afternoon, it lay calm and smooth, a good audience for silence, a seven-mile circumference that could be traveled by slow car in twenty-five minutes. It was not such a good lake for swimming. After high school, he'd caught an ear infection that had almost kept him out of the war. And the lake had drowned his friend Max Arnold, keeping him out of the war entirely. Max had been one who liked to talk about the existence of God. "No, I'm not saying *that*," he'd argue against the drone of the engine. "I'm saying it's possible as an *idea*, even necessary as an idea, a final cause in the whole structure of causation." Now he knew, perhaps. Before the war, they'd driven around the lake as friends, but now Max was just an idea, and most of Norman Bowker's other friends were living in Des Moines or Sioux City, or going to school somewhere, or holding down jobs. The high school girls were mostly gone or married. Sally Kramer, whose pictures he had once carried in his wallet, was one who had married. Her name was now Sally Gustafson and she lived in a pleasant blue house on the less expensive side of the lake road. On his third day home he'd seen her out mowing the lawn, still pretty in a lacy red blouse and white shorts. For a moment he'd almost pulled over, just to talk, but instead he'd pushed down hard on the gas pedal. She looked happy. She had her house and her new husband, and there was really nothing he could say to her.

The town seemed remote somehow. Sally was married and Max

was drowned and his father was at home watching baseball on national TV.

Norman Bowker shrugged. "No problem," he murmured.

Clockwise, as if in orbit, he took the Chevy on another seven-mile turn around the lake.

Even in late afternoon the day was hot. He turned on the air conditioner, then the radio, and he leaned back and let the cold air and music blow over him. Along the road, kicking stones in front of them, two young boys were hiking with knapsacks and toy rifles and canteens. He honked going by, but neither boy looked up. Already he had passed them six times, forty-two miles, nearly three hours without stop. He watched the boys recede in his rearview mirror. They turned a soft grayish color, like sand, before finally disappearing.

He tapped down lightly on the accelerator.

Out on the lake a man's motorboat had stalled; the man was bent over the engine with a wrench and a frown. Beyond the stalled boat there were other boats, and a few water-skiers, and the smooth July waters, and an immense flatness everywhere. Two mud hens floated stiffly beside a white dock.

The road curved west, where the sun had now dipped low. He figured it was close to five o'clock—twenty after, he guessed. The war had taught him to tell time without clocks, and even at night, waking from sleep, he could usually place it within ten minutes either way. What he should do, he thought, is stop at Sally's house and impress her with this new time-telling trick of his. They'd talk for a while, catching up on things, and then he'd say, "Well, better hit the road, it's five thirty-four," and she'd glance at her wristwatch and say, "Hey! How'd you *do* that?" and he'd give a casual shrug and tell her it was just one of those things you pick up. He'd keep it light. He wouldn't say anything about anything. "How's it being married?" he might ask, and he'd nod at whatever she answered with, and he would not say a word about how he'd almost won the Silver Star for valor.

He drove past Slater Park and across the causeway and past Sunset Park. The radio announcer sounded tired. The temperature in Des Moines was eighty-one degrees, and the time was five thirty-five, and "All you on the road, drive extra careful now on this fine Fourth of

July." If Sally had not been married, or if his father were not such a baseball fan, it would have been a good time to talk.

"The Silver Star?" his father might have said.

"Yes, but I didn't get it. Almost, but not quite."

And his father would have nodded, knowing full well that many brave men do not win medals for their bravery, and that others win medals for doing nothing. As a starting point, maybe, Norman Bowker might then have listed the seven medals he did win: the Combat Infantryman's Badge, the Air Medal, the Army Commendation Medal, the Good Conduct Medal, the Vietnam Campaign Medal, the Bronze Star, and the Purple Heart, though it wasn't much of a wound and did not leave a scar and did not hurt and never had. He would've explained to his father that none of these decorations was for uncommon valor. They were for common valor. The routine, daily stuff—just humping, just enduring—but that was worth something, wasn't it? Yes, it was. Worth plenty. The ribbons looked good on the uniform in his closet, and if his father were to ask, he would've explained what each signified and how he was proud of all of them, especially the Combat Infantryman's Badge, because it meant he had been there as a real soldier and had done all the things that soldiers do, and therefore it wasn't such a big deal that he could not bring himself to be uncommonly brave.

And then he would have talked about the medal he did not win and why he did not win it.

"I almost won the Silver Star," he would have said.

"How's that?"

"Just a story."

"So tell me," his father would have said.

Slowly then, circling the lake, Norman Bowker would have started by describing the Song Tra Bong. "A river," he would've said, "this slow flat muddy river." He would've explained how during the dry season it was exactly like any other river, nothing special, but how in October the monsoons began and the whole situation changed. For a solid week the rains never stopped, not once, and so after a few days the Song Tra Bong overflowed its banks and the land turned into a deep, thick muck for a half mile on either side. Just muck—no other word for it. Like quicksand, almost, except the stink was incredible. "You couldn't even sleep," he'd tell his father. "At night you'd find a high spot, and you'd doze off, but then later you'd wake up because you'd be buried in that slime. You'd just sink in. You'd feel it ooze up over your body and sort of suck you down. And the whole time there was that constant rain. I mean, it never stopped, not ever."

"Sounds pretty wet," his father would've said, pausing briefly. "So what happened?"

"You really want to hear this?"

"Hey, I'm your *father*."

Norman Bowker smiled. He looked out across the lake and imagined the feel of his tongue against the truth. "Well, this one time, this one night out by the river . . . I wasn't very brave."

"You have seven medals."

"Sure."

"Seven. Count 'em. You weren't a coward either."

"Well, maybe not. But I had the chance and I blew it. The stink, that's what got to me. I couldn't take that goddamn awful *smell*."

"If you don't want to say anymore—"

"I do want to."

"All right then. Slow and sweet, take your time."

The road descended into the outskirts of town, turning northwest past the junior college and the tennis courts, then past Chautauqua Park, where the picnic tables were spread with sheets of colored plastic and where picnickers sat in lawn chairs and listened to the high school band playing Sousa marches under the band shell. The music faded after a few blocks. He drove beneath a canopy of elms, then along a stretch of open shore, then past the municipal docks, where a woman in pedal pushers stood casting for bullheads. There were no other fish in the lake except for perch and a few worthless carp. It was a bad lake for swimming and fishing both.

He drove slowly. No hurry, nowhere to go. Inside the Chevy the air was cool and oily-smelling, and he took pleasure in the steady sounds of the engine and air conditioning. A tour bus feeling, in a way, except the town he was touring seemed dead. Through the windows, as if in a stop-motion photograph, the place looked as if it had been hit by nerve gas, everything still and lifeless, even the people. The town could not talk, and would not listen. "How'd you like to hear about the war?" he might have asked, but the place could only blink and shrug. It had no memory, therefore no guilt. The taxes got paid and the votes got counted and the agencies of government did their work briskly and politely. It was a brisk, polite town. It did not know shit about shit, and did not care to know.

Norman Bowker leaned back and considered what he might've said on the subject. He knew shit. It was his specialty. The smell, in particular, but also the numerous varieties of texture and taste. Someday he'd give a lecture on the topic. Put on a suit and tie and stand up in front of the Kiwanis club and tell the fuckers about all the wonderful shit he knew. Pass out samples, maybe.

Smiling at this, he clamped the steering wheel slightly right of center, which produced a smooth clockwise motion against the curve of the road. The Chevy seemed to know its own way.

The sun was lower now. Five fifty-five, he decided—six o'clock, tops.

Along an unused railway spur, four workmen labored in the shadowy red heat, setting up a platform and steel launchers for the evening fireworks. They were dressed alike in khaki trousers, work shirts, visored caps, and brown boots. Their faces were dark and smudgy. "Want to hear about the Silver Star I almost won?" Norman Bowker whispered, but none of the workmen looked up. Later they would blow color into the sky. The lake would sparkle with reds and blues and greens, like a mirror, and the picnickers would make low sounds of appreciation.

"Well, see, it never stopped raining," he would've said. "The muck was everywhere, you couldn't get away from it."

He would have paused a second.

Then he would have told about the night they bivouacked in a field along the Song Tra Bong. A big swampy field beside the river. There was a ville nearby, fifty meters downstream, and right away a dozen old mama-sans ran out and started yelling. A weird scene, he would've said. The mama-sans just stood there in the rain, soaking wet, yapping away about how this field was bad news. Number ten, they said. Evil ground. Not a good spot for good GIs. Finally Lieutenant Jimmy Cross had to get out his pistol and fire off a few rounds just to shoo them away. By then it was almost dark. So they set up a perimeter, ate chow, then crawled under their ponchos and tried to settle in for the night.

But the rain kept getting worse. And by midnight the field turned into soup.

"Just this deep, oozy soup," he would've said. "Like sewage or something. Thick and mushy. You couldn't sleep. You couldn't even lie down, not for long, because you'd start to sink under the soup. Real clammy. You could feel the crud coming up inside your boots and pants."

Here, Norman Bowker would have squinted against the low sun. He would have kept his voice cool, no self-pity.

"But the worst part," he would've said quietly, "was the smell. Partly it was the river—a dead fish smell—but it was something else, too. Finally somebody figured it out. What this was, it was a shit field. The village toilet. No indoor plumbing, right? So they used the field. I mean, we were camped in a goddamn *shit* field."

He imagined Sally Kramer closing her eyes.

If she were here with him, in the car, she would've said, "Stop it. I don't like that word."

"That's what it *was*."

"All right, but you don't have to use that word."

"Fine. What should we call it?"

She would have glared at him. "I don't know. Just stop it."

Clearly, he thought, this was not a story for Sally Kramer. She was Sally Gustafson now. No doubt Max would've liked it, the irony in particular, but Max had become a pure idea, which was its own irony. It was just too bad. If his father were here, riding shotgun around the lake, the old man might have glanced over for a second, understanding perfectly well that it was not a question of offensive language but of fact. His father would have sighed and folded his arms and waited.

"A shit field," Norman Bowker would have said. "And later that night I could've won the Silver Star for valor."

"Right," his father would've murmured, "I hear you."

The Chevy rolled smoothly across a viaduct and up the narrow tar road. To the right was open lake. To the left, across the road, most of the lawns were scorched dry like October corn. Hopelessly, round and round, a rotating sprinkler scattered lake water on Dr. Mason's vegetable garden. Already the prairie had been baked dry, but in August it would get worse. The lake would turn green with algae, and the golf course would burn up, and the dragonflies would crack open for want of good water.

The big Chevy curved past Centennial Beach and the A&W root beer stand.

It was his eighth revolution around the lake.

He followed the road past the handsome houses with their docks and wooden shingles. Back to Slater Park, across the causeway, around to Sunset Park, as though riding on tracks.

The two little boys were still trudging along on their seven-mile hike.

Out on the lake, the man in the stalled motorboat still fiddled with his engine. The pair of mud hens floated like wooden decoys, and the water-skiers looked tanned and athletic, and the high school band was packing up its instruments, and the woman in pedal pushers patiently rebaited her hook for one last try.

Quaint, he thought.

A hot summer day and it was all very quaint and remote. The four workmen had nearly completed their preparations for the evening fireworks.

Facing the sun again, Norman Bowker decided it was nearly seven o'clock. Not much later the tired radio announcer confirmed it, his voice rocking itself into a deep Sunday snooze. If Max Arnold were here, he would say something about the announcer's fatigue, and relate it to the bright pink in the sky, and the war, and courage. A pity that Max was gone. And a pity about his father, who had his own war and who now preferred silence.

Still, there was so much to say.

How the rain never stopped. How the cold worked into your bones. Sometimes the bravest thing on earth was to sit through the night and feel cold in your bones. Courage was not always a matter of yes or no.

Sometimes it came in degrees, like the cold; sometimes you were very brave up to a point and then beyond that point you were not so brave. In certain situations you could do incredible things, you could advance toward enemy fire, but in other situations, which were not nearly so bad, you had trouble keeping your eyes open. Sometimes, like that night in the shit field, the difference between courage and cowardice was something small and stupid.

The way the earth bubbled. And the smell.

In a soft voice, without flourishes, he would have told the exact truth.

"Late in the night," he would've said, "we took some mortar fire."

He would've explained how it was still raining, and how the clouds were pasted to the field, and how the mortar rounds seemed to come right out of the clouds. Everything was black and wet. The field just exploded. Rain and slop and shrapnel, nowhere to run, and all they could do was worm down into slime and cover up and wait. He would've described the crazy things he saw. Weird things. Like how at one point he noticed a guy lying next to him in the sludge, completely buried except for his face, and how after a moment the guy rolled his eyes and winked at him. The noise was fierce. Heavy thunder, and mortar rounds, and people yelling. Some of the men began shooting up flares. Red and green and silver flares, all colors, and the rain came down in Technicolor.

The field was boiling. The shells made deep slushy craters, opening up all those years of waste, centuries worth, and the smell came bubbling out of the earth. Two rounds hit close by. Then a third, even closer, and immediately, off to his left, he heard somebody screaming. It was Kiowa—he knew that. The sound was ragged and clotted up, but even so he knew the voice. A strange gargling noise. Rolling sideways, he crawled toward the screaming in the dark. The rain was hard and steady. Along the perimeter there were quick bursts of gunfire. Another round hit nearby, spraying up shit and water, and for a few moments he ducked down beneath the mud. He heard the valves in his heart. He heard the quick, feathering action of the hinges. Extraordinary, he thought. As he came up, a pair of red flares puffed open, a soft fuzzy glow, and in the glow he saw Kiowa's wide-open eyes settling down into the scum. Briefly, all he could do was watch. He heard himself moan. Then he moved again, crabbing forward, but when he got there Kiowa was almost completely under. There was a knee. There was an arm and a gold wristwatch and part of a boot.

He could not describe what happened next, not ever, but he would've tried anyway. He would've spoken carefully so as to make it real for anyone who would listen.

There were bubbles where Kiowa's head should've been.

The left hand was curled open; the fingernails were filthy; the wristwatch gave off a green phosphorescent shine as it slipped beneath the thick waters.

He would've talked about this, and how he grabbed Kiowa by the boot and tried to pull him out. He pulled hard but Kiowa was gone, and then suddenly he felt himself going too. He could taste it. The shit was in his nose and eyes. There were flares and mortar rounds, and the stink was everywhere—it was inside him, in his lungs—and he could no longer tolerate it. Not here, he thought. Not like this. He released Kiowa's boot and watched it slide away. Slowly, working his way up, he hoisted himself out of the deep mud, and then he lay still and tasted the shit in his mouth and closed his eyes and listened to the rain and explosions and bubbling sounds.

He was alone.

He had lost his weapon but it did not matter. All he wanted was a bath.

Nothing else. A hot soapy bath.

Circling the lake, Norman Bowker remembered how his friend Kiowa had disappeared under the waste and water.

"I didn't flip out," he would've said. "I was cool. If things had gone right, if it hadn't been for that smell, I could've won the Silver Star."

A good war story, he thought, but it was not a war for war stories, nor for talk of valor, and nobody in town wanted to know about the terrible stink. They wanted good intentions and good deeds. But the town was not to blame, really. It was a nice little town, very prosperous, with neat houses and all the sanitary conveniences.

Norman Bowker lit a cigarette and cranked open his window. Seven thirty-five, he decided.

The lake had divided into two halves. One half still glistened, the other was caught in shadow. Along the causeway, the two little boys marched on. The man in the stalled motorboat yanked frantically on the cord to his engine, and the two mud hens sought supper at the bottom of the lake, tails bobbing. He passed Sunset Park once again, and more houses, and the junior college and the tennis courts, and the picnickers, who now sat waiting for the evening fireworks. The high school band was gone. The woman in pedal pushers patiently toyed with her line.

Although it was not yet dusk, the A&W was already awash in neon lights.

He maneuvered his father's Chevy into one of the parking slots, let the engine idle, and sat back. The place was doing a good holiday business. Mostly kids, it seemed, and a few farmers in for the day. He did not recognize any of the faces. A slim, hipless young carhop passed by, but when he hit the horn, she did not seem to notice. Her eyes slid sideways. She hooked a tray to the window of a Firebird, laughing lightly, leaning forward to chat with the three boys inside.

He felt invisible in the soft twilight. Straight ahead, over the take-out counter, swarms of mosquitoes electrocuted themselves against an aluminum Pest-Rid machine.

It was a calm, quiet summer evening.

He honked again, this time leaning on the horn. The young carhop turned slowly, as if puzzled, then said something to the boys in the Firebird and moved reluctantly toward him. Pinned to her shirt was a badge that said EAT MAMA BURGERS.

When she reached his window, she stood straight up so that all he could see was the badge.

"Mama Burger," he said. "Maybe some fries, too."

The girl sighed, leaned down, and shook her head. Her eyes were as fluffy and airy-light as cotton candy.

"You blind?" she asked.

She put out her hand and tapped an intercom attached to a steel post.

"Punch the button and place your order. All I do is carry the dumb trays."

She stared at him for a moment. Briefly, he thought, a question lingered in her fuzzy eyes, but then she turned and punched the button for him and returned to her friends in the Firebird.

The intercom squeaked and said, "Order."

"Mama Burger and fries," Norman Bowker said.

"Affirmative, copy clear. No rootie-tootie?"

"Rootie-tootie?"

"You know, man—*root* beer."

"A small one."

"Roger-dodger. Repeat: one Mama, one fries, one small beer. Fire for effect. Stand by."

The intercom squeaked and went dead.

"Out," said Norman Bowker.

When the girl brought his tray, he ate quickly, without looking up. The tired radio announcer in Des Moines gave the time, almost eight-thirty. Dark was pressing in tight now, and he wished there were somewhere to go. In the morning he'd check out some job possibilities. Shoot a few buckets down at the Y, maybe wash the Chevy.

He finished his root beer and pushed the intercom button.

"Order," said the tinny voice.

"All done."

"That's *it*?"

"I guess so."

"Hey, loosen up," the voice said. "What you really need, friend?"

Norman Bowker smiled.

"Well," he said, "how'd you like to hear about—"

He stopped and shook his head.

"Hear *what*, man?"

"Nothing."

"Well, hey," the intercom said, "I'm sure as fuck not *going* anywhere. Screwed to a post, for God's sake. Go ahead, try me."

"Nothing."

"You sure?"

"Positive. All done."

The intercom made a light sound of disappointment. "Your choice, I guess. Over an' out."

"Out," said Norman Bowker.

On his tenth turn around the lake he passed the hiking boys for the last time. The man in the stalled motorboat was gone; the mud hens were gone. Beyond the lake, over Sally Gustafson's house, the sun had left a smudge of purple on the horizon. The band shell was deserted, and the woman in pedal pushers quietly reeled in her line, and Dr. Mason's sprinkler went round and round.

On his eleventh revolution he switched off the air conditioning, opened up his window, and rested his elbow comfortably on the sill, driving with one hand.

There was nothing to say.

He could not talk about it and never would. The evening was smooth and warm.

If it had been possible, which it wasn't, he would have explained how his friend Kiowa slipped away that night beneath the dark swampy field. He was folded in with the war; he was part of the waste.

Turning on his headlights, driving slowly, Norman Bowker remembered how he had taken hold of Kiowa's boot and pulled hard, but how the smell was simply too much, and how he'd backed off and in that way had lost the Silver Star.

He wished he could've explained some of this. How he had been braver than he ever thought possible, but how he had not been so brave as he wanted to be. The distinction was important. Max Arnold, who loved fine lines, would've appreciated it. And his father, who already knew, would've nodded.

"The truth," Norman Bowker would've said, "is I let the guy go."

"Maybe he was already gone."

"He wasn't."

"But maybe."

"No, I could feel it. He wasn't. Some things you can feel."

His father would have been quiet for a while, watching the headlights against the narrow tar road.

"Well, anyway," the old man would've said, "there's still the seven medals."

"I suppose."

"Seven honeys."

"Right."

On his twelfth revolution, the sky went crazy with color.

He pulled into Sunset Park and stopped in the shadow of a picnic shelter. After a time he got out, walked down to the beach, and waded into the lake without undressing. The water felt warm against his skin. He put his head under. He opened his lips, very slightly, for the taste, then he stood up and folded his arms and watched the fireworks. For a small town, he decided, it was a pretty good show.

NOTES

"Speaking of Courage" was written in 1975 at the suggestion of Norman Bowker, who three years later hanged himself in the locker room of a YMCA in his hometown in central Iowa.

In the spring of 1975, near the time of Saigon's final collapse, I received a long, disjointed letter in which Bowker described the problem of finding a meaningful use for his life after the war. He had worked briefly as an automotive parts salesman, a janitor, a car wash attendant, and a short order cook at the local A&W fast food franchise. None of these jobs, he said, had lasted more than ten weeks. He lived with his parents, who supported him, and who treated him with kindness and obvious love. At one point he had enrolled in the junior college in his hometown, but the course work, he said, seemed too abstract, too distant, with nothing real or tangible at stake, certainly not the stakes of a war. He dropped out after eight months. He spent his mornings in bed. In the afternoons he played pickup basketball at the Y, and then at night he drove around town in his father's car, mostly alone, or with a six-pack of beer, cruising.

"The thing is," he wrote, "there's no place to go. Not just in this lousy little town. In general. My life, I mean. It's almost like I got killed over in Nam . . . Hard to describe. That night when Kiowa got wasted, I sort of sank down into the sewage with him . . . Feels like I'm still in deep shit."

The letter covered seventeen handwritten pages, its tone jumping from self-pity to anger to irony to guilt to a kind of feigned indifference. He didn't know what to feel. In the middle of the letter, for example, he reproached himself for complaining too much:

God, this is starting to sound like some jerkoff vet crying in his beer. Sorry about that. I'm no basket case—not even any bad dreams. And I don't feel like anybody mistreats me or anything, except sometimes people act *too* nice, too polite, like they're afraid they might ask the wrong question . . . But I shouldn't bitch. One thing I hate—really hate—is all those whiner-vets. Guys sniveling about how they didn't get any parades. Such absolute crap. I mean, who in his right mind wants a *parade*? Or getting his back clapped by a bunch of patriotic idiots who don't know jack about what it feels like to kill people or get shot at or sleep in the rain or watch your body go down underneath the mud? Who *needs* it?

Anyhow, I'm basically A-Okay. Home free! So why not come down for a visit sometime and we'll chase pussy and shoot the breeze and tell each other old war lies? A good long bull session, you know?

I felt it coming, and near the end of the letter it came. He explained that he had read my first book, *If I Die in a Combat Zone*, which he liked except for the "bleeding-heart political parts." For half a page he talked about how much the book had meant to him, how it brought back all kinds of memories, the villes and paddies and rivers, and how he recognized most of the characters, including himself, even though almost all of the names were changed.

Then Bowker came straight out with it:

What you should do, Tim, is write a story about a guy who feels like he got zapped over in that shithole. A guy who can't get his act together and just drives around town all day and can't think of any damn place to go and doesn't know how to get there anyway. This guy wants to talk about it, but he *can't* . . . If you want, you can use the stuff in this letter. (But not my real name, okay?) I'd write it myself except I can't ever find any words, if you know what I mean, and I can't figure out what exactly to say. Something about the field that night. The way Kiowa just disappeared into the crud. You were there—you can tell it.

Norman Bowker's letter hit me hard. For years I'd felt a certain smugness about how easily I had made the shift from war to peace. A nice smooth glide—no flashbacks or midnight sweats. The war was over, after all. And the thing to do was go on. So I took pride in sliding gracefully from Vietnam to graduate school, from Chu Lai to Harvard, from one world to another. In ordinary conversation I never spoke much about the war, certainly not in detail, and yet ever since my return I had been talking about it virtually nonstop through my writing. Telling stories seemed a natural, inevitable process, like clearing the throat. Partly catharsis, partly communication, it was a way of grabbing people by the shirt and explaining exactly what had happened to me, how I'd allowed myself to get dragged into a wrong war, all the mistakes I'd made, all the terrible things I had seen and done.

I did not look on my work as therapy, and still don't. Yet when I received Norman Bowker's letter, it occurred to me that the act of writing had led me through a swirl of memories that might otherwise have ended in paralysis or worse. By telling stories, you objectify your own experience. You separate it from yourself. You pin down certain truths. You make up others. You start sometimes with an incident that truly happened, like the night in the shit field, and you carry it forward by inventing incidents that did not in fact occur but that nonetheless help to clarify and explain.

In any case, Norman Bowker's letter had an effect. It haunted me for more than a month, not the words so much as its desperation, and I resolved finally to take him up on his story suggestion. At the time I was at work on a new novel, *Going After Cacciato*, and one morning I sat down and began a chapter titled "Speaking of Courage." The emotional core came directly from Bowker's letter: the simple need to talk. To provide a dramatic frame, I collapsed events into a single time and place, a car circling a lake on a quiet afternoon in midsummer, using the lake as a nucleus around which the story would orbit. As he'd requested, I did not use Norman Bowker's name, instead substituting the name of my novel's main character, Paul Berlin. For the scenery I borrowed heavily from my own hometown. Wholesale thievery, in fact. I lifted up Worthington, Minnesota—the lake, the road, the causeway, the woman in pedal pushers, the junior college, the handsome houses and docks and boats and public parks—and carried it all a few hundred miles south and transplanted it into the Iowa prairie.

The writing went quickly and easily. I drafted the piece in a week or two, fiddled with it for another week, then published it as a separate short story.

Almost immediately, though, there was a sense of failure. The details of Norman Bowker's story were missing. In this original version, which I still conceived as part of the novel, I had been forced to omit the shit field and the rain and the death of Kiowa, replacing this material with events that better fit the book's narrative. As a consequence I'd lost the natural counterpoint between the lake and the field. A metaphoric unity was broken. What the place needed, and did not have, was the terrible killing power of that shit field.

As the novel developed over the next year, and as my own ideas clarified, it became apparent that the chapter had no proper home in the larger narrative. *Going After Cacciato* was a war story; "Speaking of Courage" was a postwar story. Two different time periods, two different sets of issues. There was no choice but to remove the chapter entirely. The mistake, in part, had been in trying to wedge the piece into a novel. Beyond that, though, something about the story had frightened me—I was afraid to speak directly, afraid to remember— and in the end the piece had been ruined by a failure to tell the full and exact truth about our night in the shit field.

Over the next several months, as it often happens, I managed to erase the story's flaws from my memory, taking pride in a shadowy, idealized recollection of its virtues. When the piece appeared in an anthology of short fiction, I sent a copy off to Norman Bowker with the thought that it might please him. His reaction was short and somewhat bitter.

"It's not terrible," he wrote me, "but you left out Vietnam. Where's Kiowa? Where's the shit?"

Eight months later he hanged himself.

In August of 1978 his mother sent me a brief note explaining what had happened. He'd been playing pickup basketball at the Y; after two hours he went off for a drink of water; he used a jump rope; his friends found him hanging from a water pipe. There was no suicide note, no message of any kind. "Norman was a quiet boy," his mother wrote, "and I don't suppose he wanted to bother anybody."

Now, a decade after his death, I'm hoping that "Speaking of Courage" makes good on Norman Bowker's silence. And I hope it's a better story. Although the old structure remains, the piece has been substantially revised, in some places by severe cutting, in other places by the addition of new material. Norman is back in the story, where he belongs, and I don't think he would mind that his real name appears. The central incident—our long night in the shit field along the Song Tra Bong—has been restored to the piece. It was hard stuff to write. Kiowa, after all, had been a close friend, and for years I've avoided thinking about his death and my own complicity in it. Even here it's not easy. In the interests of truth, however, I want to make it clear that Norman Bowker was in no way responsible for what happened to Kiowa. Norman did not experience a failure of nerve that night. He did not freeze up or lose the Silver Star for valor. That part of the story is my own.

12

Memory

March 1968. At My Lai, U.S. forces under Lt. William Calley slaughter hundreds of South Vietnamese civilians. The massacre is unsuccessfully covered up by the military.

The returned vet's flashback to combat experience is a common device in Vietnam writing, from the highest literary art to the basest genre thriller. Backed by veterans' testimonies as well as ample medical research into Post-Traumatic Stress Disorder (PTSD), authors conjure up memories to overwhelm and torture their heroes. This can be done subtly or clumsily depending on the author, but it's the most notable—and inescapable—use of memory in the literature.

The pieces in this chapter employ memory in other ways, although, in the end, many of the vets we see are not much different from those the popular media gives us. The gap between veterans and civilians seems even more present now, so many years after the war, and the relationships of the veterans are that much shakier. There's a loneliness, an unwillingness to speak or unearth the past. It's not merely that America won't listen, it's that for his own sake the vet hesitates to make the private public, and instead keeps it inside.

Unlike most other veterans, Yusef Komunyakaa didn't write about the war until he'd established himself as a major poet. He'd already published a number of critically acclaimed collections before bringing out *Dien Cai Dau* in 1988. The title is Vietnamese for "crazy" or "no good," and Komunyakaa or his poetic persona recalls those strange days by quietly contemplating remembered images, trying to make sense of his experience without the melodrama of the flashback. His memories are no less insistent though; as he says in "The Dead at

Quang Tri," "the grass we walk on / won't stay down." His work also probes the relationship between African American soldiers and the United States, as well as those same soldiers and the local Vietnamese prostitutes.

Nonvet and literary short-story writer Bobbie Ann Mason's first novel *In Country* (1985) explores the lack of memories its teenage hero Sam has of her father, who was killed in Vietnam. Sam attempts to reconnect with him by trying to reexperience the war, obsessively watching *M*A*S*H* and reading Vietnam books—in essence, trying to bridge the gap (not only of the war, but of gender and generation). Her uncle, Emmett, is a quirky, messed-up vet, and in the section excerpted here, he grudgingly lets Sam in on some of his own well-guarded memories of the war. What's interesting is that Sam has already collected these memories from popular sources; the individual memory of the vet is being absorbed or subsumed by the culture at large. Like Mason's stories, *In Country* is written in a style that eighties critics labeled trailer-park minimalism, a blue-collar, lightly ironic realism with an emphasis on the everyday details of domestic American life, especially the use of familiar brand-name products.

First Air Cav vet Kevin Bowen's "Incoming" from his 1994 collection *Playing Basketball with the Viet Cong* seems to be conveying the reality of what it feels like to be mortared, and then, halfway through, the poem takes us across the ocean and into the lives of those affected by the loss of loved ones, and shows us how that loss remains far beyond the physical end of the war.

In the Lake of the Woods (1994) is Tim O'Brien's fourth Vietnam book. The novel investigates the disappearance and possible murder of Kathy Wade and the life of the prime suspect, her husband, Vietnam vet and recently failed politician John Wade. In the closing days of an election, newspapers report that John took part in the My Lai massacre, and he loses badly. He and Kathy retreat to their lake house, from which Kathy disappears. O'Brien looks into three distinct mysteries in the book, all of which have already taken place—John's formative years, his participation in the massacre, and the disappearance of Kathy—by using memories and chapters the author calls "Evidence," made up of a combination of nonfiction (some of it from William

Calley's court-martial) and fictional testimony of characters who had some connection to John Wade. The novel is an examination of John's possible guilt or innocence, and by extension the conduct of the war. As in *The Things They Carried*, a first-person author figure is present, and facts and stories often blend and clash, revealing no final concrete answers. In the end, O'Brien gives us several possibilities for what could have happened to Kathy, but none excuse John Wade's (or America's) denial of his terrible past. The *New York Times Book Review* judged *In the Lake of the Woods* the best book of fiction for 1994.

In John Balaban's "Mr. Giai's Poem," Mr. Giai, a former Viet Minh soldier, shares a quiet memory he himself tried to immortalize in his own poetry. His intimate audience of three American veterans (in actuality the poets W. D. Ehrhart, Bruce Weigl, and the author himself) toasts this moment of connection, creating a new, redeeming memory.

In each piece, memory serves some other purpose than conjuring mere terror or heartrending sorrow. It seems that as the years pass and the war recedes, more Vietnam authors are questioning memory, examining how it can be at once devastating and salvific, perhaps because with the dwindling of any worthwhile popular discussion concerning the war, veterans and their families are left with little but their own intimate recollections.

Dien Cai Dau

YUSEF KOMUNYAKAA

1988

Somewhere Near Phu Bai

The moon cuts through
night trees like a circular saw
white hot. In the guard shack
I lean on the sandbags,
taking aim at whatever.
Hundreds of blue-steel stars
cut a path, fanning out
silver for a second. If anyone's
there, don't blame me.

I count the shapes ten meters
out front, over & over, making sure
they're always there.
I don't dare blink an eye.
The white-painted backs
of the Claymore mines
like quarter-moons.
They say Victor Charlie will
paint the other sides & turn
the blast toward you.

If I hear a noise
will I push the button
& blow myself away?
The moon grazes treetops.
I count the Claymores again.
Thinking about buckshot
kneaded in the plastic C-4
of the brain, counting
sheep before I know it.

Starlight Scope Myopia

Gray-blue shadows lift
shadows onto an oxcart.

Making night work for us,
the starlight scope brings
men into killing range.

The river under Vi Bridge
takes the heart away

like the Water God
riding his dragon.
Smoke-colored

Viet Cong
move under our eyelids,

lords over loneliness
winding like coral vine through
sandalwood & lotus,

inside our lowered heads
years after this scene

ends. The brain closes
down. What looks like
one step into the trees,

they're lifting crates of ammo
& sacks of rice, swaying

under their shared weight.
Caught in the infrared,
what are they saying?

Are they talking about women
or calling the Americans

beaucoup dien cai dau?
One of them is laughing.
You want to place a finger

to his lips & say "shhhh."
You try reading ghost talk

on their lips. They say
"up-up we go," lifting as one.
This one, old, bowlegged,

you feel you could reach out
& take him into your arms. You

peer down the sights of your M-16,
seeing the full moon
loaded on an oxcart.

The Dead at Quang Tri

This is harder than counting stones
along paths going nowhere, the way
a tiger circles & backtracks by
smelling his blood on the ground.
The one kneeling beside the pagoda,
remember him? Captain, we won't
talk about that. The Buddhist boy
at the gate with the shaven head
we rubbed for luck
glides by like a white moon.
He won't stay dead, dammit!
Blades aim for the family jewels;
the grass we walk on
won't stay down.

Hanoi Hannah

Ray Charles! His voice
calls from waist-high grass,
& we duck behind gray sandbags.
"Hello, Soul Brothers. Yeah,
Georgia's also on my mind."
Flares bloom over the trees.
"Here's Hannah again.
Let's see if we can't
light her goddamn fuse
this time." Artillery
shells carve a white arc
against dusk. Her voice rises
from a hedgerow on our left.
"It's Saturday night in the States.
Guess what your woman's doing tonight.
I think I'll let Tina Turner
tell you, you homesick GIs."
Howitzers buck like a herd
of horses behind concertina.
"You know you're dead men,
don't you? You're dead
as King today in Memphis.
Boys, you're surrounded by
General Tran Do's division."
Her knife-edge song cuts
deep as a sniper's bullet.
"Soul Brothers, what you dying for?"
We lay down a white-klieg

trail of tracers. Phantom jets
fan out over the trees.
Artillery fire zeros in.
Her voice grows flesh
& we can see her falling
into words, a bleeding flower
no one knows the true name for.
"You're lousy shots, GIs."
Her laughter floats up
as though the airways are
buried under our feet.

Roll Call

Through rifle sights
we must've looked like crows
perched on a fire-eaten branch,
lined up for reveille, ready
to roll-call each M-16
propped upright
between a pair of jungle boots,
a helmet on its barrel
as if it were a man.
The perfect row aligned
with the chaplain's cross
while a metallic-gray squadron
of sea gulls circled. Only
a few lovers have blurred
the edges of this picture.
Sometimes I can hear them
marching through the house,
closing the distance. All
the lonely beds take me back
to where we saluted those
five pairs of boots
as the sun rose against our faces.

Seeing in the Dark

The scratchy sound of skin
flicks works deeper & deeper,
as mortar fire colors the night
flesh tone. The corporal at the door
grins; his teeth shiny as raw pearl,
he stands with a fist of money,
happy to see infantrymen
from the boonies—men who know
more about dodging trip wires &
seeing in the dark than they do
about women. They're in Shangri-la
gaping at washed-out images
thrown against a bedsheet.

We're men ready to be fused
with ghost pictures, trying
to keep the faces we love
from getting shuffled
with those on the wall.
Is that Hawk's tenor
coloring-in the next frame?
Three women on a round bed
coax in a German shepherd—
everything turns white as alabaster.
The picture flickers; the projector
goes dead, & we cuss the dark
& the cicadas' heavy breath.

627

Tu Do Street

Music divides the evening.
I close my eyes & can see
men drawing lines in the dust.
America pushes through the membrane
of mist & smoke, & I'm a small boy
again in Bogalusa. *White Only*
signs & Hank Snow. But tonight
I walk into a place where bar girls
fade like tropical birds. When
I order a beer, the mama-san
behind the counter acts as if she
can't understand, while her eyes
skirt each white face, as Hank Williams
calls from the psychedelic jukebox.
We have played Judas where
only machine-gun fire brings us
together. Down the street
black GIs hold to their turf also.
An off-limits sign pulls me
deeper into alleys, as I look
for a softness behind these voices
wounded by their beauty & war.
Back in the bush at Dak To
& Khe Sanh, we fought
the brothers of these women
we now run to hold in our arms.
There's more than a nation
inside us, as black & white
soldiers touch the same lovers

minutes apart, tasting
each other's breath,
without knowing these rooms
run into each other like tunnels
leading to the underworld.

The Edge

When guns fall silent for an hour
or two, you can hear the cries

of women making love to soldiers.
They have an unmerciful memory

& know how to wear bright dresses
to draw a crowd, conversing

with a platoon of shadows
numbed by morphine. Their real feelings

make them break like April
into red blossoms.

Cursing themselves in ragged dreams
fire has singed the edges of,

they know a slow dying the fields have come to terms with.
Shimmering fans work against the heat

& smell of gunpowder, making money
float from hand to hand. The next moment

a rocket pushes a white fist
through night sky, & they scatter like birds

& fall into the shape their lives
have become.

"You want a girl, GI?"
"You buy me Saigon tea?"

Soldiers bring the scent of burning flesh
with them—on their clothes & in their hair,

drawn to faces in half-lit rooms.
As good-bye kisses are thrown

to the charred air, silhouettes of jets
ease over nude bodies on straw mats.

In Country

BOBBIE ANN MASON

1985

29

Moon Pie, lounging under Mrs. Biggs's forsythia bush, yawned at Sam when she slammed the car door. Emmett was usually home at this time of day, fixing supper, but the door was locked. He wasn't expecting her back from Mamaw's until tomorrow. Luckily, she had a key with her. When she opened the door, a harsh, overpowering chemical smell rushed at her, instead of the usual stale smell of cigarettes. What in the hell? Emmett couldn't have put his head in a gas oven, she thought. Their stove was electric. Her second thought was Agent Orange, although this didn't smell like oranges. She gulped a deep breath of air from outside and rushed in. When she called "Emmett!" her air rushed out. She gulped some more fresh air and raced around downstairs, calling for him. Then she found the source of the smell. In the center of the living room, between the TV and the couch, a spray can had been set on a kitchen chair. She snatched it up and read the label. It was a flea bomb, one of those spray cans that could be locked in a spray position. It was empty now. Emmett had set off a flea bomb and left the house, as though he had thrown a hand grenade inside and run away. It was just like him to do something secretive like that, without even mentioning it. It made her furious. He was so paranoid about those fleas.

She paced up and down the porch and tried to think. She had opened both doors to get cross-ventilation. She was so angry she could shit bricks. Then she had an idea. She went to the car and ripped a blank page out of her father's diary. She wrote Emmett a note and left it on the refrigerator, under a tomato magnet. The note said, "You think you can get away with everything because you're a V.N. vet, but you can't. On the table is a diary my daddy kept. Mamaw gave it to me. Is that what it was like over there? If it was, then you can just forget about me. Don't try to find me. You're on your own now. Goodbye. Sam."

Sam took a deep breath of fresh air and raced upstairs. The air in her room was tolerable. She opened the window, then searched the closet for her sleeping bag and backpack from Girl Scouts. She crammed some shorts and T-shirts into the pack, then grabbed some jeans and her cowboy boots. She got Emmett's space blanket and poncho from his footlocker. Downstairs, with a new breath from outside, she searched for food to take with her. They didn't have any ham and mother-fuckers, so she took pork and beans. G.I.s lived out of cans. They even had canned butter. She put a can of potted meat and some Doritos and granola bars in the pack, along with the Granny Cakes and the can of smoked oysters she had bought. She loaded a six-pack cooler with Pepsi and cheese and grape juice. She found some plastic utensils she had saved from the Burger Boy. Her job was supposed to start in two weeks. Where would she be in two weeks?

She imagined that the smell was Agent Orange. Her lungs were soaking up dioxin, and molecules of it were embedding themselves in the tissues, and someday it would come back to haunt her, like the foods that gave Emmett gas.

Probably dioxin wasn't in flea bombs. But for all anyone knew, they could have a chemical just as deadly. Those chemical companies didn't care.

On the way out of town, she had the appalling thought that Moon Pie might have sneaked back in the house. But she was almost sure he was still under that bush when she pulled out of the driveway.

If men went to war for women, and for unborn generations, then she was going to find out what they went through. Sam didn't think the women or the unborn babies had any say in it. If it were up to women, there wouldn't be any war. No, that was a naive thought.

When women got power, they were just like men. She thought of Indira Gandhi and Margaret Thatcher. She wouldn't want to meet those women out in the swamp at night.

What would make people want to kill? If the U.S.A. sent her to a foreign country, with a rifle and a heavy backpack, could she root around in the jungle, sleep in the mud, and shoot at strangers? How did the Army get boys to do that? Why was there war?

Her dad had no sense of humor. At least Emmett had a sense of humor. Dwayne couldn't spell, and his handwriting was bad.

Emmett's fear of fleas was silly. Sam wasn't even afraid of spending the night at Cawood's Pond, sleeping out on the ground. Cawood's Pond was so dangerous even the Boy Scouts wouldn't camp out there, but it was the last place in western Kentucky where a person could really face the wild. That was what she wanted to do.

Along the secondary road leading to the pond, bulldozers had been at work, dredging the outer reaches of the swamp. Sam drove up the bumpy lane and left the car in the center of the clearing. Her shoes crunched on the gravel. Down the path to the boardwalk, she paused at a stump. Inside the hollow, a million tiny black ants were working on a bit of plastic, ripping it up into nonbiodegradable tidbits and marching off with it. Emmett imagined the fleas were like that, crawling all over him while he slept. She thought he must have been having a flashback when he tossed in the flea-bomb grenade and ran away. The fleas were the Vietnamese. How often had she heard the enemy soldiers compared to ants, or other creatures too numerous to count? She remembered someone saying that the G.I.s would fight for a position and gain it and then the next day there would be a thousand more of the enemy swarming around them.

The Vietnamese used anything the Americans threw away—bomb casings and cigarette butts and helicopter parts and Coke cans. It was like Emmett rigging up things in the house. It was Vietnamese behavior, she thought, making do with what he could scrounge. The Vietnamese could make a bomb out of a Coke can.

Emmett had helped kill those Vietnamese, the same way he killed the fleas, the same way people killed ants. It was easy, her father wrote. But the enemy always returned, in greater numbers. Pete had practically bragged about killing. Men were nostalgic about killing. It aroused something in them.

The fleas would come back. People in cities had roaches, super-bugs resistant to chemicals.

At Cawood's Pond, bugs rose up like steam from the swamp water.

Emmett set off the flea bombs just as casually as he would have launched a mortar into the sky, the way the soldiers did in the war, the way he pumped that firing button on the Atari.

She remembered when he used to shout in his sleep. He was after Charlie. There weren't any Vietcong to hunt down now, no hills to capture, no bases to defend, but he was still doing it. He was out to kill, in spite of himself, like a habit he couldn't break. It was sick. He was all the time reliving that war. Men wanted to kill. That's what men did, she thought. It was their basic profession.

Granddad killed Japanese soldiers in World War II. Her father had been killed because that was the way the game was played. Some lived and some died. There was no other conclusion to be drawn.

Women didn't kill. That was why her mother wouldn't honor the flag, or honor the dead. Honoring the dead meant honoring the cause. Irene was saying, Fuck you, U.S.A., he's dead and it meant nothing. He went to fight and he got killed and that was the end of him. Sam thought, To hell with all of them—Lonnie, her dad, her uncle, her grandfathers, Lorenzo Jones. Tom. Maybe not Tom.

She waited on the boardwalk, sitting there for a long time, quietly, until the birds flew by unselfconsciously. This was what Emmett did, as he watched and waited, like a spider hiding in a web. A big bird whooshed through the swamp like a reconnaissance chopper, and she caught a glimpse of brown. Then she heard a blue jay squawking. The blue jay was teasing a squirrel. She saw some sparrows. She wanted to know what the big deal was, waiting for birds. It was what hunters did.

She was a runaway. There was no runaway hotline out here. Emmett had run away, too, to Lexington, so she felt justified. It wasn't as though she were running away to New York to be a prostitute in a dope ring. Her English teacher who thought Thoreau's retreat to Walden Pond was such a hot idea would probably approve. If it was in a book, there was something to it. But in Sam's opinion Thoreau was paranoid.

That rotting corpse her dad had found invaded her mind—those banana leaves, reeking sweetly. She knew that whenever she had tried to imagine Vietnam she had had her facts all wrong. She couldn't get hickory trees and maples and oaks and other familiar trees, like these cypresses at Cawood's Pond, out of her head. They probably didn't have these trees over there. Rice paddies weren't real to her. She thought of tanks knocking down the jungle and tigers sitting under bushes. Her notions came from the movies. Some vets blamed what they did on the horror of the jungle. What did the jungle do to them? Humping the boonies. Here I am, she thought. In country.

Cawood's Pond was famous for snakes, but it also had migrating birds—herons, and sometimes even egrets, Emmett claimed. She saw the egret so often in her mind she almost thought she had really seen it. It was white, like a stork. Maybe her father had seen egrets in Vietnam and thought they were storks. The stork was bringing her. Emmett went over there soon after, as though he were looking for that stork, something that brought life. Emmett didn't look hard enough for that bird. He stayed at home and watched TV. He hid. He lived in his little fantasy world, she thought. But Sam meant to face facts. This was as close to the jungle as she could get, with only a VW.

A blue jay fussed overhead. A fish splashed. She leaned over the railing of the boardwalk and watched the Jesus bugs. The place was quiet, but gradually the vacancy of the air was filled with a complex fabric of sounds—insects and frogs, and occasional whirring wings and loud honks of large birds.

The insects were multiplying, as though they were screwing and reproducing right in the air around her. A gnat flew into her eye. She went back to the car and put on her jeans and boots. She hadn't brought any Bug-Off. With the space blanket and her backpack and the picnic cooler, she followed a path through the jungle. The cypress knees, little humps of the roots sticking up, studded the swamp, and some of them even jutted up on the path. She had to walk carefully. She was walking point. The cypress knees were like land mines. There would be an invisible thread stretched across the path to trigger the mine. She waded through elephant grass, and in the distance there was a rice paddy.

She dropped her things in a clearing and returned to the boardwalk for a while, sitting on a pillow she had thought to bring from the couch, a little square of foam rubber covered with dirty green velour. She watched for snakes. They would be out in the water—water moccasins, no doubt—and their triangular heads would leave a V mark in the water. A large turtle perched on a log. It was probably too late in the day for snakes, she thought. Snakes needed sun to heat up their blood. She remembered that from a *National Geographic* special.

Before dark, she hauled her stuff farther down the path and fixed up her camp. She had to search for a flat place that wasn't interrupted by cypress knees. She found a tall oak tree that had a flat clearing under it. This area had once been water, but now the water level was lower and the ground had dried out. Even the mosquitoes seemed less annoying here. The tree had a bank of moss and a curtain of ferns. She spread out the space blanket and waited for dark while she ate pork and beans and some cheese and crackers, with a Pepsi from the cooler. In the dark, the snipers couldn't find her. She would be invisible, and no one could find her. No one, she thought, except a creature with an acute sense of smell.

Here she was, humping the boonies.

The smells returned. The flea bomb, the banana leaves, the special gook stink.

If she were a soldier, she would be wading through that swamp, with snakes winding themselves around her legs.

There were patches of ooze, like quicksand, that swallowed up people in the swamp. But she was on solid ground under this tree. There couldn't be a sinkhole next to a tree.

She pictured Emmett standing silhouetted against the Vietnam sky, standing at the edge of a rice paddy, watching a bird fly away. In the background, working in the fields, were some peasants in bamboo hats. Emmett kept watching the bird fly into the distance, and the *beat-beat-beat* of a helicopter interrupted the scene, moving in slowly on it. The peasants did not look up, and Emmett kept staring, as though the bird had been transformed into the chopper and had returned to take him away. Then in one corner of the scene a bomb exploded, sending debris and flame sky-high, but the peasants kept working, bending over their rows of rice.

Did rice grow in rows? Was it bushy, like soybeans? No, it was like grass. It was like wheat growing in water.

She felt so stupid. She couldn't dig a foxhole even if she had to, because she didn't have the tools. And could she actually dig a foxhole? She didn't know. The way Emmett had worked on his ditch for so long had irked her so much that she hadn't taken it seriously. But it might be handy to know how to dig in. It occurred to her that in this swamp any hole would fill up with water.

In Vietnam, the soldiers wouldn't have had a safe boardwalk. They would have waded through the swamp, with leeches sucking on them and big poisonous jungle snakes brushing their legs, and the splash of water would have betrayed their positions. They had to creep. They had to go with the natural sound of the water and hold their breath if they saw a snake. A startled peep could mean the end. They couldn't afford to be cowards. She wondered if there were alligators in Nam. Vietnam had a monsoon climate, Emmett had said. Sam remembered monsoons from geography.

She ate a Granny Cake. Each bite was a loud smack, like a breaking leaf. The bullfrogs had started bellyaching, like Emmett with a gas attack. It was amazing how long you could sit out in the wild and still not see many animals. They know I'm here, she thought. Even the squirrels know I'm here. Squirrels are always on the other side of the tree. That's why you need a squirrel dog to hunt squirrels, Granddad Smith had told her. A fice is best, he said.

And then something happened. It started with a chirping sound, and then some scrapes. She could see movement through some weeds on the side of the entrance to the boardwalk where the bank sloped down to the swamp. She saw a face, a face with beady eyes. It scared her. It was a V.C. Then she saw a sharp nose and streaks around the eyes. It was a raccoon. As she watched, the raccoon came into view, and then she saw a baby raccoon, and then another. They were large, almost grown, but still fuzzy. They climbed down the bank and stood in the water and drank. The mother nuzzled them. Behind her, two others wriggled down the bank.

For a long time, Sam watched as the babies chirped and the mother poked her nose at them, trying to round them up, to go back up the bank. She led two of them up and returned for the others, but then the first two followed her down again. It took her about ten minutes to get them rounded up. Twice, she stared straight at Sam. And when she had all the babies together, she led them away, through the underbrush.

After a while, there was a pattern of recognition in the night noises. There were voices, messages, in the insect sounds. "Who's next?" they said. Or "Watch out." She had read about a lizard in Vietnam that had a cry that sounded to the American soldiers like "Fuck you! Fuck you!" She recognized the owls. Like the V.C., they conducted their business at night. Sam crouched on the space blanket and thought about what people would think if they knew where she was. Lonnie would be totally disgusted with her. His mother would think Sam had lost her brains. Grandma would have a heart attack just at the idea of snakes. Sam enjoyed thinking of their reactions. Maybe her mother would think the idea wasn't so ridiculous. Her mother had done braver things. A frog belly-ooped. Sam remembered that Emmett used to go frog-gigging with Granddad at his pond. She heard rustling weeds and chirps and water splashing.

There weren't many people out here, so there was really nothing to be afraid of.

First watch. She wouldn't sleep. She'd stay on watch. The G.I.s stayed awake in the frightening night, until they fell asleep like cats, ready to bolt awake. It was hot inside the sleeping bag, but outside the bag the mosquitoes plucked at her skin, whining their little song. When she had come to the pond before, with Lonnie and Emmett, it had seemed safe. Did the soldiers feel safer with each other? Of course, she could retreat to the VW. VWs were watertight, so they would be bugtight too.

It hit her suddenly that this nature preserve in a protected corner of Kentucky wasn't like Vietnam at all. The night sky in Vietnam was a light show, Emmett had said once. Rockets, parachute flares, tracer bullets, illumination rounds, signal flares, searchlights, pencil flares. She tried to remember the description she had read. It was like fireworks. And the soundtrack was different from bugs and frogs: the *whoosh-beat* of choppers, the scream of jets, the thunder-boom of artillery rounds, the mortar rounds, random bullets and bombs and explosions. The rock-and-roll sounds of war.

It was growing darker. She wouldn't find that bird in the dark. She recalled the poem from school about the man who had to wear a dead albatross around his neck. The man in the poem was sorry he had shot the albatross, and he went around telling everybody at a wedding about it, like a pregnant woman thrusting her condition on everyone. Dawn would be like that. Sam's mother had been like that earlier this year. "You'd think she was the only person on earth who had ever had a baby," Grandma had said. But women would never really behave like that guy with the bird around his neck. Women were practical. They would bury a dead bird when it started to stink. They wouldn't collect teeth and ears for souvenirs. They wouldn't cut notches on their machetes. Sam kept thinking about the albatross, trying to remember how the poem went. Then chills rushed over her. Soldiers murdered babies. But women did too. They ripped their own unborn babies out of themselves and flushed them away, squirming and bloody. The chills wouldn't stop.

In the deepening dark, she struggled against Dracula images invading her mind. The soundtrack in the back of her mind, she realized, was from *Apocalypse Now*—the Doors moaning ominously, "This is the end . . . the children are insane."

It must have been years since she had gone so long without listening to a radio.

Dawn washed over the swamp, along with a misty fog. It was cool. The clatter of birds was like a three-alarm fire. Everything seemed alarmed by the new day. Sam lay very still on the space blanket and looked around her slowly. Her watch said five-fifteen. The soldiers would have been up before first light, creeping around, pulling up camp. She had survived.

She had many large bites on her body. One on her leg was bright red and inflamed, like a rash. She peed on a honeysuckle vine, and some splashed on poison ivy. She splattered a nondescript, hard-shelled bug crawling along.

As quietly as she could, she got some grape juice out of the cooler. She drank the juice and ate a granola bar. If she were a soldier, she'd drink hot chocolate or coffee from her canteen cup.

She cleaned up her camp. She was learning to be quiet. She could fold her sleeping bag silently. She closed the lid of the picnic cooler in slow motion. She had survived. But she didn't know what to do. She wished that bird would come. If the bird came, then she would leave.

The quality of dawn was different from the quality of dusk. Dusk lingered, and went through stages of dimness, but dawn was swift and pervasive. There must be some scientific principle behind that, she thought.

Before long, the sun blasted through the swamp. Sam actually saw some glowing rays hitting the path like those rays in religious paintings, like the ones in Aunt Bessie's *Upper Rooms*. Sam didn't think there was any upper room. Life was here and now. Her father was dead, and no one cared. That outlaw was dissolved in the swamp.

At seven-thirty, she heard noises. Low scratchings of gravel—maybe a dog, or some deer. She sat behind the tree, out of sight of the clearing, and waited as the noises grew louder. She wondered if it was Emmett, looking for her. Or was it a hunter? If a hunter saw her move, she might get shot. Hunters would shoot anything that moved. They were always shooting each other, mistaking each other for turkeys or deer.

There were peculiar new rustlings, something creeping, a sort of shuffle. It couldn't be a rapist, she thought. Rapists didn't go out into the wilderness, where there weren't likely to be any women to rape. They were calculating. Sam was defenseless. She looked around for rocks and sticks. She felt inside her backpack for a weapon. She had the can of smoked baby oysters with a roll-key opener. Hurriedly, she worked to create a weapon with the sharp edge of the can. The smell of smoked oysters sickened her. Too late, she realized the smell would give away her position. She tried to remember what she had been told about self-defense. Jab his eyes out with a key and knee him in the balls. She could take the open can, with its dangerous edge, and smash oysters all over his face and cut his nose.

The birds grew quieter, and the footsteps were on the boardwalk. She should have made her camp farther in the woods. What an idiotic thing to happen, she thought—to face the terror of the jungle and then meet a rapist. It would be like that scene in *Apocalypse Now* where the soldiers met a tiger, the last thing they expected in the guerrilla-infested jungle.

30

The footsteps on the boardwalk grew louder. Sam closed the zipper on her backpack, inching it along. She intended to leave the path and creep through the jungle back to the car. But it seemed a cheat to have a car for escape. She should have had a foxhole, with broken branches to cover it, to hide in. But the V.C. would know the jungle, and they would see where she had been. They would see the picnic cooler. The V.C. rapist-terrorist was still at the boardwalk. A bird flew over but she didn't dare glance at it. Its shadow fell on the bushes.

Here she was in a swamp where an old outlaw had died, and someone was stalking her. In her head, the Kinks were singing, "There's a little green man in my head," their song about paranoia. But this was real. A curious pleasure stole over her. This terror was what the soldiers had felt every minute. They lived with the possibility of unseen eyes of snipers. They crept along, pointing the way with their rifles, alert to land mines, listening, always listening. They were completely alive, every nerve on edge, and sleep, when it came, was like catnapping. No nightmares in the jungle. Just silent terror. During the night, she had stayed awake in the dark swamp, watching and waiting. She could make out faint rings of lights and winking lightning bugs. She put herself in Moon Pie's place. In Emmett's place. She had fantasized Tom there with her in her sleeping bag, the way her father had tried to imagine her mother. But Tom floated away.

She was in her father's place, in a foxhole in the jungle, with a bunch of buddies, all breathing quietly, daring to smoke in their quiet holes, eating their C-rations silently, their cold beans. She remembered Emmett eating cold split-pea soup from the can. She felt more like a cat than anything, small and fragile and very alert to movement, her whiskers flicking and her pupils widening in the dark. It was a new way of seeing.

Now she felt no rush of adrenaline, no trembling of knees. She knew it was because she didn't really believe this was real, after all. It couldn't be happening to her. In a few moments, everything would be clear and fine.

Her breathing was silent. Not even her eyes moved. She could see bushes stir as the rapist approached. He had left the boardwalk and was heading down the path in her direction. Her only hope was to remain hidden, with the can of oysters ready to cut his eyes out. The greasy oysters leaked onto her fingers.

A leaf moved, a color flashed. Someone whistled a tune, "Suicide Is Painless." This was a joke, after all, for it was only Emmett, in an old green T-shirt and green fatigues. He was empty-handed. His running shoes were wet with dew and his hair was uncombed. She stood up, feeling like a jack-in-the-box. In Vietnam, this scene would never have happened. It would always be the enemy behind a bush.

"Hey, Emmett," she said.

"What are you doing here?"

"How did you know I was here?"

"I saw your car out there."

"I know that. But how did you know my car would be here?"

"Just a guess."

"How'd you get here?"

"Walked."

Her knees were still trembling. She hadn't been scared. She marched ahead of him on the path, and he trailed after her. She had her backpack, and he had grabbed the cooler. She said, "It was crazy to walk all the way out here."

"Jesus fuckin'-A Christ!" Emmett yelled suddenly. "You worried me half to death! Crazy? I'd say it was crazy to camp out here. I thought you'd gone off the deep end. Man, I thought you'd lost it."

Sam reached into her car and opened the door and set her stuff in the back seat. The windows had mist on them. The car inside seemed damp and cool. It must not be watertight, after all. Emmett was haggard and unshaved, and his T-shirt was dirty. The smoke from his cigarette flooded the swamp, obliterating the jungle smells.

"You scared me," he said. "I was afraid of what you might do. You might have considered that some people would be worried about you."

"Ha! I'd talk if I's you. At least I left a note."

"I was worried. I was scared you'd get hurt."

"You didn't have to come after me."

Emmett sat on a front fender and put his hands on his face. He was trembling, and his teeth chattered. A bird flew by and Emmett didn't look up. It was a Kentucky cardinal, a brilliant surprise, a flash of red, like a train signal.

"What were you doing out here?" Emmett asked.

"Humping the boonies."

"What?"

"I wanted to know what it was like out in the jungle at night." Sam scraped the dew off the bumper with her boot.

"This ain't a jungle. It's a swamp, and it's dangerous. I thought you aimed to stay at the Hugheses' last night."

"I didn't want to. Where were you?"

"I went over to Jim's. He's back from Lexington. I thought it would be a good time to set off that bomb, with you gone. But I went back to round up Moon Pie at dark and I went in and found your note."

"Did you leave Moon Pie in the house to breathe those fumes?"

"No. I took him to Jim's. He hated riding in Jim's truck."

"When I found that stupid flea bomb, I thought you'd flipped out again."

"I had to get rid of those fleas."

"Those fleas don't even bother Moon Pie, and you know it."

He smoked his cigarette down and ground it out on the gravel. He said, "I found out something yesterday morning after you left."

"What?"

"Buddy Mangrum's in the hospital. His liver's real bad."

Sam kicked at the car. "I hate Agent Orange! I hate the Army! What about his little girl?"

"She's home. That operation went O.K., but I don't know how they're going to pay all the bills. If he dies, maybe his wife will collect some benefits, but I doubt it."

Emmett leaned against the VW hood, its prim beige forehead. He said, "Jim and me went up to the hospital for a while, but we didn't see Buddy. We hung around in the waiting room a long time arguing about Geraldine Ferraro." Emmett smiled. "I guess Jim's afraid Sue Ann might decide to run for President or something." Emmett seemed old and worn out. He said, "I know why you were out there. You think you can go through what we went through out in the jungle, but you can't. This place is scary, and things can happen to you, but it's not the same thing as having snipers and mortar fire and shells and people shooting at you from behind bushes. What have you got to be afraid of? You're afraid somebody'll look at you the wrong way. You're afraid your mama's going to make you go to school in Lexington. Big deal."

"I slept out here in the swamp and I wasn't afraid of anything," she said. "Some people are afraid of snakes, but not me. Some people are even afraid of fleas. I wasn't afraid of snakes or hoot owls or anything."

"Congratulations."

"And when you came, I thought it might be a hunter, or a rapist. But I wasn't scared. I was ready for you." She had left the can of smoked oysters behind, but her hands still smelled.

Emmett lit another cigarette and the sun came up some more. The fog was burning off. Emmett's pimples were crusted with yellow salve. Bile was yellow. Maybe his bile was oozing up from his liver. His liver would go next.

"I wanted to see that bird," she said. "That bird you're looking for." He shrugged, and she went on. "I saw a cardinal. And some raccoons. And a blue jay teasing a squirrel."

"Good for you."

She breathed deeply and kicked at the fender. She was bored with

Cawood's Pond. How could that outlaw have stayed out here in hiding? What did he eat? What did he do for recreation? She said, "How did you know I was here?"

"I called around."

"Nobody knew I was here."

"I thought you might have gone to Lexington, but I called Irene this morning and she hadn't seen you."

"You didn't tell her I was missing, did you?"

"No. I just talked about something else. I knew she'd mention it if you were there. I finally figured out you were here from your note. For one thing, I figured you'd go someplace to escape. And also someplace dramatic, because that's like you. Also, you took my poncho and space blanket. When I read that diary I tried to imagine what I would have done, and this is what I would have done. Once when I was little and Daddy gave me a whipping because I didn't feed the calves on time, I ran away from home. I ran to the creek and stayed there till it got dark, and while I was there I thought I was getting revenge, for some reason. It's childish, to go run off to the wilderness to get revenge. It's the most typical thing in the world."

"That explains it, then," Sam said disgustedly. "That's what you were doing in Vietnam. That explains what the whole country was doing over there. The least little threat and America's got to put on its cowboy boots and stomp around and show somebody a thing or two."

Emmett walked down the path to the boardwalk, and Sam followed him. She watched her feet, carefully avoiding a broken plank. He flung his cigarette into the water.

She asked, "What did you think of the diary?"

"I didn't sleep none after I read it."

"He couldn't even spell 'machete.' "

"Are you disappointed?"

She fidgeted. "The way he talked about gooks and killing—I hated it." She paused. "I hate him. He was awful, the way he talked about gooks and killing."

Emmett shook her by the shoulders, jostling her until her teeth rattled. "Look here, little girl. He could have been me. All of us, it was the same."

"He loved it, like Pete. He went over there to get some notches on his machete."

"Yeah, and if he hadn't got killed, then he'd have had to live with that."

"It wouldn't have bothered him. He's like Pete."

"It's the same for all of us! Tom and Pete and Jim and Buddy and all of us. You can't do what we did and be happy about it. And nobody lets you forget it. Goddamn it, Sam!" He slammed the railing of the boardwalk so hard it almost broke. He would have fallen into the murky swamp. Emmett was shuddering again, close to sobbing.

"Oh, Emmett!" cried Sam. She was standing with her arms branched out, like the cypress above, but she was frozen on the spot, unable to reach him. She waited. She thought he was going to come out with some suppressed memories of events as dramatic as that one that caused Hawkeye to crack up in the final episode of *M*A*S*H*. But nothing came.

"Are you going to talk, Emmett? Can you tell about it? Do the way Hawkeye did when he told about that baby on the bus. His memories lied to him. But he got better when he could reach down and get the right memories." Sam was practically yelling at him. She was frantic.

Emmett said, "There ain't no way to tell it. No point. You can't tell it all. Dwayne didn't begin to tell it all."

"Just tell one thing."

"O.K. One thing."

"One thing at a time will be all right."

Emmett lit a cigarette and started slowly, but then he talked faster and faster, as though he were going to pour out everything after all. He said, "There was this patrol I was on and we didn't have enough guys? And we were too close together and this land mine blew us sky-high. We was too close. We had already lost a bunch and we freaked out and huddled together, which you should never do, so we was scrambling to an LZ to meet the chopper. And first we hit this mine and then this grenade come out of nowhere, and I played like I was dead, and I was underneath this big guy about to smother me. The NVA poked around and decided we were all dead and they left, and I laid there about nine hours, and I heard that chopper come and go, but it was too far away and it didn't spot me. I was too scared to signal, because the enemy was there. I could hear 'em. They shot at the chopper. What do you think of that? For hours, then, until the next day, I was all by myself, except for dead bodies. The smell of warm blood in the jungle heat, like soup coming to a boil. Oh, that was awful! They got the radio guy and the radio was smashed. I couldn't use it. I was petrified, and I thought I could hear them for a long time."

"That sounds familiar. I saw something like that in a movie on TV." Sam was shaking, scared.

"I know the one you're thinking about—that movie where the camp got overrun and the guy had to hide in that tunnel. This was completely different. It really happened," he said, dragging on his cigarette. "That smell—the smell of death—was everywhere all the time. Even when you were eating, it was like you were eating death."

"I heard somebody in that documentary we saw say that," Sam said.

"Well, it was true! I wasn't the only one who noticed it. Dwayne smelled it."

"He probably liked it."

"Oh, shit-fire, Sam! We were out there trying to survive. It felt good when you got even. You came out here like a little kid running away from home, for spite. Now didn't it feel good? That's why you weren't afraid. 'Cause it felt good to worry me half to death."

Sam said, "If you ran away when you were little, and you think it's childish to run out here, don't you think you do the same thing? Don't you think it's childish to do what you do, the way you hide and won't get a job, and won't have a girlfriend? Anita's a real pretty woman and it just kills me that you won't go with her."

Emmett's head fell forward with sobs. He cried. Sam hadn't seen him cry like that. The sobs grew louder. He tried to talk and he couldn't. He couldn't even smoke his cigarette.

"Don't talk," she said. He kept crying, his head down—long throaty sobs, heaving helplessly. Sam let him cry. She heard him say "Anita." She was afraid. Now, at last. She went into the woods to pee and when she got back he was still crying. He sounded exactly like a screech owl. She touched his shoulder, and he shoved her hand away and kept crying—louder now, as though now that they were out in the woods, and it was broad daylight, and there were no people, he could just let loose.

His cry grew louder, as loud as the wail of a peacock. She watched in awe. In his diary, her father seemed to whimper, but Emmett's sorrow was full-blown, as though it had grown over the years into something monstrous and fantastic. His cigarette had burned down, and he dropped it over the railing.

They walked back to the car. Sam sat in the car and Emmett, still crying, sat on the hood. His bulk made the car shake with his sobs. Sam reached in her backpack and wormed out a granola bar. She resisted the temptation to turn on the car radio. An old song, "Stranded in the Jungle," went through her mind. A flash from the past. A golden oldie. It would be ironic if the car wouldn't start. But Cawood's Pond was beginning to seem like home. She and Emmett could stay out here. Emmett's ability to repair things would come in handy. He could rig them up a lean-to. He could dig them a foxhole. It still made her angry that she couldn't dig a foxhole. That woman Mondale nominated could probably dig one.

She had left the car door open. Emmett hung on the door and bent down to speak to her through the window. He said, "You ran off. When you ran off I thought you were dead."

"No, I wasn't dead. What made you think that?"

"I thought you'd left me. I thought you must have gone off to die. I was afraid you'd kill yourself."

"Why would you think that?"

"So many kids these days are doing it. On the news the other day, those kids over in Carlisle County that made that suicide pact—that shook me up."

"I wouldn't do that," Sam said.

"But how was I to know? You were gone, and I didn't know what might have happened to you. I thought you'd get hurt. It was like being left by myself and all my buddies dead. I had to find you."

"Thank you." She wadded up the granola wrapper and squeezed it in her hand. She said, "You've done something like that before, Emmett. When you went to Vietnam, you went for Mom's sake—and mine."

He nodded thoughtfully. He said, "It wasn't what you wanted, was it? It wasn't what Irene wanted. Then she got stuck with me because of what I did for her. Ain't life stupid? Fuck a duck!"

"Get in, Emmett," she said, reaching to open the door on the passenger side.

"No. I ain't finished." His face was twisted in pain and his pimples glistened with tears. He said, "There's something wrong with me. I'm damaged. It's like something in the center of my heart is gone and I can't get it back. You know when you cut down a tree sometimes and it's diseased in the middle?"

"I never cut down a tree."

"Well, imagine it."

"Yeah. But what you're saying is you don't care about anybody. But you cared enough about me to come out here. And you cared about Mom enough to go over there."

"But don't you understand—let me explain. This is what I *do*. I work on staying together, one day at a time. There's no room for anything else. It takes all my energy."

"Emmett, don't you want to get married and have a family like other people? Don't you want to do something with your life?"

He sobbed again. "I *want* to be a father. But I can't. The closest I can come is with you. And I failed. I should never have let you go so wild. I should have taken care of you."

"You cared," she said. "You felt something for me coming out here." She felt weak. Now her knees felt wobbly. She got out of the car and shut the door.

"I was afraid," he said. "Come here, I want to show you something." He led her to the boardwalk, and they looked out over the swamp. He pointed to a snake sunning on a log. "That sucker's a cottonmouth."

"I wish that bird would come," Sam said.

"You know the reason I want to see that bird?"

"Not really."

"If you can think about something like birds, you can get outside of yourself, and it doesn't hurt as much. That's the whole idea. That's the whole challenge for the human race. Think about that. Put your thinking cap on, Sam. Put that in your pipe and smoke it! But I can barely get to the point where I can be a self to get out of."

Sam picked a big hunk of fungus off a stump and sniffed it. It smelled dead. Emmett said, "I came out here to save you, but maybe I can't. Maybe you have to find out for yourself. Fuck. You can't learn from the past. The main thing you learn from history is that you can't learn from history. That's what history *is*."

Emmett flung a hand toward the black water beside the boardwalk. "See these little minnows? It looks like they've got one eye on the top of their heads. They're called topwaters. They're good for a pond. Catfish whomp 'em up. See that dead tree? That's a woodpecker hole up there. But a wood duck will build a nest there."

"How do you know all that?"

"I've watched 'em. There are things you can figure out, but most things you can't." He waved at the dark swamp. "There are some things you can never figure out."

He turned and walked ahead of her, walking fast up the path from the boardwalk. She followed. He entered a path into the woods and walked faster. Poison ivy curled around his shoes. From the back, he looked like an old peasant woman hugging a baby. Sam watched as he disappeared into the woods. He seemed to float away, above the poison ivy, like a pond skimmer, beautiful in his flight.

Incoming

KEVIN BOWEN

1994

Incoming

Don't let them kid you—
The mind no fool like the movies,
doesn't wait for flash or screech,
but moves of its own accord,
even hears the slight
bump the mortars make
as they kiss the tubes good-bye.
Then the furious rain,
a fist driving home a message:
"Boy, you don't belong here."
On good nights they walk them in.
You wait for them to fall,
stomach pinned so tight to ground
you might feel a woman's foot
pace a kitchen floor in Brownsville;
the hushed fall of a man lost
in a corn field in Michigan;
a young girl's finger trace
a lover's name on a beach along Cape Cod.
But then the air is sucked
straight up off the jungle
floor and the entire weight
of Jupiter and her moons

presses down on the back of a knee.
In a moment, it's over.
But it takes a lifetime to recover,
let out the last breath
you took as you dove.
This is why you'll see them sometimes,
in malls, men and women off in corners;
the ways they stare through the windows in silence.

In the Lake of the Woods

TIM O'BRIEN

1994

THE NATURE OF THE BEAST

The war was aimless. No targets, no visible enemy. There was nothing to shoot back at. Men were hurt and then more men were hurt and nothing was ever gained by it. The ambushes never worked. The patrols turned up nothing but women and kids and old men.

"Like that bullshit kid's game," Rusty Calley said one evening. "They hide, we seek, except we're chasin' a bunch of gookish fucking ghosts."

In the dark someone did witch imitations. Someone else laughed. For Sorcerer, who sat listening at his foxhole, the war had become a state of mind. Not bedlam exactly, but the din was nearby.

"Eyeballs for eyeballs," Calley said. "One of your famous Bible regulations."

All through February they worked an AO called Pinkville, a chain of dark, sullen hamlets tucked up against the South China Sea. The men hated the place, and feared it. On their maps the sector was shaded a bright shimmering pink to signify a "built-up area," with many hamlets and paddy dikes and fields of rice. But for Charlie Company there was nothing bright about Pinkville. It was spook country. The geography of evil: tunnels and bamboo thickets and mud huts and graves.

On February 25, 1968, they stumbled into a minefield near a village called Lac Son.

"I'm killed," someone said, and he was.

A steady gray rain was falling. Thunder advanced from the mountains to the west. After an hour a pair of dustoff choppers settled in. The casualties were piled aboard and the helicopters rose into the rain with three more dead, twelve more wounded.

"Don't mean zip," Calley said. His face was childlike and flaccid. He turned to one of the medics. "What's up, doc?"

Three weeks later, on March 14, a booby-trapped 155 round blew Sergeant George Cox into several large wet pieces. Dyson lost both legs. Hendrixson lost an arm and a leg.

Two or three men were crying.

Others couldn't remember how.

"Kill Nam," said Lieutenant Calley. He pointed his weapon at the earth, burned twenty quick rounds. "Kill it," he said. He reloaded and shot the grass and a palm tree and then the earth again. "Grease the place," he said. "Kill it."

In the late afternoon of March 15 John Wade received a short letter from Kathy. It was composed on light blue stationery with a strip of embossed gold running along the top margin. Her handwriting was dark and confident.

"What I hope," she wrote him, "is that someday you'll understand that I need things for myself. I need a productive future—a real life. When you get home, John, you'll have to treat me like the human being I am. I've grown up. I'm different now, and you are too, and we'll both have to make adjustments. We have to be looser with each other, not so wound up or something—you can't *squeeze* me so much—I need to feel like I'm not a puppet or something. Anyway, just so you know, I've been going out with a couple of guys. It's nothing serious. Repeat: nothing serious. I love you, and I think we can be wonderful together."

Sorcerer wrote back that evening: "What do you get when you breed VC with rats?"

He smiled to himself and jotted down the answer on a separate slip of paper.

"Midget rats," he wrote.

. . .

At 7:22 on the morning of March 16, 1968, the lead elements of Charlie Company boarded a flight of helicopters that climbed into the thin, rosy sunlight, gathered into assault formation, then banked south and skimmed low and fast over scarred, mangled, bombed-out countryside toward a landing zone just west of Pinkville.

Something was wrong.

Maybe it was the sunlight.

Sorcerer felt dazed and half asleep, still dreaming wild dawn dreams. All night he'd been caught up in pink rivers and pink paddies; even now, squatting at the rear of the chopper, he couldn't flush away the pink. All that color—it was wrong. The air was wrong. The smells were wrong, and the thin rosy sunlight, and how the men seemed wrapped inside themselves. Meadlo and Mitchell and Thinbill sat with their eyes closed. Sledge fiddled with his radio. Conti was off in some mental whorehouse. PFC Weatherby kept wiping his M-16 with a towel, first the barrel and then his face and then the barrel again. Boyce and Maples and Lieutenant Calley sat side by side in the chopper's open doorway, sharing a cigarette, quietly peering down at the cratered fields and paddies.

Pure wrongness, Sorcerer knew.

He could taste the sunlight. It had a rusty, metallic flavor, like nails on his tongue.

For a few seconds, Sorcerer shut his eyes and retreated behind the mirrors in his head, pretending to be elsewhere, but even then the landscapes kept coming at him fast and lurid.

At 7:30 the choppers banked in a long arc and approached the hamlet of Thuan Yen from the southwest. Below, almost straight ahead, white puffs of smoke opened up in the paddies just outside the village. The artillery barrage swept across the fields and into the western fringes of Thuan Yen, cutting through underbrush and bamboo and banana trees, setting fires here and there, shifting northward as the helicopters skimmed in low over the drop zone. The door gunners were now laying down a steady suppressing fire. They leaned into their big guns, shoulders twitching. The noise made Sorcerer's eyelids go haywire.

"Down and dirty!" someone yelled, and the chopper settled into a wide dry paddy.

Mitchell was first off. Then Boyce and Conti and Meadlo, then Maples, then Sledge, then Thinbill and the stubby lieutenant.

Sorcerer went last.

He jumped into the sunlight, fell flat, found himself alone in the paddy. The others had vanished. There was gunfire all around, a machine-gun wind, and the wind seemed to pick him up and blow him from place to place. He couldn't get his legs beneath him. For a time he lay pinned down by things unnatural, the wind and heat, the wicked sunlight. He would not remember pushing to his feet. Directly ahead, a pair of stately old coconut trees burst into flame.

Just inside the village, Sorcerer found a pile of dead goats.

He found a pretty girl with her pants down. She was dead too. She looked at him cross-eyed. Her hair was gone.

He found dead dogs, dead chickens.

Farther along, he encountered someone's forehead. He found three dead water buffalo. He found a dead monkey. He found ducks pecking at a dead toddler. Events had been channeling this way for a long while, months of terror, months of slaughter, and now in the pale morning sunlight a kind of meltdown was in progress.

Pigs were squealing.

The morning air was flaming up toward purple.

He watched a young man hobbling up the trail, one foot torn away at the ankle. He watched Weatherby shoot two little girls in the face. Deeper into the village, in front of a small L-shaped hootch, he came across a GI with a woman's black ponytail flowing from his helmet. The man wiped a hand across his crotch. He gave a little flip to the ponytail and smiled at Sorcerer and blooped an M-79 round into the L-shaped hootch. "Blammo," the man said. He shook his head as if embarrassed. "Yeah, well," he said, then shrugged and fired off another round and said, "Boom." At his feet was a wailing infant. A middle-aged woman lay nearby. She was draped across a bundle of straw, not quite dead, shot in the legs and stomach. The woman gazed at the world with indifference. At one point she made an obscure motion with her head, a kind of bow, inexact, after which she rocked herself away.

There were dead waterfowl and dead house pets. People were dying loudly inside the L-shaped hootch.

Sorcerer uttered meaningless sounds—"No," he said, then after a second he said, "Please!"—and then the sunlight sucked him down a trail toward the center of the village, where he found burning hootches and brightly mobile figures engaged in murder. Simpson was killing children. PFC Weatherby was killing whatever he could kill. A row of corpses lay in the pink-to-purple sunshine along the trail—teenagers and old women and two babies and a young boy. Most were dead, some were almost dead. The dead lay very still. The almost-dead did twitching things until PFC Weatherby had occasion to reload and make them fully dead. The noise was fierce. No one was dying quietly. There were squeakings and chickenhouse sounds.

"Please," Sorcerer said again. He felt very stupid. Thirty meters up the trail he came across Conti and Meadlo and Rusty Calley. Meadlo and the lieutenant were spraying gunfire into a crowd of villagers. They stood side by side, taking turns. Meadlo was crying. Conti was watching. The lieutenant shouted something and shot down a dozen women and kids and then reloaded and shot down more and then reloaded and shot down more and then reloaded again. The air was hot and wet. "Jeez, come *on*," the lieutenant said, "get with it— *move*—light up these fuckers," but Sorcerer was already sprinting away. He ran past a smoking bamboo schoolhouse. Behind him and in front of him, a brisk machine-gun wind pressed through Thuan Yen. The wind stirred up a powdery red dust that sparkled in the morning sunshine, and the little village had now gone mostly violet. He found someone stabbing people with a big silver knife. Hutto was shooting corpses. T'Souvas was shooting children. Doherty and Terry were finishing off the wounded. This was not madness, Sorcerer understood. This was sin. He felt it winding through his own arteries, something vile and slippery like heavy black oil in a crankcase.

Stop, he thought. But it wouldn't stop. Someone shot an old farmer and lifted him up and dumped him in a well and tossed in a grenade.

Roschevitz shot people in the head.

Hutson and Wright took turns on a machine gun.

The killing was steady and inclusive. The men took frequent smoke breaks; they ate candy bars and exchanged stories.

A period of dark time went by, maybe an hour, maybe more, then Sorcerer found himself on his hands and knees behind a bamboo fence. A few meters away, in the vicinity of a large wooden turret, fifteen or twenty villagers squatted in the morning sunlight. They were chattering among themselves, their faces tight, and then somebody strolled up and made a waving motion and shot them dead.

There were flies now—a low droning buzz that swelled up from somewhere deep inside the village.

And then for a while Sorcerer let himself glide away. All he could do was close his eyes and kneel there and wait for whatever was wrong with the world to right itself. At one point it occurred to him that the weight of this day would ultimately prove too much, that sooner or later he would have to lighten the load.

He looked at the sky.

Later he nodded.

And then later still, snagged in the sunlight, he gave himself over to forgetfulness. "Go away," he murmured. He waited a moment, then said it again, firmly, much louder, and the little village began to vanish inside its own rosy glow. Here, he reasoned, was the most majestic trick of all. In the months and years ahead, John Wade would remember Thuan Yen the way chemical nightmares are remembered, impossible combinations, impossible events, and over time the impossibility itself would become the richest and deepest and most profound memory.

This could not have happened. Therefore it did not.

Already he felt better.

Tracer rounds corkscrewed through the glare, and people were dying in long neat rows. The sunlight was in his blood.

He would both remember and not remember a fleet human movement off to his left.

He would not remember squealing.

He would not remember raising his weapon, nor rolling away from the bamboo fence, but he would remember forever how he turned and shot down an old man with a wispy beard and wire glasses and what looked to be a rifle. It was not a rifle. It was a small wooden hoe. The hoe he would always remember. In the ordinary hours after the war, at the breakfast table or in the babble of some dreary statehouse hearing, John Wade would sometimes look up to see the wooden hoe spinning like a baton in the morning sunlight. He would see the old man shuffling past the bamboo fence, the skinny legs, the erect posture and the wire glasses, the hoe suddenly sailing up high and doing its quick twinkling spin and coming down uncaught. He would feel only the faintest sense of culpability. The forgetting trick mostly worked. On certain late-night occasions, however, John Wade would remember covering his head and screaming and crawling through a hedgerow and out into a wide paddy where helicopters were ferrying in supplies. The paddy was full of colored smoke, lavenders and yellows. There were loud voices, and many explosions, but he couldn't seem to locate anyone. He found a young woman laid open without a chest or lungs. He found dead cattle. All around him there were flies and burning trees and burning hootches.

Later, he found himself at the bottom of an irrigation ditch. There were many bodies present, maybe a hundred. He was caught up in the slime.

PFC Weatherby found him there.

"Hey, Sorcerer," Weatherby said. The guy started to smile, but Sorcerer shot him anyway.

EVIDENCE

Q: How do you evacuate someone with a hand grenade?

A: I don't have any idea, sir.

Q: Why did you make that statement?

A: It was a figure of speech, sir.

Q: What did you mean when you said it?

A: I meant just—I meant only that the only means I could evacuate the people would be a hand grenade. And that isn't exactly evacuating somebody.[37]

   —William Calley (Court-Martial Testimony)

Son My Village is located approximately 9 kilometers northeast of Quang Ngai City and fronts on the South China Sea. In March 1968, the village was composed of four hamlets, Tu Cung, My Lai, My Khe, and Co Luy, each of which contained several subhamlets . . . The Vietnamese knew many of these subhamlets by names different from those indicated on US topographic maps of the area. . . . For example, the subhamlet identified on the topographic map as My Lai (4) is actually named Thuan Yen.[38]

—The Peers Commission

Q: What did you do?

A: I held my M-16 on them.

---

[37] In Richard Hammer, *The Court-Martial of Lt. Calley* (New York: Coward, McCann & Geoghegen, 1971), p. 272.

[38] *Report of the Department of the Army, Review of the Preliminary Investigations into the My Lai Incident*, Volume I, Department of the Army, March 14, 1970, p. 3–3. Hereafter referred to as The Peers Commission.

Q: Why?

A: Because they might attack.

Q: They were children and babies?

A: Yes.

Q: And they might attack? Children and babies?

A: They might've had a fully loaded grenade on them. The mothers might have throwed them at us.

Q: Babies?

A: Yes.

Q: Were the babies in their mothers' arms?

A: I guess so.

Q: And the babies moved to attack?

A: I expected at any moment they were about to make a counterbalance.[39]

— Paul Meadlo (Court-Martial Testimony)

I raised him up to be a good boy and I did everything I could. They come along and took him to the service. He fought for his country and look what they done to him. Made a murderer out of him, to start with.[40]

— Mrs. Myrtle Meadlo (Mother of Paul Meadlo)

. . . there is a line that a man dare not cross, deeds he dare not commit, regardless of orders and the hopelessness of the situation, for such deeds would destroy something in him that he values more than life itself.[41]

— J. Glenn Gray (*The Warriors*)

John had his own way of handling it all. It destroyed him, you could say. But maybe in a lot of ways he was already destroyed.

— Anthony L. (Tony) Carbo

[39] In Hammer, *The Court-Martial of Lt. Calley*, pp. 161–162.

[40] CBS Evening News, Nov. 25, 1969, in Michael Bilton and Kevin Sim, *Four Hours in My Lai* (New York: Viking, 1992), p. 263.

[41] J. Glenn Gray, *The Warriors: Reflections on Men in Battle* (1959; reprint, Harper Torchbooks, 1970), p. 186.

I am struck by how little of these events I can or even wish to remember . . .[42]

— Colonel William V. Wilson (U.S. Army Investigator)

Look, I don't remember. It was three years ago.[43]

— Ronald Grzesik (Court-Martial Testimony)

Q: Did you ever tell any officer about what you'd seen?
A: I can't specifically recall.[44]

— Ronald Haeberle (Court-Martial Testimony)

Q: How many people were in the ditch?
A: I don't know, sir.
Q: Over how large an area were they in the ditch?
A: I don't know, sir.
Q: Could you give us an estimate as to how many people were in the ditch?
A: No, sir.[45]

— William Calley (Court-Martial Testimony)

Q: What happened then?
A: He [Lieutenant Calley] started shoving them off and shooting them in the ravine.
Q: How many times did he shoot?
A: I can't remember.[46]

— Paul Meadlo (Court-Martial Testimony)

All I remember now is flies. And the stink. Some of the guys made these gas masks — dunked their T-shirts in mosquito juice and Kool-

---

[42] Col. William V. Wilson, *American Heritage*, February 1990, p. 53.
[43] In Hammer, *The Court-Martial of Lt. Calley*, p. 151.
[44] *Ibid.*, p. 91.
[45] *Ibid.*, p. 269.
[46] *Ibid.*, p. 155.

Aid. That helped a little, but it didn't help with the flies. I can't stop dreaming about them. You think I'm crazy?

—Richard Thinbill

The ordinary response to atrocities is to banish them from consciousness.[47]

—Judith Herman (*Trauma and Recovery*)

John really suffered during the campaign. Those terrible things people said, it wasn't right. I don't believe a word.

—Eleanor K. Wade

Q: Did you see any dead Vietnamese in the village?

A: Yes, sir.

Q: How many?

A: Most of them. All over.[48]

—Gene Oliver (Court-Martial Testimony)

Persons taking no active part in the hostilities, including members of armed forces who have laid down their arms and those placed *hors de combat* by sickness, wounds, detention, or any other cause, shall in all circumstances be treated humanely . . .[49]

—The Geneva Convention on the Laws of War

Q: Can you describe what you saw?

A: There was a large mound of dead Vietnamese in the ditch.

Q: Can you estimate how many?

A: It's hard to say. I'd say forty to fifty.

Q: Can you describe the ditch?

A: It was seven to ten feet deep, maybe ten to fifteen feet across. The

---

[47] Herman, *Trauma and Recovery*, p. 1.

[48] In Hammer, *The Court-Martial of Lt. Calley*, p. 101.

[49] *The Geneva Convention on the Laws of War*, 1949, article 3, section 1.

bodies were all across it. There was one group in the middle and more on the sides. The bodies were on top of each other.[50]

    —Richard Pendleton (Court-Martial Testimony)

Q: How did you know they were dead?
A: They weren't moving. There was a lot of blood coming from all over them. They were in piles and scattered. There were very old people, very young people, and mothers. Blood was coming from everywhere. Everything was all blood.[51]

    —Charles Hall (Court-Martial Testimony)

Q: Did you see any bodies shot?
A: Right, sir.
Q: Women and children?
A: Right, sir, women and children, about twenty-five of them in the northeastern part of My Lai (4).
Q: Did you see any other bodies?
A: Right, sir. About ten of them, in that place north of My Lai. They were all women and they were all nude.
Q: Were there any soldiers from your platoon there?
A: Right, sir. Roshevitz, he was there. He had an M-79. Those women, they died from a canister round from his M-79.[52]

    —Leonard Gonzalez (Court-Martial Testimony)

Exhibit Eight: John Wade's Box of Tricks, Partial List
    Deck of playing cards (all the jack of diamonds)
    Thumb tip feke
    Photographs (12) of father
    Pack of chewing gum
    Bronze Star with V-device
    Purple Hearts (2)
    Army Commendation Medal

[50] In Hammer, *The Court-Martial of Lt. Calley*, p. 104.
[51] *Ibid.*, p. 177.
[52] *Ibid.*, p. 193.

Combat Infantryman's Badge
Waxed rope
Adhesive false mustache
Vodka bottle (empty)
Book: *Mental Magic*
Book: *Feats of Levitation*

Q: What were they firing at?
A: At the enemy, sir.
Q: At people?
A: At the enemy, sir.
Q: They weren't human beings?
A: Yes, sir.
Q: They were human beings?
A: Yes, sir.
Q: Were they men?
A: I don't know, sir. I would imagine they were, sir.
Q: Didn't you see?
A: Pardon, sir?
Q: Did you see them?
A: I wasn't discriminating.
Q: Did you see women?
A: I don't know, sir.
Q: What do you mean, you weren't discriminating?
A: I didn't discriminate between individuals in the village, sir. They were all the enemy, they were all to be destroyed, sir.[53]
  —William Calley (Court-Martial Testimony)

It is a crucial moment in a soldier's life when he is ordered to perform a deed that he finds completely at variance with his own notions of right and good. Probably for the first time, he discovers that an act someone else thinks to be necessary is for him criminal . . . Suddenly the soldier feels himself abandoned and cast off from all security. Conscience has isolated him, and its voice is a warning. If you do

[53] *Ibid.*, p. 263.

this, you will not be at peace with me in the future. You can do it, but you ought not. You must act as a man and not as an instrument of another's will.[54]

—J. Glenn Gray (*The Warriors*)

The violation of human connection, and consequently the risk of a post-traumatic stress disorder, is highest of all when the survivor has been not merely a passive witness but also an active participant in violent death or atrocity.[55]

—Judith Herman (*Trauma and Recovery*)

Q: Did you receive any hostile fire at all any time that day?
A: No, sir.[56]

—Frank Beardslee (Court-Martial Testimony)

Q: Did you obey your orders?
A: Yes, sir.
Q: What were your orders?
A: Kill anything that breathed.[57]

—Salvatore LaMartina (Court-Martial Testimony)

John! John! Oh, John![58]
—George Armstrong Custer

Fucking flies!
—Richard Thinbill

I just went. My mind just went. And I wasn't the only one that did it. A lot of other people did it. I just killed. Once I started the . . . the

---

[54] Gray, *The Warriors: Reflections on Men in Battle*, pp. 184–185.

[55] Herman, *Trauma and Recovery*, p. 54.

[56] In Hammer, *The Court-Martial of Lt. Calley*, p. 93.

[57] *Ibid.*, p. 188.

[58] Evan S. Connell, *Son of the Morning Star* (San Francisco: North Point Press, 1984), p. 307. Connell writes that "John" was the name "ordinarily used by whites when addressing an Indian." At the Little Big Horn, on June 25, 1876, one terrified trooper "was heard sobbing this name, as though it might save his life. *John! John! Oh, John!* This plea echoes horribly down a hundred years."

training, the whole programming part of killing, it just came out . . .
I just followed suit. I just lost all sense of direction, of purpose. I just
started killing any kinda way I could kill. It just came. I didn't know I
had it in me.[59]

   —Varnado Simpson (Charlie Company, Second Platoon)

Q: Then what happened?
A: Lieutenant Calley came out and said take care of these people. So
we said, okay, so we stood there and watched them. He went away,
then he came back and said, "I thought I told you to take care of
these people." We said, "We are." He said, "I mean kill them." I
was a little stunned and I didn't know what to do. . . . I stood
behind them and they stood side by side. So they—Calley and
Meadlo—got on line and fired directly into the people . . . It
was automatic. The people screamed and yelled and fell. I guess
they tried to get up, too. They couldn't. That was it. The people
were pretty well messed up. Lots of heads was shot off. Pieces of
heads and pieces of flesh flew off the sides and arms.[60]

   —Dennis Conti (Court-Martial Testimony)

The dismounted troopers then ran downhill and slid into the ravine
where their bodies were found . . . [T]hey must have felt helplessly
exposed and rushed toward the one place that might protect them. Yet
the moment they skidded into the gully they were trapped. All they
could do was hug the sides or crouch among the bushes, looking
fearfully upward, and wait. A few tried to scramble up the south wall
because the earth showed boot marks and furrows probably gouged by
their fingers, but none of these tracks reached the surface.[61]

   —Evan S. Connell (*Son of the Morning Star*)

Q: Can you describe them?
A: They was women and little kids.

---

[59] In Bilton and Sims, *Four Hours in My Lai*, p. 7.
[60] In Hammer, *The Court-Martial of Lt. Calley*, pp. 122–124.
[61] Connell, *Son of the Morning Star*, p. 309.

Q: What were they doing?

A: They were lying on the ground, bleeding from all over. They was dead.[62]

— Rennard Doines (Court-Martial Testimony)

Q: Did you have any conversation with Lieutenant Calley at that ditch?

A: Yes.

Q: What did he say?

A: He asked me to use my machine gun.

Q: At the ditch?

A: Yes.

Q: What did you say?

A: I refused.[63]

— Robert Maples (Court-Martial Testimony)

Q: Did you ever open your pants in front of a woman in the village of My Lai?

A: No.

Q: Isn't it a fact that you were going through My Lai that day looking for women?

A: No.

Q: Didn't you carry a woman half-nude on your shoulders and throw her down and say that she was too dirty to rape? You did that, didn't you?

A: Oh, yeah, but it wasn't at My Lai.[64]

— Dennis Conti (Court-Martial Testimony)

Every man has some reminiscences which he would not tell to every-one, but only to his friends. He has others which he would not reveal even to his friends, but only to himself, and that in secret. But finally there are still others which a man is even afraid to tell himself, and

---

[62] In Hammer, *The Court-Martial of Lt. Calley*, p. 112.

[63] *Ibid.*, p. 114.

[64] *Ibid.*, p. 127.

every decent man has a considerable number of such things stored away. . . . Man is bound to lie about himself.[65]
—Fyodor Dostoevsky *(Notes from Underground)*

Married veterans or guys who married when they got back had difficulties, too. Waking up with your hands around your wife's throat is frightening to the vet and to the wife. Is he crazy? Does he hate me? What the hell's going on?[66]
—Patience H. C. Mason *(Recovering from the War)*

Like I told you, he used to yell things in his sleep. Bad things. Kathy thought he needed help.
—Patricia S. Hood

Something was wrong with the guy. No shit, I could almost smell it.
—Vincent R. (Vinny) Pearson

. . . the crimes visited on the inhabitants of Son My Village included individual and group acts of murder, rape, sodomy, maiming, assault on noncombatants, and the mistreatment and killing of detainees.[67]
—Colonel William V. Wilson (U.S. Army Investigator)

[65] Fyodor Dostoevsky, *Notes from Underground*, translated by Ralph E. Matlaw (New York: E. P. Dutton, 1960), p. 35.

[66] Mason, *Recovering from the War: A Woman's Guide to Helping Your Vietnam Vet, Your Family, and Yourself*, p. 181.

[67] Wilson, *American Heritage*, p. 53. The number of civilian casualties during operations in Son My Village on March 16, 1968, is a matter of continuing dispute. The Peers Commission concluded that "at least 175–200 Vietnamese men, women, and children" were killed in the course of the March 16th operation. The U.S. Army's Criminal Investigation Division (CID) estimated on the basis of census data that the casualties "may have exceeded 400." At the Son My Memorial, which I visited in the course of research for this book, the number is fixed at 504. An amazing experience, by the way. Thuan Yen is still a quiet little farming village, very poor, very remote, with dirt paths and cow dung and high bamboo hedgerows. Very friendly, all things considered: the old folks nod and smile; the children giggle at our white foreign faces. The ditch is still there. I found it easily. Just five or six feet deep, shallow and unimposing, yet it was as if I had been there before, in my dreams, or in some other life.

Mr. Giai's Poem

JOHN BALABAN

1991

Mr. Giai's Poem

The French ships shelled Haiphong then took the port.
Mr. Giai was running down the road, mobilized
with two friends, looking for their unit in towns
where thatch and geese lay shattered on the roads
and smoke looped up from cratered yards. A swarm
of bullock carts and bicycles streamed against them
as trousered women strained with children, chickens,
charcoal, and rice towards Hanoi in the barrage lull.
Then, Giai said, they saw just stragglers.
Ahead, the horizon thumped with bombs.

At an empty inn they tried their luck
though the waiter said he'd nothing left.
"Just a coffee," said Mr. Giai. "A sip
of whisky," said one friend. "A cigarette," the other.
Miraculously, these each appeared. Serene,
they sat a while, then went to fight.
Giai wrote a poem about that pause for *Ve Quoc Quan*,
the Army paper. Critics found the piece bourgeois.

Forty years of combat now behind him
—Japanese, Americans, and French.
Wounded twice, deployed in jungles for nine years,
his son just killed in Cambodia,

Giai tells this tale to three Americans
each young enough to be his son:
an ex-Marine once rocketed in Hue,
an Army grunt, mortared at Bong Son,
a c.o. hit by a stray of shrapnel,
all four now silent in the floating restaurant
rocking on moor-lines in the Saigon river.
Crabshells and beer bottles litter their table.
A rat runs a rafter overhead. A wave slaps by.
"That moment," Giai adds, "was a little like now."
They raise their glasses to the river's amber light,
all four as quiet as if carved in ivory.

13

The Wall

1985. A veteran at the Vietnam Memorial.

Now a national shrine, the Vietnam Veterans Memorial at first aroused bitter controversy. In 1981, Yale architecture student Maya Lin's winning design (the judges' decision was unanimous) was called "a black ditch of shame," and opposed vigorously by many in the Reagan administration, including James Webb. Though private money funded the construction, in a flurry of political dealing— much of it involving the government land and corporate funding for the Wall—Ross Perot's contingent managed to get Jan Scruggs and the other founders of the Memorial to add the more heroic statue of the three grunts. It was fitting, cultural critics said, that even the memorial to this war would divide the country; literary critics noted the typical representational split between the figurative and the literal.

The dedication of the Wall in 1982 dispelled any controversy, as veterans and their relatives found the Memorial a powerful and apt remembrance of their friends and loved ones. Legends sprang up around the Wall, the most famous alleging that names carved in the black granite could be seen shedding tears. The Wall is now Washington's most popular tourist destination, and thousands of Americans visit it each day, many leaving behind offerings for the war's dead.

W. D. Ehrhart's 1984 "The Invasion of Granada," written on the occasion of the Reagan administration's contemporary use of the military, opens up a different controversy, wondering what good the sudden acceptance of the veteran is without a similar understanding of

677

why the Vietnam War was wrong. Again, the veteran and what he or she represents has been forgotten; the symbol of the Wall, it seems, is easier to embrace than the real lessons of the war.

In the literature of Vietnam, as in life, the Wall has become a final destination for veterans and family members. The long journey to it—emotionally and physically—ends a great number of oral histories, memoirs, and novels. In my own *The Names of the Dead* (1996), medic Larry Markham takes his mentally disabled son Scott to the Wall, along with the offerings his veterans-outreach group has asked him to leave. Like many vets, Larry resists going to the Wall yet feels it's necessary; he's not sure how it's going to hit him, if—like the stories his rap group tells and the memories he himself examines—it will help him or only hurt him more. *The Names of the Dead* is distinctive in that it's the first Vietnam novel from a vet's perspective written by a nonvet from the next generation.

Yusef Komunyakaa's "Between Days" and "Facing It" from *Dien Cai Dau* (1988) concern memorials, the first a mother's inability to give up her dead son, the second the poet's own thoughts on seeing the Wall for the first time. In both, the power of hope and memory fuses the present with the past, the last generation to the next one. Unlike the casual visitor, the vet has to figure out what the Wall means and, symbolically, where he stands in relation to his memories of the war—trapped inside them, free to leave, or both.

The Invasion of Grenada

W. D. Ehrhart

1984

The Invasion of Grenada

I didn't want a monument,
not even one as sober as that
vast black wall of broken lives.
I didn't want a postage stamp.
I didn't want a road beside the Delaware
River with a sign proclaiming:
"Vietnam Veterans Memorial Highway."

What I wanted was a simple recognition
of the limits of our power as a nation
to inflict our will on others.
What I wanted was an understanding
that the world is neither black-and-white
nor ours.

What I wanted
was an end to monuments.

The Names of the Dead

Stewart O'Nan

1996

It wasn't just the names. They wanted him to take pictures. They wanted him to leave things. Trayner gave him a boonie hat soft as a chamois, Mel White a pair of mirrored shades missing a stem. Meredith sent a pocket chess set, Sponge a plastic grass skirt. Larry wanted to take the ace and the pistol, but Clines needed them for evidence. He'd kept Larry's name out of the paper. Creeley was a suicide, the wound self-inflicted, which was the truth. Larry emptied the trunk upstairs. He had Magoo's pictures and Leonard Dawson's cards in a bag in the back of Number 1, along with all of the ward's stuff. His class A's swung from a hanger in the empty racks.

He wasn't carrying anything else. He'd checked the truck out before Marv got in, and now he was well south of Ithaca, tooling through the hills. In the passenger seat, Scott followed the arc of the wipers, cocking his head like a dog. Vicki had forbidden him to go, and Larry had to kidnap him out of class. He kept to the right lane, watched for cops in the grassy meridian, the islands of trees.

He'd thought of taking his father but he needed a few days to recuperate. Though the beating had left no visible scars, his body was thick with fluid, his knees and elbows swollen. Mrs. Railsbeck took a tray up to his bedroom. His father remembered Creeley saying something about his mother but exactly what he could honestly not recall. He thought Larry should have killed him but understood; maybe Larry was right. It was an argument for another time. Scott was a better choice, Larry thought; his father already knew the price of war, the hardest lessons.

It was Wednesday, there was no one on the road, only muddy logging trucks, campers quilted with bumper stickers. They slowed for the little cities—Horseheads, Corning—moved through them anonymously, camouflaged, then turned south into the emptiness of central Pennsylvania. Peeling billboards stood in cornfields; churches advertised their sermons. Miles outside of Mansfield an adult bookstore beckoned to truckers, its front windowless, a heavy grille over the door. Blossburg came, and Covington—towns without stores, houses falling in on themselves. SPEED CHECKED BY AIRCRAFT, a sign claimed.

"I spy with my little eye," Larry said, "something green."

"Tree," Scott guessed, and then it was his turn.

They used up the yellow line, the bridges, the other cars' license plates. In the mountains the radio stations broke up. "Chances are," Larry whistled. The truck labored up the long grades, the needle dipped toward empty. They coasted through the high hunting country, curving above the great reservoirs, the signs promising Williamsport. It cost him thirty dollars to fill up.

They stopped at a Friendly's above Harrisburg for lunch. Larry checked his wallet, then helped Scott down and held his hand across the parking lot. The waitress gave Scott crayons in a cup and an E.T. placemat; she called him darlin'.

"Nothing for Dad?" she asked, and Larry smiled as if he had to resist her. A free sundae came with the meal; Larry helped him with it.

They got back in the truck and drove, the Susquehanna on their left, the low stone bridges and railroad tracks. Larry hoped for a train to show Scott, but when they caught up with one, he'd fallen asleep, his head bent forward, one eye vigilant, the other closed. Larry wedged his jacket under his chin, but a minute later it fell out. He hadn't invited Vicki; now he wished she had come. She was better at planning things.

The rain grew worse as the day faded. South of York, traffic on the interstate stopped, a field of taillights. For half an hour they inched along, merging left. Ahead, a galaxy of police cars blocked the road, their lightbars strobing over the pines. Trucks headed the other way slowed to see what was going on. Larry expected to be stopped and questioned, Scott pulled from the truck. Finally the file slid past an accident, a yellow Corvette broken over the guardrail, its fiberglass nose cracked. The EMTs were working over someone, their elbows jerking. He thought of the grip they'd taught him at Fort Sam, and for an instant, Salazar, then held himself back. If he started now, he wouldn't stop. He wanted to leave everything there, dump it all in one spot like an Arc Light.

Scott slept through dinner. At the Maryland line, a trooper had a Mercedes on the berm, its owner walking a tightrope in the lights. High above a cloverleaf, a Sunoco sign hung in the black sky like a planet. Farther on, high magnesium stanchions bathed a major exchange the color of weak tea; the interstates poured into each other, widening, gaining strength. Semis whined past a few feet beside him, nose to tail like the cars of a train. It was eight, the professionals were out now, the nationwide lines—Roadway and Carolina, Consolidated Freightways, Red Ball Express. Signs for Virginia appeared, the traffic clotted, and the big rigs veered off, bypassing the Capitol.

On the outskirts, the motel rates tempted him, the truckstops and gas plazas. He didn't know where he was going and he needed to fill up. His eyes burned and his back hurt and he was hungry, but he stayed in the middle lane, avoiding the on-ramps, pointing Number 1 for the city. The signs took him along the river, toward the Lincoln Memorial. He got off and stopped at a gas station, waking Scott.

"Home?" Scott guessed.

It was warmer here, the air rich with mud, as after a thaw. Larry got the pump started and walked to the lit office. The attendant wore a union suit, under it a sweatshirt with a hood. He was younger, his hair in cornrows; he kept a toothpick in one corner of his mouth but didn't chew it. He unfurled a map on the counter but said nothing, and Larry had to ask.

"You mean the ditch," the attendant said, and removed the toothpick. His finger lit on it immediately. "There you go. You won't see nothing though."

Larry bought the map and the attendant drew the route on it with a marker.

Larry had only seen Washington on TV, the protestors and limousines, the marble facades. He remembered the gaslamps from JFK's cortège, the boots turned backwards in the stirrups. It was a disappointment to see it was a city. The corners bristled with convenience stores and panhandlers. Traffic rushed madly from light to light, buses cutting in front of him. He had the map folded into a square, pinning it to the wheel with one thumb.

On the way, they passed a McDonald's. Scott was hungry.

"After," Larry said, and he whined. Larry was trying to placate him when he saw the Washington Monument, the two warning lights on top blinking like eyes. He signaled and pulled to the curb.

The map told him to go around, but the park entrance was closed. They sat idling by the chain with their lights off. The Wall was supposed to be through these trees, but he didn't see anything and double-checked to make sure.

"Okay," he said, and unbuckled Scott.

He helped him down, then went into the back for the bag. He draped his class A's over his shoulder and took Scott's hand. It was still raining, but not hard; under the trees they couldn't feel it. The ground was spongy beneath his feet; he stepped lightly, wary of the roots. In the blackness, Scott squeezed his hand, and Larry wondered how safe the park was. He was too used to Ithaca.

They came to a clearing and stumbled onto a cobblestone path. The bag bumped against his leg. The Wall was supposed to be there, in front of them, but all he saw was an opening and another grove of trees. They crossed the path and a tripwire snagged his shin.

It was a string to keep people off the new grass. Beyond it leaned a snow fence, a slope leading down.

Ahead, below them, a lighter flared, and he could see a figure silhouetted against the Wall. The flame touched a candle, illuminating a face, then just a pair of jungle boots mirrored in the polished stone.

His eyes grew accustomed to the wet reflection. On either side of the candle the Wall stretched indefinitely. It was sunken, the earth contoured to reveal it, ten feet thick in the center, the edges tapering away. It loomed like a whale over the candle, the granite soaking up most of the light. He was too far away to see the names, and wondered how large they were, how small, how many. All, they'd said.

"I'm hungry," Scott whined.

"I know," Larry answered.

They followed the path down to the Wall. It seemed to rise out of the ground in front of them. As they descended, the rush of traffic in the distance softened, then disappeared, leaving only the rain, their shoes scuffing the path. The man at the candle stepped into darkness and vanished as if they'd scared him away.

They moved to the flame and stood before it, holding hands. Larry didn't know the names he was seeing. They looked gray in the flickering light, separated by diamonds. They were small, and most had a middle initial. Someone had loved all of them—mothers, fathers, girlfriends. They had come from towns like Ithaca, from high school, leaving everything they knew. The waste seemed plain. In the tiny patch of light there had to be a hundred. Behind them, looking out, stood the reflection of himself and Scott.

The candle rested on a ledge jutting from the base of the Wall. Between the path and the ledge stretched a few feet of sod heaped with wreaths and flags and heart-shaped pillows, teddy bears and keychains, framed pictures. There were boots and OD T-shirts, helmets with scrawled-on liners, medals in their cases, unopened beer cans and packs of cigarettes. Scott sloughed off his hand and leaned down to pick up a stuffed rabbit, and Larry gently said, "No, champ."

"Here," he said, and gave him his class A's. He had to convince Scott to add them to the pile.

He opened the bag and let Scott take some of his things out— Magoo's pictures and Leonard Dawson's cards, Salazar's list. They walked down toward the meeting of the V, dropping off Rinehart's fatigue jacket and Cartwright's cigar box. In the cracks between the panels, people had wedged snapshots and letters; a few had fallen to the wet grass. They walked slowly, doling out the contents of the bag—the .50 caliber rounds and paper fans, the jingling dogtags.

When they reached the end, there was nothing left but the lists and Larry's camera.

He shuffled the lists, though they were impossible to see. In the darkness, he couldn't make out the names on the Wall, and he wasn't going to take the man's candle. He leaned across the offerings and touched the granite, his fingertips tracing the letters. All of them, he thought. They were arranged by date. Somewhere in the middle were his—Salazar and Smart Andy, Leonard Dawson and Bates. The Martian, the LT. He didn't have to look at any list. He knew their names.

Larry took out the camera and handed Scott the bag. They'd given him money to buy film. He stood back, framing the blackness. He pressed the button and the flash exploded off the stone, dazzling him. He moved a few steps to his right and took another. The letters stayed with him, burned purple in the dark. He made his way down the Wall, flipping the flashbar, jamming it in like a clip. He worried that the pictures wouldn't come out, and at the far end he turned and came back, taking a second set. He wanted to make sure he got Carl Metcalf and Dumb Andy, Nate and Pony and Bogut. He'd get Fred the Head and Magoo. He'd even get Creeley. This time Larry wouldn't miss anyone. This time he would bring them all home.

Dien Cai Dau

Yusef Komunyakaa

1988

Between Days

Expecting to see him anytime
coming up the walkway
through blueweed & bloodwort,
she says, "That closed casket
was weighed down with stones."
The room is as he left it
fourteen years ago, everything
freshly dusted & polished
with lemon oil. The uncashed
death check from Uncle Sam
marks a passage in the Bible
on the dresser, next to the photo
staring out through the window.
"Mistakes. Mistakes. Now,
he's gonna have to give them this
money back when he gets home.
But I wouldn't. I would
let them pay for their mistakes.
They killed his daddy. & Janet,
she & her three children
by three different men, I hope
he's strong enough to tell her
to get lost. Lord, mistakes."
His row of tin soldiers
lines the window sill. The sunset
flashes across them like a blast.
She's buried the Silver Star
& flag under his winter clothes.
The evening's first fireflies

dance in the air like distant tracers.
Her chair faces the walkway
where she sits before the TV
asleep, as the screen dissolves
into days between snow.

Facing It

My black face fades,
hiding inside the black granite.
I said I wouldn't,
dammit: No tears.
I'm stone. I'm flesh.
My clouded reflection eyes me
like a bird of prey, the profile of night
slanted against morning. I turn
this way—the stone lets me go.
I turn that way—I'm inside
the Vietnam Veterans Memorial
again, depending on the light
to make a difference.
I go down the 58,022 names,
half-expecting to find
my own in letters like smoke.
I touch the name Andrew Johnson;
I see the booby trap's white flash.
Names shimmer on a woman's blouse
but when she walks away
the names stay on the wall.
Brushstrokes flash, a red bird's
wings cutting across my stare.
The sky. A plane in the sky.
A white vet's image floats
closer to me, then his pale eyes
look through mine. I'm a window.
He's lost his right arm
inside the stone. In the black mirror
a woman's trying to erase names:
No, she's brushing a boy's hair.

April 1975. As Saigon falls, helicopters evacuate the U.S. embassy.

Glossary

AIT—advanced individual training

amtrac—amphibious tractor; a landing craft

AO—area of operations

ao dai—traditional dress of Vietnamese women: slacks and a tunic slit up the sides

APC—armored personnel carrier

arty—artillery

ARVN, or Arvin—Army of the Republic of Viet Nam (South Vietnam), or any regular South Vietnamese Army soldier

AWOL—absent without leave

babysan—Vietnamese child; also, very young woman

bac-si, also *bac se*—doctor

BCD—bad conduct discharge

BMB—brigade main base

Brown Bar—second lieutenant

CA—combat assault; inserting troops by helicopter into a hot landing zone, usually with gunship support

C-4—plastic explosive, small chunks of which burned like Sterno and were used to heat C-rations

Charlie, also **Charles**—Viet Cong, from the military phonetic spelling of the acronym VC, or Victor Charlie

cherry—a new guy

Chinook—the CH-47 helicopter, a large, twin-rotor job used to move troops and cargo; also called a Shithook

Class A's—the Army dress uniform

Claymore—a command-detonated antipersonnel mine packed with steel pellets

click (see **klick**)

Cobra—a helicopter gunship with rockets and mini-guns

CP—command post

crispy critters—severely burned victims of napalm; named after a popular children's cereal of the time

DEROS—Date of Expected Return from Overseas

deuce-and-a-half—a two-and-a-half ton truck

didi mau—go or leave quickly, take off, scram

DMZ—demilitarized zone; the fifteen miles on either side of the border between North and South Vietnam designated by the Geneva accords

DTs—defensive targets

dung lai—stop, halt, don't move

dustoff—medical evacuation, or medevac; also, any helicopter pickup

DZ—drop zone

EOD—Explosive Ordnance Disposal (or Demolition)

FDC—Fire Direction Control Center; coordinated artillery

fire for effect—command meaning that rounds are hitting the target and to pour it on

FNG, also **fenugie**—fucking new guy

FO—1. fire officer 2. field officer 3. forward observer

frag—a fragmentation grenade; to kill using a grenade; to assassinate a despised superior

H & I—harassment and interdiction fire; artillery fired to discourage enemy movement

HE—high-explosive rounds

hootch, also **hooch**—a hut or tent; any small building

Huey—Bell's UH-1A, -1B, and other utility helicopters of that series, the most prevalent in Vietnam

jarhead—a Marine

KIA—Killed in Action

klick, or **click**—a kilometer

laager, also **lager**—a night defensive position or camp

LAAW—light antiarmor assault weapon, or light antitank assault weapon; a shoulder-launched rocket in a disposable fiberglass tube

liftship—a Huey

little people, the—the Viet Cong; also, any Vietnamese

loach, also **LOH**—light observation helicopter

LP—listening post

LZ, or **lz**—landing zone

MACV—Military Assistance Command, Vietnam; the American military headquarters for Vietnam

Marvin—slang for any ARVN or South Vietnamese soldier

medevac—a medical evacuation flight by a helicopter, usually a Huey

MLR—main line of resistance

NCO—noncommisioned officer

NDP—night defensive position

nuocmam—a powerful-smelling fish sauce

NVA—North Vietnamese Army, or any soldier belonging to the PAVN, or People's Army of Vietnam

OD—olive drab

PBR—patrol boat, river

poge—support personnel at rear area bases, also known as REMFs

PT—physical training

Puff the Magic Dragon—a C-47 cargo plane outfitted with mini-guns

punji stakes, also pungi—sharpened stakes, usually of bamboo, anchored in pits to injure foot soldiers

PZ—pickup zone

recoilless rifle—a portable heavy weapon much like a bazooka

REMF—rear-echelon motherfucker; anyone stationed in the rear

re-up—to enlist for another tour, usually with the (shaky) promise that you won't have to serve as many months in combat

ricky-tick—fast, quickly

Rome plow—huge bulldozer used to clear away forest

RPD—Soviet light machine gun used by the VC and the NVA; similar to the U.S. M-60

RPG—rocket propelled grenade

RTO—Radio-Telephone Operator

ruck, or rucksack—the Army-issue backpack

Saigon cowboy—young South Vietnamese male involved in the street life and black market of Saigon, usually taking on Western styles

sapper—enemy commando who sneaks into American facilities, often on a suicide mission

SDS—Students for a Democratic Society; vocal, high-profile antiwar protesters

Shithook (see **Chinook**)

short, also short-timer—a U.S. soldier with few days left in-country

short round—an artillery round or bomb that falls short of the target, often on one's own troop positions

sit-rep—situation report

six—radio call sign for any unit commander

slack—the number-two man in a patrol, walking immediately behind the point man

slick—a UH-1 helicopter with no protruding armament; or, any Huey

slope—racial slur, applied to Vietnamese; or any Asian person

SOP—standard operating procedure

squid—a member of the Navy

Starlight scope—an optical device that amplifies moonlight and starlight to allow the user to see in the dark

TAOR—Tactical Area of Operational Responsibility

thumper—M-79 grenade launcher

ti-ti, also *titi*—little, tiny, small

TOC—Tactical Operations Center

TOT—time on target

Victor Charlie—the military phonetic spelling of VC, or Viet Cong

web gear, also **webb gear**—the belt and harnesslike suspenders from which a soldier's ammo, grenades, smoke canisters, canteen, etc., hang

WIA—Wounded in Action

Willie Peter, also **WP**—white phosphorous

XO—executive officer

zip, also **zipperhead**—racial slur, applied to Vietnamese; or to any Asian person

zoomie—a member of the U.S. Air Force

Selected Additional Bibliography

Anderson, Douglas. *The Moon Reflected Fire*. Cambridge, Mass.: Alice James Books, 1994.

Balaban, John. *After Our War*. Pittsburgh, Pa.: University of Pittsburgh Press, 1974.

———. *Coming Down Again*. New York: Harcourt Brace Jovanovich, 1985.

Beidler, Philip. *American Literature and the Experience of Vietnam*. Athens, Ga.: University of Georgia Press, 1982.

———. *Re-Writing America: Vietnam Authors in Their Generation*. Athens: University of Georgia Press, 1991.

Broyles, William. *Brothers in Arms*. New York: Knopf, 1986

Bryan, C. D. B. *Friendly Fire*. New York: G. P. Putnam's Sons, 1976.

Butler, Robert Olen. *A Good Scent from a Strange Mountain*. New York: Holt, 1992.

———. *On Distant Ground*. New York: Knopf, 1985.

Caputo, Philip. *Indian Country*. New York: Bantam, 1987

Currey, Richard. *Crossing Over*. Cambridge/Newton, Mass.: Apple-wood Press, 1980.

———. *Fatal Light*. New York: E. P. Dutton/Seymour Lawrence, 1988.

Dodge, Ed. *Dau*. New York: Macmillan, 1984.

Ehrhart, W. D. *To Those Who Have Gone Home Tired*. New York: Thunder's Mouth Press, 1984.

Emerson, Gloria. *Winners and Losers*. New York: Harcourt Brace Jovanovich, 1976.

FitzGerald, Frances. *Fire in the Lake*. New York: Random House, 1972.

French, Albert. *Patches of Fire*. New York: Anchor, 1997.

Greene, Graham. *The Quiet American*. Harmondsworth, England: Penguin, 1955.

Groom, Winston. *Better Times Than These*. New York: Summit Books, 1978.

Halberstam, David. *The Best and the Brightest*. New York: Random House, 1972.

———. *The Making of a Quagmire*. New York: Random House, 1965.

Hasford, Gustav. *The Short-Timers*. New York: Bantam Books, 1979.

Heinemann, Larry. *Close Quarters*. New York: Farrar, Straus and Giroux, 1977.

Hellman, John. *American Myth and the Legacy of Vietnam.* New York: Columbia University Press, 1986.

Karlin, Wayne, Le Minh Khue, and Truong Vu, eds. *The Other Side of Heaven.* Willimantic, Conn.: Curbstone Press, 1995.

Karlin, Wayne, Basil T. Paquet, and Larry Rottmann, eds. *Free Fire Zone: Short Stories by Vietnam Veterans.* New York: McGraw-Hill, 1973.

Karnow, Stanley. *Vietnam: A History.* New York: Viking Press, 1983.

Klein, Joe. *Payback.* New York: Knopf, 1984.

Kopit, Arthur. *Indians.* New York: Hill & Wang, 1969.

Lang, Daniel. *Casualties of War.* New York: McGraw-Hill, 1969.

Lomperis, Timothy J. *Reading the Wind: The Literature of the Vietnam War.* Durham, N.C.: Duke University Press, 1987.

Marshall, Kathryn. *In the Combat Zone: An Oral History of American Women in Vietnam.* New York: Harper and Row, 1984.

McDonald, Walter. *After the Noise of Saigon.* Amherst, Mass.: University of Massachusetts Press, 1988.

Moore, Harold G., and Joseph L. Galloway. *We Were Soldiers Once . . . and Young.* New York: Random House, 1992.

Myers, Thomas. *Walking Point: American Narratives of Vietnam.* New York: Oxford University Press, 1988.

Page, Tim. *Tim Page's Nam.* New York: Knopf, 1983.

Pratt, John Clark, ed. *Vietnam Voices.* New York: Penguin, 1984.

Rabe, David. *Streamers.* New York: Knopf, 1977.

Ringnalda, Donald. *Fighting and Writing the Vietnam War.* Jackson, Miss.: University Press of Mississippi, 1994.

Rottmann, Larry, Jan Barry, and Basil Paquet, eds. *Winning Hearts and Minds.* Brooklyn, N.Y.: 1st Casualty Press, 1972.

Schroeder, Eric James, ed. *Vietnam, We've All Been There: Interviews with American Writers.* Westport, Conn.: Praeger, 1992.

Searle, William J., ed. *Search and Clear: Critical Responses to Selected Literature and Films of the Vietnam War.* Bowling Green, Ohio: Bowling Green State University Popular Press, 1988.

Sheehan, Neil. *A Bright Shining Lie: John Paul Vann and America in Vietnam.* New York: Random House, 1988.

Stone, Robert. *Dog Soldiers.* Boston, Mass.: Houghton Mifflin, 1973.

Weigl, Bruce. *Song of Napalm.* New York: Atlantic Monthly Press, 1988.

Selected Additional Filmography

The Anderson Platoon (1966)
Bat 21 (1988)
Dear America: Letters Home from Vietnam (1988)
84 Charlie MoPic (1989)
Gardens of Stone (1987)
Go Tell the Spartans (1978)
Hearts and Minds (1974)
In Country (1988)
Jackknife (1989)
Streamers (1984)
Vietnam: A Television History (1983)
Vietnam: The Ten Thousand Day War (1980)
Vietnam: The War at Home (1978)

Reading Questions

I've gathered these sample reading questions for students as well as general readers as a way of interrogating these pieces. They're only leads, possible directions to pursue, not a prescription. I'll be the first to admit that their concerns are mine, and that readers, teachers, and students all can come up with better ones. Mine are just an easy way into the work, a first step. The important thing is to question the texts.

Early in the war, the opposition to the U.S. involvement accused the government of lying, falsely representing both America's actions and motives. Likewise, supporters of the war alleged that the antiwar movement grossly overstated its case, blowing isolated incidents out of proportion. Though the official story of the war seems to have been discredited early on (and continues, with Kennedy and Johnson administration officials such as Clark Clifford and Robert McNamara recently confessing that well before Tet the inner circle knew it was a losing cause), it was clear then and it's clear now that both sides bent the facts in hopes of enforcing their political points. The ends, it seemed, would justify the means.

That is no less true today, as each author—participant or not—creates and relates his or her version of the war. It's no coincidence that Tim O'Brien's "How to Tell a True War Story" is this anthology's keystone. With so many issues of truth and authority swirling around any representation of America's involvement in Vietnam, it's important that the reader not simply accept at face value what one or even several authors claim. As in any popular literature, stereotypes abound here. The veteran and the conduct of the war itself are continually subject to a dramatic warping. Twenty-five years after the last ground troops pulled out, Americans are still fighting to legitimize their mutually exclusive views of the war and what it meant, whose fault it was, why it happened the way it did, and even—astonishingly—the ques-

701

tion of who really won. Because it split American society so deeply, the war will continue to be heatedly debated, perhaps always. By questioning the selections in this book, the reader will not only be able to join in that debate but to understand the issues that created and sustain it.

1. Green

1. Compare the narrators' attitudes toward soldiers and soldiering.

2. What are the two first-person narrators' jobs? Paul Berlin's? How might this affect their views?

3. Every narrative has a main character or "hero." How are the heroes of these three war narratives typical or atypical? Whom are we asked to identify with, and why? What traits do these heroes share with other American heroes?

4. What implicit criticisms of the way the war is being fought or handled by the American military and political systems can you find in these pieces?

5. Compare the welcome the central characters of *Going After Cacciato* and *The Green Berets* receive and how they react to it.

6. What do these narratives imply about American innocence and nobility, especially that of the combat soldier? Compare O'Brien's Paul Berlin to any of the others.

7. Examine the use of language in *Cacciato* and *The Green Berets*, especially profanity and military jargon. Who uses it and in what context?

8. How would the hero of *The Green Berets* view the hero of *Cacciato?*

9. How would the Tim O'Brien of *If I Die in a Combat Zone* see Sven Kornie's views?

10. Discuss the abundance or lack of irony and comedy across the three works. Why is there so much or so little?

11. How are the Vietnamese portrayed?

12. How do the soldiers in each piece fit into the military?

13. Examine the two in-country settings and what they say about the war.

14. What do the three texts say about courage and fear?

15. How do these pieces address concepts of masculinity?

2. Early Work

1. Contrast Casey's, O'Brien's, and Rabe's use of irony and twisted humor.

2. Examine pieces that comment on the very act of trying to relate the experience of Vietnam. What do these pieces say about the possibility or impossibility of relating that experience?

3. How are the Vietnamese treated by American personnel in these five readings? Especially look at Halberstam's use of Thuong as a point-of-view character and at Rabe's very different use of Zung.

4. How are Americans who stayed home viewed?

5. Discuss how women are portrayed in the five selections.

6. How do the authors make use of pop culture?

7. How is the body (or bodies) used?

8. With whom are we supposed to identify in *Sticks and Bones?* How does Rabe achieve this effect, and why?

9. How do the authors portray previous generations?

10. How do the authors employ language and formal innovation (or conversely, traditional methods) to convey this new material?

11. How (and where) does David's return in *Sticks and Bones* challenge American myths? How does Rabe attempt to indict the culture as a whole?

12. In what ways is this protest literature? What judgment do these works pass on the war and on America, and how?

13. Examine the relationship of the individual to the group in two or more pieces.

14. Compare the views of the war given by the minor characters in *If I Die in a Combat Zone.* Taken as a group, do they offer the FNG O'Brien a coherent or consistent picture of the war (or of their own ability to make sense of it)?

15. Where do the authors attack what they see as the gaps between the professed virtues of the American system and the realities?

16. Again, how do these authors present soldiers and soldiering? How are these versions different from the typical warrior-hero model?

17. Find examples of or allusions to American innocence and American evil. To whom (or what) are they attributed, and why?

18. In Casey's "Learning," the narrator says he enjoyed reading about Caesar's fighting. Discuss the aesthetic allure of combat violence—why people like to read about it—and some of the moral challenges this poses to the writers of these five pieces.

19. Contrast Halberstam's use of history with the other authors'.

3. First Wave of Major Work

1. Compare the end of Caputo's prologue to O'Brien's *If I Die in a Combat Zone* and discuss the paradox inherent in their resignation concerning the power of their separate testimonies. Examine their claims to be writing fiction or nonfiction, reportage or stories.

2. Discuss the very different literary techniques used by these five authors.

3. How do Kovic, Caputo, and the men in *Fields of Fire* and *Dispatches* fit into the stereotypical categories of American soldier?

4. How do Kovic, Caputo, and Herr explain the attraction or thrill of war? "You know how it is, you want to look and you don't want to look."

5. Examine Philip Caputo's musings on the morality or culpability of the American combat soldier in Vietnam. Now Paul Berlin's. How might Michael Herr criticize Caputo's or Berlin's explanations? How might Webb's Goodrich agree with them?

6. Though these pieces come from the first wave of major literary works about the American war, all five postdate their authors' tours of duty by at least five years. Examine Caputo's prologue (especially his claim that *A Rumor of War* is not a political document) and Paul Berlin's imagining with this quotation from *Dispatches* in mind: ". . . afterward you can make up any kind of bullshit you want to about it . . ." How does this serve as an analogy for any vet writing about the war (and how we as American readers must approach their work)?

7. In all five pieces, find instances where the authors question the nature of truth, reality, facts, lies, etc.

8. Discuss Caputo's view of Vietnam and the Vietnamese. How might this influence a civilian jury's evaluation of his guilt or innocence as the defendant in a murder trial (the victims being Vietnamese)? Examine his statement about the killings being substantially and fundamentally different from killings in Los Angeles. Now look at Paul Berlin's view of civilians. How about Goodrich's musings on the one hundred NVA dead and the old lady?

9. Discuss Herr's portrayal of Americans in Vietnam.

10. Herr cites Hemingway's title "A Way You'll Never Be." Discuss how Kovic, Webb, Caputo, and Herr show the difficulty (impossibility?) of bridging the gap between combatant and noncombatant, soldier and American civilian. How is this an analogy for the writer and America?

11. Locate instances of participants feeling a nostalgia for the war or unable to reconnect with society. How does this play into contemporary (1976–78) clichés about the Vietnam vet?

6. The Oral History Boom

1. In contrast to "the gap," or the impossibility of relating the experience of the war to the American public found in earlier texts, these oral histories purposely attack that very problem. How do they try to bridge the gap? What do they do that previous texts could not? Do they run into the same problems or adopt the same tactics as earlier work?

2. Discuss the problems of authority in these oral histories. How do the editors establish the speakers' right (even duty) to relate their stories?

3. Fiction versus nonfiction: Look at *Nam*'s uncredited epigraph. Examine the contradictions of the oral history and the oral tradition of storytelling. (It wouldn't hurt to keep Michael Herr's *Dispatches* in mind here, and his penchant for telling emblematic yet way-over-the-top stories, then attributing them to someone else, or even no one in particular.)

4. What do the people in the one section of *Nam* say about America? How do they fit into the culture?

5. What do they say about going to Vietnam? How do they fit or explode the easy categories of reluctant draftee, professional warrior, psycho killer?

6. What is their grasp of American foreign policy? How does America fit into the world?

7. Discuss the radicalization of Malik Edwards, his views of the war, the American military, and America itself. Find other participants, fictional and otherwise, who share his views—especially Robert Santos's comments about the Detroit riots, and his quote: "I just thought I was white like everyone else." Address the issue of the soldier-protester, a quintessential Vietnam figure.

8. Examine how the speakers apprehend the roles of men and women in American society.

9. Critics have said there seems to be an implicit view of the speakers in these oral histories as guiltless victims of the war (which in many cultural circles is now the prevailing truth). Do you find this to be true, and if so, why? What previous stereotypes do the editors and speakers hope to overthrow or replace? In whose works have we previously seen this new version of the American soldier in Vietnam?

10. Pop versions: Several men in *Nam* cite John Wayne. Search for instances where vets discuss film or other media versions of the war. How do they see them? Examine Robert Santos's saying: ". . . it was like a goddamn movie."

11. Contrast the group of letter writers in *Dear America* with the speakers in *Nam*. On the whole, do their views of the war differ? Their politics (or lack of)? What might this have to do with the time when the letters were written and the pieces taped? How do the editors' choices affect our view of Americans in Vietnam?

12. Compare Anne Simon Auger's life after the war with those of other vets—Ron Kovic; Michael, Nick, and Steven from *The Deer Hunter*; David in *Sticks and Bones*, etc.

13. Discuss instances of the individual caught in the system.

14. How do these testimonies fit the *Bildungroman* trajectory from innocence to experience? What have the speakers learned?

7. Second Wave of Major Work

1. Examine Del Vecchio's use of dialect spellings and his portrayal of Doc Johnson. Compare this use of language and cultural history with that of Wallace Terry in Malik Edwards's section of *Bloods*. Use this comparison as the kernel of a larger discussion on the representation of minority servicemen (and -women, if you can find the evidence).

2. Rufus Brooks's R&R: How does Del Vecchio's portrayal of Lila fit with other female characters we've seen? Examine the assumptions the male characters (and, perhaps, the male authors) make about women in general and, more specifically, women in U.S. society. Keep in mind that the Women's Lib movement was contemporary with the end of the war.

3. The usual question we ask of an American text: How do these three books portray the U.S. involvement in Vietnam? Sympathetically or not? Who do these books praise or blame?

4. How is Wright's veteran at home different from others we've seen? In what ways is he the same?

5. Examine how Wright and Heinemann push their language compared to Del Vecchio. Look at the form of the novels as well. Compare the techniques used with those of Kovic or O'Brien, Herr or Baker. What similarities do you find?

6. Discuss Wright's and Heinemann's use of pop culture.

7. Discuss Wright's view of American technology and society.

8. Dissect Heinemann's first paragraph and the next few ensuing pages in light of other disclaimers (Caputo's, O'Brien's, Moore's) or questionable claims of authenticity (Herr's, Terry's, Baker's).

9. What about Heinemann's narrator's claim that most folks will shell out to see artful carnage? Discuss whether you find this true or not and why, using evidence gleaned from the other texts and films, as well as from American culture at large.

10. How and where does Heinemann indulge in—even celebrate in an over-the-top way—the stereotypes of Americans in Vietnam?

Examine his use of caricatures and other elements of the tall tale rather than the relatively straight-ahead realism of Del Vecchio.

11. Going back to Question 1, how is Heinemann's portrait of Jonesy different from Del Vecchio's Jackson or Johnson?

12. Who is this James that Heinemann's narrator addresses? What is the significance of this story being told to a particular audience?

13. Compare Heinemann's narrator's discussion of war correspondents with other authors' views of the media, especially Herr's, who seems to be at least partly the target of these jibes. Tie in the line about the impossibility of a movie getting the truth about the war across that ends that section.

9. Memoirs

1. Usually memoirs are first-person accounts of lived experience. Examine Glasser's use of fictional techniques, as well as his choice of a third-person narrator.

2. Once again, the usual question: How do these personal narratives portray the U.S. involvement in Vietnam—sympathetically or not? Compare Glasser's view of war with Lanning's and Downs's.

3. What, ostensibly, is the purpose of each text—that is, what does it appear the author wants from his audience? Who is that audience?

4. Continuing issue: How are the heroes of these narratives similar to those we've seen in other Vietnam books? How do they differ from standard American heroes?

5. How might the authors' relationship to the Army influence their view of the war? Think of the authors in terms of our categories of soldiers—damaged vet, psycho killer, professional, reluctant draftee, protest vet, frontier hero, etc.

6. These works focus on very different events and operations to represent the Vietnam experience. Discuss the emphasis each writer has chosen, and possible reasons for that choice.

7. What implicit critiques of American tactics and strategies do these narratives contain?

8. How America chooses its war: Glasser published his book in 1971, Downs in '78, Mason in '83, Lanning in '87. Keeping in mind that the antiwar movement was huge by '68 and the Memorial was dedicated in '82, explain how the political climate of the country may fit each text—that is, how the way the culture was seeing the war and the vet at that particular time may have matched what the author had to say.

9. Examine how the authors use atrocities or war crimes. Compare the treatment of VC prisoners in Downs's and Mason's work.

10. Examine the authors' views of relations between Americans and the Vietnamese.

11. Compare these personal narratives with literary fiction from the war. Examine how different texts emphasize action over character or vice versa. What or whom are we supposed to be concerned about? How do these pieces of nonfiction conform to or explode the conventions of the heroic battle narrative or its twin, the protest memoir?

12. Recurring themes: Views of women, definitions of masculinity.

13. Critics often charge that American Vietnam War narratives— especially those written years after the war—focus on the personal or technical at the expense of judging the larger political and moral realities of our involvement. Do you find this criticism valid for these texts or not, and why?

10. Masterwork

1. Is this just a batch of stories strung together? A novel? Comment on O'Brien's use of form. You might compare this fractured form with that of his own *Going After Cacciato*. Or, on a grander scale, you might look at how so many Vietnam narratives have nonlinear or exploded structures.

2. Fiction or nonfiction? At times, O'Brien interrupts, often to correct or undercut the effect of a story. Discuss this odd metafictional tactic and its effect on the reader. Also, comment on O'Brien's use of himself as a (possibly fictional) character.

3. Examine the story "How to Tell a True War Story" in the context of the opening pages of Heinemann's *Paco's Story*.

4. Explain the line "It *wasn't* a war story, it was a *love* story."

5. Discuss the different audiences O'Brien is telling his stories to

and what he says (or implies) about them. Compare this with Heinemann's narrator's view of Americans' thirst for war stories.

6. Innocent kids or psycho killers? How does O'Brien view the American soldier, and how does this differ from the views of other authors?

7. Views of the enemy. Compare "The Man I Killed" with other versions of VC or NVA regulars.

8. The reluctant draftee kills the reluctant draftee: Compare "The Man I Killed" with O'Brien's self-portrait in *If I Die in a Combat Zone*.

9. Examine the reactions of other platoon members to O'Brien killing the man. How might these be read as allegories for the veteran's reception by America? Look for evidence of this theme (views of the vet) in the other stories.

10. Discuss the significance of O'Brien's titles.

11. "This is true." Truth is such a loaded issue when it comes to Vietnam, yet O'Brien purposely and continually plays up the fact that he's inventing what we're reading. Contrast this with all the odd prefaces and disclaimers other authors have used to prove their authority.

12. The tall tale as a major Vietnam genre: Compare fabulous tales (*Paco's Story*, *Going After Cacciato*, some of the more outrageous whoppers from *Dispatches*, parts of *The Things They Carried*) with scrupulous realism (*The 13th Valley*, *The Green Berets*, oral histories, and other supposedly objective nonfiction).

13. The kid with one leg and the chocolate bar: Throughout *The Things*, O'Brien uses ready-made and sentimental images and then finds a way to overcome them, put a different spin on them. Find examples and compare this effect with how he uses the reader's conventional expectations against us.

14. Look at how O'Brien uses games and toys both to characterize the soldiers as children and to comment on how his choice of form (and the war) works.

11. Homecoming

1. What are these returned vets like? How do the authors' characterizations fit into previous categories we've seen? Compare them with first-person accounts of life after service in Vietnam (oral histories, nonfiction). Have we seen these same traits from Hollywood films, TV shows, popular literature? Would you say they're stereotypes or true to life—and how can one tell?

2. Paco in his rented room, Norman Bowker in his father's car: How is the vet's relationship with America (or his community) represented? How do the authors portray the vet's view of America?

3. Look at all the instances of returned vets trying to connect with women. Examine their relationships.

4. A related question: Compare Paco's (and the narrator's) imagining Cathy having sex with Marty-boy and the gang rape of the captured VC. You might also look at the execution of the imaginary male VC.

5. Collect evidence of the gap between veteran and civilian.

6. How do the different authors and narrators (and characters) try to bridge the gap?

7. Flashbacks: Discuss how most if not all of these vets seem to be haunted by the past. Look at the many ways the authors show the power of memory and the mind.

8. My Lai: Civilians (read: readers) agree on the insanity and immorality of war, and especially war crimes. Comment on the authors' use of atrocities.

9. The Ivy League English major ROTC lieutenant: Examine how Heinemann uses the character Lieutenant Stennett.

10. In "Speaking of Courage" and its companion "Notes," examine vets' views of other vets. Consider the position of the character Tim O'Brien looking at the character Norman Bowker, as well as Bowker's thoughts in his letter.

11. "The town did not know shit about shit." Compare Norman Bowker's view of the town to O'Brien's view of the actual Worthington, Minnesota, in *If I Die in a Combat Zone*.

12. Note the emphasis: "After *Our* War." Self-accusation: Find instances where these works force the American reader to look at America, to admit complicity. Is this a form of bridging the gap?

13. Analyze Bruce Weigl's "Monkey" in the light of Paco, Norman Bowker, and Henry Lamartine of Louise Erdrich's "A Bridge."

12. Memory

1. Once again, examine the returned vets. How do they differ from other popular versions we've seen? In what ways are they the same?

2. Discuss the personae in Yusef Komunyakaa's poems and their relationship with the Vietnamese — male and female, enemy and ally.

3. And again, the relationship of vets and women: Look especially at *In Country*, in which one vet, Tom (only briefly mentioned in these sections), is Sam's impotent lover; Emmett is her bachelor uncle; and her dead father's relationship with her mother was strained by her antiwar leanings.

4. Race and the military. Examine Komunyakaa's portrayal of African American soldiers. Compare his versions with, say, Heinemann's Jonesy or Del Vecchio's Doc Johnson.

5. We see the gap from both sides in *In Country*. Compare how Sam and Emmett see it differently.

6. How does Sam try to bridge this gap?

7. How about the generation gap? Norman Bowker and his father, Sam and Emmett — or Sam and her lost father.

8. Is that you, John Wade? Is this me? How does O'Brien frame his character's guilt or innocence in Thuan Yen? American innocence? How does he explain the evils of war, and how does this fit with Caputo's defense?

9. Fact or fiction? Again, O'Brien is walking the line between documented truth and the imaginary, and includes a possibly fictional narrator/author. What effect does this situating of an overtly fictional story in a documented historical event have upon our unavoidably politicized reading?

10. Examine the position of women in *In the Lake of the Woods*.

11. Discuss memory or conscience with respect to *In Country* and *In the Lake of the Woods*. How about complicity, denial, America's historical conscience? Who does the war continue to affect?

12. Look at Emmett's big emotional scene in *In Country*. How does this fit with stereotypes of the Vietnam vet? Examine Emmett saying, "It's the same for all of us."

13. How does Balaban use history and time in "Mr. Giai's Poem"? What might he be implying about the consolations of memory? Of poetry? How might Tim O'Brien or Norman Bowker refute or agree with this view of the salvific power of memory? That is, does memory save us or condemn us? Include Kevin Bowen's "Incoming" in this discussion.

13. The Wall

1. How do the veterans in these pieces view the Wall? The war?

2. In *The Names of the Dead* and Komunyakaa's poems, examine the differences between generations and how they connect with the Wall and the war.

3. "I'm inside the Vietnam Veterans Memorial," Komunyakaa's narrator says. Compare this with Larry Markham's vision of himself and his son "looking out" of the Wall, and discuss how many of the vets we've seen have felt trapped or still caught inside the war.

4. Look at the mother's mementos in "Between Days" and the offerings Larry Markham leaves at the Wall. How have veterans and civilians in these and other pieces chosen to memorialize the war— keep it present and with them? How might this relate to the number of books written about the war?

5. Consider ". . . framing the blackness." Note the confusion both Komunyakaa's narrator and Larry Markham struggle with, trying to place themselves and figure out what they're seeing, where they fit in it, what it means to them.

Acknowledgments

Songs

Photographs

rance. Copyright © 1989 by Dick Durrance. Reprinted by permission of Hill and Wang, a division of Farrar, Straus, & Giroux, Inc.
Chapter 11: Ray Mews, AP/Wide World Photos
Chapter 12: Ron Haeberle, Life Magazine © Time, Inc.
Chapter 13: Magnum Photos, Inc. © 1985 Peter Marlow
Appendices: Used by permission of UPI/Corbis-Bettmann

Index

719